8/19

PRESIDENTIAL MISCONDUCT

PRESIDENTIAL MISCONDUCT

FROM GEORGE WASHINGTON *TO TODAY*

EDITED BY

JAMES M. BANNER, JR.

THE
NEW
PRESS

NEW YORK
LONDON

"A Measure of Executive Misdeeds" © 2019 James M. Banner, Jr.
"Richard M. Nixon," "George H. W. Bush," and "George W. Bush" © 2019 Kathryn S. Olmsted
    and Eric Rauchway
"Gerald R. Ford, Jr." © 2019 Joan Hoff
"James E. Carter, Jr." © 2019 Kevin M. Kruse
"Ronald Reagan" © 2019 Jeremi Suri
"William J. Clinton" © 2019 Kathryn Cramer Brownell
"Barack Obama" © 2019 Allan J. Lichtman

Requests to reproduce the nine selections written expressly for this 2019 edition should be made
through our website: https://thenewpress.com/contact.

The introduction by C. Vann Woodward and the chapters from George Washington through Lyndon
B. Johnson were originally published in the United States as *Responses of the Presidents to Charges of
Misconduct* by Dell Publishing Co., Inc., New York, 1974.

This edition with new material published in the United States by The New Press, New York, 2019.
Distributed by Two Rivers Distribution.

ISBN 978-1-62097-549-7 (hc)
ISBN 978-1-62097-550-3 (ebook)
CIP data is available

The New Press publishes books that promote and enrich public discussion and understanding of
the issues vital to our democracy and to a more equitable world. These books are made possible by
the enthusiasm of our readers; the support of a committed group of donors, large and small; the
collaboration of our many partners in the independent media and the not-for-profit sector; booksellers,
who often hand-sell New Press books; librarians; and above all by our authors.

www.thenewpress.com

Composition by dix!

Printed in the United States of America

10   9   8   7   6   5   4   3   2   1

CONTENTS

A MEASURE OF
EXECUTIVE MISDEEDS

James M. Banner, Jr.

Like the report and book that preceded it in 1974, this book is occasioned by a grave crisis in the nation's affairs.

In 1974, President Richard M. Nixon was facing impeachment by the House of Representatives for acts brought to light during the Watergate crisis. Those events led the House Committee on the Judiciary, as part of its investigation into the grounds for the President's impeachment, to seek the production of a historical account of presidential misconduct reaching back to the administration of George Washington. In 2019, another president and his associates and subordinate officers are under scrutiny for a wide range of possible legal and constitutional offenses: collusion with a foreign power to affect the outcome of his election, financial ties with foreign interests that interfere with his ability to act in the national interest, obstruction of justice, suppression of evidence, disregard of campaign finance laws, money laundering, tax evasion, breaches of the emoluments clause of the Constitution, and other offenses, such as abusing power, directing the commission of felonies, and undermining the rule of law and norms of democratic governance. Already, some of the President's close associates have pled guilty to perjury, violation of campaign finance laws, and other crimes. Since the parallel gravity of the two crises is apparent, an expanded historical survey of presidential misconduct since 1789, one updated to cover the eight presidential administrations since 1974, including Nixon's, is clearly needed. It must of course be borne in mind that, as of the early days of 2019, the present crisis remains unresolved. But we can at least say that today's crisis poses enough threats to constitutional government and normal political practices to demand comparison with previous instances of known presidential misconduct. This book renews efforts by historians to provide the basis for that comparison.

The 1974 report to the Impeachment Inquiry took shape with the same urgency as this one. In April of that year, during hearings on potential articles of impeachment against President Nixon, John Doar, Special Counsel to the Impeachment Inquiry, asked C. Vann Woodward, a Yale historian, to direct a study of presidential misconduct from the administration of George Washington through that of Nixon's predecessor, Lyndon B. Johnson. A historical frame of reference, Doar believed, would help members of the Judiciary Committee judge the gravity of accusations against Nixon and senior administration officials. Woodward recruited three other historians—William E. Leuchtenburg, William S. McFeely, and Merrill D. Peterson—to help manage the production of the report. Under their direction, eleven other historians, among whom I was one, placed on record how earlier presidents had responded to charges of misconduct against themselves, senior members of their administrations, and employees of the federal bureaucracy. Within an eight-week deadline, we managed to prepare our respective segments of the report.

Participants in the study understood from the start that the study might be published as part of the official record of the Inquiry. But since the President resigned in August 1974 only weeks after we submitted our report in late June, our work was not included in the investigation's formal record. What use, if any, the committee and its staff members made of the study was never made clear to us. Subsequently, the report fell into the public domain and was published the same year by Delacorte Press as a book bearing the title of the original report: *Responses of the Presidents to Charges of Misconduct.* For that book, Woodward added an introduction, "The Conscience of the White House," which is included here. With Nixon out of office, few took notice of the book; even today, most historians are unaware of its existence.

Those of us who participated in the original study were confident that, consistent with the intent behind Doar's invitation, the report contributed to knowledge about a largely neglected aspect of the nation's political and constitutional history—that is, presidential misconduct.

We also thought that, if it were needed, a continued study would provide Americans with a means of assessing the performance of later White House occupants. This extension of the original work offers the grounds for that assessment.

As Woodward stated in 1974, our study of presidential misconduct was "without precedent." It seemed, to both the Impeachment Inquiry and our group of historians, that the political and constitutional circumstances of the time had no parallel in American history. The study was also unprecedented in that no other general survey of the subject then existed. That, to our knowledge, remains the case, although discrete studies of particular scandals continue to appear. Like its predecessor, this expanded study is distinctive in its content and similarly urgent in the need that makes it relevant. But its value must also be measured by its utility in providing grounds for assessing the conduct of each presidential administration. Under normal circumstances, historians, journalists, and others involved in law and politics might constitute the limited audience for such an assessment. But these extraordinary times require another effort to provide a wider audience with a rough kind of metric by which the current crisis can be broadly understood. Like the original report, this one ends with the most recently completed administration, that of Barack Obama.

The book is unusual, as well as unprecedented, because, unlike most historical works, its core contents—a series of brief essays, organized chronologically by administration, of charges and findings of misconduct faced by successive presidencies—deliberately lack interpretation. The essays are episodic and almost without exception self-contained; even Woodward's original introduction is spare in its interpretive suggestions. Moreover, the historians who have prepared the materials added to those written in 1974 have, like the original authors, undertaken no new research; as in 1974, the new authors have grounded their work in what is already known from existing secondary sources and published public documents. While all chapters reflect a normal alertness to relevance and context, they are not meant to be exploratory or argumentative. Any breaches in these guidelines are inadvertent.

What standard has been used to determine what does and does not constitute presidential misconduct? For instance, should our work encompass charges of a partisan or ideological nature or of unconstitutional conduct that did not raise questions of corruption? If the original report had included partisan, ideological, and constitutional issues, it could have examined James Madison's attempts to enlist New England militias in national service during the War of 1812 or Harry S. Truman's seizure of the steel mills in 1952, the latter of which was rebuffed by the Supreme Court. These and similar events that constitute legitimate disputes about matters of judgment, decision, or execution are omitted here. Such episodes raised questions of prerogative—what we now call executive power—as, for instance, did the Obama administration's decision to allow those brought as young children to the United States by illegal immigrant parents to gain legal status, avoid deportation, complete their education, and gain work permits. But these acts, all disputed still, did not constitute instances of misconduct commonly understood as wrongdoing. Consequently, like the 1974 report, this augmented study limits its scope, as Woodward wrote in his original introduction, to the "responses of the President, on his part or on the part of his subordinates, to charges of misconduct that was alleged to be illegal and for which offenders would be culpable." In effect, this book's authors have been asked to set down instances in which presidents, members of their "official families," and other federal officers acting in their official capacities were charged with illegal or criminal conduct that benefited them directly or personally or that injured others. As far as is known, all major charges of such misconduct are included here. When charges were dropped or the basis for them found lacking, the authors have so indicated. All accusations of misconduct that took place solely in private life and did not impinge on public affairs, save for the most egregious ones, are excluded, as are any alleged or proved misdeeds of the presidents and their senior officials before or after their terms in office.

Despite its limitations, this new study uniquely reveals the nature of personal misconduct and major suspected and substantiated offenses against law and public ethics in our national history. Starting with William Duer's frauds with public moneys during Washington's administration, misconduct has marked the record of the American state. The manner in which presidents have responded to charges of misconduct against themselves or their senior subordinates discloses both changing standards of executive expectations and conduct and similarities in charges of presidential misconduct since the launching of constitutional government in 1789.

The first decade of government under the Constitution of 1787 set a pattern for events to come. Much of that day's executive branch misconduct, starting with Duer's acts, stemmed from greed for personal enrichment and political power, motivations that have had loud echoes ever since. Washington's Secretary of the Treasury, Alexander Hamilton, was accused of conspiring with officers of foreign governments and was caught up in a sex scandal that involved the payment of blackmail, while his Cabinet colleague Secretary of State Thomas Jefferson failed to act forthrightly in seeking the recall of the French Ambassador who tried to undercut American neutrality in the continental wars of the French Revolution. It was then, too, that the House opened its first inquiry into the conduct of a Cabinet officer (Hamilton again); that an official, Edmund Randolph, Jefferson's successor as Secretary of State, resigned after being accused (unjustly it turned out) of accepting a French bribe; and that an administration (John Adams's) and a Congress in control of the Federalist Party was attacked for violating young norms of free speech and assembly and criticism of government with the infamous Alien and Sedition Acts of 1798. The opening years of the next century saw the first successful attempt to impeach and remove from office a federal official—Judge John Pickering—as well as the first failed impeachment—that against Supreme Court Justice Samuel Chase.

Impeachment has since proved to be a blunt instrument against alleged wrongdoing—as it proved later against Presidents John Tyler, Andrew Johnson, and William J. Clinton. An indictment for treason against Vice President Aaron Burr also failed before a federal court presided over by Chief Justice John Marshall. Yet charges against federal officers and the means to investigate them and gain restitution and punishment for official misdeeds nonetheless continued to grow in number and variety, if not always in effectiveness. The modern age of alleged and proved misconduct made its appearance, as this book makes clear, toward the close of Andrew Jackson's presidency. It achieved its initial peak under James Buchanan, then re-emerged during the days of Ulysses S. Grant and Warren G. Harding, and displayed notable strength during the presidencies of Harry Truman and Ronald Reagan. Nevertheless, in many respects those charges and acts of corruption seem quaint when set against some of the misconduct of the years since 1968. It is only since then that the acts of two presidents, the only two in American history, have led them to be named—as disputed as the use and legal standing of the term may be—as explicit or implicit unindicted co-conspirators in filings in courts of law.

How are we to understand the record of misconduct since the nation's earliest days? Perhaps, given the size, complexity, and age of the United States, we should conclude that, overall, American government has been remarkably free of corruption, especially in comparison with other nations. Yet not all presidential administrations have been equally free of illegal and illicit conduct. As Woodward pointed out in 1974, it is difficult to assess administrations on a good-conduct scale. Many factors play into the record of any administration—not just breaches of public trust, but also criteria like an administration's political and policy goals, the obstacles it encounters in achieving them, and the skills it musters to succeed in doing so. Some figures in the past—James Wilkinson and Orville E. Babcock come immediately to mind—proved so irredeemably corrupt throughout their federal service in more than a single administration that their misbehavior falls into a special category of malfeasance. Across time, the number and nature of charges of corruption and the means each administration has used to address them have also turned on such external circumstances as the size of the government, the length of an administration, the contemporary canons of official conduct, the vigilance of citizens and officeholders, and the existing partisan climate.

For instance, length of time in office is a variable that must figure into any evaluation of official misdeeds. Thus while the administration of William Henry Harrison was the sole presidency to escape all charges of misconduct, the reason lies close to hand: Harrison died only one month after assuming office. As Joan Hoff shows, the brief administration of Gerald R. Ford, Jr., was similarly devoid of misconduct. Yet Harding's similarly short presidency proved among the most corrupt in American history. Alterations in law should also play a part in assessing presidential conduct. For instance, legally required competitive bidding for federal contracts has reduced, even if it has not ended, corruption in federal procurement practices, and civil service reform has gradually eroded the spoils system for appointment to the federal service. But the failure to control the intrusion of excessive amounts of private money into campaigns, the sources of those funds often hidden, has continued to lead to the repeated corruption of state and federal elections, with campaign contributions buying access to political influence and favors from public agencies. Such contextual and historical realities must guide the evaluation of each administration.

Yet all efforts at comparison are necessary and appropriate. For example, many presidents entered office with a determination to end their tenure with records unsullied by corruption and worked to achieve that goal. They established standards of good conduct for administration officials, set an example through their own good conduct, and left office with a relatively clean slate (as, in Allan J. Lichtman's telling, did Barack Obama). But the record of events recounted here by historians also shows that neither good intentions, good examples, presidential exhortations, nor existing laws dependably prevent misconduct. If, as the history of the Harding and Reagan administrations shows, a president falls victim to his good-natured naiveté, fails to control his political appointees, quails before dismissing them, or holds back from disciplining those suspected of corruption, misconduct is the likely result. Some presidents, like George H.W. Bush (as Kathryn S. Olmsted and Eric Rauchway indicate), fall victim to misconduct originating in the previous administration. Many presidents, as Jeremi Suri and Kevin M. Kruse show in the cases, respectively, of Reagan and Jimmy Carter, have more often than not been victims of malfeasance originating within their administrations rather than the instigators of it.

Some White House occupants—take Clinton, for instance, in Kathryn Cramer Brownell's telling—find themselves ensnared in controversy for failing to be truthful about private acts, embarrassing as they might be, that, owned directly up to, would not run afoul of the law save for the attempt to hide knowledge of them. Nor should the corrosive effects of sheer ideological and partisan attacks on a presidency—Clinton again—be discounted as the cause of many acts that lead an administration into a thicket of difficulties. But many administrations have also inflicted harm on themselves and others by deliberately misconstruing existing law or by covering up questionable conduct. Such was the case, as Olmsted and Rauchway make clear, during the presidency of George W. Bush. Richard Nixon's administration went further. It not only concealed knowledge of its actions, many of which were criminal; the President, whose misdeeds are recounted also by Olmsted and Rauchway, himself directed and fully participated in the misdeeds of his subordinates. A look back forty-five years to the political and constitutional turmoil in which the 1974 report was written leads to the inescapable conclusion that, through the end of the Obama presidency, Nixon's administration perpetrated the worst breaches of law and custom in the history of the presidency.

Until Nixon's administration, none of the corruption and misconduct detailed in this book precipitated a constitutional emergency. Those emergencies originated from other sources. Previous national crises did not arise from corruption, and they lacked the severity of the Watergate scandal. It was political deadlock and flaws in the system for electing presidents that brought American government to the brink of chaos. In the first of these emergencies, in 1801, an electoral vote tie between Thomas Jefferson and Aaron Burr, both of the same political party, required the House of Representatives to choose the president. Only after thirty-six votes did the House elect Jefferson on the eve of inauguration day, thus only narrowly ensuring the peaceful transfer of power from one administration to another and preserving constitutional order. In the fraud-ridden election of 1876, Democrat Samuel J. Tilden won the popular vote, but Republican Rutherford B. Hayes carried the Electoral College by a single ballot. Required to recount the electoral votes, a divided and deadlocked Congress, with the House and Senate controlled by opposing parties, improvised the appointment of a special commission to settle the crisis. Again, just short of inauguration day, the commission's members, by a partisan 8 to 7 vote, put Hayes in office but at the price of arranging for the final withdrawal of federal troops from what would become the solidly Democratic South, which dedicated itself thereafter to the oppression of African Americans. In the third analogous electoral crisis, that of 2000, the Supreme Court halted a recount of disputed votes from Florida and handed the presidency to George W. Bush. Although each of these crises raised grave constitutional issues—for example, what should be done if a presidential election remained unresolved by the date stipulated in the Constitution?—personal misconduct, the subject of this book, was not involved in any of them.

Short of civil war, the gravest threats to American democracy and government may be those brought on by a chief executive himself, as it was by Nixon, through deliberate illegal and unconstitutional conduct. The historians who prepared the 1974 report knew the general elements of that administration's misdeeds but, when they submitted their report to the Impeachment Inquiry, not its full extent. The Nixon presidency's complete record has only gradually appeared in the years since then, most recently through evidence that during the 1968 campaign and before he was inaugurated, Nixon illegally intervened to scuttle ongoing Johnson administration diplomatic negotiations to conclude the war in Vietnam. What is striking about the Nixon administration from the vantage of 2019 is the extent and willfulness of its illegal acts, acts that were prefigured before Nixon took office.

In the nation's formative years—the era of the American Revolution and the constitution-making that followed it—leading Americans warned of the dangers of a corrupt chief executive. By "corruption," eighteenth-century American patriots, with examples of European monarchs in mind, above all else meant undue executive influence over the levers of government. They wrote their federal and state constitutions to fence in presidents and governors. Fearing, in Washington's later words in his celebrated Farewell Address of 1796, "the insidious wiles of foreign influence," they placed in the Constitution a ban on the acceptance of outside emoluments by the chief executive. They provided for impeachment, gave Congress the sole power to declare war, put federal judges confirmed to office outside executive reach, and gave Congress the power to override presidential vetoes. Since then, presidential power has been further restricted by Supreme Court decisions and the addition by constitutional amendment of a two-term limit on presidential service.

But what Madison termed "parchment barriers"—mere words on paper—have never alone sufficed to check rogue presidents and their subordinate officers. Nor have these barriers prevented the growth of greatly heightened executive authority into what has been called the imperial presidency. Try as they may to discover, thwart, and punish executive misdeeds, members of Congress and the federal bench have never succeeded in deterring misconduct by determined perpetrators. Nor has the risk of exposure and risk to the legacy of a president and his appointees served as a firm deterrent.

In fact, as this book reveals, remedies for illicit and illegal conduct by presidential administrations have had a mixed record of success. Congressional oversight may expose corruption and prompt resignations, legal proceedings, and impeachments, but it often fails to offer solutions and punishments in instances of ambiguous cases of misconduct by public officials. Court proceedings, with their strict rules of standing, evidence, and verdicts, also offer no sure outcomes. Partisanship can impede, as well as advance, remedial measures. Most worrisome is that long experience has thrown doubt on the Founders' conviction that an informed and active citizenry backed by a robust free press and represented by a responsible Congress will always or easily prevail against corruption at the highest reaches of government.

Moreover, even after the passage of 230 years of government under the Constitution, some forms of misconduct have yet to be formally investigated, judged, and punished. For example, the Logan Act of 1799, which makes it a crime to negotiate with foreign powers on behalf of the United States without governmental authorization, has led to only a handful of indictments and to no successful prosecutions. Nor has the emoluments clause of the Constitution, which forbids members of the government from receiving gifts, payments, offices, or titles from foreign powers without congressional consent, ever been wielded against a sitting president. The failure to use such existing means to prevent and correct illegal and corrupt behavior is a reminder of how failures of political and legal will have enabled wrongdoers to slip out of accountability for their illegal acts.

Historical knowledge can help illuminate the context, motives, and means of presidential scandals and the successes and failures of remedial measures. But historical study is no armchair pursuit, and historians are not immune from the history they seek to understand. There comes a point at which, faced with the most severe constitutional crisis of our time, historians must put their professional knowledge and considered judgment about the state of their nation at the service of their fellow citizens. Historians may not be able to change the course of current events, but they can help decision makers avoid past mistakes and distinguish between genuine corruption and political and policy disputes. To stand by without some attempt to provide a full record against which the activities of the present administration can be compared would be a dereliction of historians' civic office. We provide this book and its factual record in the hope that everyone trying to make that comparison today will find the book of use in doing so.

ACKNOWLEDGMENTS

From the start of this project, I have had the support and dedication of people located far and wide, in different situations, and of different skills.

Unbidden good fortune played a large part in both its origin and completion. By recently, and accidentally, coming upon a reference to the 1974 report on which this book is based—while, like most historians, knowing nothing previously about it—historian Jill Lepore, subsequently writing about it for the *New Yorker*, set off the events that have led to the publication of this expanded version of the earlier study. Spotting Lepore's article, Bill Moyers brought it to the attention of Diane Wachtell, executive director of The New Press. By somewhat miraculous coincidence, she and Robert L. Bernstein, former president of Random House, had a chance conversation about Lepore's article. Bernstein passed along to Wachtell his knowledge of a then young plan, spearheaded by his son, the literary agent Peter W. Bernstein, to reawaken the former project under my direction. Wachtell conveyed to Robert Bernstein her already formed independent determination to see to the project's rebirth. That conversation led back to Peter Bernstein, who, since then, has devoted himself tirelessly and beyond the conventional responsibilities of his craft to the book's realization.

Diane Wachtell has fiercely championed and promoted the project from the start. Others at The New Press—Benjamin Woodward, Maury Botton, Brian Ulicky, Sharon Swados, Beverly Rivero, Ashia Troiano, and their many skilled associates—have proven themselves unsurpassed in their skill in bringing it to completion. The Press and I have benefited

along the way from the advice of Karol A. Kepchar, Douglas B. May-
nard, and Katherine Porter of Akin Gump. Michael Lotstein of the Yale
University Archives, unstinting in his assistance, has proven once again
how invaluable is the knowledge and dedication of archivists the world
over. Susan Woodward eased my way through some potential difficulties by her familiarity with the records of her late father-in-law, C. Vann
Woodward, and never flagged in her enthusiasm for this follow-up to
the earlier effort he managed. Eric Arnesen, Brian H. Balogh, John M.
Belohlavek, Norman S. Fiering, Meg Jacobs, Arnita Jones, Linda K. Kerber, Gerald W. McFarland, Timothy Naftali, the late Leo P. Ribuffo, Donald A. Ritchie, Bruce J. Schulman, Thomas J. Sugrue, Harry L. Watson,
Sean Wilentz, and Julian E. Zelizer gave me astute counsel or assisted
me in other ways. The essays in this book added since the 1974 edition
benefited greatly from the attentive and detailed review by Jeffrey A.
Engel.

All eight other surviving authors of the original 1974 report—James
Boylan, John W. Chambers, Mark I. Gelfand, Michael F. Holt, Robert P.
Ingalls, William E. Leuchtenburg, William S. McFeely, and Stephen B.
Oates—have backed the new project and assisted me in exhuming materials from their files not in my own. I single out especially James Boylan,
who, as always, along with Betsy Wade, gave unstintingly of his time and
energy to read and, where necessary, correct the galleys of this new edition; he also fact-checked some parts of the added material and offered
sage advice on a variety of matters. And of course this edition would
not exist save for the work, under an exacting deadline, of the authors
of the fresh sections of the book: Kathryn Cramer Brownell, Joan Hoff,
Kevin M. Kruse, Allan J. Lichtman, Kathryn S. Olmsted, Eric Rauchway,
and Jeremi Suri. Professors Olmsted and Rauchway will recognize the
grounds for my special gratitude to them. I salute them all for putting
much aside to bring to realization the book—a product of their civic
commitment as much as of their authoritative historical knowledge.

James M. Banner, Jr.
Washington, D.C.
March 4, 2019

THE CONSCIENCE OF
THE WHITE HOUSE

C. Vann Woodward

(This introduction, not included in the 1974 study submitted to the House Committee on the Judiciary, appeared subsequently in a trade edition of the report published by Delacorte Press.)

A whole book devoted exclusively to the misconduct of American presidents and their responses to charges of misconduct is without precedent. The presidents have been studied for their policies, their theories, their achievements, their character and personality, for their concept of executive power, and for comparative assessment in these and other respects. A substantial library of such works exists. Misconduct and response to charges of misconduct in the White House, however, have never before inspired a general treatment by historians.

The present work was prepared for the use of the Impeachment Inquiry Staff of the House Committee on the Judiciary in connection with the staff's study of the grounds for impeachment of the president of the United States. Members of the staff found that their investigations took them to the past as well as to the present, to the records of former presidents as well as to those of Richard M. Nixon. It was their belief that historians could provide a study which would prove useful in debates in the House of Representatives should resolutions of impeachment be recommended and, if such resolutions were adopted, also in the trial proceedings in the Senate.

Since it was impossible to know just what historical questions might arise, the historians were directed to provide a factual account without evaluation and without attempting to anticipate specific questions. Certain broad lines of historical relevance, however, could be taken for granted. Some of the allegations of misconduct and corruption brought against Richard M. Nixon had been leveled at previous presidents. Often these charges had been proved valid, either by investigation at the time or later by historians. None of the previous presidents save the first of the two Harrisons, who died after only a month in office, entirely escaped charges of some sort of misconduct or corruption. Yet none of them were removed from office because of these charges, and only one was impeached and tried, though not convicted. If all previous offenders escaped punishment, why make an exception of the most recent? If all the presidents at one time or another became involved in such charges, was it not simply "politics as usual"? What was so distinctive about the offenses of President Nixon as to justify very special treatment and set him apart from all the others?

We shall return to these questions later for what light the present study can shed upon them. Before attempting that, however, it would be well to point out certain limitations of this approach and certain dangers of making comparisons and drawing conclusions within these limits. Although it was quite incidental to the purposes of the Committee on the Judiciary, its staff's commission has resulted in the production of a work of history by professional historians. They certainly hoped that their work might prove useful for the purposes of those who commissioned it. But as historians, they have other and quite independent criteria to meet and standards to satisfy in their work.

To single out one aspect—misconduct, or any other—in the history of the American presidency from 1789 to 1969 and treat it to the exclusion of all else is to incur risks of abstraction and distortion. Though all the presidents had allegations—many of them, the realities—of misconduct to cope with in their administrations, for the great majority of them the problem was a minor concern among many larger concerns. The affliction could be compared with a slight cold or a passing headache in the medical history of a healthy man. In few administrations could this ailment—to continue the medical figure—be thought of as chronic or debilitating, and in none of them as fatal—as a cancer, for example. At least they all survived.

It would also be misleading to form any firm impressions of the relative health or virtue of presidential administrations on the basis of the number of allegations of misconduct filed against them, and certainly on the basis of the comparative space devoted to the treatment of such charges in these pages. On that basis, some of the most virtuous administrations, those of Washington and Jefferson, for example, and some of the more vigorous, such as those of Theodore Roosevelt and Harry Truman, would come off very poorly in comparison with some administrations that were exceptional for neither virtue nor vigor. Warren G. Harding had few critics. To have any validity, such comparisons would have to take into account the rigor of standards to which a particular president was held at a particular time. Allegations are not proof, and the volume of allegations may be more an index of the strength of congressional opposition, or the zeal of critics and the austerity of their standards than of the culpability of the accused. Fairness would also require some weighing of the effectiveness of a president's response to criticism and what he did about the crimes and misdemeanors with which he or his subordinates were charged. An equitable judgment would also seem to require assessment of the positive achievements of an administration against the weight of charges of misconduct.

A history of the abuses of the office of the presidency might also be subject to misuse in judgments of the institution itself. In recent years it has been not merely the occupants of the office that have come under attack, but to a lesser extent the office itself. This criticism in perhaps its most extreme form has been expressed by one historian who declares that "history plainly shows that the American presidency is the most defective major institution in any 'developed' political system."[1] Lest this study of the abuses of the presidency be construed as support for any such conclusion, it should be pointed out that its limitations preclude comparative judgment of the institution. Until the delinquencies of the heads of state in other countries between 1789 and 1969 have been similarly studied, no valid comparative judgment of the American institution is warranted. It is at least possible that the shortcomings of rulers abroad were even worse than those of rulers at home.

The only foreign contemporary model (they were uncommonly aware of ancient examples) available to the former British colonists who founded and ran the new republic during the first generation of its existence was the mother country. That model in the late eighteenth and early nineteenth centuries was not very edifying, though it was not untypical of the moral standards of the age. The sale of office was accepted and assumed as a matter of course, and sinecures abounded. The great families thought nothing of nominating worthless incompetents to office, and the civil lists were packed with their abandoned retainers and mistresses, their illegitimate children, and their poor relations. Administrative standards were generally lax, corrupt, and class-ridden. The revolt against the mother country was at least in part a revolt against those standards. One firm tenet of the revolutionists was that corruption led inevitably to tyranny and the loss of liberty. They thought this had been the history of all governments and were prepared to expect the worst of their own. Their revolutionary puritanism inspired the direst suspicions and an excessive zeal in criticism. With this spirit the early presidents of the republic had constantly to contend.[2]

It is difficult now to avoid the "golden age" fallacy in thinking of the era of the Founders and early presidents. Men of enormous prestige and formidable integrity, they held rigid standards of conduct and scrupulous regard for the Constitution. They or their friends had written it. Yet to the first presidents as well as to their critics, the early years of the republic probably seemed more like a time of troubles than a golden age. The vocabulary of criticism leveled at them was that of suspicion and resentment, and back of it were the revolution-bred fears of usurpation, monarchy, tyranny, despotism, and the "corruption" that led inevitably to decay of liberty. No one was above suspicion until he left office. A few at secondary levels deserved it, but the Federalist administrations on the whole maintained standards of conduct that were lofty, and endured abuse for offenses that were petty, in comparison with later experience. Yet Washington retired under a torrent of abuse, and John Adams fared little better.

The Jeffersonian "revolution" of 1800 did not alter in essentials the high tone of conduct set by the Federalists. The standards of their predecessors were equally acceptable to the Virginia gentlemen who succeeded them, among whom personal integrity was taken as a matter of course. Jefferson, Madison, and Monroe were no more culpable of executive misconduct, but neither were they much freer of criticism and charges of corruption. If ethical standards had not relaxed appreciably, neither had the concern of critics and the suspicions of misconduct. The latter were fed by instances of abuse among lower-level officials, but on the whole the record was still admirable from a later perspective.

Circumstances outside of government favored maintenance of high standards during the first three or four decades of presidential history. Citizens had little to ask of the federal government, and the White House had few favors to distribute. It had relatively little contact with citizens, who were generally content to be let alone. Charges of neglect, favoritism, or malfeasance were not unknown, but they were rare. The scale of operations was so small that most transactions were widely known and discussed, and relations were highly personal.

Deterioration of traditional standards set in toward the end of Andrew Jackson's administration and continued—with many exceptions and countercurrents—through the rest of the ante-bellum period. The change in government ethics was accompanied by social and economic changes. The increasing scale of business enterprise multiplied impersonal dealings as well as opportunities for unscrupulous operations and pressures that lowered business morality. The impersonal quality of life was enhanced by the growing population of cities. Government also became more impersonal and, with greater budgets and more favors to grant, more prone to corruption. Citizens grew more demanding of government. President Polk complained in 1846 that "The City is swarming with manufacturers," and six years later James Buchanan wrote Franklin Pierce of "hosts of contractors, speculators, stock jobbers, & lobby members which haunt the halls of Congress . . . to get their arms in the public Treasury."[3]

Although some members of the old ruling class still remained in high office, their numbers declined with the democratization of politics. Gentlemen in office became rarer, and the class of politicians who replaced them did not improve ethical standards. As the arm of the government extended, White House control over remote field services grew lax. Machines and swindlers took over the long payrolls of several custom houses, post offices, and revenue collectors. Men were often retained in office long after they were proved guilty of gross and repeated violations of the law either on the ground that alternative appointments would be even more corrupt or, as a congressional committee report said in 1839, "because they possessed extensive political influence, and were useful and active partisans." After Andrew Jackson's customs collector of the Port of New York defaulted and fled to Europe, President Van Buren appointed a successor who outdid his predecessor in several respects before he also decamped.[4]

The amount of corruption exposed in a particular administration did not necessarily indicate the amount that occurred. The exposure might coincide more closely with the opportunities of the exposers and the thoroughness of their investigations. In James Buchanan's ill-starred administration, however, the extent of misconduct and zeal for its exposure coincided remarkably. Congressmen of the new Republican Party took the lead in uncovering Democratic misconduct. Much of the improper conduct had been practiced since Jackson's time, but it culminated and flourished most luxuriantly under Buchanan. Corruption of the public press and the election process and of government agencies was uncovered in appalling amounts. Buchanan had made no serious attempt to stop known malfeasance in custom houses, navy yards, post offices, and public printing contracts, and he vehemently resisted congressional investigation. His administration marked the low point before the Civil War and somewhat approached later levels of corruption.

In the post-war period a new record was set by President Grant's administration, though its distinction was more in pervasiveness and extent than in depth of corruption. In kind, the corruption was much the same, only much more extensive. It pervaded every executive department and involved Cabinet members, White House staff, members of the Grant families, and many thought the President himself. The exposure came this time at the hands of Democratic investigators with the aid of the dissident Republicans. As indefensible and degrading as it was, the corruption typical of the Grant era had no more sinister purpose than self-aggrandizement of the officials concerned or of their associates outside the government. It involved no scheme to subvert constitutional rights and liberties and no plan to aggrandize the power of one branch of the government over another. Nor was there evidence of any general conspiracy—certainly none attributable to the President himself.

The contours of the next peak of disgrace in the White House are roughly similar. President Warren G. Harding, however, was in office only two and a half years before his death. The proliferation of graft that characterized Grant's eight years was not only limited in Harding's brief term by time but also by the presence in his Cabinet of such formidable figures of probity as Charles Evans Hughes, Herbert Hoover, and the earlier Henry Wallace. In spite of the limitations of time and opportunity, however, corruption at high level rivaled any previously recorded, though Harding probably died unaware of the worst of it. Later revelations landed one cabinet member in jail and destroyed the reputations of two more. Even so, the flagrant corruption of the Harding era partook of much the same quality of "innocence" that characterized the greed and self-aggrandizement of Gilded Age miscreants.

So accustomed are we to identifying presidents with their times, to making them symbols of their moment in national history and expressions of its spirit, that we find it difficult to separate the man from the age. It is as impossible to divorce U.S. Grant from the grossness depicted in Mark Twain's *Gilded Age* as to divorce Harding from the laxity and apathy of Sinclair Lewis's *Main Street.* Certainly the delinquencies for which their administrations were best known were no major cause of alienation from their contemporaries. After the worst was exposed about his two terms in office, Grant seriously expected, and came near winning, election to a third term. It might well have been the same for Harding. Death intervened before the worst was known, but the outpouring of grief accompanying the train bearing his body back to Washington from the West Coast was described by the New York *Times* as "the most remarkable demonstration in American history of affection, respect, and reverence for the dead."[5]

It is easy to slip from identification of the man with his times to adoption of a vulgar fallacy of determinism—the popular theory that the quality of the presidency is determined by the character of the age and its spiritual climate. With due concession to the plausibilities of the theory, it is hard to reconcile with fact. Grant was preceded by Lincoln and Johnson and followed by Rutherford B. Hayes. Each had shortcomings of his own, different from those of the others, and all quite different from those of Grant. Then, too, Harding followed immediately upon the heels of a stern Calvinist named Woodrow Wilson and was succeeded by a "Puritan in Babylon," Calvin Coolidge. The spirit of the times does not always obligingly change with the change of guard at the White House.

One incident in February, 1881, related by John Sproat in his account of Hayes, brilliantly illustrates the level of public ethics on which four presidents and one perennial aspirant for the office found themselves simultaneously equated. It was a dinner in honor of the manager of the campaign that had recently elected Garfield president. Former President Grant presided, and future President Chester A. Arthur, then Vice

President-elect, made the chief address. Would-be President James G. Blaine wrote President-elect Garfield that the "true intent and meaning" of the dinner was to enable "a small cabal to steal half a million a year during your administration." Neither Blaine nor Garfield thought of informing incumbent President Hayes (nor did Grant or Arthur), since it was assumed that he already knew of and tolerated the cabal's fraudulent operations in his own administration.

Periodic jeremiads and lamentations over the decline of the republic and its morals have been inspired by misconduct in the White House. For if some believed the ethical standards of the presidency were determined by the times, others considered the moral level in the White House a faithful barometer of the climate of national morals. One such jeremiad in 1884 is not untypical:

> In whatever direction we turn, this phenomenon meets our eye; and there is no branch of business, no department of government, and no class in society in which it does not appear. . . . Fraudulent contracts, sinister legislation, bought and paid for by those whom it benefits, trading of offices and votes, and all the various methods of robbing the public for the benefit of a few, have become so common among us as hardly to awaken surprise when exposed to public view.[6]

Yet these lamentations came on the eve of Grover Cleveland's first administration, one noted for the relative rarity of the evils lamented. Moralists have, in fact, not been able to establish any linear progression of national morals or any firm correlation between the state of the nation and the state of the presidency.

Comparing the ethical standards of William McKinley's administration with those during Grant's, Leonard D. White finds the change for the better to be "marked and dramatic."[7] With Cleveland's second administration and the presidencies of Herbert Hoover and Franklin Roosevelt in mind, it is tempting to suggest a correlation between hard times and high standards in the White House. The trouble is that depressions have not invariably produced presidents with the ethical standards of Cleveland, Hoover, and Roosevelt. Depression overtook Buchanan and swamped Grant's second term, and whether the economic troubles of the 1970s are rightly called "depression" or something else, they do not seem to have fostered the highest level of purity in the White House.

Since reformers are often prominent in the uncovering of presidential misconduct, a correlation has been suggested between periods of reform and disgraced administrations—with the implied corollary that the disgraced are those who get caught and that reformers catch them. The acceptability of that correlation, however, is embarrassed by the instance of Wilson, who presided over a period of reform and was not disgraced by scandal, and the instance of Harding, who did not coincide with a reform period and yet was covered with disgrace.

One of the favorite gambits in the game of presidential typology is dividing the "weak" from the "strong" chief executives. Nearly all American presidents have been tagged, rightly or wrongly, as one or the other, though some continue to be perpetually in dispute. In popular favor, the "strong" presidents almost invariably outrank the "weak." Professor E. S. Corwin, one of the most confident typologists, goes so far as to say that "the history of the Presidency has been a history of aggrandizement" and to assume executive expansion to be an index of national unity and well-being.[8] A shrewd English observer has noted the growing American assumption "that what has been good for the Presidency has been good for the country."[9] The national predilection for the "strong" presidents has naturally fathered the wish to see them as rising above allegations of misconduct, and the "weak" as typically prone to such charges. Comfort for these identifications is derived from thinking of the "weak" Buchanan, Grant, and Harding and the "strong" Polk, Wilson, and Franklin Roosevelt. On the other hand, little but discomfort for the theory comes of contemplating the administrations of the "weak" William McKinley and Herbert Hoover and the allegations that plagued the "strong" Theodore Roosevelt and Harry Truman. Correlation between corruption and post-war periods is also troubled by exceptions.

Such reflections tend to discourage attempts at broad generalization about presidential morals. And they do not particularly encourage efforts to establish correlations between changes in White House ethical standards and the shifting tides of the business cycle, political reform, social malaise, and health of national morals. Further study may establish such correlations. Until then contemplation of the whole matter tends rather to point to the need for knowledge of individual presidents,

the ethical standards to which they held themselves and their subordinates accountable, the relative gravity of the offenses of which they
were accused, and the different ways in which they responded to allegations of misconduct, as well as the dispatch with which they dealt with
miscreants.

There was the case of President Monroe's furniture, which James
Banner relates. Congress had appropriated money to furnish the White
House, burnt out by British troops. But the furniture was slow in com-
ing from abroad, and Monroe moved in with his own French furniture.
He had intended to sell the collection privately in order to finance pres-
idential travels, for which there were no government appropriations.
Instead he received small advances from the Treasury on his furniture.
The loans bore no interest, but Monroe had agreed to absorb costs of
wear and tear on his furniture. Yet concern over the use of public funds
for private ends prompted two congressional investigations.

The Lincoln family also had furniture problems, recounted by Stephen Oates. The furniture appropriation for the White House in 1861
was the same as that of 1817, $20,000. But Mary Todd Lincoln, a com-
pulsive spender, overshot the limit by $6,700 and surreptitiously tried
to get the government to cover the excess. Declaring that this would be
a "stink in the nostrils of the American people," Lincoln paid the bill
out of his own pocket. Such antique punctilio did not wholly disappear
with the Monroes and Lincolns. Franklin Roosevelt's Secretary of the
Interior, Harold Ickes, for example, could work up unfeigned concern
over allegations that the PWA had mishandled $47 worth of cement in
the Virgin Islands.

Personal gifts were a recurrent problem for presidents, some of whom
were more sensitive than others on the matter. John Quincy Adams was
determined to return a gift of soap to a manufacturer until dissuaded by
his wife. President Jackson was extremely annoyed by the gift of a lion
and two horses from the Emperor of Morocco and asked Congress how
to dispose of the animals. President Polk drew the line against any gift
of more value than a book or a cane. Buchanan ruled out any gifts at all,
even from intimate friends, and sternly reproved his niece Harriet Lane
for entertaining friends on the Potomac in the public vessel named in
her honor.[10] Presidential attitudes on gifts had undergone considerable
change by the era of Eisenhower, who deemed a gift "not necessarily a

bribe," but "a tangible expression of friendship." The general declared the conduct of a public servant had "to be impeccable both from the standpoint of law and the standpoint of ethics," but he was able to reconcile that belief with the acceptance of an estimated $300,000 worth of gifts in livestock and agricultural machinery for his Gettysburg farm. His aide, Sherman Adams, was less fortunate in reconciling gifts with current ethical standards.

American presidents have differed widely in their manner of responding to charges of misconduct against themselves and their subordinates. The differences occur in the degree of their cooperativeness with congressional investigators, in the speed with which they have acted to correct abuses, in the limits to which they have gone to protect offenders and cover up their offenses, and in the severity with which they have dealt with offenders.

The shattering experience of President Washington's secretary of state Edmund Randolph will illustrate one extreme of severity. A shining light among the framers of the Constitution, former governor of Virginia, and personal friend of both Washington and Jefferson, Randolph was suddenly called on the carpet by the President and confronted with a captured document that seemed to implicate him in treasonous dealings with the French. When he was unable to give a satisfactory explanation on the spot, his resignation was summarily accepted. Much later it appeared that Randolph had been the victim of an injustice, but he left George Washington's terrible presence with his political career in ruins and his reputation darkened for life.

Lincoln also dealt with a charge of treason, but in a manner characteristically his own. A congressional committee was meeting secretly, without notice to the President, to investigate reports that Mary Todd Lincoln was passing state secrets to some of her numerous Confederate kin. With no warning at all, the President suddenly entered the meeting room alone. A silence fell, which Lincoln finally broke by saying, "It is untrue that any of my family hold treasonable communication with the enemy." He then left the room as quietly as he had entered it. The silence continued until the chairman declared the committee adjourned and the matter under consideration dropped.

Too frequently presidents under fire proved less than cooperative with congressional investigating committees. Few defied demands for relevant documents for long, but compliance was often slow-footed and reluctant. Defenders of Buchanan, Coolidge, and Eisenhower protested that congressional investigators were engaging in a "fishing expedition" by extensive demand for documents. The minority report of the committee giving Buchanan so much trouble pronounced the investigation a "witch hunt," and Buchanan protested that he was not seeking to save his own reputation, but "the Presidential office itself," which his critics were degrading by their slander. None of the presidents cited as protesting innocence and resisting exposure could say, as John Quincy Adams said of James Madison, that it was like asking "a blooming virgin to exhibit herself before a multitude." (Adams himself, of all people, had been charged with "pimping" to the Emperor of All the Russias while a minister to his court.)

A besetting fault of presidents under fire was a dogged and frequently misplaced loyalty to subordinates drawing the fire. Sometimes the forgivable quality of loyalty was mixed with political timidity and something like moral cowardice. Only such a mixture could explain Buchanan's failure to demand the resignation of his secretary of war John B. Floyd. The Virginian's incompetence, carelessness, favoritism, and weak compliance with war contract swindlers had discredited him with congressmen of both parties. Yet long after Floyd's disgrace was public knowledge and self-confessed, Buchanan continued to tolerate his attendance at cabinet meetings. Floyd finally resigned at the end of December, 1860, with a charade of righteous indignation over the President's policy toward South Carolina in the secession crisis.

A special point of vulnerability for several presidents was the personal aide and his chief's loyalty to him. A few of the numerous examples that come to mind are Grant and his Orville Babcock, Coolidge and his C. Bascom Slemp, Truman and his Harry Vaughan, Eisenhower and his Sherman Adams. None of these latter presidential aides remotely rivaled Babcock for persistent and repeated malfeasance and the utterly blind loyalty he commanded from a president. Babcock joined Grant's staff at Vicksburg in 1863, and after that bloody bond he could do no wrong, and Grant would hear no wrong of him. Year after year Babcock's name cropped up in scandal after scandal, sometimes at the center of it, yet through it all and to the bitter end the trusting general maintained that his friend was innocent.

It is only fair to the more recent presidents to remember that the opportunities for abuse of confidence expanded with the expansion of those in whom confidence had to be invested. The growth of White House staff had been quite slow during its first century. Jefferson made do with one messenger and a secretary. Grant had only two professional staff members, and Wilson fought the First World War with the assistance of seven aides. The expansion started under Franklin Roosevelt, and since 1939 more than 170 professional aides have moved in and out of the White House. But the great escalation occurred only since the Second World War. By 1970 the White House staff alone totaled nearly 550 members of all grades, not to mention hundreds in the Bureau of the Budget and elsewhere. By 1971 the budget for "special functions" and "clerical assistance" of the vice president alone was considerably larger than funds for the entire White House staff less than twenty-five years before.[11] This is not to suggest that increases in staff delinquencies were proportional to increases in staff numbers. The recent record, however, of seven former staff members in one administration serving jail sentences and others awaiting trial is without precedent.

Serious considerations of the impeachment of presidents—including the only bill of impeachment adopted by the House and brought to trial in the Senate—were not prompted in Congress by graft and misconduct of the sort that disgraced the more unfortunate administrations. Rather, they were prompted by head-on clashes between a president and Congress over grave constitutional and political issues. If it had commanded the necessary votes, Congress would have impeached Andrew Jackson over the removal of government deposits from the Second Bank of the United States. Instead, the Senate voted 26–20 to "censure" him and provoked from Jackson a demand for impeachment that he might defend himself at trial. Others have—more or less ingenuously—demanded it on the same ground.

Congress did invoke the impeachment process against two later presidents, John Tyler and Andrew Johnson. In the first instance, it sheathed the formidable weapon it had half drawn before bringing it to bear, and in the second it followed through with the stroke but fell short of decapitation by one vote in the Senate trial. The issues that brought things to this pass were similar in both crises, and so were the peculiar political circumstances of the presidents. Both Tyler and Johnson were elected vice president and succeeded to the White House on the death of a president, and both quickly found themselves irreconcilably alienated from the congressmen of the party that had elected them and that they then headed.

By repeated use of his veto power and his appointing and removal powers, Tyler completely frustrated the legislative program of the Whig Party and its congressmen. Enraged by his obstructionist tactics and his claim of executive privilege, the Whigs read Tyler out of the party. A committee headed by former president John Quincy Adams, then a member of the House, reported that Tyler's misconduct deserved impeachment, but failed to recommend the process because of the lack of votes to convict in the Senate. The House accepted the report by a majority of 100 to 80, thus clearly implying that Tyler was impeachable. When nine formal articles of impeachment were presented, however, the House defeated a motion to appoint a committee to investigate, again because of expected failure of conviction in the Senate.

Andrew Johnson faced the same kind of charges—the abuse of presidential powers of veto, appointment, and removal from office to obstruct and frustrate the legislative program of Congress—in this case the laws for the Reconstruction of the former Confederate states. For such obstruction, Johnson was undoubtedly responsible. Unable to marshal adequate support for impeachment on these grounds, or to find evidence to sustain charges of crime or misdemeanor, or to support the absurd allegation that he had conspired to murder Lincoln, the impeachers finally rested their case on a technical charge of violation of the Tenure of Office Act in removing Secretary of War Edwin M. Stanton from office. It was a flimsy case. For one thing it was doubtful that the law was constitutional, and for another it was doubtful that it covered Stanton, or if it did, that Johnson had violated it. Even so, the impeachers came within one vote of getting the two-thirds majority required to convict in the Senate.

It is significant that neither of the presidents heretofore seriously threatened by impeachment could be found culpable for the sort of misconduct that has been the main preoccupation of congressional investigations of other administrations, the sort that crowds the following pages. That is, the favoritism and graft and corruption that feed individual and corporate greed and have been perpetrated surreptitiously.

Typically, the American president under attack for, shall we say, the "traditional" kind of misconduct was the victim, not the perpetrator, of malfeasance. He was the victim of a subordinate's indiscretion or duplicity, or the greed of his friends or subordinates' friends. In short, the president was typically the victim of some manner of betrayal. Apart from the offices of overzealous solicitors of campaign contributions and numerous fixers of elections, the president was not the beneficiary of misconduct. Nor was the misconduct directed by him, or the result of his plan or conspirational purpose. More often than not, he remained unaware, or dimly aware, of the misdemeanors until they were publicly exposed. His offense usually lay in negligence or in indecision about correcting the offensive practices or discharging the accused.

Heretofore, no president has been proved to be the chief coordinator of the crime and misdemeanor charged against his own administration as a deliberate course of conduct or plan. Heretofore, no president has been held to be the chief personal beneficiary of misconduct in his administration or of measures taken to destroy or cover up evidence of it. Heretofore, the malfeasance and misdemeanor have had no confessed ideological purpose, no constitutionally subversive ends. Heretofore, no president has been accused of extensively subverting and secretly using established government agencies to defame or discredit political opponents and critics, to obstruct justice, to conceal misconduct and protect criminals, or to deprive citizens of their rights and liberties. Heretofore, no president has been accused of creating secret investigative units to engage in covert and unlawful activities against private citizens and their rights.

For all the great variations in style and sensitivity in the conscience of the White House from 1789 to 1969, they do little to prepare us for the innovations of the ensuing period of five and a half years. A search of the long history of misconduct charged against the presidents down to 1969—the record that follows—will fail to disclose many of the abuses of that office, many combinations and concentrations of abuses, and many new uses and purposes of such abuses, that have subsequently become increasingly familiar to American citizens.

NOTES

[1]Lee Benson, *Toward the Scientific Study of History* (Philadelphia, 1972), 318–319.

[2]Leonard D. White, *The Federalists* (New York, 1961), 468–469.

[3]Leonard D. White, *The Jeffersonians* (New York, 1951), 412–13, 422; *The Jacksonians* (New York, 1954), 411–416.

[4]White, *Jacksonians,* 411–428.

[5]Emmet John Hughes, *The Living Presidency* (New York, 1973), 85–86, 94–95, 273–274.

[6]*Century Magazine,* XXVIII (1884), 463.

[7]Leonard D. White, *The Republican Era: 1869–1901* (New York, 1958), 379.

[8]E. S. Corwin, *The President: Office and Powers* (New York, 1957), 29–30.

[9]Marcus Cunliffe, *American Presidents and the Presidency* (London, 1969), 111.

[10]White, *The Jacksonians,* 431–33.

[11]Hughes, *The Living Presidency,* 138–139, 143.

A NOTE ON THE TEXT

The text on which much of this book is based is a report submitted to the Impeachment Inquiry of the House Committee on the Judiciary in June 1974. The original text resides in the archives of the committee, unavailable for examination, under House rules, for fifty years after its preparation. No other original copy of the report is known to exist.

Because the report was commissioned by, submitted to, and accepted by the Judiciary Committee, its text fell into the public domain. Possibly from a copy retained by C. Vann Woodward, who directed the original study, the report's contents were subsequently published in book form by Delacorte Press as *Responses of the Presidents to Charges of Misconduct*. Woodward wrote an introduction for the Delacorte edition that was not part of the text submitted to the Judiciary Committee. The contents of the Delacorte book, including Woodward's introduction, are fully embodied in this one and appear as originally published. No changes to them—save for necessary corrections to typographical errors, small alterations to format, or rare inappropriate wordage—have been made, even changes that might now, under other circumstances, be occasioned by the more recent discovery of additional evidence. The notes to the original text also remain as they were and have not been brought up to date.

What is new to this volume is coverage of the eight completed administrations that have followed that of Lyndon B. Johnson, plus an introduction by this edition's editor. The approach to these additions follows that of the original report. Notes serve principally to lead readers to sources, not to introduce them to every element of the existing scholarly literature on each presidency.

PRESIDENTIAL MISCONDUCT

GEORGE WASHINGTON
1789–1797

Lance Banning

Introduction

Historians have reached no consensus in their interpretations of the administrations of George Washington and John Adams, but two statements can be made with little fear of contradiction. At the senior levels of the executive department during the first decade of the national government, there was no behavior that can unequivocally be described as misconduct in office. Yet there has never been a time in the American past when allegations of misuse of executive power and suspicions of administration motives have assumed a tone more extreme.

These paradoxical statements can be understood only by reference to the context of a distinctive age. The Federal Period was a stage in the American Revolution, the time when the Founders sought to put their political principles into effect on the national level. To them, this was a project for the ages, one that would determine the future of liberty in the world. Every important action had to be taken in light of revolutionary principle and with a view toward the many generations who would live with the results. The nature of the age thus shaped its leaders' conduct. It also made certain that their actions would be judged in the harshest light.

Washington and the men around him came to their national offices as heroes of a great revolution, their places in history already secure. Valuing so highly their reputations with the people and posterity, Presidents Washington and Adams and their advisers seldom slipped from a rigid standard of personal integrity and scrupulous regard for the laws.

As much, perhaps, as men can be, they were simply above the kinds of conduct that later generations have come to associate with the abuse of power.[1]

But this did not shield them from accusations such as few American leaders have ever had to hear. In 1789, when the federal government went into effect, Americans shared no agreement about what a federal republic should be like. The new constitution was a piece of parchment which a majority of the people may well have opposed. It provided, at best, only an outline of a working government, and the outline meant different things to different men. There was one point on which most Americans did agree: it would be extremely difficult—perhaps impossible—to provide a single, republican government over so vast and varied a country. Certainly, each step at this beginning would have to be watched with the most conscientious suspicion, so that a hard-won liberty would not be lost. Such was the atmosphere of the Federal years, 1789–1801, and in this atmosphere it proved impossible for leaders to avoid the charge that their conduct was not only corrupt but deliberately inimical to the liberty they were sworn to preserve.[2]

"Corruption" is a hateful word in any age, but the word had larger meaning in the time of the Founders than it does today. To them, any uses of public trust for private ends were indications of a deeper malaise. Corruption referred not just to these practices, but also to a larger process of which they were commonly a part. The word suggested a progressive degeneration of the body politic, a process often compared with growth of cancer in organic bodies. There was nothing the Founders feared so much as corruption in their special sense. Once started, corruption was all but impossible to reverse. The state so infected ran its course to political death. And the revolutionary heritage assured the Founders that corruption was the normal direction of political change, the fate of every previous state.[3]

In one of its aspects, the American Revolution was the last great expression of a current in political thought that came down to the Founders from classical times. Transmitted to America by way of the English inheritance, this neoclassical politics sought a way to combine liberty with stability in a state.[4] Following its precepts, the Founders believed that no simple form of government could achieve this end. Because men will pursue their selfish interests at other men's expense, no single man or single group of men—not even a majority—can be wholly trusted with the welfare of a state. Absolute control by a majority will prove oppressive to minorities just as surely as control by a single individual will prove oppressive to all the rest. History will be an endless cycle of governmental degeneration, oppression, and revolt. Escape from instability and liberty for all depends on a form of government in which the powers of different branches and different principles are balanced against one another in a system of complicated checks. In this form only can the strength of a single executive be combined with wisdom and concern for the common good into a just and stable government where the law is supreme.

Even a balanced government must be constantly guarded against corruption or decay. It is hard to strike the proper balance between the parts, harder still to see that the original equilibrium is maintained. The very independence and self-interest which assure that each branch will check the others make it certain that each will also seek a larger share of power for itself. Success by any branch in the inevitable quest for larger power means constitutional decay. The government will increasingly approximate a simpler form. The rule of law will tend increasingly to become a rule of men, and liberty will be lost.

Thirteen years before the First Federal Congress assembled in New York, America had severed its ties with England. In no small part, independence had come because Americans had concluded that the supposedly balanced constitution of England had become an executive tyranny in disguise. By corrupting the members of Parliament, Americans believed, the men around the King had achieved complete control. That done, the tyrants of Britain planned to destroy American liberty as well. The American Revolution was an effort to defeat this plot and to secure the lasting happiness of an independent people by once more returning to a government of laws—this time, a republican government, with equal rights and equal laws, which might be more secure against the ravages of conspiracy and decay.[5]

The Federal Constitution was the last in a series of efforts to achieve a balanced government that would fulfill the republican ideal.[6] To the classic defense of checks and balances, its framers had added a further protection for liberty in the division between state and federal power. But no one could be certain that the experiment would succeed. The new government must become a fact. It must do so under the steady stare of a generation who could not yet define what "republicanism" would mean, but who had been reared and blooded in the belief that the balance between liberty and stability is a very fragile thing. These men had grown up in the conviction that governments are prone to decay. All their thought and experience taught them that power is subject to conspiratorial abuse. The administrations of Washington and John Adams, and to a lesser extent of the Jeffersonians which followed, are incomprehensible without an awareness of this heritage of thought.

Pater Patriae

George Washington came to the presidency by unanimous vote of the Electoral College. In 1789 his presence at the head of the government was sufficient by itself to assure the new constitution a period of trial. He was the savior of his people's liberty, *pater patriae* in the classical phrase so full of meaning in his time. He was a modern Cincinnatus, who had left his farm to save his country and had retired when the struggle was over, though he might conceivably have made himself a dictator or king. But then he had to place his reputation at risk by trying to make himself a model for republican heads of state.[7] The result was as he feared. The old hero left office in a storm of vituperative abuse.

Washington would appear to have been almost immune. His reputation with the people made opponents wary of direct attacks. Circumstances further strengthened his position. In the first years of the federal government, no one knew for certain what a president was supposed to be. It was not clear whether governmental policy should be attributed to the president or, as in England, to the cabinet ministers who served the head of state.[8] Washington himself was modest about his talents and about the chief executive's constitutional role. He made it a consistent policy never to comment on matters pending in Congress. He surrounded himself with a brilliant cabinet and listened to them carefully, reserving his own opinion until all the advice was in. Decisions were ultimately the President's, but the planning or policy and its management through Congress usually were not.[9]

In these circumstances, Washington maintained for several years a position largely above the political battles which rose with mounting fury in the country. It was small satisfaction. The President necessarily saw attacks on administration policies as criticisms of himself, and he was sorely stung by the infrequent reflections on his own conduct. Soon, moreover, the members of his cabinet were forming rival parties, accusing one another of evil designs. He struggled hard for unity, without success. Then, gradually, events required decisions that were undeniably his own. In the end, the first president was subjected almost daily to charges that he was bent on betraying the country he loved.

Alexander Hamilton and the Financial Program (1790–1792)

Apart from the organization of its own agencies and provision of an adequate revenue for the country, the most important task before the new federal government was the establishment of public credit by the funding of the revolutionary debt. Congress gave the task to Alexander Hamilton, Secretary of the Treasury.

Hamilton's solution to the problem was a brilliant one. The federal debt was re-funded at full value with permanent provision for regular payment; state debts were assumed by the federal government; a national bank was erected partly on the solid securities thus obtained by private investors. The bank's notes and the federal securities gave the country an adequate currency at last, and the fiscal program restored the power to borrow to a bankrupt state. The Secretary of the Treasury had reason for his hope that the new financial structure might encourage economic power that would eventually rival Britain's own.[10]

But Hamilton met fierce opposition from areas and interests that might be adversely affected by his plan. Assumption of state debts was almost defeated in Congress, where the opposition was led by James Madison, the most respected member of the House. The national bank became a fact only after Hamilton convinced the President that Madison and Thomas Jefferson, Madison's friend in the cabinet, were mistaken in their argument that the Constitution gave Congress no power to charter an institution of this sort. By the summer of 1791, these two famous Virginians had concluded that Hamilton's plans and constitutional constructions threatened a dangerous augmentation of federal power, which must ultimately prove oppressive. Offering Philip Freneau a part-time position as translator in Jefferson's Department of State, they encouraged the revolutionary poet to come to the capital to start a news-paper which would counteract the pro-Hamiltonian press. During the fall and winter, as Freneau's *National Gazette* added its voice to those of other critics of the fiscal program, the emerging opposition concluded that the threat from the Treasury was even more serious than Jefferson and Madison had originally believed.[11]

Many Americans entered into the new government fully expecting that it might quickly suffer corruption and decay. Among the signs an-ticipated were a financial system resting on a funded debt and a priv-ileged bank. It was a matter of general belief that the British financial system was one of the contrivances that wicked ministers had used to destroy the balanced constitution of England. In essentials, Hamilton's financial program was a duplicate of Britain's. Critics decided that it was intended to have the same effect.[12]

During the first half of 1792, led by the *National Gazette,* the opposi-tion press began to advance a grave indictment of administration policy. The newspapers charged that Alexander Hamilton, acting virtually as a prime minister, was engaged in nothing less than a conspiracy to sub-vert the liberty of his country. Hamilton's program, the accusation ran, enriched a few public creditors and holders of bank stock at the pub-lic's expense. Dependent for their fortunes on the favor of the Treasury, these powerful men were committed to follow the Secretary's every whim. There were enough of them in Congress to assure that the legis-lature would invariably follow the executive's command. In the country at large, it was said, their corrupt example subverted habits of honesty and honest work, while their tax-supported riches opened a chasm be-tween rich and poor which could only be disastrous for a republican state. The intentions behind developments were as plain as their results. Hamilton's constitutional opinions, his critics held, tended to transform a federal government into a national state. His economic program, they charged, subverted the will of the people by creating in the legislature a "corrupt squadron" that tended to deliver the whole power of the cen-tral government to the feared executive branch. In this way, Hamilton had found an underhanded means to secure a change of government. He had often expressed his suspicion of the people and his admiration of the British system. Now he was directing a workable conspiracy to return to the rule of aristocrats and kings.[13]

This was the burden of charges in newspapers which spoke for an opposition that called itself "Republican," because it feared a conspiracy to destroy a government of the popular sort. It was the same accusation which, in letters and private conversations, Secretary of State Thomas Jefferson was repeating to the President himself.[14]

Washington did not yet act. He could not take seriously the accusations that there was a design to create an American monarchy, though he did ask Hamilton to respond to the criticism of his program. Washington was irritated by newspapers which tended to incite opposition to the infant government and necessarily implied an indirect criticism of the man who signed the laws, but he made it a policy not to reply to the press. He was worried by the growing evidence of political division, for he hoped above all to hold together both the cabinet and the country. Perhaps he would have to abandon his hope of retiring at the end of his first term.[15]

Hamilton, Jefferson, and the Newspaper War (1792)

The political storm that had been forming burst upon Washington and the country in the summer of 1792. Having concluded that Jefferson and Madison were "at the head of a faction decidedly hostile to me and my administration and actuated by views ... subversive of the principles of good government," Hamilton felt he must reply to the opposition's mounting attacks.[16] On July 25, 1792, writing under a pseudonym for the *Gazette of the United States*, he hit squarely at the connection between Jefferson and the Republican press. "The editor of the *National Gazette* receives a salary from government," he charged, asking "whether this salary is paid him for translations or for publications the design of which is to vilify those to whom the voice of the people has committed the administration of public affairs."[17]

Over the next weeks, Hamilton pushed forward his counterattack, calling on the Secretary of State to resign his office if he could not support the administration. Jefferson's friends came immediately to his defense, while Freneau began a bitter feud with the *Gazette of the United States* over the relative independence of the rival editors.[18] The fact was that both Hamilton and Jefferson habitually supported, if they did not exactly control or manage, a partisan press.[19]

In the newspaper battles that summer, the identity of the various writers was poorly disguised, and citizens everywhere felt a growing pressure to take sides in the spectacular warfare between the officers of government. In August, increasingly alarmed, Washington appealed to both principals for tolerance and an end to the public dispute.[20] Though both men were chastened by the presidential appeal, neither was willing to withdraw. Hamilton explained that his quarrel was not simply personal. It was with a "formed party" in Congress and in the country which meant to destroy the federal government by overturning the fiscal program.[21] In much the same spirit, Jefferson denied that he controlled Freneau and once again insisted that Hamilton's system "was calculated to undermine and demolish the republic."[22]

Despite Washington's appeal, the public dispute continued to widen, as Hamilton and others questioned Jefferson's attitude toward the Constitution while the Republicans developed their theme of a Hamiltonian conspiracy against the republic. The President watched in resigned concern, reluctantly giving up his hope for retirement. No other man, both sides told him, could hold the country together in the face of sectional disagreements and party strife.[23] The newspaper war went on unabated until the end of the year, when Hamilton was confronted with Republican knowledge of the Reynolds Affair and decided to desist.[24]

The Investigation of Hamilton (1793)

For some time Republican attacks on the Hamiltonian system had occasionally been repeated on the floor of Congress. But the second session of the Second Congress was a party battleground. In January, 1793, Republicans in the House began to flood the Treasury with demands for reports on its activities, probing for a weakness they could hit. Understandably annoyed, Hamilton exhausted himself to meet the demands, but not without a biting reference to the harassment. Legislative sensibilities were provoked by his reply, and the Republicans pressed forward their inquiry into his conduct.

The results were disappointing. Had the investigative arm of Congress been better developed—it was, in fact, virtually nonexistent—the outcome might have been different. Hamilton was not above reproach.

Years later he would publicly confess to sexual misconduct while he was Secretary of the Treasury—the Reynolds Affair—and this involved possible ramifications of an official nature.[25] He could be blamed for giving the second position in the Treasury to William Duer, a bosom friend as well as a notorious speculator who might have been expected to use his office for private gain. After Duer voluntarily resigned, Hamilton and the Treasury failed to press him for $200,000 owed to the government, thereby enabling Duer to engage in gigantic speculations and frauds that caused in 1792 the first financial panic in the nation's history.[26] But when the comptroller of the Treasury finally brought suit against Duer, hastening his collapse, Hamilton did nothing to protect him and, of course, never profited from his schemes.

As part of his campaign to promote manufacturing enterprise in the United States, Hamilton, with Duer and others, established the Society for Useful Manufactures—a gigantic industrial corporation—under a privileged New Jersey charter in 1791. In this connection Hamilton prevailed upon the Bank of New York, a favored depository of federal funds, to extend low interest loans to the Society with explicit assurances that Treasury generosity to the bank would continue. The evidence was sufficiently incriminating on the relations between the Treasury and banks and corporations, in the judgment of Hamilton's recent biographer, that had it become known the Republicans "perhaps could have driven him from the administration."[27] But the evidence was not known to Congress or to the President, whose confidence in Hamilton was never shaken. It was part of Hamilton's wisdom in statecraft to associate private gains with public benefits, but he was above profiting for himself from such arrangements. He sought fame, not lucre, and he lived by a code which placed too high a value on public service and personal honor to engage in self-serving misconduct.[28]

The Republicans' quarrel with Hamilton was fundamentally ideological, but they needed some specific incident of misconduct if they were to secure the congressional censure that might force him to resign. For lack of any evidence that the Secretary was involved in speculation or in improper relationships with corporations and banks, they settled for a technical charge of illegality in the administration of certain loans authorized by Congress. In 1790 Hamilton had mixed together two loans which Congress had meant to keep separate, applying monies intended for payment of the foreign debt to domestic operations and domestic monies to the foreign debt. This exercise of discretion was hardly more culpable than his impolite response to congressional harassment, but it was all the Republicans had. So, on February 27, 1793, working from a draft supplied by Jefferson, William Branch Giles of Virginia introduced a series of nine resolutions which asked the House to condemn Hamilton's handling of the loans and his disrespect for Congress.[29] The Secretary was comfortably vindicated on all charges, their weakness having combined with a dread of implying some criticism of the Chief Executive to shatter Republican ranks.[30]

Washington himself had remained aloof, confident that the Secretary would vindicate himself but unwilling to hazard his own prestige. He may have wounded Hamilton's feelings by refusing to provide a statement that he approved the Secretary's handling of the loans, but he was pleased by Hamilton's triumph.[31] Of course, the defeat of Giles's Resolutions brought no peace. The Republicans simply concluded that the phalanx of congressional stockholders had protected their chief.[32]

The French Revolution and the Fear of Foreign Influence

Near the end of March, 1793, news arrived that the revolutionary French Republic had declared war on Great Britain. This marked the beginning of the most difficult period of Washington's administration. The President was determined to maintain the strictest neutrality, but to do so would necessitate a battle against long odds. Locked in a struggle for survival, both France and Britain interfered with American neutral trade. Moreover, few Americans could be impartial about the war. The two political parties were involved in a struggle between liberty and order at home, and both saw a similar struggle in the conflict abroad. Republicans were certain that domestic conspirators desired a connection with Great Britain in order to advance their plot and to bring the United States into the war against liberty in Europe. Similarly, Federalists suspected a connection between the Republicans and the French which might involve America in the war and bring about a second and more violent revolution in the United States.[33] Public opinion was inflamed by the contest between "French" and "British" factions, and political division assumed a ferocity seldom equaled. Washington found it impossible to maintain the national harmony he desired and increasingly difficult to stay above the fray.[34]

During the course of 1793, the President issued a Neutrality Proclamation and the administration pulled together to defeat the attempts of the inept French minister Edmond Genêt to compromise the country's neutral course.[35] Each political party became more and more convinced that its opponents were unduly influenced by affection for a foreign power if not by foreign money. Accusations of foreign bribery have never been substantiated, at least as to high executive officers; and although historians would later turn up evidence of questionable conduct on the part of Jefferson and more especially Hamilton, none of this evidence was known in the 1790s. The Secretary of State, for example, allowed himself to be used by Genêt in the minister's project to employ western Americans in an expedition against Spanish Louisiana. Hamilton was more or less constantly involved in confidential, even clandestine, communications with British agents or ministers from 1789. Jefferson came to suspect that Hamilton was secretly sabotaging his negotiations with foreign powers, particularly Britain, and this contributed to the frustrations that led him to resign his post at the end of 1793. Most historians have found Hamilton's actions improper, perhaps even damaging to the country's foreign relations, but have acquitted him of culpable misconduct.[36] In the ideology of the new republic, no danger was greater than the corruption of foreign intrigue and influence. Washington in the Farewell Address solemnly adjured his countrymen to be constantly awake against "the insidious wiles of foreign influence . . . since history and experience prove that foreign influence is one of the most baneful foes of republican government."

Britain's attempt to deny the French the benefits of American trade resulted in a war crisis of serious proportions in 1794. To frustrate Republican demands for economic retaliation, Hamilton and other Federalists persuaded the President to combine preparations for defense with appointment of a special envoy to negotiate the differences with Britain. Chief Justice John Jay, one of the great diplomats of the Revolution, was commissioned minister plenipotentiary in March, 1794.

His negotiations extended through the summer and fall. The terms of the completed treaty remained secret until June 1795, when a copy was leaked to the press on the eve of the Senate's ratification.[37]

Jay's Treaty and Edmund Randolph's "Treason" (1795)

When the terms of Jay's Treaty were finally revealed, the worst fears of Republicans seemed to be confirmed. Most, though not all, modern students think that Jay could not have obtained better terms, but contemporary reaction was decidedly adverse. The Senate ratified the treaty without a vote to spare, and the country flooded Philadelphia with petitions beseeching the President to refuse to put it into effect. Washington had swallowed his own original doubts, deciding to accept the judgment of the Senate. But now he hesitated to sign the treaty into law, worried by the public reaction and deeply angered by new British seizures of provisions bound for France. Federalists urged him to seek redress after the treaty became law, but the President was strengthened in his inclination to refuse his consent by Edmund Randolph, an old Virginia friend and Jefferson's successor as secretary of state.[38]

With the Federalists all suspecting that only Randolph's influence impeded efforts to put the treaty into effect, the British minister delivered to Timothy Pickering and Oliver Wolcott, successors to Henry Knox and Hamilton, respectively, in the War and Treasury Departments, captured French documents which gave rise to the most serious accusation any of Washington's advisers ever faced. In one of French minister Fauchet's reports to his government, the Federalist cabinet members saw evidence that at the time of the Whiskey Rebellion, in 1794, Randolph had offered to foment civil strife in exchange for a French bribe.

Eager to believe that any Antifederalist might be in French pay, Pickering and Wolcott showed the captured report to the President, accusing their colleague of corruption and treason. Knowing that Randolph's personal finances had long been precarious, and feeling his own integrity offended, Washington deferred to the Federalists' opinion that he should not ask the French for additional documents that might have clarified the vague references in the captured dispatch. Apparently, no one even paused to refresh his own memory of Randolph's actions during the time in dispute. Instead, Washington at once signed the British treaty, meanwhile concealing his suspicions of Randolph in order to use him to put the treaty into effect, then arranged a summary hearing. The President, with Pickering and Wolcott to help him judge the reaction, summoned Randolph, confronted him with the captured document, and asked for an explanation. The Secretary did his best, though he could not recall with precision the circumstances to which Fauchet seemed to have referred. Then Randolph was asked to leave the room while the others discussed his response. When called back, he was visibly shaken. Protesting the humiliating treatment, he summarily resigned. The explosion served only to convince the others of his guilt, and Randolph left to prepare a public vindication, which would prove a turgid and confusing combination of his own defense with an attack on Washington's dissembling conduct. It convinced Republicans of his innocence, but confirmed Federalist suspicions of his guilt.[39]

Though Edmund Randolph was never convicted in a court of law, he was destroyed as a public figure and ruined financially by a voluntary effort to make up shortages which Pickering and Wolcott managed to discover in State Department accounts. For many years, accusations of bribery, defalcation, and treason continued to blacken his name. He was, historians are now generally agreed, the victim of injustice, condemned too quickly by a president whose own fierce integrity was used by malevolent partisans to remove a barrier to their desires. Shortages in accounts were Randolph's responsibility only as a technical matter of contemporary law. He solicited no bribe: examined in the light of other evidence, the damning phrases in the captured dispatch made reference to a suggestion on his part that Fauchet might uncover evidence of British complicity in the Whiskey Rebellion if he could protect some flour merchants from their British creditors by advancing them money on their contracts. Randolph did not deliver, or promise to deliver, government secrets to the French. Ironically, he was probably more correct in his dealings with foreign envoys than others, like Jefferson and Hamilton, who were never accused.

The Assault on the President (1796–1797)

Jay's Treaty put an end to serious danger of war with Great Britain. But as 1795 became 1796, French retaliation for the British treaty posed a growing danger of war with the other great power of the world. In direct proportion, the President found himself the target for Republican attack.

In the early years of his presidency, Washington had not been subjected to direct assault. Critics began to close on the President himself only very gradually and with considerable caution, since Federalists had always found it useful to defend governmental policies by invoking the hero's prestige. In time, however, it became increasingly difficult to deny that some decisions came from Washington, and a minority of Republicans concluded that they could destroy the policies only by damaging the President's prestige.

The first target was the Neutrality Proclamation of 1793, which many Americans considered a betrayal of revolutionary France. Few critics, as yet, impugned the President's motives. From the first days of the new government, however, one form of criticism had particularly angered the head of state. Some writers had periodically worried about the tone of the new government, denouncing a kind of pageantry that seemed better suited to a monarchy than a republican state. Robes for judicial officers, honorary forms of address for public officials, high government salaries, extravagant private entertainments, and celebration of the President's birthday had all been attacked. So had the President's official dinners and formal receptions, which too much resembled "courtly" levees. At the end of 1792, "Mirabeau," "Cornelia," and other anonymous writers in the *National Gazette* mounted a campaign against these practices. Such criticisms provoked Washington's impassioned outburst against "that rascal Freneau" in a cabinet meeting in August, 1793.[40] The President was infuriated by hints that he displayed monarchical leanings, although, to this point, most critics of the high tone of government would have agreed with Senator William Maclay: "the creatures that surround him would place a crown on his head that they may have the handling of its jewels."[41]

Another long stride toward involvement of the President in opposition charges came in the aftermath of the Whiskey Rebellion, when Washington included in his annual address to Congress a criticism of "certain self-created societies." Reluctant though they were to challenge the President, even congressional Republicans saw this rebuke of the democratic-republican societies as a party act and a dangerous interference with the right to censure the government.[42] Still, most critics avoided a direct confrontation. It was only when he signed Jay's Treaty that Washington wrote an end to his immunity to the sharpest barbs of critical assault.

To Republicans, Jay's Treaty was the penultimate confirmation of their fears that a "British interest" was involved in a Federalist conspiracy to destroy republican government in the United States. It was impossible to deny the President's agency in putting the treaty into effect, particularly after he refused on constitutional grounds to deliver papers relating to the negotiations to the House. Thus a minority of Republican writers deliberately set out to destroy the President's reputation with the people.[43] "Belisarius," "Valerius," "Pittachus," and others filled the Philadelphia *Aurora* with direct attacks on the President, sometimes going so far as to advocate his impeachment. The New York *Argus* and Boston's *Independent Chronicle* joined the campaign, along with a few pamphleteers.[44] From France, Thomas Paine took a hand in the assault.[45] Even Jefferson was involved, when a Federalist newspaper published his famous accusation that "men who were Samsons in the field and Solomons in the council . . . have had their heads shorn by the harlot England."[46]

Jay's Treaty occasioned the assault, but the Republicans reexamined Washington's conduct as a whole. They rewrote their history of the Federalist conspiracy in such a manner as to impugn the President himself. "Belisarius," for example, addressed the President directly, charging that his administration had entailed upon the country "deep and incurable public evils." The administration had created a distinction between the people and the executive through monarchical pageantry, sanctioned the plunder of revolutionary veterans by avaricious speculators, mortgaged the revenue to an irredeemable public debt, formed a "monied aristocracy" by chartering a national bank, created a dangerous standing army, and incited the people to rebellion with excise laws. Now it had approved an unconstitutional treaty "deeply subversive of republicanism and destructive to every principle of free representative government."[47] Would Washington, asked one of the most important pamphleteers, end his term "the tyrant instead of the savior of his country?"[48]

Washington's last years in office were made an agony by such abuse. He was charged with exceeding his expense account. Old revolutionary forgeries were revived to impugn his patriotism. For a man whose sole remaining ambition was to retire, who felt he had sacrificed a lifetime to his country, the assault was absolutely insufferable. It was no consolation that his enemies probably damaged their own cause more than himself. It required considerable restraint, when he prepared his Farewell Address, to confine himself to warnings against the evils of faction, the threat of sectional confrontation, and the dangers of undue affection for a foreign state.[49] But this was Washington's only public response to the opposition attacks.

NOTES

[1] Douglas Adair, *Fame and the Founding Fathers* (New York, 1974).

[2] This understanding of the atmosphere of the Federal years has been most influenced by: John R. Howe, Jr., "Republican Thought and the Political Violence of the 1790's," *American Quarterly*, XIX (1967), 147–165; James M. Banner, Jr., *To the Hartford Convention: The Federalists and the Origins of Party Politics in Massachusetts, 1789–1915* (New York, 1970); Linda K. Kerber, *Federalists in Dissent: Imagery and Ideology in Jeffersonian America* (Ithaca, N.Y., 1970); Richard Buel, Jr., *Securing the Revolution: Ideology in American Politics, 1789–1815* (Ithaca, N.Y., 1972).

[3] Lance Banning, "Republican Ideology and the Triumph of the Constitution, 1789 to 1793," *William and Mary Quarterly*, 3rd ser., XXXI (1974), 167–188.

[4] The most important sources for an understanding of the heritage of neoclassical politics include: J. G. A. Pocock, "Machiavelli, Harrington, and English Political Ideologies in the Eighteenth Century," *William and Mary Quarterly*, 3rd ser., XXII (1965), 549–583; Isaac Kramnick, *Bolingbroke and His Circle: The Politics of Nostalgia in the Age of Walpole* (Cambridge, Mass., 1968); and Caroline Robbins, *The Eighteenth-Century Commonwealthman* (Cambridge, Mass., 1959).

[5] Bernard Bailyn, *The Ideological Origins of the American Revolution* (Cambridge, Mass., 1967); Pauline Maier, *From Resistance to Revolution: Colonial Radicals and the Development of American Opposition to Britain, 1765–1776* (New York, 1972).

[6] Gordon S. Wood, *The Creation of the American Republic, 1776–1787* (Chapel Hill, N.C., 1969).

[7] Washington compared himself to "a culprit who is going to the place of execution" in a letter to Henry Knox, April 1, 1789. John C. Fitzpatrick, ed., *The Writings of George Washington* (39 vols., Washington, D.C., 1931–1944), XXX, 268.

[8] For an overview, see Edward S. Corwin, *The President: Office and Powers, 1787–1948* (3rd ed., New York, 1948), chap. i; Leonard D. White, *The Federalists* (New York, 1948).

[9] Douglas Southall Freeman, *George Washington: A Biography* (6 vols., New York, 1948–1954), VI: *Patriot and President*.

[10] For Hamilton's motives and the nature of his plans, see Gerald Stourzh, *Alexander Hamilton and the Idea of Republican Government* (Stanford, 1970); John C. Miller, *Alexander Hamilton: Portrait in Paradox* (New York, 1959), pt. 3; E. James Ferguson, *The Power of the Purse: A History of American Public Finance, 1776–1790* (Chapel Hill, N.C., 1961).

[11] The emergence of political parties may be followed in John C. Miller, *The Federalist*

Era, 1789–1801 (New York, 1960); Noble E. Cunningham, Jr., *The Jeffersonian Republicans: The Formation of Party Organization, 1789–1801* (Chapel Hill, N.C., 1957); William Nesbit Chambers, *Political Parties in a New Nation* (New York, 1963).

[12]The best source for the inherited critique of the British financial system is Kramnick, *Bolingbroke and His Circle.*

[13]The emergence of this theme in contemporary newspapers can be followed in Lance Banning, "The Quarrel with Federalism: A Study in the Origins and Character of Republican Thought" (unpublished Ph.D. dissertation, Washington University, 1971), 243–272.

[14]See Jefferson's record of conversations with the President in Paul L. Ford, ed., *The Writings of Thomas Jefferson* (10 vols. New York, 1892–1899), I, 192–198, 227–231, 233–237; Jefferson to Washington, May 23, 1792, *ibid.*, VI, 309–312.

[15]Freeman, *Washington,* VI, chap. xvi.

[16]Hamilton to Edward Carrington, May 26, 1792, in Harold C. Syrett and Jacob Cooke, eds., *The Papers of Alexander Hamilton* (13 vols. to date, New York, 1961—), XI, 426–445.

[17]This and subsequent pseudonymous pieces are available *ibid., XII.*

[18]Philip M. Marsh, ed., *Monroe's Defense of Jefferson and Freneau against Hamilton* (Oxford, Ohio, 1948).

[19]Hamilton's support of Federalist newspapers is examined in Miller, *Hamilton, passim.* Jefferson's relationship with the press is discussed in Dumas Malone, *Jefferson and His Time,* (5 vols. to date, Boston, 1948–1974), II and III.

[20]Washington to Jefferson, August 23, 1792, Fitzpatrick, *Writings of Washington,* XXXII, 130–131; Washington to Hamilton, August 26, 1792, *ibid.,* 132–134.

[21]Hamilton to Washington, September 9, 1792, Syrett and Cooke, *Papers,* XII, 347–349.

[22]Jefferson to Washington, September 9, 1792, Ford, *Writings of Jefferson,* VII, 101–109.

[23]Freeman, *Washington,* VI, chap. xvi.

[24]In December, 1792, Congressman Frederick Muhlenburg received a message from a pair of confidence men, James Reynolds and Jacob Clingman, who were lodged on a federal warrant in the Philadelphia jail. The pair claimed to have information that would "hang" Alexander Hamilton, implicating him in speculation in the public funds. With Senator James Monroe and fellow congressman Abraham Venable, Muhlenburg met with Reynolds and also with his wife, emerging with letters and other information which seemed to confirm the charge. On the morning of December 15, this trio confronted Hamilton at his office and agreed to an evening meeting at his home, where Hamilton promised to present evidence that would refute the charge. That evening the Secretary displayed his own bundle of correspondence and convinced the congressmen that he had been the victim of blackmail that had nothing to do with speculation in the funds. He said he had been the mark in a confidence game, having been drawn into an adulterous relationship with Maria Reynolds and then confronted by her husband with demands for compensation and loans. Reynolds had used this money for speculation and fraud, but Hamilton had refused Reynolds' demands for a position in the Treasury and ignored his threats to expose the Secretary unless he used his position to end the federal prosecution.

Since the affair seemed to involve personal misconduct, not misuse of Hamilton's office, the congressional gentlemen dropped their plan to lay it before the President and agreed to bury their knowledge. The business remained secret until after Hamilton's retirement. By 1797, however, the story had leaked to James Thompson Callender, a scurrilous pamphleteer, who exposed the tale in his *History of the United States for the Year 1796.* Callender revived the original charge that Hamilton and Reynolds had conspired in speculations, and the former official decided to protect his public reputation by confessing his private transgression. His *Observations* on Callender's pamphlet was a detailed confession of sexual indiscretion, opening him to public ridicule but preserving his valued reputation for official integrity.

Historians have overwhelmingly accepted Hamilton's own account of the affair. See, for example, Miller, *Hamilton,* 332–340, 458–464. Recently, however, in an appendix to vol. XVIII of his *Papers of Thomas Jefferson* (Princeton, 1973), Julian P. Boyd has argued that Hamilton's confession avoids the more serious charge of official misconduct and cannot be accepted as straightforward and disingenuous. Boyd does not assert that official misconduct can be shown, but he believes that Hamilton may have forged the letters he showed to the congressmen and that the affair proves that Hamilton was by no means as vigilant as he claimed in tracking down misconduct among subordinates in his department.

[25]See note 24.

[26]Miller, *Hamilton,* 244–246, 270–271; Joseph S. Davis, *Essays in the Earlier History of American Corporations* (2 vols., Cambridge, Mass., 1917), I, 278–315.

[27]*Ibid.,* 274–276, 302.

[28]Although, on several occasions, Hamilton did attempt to persuade Federalist governors or electors to interfere with the people's choice in elections, the most important of these attempts occurred when he was out of office, and all failed.

[29]Jefferson's original draft is presented alongside the resolutions as actually introduced in Ford, *Writings,* VII, 222–223.

[30]A good short account is Miller, *Hamilton,* 327–332.

[31]Washington to Hamilton, July 27, 1793, Fitzpatrick, *Writings of Washington,* XXXIII, 18.

[32]For example, Jefferson to Thomas Mann Randolph, March 3, 1793, Ford, *Writings of Jefferson,* VI, 195.

[33]Lance Banning, "Republican Ideology and the French Revolution: A Question of Liberticide at Home," *Studies in Burke and His Time,* 17 (Winter 1976), 5–260. A standard account is Charles M. Thomas, *American Neutrality in 1793* (New York, 1931).

[34]See the seventh volume of Freeman's *Washington* entitled *George Washington: First in Peace* (New York, 1957), which was written after Freeman's death by John Alexander Carroll and Mary Wells Ashworth. See also James Thomas Flexner, *George Washington: Anguish and Farewell* (Boston, 1972).

[35]Harry Ammon, *The Genêt Mission* (New York, 1973).

[36]For a critical view of Hamilton, see Julian P. Boyd, *Alexander Hamilton's Secret Attempts to Control American Foreign Policy* (Princeton, 1964). For Jefferson on Genêt, see Dumas Malone, *Jefferson and the Ordeal of Liberty* (Boston, 1962), 104–113.

[37]Samuel Flagg Bemis, *Jay's Treaty* (New York, 1924); Jerald A. Combs, *The Jay Treaty: Political Battleground of the Founding Fathers* (Berkeley, 1970); Charles R. Ritcheson, *Aftermath of Revolution* (Dallas, 1969). For a critical view, see Alexander DeConde, *Entangling Alliance: Politics and Diplomacy under George Washington* (Durham, N.C., 1958).

[38]This narrative follows Carroll and Ashworth, *Washington;* Flexner, *Washington,* III; Irving Brant, "Edmund Randolph, Not Guilty!", *William and Mary Quarterly,* 3rd ser., VII (1950), 179–198.

[39]*A Vindication of Mr. Randolph's Resignation* (Philadelphia, 1795).

[40]Ford, *Writings of Jefferson,* I, 242–243.

[41]Edgar S. Maclay, ed., *The Journal of William Maclay* (New York, 1927), 119–120.

[42]A brief treatment is in Miller, *Federalist Era,* 160–162.

[43]The campaign was concocted by Benjamin Franklin Bache, William Duane, and John Beckley. See Mathew Carey, *Autobiography,* 39.

[44]Most notably, Albert Gallatin, anonymously, in *Examination of the Conduct of the Executive and Remarks Occasioned by the Late Conduct of Mr. Washington as President of the United States* (Philadelphia, 1797).

[45]"Letters to George Washington," in Philip S. Foner, ed., *The Complete Writings of Thomas Paine,* (2 vols., New York, 1945), II, 689–723.

[46]Jefferson to Philip Mazzei, April 19, 1796, Ford, *Writings of Jefferson,* VIII, 238–241.

[47]"Belisarius," *Aurora,* September 11, 1795. Compare "Pittachus," *ibid.,* September 28, 1795, and "Casca," *ibid.,* October 16, 1795.

[48][Gallatin], *An Examination,* 44.

[49]Flexner, *Washington,* III, chap. xxxii.

JOHN ADAMS
1797–1801

Lance Banning

Although John Adams had been vice president under Washington and was a firm Federalist, he had had virtually no involvement in Washington's administration. Because of his voluminous writings on government, Republicans suspected him of "monarchical" proclivities; but Adams was never an advocate of Hamiltonian finance, and despite his well-known hostility to the French Revolution, he was equally jealous of American independence of British influence. As the new administration began, Jefferson, the defeated Republican candidate, who now succeeded his old friend as vice president, dared to hope for a political reconciliation under Adams. But this was not to be.

The Quasi-War and the Republican Attack (1798–1800)

Washington had left his successors a war crisis of serious proportions, and on May 16, 1797, Adams's address to a special session of the Fifth Congress made it clear that new attempts to settle the differences with France would be accompanied by stronger defense preparations. Quickly the Republicans resumed their attacks. War with France, the critics had long believed, would be the final step in the Federalist plot. In 1798, in the aftermath of the "XYZ" Affair, hostilities widened into an undeclared naval war, and Republicans placed a large share of the blame on Adams.[1]

With Adams, as clearly as with Washington, the Republican quarrel was fundamentally ideological. New accusations did appear. Adams was prone to bellicose extremes in public statements and to sudden shifts

of course, which gave rise to occasional assertions that he was temper-
amentally unsuited for office—perhaps even senile or insane.² Charges
of nepotism or even desire to found a dynasty of American kings were
raised against Adams, not only because he allowed his son John Quincy
to continue his diplomatic career but also because he forced the nomination of his son-in-law, William S. Smith, as an adjutant general in the
army and, when this was defeated by the Senate, managed to get him
appointed to the post of surveyor of customs in New York.³

As before, however, specific accusations of misconduct were a very
minor part of the opposition theme. The Republicans were principally
concerned with what they considered a far more dangerous thing. The
Adams administration and the war with France seemed logical continu-
ations of a Federalist plot which many Republicans believed to be aimed
at establishing monarchical rule.

The Alien and Sedition Acts (1798)

The best support for Republicans' condemnation of the motives of their
foes was the repressive legislation adopted in the crisis with France. Hostilities had commenced in a wave of patriotic hysteria, during which old
suspicions of a connection between the Republicans and the French had
flamed into widespread belief in treasonous plots. Taking advantage of
this popular feeling, the Federalist majority in Congress adopted measures meant to cripple or destroy the domestic opposition.⁴ French and
Irish immigrants tended to support the Republicans and to favor the
French in the war with Britain. Congress extended to fourteen years the
period of residence necessary for naturalization and gave the president
power summarily to deport any alien whose residence he considered
dangerous to the United States. In a more direct blow at the opposition,
the Sedition Act made it a criminal offense to incite opposition to the
laws or to

> write, print, utter, or publish . . . any false, scandalous, and ma-
> licious writing or writings against the government of the United
> States, or either house of the Congress of the United States, or the
> President of the United States with intent to defame them or to
> bring them . . . into disrepute.⁵

Enforced by a partisan judiciary and by Timothy Pickering, the High Federalist Secretary of State, these Alien and Sedition Laws established a bloodless reign of terror. Although no one was actually deported under the Alien Friends Law, it had an intimidating effect, and administration officials did not escape censure for it. The Sedition Law, however, was enforced with partisan vengeance. William Duane of the *Aurora* in Philadelphia, Thomas Adams of the *Independent Chronicle* in Boston, and pamphleteers such as Thomas Cooper and James Thompson Callender all faced prosecution. The *Time Piece* and the *Argus,* the only Republican newspapers in New York City, were forced out of business. Republican congressman Matthew Lyon of Vermont was imprisoned for a publication incident to his reelection campaign in the fall of 1798. Men were prosecuted under the Sedition Law for offenses as diverse and as trivial as circulating a petition for its repeal, erecting a liberty pole, and expressing a drunken wish that a cannon ball had struck the President in the behind. Not only did the act seem to violate the First Amendment, but it was a formidable danger to the political process as it was coming to be known in the United States. Republicans were quick to concentrate their fire on a measure that seemed so obviously intended to undermine representative government by impeding the people's right to criticize official acts and enforce changes through a free electoral system.

Although Adams approved the Alien and Sedition Acts, Congress rather than the administration had taken the initiative in writing the laws. Criticism of these "unconstitutional" measures thus fell mainly on the Federalists in general and on partisan enforcement in the courts. Of course, they were a problem to the administration as well. Republicans were not silenced. On the contrary, they were given a crop of martyrs and an issue which became more effective as time passed, since enforcement of the laws became more stringent and more obviously partisan as the emergency eased.

Insubordination in the Cabinet (1798–1799)

More partisan than Washington,[6] Adams was still not really a party man. Fearing his independence, Hamilton had maneuvered to persuade the Federalists to slip their vice-presidential candidate in ahead of Adams in the Electoral College in 1796. Adams, in turn, was capable of considering the Hamiltonian wing of his own party nearly as dangerous as their mutual foes. In the last two years of his administration, this peculiar situation produced a crisis within the executive and bitter criticism of the President from Federalist ranks.[7]

From Washington, Adams had inherited a cabinet whose most important figures were more loyal to Hamilton than to the President himself: Pickering, Secretary of State; Wolcott, Secretary of the Treasury; and James McHenry, Secretary of War. The relationship between the President and the cabinet was still not clear. Were members of the cabinet part of the President's "family," or did they hold their offices by merit in some degree of independence from the head of the executive branch? Adams had kept Washington's appointees, though it was soon evident that they consulted Hamilton on most matters and often repeated his advice to the President. McHenry, the least competent, was particularly subservient to Hamilton, and he had been involved more obviously than the others in persuading the aged Washington, brought out of retirement, to force President Adams to appoint Hamilton second-in-command of the provisional army created during the crisis with France. With Hamilton effectively at the head of the army—and Republicans asking against whom this army was going to be employed—Adams's enthusiasm for hostilities steadily cooled.

Indicative of the independence, if not outright insubordination, shown by High Federalist officials loyal to Hamilton was their covert cooperation in the project of Francisco de Miranda, the Latin American adventurer and revolutionary, for the liberation of Spanish dominions in the Americas. Miranda had been encouraged in his scheme by the British government. Under cover of war against France, the American army and the British fleet would descend upon the tottering Spanish empire. Rufus King, the United States minister to Great Britain, Pickering, McHenry, and Hamilton, who expected to command the invading army, were the principal conspirators on the American side. The project was matured behind Adams's back, but it depended ultimately upon his assent as well as an open declaration of war. When the plan was finally broached to him in August, 1798, Adams would have nothing to do with it. As he later wrote:

> It was impossible not to perceive a profound and artful plot hatching in England, France, Spain, South and North America, to draw

me into a decided instead of a *quasi* war with France, Spain, Holland, and all the enemies of England, and a perpetual alliance, offensive and defensive, with Great Britain; or in other words, to entangle us forever in the wars of Europe.[8]

Partly because he was determined to arrest this plot, and partly because of the assurances he was receiving from various sources of the French government's desire for peace in the later months of 1798, Adams seized the olive branch and prepared to negotiate an end to the country's troubles. On February 18, 1799, without consulting his cabinet or the Federalists in Congress, he nominated William Vans Murray to try again to settle the differences with France. The Hamiltonian wing of his party, who were committed to war partly as a means of maintaining their political supremacy, were thoroughly outraged. Over the next months, as Adams tried to get the diplomatic mission off, he was repeatedly obstructed by his cabinet. Ultimately he boiled over with anger at the insubordination and intrigue. On May 6, 1800, with McHenry before him on a matter of routine, Adams lost control, berating the Secretary for his subservience to Hamilton and forcing him to resign. Four days later, when Pickering refused to submit his resignation, he was summarily dismissed.[9] The role of cabinet officers was settled, and Adams's break with the Hamiltonians was complete.

Split in the Federalist Party (1799–1800)

Since February, 1799, when Adams nominated Murray as minister to France, Republican attacks on the President had noticeably eased. Hamilton, Pickering, a partisan judiciary, or Federalism in general caught the brunt of opposition attacks. In the aftermath of the cabinet purge, the situation became odder still. The sharpest criticism of the administration now came from the Federalist side. Most of this was confined to private correspondence, but its tenor was revealed to all when the Republicans managed to intercept and publish a letter that Hamilton had been circulating among his Federalist friends. Hamilton wrote:

> Not denying to Mr. Adams patriotism and integrity and even talents of a certain kind, he does not possess the talents adapted to the

administration of government . . . and there are great and intrinsic defects in his character which unfit him for the office of chief magistrate. . . . He is a man of imagination sublimated and eccentric, propitious neither to the regular display of sound judgment nor to steady perseverance in a systematic plan of conduct; and . . . to this defect are added the foibles of a vanity without bounds and a jealousy capable of discoloring every object.[10]

President Adams ended the undeclared war with France and destroyed in the seed any danger to liberty that extremists in his own party may have posed. At the same time, however, he and his administration had imposed upon the country a large standing army, wartime taxes, and a program of repression—all designed to meet an emergency that had passed. The Federalists approached the election of 1800 thoroughly demoralized and as angry with one another as any of them were with their Republican foes.

NOTES

[1]Page Smith, *John Adams* (New York, 1962), II; Steven Kurtz, *The Presidency of John Adams: The Collapse of Federalism, 1795–1800* (Philadelphia, 1957); Alexander DeConde, *The Quasi-War: The Politics and Diplomacy of the Undeclared Naval War with France, 1797–1801* (New York, 1966).

[2]For example, James Thompson Callender, *The Prospect before Us* (Philadelphia, 1800).

[3]Abundant examples are in Smith, *Adams*, II.

[4]The "Black Cockade Fever" and Federalist motives are described in DeConde, *Quasi-War*, chap. iii, and James Morton Smith, *Freedom's Fetters: The Alien and Sedition Laws and American Civil Liberties* (Ithaca, N.Y., 1956), pt. I.

[5]Smith, *Freedom's Fetters*, is the definitive history of the repressive legislation.

[6]Adams was also more willing to use his public addresses as occasions for attacking his political foes. In the aftermath of the "XYZ" Affair, some of Adams's attacks on the Republicans and their affection for France were so strong that even Hamilton called them "revolutionary." Smith, *Adams*, II, 963–964.

[7]Kurtz, *Presidency of Adams*, is the best account, although he may overemphasize the degree to which Adams was influenced by political considerations. Smith, *Adams*, II, is a corrective.

[8]Adams to James Lloyd, March 30, 1815, in Charles Francis Adams, ed., *The Life and Works of John Adams* (10 vols., Boston, 1856), X, 151.

[9]Not long after the executive offices were moved to Washington in 1800, fires occurred in both the War and Treasury Departments, consuming many valuable papers. Rabid partisans were already charging Pickering's dismissal to pecuniary deficiencies in

his accounts; inevitably, it was now charged that the fires had been deliberately set to destroy damaging evidence against high officials in the War and Treasury Departments. A House investigating committee reported on February 28, 1801, that it found no evidence whatever that the fire in the War Office originated in corrupt design or negligence; as to the Treasury, the committee found no evidence which entitled it to "a satisfactory conjecture." And there the matter ended. See the account in George Gibbs, *Memoirs of the Administrations of Washington and Adams* (2 vols., New York, 1846), II, 478ff.

[10]"The Public Character and Conduct of John Adams, Esq., President of the United States," in Henry Cabot Lodge, ed., *The Works of Alexander Hamilton* (12 vols., New York, 1904), VII, 310–311, 314.

THOMAS JEFFERSON
1801–1809

James M. Banner, Jr.

A survey of the administration of Thomas Jefferson, and indeed of the entire Virginia triumvirate, including Madison and Monroe, shows them to have been relatively free of proved instances of executive misconduct. Only one verified instance of corruption—that of James Wilkinson—mars the record, and its occurrence was not conclusively demonstrated until the twentieth century. Charges of malfeasance, unconstitutional or illegal action, and duplicity were, of course, frequently lodged against these three presidents and against members of their official families. Furthermore, proved examples of misconduct and corruption in the lower echelons of the executive branch seem to have been somewhat more numerous. However, the record all in all was a good one.[1]

Charges of corruption nevertheless abounded, principally because of the contemporary conception of corruption—which was taken to encompass not only personal depravity but also abuses of public and private power. These included executive removals from office, nomination by caucus, lobbying, and the partisan award of patronage. Contemporary charges of such kinds of purported misconduct have not been considered below, inasmuch as most were of a purely partisan nature and did not involve any suspicion of efforts to benefit high administration officials by criminal or clandestine means.

From 1800 to 1825, however, a subtle but important change occurred in both the charges and investigations of misconduct. Whereas in the early years of the century they generally concerned suspicion of assaults against the state, after 1815 they more frequently had to do with suspected wrongdoing in the interest of personal benefit or gain. By then, the government and its budget had become larger and more complex. Maneuvering for partisan advantage had become more open and competitive, and efforts to sniff out wrongdoing therefore more concerted. In addition, a democratic sensitivity to the exploitation of government for private ends had begun to spread. Inquiries into Burr's conspiracy and the controversy over the Two Million Act were thus characteristic of the early years. Later the allegations of misuse of public funds lodged against Calhoun, Crawford, and Monroe were more representative. The canons by which allowable conduct was measured had broadened considerably by the 1820s. Office-bidders were now judged by their determination not only to protect the integrity of the government and the Union but also to protect the average citizen against being placed at a disadvantage in the competition for personal fortune by those who held or benefited from public office.

The Election of 1800–1801

In the absence of well-developed political parties and without long experience with partisan give-and-take, contemporaries tagged as "corrupt" what today would be considered the normal, expected, and legitimate transactions of party politics. Thus the conditions under which Thomas Jefferson won the presidency in 1801 exposed him to charges of misconduct in the very act of gaining office.

The facts were these:[2] Through a series of inadvertencies, Jefferson and Aaron Burr received an equal number of electoral votes in the fall election of 1800. Under the Constitution, this threw the choice of candidates into the House of Representatives, where each state had one vote. Although it had always been assumed that Burr was running for the vice presidency, the accident of the tie vote whetted his substantial ambitions for the presidency. (The Twelfth Amendment, designed to forestall a recurrence by distinguishing between presidential and vice-presidential aspirants, was enacted after this episode.) Despite charges that Burr or his agents tried to strike a bargain with the Federalist congressmen who were numerous enough to prevent Jefferson's election, if not to elect Burr, no substantial evidence of such negotiations has come to light.

Instead, rather than conceding the election to Jefferson by some un-equivocal public declaration or by withdrawing his name, Burr sim-ply did nothing—which was enough to keep anti-Jefferson hopes alive among the Federalists. Therefore the initiative to resolve the impasse passed in effect to Jefferson and his colleagues.

The votes of nine states out of sixteen were needed for Jefferson's elec-tion by the House. For thirty-five ballots the vote stood 8–6 in Jeffer-son's favor, with the votes of two state delegations, those of Vermont and Maryland, evenly divided and thus not counted. On the thirty-sixth ballot the Federalist members of these two state delegations abstained, thereby throwing their states' votes to Jefferson. Delaware and South Carolina also formally abstained. Jefferson was president.

The circumstances of some sort of arrangement surrounding the outcome were rumored at the time but did not become controversial until about 1805. A bargain, it was alleged, had been struck in 1801 be-tween Jefferson and James A. Bayard, the Federalist congressman from Delaware. It now, however, seems clearly substantiated that the "negoti-ations" were complex and probably misapprehended. Through the me-diation of Jefferson's friend Representative Samuel Smith of Maryland, Bayard sought assurances and was led to believe that Jefferson would not disturb the fiscal system or the naval administration created by the Federalists in the 1790s and would not make a massive sweep of Feder-alists from public office. (Bayard was especially concerned about some of his own friends and associates.) Assuming that he had received such assurances from Jefferson through Smith, Bayard then convinced other Federalists of the inadvisability of holding out longer for Burr.

Jefferson steadfastly labeled charges of a bargain "absolutely false." The truth is probably that, in Albert Gallatin's words, Smith "under-took to act as an intermediary, and confounding his own opinions and wishes with those of Mr. Jefferson, reported the result [to Bayard] in such a manner as gave subsequently occasion for very unfounded sur-mises."[3] At any rate, whether or not such an understanding was in fact concluded, Jefferson's future policies were in accord with its general outlines—which also conformed rather closely to his own moderate views. There is no reason to believe that Jefferson gained the presidency with any fetters upon his freedom of action.

The Burr-Hamilton Duel

On July 11, 1804, Aaron Burr, Vice President of the United States, met Alexander Hamilton on a secluded dueling ground in Weehawken, New Jersey, and mortally wounded the former secretary of the Treasury.[4] Their enmity and competition, reaching back many years, had recently been capped by Hamilton's intercession in behalf of Burr's opponent in the New York gubernatorial race, which Burr lost. Disparaging remarks about Burr made by Hamilton at the time quickly became known to the Vice President. Burr, under the ancient and still observed code duello, therefore moved to protect his honor. Hamilton accepted the challenge and the fatal duel ensued. Many men had previously fallen, and many more would fall, before an opponent's pistol. In this case, private action had been taken to preserve the honor of two men long locked in public combat.

A New York City coroner's jury (lacking any jurisdiction in New Jersey) handed down a verdict that Burr and his accessories "feloniously wilfully and of their Malice aforethought did kill and Murder" Hamilton.[5] A New York City grand jury changed the charge to challenging to a duel—a misdemeanor. The Bergen County, New Jersey, grand jury then indicted Burr for murder, and the state governor, though petitioned by a group of notables, disclaimed jurisdiction to quash the indictment. Burdened by these two charges, Burr nevertheless returned to Washington to preside calmly, as president of the Senate, over the impeachment trial of Justice Samuel Chase. Subsequently, both indictments were quietly allowed to die. A test of whether an incumbent vice president could stand trial under criminal law was thus not made.

Aaron Burr and the New England Federalist Conspiracy of 1804

Smarting under their loss of national power to the Republicans and what they called their bondage to Virginia policies, a small group of frustrated New England Federalist leaders launched a secret and misguided effort in 1804 to separate the northeastern states from the rest of the Union. Popular support for secession was scarcely abundant; but perhaps with the association of New York, they reasoned, their scheme would succeed—at least to the point of checking Jefferson's initiatives.

They approached Vice President Aaron Burr, then running for governor of New York. Burr received their visits and views and may have heard them intimate that the future leadership of the new confederacy would be his; but he remained studiously equivocal and noncommittal. How he would have responded had he been elected governor is uncertain: but he lost the race and soon thereafter killed Hamilton, rendering himself useless to the schemers' purpose. No evidence has ever come to light implicating Burr further in the matter. The conspiracy, weak to begin with, evaporated quickly and did not become generally known for many years.[6]

James Wilkinson in the Pay of Spain

James Wilkinson—ranking general of the U.S. Army after 1796, commanding general of the Army under Jefferson, and, from March, 1805, governor of the Louisiana Territory by Jefferson's appointment—has been called "the most skillful and unscrupulous plotter this country has ever produced."[7]

During the administrations of Washington and Adams, Wilkinson was rumored to be in the pay of Spain, allegedly helping to effect the separation of Kentucky from the United States. Early in 1806 Jefferson and others were told that he was again on a Spanish retainer. Not until the twentieth century was convincing proof brought forth on both charges, from papers discovered in the Spanish archives. Regarding Wilkinson's intrigues while commanding general and governor under Jefferson, the facts are as follows:[8]

When in New Orleans in 1804, Wilkinson, always short of funds, resumed his covert dealings with Spanish authorities in West Florida. He received 12,000 pesos as payment toward arrears on his pension in return for information on American boundary policies, military conditions, and diplomatic plans. From this arrangement, the Spanish probably never learned much they did not already know. At the same time, he was receiving questionable advances on his salary and payments of submitted claims under authorization of Secretary of War Henry Dearborn. Jefferson was not involved.

In January, 1806, Joseph H. Daveiss, U.S. attorney for Kentucky, charged in a letter to Jefferson that Wilkinson was on the Spanish payroll and that, in addition, a large-scale western plot was in the offing. Because Daveiss was a Federalist and brother-in-law of Jefferson's bitter enemy Chief Justice John Marshall, and because his increasingly excessive charges were unsubstantiated, Jefferson, on the advice of Treasury Secretary Albert Gallatin, took no action against Wilkinson.

By this time Wilkinson was enmeshed in the Burr conspiracy, from which he extricated himself only with further blots on his already tarnished reputation. For this, Jefferson removed him in March, 1807, as governor of the Louisiana Territory.

In late December, 1807, John Randolph, now the administration's most bitter and persistent critic, prompted an investigation into Wilkinson's purported relations with the Spanish. The inquiry was not meant to reflect on Jefferson, and he cooperated with it by supplying relevant documents from executive files. Most of the House sessions of January and February, 1808, were taken up with debate on Wilkinson's conduct. Given the absence of proof—the Spanish governor of West Florida had obligingly transferred all incriminating papers to Havana, whence they were later sent to Spain—the debate was inconclusive.

Simultaneously, in 1808, a military court of inquiry was convened by Dearborn to examine the same charges. Wilkinson—a man of winning and cunning ways—ran his own defense before three lower-ranking officers, who were unlikely to find against him. The court, lacking other evidence, believed Wilkinson's tale that the money he had received was due him on an old tobacco contract. He was again exonerated. Because of his exculpation, the House refused to begin its own formal inquiry but made known its wish that the President do so. Jefferson, always too trusting, took no action but reassigned Wilkinson to a New Orleans command.

That Jefferson would not act has long remained a puzzle. No evidence has ever come to light—nor has anyone ever charged—that Jefferson retained his loyalty to this rogue for some suspect reason. It seems instead that Jefferson's overly trusting ways, his respect for Wilkinson's capacity for hard work, and his desire to use Wilkinson against Aaron Burr in the latter's treason trial led Jefferson to keep him on though not to protect him. As a result, the problem of James Wilkinson was passed on to Jefferson's unlucky successor, James Madison.

Burr, Wilkinson, and the Burr Conspiracy

Shortly after killing Hamilton and while still vice president, Aaron Burr began to lay plans to separate the western states from the Union. Most of his vain plottings and actions—for which he was later tried for treason and acquitted—took place, however, after he was out of office.

Joined with Burr at the outset was that other notorious schemer James Wilkinson, commanding general of the U.S. Army and governor of the Louisiana Territory. Wilkinson went along with Burr's conspiracy through 1805; but in 1806, for obscure but apparently self-interested motives, he decided to renounce the plot and betray its leader. This he did, beginning with a letter to Jefferson in the autumn of 1806. Subsequently he unsuccessfully tried to seize Burr but did manage to round up some of Burr's accessories in moves that involved improprieties if not minor illegalities. Jefferson removed him as territorial governor in March, 1807.

Appearing as the chief government witness in Burr's 1807 treason trial before John Marshall, Wilkinson himself narrowly escaped indictment before the grand jury for misprision of treason. Always trafficking in duplicity, he also deleted from documents submitted to the court evidence which suggested his earlier knowledge of, and collaboration in, the western conspiracy.[9] Jefferson, however, continued to trust this faithless plotter.

The Two Million Act

The Two Million Act led to serious charges of executive duplicity. On December 3, 1805, Jefferson submitted to Congress an annual message which belligerently assailed Spanish depredations on the borders of Florida, then in Spanish hands. The strong tone of the message may have been designed to enhance Secretary of State Madison's standing with the public in his coming bid for the presidency, as well as to bring pressure on Spain to surrender the Floridas. Three days later, however, Jefferson sent a milder secret message which, while along the same lines, also suggested a disposition on the part of France to press Spain to relinquish the Florida territories. He also requested the appropriation of an unspecified sum of money without indicating its specific use, thereby laying the responsibility for diplomatic initiative upon Congress and laying himself open to later charges of deception. Treasury Secretary Gallatin apparently had in mind using any funds appropriated as an earnest of American intentions once possession of the Floridas had been assured and as a means of obviating a dangerous wait for Senate ratification of a treaty. In short, candor was lacking, and the administration seems to have been seeking a way around the potentially troublesome prospect of protracted or delayed Senate consideration.[10]

When informed privately that Jefferson sought $2,000,000 to purchase the Floridas, John Randolph, the sulfurous chairman of the powerful House Ways and Means Committee, protested. He approved neither the goal—a swollen national debt was anathema to him—nor the secrecy of the request nor Jefferson's apparent attempt to put the onus on Congress. Randolph also believed the funds would be used, as Madison privately hinted they might be, to bribe France into pressuring Spain, since Monroe's missions to France and Spain had recently failed. Acting to avoid anticipated Federalist Party protests against "French influence" if his request for funds were made public, Jefferson instead had kicked up strong opposition within his own Republican ranks.

Despite the opposition, the Two Million Act passed both houses of Congress, but only after Jefferson maneuvered to replace Randolph as floor leader with Barnabas Bidwell of Massachusetts, thereby arousing charges of "executive influence"—a form of corruption eighteenth-century republicans had so feared. The bill received Jefferson's signature in February, 1806. Six weeks later it was made public. France, which virtually controlled Spain, did not yield to the blandishments of money, and the Floridas remained in Spanish hands.

Randolph, ever suspicious and increasingly antagonistic to the presidential aspirations of fellow Virginian James Madison, would probably have opposed Jefferson's proposal on any grounds. (In fact, this episode was the occasion for Randolph's formal break with the administration and for Randolph's untrue charge that Madison had tried to draw funds from the Treasury without authorization.[11]) But by his not entirely candid actions, Jefferson had squandered the trust of political friends as well as foes. And most ironically, he did so in part by an overscrupulous regard for the separation of powers. Concluding that Congress should alone make determinations regarding appropriations, he would not openly propose a sum to the House of Representatives.

The Post Office Investigation (1805–1806)

During the Eighth and Ninth Congresses, Gideon Granger of Connecticut, Jefferson's postmaster general (a position not then carrying cabinet status but commanding great patronage), was charged by John Randolph and others with exercising the patronage of the Post Office in behalf of himself and other shareholders in the New England Mississippi Land Company. This group had pending then before Congress claims which grew out of the tangled history of the Yazoo land grants in Georgia. Granger, it was asserted, had tried to get William Duane, the influential editor of the Philadelphia *Aurora*, to back the Yazoo claims (to which Duane was violently opposed); had employed a secret accessory whose job it was to lobby House members to support the claims in which Granger had an interest; and was bribing congressmen with mail contracts.[12]

Granger, who with other Democratic-Republicans of New England had earlier presented an open memorial for the Yazoo claimants, steadfastly maintained his innocence of the charges of patronage dealing and clandestine pressure and on February 1, 1805, requested a House investigation. After postponing a decision to investigate for a year, in March, 1806, the House appointed a committee of investigation, which in mid-April requested a postponement of its report until the next session of Congress. The House granted an indefinite postponement and the matter—neither examined nor proved or disproved—was not heard of again.

Jefferson seems to have ignored the matter, although he may have spoken with Granger about it. The Postmaster General, one of the few prominent New England Republicans, was at the time the administration's eyes and ears in the Northeast, and his further embarrassment would have given a major check to Jefferson's plans to build Republican strength in the Federalist Party strongholds of Connecticut and Massachusetts.

It was also rumored that Granger, "in conformity to the special direction of the President," had awarded a mail contract in Connecticut to a high-bidding Republican instead of to the lowest bidder, a Federalist of proved dependability. These charges seem never to have been publicly aired or investigated.[13]

The Miranda Expedition

In February, 1806, General Francisco de Miranda, a captivating Latin American revolutionary, sailed from New York aboard an American vessel loaded with troops and munitions to liberate Venezuela, his native land, from Spain. He believed that he carried with him the private assurances of the administration that it would not obstruct his venture; for by fitting out an American ship for an assault against a nation with which the United States was at peace and by raising troops among American citizens, the expedition was in violation of the law. However, Miranda assumed incorrectly. After ordering an investigation of the sailing, the government under Jefferson's orders arrested, and had indicted, for abetting Miranda's activities Samuel G. Ogden and William S. Smith, John Adams's son-in-law, both of New York.

These two men defended themselves by charging the administration with reneging on its purported promise of support and with sacrificing them to save the reputation of cabinet officers. The House refused by an overwhelming vote to credit the charges. During their trial, however, Ogden and Smith succeeded in having Secretaries Madison, Henry Dearborn, and Robert Smith served with subpoenas requiring their testimony in New York. The three, not disposed to answer the subpoenas, alleged the difficulty of leaving official business but, in order to avoid a directed acquittal, offered to submit written testimony by affidavits made in Washington. Madison also feared disclosing information prejudicial to negotiations with Spain. The court rendered these issues moot when it held in effect that testimony of the cabinet members would in any case be immaterial. The jury then acquitted the defendants. Jefferson, who appears to have approved the stance of his cabinet officers, later expressed satisfaction with the outcome of the trial of two men toward whom he bore little ill will.[14]

Josiah Quincy's Attempted Impeachment of Jefferson

On January 25, 1809, Congressman Josiah Quincy, a Massachusetts Federalist, charged that a "high misdemeanor has been committed against this nation" by Jefferson. Seeking the Republican president's impeachment, Quincy specifically charged that although Benjamin Lincoln, the collector of the Port of Boston, had for two years importuned Jefferson to allow him to resign for reasons of age and incapacity, Jefferson had refused to accept the resignation, hoping instead to preserve the lucrative post for his then secretary of war, Henry Dearborn of Massachusetts. Quincy offered resolutions that Jefferson be requested to submit to the House all correspondence on the matter of the collectorship and that a committee of investigation be appointed. The House agreed, 93–24, to consider the resolutions. But after a debate in which it was argued, among other things, that Lincoln could resign, that Jefferson's stance did not constitute a high misdemeanor, and that the House had no jurisdiction, the resolutions were overwhelmingly defeated, 117–1. Quincy's attempt to embarrass the administration had failed, and the question was permanently dropped.[15]

Dearborn, to whom Jefferson was committed, soon became collector of the Port of Boston. And the issue of appointments in the absence of statutes otherwise regulating tenures of office and the removal power (for alleged violations of which President Andrew Johnson was impeached and acquitted) seems never again to have arisen as a matter falling within the jurisdiction of the House to impeach.

Jefferson and the New Orleans "Batture" Case

When president, Jefferson had directed, with the concurrence of his cabinet, that Edward Livingston, an admitted defaulter to the Treasury, be removed from some Mississippi River alluvial lands (a *batture*) near New Orleans which he claimed but which the administration chose to treat as public domain. Livingston was forcibly evicted by a federal marshal, even though the territorial court at New Orleans had upheld his claim. After Jefferson's retirement, Livingston entered a suit for trespass against Jefferson and sought personal damages of $100,000. Among the many legal questions arising out of this complex and protracted affair—it had originated in 1805—was whether a former high official could be sued and judged adversely as a private citizen for actions taken in presumed pursuit of the public interest when an officer of government.

Livingston brought suit in the Federal Circuit Court at Richmond, Virginia, on which sat Chief Justice John Marshall, Jefferson's distant kinsman and enemy. The court, with Marshall reluctantly concurring, threw out the case for lack of jurisdiction. Livingston later won title to the property, made up his Treasury debt, enjoyed a respectable public career, and resumed cordial relations with Jefferson.[16] The question of private responsibility for alleged executive misconduct in public office was not resolved. Yet the case—the first known suit against a former president—has served as a deterrent against similar suits, despite the technical nature of the dismissal.

NOTES

[1]This conclusion is also that of Leonard D. White, *The Jeffersonians: A Study in Administrative History, 1801–1829* (New York, 1959), who also examines major instances of fraud and wrongdoing in lower levels of the executive branch.

[2]The best sources are Dumas Malone, *Jefferson and the Ordeal of Liberty*, vol. III of *Jefferson and His Time* (Boston, 1962), chap. xxx; Malone, *Jefferson the President: First Term, 1801–1805*, vol. IV of *Jefferson and His Time* (Boston, 1970), chap. i and app. i; Morton Borden, *The Federalism of James A. Bayard* (New York, 1955), chap. vii; Irving Brant, *James Madison, Secretary of State, 1800–1809* (Indianapolis, 1953), chap. ii; Merrill D. Peterson, *Thomas Jefferson and the New Nation: A Biography* (New York, 1970), 625–51; and John S. Pancake, "Aaron Burr: Would-be Usurper," *William and Mary Quarterly*, 3rd ser., VIII (April, 1951), 204–213.

[3]Borden, *Bayard*, 93.

[4]The major studies and documents about this episode are Nathan Schachner, *Aaron Burr: A Biography* (New York, 1937), chap. xvii; Broadus Mitchell, *Alexander Hamilton: The National Adventure, 1788–1804* (New York, 1962), chap. 26; Herbert S. Parmet and Marie B. Hecht, *Aaron Burr: Portrait of an Ambitious Man* (New York, 1967), chaps. 14 and 15; and Harold C. Syrett and Jean G. Cooke, eds., *Interview in Weehawken: The Burr-Hamilton Duel as Told in the Original Documents* (Middletown, Conn., 1960).

[5]Syrett and Cooke, *Interview in Weehawken*, 156–159.

[6]The conspiracy is reviewed in Henry Adams, *History of the United States of America during the Administrations of Jefferson and Madison* (9 vols., New York, 1889–1898), II, chap. viii; Schachner, *Burr*, 243–245; Samuel Eliot Morison, *Life and Letters of Harrison Gray Otis, Federalist, 1765–1848* (2 vols., Boston, 1913), I, 264–267; Lynn W. Turner, *William Plumber of New Hampshire, 1759–1850* (Chapel Hill, N.C., 1962), chap. viii.

[7]Thomas Perkins Abernethy, *The Burr Conspiracy* (New York, 1954), 15.

[8]In addition to *ibid.*, evidence of Wilkinson's intrigues can be found in Isaac Joslin

Cox, "General Wilkinson and His Later Intrigues with the Spaniards," *American Historical Review,* XIX (July, 1914), 794–812; Malone, *Jefferson the President: Second Term, 1805–1809,* vol. V of *Jefferson and his Time* (Boston, 1974), chap. xiii and pp. 361–367; James Ripley Jacobs, *Tarnished Warrior: Major-General James Wilkinson* (New York, 1938).

⁹The complex history of the conspiracy, Burr's trial, and Wilkinson's role is related in Abernethy, *Burr Conspiracy;* Jacobs, *Tarnished Warrior;* Malone *Jefferson the President: Second Term,* chaps. xiv–xix; Adams, *History,* III, chaps. x–xiv, xix; Walter Flavius Mc-Caleb, *The Aaron Burr Conspiracy* and *A New Light on Aaron Burr* (comp. ed., New York, 1966); Albert J. Beveridge, *The Life of John Marshall* (4 vols., Boston, 1919), III, chaps. vi–ix; Bradley Chapin, *The American Law of Treason: Revolutionary and Early National Origins* (Seattle, 1964), chap. 7. On Jefferson's role, see in addition Raoul Berger, *Executive Privilege: A Constitutional Myth* (Cambridge, Mass., 1974), 179–181, 187–194, 356–361; Peterson, *Thomas Jefferson and the New Nation,* 841–874.

¹⁰This episode is explored in Adams, *History,* III, chaps. v and vi; Malone, *Jefferson the President: Second Term,* 69–78; and Peterson, *Thomas Jefferson and the New Nation,* 815–820.

¹¹For Randolph's charge, see Henry Adams, *The Life of Albert Gallatin* (New York, 1879), 340–342.

¹²Details and documents will be found in C. Peter Magrath, *Yazoo: The Case of Fletcher v. Peck* (New York, 1966), 15, 38–39, 44, 98–99, 172–180; White, *Jeffersonians,* 311–312; Malone, *Jefferson the President: First Term,* 453–455; *Annals of Congress,* 8th Cong., 2nd Sess., 725, 1031–1032, 1106, 1110–1118, and 9th Cong., 1st Sess., 831–833, 1065–1066, 1116; *American State Papers: Post Office,* 40.

¹³This charge was recorded by William Plumber. Everett Somerville Brown, ed., *William Plumber's Memorandum of Proceedings in the United States Senate, 1803–1807* (New York, 1923), 485–486.

¹⁴These events are reviewed in Malone, *Jefferson the President: Second Term,* 80–88; Brant, *James Madison, Secretary of State,* chap. xxiv.

¹⁵Robert A. McCaughey, *Josiah Quincy, 1772–1864: The Last Federalist* (Cambridge, Mass., 1974), 54; Malone, *Jefferson the President: Second Term,* 660; *Annals of Congress,* 10th Cong., 2nd Sess., 1173–1183.

¹⁶This complex case is treated by Richard Hildreth, *The History of the United States of America from the Adoption of the Federal Constitution . . .* (3 vols., New York, 1852), III, 143–148; William B. Hatcher, *Edward Livingston: Jeffersonian Republican and Jacksonian Democrat* (University, La., 1940), chap. viii; Beveridge, *Marshall,* IV, 100–116; Peterson, *Thomas Jefferson and the New Nation,* 944–947.

JAMES MADISON
1809–1817

James M. Banner, Jr.

In 1810 the House again launched an investigation into James Wilkinson's links to the Spanish. A House committee chose not to make a formal report but turned its documents over to the entire House, which then transmitted them to the President. James Madison, however, turned down as irregular Wilkinson's request for a military court of inquiry. Wilkinson then requested Madison to order fourteen army officers to Washington to offer evidence in his behalf. Madison refused.

In late 1810 the House again debated Wilkinson's record, this time including charges holding him responsible for the high mortality among troops in his command. Again he was cleared.

In 1811 Madison finally authorized a court-martial of Wilkinson on the charges lodged against him before the House in 1810 and later referred to the President. The military court absolved him of misconduct in December, 1811, after which Madison approved the findings and restored Wilkinson to active duty.[1]

Poor judgment alone can be charged against Madison, as it can against Jefferson, for keeping Wilkinson so long in the service and in responsible commands. But Madison was not yet done with the general. Wilkinson bungled a command during the War of 1812 and was dismissed, this time—at last—for incompetence. After facing one of his periodic courts-martial in 1815, he was again acquitted, but not reinstated in the service.

NOTES

[1]This phase of Wilkinson's career is reviewed in James Ripley Jacobs, *Tarnished Warrior: Major-General James Wilkinson* (New York, 1938), 263–274; Irving Brant, *James Madison: The President, 1809–1812* (Indianapolis, 1956), 177, 345, 352. It is documented in *Journal of the House of Representatives,* 11th Cong., 306, 339–348, 450–453, 578–582; *American State Papers: Miscellaneous,* II, 79–127, and *Military Affairs,* I, 268–295.

JAMES MONROE
1817–1825

James M. Banner, Jr.

Monroe's "Furniture Fund"

The White House and its furnishings had been destroyed by British troops in 1814. To accompany the building's restoration, Congress appropriated $20,000 for furnishings shortly before James Monroe's inauguration in 1817. Because the furnishings would take time to secure, the new president suggested that he sell to the government on the basis of two expert appraisals his own collection of furniture, purchased earlier in France and intended for private sale. He did not request immediate compensation, agreeing instead to await further congressional appropriations; should they not be voted, Monroe would reclaim the furniture and bear the costs of wear and tear. This agreement was readily accepted by William Lee, second auditor of the Treasury, and Samuel Lane, commissioner of public buildings, two friends whom Monroe had appointed to manage the Furniture Fund. Lane also, in effect, became a member of the White House staff and manager of Monroe's personal accounts.

Contrary to his initial disposition, Monroe quickly borrowed against his furniture $6,000, probably to finance his celebrated 1817 northern tour—such semi-official trips at the time not being underwritten by the government—which he had expected to underwrite from the private sale of his furniture. The loan bore no interest, but was considered an advance against congressional appropriations. Monroe repaid the loan from personal funds in late 1817. But he had—if only briefly—put public funds to use for private ends.

New appropriations were made to the Furniture Fund in 1818 to make up deficiencies and provide additional sums. This time Monroe decided not to sell his furniture to the government but sought and received another advance, this time for about $9,000 (the value of the appraisal), to be returned when the new furniture arrived from abroad. Monroe later explained that he did this wishing to protect his estate against his untimely death. He again used the advance for presidential travel. By 1821 he agreed to transform the advance from government moneys into an outright but provisional payment for his goods and to leave his furniture in public possession. He still intended, however, to seek approval of his actions from Congress and, if thwarted, to reclaim the furnishings and repay the government.

None of this would have come to light had not Lane died insolvent with $20,000 of public building funds unaccounted for. Moreover, it was discovered that Monroe was indebted to Lane's estate because the deceased had advanced moneys in Monroe's behalf (in one case to a dishonest White House steward) without his knowledge. Two inconclusive congressional investigations followed in 1822 and 1823; and Monroe, correctly viewing the Furniture Fund as a discretionary presidential fund over which he had full control, refused to attend committee hearings or to answer questions in writing. In any case, the Furniture Fund was never found to have any deficiencies.

Monroe's conduct was questioned again in the hearings about Secretary William H. Crawford's management of the Treasury when it was said without further substantiation that Ninian Edwards had claimed Monroe to be in his control through Lane. Monroe then asked for a full congressional investigation of his conduct and, when it was authorized in 1825, provided appropriate documents, along with a defense of his actions. But the House preferred merely to accept information and made no report of findings. Monroe's reputation was thus not fully cleared. But if he was guilty of impropriety in the original matter, no evidence of malversation has ever turned up.

John Quincy Adams commented in his diary that the House investigation had humiliated the President, if not the presidency, and likened it to asking a "blooming virgin to exhibit herself naked before a multitude."[1] Adams may not have understood that the standards of expected political behavior were rapidly changing. The people now wished to know more about the lives and actions of their chief executives. Monroe, the last president of the revolutionary generation, sensed this and was forthcoming but did not escape embarrassment.

The Yellowstone Expedition Contracts

As part of his strategy of advancing government military posts farther westward in order to promote the Indian fur trade, encourage and protect settlement, and spread Christianity among the tribes, Secretary of War John C. Calhoun laid plans in 1818 for an expedition 1,800 miles up the Missouri River to the mouth of the Yellowstone. The quartermaster general granted the contracts for supplying and transporting the expedition to James Johnson, the brother of Calhoun's friend Kentucky congressman Richard M. Johnson, who was chairman of the House Committee on Military Affairs and was acting as James Johnson's attorney.

James Johnson, a known and previously dependable contractor to the United States, received the usual advance from the War Department, soon requested and received a second to offset funds lost by the default of a debtor, and then received a third in the sum of $12,000 to pay a debt to the Bank of the United States in order to preserve his own credit. Probably to save the expedition. Calhoun approved the third advance, although it was both irregular and unwise.

Given the problems inherent in such a venture, especially in the West during the financial crisis which struck the nation in 1819, James Johnson, with the aid of the importuning Richard M. Johnson, was soon back for $50,000 more. The contractor had not yet overdrawn the appropriation, but neither had the expedition gotten far. Calhoun authorized another $35,000—but only if essential to provide the funds now almost impossible to secure from western banks. In the meantime, President Monroe, touring the West, found the popularity of the expedition high and directed Calhoun to advance still another $142,500! Calhoun tried vainly to stop the spiraling crisis. But given the continuing difficulties of communication and credit, Johnson already had drawn against the latest advances. Monroe finally agreed to a halt, but not before Johnson had secured more funds, and the expedition had finally to be given up.

By December, 1819, the enemies of military appropriations and swollen budgets in the House, seeing an opportunity to charge extravagance, began calling for explanations. A series of resolutions directed Calhoun to provide information on the entire Yellowstone affair, especially regarding the sums paid to and claimed by James Johnson. Though no one seems to have charged Calhoun with fraud, his entire policy was vulnerable. Furthermore, when the Johnsons repeatedly tried to draw Monroe into authorizing further advances, the President turned the requests over to Calhoun. Although he refused additional moneys and suggested instead that thenceforth all contracts be let through competitive bidding—not yet the customary procedure—Calhoun was being held accountable for any errors. Meanwhile the matter had been submitted to arbitration. By late 1820 and 1821, the congressional partisans of Henry Clay and Treasury Secretary Crawford were still hounding Calhoun. But, once the enemies of Calhoun's overall military policy had succeeded in sharply cutting the War Department budget, the Yellowstone issue was allowed to drop.

Mismanagement and ill judgment—from which it is difficult to dissent—but never fraud or corruption, had been alleged against Monroe and Calhoun. Surely, both the President and the Secretary were overly concerned not to alienate the influential Richard M. Johnson and too protective of the Johnsons' private affairs. As for the Johnsons, they earnestly tried to meet their obligations. They also won a further claim against the federal government. Fraudulent actions or claims on their part were never alleged.[2]

The Elijah Mix Contracts

In July, 1818, the engineering section of Calhoun's War Department signed a contract with Elijah Mix, brother-in-law of the department's chief clerk, Major Christopher Van Deventer, to provide stone for the construction of fortifications near Old Point Comfort, Virginia. Under then current practices, bids were not publicly advertised. Instead, a few people known to the contracting agency were requested to submit bids. In this case, because Mix submitted the lowest bid, the award went to him.

Because the bid was recklessly low under existing market conditions, Mix could not secure bond. He therefore offered to sell a quarter interest in the contract to Van Deventer. Calhoun warned the clerk that although such a purchase would be within the law, it lacked propriety and would further expose the already harassed department to investigation. Ignoring these cautions, Van Deventer made the purchase. In April, 1819, he bought another quarter share. By autumn, however, he was able to dispose of his full interest in the contract. Calhoun was apparently unaware of the entire transaction.

Shortly, however, President Monroe received an anonymous letter, which he turned over to Calhoun, charging the department with maladministration and Van Deventer with a personal interest in his brother-in-law's contract. Calhoun warned the clerk with a witness present that, if the department were forced to take any action on the Mix contract, Van Deventer would be dismissed. Soon after, the matter became public. And the House, as Calhoun had anticipated, called for relevant documents from Calhoun, which he submitted.[3]

The issue dragged on. An 1822 House inquiry censured Van Deventer and criticized procurement procedures, which Calhoun had already reformed. And then in late 1825, after Calhoun had become vice president, a series of public letters again implicated Calhoun in various conflict-of-interest affairs of his erstwhile chief clerk. (See section on John Quincy Adams.)

The "A.B. Plot"

In late January, 1823, a letter, signed "A.B." and published in a Washington newspaper, charged Treasury Secretary Crawford, a candidate for the presidency in 1824, with suppressing documents relating to the transactions of banks in which federal moneys from land sales had been placed. Further letters over the same signature subsequently charged Crawford with the mismanagement of public funds, with illegally clearing the Treasury's books with nonlegal tender notes of debts to favored western banks, with misstating the amounts of these notes, with misrepresenting the obligations of these favored banks, with depositing federal funds in local banks without notifying Congress, and with withholding information from Congress. A special House committee, evidently sympathetic to Crawford, found exclusions in documents Crawford had earlier submitted to Congress and favoritism toward some western banks, but exculpated the Secretary. A second committee, again under Craw-fordite control, justified the Treasury's actions as necessary to relieve western banking and financial difficulties in a time of financial stress. To all of these accusations, Crawford, now seriously ill and out of the presidential race, responded in a lengthy document of March, 1825.

The author of the "A.B." letters was probably Senator Ninian Edwards of Illinois, confirmed in early 1824 as ambassador to Mexico. At least, Edwards, an opponent of Crawford's presidential aspirations, claimed authorship in a riposte to Crawford's March counterattack. But later, during another investigation before a more evenly balanced House com-mittee, it was brought out that Edwards had privately denied authorship, perhaps to enhance the chances of his appointment as ambassador. As a result of this revelation, Edwards resigned his diplomatic post, and his reputation was tainted with duplicity and dishonesty. The full House report on this affair found loose administration and many oversights in the Treasury, but exonerated Crawford of wrongdoing and corruption.

No evidence of a "plot" against Crawford has been found. But neither have the charges against Crawford ever been fully examined or disproved. In fact, the preliminary report of the third House inquiry accepted the facts alleged against Crawford while absolving him of conscious intent. It is generally agreed that the evidence against Edwards was weak and that further probing of Crawford's action in the Treasury might have brought wrongdoing to light. Surely the acceptance of nonlegal tender (as the second of three House committee reports acknowledged had been done) was contrary to law, and the loss to the government was ev-idence of mismanagement. But bitter presidential politics governed all decisions in this case, and outgoing President Monroe was loath to seek a full-fledged and fourth congressional investigation, which would no doubt have become similarly entangled in partisanship.

Monroe—as well as cabinet members John C. Calhoun and John Quincy Adams, both with presidential ambitions—was involved in this affair from the outset. Monroe's appointment of Edwards to Mex-ico seemed to the Crawfordites an indication of the President's enmity. But Monroe, who would not have named Edwards had he considered him implicated, was deeply embarrassed by Edwards's actions, which the Crawfordites thought showed Monroe's hand. Only strong oppo-sition within the cabinet prevented his dismissing Edwards in place of seeking, and getting, his resignation. Monroe himself was bitter against the Crawfordites for earlier attacks on the administration and for pressing this matter to a third congressional hearing, which may have been motivated by a desire to embarrass the President. Adams and Calhoun, who had provided some documents for Edwards's defense, remained unconvinced by the House committee's clearing of Crawford. In short, Monroe was never directly implicated, but he and almost everyone involved emerged with increased political liabilities.[4]

NOTES

[1]This episode is analyzed in Lucius Wilmerding, Jr., "James Monroe and the Furniture Fund," *New York Historical Society Quarterly*, XLIV (April, 1960), 133–149, as well as in Wilmerding, *James Monroe, Public Claimant* (New Brunswick, N.J., 1960), chap. ii; Harry Ammon, *James Monroe: The Quest for National Identity* (New York, 1971), 533–536; *House Report 79*, 18th Cong., 2nd Sess.

[2]The expedition and related inquiries are documented in Charles M. Wiltse, *John C. Calhoun, Nationalist, 1782–1828* (Indianapolis, 1944), 166–168, 182–185, 201–203, 214–216, 224–227; Leland Winfield Meyer, *The Life and Times of Colonel Richard M. Johnson of Kentucky* (New York, 1932), chap. v; Ammon, *Monroe*, 470–471; *Annals of Congress*, 16th Cong., 1st Sess., 750, 848, 936, 1047, 1594, and Doc. 65; 2nd Sess., Doc. 110; *House Report 109*, 17th Cong., 1st Sess.; *American State Papers: Military Affairs*, II, 324–325.

[3]The relevant sources are Wiltse, *Calhoun*, 203–205, 253, 344–346; *House Report 109*, 17th Cong., 1st Sess. (also printed in *American State Papers: Military Affairs*, II, 431–449); *House Report 79*, 19th Cong., 2nd Sess. (reprinted in U.S. House, Committee on the Judiciary, 93rd Cong., 1st Sess., *Impeachment: Selected Materials*, 311–600).

[4]Details about this affair are found in Chase C. Mooney, *William H. Crawford, 1772–1834* (Lexington, Ky., 1974), 242–248, 319; Charles M. Wiltse, "John C. Calhoun and the 'A.B. Plot,' " *Journal of Southern History*, XIII (February, 1947), 46–61; Wayne Cutler, "The A. B. Controversy," *Mid-America*, LI (January, 1968), 24–37; Ammon, *Monroe*, 512–513, 531–533; Wiltse, *Calhoun*, 262–263, 292–293; *Annals of Congress*, 17th Cong., 2nd Sess., 652–656, 735–739, app. 1324–1335; 18th Cong., 1st Sess., app. 2713–2915; *House Report 133*, 18th Cong., 1st Sess.; *American State Papers: Finance*, V, 1–146.

JOHN QUINCY ADAMS
1825–1829

Richard E. Ellis

The years 1824 to 1840 were marked by a series of bitter presidential contests and the permanent establishment in the United States of a two-party system of politics. An important part of the background of the period was the rapid economic and social change which followed the development of a national economy after the War of 1812. At first there was widespread prosperity, but then came the Panic of 1819 and with it America's first national depression. The 1820s were a decade of hard times and mounting distrust of government. Beginning on the state level and spreading to the national scene, widespread concern developed over the power of special-interest groups, the corruptness of politicians, the need to make the government more responsive to the popular will, and the country's general moral decay. Despite the return of prosperity in the 1830s, the attitudes formed during the earlier years tended to dominate politics through 1840 and beyond.

The Election of 1824

The symbol of the older style of politics was the congressional caucus. Made up of Republican (Jeffersonian) senators and representatives, it met in Washington every four years to designate the party's presidential candidate. After 1800 and until 1824, nomination by this caucus was tantamount to election. In 1824 William H. Crawford received the nomination from a sparsely attended caucus, but the other Republican candidates, Andrew Jackson, John Quincy Adams, and Henry Clay, refused to acquiesce in the decision and took their cause to the public. In the ensuing election, Jackson won a plurality of both the popular and electoral votes; however, the Constitution provides that if no one receives a majority in the Electoral College, the election goes into the House of Representatives, where the congressional delegation from each state casts one vote among the three highest candidates. This eliminated Clay, who came in fourth. Crawford, who came in third, had just suffered a stroke and was no longer seriously considered; thus the choice was between Jackson and Adams. Clay, who was also Speaker of the House of Representatives, played an important role in the proceedings that followed. In their appeal for Clay's support, Jackson's followers argued that he should be selected because he had received the largest popular vote, but after a lengthy private interview with Adams, Clay used his influence to bring about Adams's election. When, a short time afterward, Adams appointed Clay secretary of state, the cry, led by Andrew Jackson, of "bargain and corruption" immediately went up throughout the country and continued until Jackson's victory in 1828.[1]

Although the Jacksonians were successful in convincing most of the country that the popular will had been betrayed by the result of the election of 1824, they were never able to make their charge of a "corrupt bargain" stick officially. Even before Clay was appointed secretary of state, a pro-Jackson newspaper in Philadelphia, the *Columbian Observer,* published an anonymous letter suggesting that a bargain had been struck between Clay and Adams. Clay denied the charge and demanded that the author identify himself, even challenging him to a duel. Authorship was acknowledged by George Kremer, a representative from Pennsylvania. The duel never came off, and although Kremer indicated that he was prepared to substantiate his charges, he failed to testify before a House investigatory committee.[2] In 1827 Jackson publicly charged that a congressman at the time of the House election had tried to make a bargain with him on Clay's behalf. The particular congressman was eventually identified as James Buchanan (who was to become the fifteenth president of the United States). Buchanan, however, refused to corroborate Jackson's claim. In a public letter, he asserted that he had acted "solely as his [Jackson's] friend, upon my individual responsibility and not as the agent of Mr. Clay or any other person."[3]

Historians have generally been partial to Clay and Adams, denying that a corrupt bargain took place. They stress Clay's fear of Jackson's military background and his concern over the general's lack of political experience. They also point out that although Clay and Adams had personal differences in the past, they were in agreement on the most important issues of the day: a protective tariff and federal aid to internal improvements. These historians assert that Clay probably made up his mind to support Adams even before he left Kentucky to attend the House election.[4] One has gone so far as to say that Jackson actually knew that no deal had taken place, but deliberately propagated the charge for political reasons.[5] Yet one of the most careful students of the period, Samuel Flagg Bemis, in his biography of John Quincy Adams, believes some kind of "implicit bargain" or "gentlemen's agreement" did occur. Bemis stresses in particular Adams's strong desire to become president and details a number of assurances, arrangements, promises, and political deals that Adams made with people who were in a position to help his cause. He concludes, however, that what was involved was "nothing corrupt, nothing unconstitutional, if nothing to be proud of."[6] But the "corrupt bargain" charge crippled the Adams administration from the start.

Corruption in Adams's Administration

No scandals of any magnitude occurred during Adams's administration. When the Jacksonians assumed power in 1829, they scoured the records hoping to find something that would embarrass their predecessors, but they came up with very little, discovering only several cases of embezzlement by customs collectors in areas far away from Washington. Their big find was that Dr. Tobias Watkins, a close personal friend of Adams, had embezzled over $7,000 to cover gambling debts after the President had appointed him fourth auditor of the Treasury. Watkins tried to escape, but he was caught, tried, convicted, and imprisoned. Although the Jacksonians made much of the episode, they were not able to incriminate Adams. These revelations took place after Adams had left office in 1829 and so did not affect his presidency.[7]

The Investigation of Vice President Calhoun

John C. Calhoun was vice president of the United States during John Quincy Adams's administration. He was not, however, an Adams supporter. Calhoun had been an early candidate for the presidency but had withdrawn when it became clear that he had no chance of winning. Instead, he ran unopposed for the second position. Shortly after Adams's election, he became one of Jackson's leading supporters. The investigation of Vice President Calhoun was therefore not an attack upon the Adams administration, but an attempt by some of Adams's supporters to embarrass one of the President's most important opponents. The specific incident had to do with a contract, the Mix contract, made by the War Department in 1818 when Calhoun was its secretary. In December, 1826, the Alexandria *Gazette* charged that although Calhoun did not personally benefit from the contract, he was guilty of complicity in the profits made by his chief clerk, Christopher Van Deventer. Calhoun immediately demanded and received a full investigation from the House. He also voluntarily stopped presiding over the Senate until the matter was cleared up. The House report concluded that Calhoun was not himself responsible for the particular contract in question, but it was equivocal about totally exonerating him, thus allowing the Vice President's friends and enemies to interpret the report differently. The main result of the investigation was that Van Deventer was relieved of his duties.[8] President Adams seems not to have concerned himself in the investigation in any way.

The Election of 1828

It was a particularly scurrilous campaign. The irresponsible elements of the Adams press claimed that Jackson's mother had been a prostitute, that he was the son of a mulatto named Jack (thus the name Jackson), and that he had an older brother who was a slave. They reviewed his military career to picture him as a butcher who used his power in sadistic fashion. They described him as a common ruffian who had wasted away his youth in gambling, cockfighting, horse racing, and dueling. Jackson also was accused of being a home wrecker and a seducer who had persuaded his wife Rachel to desert her first husband and to "live with him in the character of a wife." Further, Rachel was accused of adultery and bigamy. The latter charge was technically true since she had married Jackson in 1791 in the Natchez Territory before the divorce from her first husband went through in Virginia. This was the consequence of a legal misunderstanding, a somewhat common occurrence in an era when the legal process was slow and communication haphazard and poor. Discovering what had happened, the couple remarried in 1794.

The Jacksonian press was equally vicious. In addition to playing up the "corrupt bargain" of 1824, it accused Adams of being a monarchist and also a Unitarian. It reported that he and his wife had had pre-marital relations and that she was illegitimate. Further, Adams was charged with having "pimped" for Czar Alexander I when he was United States minister to Russia (1809–1814) by procuring for the Czar one of the nursemaids on his staff. An explanation of the episode was provided by one of Adams's supporters on the floor of the House of Representatives. (It seems the innocent and very respectable nursemaid had written home a number of letters describing the gossip about the Czar's love life. One of the letters came to the Czar's attention, and later, when in the company of his wife, the Czar met the nursemaid, it "afforded them some amusement.") Finally, Adams was accused of introducing gambling in the White House by installing a billiard table and of occasionally swimming nude in the Potomac.[9]

The campaign caused considerable hard feeling between the candidates, but no formal action was taken to make either of them accountable.

NOTES

[1]Background on the election is to be found in George Dangerfield, *The Era of Good Feelings* (New York, 1953), 331–345; Frederick Jackson Turner, *Rise of the New West, 1819–1829* (New York, 1906), 245–264.

[2]James F. Hopkins, ed., *The Papers of Henry Clay* (5 vols., Lexington, Ky., 1959–), IV, 53–54 n. 2; *Register of Debates,* 18 Cong., 2nd Sess., 441–444, 463–486, 522–525.

[3]John Bassett Moore, ed., *The Works of James Buchanan* (12 vols., Philadelphia, 1908–1911), I, 266; Philip S. Klein, *President James Buchanan: A Biography* (University Park, Pa., 1962), 56–59.

[4]William G. Morgan, "John Quincy Adams versus Andrew Jackson: Their Biographers and the 'Corrupt Bargain' Charge," *Tennessee Historical Quarterly,* XXVI (Spring, 1967), 43–58.

[5]Richard R. Stenberg, "Jackson, Buchanan, and the 'Corrupt Bargain' Calumny," *Pennsylvania Magazine of History and Biography,* LVII (January, 1934), 61–85.

[6]Samuel Flagg Bemis, *John Quincy Adams and the Union* (New York, 1956), 32–53, 130–131; Dangerfield, *Era of Good Feelings,* 339–342; Shaw Livermore, *The Twilight of Federalism* (Princeton, 1962), 172–182.

[7]Bemis, *John Quincy Adams,* 158–160; Leonard White, *The Jeffersonians* (New York,

1951), 412–422; Carl Russell Fish, *The Civil Service and the Patronage* (Cambridge, Mass., 1905), 128.

[8]Charles M. Wiltse, *John C. Calhoun, Nationalist, 1782–1828* (Indianapolis, 1944), 203–205, 344–346; *House Report 79*, 19th Cong., 2nd Sess.

[9]Bemis, *John Quincy Adams*, 140–147; Robert V. Remini, *The Election of Andrew Jackson* (Philadelphia and New York, 1963), 102–103, 117–119.

ANDREW JACKSON
1829–1837

Richard E. Ellis

Rotation of Office and the Spoils System

Andrew Jackson's accession to the presidency in 1829 was only the second time under the United States Constitution that the reins of power were transferred from one political party to another. The first time was when Jefferson became president in 1801, and although he removed a number of Federalist officeholders, he was in principle opposed to wholesale removals for party reasons. Madison held these principles, as did Monroe and Adams, both of whom refused to take advantage of the opportunity that the Tenure of Office Act of 1820 gave them to appoint their political friends. When Jackson became president, he reversed this policy. He argued that the former system was undemocratic, for under it "office is considered as a species of property, and government rather as a means of promoting individual interests than as an instrument created solely for the service of the people."[1] As Jackson conceived of the theory of rotation of office, it was a democratic reform designed to prevent the all too frequent passing of office from father to son and the support of the few at the expense of the many. In short, Jackson argued for rotation on the grounds that it made the civil service more responsive to the popular will.

Rotation of office in theory was one thing; in practice it was something else. Although Jackson never justified the idea of rotation in terms of partisan politics, some of his more practical-minded supporters did. There is no question but that Jackson's theory of rotation spawned what was later to be called the "spoils system." Yet most historians have not been particularly hard on Jackson on this point. Specifically, they point out that the number of removals during his administrations was not nearly as great as his opponents claimed. In point of fact, he removed only about 20% of the officeholders under his authority, and a number of these removals were for dereliction of duty and not for political reasons. Also the perversions of the spoils system—the buying of offices, the forced political activity of officeholders and the collection of party assessments from them, as well as the loss of efficiency and prestige that the federal civil service suffered—did not really begin until Jackson left office.[2]

Nonetheless, Jackson's policy of rotation acutely altered the style and tone of politics, and it was denounced during his administrations by his opponents and even by some of his more old-fashioned supporters. Many people expressed uneasiness over the unjustness of indiscriminate removals and the replacement of experienced civil servants with party stalwarts. Jackson's opponents vigorously denounced the president's removal power on the grounds that it dangerously increased executive authority, and they argued that it was neither a specifically delegated power nor an inherent part of the president's office. Long suspicious of Jackson's military background, they were fearful that like Caesar he would continually arrogate power to himself until he put an end to the republic. They complained constantly of the "reign of King Andrew I" and called themselves "Whigs" after the English party that had opposed monarchical authority in the eighteenth century. All efforts to check the president's power of removal, by making him accountable to the Senate and giving Congress the right to prescribe the tenure of officeholders, proved futile, however; finally, the opposition stopped when the Whigs adopted the system upon assuming power in 1840.[3]

The Removal of the Deposits from the Second Bank and the Censure of President Jackson

The most significant confrontation between Jackson and Congress came when the President removed William J. Duane as secretary of the Treasury. The specific episode was not part of the broader debate over Jackson's rotation policy, for Duane had received his appointment from

Jackson. Rather it raised the complicated question of the president's authority to control the actions of his cabinet members and to fire them.

When Jackson vetoed the rechartering of the Second Bank of the United States in July, 1832, the Whigs, under Henry Clay's leadership, made it the leading issue of the presidential election of 1832. Jackson, however, won a decisive victory and interpreted it as a popular mandate for further action against the bank by removing the federal deposits from it. This meant spending the federal money in the bank to meet government expenses and depositing all future income in state-chartered or "pet" banks. Jackson justified this action on the grounds that the bank had used its enormous wealth, much of which had been acquired through the use of government funds, to influence congressmen and other government officials, as well as the outcome of the presidential election.

The problem was that the president, personally, did not have the authority to remove the deposits. The act creating the Second Bank of the United States in 1816 had clearly vested this authority in the secretary of the Treasury. According to the act,

the deposits of the money of the United States . . . shall be made in said bank or branches thereof, unless the Secretary of the Treasury shall at any time otherwise order and direct. . . . [4]

The Whigs were opposed to Jackson's policy of removing the deposits, arguing that the money was safe and useful in the Second Bank of the United States and would not be so in the state banks. This point of view was shared by Louis McLane, Jackson's secretary of the Treasury as his second term began. McLane, however, agreed to resign, becoming secretary of state, and on June 1, 1833, William J. Duane of Pennsylvania was appointed secretary of the Treasury. Much to Jackson's chagrin, Duane also questioned the wisdom and legality of removing the deposits. He suggested instead a congressional inquiry into the matter. Jackson rejected this idea and tried by means of a series of letters and conferences to bring Duane around to his point of view. But Duane proved intransigent; he also refused to resign.[5] On September 18 Jackson read to his cabinet a paper (drafted by Attorney General Roger Brooke Taney) in which he listed his reasons for wanting a removal of the deposits and in effect said that cabinet members were personally responsible to him for their actions. When Duane remained adamant, he was removed and replaced by Taney as acting secretary of the Treasury, who promptly began to place the federal deposits in the hands of the state banks chosen for that purpose.[6]

In his annual message of December 3, 1833, Jackson assumed full responsibility for the removal of the deposits. The Senate responded on December 11 by a written resolution calling for the paper he had read to the cabinet on September 18. Jackson refused to comply on the following grounds:

> The executive is a coordinate and independent branch of the Government equally with the Senate, and I have yet to learn under what constitutional authority that branch of the Legislature has a right to require of me an account of any communication, either verbally or in writing, made to the Heads of the Departments acting as a Cabinet council. As well might I be required to detail to the Senate the free and private conversations I have held with those officers on any subject relating to their duties and my own.[7]

The Whig response was that under the Constitution Congress had been granted control of the public funds, and that the Act of 1789 creating the Treasury Department had made it responsible to Congress rather than to the executive. On March 28, 1834, a resolution censuring the President, introduced by Henry Clay, passed the Senate by a 26-to-20 vote. It stated:

> *Resolved,* that the President, in the late Executive proceedings in relation to the public revenue, had assumed upon himself authority and power not conferred by the Constitution and laws, but in derogation of both.[8]

The Senate also refused to confirm Taney's appointment as secretary of the Treasury.

In reply, Jackson issued a solemn protest on April 15, 1834. In it he argued that his public censure was unconstitutional, for the resolution censuring him indicated that he had committed a high crime, and that if this were true he should have been impeached, which was the only way provided by the Constitution for Congress to call a chief executive to account, and which would have given him an opportunity to defend himself. The Senate, however, refused to accept the protest, and no effort was ever made in the House to impeach Jackson despite his vigorous exercise of presidential power and influence. The censuring resolution remained a heated political issue throughout Jackson's second administration, until January 16, 1837, when the President's supporters had it expunged from the *Senate Journal* over the objections of both those who wanted it to remain and those who simply wanted it rescinded.[9]

Corruption during Jackson's Administration

Convinced that corruption had been rife in the previous administration, Jackson was determined that none should occur in his own, and upon assuming office he launched a full-scale investigation of all the executive departments. To a certain extent, Jackson was successful, for when he left office he was able to note with considerable pride that although his enemies had accused him and his subordinates of all sorts of misconduct, they had not been able to make their charges stick.[10] Still, scholars generally see Jackson's administration as the beginning of an era of decline in public ethics. Although they do not hold Jackson personally culpable, they point out that changing times in terms of the development of lobbies and special-interest groups, the growth of political machines in urban areas such as New York, Boston, and Philadelphia, the development of different standards of morality as a consequence of a massive increase in the number of immigrants, the fact that government officials were handling increasingly large sums of public money, the wild speculations of the 1830s as prosperity returned, and the growing impersonalization of business contracts as banks and corporations began to dominate the economy, all contributed to a decline of public morality.[11]

For his part, Jackson always insisted that all new appointments to office should be made on the basis of merit. He withdrew from nomination for public office a number of people who in the past were supposed to have been lax in their handling of public funds, and he was highly critical of all federal employees who used the insolvent debtor's act to avoid payment of their private debts. Further, he requested Congress to tighten up the laws dealing with civil servants involved in embezzlement, expressed concern over the fraudulent nature of many applications for pensions, urged that the revenue laws be revised to prevent the evasion of customs duties, and pressed for an improvement in the existing system of government accounting.[12]

Nonetheless, congressional investigating bodies were able to come up with various examples of misuse of public money by officers under Jackson's authority. The main problem was with those departments and bureaus that operated in the field, away from Washington, where supervision was very difficult. These included the custom houses, particularly the one in New York City, the Post Office, the War and Navy Departments, and especially the Bureau of Indian Affairs, whose budget had increased enormously over the past two decades.[13] Writing after he left office, Jackson observed of the Indian Bureau:

> I found it the most arduous part of my duty. . . . I watched over it with great vigilance, and could hardly keep it under proper restraint, and free from abuses and inquiry to the administration.[14]

The greatest embarrassment to Jackson came from an investigation of the Post Office. The department was headed by William T. Barry, a loyal supporter of the President but a very poor administrator. The investigation revealed that not only had mail service deteriorated but gross mismanagement had taken place in letting contracts for the delivery of the mail. This involved favoritism in awarding contracts, collusion between contractors and a number of important subordinates in the Post Office Department entailing excessively high rates for services, and permitting of extra allowances for improvements in service after the contract was awarded. The department was also criticized for sweeping partisan removal of postmasters, for failing adequately to supervise contract performances, audit its accounts, collect its debts, and enter into legal proceedings when necessary. Barry, however, was not charged with any kind of criminal activity, and even Henry Clay testified to his personal honesty. The department's difficulties stemmed rather from Barry's incompetence and negligence. Following Barry's resignation, Jackson appointed Amos Kendall postmaster general, who proceeded to implement a series of long-needed reforms. Although the episode provided considerable political ammunition for the President's enemies, he was never found to be personally involved in what had occurred.[15]

NOTES

[1]J. D. Richardson, ed., *A Compilation of the Messages and Papers of the Presidents, 1789–1897* (10 vols., Washington, D.C., 1900), II, 448–449.

[2]Leonard D. White, *The Jacksonians* (New York, 1964), 300–346; Albert Somit, "Andrew Jackson as Administrative Returner," *Tennessee Historical Quarterly*, XIII (September, 1954), 204–223; Erik M. Eriksson, "The Federal Civil Service under President Jackson," *Mississippi Valley Historical Review*, XIII (1926–1927), 517–540.

[3]White, *Jacksonians*, 40–42, 106–111; Carl Russell Fish, *The Civil Service and the Patronage* (Cambridge, Mass., 1905), 140–145; Edwin A. Miles, "The Whig Party and the Menace of Caesar," *Tennessee Historical Quarterly*, XXVII (Winter, 1968), 361–379.

[4]3 Stat. 266, Sec. 16 (April 10, 1816).

[5]William J. Duane, *Narrative and Correspondence Concerning the Removal of the Deposits* . . . (Philadelphia, 1838).

[6]Richardson, *Messages and Papers of the Presidents*, III, 5–19.

[7]*Ibid.*, 36.

[8]*Senate Journal*, 23rd Cong., 1st Sess., 197.

[9]Richardson, *Messages and Papers of the Presidents*, III, 69–93, 93–94.

[10]Jackson to Henry A. Wise, January 26, 1837, in John Spencer Bassett, ed., *The Correspondence of Andrew Jackson* (7 vols., Washington, D.C., 1826–1833), V, 452–453.

[11]White, *Jacksonians*, 411–436.

[12]Albert Somit, "Andrew Jackson as Administrative Reformer," *Tennessee Historical Quarterly*, XIII, 204–223.

[13]White, *Jacksonians*, 411–436.

[14]Jackson to Francis P. Blair, June 4, 1838, in Bassett, *Correspondence*, V, 553.

[15]White, *Jacksonians*, 251–283; Dorothy Ganfield Fowler, *The Cabinet Politician* (New York, 1943), 1–20; William Stickney, ed., *Autobiography of Amos Kendall* (Boston, 1872), 331–347; *Senate Document 422*, 23rd Cong., 1st Sess.; *House Report 103*, 23rd Cong., 2nd Sess.

MARTIN VAN BUREN
1837–1841

Richard E. Ellis

Martin Van Buren was widely viewed in his own time as a sly politician and manipulator of men (unjustly, many historians feel), but no formal charges of any significance involving corruption or misuse of power were brought directly against him as president. As Jackson's hand-picked successor, Van Buren did not engage in sweeping removals. The question of depositing federal funds in the state banks had been settled by the passage of the Deposit Act of 1836 and subsequently by Van Buren's policy of divorcing federal funds from all banks. Also, the Panic of 1837, followed by a depression, gave the Whigs a more effective set of issues with which to attack the President. Certain problems remained, however. In particular, it continued to be difficult to supervise those departments and bureaus that operated in areas away from Washington. The biggest scandal had to do with Samuel Swartwout, collector of the Port of New York. Van Buren had opposed his original appointment in 1829, and when Swartwout's second term expired in 1838, Van Buren did not renominate him. Swartwout sailed for Europe, and a short time later an audit of his books revealed that he had defaulted on about $2,250,000. It was an embarrassing disclosure, to be sure, and Van Buren suffered politically from it, but there never was any serious question of his personal involvement. Swartwout's successor was Jesse D. Hoyt. Appointed by Van Buren, he too embezzled funds and engaged in other corrupt practices, though his misconduct was not disclosed until later. Hoyt's appointment is viewed by scholars as a case of poor judgment on Van Buren's part.[1]

NOTES

[1]Leonard D. White, *The Jacksonians* (New York, 1964), 424–428; Carl Russell Fish, *The Civil Service and the Patronage* (Cambridge, Mass., 1905), 139–140; J. C. Fitzpatrick, ed., *Autobiography of Martin Van Buren,* American Historical Association, *Annual Report for the Year 1918,* II, 262–272, 536; James C. Curtis, *The Fox at Bay: Martin Van Buren and the Presidency, 1837–1841* (Lexington, Ky., 1970), 138–140.

WILLIAM HENRY HARRISON
MARCH–APRIL, 1841
JOHN TYLER, 1841–1845

Michael F. Holt

The Whig Party came to power in 1841 behind William Henry Harrison, but Harrison died one month after assuming office. He was succeeded by Vice President John Tyler of Virginia, who thereby became not only the first man to attain the office under those circumstances but also the nominal head of the Whig Party. He quickly broke with the party, however, by vetoing the heart of its economic program. In September, 1841, all but one member of his cabinet resigned in unison, and a congressional Whig caucus read him out of the party. Outraged feelings of betrayal, therefore, engendered much of the Whig opposition to him during the remainder of his administration. Tyler's effective use of the appointive power to fill the executive branch with men loyal to him and his frequent recourse to the veto especially infuriated the Whigs, for they had organized as a party to oppose the strong presidential actions of "King Andrew" Jackson, actions they considered constitutionally illegitimate. Despite the obviously vindictive motivations and questionable constitutional interpretations of Tyler's Whig foes, their allegations against the President help illuminate contemporary thinking about the propriety of secrecy in presidential conduct, the limits of executive privilege, and the acceptability of the president's unauthorized use of federal funds to hire private agents to do his bidding. Tyler's responses to congressional allegations, in turn, reveal how easily the president could defy Congress to enlarge his powers. The confrontations between the two branches, finally, went far toward defining what officeholders considered the proper boundaries of the impeachment process itself.

The Poindexter Commission

In May, 1841, Tyler appointed three private citizens to investigate rumors of fraud in the New York Custom House during the administration of his predecessor, Martin Van Buren. Led by George Poindexter, a former governor and a United States senator from Mississippi, this group eventually unearthed the fraudulent activities of Jesse D. Hoyt, New York collector under Van Buren.[1] By February, 1842, the Whig-controlled House learned of the Poindexter commission and requested Tyler to inform the House under what authority he had appointed the commissioners, how much they were being paid, from what funds they were being paid, and what their purpose was. Tyler's reply defended the legality of his action as a function of his constitutional duty to enforce the laws and promised he would send more information about the investigation later. He said nothing about the funding of the agents.[2] At the same time, Tyler privately wrote Poindexter that the commission's report would be seen only by the President and that he alone would decide what information, if any, would be forwarded to Congress.[3]

Congressmen were clearly disturbed by two distinct but related issues: Tyler's right to pay unauthorized private agents with federal funds and his right to withhold information from a congressional committee. Stymied by the President's stall tactics, the House Committee on Public Expenditures subpoenaed information from Poindexter himself. On April 29, 1842, when the commission had completed its investigation, the House again asked Tyler for the commission report, and the President complied the following day. His message to the House again defended the necessity and legality of his action. The House, which knew of Tyler's earlier promise to Poindexter to withhold information, was not appeased by the President's compliance and was further angered by the fact that Poindexter's report proved embarrassing to the Whig incumbent in the New York custom house as well as to the Democrat Hoyt. In early May the House passed by a vote of 86 to 83 an extraordinary resolution that

> the President has no rightful authority to appoint and commission officers to investigate abuses, or to provide information for the

President to act upon, and to compensate such officers at public expense, without authority given by law.

During the debate on these resolutions, Whigs denounced Tyler's rationale as a "monstrous doctrine," and Edward Stanley of North Carolina insisted that the activities of all persons in the pay of the government should be public knowledge.[4] At the urging of John Quincy Adams, the House tabled this resolution as soon as it had passed, but added a proviso to an appropriation bill, which eventually became law, forbidding the payment of any agents or commissioners appointed by the president to conduct investigations until Congress specifically appropriated funds for such payments.[5]

Other Clashes over Executive Privilege

The episode with the Poindexter commission did not end congressional attempts to pry information from the executive. In March, 1842, the House unsuccessfully requested information from Tyler concerning patronage applications from incumbent or former congressmen. Tyler refused and denounced the request as an encroachment upon the confidentiality of the executive branch and upon his power of appointment. It was, he fumed, "dangerous, impolitic, and unconstitutional."[6] The House apparently acquiesced in this denial.

But it was not ready to concede the principle, and in May, 1842, the House demanded information from the Secretary of War about investigations being conducted by the army concerning alleged frauds against the Cherokee Indians. Upon direct instructions from Tyler, the Secretary refused to comply, insisting that the information gathered was *ex parte* and that its disclosure would not be in the public interest. This refusal in June provoked a six-day debate in August. Eventually the House passed three resolutions. The first insisted that "the House of Representatives has a right to demand from the Executive or heads of Departments such information as may be in their possession, relating to subjects of the deliberations of the House and within the sphere of its legitimate powers." The third again "requested" Tyler to order the army officer investigating the case to turn over all the facts he had discovered. It also "requested . . .

all facts in the possession of the Executive, 'from any source, relating to the subject.' "[7] In part because Congress adjourned shortly after passing these resolutions, Tyler made no attempt to respond until the next session, in January. But Tyler also refrained because he faced a far more serious allegation from Congress that August.

Demands for Impeachment

While the House was debating Tyler's obstreperous refusal to cooperate, the President returned his fourth veto of a major Whig economic measure. Rather than placing the veto message on the record, the House appointed a select committee headed by former president John Quincy Adams of Massachusetts and John Minor Botts of Virginia to report on the veto. The committee's majority report vented the accumulated frustration of the long-suffering Whigs. The Constitution, it insisted, made the president "dependent upon and responsible to" Congress, yet Tyler's vetoes had nullified "the whole action of the Legislative authority of this Union." The committee charged that Tyler had formally pledged to a congressman that he would sign an earlier bill and then had violated the pledge by vetoing the measure. It criticized as "anomalies of character and conduct rarely seen upon earth" Tyler's "effusions of temper and sentiment divulged at convivial festivities," his obtrusion "upon the public eye by the fatal friendship of sycophant private correspondents," and his usurpation of legislative and judicial power, by which it apparently meant the vetoes. The committee's majority, the report stated, thought Tyler's actions merited invocation of the impeachment process, but they did not recommend it because impeachment would fail at that time. By a vote of 100–80, the House accepted this report with its implications that Tyler had indeed committed impeachable offenses.[8]

Tyler responded with a formal protest to the House on August 30, 1842. Using language not found in the report itself, he accused the committee of "Arraign[ing]" his motives, "assail[ing] [his] whole official conduct," and charging him with impeachable offenses without impeaching him. The House must impeach him, protested Tyler, if it was willing to vote him guilty of such offenses, so he could defend his honor in a Senate trial. Denying the truth of any of the charges, Tyler seemed to concur with the committee that if they were true, he deserved both impeachment and removal from office:

> I am charged with offenses against the country so grave and hei-
> nous as to deserve public disgrace and disfranchisement. I am
> charged with violating pledges which I never gave, with usurping
> powers not conferred by law, and above all, with using the pow-
> ers conferred upon the President by the Constitution from corrupt
> motives and for unwarrantable ends.[9]

Tyler, that is, agreed that duplicity, lying to Congress, was grounds for conviction.

To Tyler's dismay, the House refused even to accept his protest and put it on the record. Instead, the House denounced the protest itself as a breach of House privileges.[10] Nor had Tyler heard the last cry for impeachment.

The House vote in August to accept the critical Adams report pro-vided the justification for Botts, a bitter foe of Tyler, to present in January nine formal articles of impeachment for "high crimes and misdemeanors."[11] Botts assailed as impeachable Tyler's entire record in office. His first six charges listed as abuses of power presidential pre-rogatives like appointments, removals, and the veto which had long been accepted as constitutional. The last three charges merit extensive quotation because they summarize so well what many congressmen considered misbehavior.

> I charge him with gross official misconduct, in having been guilty of
> shameless duplicity, equivocation, and falsehood, with his late Cab-
> inet and Congress . . . by which he has brought such dishonor on
> himself as to disqualify him from administering the Government
> with advantage, honor, or virtue, and for which alone he would de-
> serve to be removed from office.
>
> I charge him with an illegal and unconstitutional exercise of
> power, in instituting a commission to investigate past transactions
> under a former administration of the custom house in New York,
> under the pretense of seeing the laws faithfully executed . . . with
> having directed or sanctioned the appropriation of large sums of

the public revenue to the compensation of officers of his own creation, without the authority of law; which, if sanctioned, would place the entire revenues of the country at his disposal.

I charge him with the high misdemeanor of having withheld from the Representatives of the people information called for, and declared to be necessary to the investigation of stupendous frauds and abuses alleged to have been committed by agents of the Government, both upon individuals and the Government itself, whereby he becomes accessory to those frauds.

Little came of Botts's articles of impeachment. On January 18, 1843, the House defeated his motion to appoint a committee to investigate them by a vote of 127–83.[12] Tyler, therefore, never had to respond formally. But he did so indirectly in a message of January 31, 1843, when he finally answered the House request for information on the War Department investigations of the Cherokee frauds. While he sent in all the findings, he vigorously defended his earlier refusal to comply. His constitutional obligation to enforce the laws dictated his undertaking executive investigations, he argued, and those inquiries could succeed only if the information remained confidential. Citing the House's previous acquiescence in his refusal to turn over patronage papers as implicit recognition of executive privilege, he specifically addressed the House resolutions limiting that privilege passed the previous August. He firmly denied that the House's right to demand information meant that the president had to comply with such a demand or that any papers in the hands of the president or cabinet members "must necessarily be subject to the call of the House of Representatives *merely* because they related to a subject of the deliberations of the House." "Certain communications" were "privileged," and "the general authority to compel testimony must give way in certain cases to the paramount rights of individuals or of the Government." Tyler also took the opportunity to denounce the new law forbidding payment of presidential investigations without specific congressional authorization. That law, he protested, "virtually denied to the Executive" the power to undertake investigations of executive departments no matter how urgent the necessity or flagrant the abuse.[13]

Secret Activities in Maine before the Webster-Ashburton Treaty

The allegations of misbehavior against Tyler that emerged during his presidency primarily concerned the impropriety of his secrecy itself and his defiance of Congress. Unknown to his Whig foes at the time, Tyler was also engaged in secret maneuvers that eventually involved all the questionable precedents aired publicly during his administration: the use of unauthorized agents, their payment with funds appropriated for other purposes, and the limits of executive privilege in national security matters. These activities, moreover, would later engender far graver charges of corruption and perversion of the political process. They were discovered in part by Democratic congressmen in 1846, during the Polk administration, when charges were raised against Tyler's Secretary of State Daniel Webster. The full story of these activities, however, has only recently been unraveled by historians, and the extent of Tyler's culpability is clearer now than it was then.[14]

By the early 1840s disputes about the exact location of the Maine-Canadian boundary threatened to provoke war between England and the United States. Both nations hoped to avoid conflict through a treaty, but the state of Maine, itself a legal party to the dispute, refused to enter negotiations. Until Maine agreed, nothing could be done. To prompt Maine's attendance at the proposed parley, Tyler authorized Secretary of State Webster to hire private agents in Maine to persuade local newspaper editors and state legislators to support the impending talks between Webster and Lord Ashburton. Employed secretly, these agents were paid from a presidential contingency fund, known as "the secret service fund," authorized yearly by Congress since 1810 for secret activities *abroad* in connection with foreign relations. In effect, as Frederick Merk demonstrates so forcefully, private citizens were secretly employed with funds specifically appropriated for activities outside the nation to influence domestic political decisions. "It meant federally subsidized electioneering to manage the sentiment of a state of the union."[15]

Even more dubious activities may have been involved. New York was at the time prosecuting a Canadian citizen named McLeod for murder in its state courts. Conviction would utterly disrupt Anglo-American relations, and the Tyler administration badly wanted McLeod released.

When the case came to trial, the two main witnesses against the Canadian failed to appear, and he was acquitted. In Webster's records of payments was an expenditure of $1,000 to the Attorney General of the United States for services in New York at the time of the trial. Historians have never been able to determine how this money was spent, but it seems possible that members of the cabinet bribed the witnesses. The closest students of the affair, however, doubt that this obstruction of justice took place.[16]

When the Democrats learned of the secret expenditures in 1846, after Tyler had left office, they seized the opportunity to embarrass the Whig Webster, once again senator from Massachusetts. In February, 1846, a New York Democratic senator charged Webster with "palpable and direct" interference in the McLeod trial: "an attempt on the part of the authorities at Washington to arrest the ordinary course of justice, and prevent a trial upon the merits." In April Charles J. Ingersoll, Democratic chairman of the House Committee on Foreign Affairs, accused Webster of unlawfully spending the President's contingency fund without Tyler's permission, of keeping that money for long periods of time and perhaps using it for private profit, of being in default to the government for over $2,000 when he left the State Department in 1843, and, with the aid of his Maine agents, of using government funds to "corrupt party presses" in Maine.[17] Upon Ingersoll's demand, a special committee of five was appointed to investigate his charges against the former secretary.

The House investigation of Webster evoked a new defense of executive privilege from President James K. Polk, but it produced a significant agreement between Polk and the House about the limits of that privilege should impeachment proceedings be started. The House, moreover, successfully summoned testimony from former president Tyler. Finally, in its report absolving Webster of all charges against him, the committee consciously refused to pass judgment on the most critical issue in the case—the use of funds appropriated for secret activities abroad to influence internal political events.

On April 9, 1846, the House committee asked Polk to send it Tyler's record of all payments made from the contingency fund during Webster's term as secretary of state. Polk refused on the grounds that the 1810 law creating the fund had specifically differentiated between public and secret expenditures. For the latter, the president merely had to provide certificates that he had authorized such expenditures, but he did not have to itemize them or state their purpose. By providing Tyler's records, Polk argued, he would violate the law. Polk, however, noted a major exception to this rule of executive privilege in national security matters. His reasoning merits extensive quotation.

> It may be alleged that the power of impeachment belongs to the House of Representatives, and that, with a view to the exercise of this power, the House has a right to investigate the conduct of all public officers under the Government. This is cheerfully admitted. In such a case the safety of the Republic would be the supreme law, and the power of the House in the pursuit of this object would penetrate into the most secret recesses of the Executive Departments. It could command the attendance of any and every agent of the Government, and compel them to produce all papers, public and private, official and unofficial, and to testify on oath to all facts within their knowledge. But even in a case of that kind they would adopt all wise precautions to prevent the exposure of all such matters the publication of which might injuriously affect the public interest, except so far as this might be necessary to accomplish the great ends of public justice. If the House of Representatives, as the grand inquest of the nation, should at any time have reason to believe that there has been a malversation in office by an improper use or application of the public money by a public officer, and should think proper to institute an inquiry into the matter, all the archives and papers of the Executive Departments, public or private, would be subject to the inspection and control of a committee of their body and every facility in the power of the Executive be afforded to enable them to prosecute the investigation.

Because impeachment proceedings were not under way, however, Polk would not turn over the records of Webster and Tyler.[18]

Democrats controlled the House, and they refused to challenge their leader, Polk, any further. But, armed with Ingersoll's stealthily acquired information, the investigating committee summoned former president Tyler to testify, and he appeared before it. Tyler refused to name any of the agents operating in Maine, claiming the confidentiality of presidential dealings in sensitive security matters. He intimated, however, that he might surrender even this privilege if the committee made a further ruling. It apparently made no such ruling. Tyler testified that he had authorized Webster's payments, thus refuting Ingersoll's first charge. Citing the McLeod case and the tensions along the Maine-Canadian frontier, he asserted that "the peace of the country was most seriously threatened," and therefore his actions were justified. The money was spent, he insisted, to pay agents in Maine to persuade editors and politicians, not to bribe them by direct payoffs. In later testimony F. O. J. Smith, Webster's principal operative in Maine, reaffirmed this distinction. Tyler further noted that Webster had appeared to be in arrears to the contingency fund by a sum over $2,000 when he left the State Department in 1843, but returned the money out of his own pocket on the understanding that the government would repay him when he produced vouchers that the money had been spent in government service.[19]

Splitting four to one, the Committee on Official Misconduct of the Late Secretary of State exonerated Webster of all charges. Webster had spent the money legally, had accounted for it, and had not attempted to "corrupt party presses" in Maine. The majority report explicitly dodged the most serious issue in the whole affair—the misuse of funds allocated for foreign relations. The committee did "not deem it necessary or expedient . . . to inquire into the propriety of employing agents for secret service within the United States, and paying them out of a contingent fund for foreign intercourse." Equally important, the committee endorsed Polk's view that executive privilege should be entirely suspended in case of impeachment, but since there were no grounds for impeachment, they urged that much of the testimony remain secret.[20]

NOTES

[1]For the reports, see *House Document 210,* 27th Cong. 2nd Sess.; *House Report 669,* 27th Cong., 2nd Sess.

[2]Robert J. Morgan, *A Whig Embattled: The Presidency under John Tyler* (Lincoln, Neb., 1954), 90–93; James D. Richardson, *A Compilation of the Messages and Papers of the Presidents* (11 vols., Washington, D.C., 1913), 1952–1953.

[3]*Congressional Globe,* 27th Cong., 2nd Sess., 476.

[4]Richardson, *Messages,* 2005–2007. For the House resolution and the fascinating

debates, which include a copy of Tyler's letter to Poindexter, see *Congressional Globe*, 27th Cong., 2nd Sess., 475–479.

[5]Morgan, *Whig Embattled*, 92–93. Morgan points out that this clause prohibited only the payment of private agents, not their use if the investigators went unpaid or if their office were established by law. The law was passed August 26, 1842.

[6]Richardson, *Messages*, 1958–1959.

[7]Morgan, *Whig Embattled*, 93–94; *House Journal*, 27th Cong., 2nd Sess., 1290.

[8]*House Journal*, 27th Cong., 2nd Sess., 1347–1353.

[9]Richardson, *Messages*, 2043–2046.

[10]*Congressional Globe*, 27th Cong., 2nd Sess., 974.

[11]These charges can be found in *Congressional Globe*, 27th Cong., 3rd Sess., 144.

[12]*Ibid.*, 144–146.

[13]Richardson, *Messages*, 2073–2078.

[14]Frederick Merk, *Fruits of Propaganda in the Tyler Administration* (Cambridge, Mass., 1971).

[15]*Ibid.*, 89 and *passim.*

[16]A very careful analysis can be found *ibid.*, 10–15.

[17]*Ibid.*, 69–70. Merk reproduces Ingersoll's charges and speech, 180–185. Ingersoll himself had clandestinely gained access to secret State Department archives and had found Webster's record of expenditures as well as his correspondence with agents in Maine.

[18]Richardson, *Messages*, 2281–2286.

[19]Tyler's testimony and that of Smith are reprinted in Merk, *Fruits*, 191–210.

[20]The committee report can be found *ibid.*, 185–191.

JAMES K. POLK
1845–1849

Michael F. Holt

Aside from the Investigation of Webster, few charges of criminal misconduct arose during the presidency of James K. Polk, and none of these involved Polk himself or men close to him. Indeed, Polk had a reputation of unimpeachable personal integrity, and he was an incredibly vigilant watchdog over almost all activities within the executive branch. He moved quickly and ruthlessly against any officeholders guilty of peculation or corruption, at least against men so charged. He even wanted to remove General Winfield Scott from command of American forces in Mexico when he heard rumors that Scott had tried to bribe the Mexicans to make peace.[1] When Secretary of State James Buchanan was accused of leaking secret documents to the press, Polk urged the Senate to investigate, and Buchanan was cleared. Polk was often criticized for duplicity, highhanded usurpation, and unconstitutional behavior in his conduct of foreign affairs. His role in provoking war with Mexico especially brought censure from his Whig foes. Partisan opposition to Polk was fierce, but charges of corrupt behavior simply were not raised during his presidency.[2]

The Purchase of the Washington Globe

Actually, there was an incident of clear corruption and favoritism during Polk's administration that came close to the President and that would have tarnished his reputation had it been known. Even now, all the details are mysterious. The episode involved the use of government funds to help the Democrats buy a newspaper in Washington to serve as an administration organ during Polk's tenure. Partisan control of newspapers was the rule rather than the exception in the nineteenth century, and until the spectacular revelations of the Covode Committee in 1860, almost every administration awarded government contracts for printing to its newspaper in Washington. Such contracts were enormously lucrative, and part of the profits was regularly plowed back into the party coffers for campaign expenses. What was unusual about the incident in Polk's term concerned the initial purchase of the paper, not the later letting of printing contracts.

When Polk came to Washington in 1845, he was determined to replace the old Democratic sheet, the *Globe,* and its editor, Francis P. Blair, with a new spokesman, the Richmond editor Thomas Ritchie. Ritchie, however, lacked the $35,000 necessary to purchase the *Globe.* The deal was effected with the use of government funds. Half was advanced by the Treasurer of the United States against prospective payments he would make to Ritchie for government printing, and half came from a government deposit in a Pennsylvania bank owned by a Democratic senator, Simon Cameron. Polk's secretary of the Treasury, Robert J. Walker, made no attempt to recall this deposit from the bank until 1847, after the final installment on the *Globe* had been paid. How much Polk knew of these details is unclear. Apparently he tried to insulate himself from the facts. His biographer concludes, "Polk must have taken pains to know as little as possible about the transaction."[3] Apparently no public charges were ever raised about this affair during Polk's term, and he was required to make no response.

NOTES

[1]For defense of Polk's honesty, see Charles A. McCoy, *Polk and the Presidency* (Austin, 1960), 73, 76–81, 200–201; Eugene Irving McCormac, *James K. Polk: A Political Biography* (Berkeley, 1922), 331, 531.

[2]For an account of opposition to Polk's war policies, which is itself unsympathetic to Polk but still fails to list charges of corruption in its extensive catalogue of accusations, see John H. Schroeder, *Mr. Polk's War: American Opposition and Dissent, 1846–1848* (Madison, Wis., 1973). Polk's most able biographer, Charles G. Sellers, accuses the President of almost "congenital" deception in his dealings with Congress, but he too defends Polk's integrity: *James K. Polk, Continentalist, 1843–1846* (Princeton, 1966), 219, 359–362, and *passim.*

[3]Sellers, *Polk,* 274–279; McCoy, *Polk and the Presidency,* 187.

ZACHARY TAYLOR
1849–1850

Michael F. Holt

D amaging charges of conflict of interest were raised in the spring of 1850 against three members of Zachary Taylor's cabinet and acutely embarrassed the President. Democratic newspapers also accused a fourth member, Secretary of the Interior Thomas Ewing, of making illegal payments on several large claims against the government and of employing large numbers of clerks without congressional authorization. Historians, however, have had difficulty reconstructing Taylor's response to these allegations because his private papers were largely destroyed. They have had to rely on the accounts of others. A further hindrance to ascertaining his response is that the charges of corruption became inextricably entwined in a larger battle between the President and Congress over the Compromise of 1850. Thus it is difficult to say precisely why he acted as he did. From the available evidence of his thoughts and actions, however, Taylor seems to have been guilty at least of stubborn delay in purging his cabinet of the stigma of scandal, and guilty perhaps also of moral obtuseness.

The Galphin Claim

The actions of the executive in paying off a claim against the government by the Galphin family of Georgia constituted the most serious scandal of Taylor's term, and the word "Galphinism" became a slogan used by administration foes to symbolize all the rumored corruption in the executive branch. The details behind this affair are complex. Essentially it involved the pre-Revolutionary War claim of a Georgia Indian trader named George Galphin against the British government. The British recognized the legitimacy of the claim for approximately $43,500, but the Revolutionary War intervened before payment could be made. After the war Galphin and his family pressed the claim against both the state of Georgia and the United States. Finally, in 1848, Congress passed a law directing the Secretary of the Treasury to adjust the claim and pay the amount due the Galphin heirs. Polk's Treasury secretary, Walker, thereupon paid the principal to the Galphin estate, but he deferred any action on the accumulated interest on the debt, an amount over four times as large as the principal.

The decision on the interest fell to the Taylor administration. Secretary of the Treasury William Meredith referred the claim to the Comptroller, who ruled against payment of any interest. Then Meredith sought an opinion from Attorney General Reverdy Johnson, who ruled early in 1850 that the interest must be paid. Meredith then ordered interest amounting to over $191,000 paid to the Galphins, bringing the total settlement to about $235,000.

The size of this payment alone provoked criticism of a raid on the Treasury. More embarrassing, Taylor's secretary of war, George W. Crawford, profited from the settlement. Since 1832 Crawford had been the attorney for the Galphin family, and he had been promised as a fee half of any payment from the government on the claim. When he joined the cabinet, this agreement continued, although Crawford was no longer the attorney of record for the family. Crawford therefore received about $95,000 as a result of the decision of Meredith and Johnson. Democratic newspapers shrieked of a Whig conspiracy to plunder the public purse. Even Whig papers condemned the cabinet for not holding a meeting on so large a claim in order to avoid both the substance and the appearance of impropriety. Confronted with these accusations, Crawford himself asked the House to investigate his role in the matter on April 2, 1850.[1]

Crucial questions were raised. How much had Taylor known about Crawford's interest in the claim when he appointed him? Did Meredith and Johnson know when they made the decision? How could they not have known? Did Crawford exploit his position to speed and shape the decision? Finally, what was Taylor going to do about this flagrant conflict of interest?

The Whig administrators protested their innocence. When a cabinet meeting was finally held on the claim, after public charges had been raised, both Meredith and Johnson denied any knowledge of Crawford's stake in the claim. The culpability of Taylor and Crawford is more difficult to ascertain. Crawford told the House committee that he first informed Taylor of his connection to the claim in May, 1849, although he evidently did not make clear to Taylor that Congress had already handed the decision to the Treasury Department or that he would receive approximately half of any award. According to Crawford, Taylor told him then that "none of [his] pre-existing individual rights . . . had been curtailed by his acceptance of office." During a second discussion of the matter in March, 1850, Crawford testified, Taylor told him that he now understood the matter more clearly but that his opinion had not changed: "that being at the head of the War Department, and agent of the claimants, did not deprive him of the rights he may have had as such agent, nor would have justified him [Taylor] in having the examination and decision of the claim by the Secretary of the Treasury suspended."[2] This, of course, is only Crawford's testimony about what Taylor said. What is clear is that when the rest of the cabinet demanded Crawford's dismissal, Taylor refused.[3]

Later in the spring, the House investigating committee reported, and there was a sharp debate on its report in early July. The committee divided along partisan lines over whether the interest should have been paid, but they were unanimous that the 1848 law compelled Walker to pay the principal. The debate was very confused. Some Democrats demanded laws prohibiting cabinet members from deciding on claims to which any other cabinet member was a party. At various times amendments were passed and then buried that criticized Meredith and Johnson and condemned what Taylor had supposedly told Crawford about the propriety of his continued interest in the claim while in high executive office. Eventually, the House voted to accept the three resolutions accompanying the majority report. These held that the entire Galphin claim was unjust, that the law compelled Walker to pay the principal, and that Meredith's payment of the interest was unauthorized. In accepting these resolutions, the House acquiesced in the majority report, which also found that Crawford had not used his position to influence the decision and that Johnson and Meredith had not known of Crawford's interest.[4]

Even before this final House action, pressure was mounting on the seemingly impervious Taylor to dismiss the three cabinet officers and Ewing as well. Much of this pressure was political and had more to do with Taylor's fight against the Compromise than with the Galphin claim itself. By early July, Taylor, who was terribly pained by the uproar even if he was unconvinced any wrong had been done, had apparently decided to remake the cabinet. But he wanted to wait until the end of the regular session of Congress that summer or at least until after the July 4th recess. Taylor's sudden death on July 9, 1850, intervened before he could take action. His successor, Millard Fillmore, who wanted to reverse the White House's position on the Compromise, demanded the resignations of the entire cabinet, and he replaced them with new men.[5]

NOTES

[1] Allan Nevins, *Ordeal of the Union* (2 vols., New York, 1947), I, 324–327; Holman Hamilton, *Zachary Taylor: Soldier in the White House* (Indianapolis, 1951), 345–356.

[2] The quotations are taken from the committee report on the Galphin Claim. See *Congressional Globe*, 31st Cong., 1st Sess., Appx., 546–549.

[3] Hamilton, *Zachary Taylor*, 347.

[4] *Congressional Globe*, 31st Cong., 1st Sess., 1340–1360.

[5] The evidence that Taylor was prepared to reorganize his cabinet rests primarily on the account of an interview with the President on July 3, 1850, by New York editor and Whig boss Thurlow Weed. Weed recorded this account many years later in his autobiography. Historians, therefore, differ in their certainty about Taylor's decision. His biographer Holman Hamilton, *Zachary Taylor*, 355–356, says Taylor "almost surely" planned a cabinet shakeup, while Allan Nevins and Robert Rayback state much more positively that he did. Nevins, *Ordeal*, I, 327; Rayback, *Millard Fillmore: Biography of a President* (Buffalo, 1959), 236–237.

MILLARD FILLMORE
1850–1853

Michael F. Holt

A s was the case with almost every ante-bellum administration, Millard Fillmore's was not entirely free of corruption or improper behavior. Most of this occurred at lower levels of the executive branch, such as custom houses, and Fillmore probably never knew of it. He may have been more aware that his secretary of the Treasury, Thomas Corwin, was flouting the letter of the Independent Treasury Act by using private Whig bankers, rather than Treasury officials, to buy back government bonds to reduce the debt. These practices, however, were not discovered until 1853 when Corwin's Democratic successor, James B. Guthrie, took over the Treasury.[1] During Fillmore's term itself, no serious allegations of misconduct appear to have been raised, and Fillmore was therefore required to make no response.[2]

NOTES

[1] Roy F. Nichols, *Franklin Pierce: Young Hickory of the Granite Hills* (2nd ed. rev., Philadelphia, 1958), 270–272.

[2] Excluded here is a charge raised by a Massachusetts foe of Fillmore's secretary of state, Daniel Webster, that Webster was corrupt for accepting a fund raised by wealthy Bostonians to defray his expenses in that office. Webster denied that he even knew the names of the donors, although he accepted such funds throughout his public career. Allan Nevins, *Ordeal of the Union* (2 vols., New York, 1947), I, 394.

FRANKLIN PIERCE
1853–1857

Michael F. Holt

On the surface, Franklin Pierce's administration was relatively free of corruption. He appointed several vigorous cabinet members like Guthrie who attempted to stop questionable practices in their departments, and Pierce assumed a public pose of rectitude.[1] As a result, Pierce and his men escaped any serious allegations of misbehavior even though their policies drew stormy political opposition. Beneath the surface, however, there seems to have been widespread corruption, favoritism, and fraud, much of which would be exposed only during the term of Pierce's successor, James Buchanan. Pierce, for example, appointed Isaac Fowler as postmaster of New York, and Buchanan reappointed him. During his whole term in office, Fowler stole postal revenues and gave them to Democratic candidates during elections. By 1860 Fowler had to flee the country when his accounts were short about $160,000.[2] Similarly, navy yards frequently favored political contributors in the awarding of contracts, and those practices were exposed in 1859. Finally, the Pierce administration gave the executive printing to Cornelius Wendell, part-owner of the Democratic organ in Washington, the *Union,* and Wendell in turn contributed some of his huge profits to Democratic newspapers and candidates. Wendell's whole operation would be exposed at the end of Buchanan's term. The absence of detailed allegations against, and congressional investigations of, Pierce's administration, then, is not an accurate index of its ethics.

Speculation in Kansas by Governor Reeder

On at least one occasion, however, Pierce displayed morally dubious behavior in response to allegations against a government official. Rather than acting immediately to dismiss the individual, he delayed and then tried to use the charges as leverage in dealing with a difficult political situation. The charges involved illegal or at least improper land speculations by Andrew Reeder, the man Pierce had appointed governor of the Kansas Territory. Normally, the activities of a territorial governor would not come close enough to a president to cause him embarrassment, but the organization and administration of Kansas was the central political issue of Pierce's entire term; he had carefully picked the Pennsylvanian Reeder to provide balance between the North and South in the disputed territory, and he himself dealt directly with Reeder when charges were raised.

When Reeder arrived in Kansas, he began to arrange the purchase of land on a reservation granted to some Indians by a treaty in 1825. Dealing directly with the Indians rather than through Indian agents and buying reservation land violated long-standing rulings of the government, the treaty of 1825, and the settled policy of officials in the Bureau of Indian Affairs in Washington. Reeder's purpose was purely speculative, for he hoped, and later tried, to establish the territorial capital at Pawnee City on the lands he had contracted to buy, so the price of his lots would rise. Reeder sent his land contracts to the Indian Affairs Commissioner in Washington in January 1855, and that official quickly disallowed them and informed President Pierce they were illegal. Pierce simply returned the contracts to Reeder without approval. In the meantime, allegations were raised in newspapers about Reeder's activities. The situation became vastly complicated by the sectional competition over Kansas. Southern Democrats, who hoped to establish slavery in the territory, demanded Reeder's removal because he was considered pro-northern. Pierce hesitated to act because removing Reeder might offend the North.

The situation was at an impasse when Reeder came east in April to defend his record and secure approval of his land contracts from the Commissioner of Indian Affairs. In early May he confronted Pierce directly. The President chastised Reeder for his actions. Trying to establish the territorial capital on Indian lands only compounded Reeder's sins, he told the governor. Then, primarily because of the southern political pressure, not the illegality of Reeder's actions, Pierce tried to persuade Reeder to resign. According to Reeder's account of the interview, which Pierce never refuted when it became public, the President assured Reeder that he not only would approve of his record as governor but also would make arrangements to "promote [Reeder's] private interests" if Reeder agreed to step down. If Reeder refused, however, he would use the improper land deals as justification for firing him.

Reeder refused to step down, and he returned to Kansas. He even re-submitted his land contracts to Pierce for approval. Finally, in July, 1855, Pierce again sent them to the Indian Office for an opinion on their legality. They were again rejected, and on July 28, at least six months after the speculations had been discovered, Pierce ordered Reeder's dismissal on the ground that his explanation of the land deals was unacceptable.[3]

NOTES

[1]Roy F. Nichols, *Franklin Pierce: Young Hickory of the Granite Hills* (2nd ed. rev., Philadelphia, 1958), 383.

[2]Roy F. Nichols, *The Disruption of American Democracy* (New York, 1948), 311; Leonard D. White, *The Jacksonians: A Study in Administrative History, 1829–1861* (New York, 1965), 429.

[3]Nichols, *Pierce,* 408–418. Allan Nevins in his generally pro-northern account denies that Reeder acted dishonestly in his land deals, and points out that contemporaries such as Thomas Hart Benton recognized that the speculations were only a pretext, not the real reason, for Reeder's dismissal. Nevins, *Ordeal of the Union* (2 vols., New York, 1947), II, 389–390.

JAMES BUCHANAN
1857–1861

Michael F. Holt

The closest student of public administration before the Civil War points to the presidency of James Buchanan as the nadir of antebellum public ethics.[1] All of the trends of corruption at the lower ranks of the government seemed to culminate in three years, and the rate of exposure increased dramatically. Republicans—the new Republican Party had become the nation's second party by 1856—and antiadministration Democrats alike fostered a multitude of congressional investigations of custom houses, navy yards, post offices, and the public printing. These revealed not only executive turpitude but also congressional corruption, not only activities during Buchanan's term but sleazy practices during the entire 1850s and even earlier.

Corruption of the Political Process

There is ample evidence of improper, if not outrightly illegal, Democratic actions to carry the elections of 1856 and 1858, actions of which Buchanan apparently was aware and in which some of his closest friends participated. Whether or not Buchanan directed or approved these activities, he apparently condoned them, for he made no attempt to stop them. Many of these would be exposed by the Covode Committee in 1860.

To raise money for the 1856 campaign, the Democrats employed a host of dubious practices. For example, Buchanan's close personal friend, George Plitt of Philadelphia, promised naval contracts in return for campaign contributions, and such contracts were later awarded.[2] Isaac

Fowler, Democratic postmaster in New York City under both Pierce and Buchanan, directly funneled large sums of government money into Democratic coffers in New York for the campaign.[3] Finally, the major printer of government documents under the two Democratic presidents, Cornelius Wendell, channeled large shares of his inflated profits into the Democratic war chest, as he would again in 1858 and 1860. Wendell later told Congress that between 1856 and 1860 he contributed over $100,000 to Democratic campaigns over and above the portions of his profits he used to support Democratic newspapers in Washington and elsewhere.[4] In addition to the normal antebellum practice of assessing officeholders for campaign contributions, therefore, the Democrats made startlingly effective use of their control of the federal government.

Most of this war chest was spent for perfectly legitimate purposes: subsidization of party newspapers, printing of campaign documents, payment of touring speakers, and printing and distribution of ballots. Getting ballots to the voters was a party, not a governmental, function in the mid-nineteenth century, and it was expensive. Evidence exists, however, that some of the money at least was used to buy votes in Indiana and Pennsylvania. Thousands of aliens, moreover, were illegally naturalized and marched to the polls by the Democrats. Elsewhere the Democratic machine transported immigrant voters to crucial states, where they were not legal residents. Before the important congressional elections in October, 1856, Buchanan's henchman in Philadelphia, John Forney, wrote him, "We have naturalized a vast mass of men and assessed many of the native-born citizens. The Opposition are appalled. They cry fraud. Our most experienced men say *all is well*."[5] Only taxpayers could vote in Pennsylvania, and when Forney spoke of assessing citizens, he probably meant that the Democrats either paid taxes for them or provided them with fraudulent tax assessment records so they could vote. After the election, Virginia fire-eater Edmund Ruffin heard in Washington "that enormous sums of money were sent from the city of New York and a good deal also from the Democrats of New England to buy votes in Pennsylvania and which turned the vote in that state."[6]

Further evidence of Buchanan's acquiescence in corrupt political methods emerged in 1858 during the battle over the Lecompton Constitution in Congress. Buchanan desperately wanted Congress to vote Kansas's admission as a state with that proslavery constitution, and he used almost every means at his disposal to pressure hesitant Democratic congressmen from the North to support the measure. Even Buchanan's sympathetic biographer admits that the President dismissed the friends of anti-Lecompton Democrats from federal jobs, promised new appointments in return for votes, and offered "contracts, commissions, and in some cases cold cash" to wavering congressmen.[7] Cabinet members were especially prominent in dangling government contracts to secure support, and in some cases they abetted corrupt officeholders. To chastise Illinois senator Stephen A. Douglas, for example, Buchanan removed his man in the Chicago post office and replaced him with Douglas's arch foe, Isaac "Ike" Cook. A notorious thief, Cook had held that office before but had left in public disgrace as a defaulter to the government. He still had not paid what he owed the government when Buchanan nominated him in 1858. To meet his debt, Cook had offered the government a plot of land in Chicago to which his title was unclear. Secretary of the Treasury Howell Cobb had previously refused to accept the land as payment. When the administration wanted Cook in office to pursue his feud with Douglas, however, Attorney General Jeremiah S. Black ruled Cook's title valid, and Cobb accepted the land as payment. Cook and his cronies in Chicago then proceeded to rob the post office blind, even pilfering registered mail. Despite cries of outrage, the administration benignly turned its head and kept Cook in office. He was too valuable a foe of the hated Douglas to remove.[8]

Public Printing Scandals

One source of Democratic funds was the public printing rake-off. Until Congress established a government printing office in 1860, government documents from both the executive branch and Congress were published by private printers. During the ante-bellum period, Congress experimented with different methods of awarding those lucrative contracts, and theoretically they should have gone to the lowest bidder. In practice, however, since the days of Jackson they had gone to the political friends of the president and of the majority party in each house of Congress. Often they were given directly to party newspapers in Washington and the hinterland. At other times, they were awarded to friendly printers or simply to favorites who then subcontracted the work to jobbers after keeping a share of the profit for getting the original contract. Although laws gave the dispensation of executive printing to individual department heads, the president effectively controlled it, and he almost always awarded it to the party organ in Washington. Profits were scandalously high. Cornelius Wendell was said to have made millions through direct contracting and subcontracting between 1853 and 1860. Buchanan, then, inherited a system of long duration which involved the entire federal government, not just the executive branch. Nor was the President the specific target of all the congressional investigations between 1858 and 1861 which exposed this methodical bilking of the government. His name was linked to those involved, however, and his response to the cry for reform reveals much about the man.[9]

In the summer of 1858, a congressional committee attempted to curb some of the worst abuses in the printing system. Unearthing graft and gross overpayment for printing services, it persuaded Congress to pass laws forbidding double payment for printing the same document for the House and the Senate and, more important, prohibiting the subcontracting of printing which had pushed prices to such unreasonable heights. The law forbade the men awarded congressional printing contracts from selling them out to jobbers like Wendell. Indeed, the law was probably aimed specifically at Wendell. The committee had also discovered that the superintendent of public printing, an official appointed by the president to oversee the distribution of government contracts, had consistently extorted bribes or kickbacks from bidders before awarding them government business. Wendell, too, apparently shared these "commissions" for distributing business to printers outside Washington. Because low and honest bidders were ignored, this extortion only drove up printing prices. The superintendent who had been appointed by Pierce and retained by Buchanan was indicted and convicted.[10]

The jailing of the incumbent allowed Buchanan to pick the new superintendent, and he chose an honest Pennsylvania editor named George Bowman. Bowman cracked down on illegal practices, and had the incident ended here, Buchanan would deserve applause. The new laws, however, immediately cut into Wendell's profits, and he announced that he would no longer support the *Union*, the administration paper. That sheet would lose money without funds from the printing rake-off. Buchanan then became involved in the same kind of bargaining that occurred under Polk when Thomas Ritchie bought the *Globe* and re-named it the *Union*. The President pressured Bowman to leave his new post and take over the paper. Bowman could not afford to do so. A contract was therefore arranged under the auspices of Attorney General Black, which violated the spirit if not the letter of the new law against subcontracting. Bowman would take over the *Union,* and Wendell would pay him $10,000 a year to run it. In return, Bowman would give Wendell the Senate printing, which it was assumed he as the administration editor would get, and Wendell would do that printing in the *Union* plant. Wendell, that is, would receive the profits of a contract naming Bowman as printer. Wendell would in turn share some of his profits with two Pennsylvania newspapers that supported Buchanan. Buchanan apparently absented himself from the actual negotiations, leaving them to his friend from Pennsylvania, Black. Wendell later testified, however, that Buchanan was aware of each step of the negotiations and that the division of largesse between the Pennsylvania papers came at his suggestion, if not at his direct order. These revelations came during the investigations of the Covode Committee in 1860.[11]

The Covode Investigations

In the spring of 1860, the Republicans, who took control of the House the previous year, set out directly after Buchanan's scalp. Despite Democratic protests that it was launching a fishing expedition on the basis of unspecified charges, the House on March 5 approved resolutions of a Republican representative, John Covode of Pennsylvania to appoint a select committee to investigate "whether the President of the United States, or any other officer of the Government, has, by money, patronage, or other improper means sought to influence the action of Congress, or any committee thereof, for or against the passage of any law pertaining to the rights of any State or territory." The committee, which Covode himself would head, was also empowered to investigate whether the President or other officials had sought to prevent the execution of laws and to inquire into abuses in post offices, navy yards, and other public works. Finally, it was authorized to check into illegal campaign expenditures in Pennsylvania and other states.[12]

The committee dragged witnesses into its secret hearings throughout the spring and issued a report on June 16, 1860. It uncovered just about every improper practice of the Buchanan years, as well as the scandalous printing mess, which dated back to Jackson's day. It publicized the malodorous record of Ike Cook in Chicago and the way he secured the postmastership. It revealed that the brother of the Philadelphia customs collector remained on the government payroll while editing a Democratic newspaper there.

The committee's major focus, however, was on Buchanan's connection with the printing and his efforts to ram the Lecompton Constitution through the House. Stripped of most of his profits by 1860, Cornelius Wendell became the star witness for the Republicans. Claiming intimate friendship with the President, Wendell exposed the enormous profits of the printing, as well as how they were divided among Democratic candidates and newspapers, often at the President's suggestion. His most damaging testimony was that $30,000–40,000 had been spent in 1858 to bribe congressmen to pass the Lecompton Constitution. John W. Forney, once Buchanan's principal lieutenant in Pennsylvania but now alienated from the administration, asserted that he had been offered $80,000 worth of post office printing in return for endorsing Lecompton in his editorial columns. On top of Buchanan's other woes, May brought announcement of New York postmaster Fowler's defalcation and flight. Buchanan's appointment of John A. Dix to clean up the mess in New York did little to mitigate the impact of this bombshell.[13]

The Republicans seem to have been primarily interested in manufacturing ammunition for the 1860 presidential campaign. During the secret hearings, charges against Buchanan were systematically leaked to the New York press while testimony in the President's defense was suppressed until the final report. Perhaps because of the clear biases of the witnesses or the lack of substantiating evidence, the committee did not recommend impeachment or even censure of the President or his men. Instead, the dominant Republicans contented themselves with printing thousands of copies of the huge report, which seemed to convict the President by its size alone. The party also printed separately hundreds of thousands of copies of a thirty-page summary of the majority report and disseminated them widely as a campaign document.

From the committee's inception in March, Buchanan had moved covertly to undermine its efforts and publicly to denounce the legitimacy of its proceedings. Privately he attempted to muster newspapers to his defense, to discredit the witnesses against him, and to defuse the impact of their testimony. Wendell's testimony, Buchanan wrote a New York editor, contained "nothing but falsehoods." Nor could Forney be believed, he wrote another. They should be denounced. As a result, Democratic papers correctly blasted Covode as a biased personal foe of Buchanan, and did what they could to protect the President. While he marshaled a defense in the press, Buchanan, with the aid of his attorney general, secretly prepared questions for the lone Democrat on the committee, Warren Winslow of North Carolina, with which he could embarrass witnesses like Wendell. Winslow later wrote a minority report attacking the entire proceeding as a partisan witch hunt that, even with the testimony of clearly biased and unreliable witnesses, could find no grounds to impeach or censure the President.[14]

Publicly Buchanan sent two formal protests to the House, on March 28 and then on June 22, after the House had ordered the report printed. In these remarkable messages, Buchanan developed a three-pronged defensive strategy. Failing to denounce the improprieties disclosed and ignoring as much as possible the substance of the charges against him, he protested instead the procedures of the House. Pillorying the motives of his investigators and of the witnesses against him, he openly appealed to an American distaste for tattletales. Finally, wrapping himself in history and the Constitution, he insisted that he was not trying to protect his own skin but was trying to protect the presidency itself from legislative incursion.

Buchanan vehemently attacked the methods employed by the House. While the House could legitimately scrutinize the activities of executive departments, he protested, it could investigate the president himself only when acting as an "impeaching body." In that case, precedent demanded open hearings before the impartial Judiciary Committee, where the accused could confront and cross-examine his accusers. Instead, "the House have made my accuser [Covode] one of my judges," and permitted him to conduct secret hearings where the President's character could be defamed without his knowing what the charge was. Moreover, impeachment proceedings required precise charges against specific actions of the President, not the impossibly vague and broad allegations Covode had made. In June Buchanan angrily accused the committee of going beyond even those unfairly broad allegations. In one of his few references to the substance of the committee's work, he demanded to know "by what authority" Covode had inquired into such irrelevant matters as printing contracts and patronage matters. Worse still, he protested justly, accusations against him had been selectively given to the press for publication. "It was a secret committee in regard to the testimony in my defense, but it was public in regard to all the testimony which could by possibility reflect on my character. The poison was left to produce its effect upon the public mind, whilst the antidote was carefully withheld."

What manner of men were his accusers, Buchanan asked. "Interested parasites and informers," disappointed office seekers, and "vindictive" and prejudiced men, he complained, men who were free to vent their spleen against him. No honorable man would ever divulge the confidentiality of private discussions and correspondence as these men had. These maligners, therefore, could testify with impunity, secure in the knowledge that the President could refute them only by emulating their violations of confidences. No president could do that. "His lips are sealed and he is left at their mercy. He cannot, as a coordinate branch of the Government, appear before a committee of investigation to contradict the oaths of such witnesses." Americans would never believe such men. The people, he asserted in June, "detest delators and informers."

In June Buchanan trumpeted, "I have passed triumphantly through this ordeal. My vindication is complete." Still, he protested in both messages, his concern had never been for himself but for his office and his successors. The Covode Committee had "acted as though they possessed unlimited power . . . to degrade the Presidential office itself to such a degree as to render it unworthy of the acceptance of any man of honor or principle." The Constitution gave the House no power to remove a president, only to impeach him. Yet if the House were permitted to continue such proceedings, to pry into private presidential conversations, to defame presidential honor through slanderous testimony and resolutions of censure, no man could conduct the office. Such a precedent would begin what the Founding Fathers had most feared, "the aggrandizement of the legislative at the expense of the executive and judicial departments" of the government.[15]

John B. Floyd and the War Department

The wide net cast by the Covode Committee did not cover all the abuses of Buchanan's cabinet, nor did it raise the most embarrassing allegations against the men around the President. A Democratic investigation of graft in the dispensation of naval contracts, for example, exculpated the Secretary of the Navy, but a minority wanted to censure both the Secretary and Buchanan for their sanctioning of gross favoritism.[16]

The most discomforting problems, however, came with Secretary of War John B. Floyd. Buchanan's egregious weakness in dealing with that cabinet officer and delay in decapitating him are as incomprehensible as they are reprehensible.

The Virginian Floyd does not appear to have profited personally from the War Department contracts or to have realized always how he was exploited. He was simply a careless administrator who tried too hard to please his friends and fellow party members. In 1858, for example, a congressional committee discovered some shady deals that Floyd had arranged to benefit his friends. When the army decided to build a new fort near New York City, Floyd asked some Democratic politicians there to find a suitable site. They quickly formed a syndicate, bought at a price of $130,000 some land which army engineers had earlier rejected, and sold it to Floyd for $200,000. Equally suitable sites were readily available at half the price. It was also discovered that summer that Floyd had arranged the sale of the 7,000-acre Fort Snelling reservation in Minnesota to some Virginia friends for $90,000 when the property was worth considerably more.[17] Despite these exposures of incompetence and favoritism, Buchanan kept the hapless Floyd on.

Similarly, in the spring and summer of 1860, Congress in effect voted no confidence in the Secretary by attaching provisos to appropriations bills restricting his flexibility in awarding contracts. Yet another committee had learned of Floyd's efforts to favor some Virginia builders with contracts for construction projects in Washington which the army was directing. An open fight had developed between Floyd and influential senators over Floyd's efforts to remove the army engineer in charge of that construction when he refused to deal with the Secretary's cronies. Congress actually included in the appropriation for the project a stipulation that the engineer, Captain Montgomery Meigs, must supervise it in order to prevent Floyd from exiling Meigs to a barren army post in Florida. Floyd was totally discredited with congressmen of both parties. Still Buchanan kept him on.[18]

In December, 1860, when the Buchanan administration was grappling with the tense secession crisis in South Carolina, the roof finally fell in on Floyd. Throughout Buchanan's term, Congress had delayed and cut army appropriations. As a result, the contractors who supplied the army had, since 1857, been presenting bills to Floyd for the goods sold to the army before Floyd had the appropriations to pay them. Without authorization Floyd had signed these bills, thereby indicating the government intended to pay them, and the contractors, especially the New York firm of Russell, Majors, and Waddell, had used the endorsed bills as collateral to obtain bank loans. Floyd simply assumed that Congress would make contingency appropriations for the army to meet these debts, but he had no guarantee. Buchanan learned of this practice in 1859 and was appalled. He reprimanded Floyd and ordered him to stop. But Floyd continued the practice, just as he continued in office.

Had the contracts been legitimate, Floyd would have had some justification. The army, after all, had to be supplied. Russell soon learned, however, that Floyd would sign anything, and he began to present fictitious bills for supplies never provided. Floyd continued to endorse them, and Russell continued to take out bank loans with the bills as collateral. There were eventually some $5,000,000 worth of bogus bills endorsed by Floyd in circulation. Finally, the bankers refused to accept any more until the government paid up. Russell, whose demand for cash to repay old loans was insatiable, then learned of an Indian trust fund of $3,000,000 in negotiable bonds in the Interior Department. Spurned by the bankers, he now bribed the clerk in charge of the fund, a man named Bailey, to "loan" him the bonds temporarily with the Floyd-endorsed bills as collateral. Inevitably, the bonds were never returned. Soon Russell would present Floyd with a phony bill any time he needed cash and then march over to the Indian Office to exchange the note for bonds which he then sold for cash. Incredibly, Floyd never seems to have known what was going on.

By December, 1860, Bailey was growing nervous. His accounts were due to be audited on January 1, and he was missing $870,000 in bonds.

On December 19 Bailey wrote a confession to Secretary of the Interior Jacob Thompson and sent a copy to Floyd. Buchanan learned of the whole affair on December 22 from Thompson. Thompson was livid with rage and had Russell arrested. He wanted Floyd dismissed, and by now even Buchanan thought the Virginian had to go. Still he hesitated. Unwilling to confront Floyd personally, he sent Thompson and Black to see Floyd, who was sick in bed. Floyd confessed all. Buchanan, however, could not bring himself to fire the man. He asked Black to seek Floyd's resignation: Black refused. Next, Buchanan persuaded Vice President John C. Breckinridge to ask Floyd for his resignation. Floyd indignantly refused and, despite his disgrace, continued to attend crucial cabinet meetings on events in the secession crisis. Buchanan appeared powerless. Finally, on December 29, 1860, Floyd resigned, using as his excuse disagreement with administration policy in Charleston harbor. The administration had reneged on pledges to South Carolina, he proclaimed righteously, and he refused to remain associated with such a dishonored regime.[19]

Thus a man who had embarrassed and disgraced the Buchanan administration since 1857, a man whose ineptitude and conniving had been well publicized since at least 1858, finally left the cabinet. Buchanan's weakness vis-à-vis Floyd, his apparent apathy about, if not obliviousness to, the appearance as well as the substance of impropriety in the conduct of government affairs, and his abdication of his responsibilities as chief administrator, reflect too well his role during his entire presidency.

NOTES

[1]Leonard D. White, *The Jacksonians: A Study in Administrative History, 1829–1861* (New York, 1965), 411.

[2]Roy F. Nichols, *The Disruption of American Democracy* (New York, 1948), 59–94.

[3]Allan Nevins, *Ordeal of the Union* (2 vols., New York, 1947), II, 495.

[4]White, *Jacksonians*, 294–297.

[5]Nevins, *Ordeal*, II, 505–509; Nichols, *Disruption*, 59–60.

[6]Nichols, *Disruption*, 80.

[7]Philip Shriver Klein, *President James Buchanan: A Biography* (University Park, Pa., 1962), 311. See also Nichols, *Disruption*, 170–171; Allan Nevins, *The Emergence of Lincoln* (2 vols., New York, 1950), I, 290–291. For a dissenting view concerning the use of patronage—but not contracts and bribes—to win support for Lecompton, see

David E. Meerse, "James Buchanan, the Patronage, and the Northern Democratic Party, 1857–1858" (unpublished Ph.D. dissertation, University of Illinois, 1969).

[8]Nichols, *Disruption,* 216, 248.

[9]This whole system is described in White, *Jacksonians,* 284–299.

[10]Nichols, *Disruption,* 248–249.

[11]Ibid., 249–250; White, *Jacksonians,* 294–299.

[12]*Congressional Globe,* 36th Cong., 1st Sess., 997.

[13]Nevins, *Emergence of Lincoln,* II, 196–200; Nichols, *Disruption,* 170–171, 285–286; White, *Jacksonians,* 295–299; Klein, *Buchanan,* 338–339. The Covode Committee report can be found in *House Report 648,* 36th Cong., 1st Sess.

[14]Nichols, *Disruption,* 285, 328–330; Klein, *Buchanan,* 338–339.

[15]These protests can be found in Richardson, *Messages,* 3145–3156.

[16]White, *Jacksonians,* 220.

[17]Nevins, *Emergence of Lincoln,* II, 199; Nichols, *Disruption,* 194–195.

[18]Nichols, *Disruption,* 326–328; Nevins, *Emergence of Lincoln,* II, 199–200.

[19]Nichols, *Disruption,* 418–425; Klein, *Buchanan,* 377–381.

ABRAHAM LINCOLN
1861–1865

Stephen B. Oates

There were instances of misconduct in Abraham Lincoln's administration, especially in the War Department and the army. And there were scandals, too, though none was ever linked to the President himself or to any member of his official family except Simon Cameron, first secretary of war. Historians regard much of the administrative irregularities as perhaps inevitable, given the chaos and confusion, waste and inefficiency, that characterized the Union war effort in the first two years of hostilities. In 1861 the government was almost totally unprepared to fight a massive civil war: it had never before had to raise, equip, and supply such large field armies; and it had never had to cope with problems of internal security at a time of domestic rebellion. Lincoln himself, without previous administrative experience, thus confronted a national emergency for which precedents and guidelines were virtually nonexistent. His cabinet members, moreover, lacked clear lines of authority in managing a war of this kind and often worked at cross-purposes. It is in this context of confusion and genuine national peril that the following chronicle of administrative abuses must be understood.

Frémont's Western Department

In July, 1861, Lincoln appointed Major General John Charles Frémont, former Republican candidate for president, as commander of the Western Department with headquarters in St. Louis. Soon Frémont became involved in a political feud with Frank Blair, Jr., whose brother was in Lincoln's cabinet and whose father was one of Lincoln's closest advisers.

As Blair and Frémont struggled for control of Missouri politics, Blair and other officials reported to Washington that Frémont was "extravagant" and that his command was brimming with a "horde of pirates" who were defrauding the army.[1] Alarmed, Lincoln dispatched Adjutant General Lorenzo Thomas to check on Frémont, and Thomas wrote back that the general was incompetent and that dubious army purchases had been made.[2]

Meanwhile, a Congressional subcommittee headed by Elihu B. Washburne—followed later by a Commission on War Claims—conducted an investigation of the Western Department and found that much of what Blair had charged was true. Frémont, for example, had established his headquarters in a mansion which cost the government $6,000 a year in rent—the equivalent of many times that amount today. Moreover, the general had surrounded himself with a retinue of California cronies who made extortionate profits by securing army contracts without competitive bidding as prescribed by law. For instance, a contract went to one Californian for the construction of thirty-eight mortar boats at $8,250 apiece—about twice what they were worth. Another Californian, a friend of Frémont's who had no experience in fort construction, nevertheless received $191,000 to build a series of forts that should have cost about one-third that much. In addition, Frémont had given favorite sellers "the most stupendous contracts" for railroad cars, horses, mules, tents, and other equipment, much of it inferior in quality.[3]

On top of that, Frémont had also abolished slavery in Missouri by a military decree—a move that violated Lincoln's own explicit policy in 1861 of fighting a war only to save the Union and not to free the slaves. Because Lincoln considered Frémont both a poor administrator and an insubordinate officer, the President in October of 1861 relieved him of command. Still, Lincoln did not think Frémont personally dishonest. "His cardinal mistake," the President remarked, "is that he isolates himself, and allows nobody to see him; and by which he does not know what is going on in the very matter he is dealing with."[4]

Most historians have agreed with Lincoln. On the other hand, Allan Nevins has stressed that many of Frémont's troubles were inherent in the newly established Western Department—one without organization, war materiel, and trained recruits—and that the waste, corruption, and extravagance there was characteristic of Cameron's War Department as a whole.[5]

Cameron's War Department

From the outset, Cameron was responsible for spending enormous sums of money to supply and equip Union armies. But the War Department was so understaffed that the Secretary turned to state governors and private citizens for help. The result was widespread chaos, as agents representing state governors as well as the Ordnance, Quartermaster, and Commissary Bureaus of the War Department vied with one another in spending federal funds for war materiel.

Apprised of certain irregularities in War Department spending, Congress in July, 1861, twice demanded that Cameron provide specific information on all government contracts awarded since March 4. But Cameron refused both times to comply. As a consequence, the House established a special committee on contracts to investigate; and the committee, after hearing testimony and examining war expenditures, produced a 1,109-page indictment of maladministration in Cameron's office. The committee's principal complaint was that the Secretary and his maze of agents—some unscrupulous, others inept—had thrown competitive bidding to the winds and had bought exclusively from favorite middlemen and suppliers, many of them "unprincipled and dishonest." Thanks to a combination of inefficiency and fraud, the War Department had purchased huge quantities of rotten blankets, tainted pork, knapsacks that came unglued in the rain, uniforms that fell apart, discarded Austrian muskets, and hundreds of diseased and dying horses—all at exorbitant prices. In one instance, the War Department had sold a lot of condemned Hall carbines for a nominal sum, bought them back at $15 apiece, sold them at $3.50 apiece, and bought them back again at $22 apiece.

The list of abuses seemed endless. One Boston agent, charging the government a percentage of the contracts he arranged, made $20,000 in one week. Another agent acquired two boats for the War Department at a price of $100,000 each—after the navy had rejected them as unsafe—and one of the vessels sank on its first voyage. Then there were the activities of one of Cameron's own political lieutenants, Alexander Cummings, whom the Secretary had appointed as supervisor of army purchases in New York City. By Cummings's authority, the government spent $21,000 for straw hats and linen pantaloons and bought such "army supplies" as Scotch ale, selected herring, and barreled pickles. In addition, Cummings had contracted for 75,000 pairs of overpriced shoes from a firm that occasionally loaned him money.

The House committee, of course, bemoaned such "prostitution of public confidence to purposes of individual aggrandizement" and castigated Cameron's office for treating congressional law as "almost a dead letter," for awarding contracts "universally injurious to the government," and for promoting favoritism and "colossal graft." [6]

By January, 1862, Lincoln had decided that Cameron was not the man to run the War Department. While Cameron had not enriched himself in the contracts scandals, he was plainly an incompetent administrator. In addition, he too had violated Lincoln's policy regarding slaves and Negroes: without the President's approval, Cameron had released a War Department report in which he called for the enlistment of black soldiers, a move the President at this time officially opposed. In mid-January, when the Russian ministry became vacant, Lincoln appointed Cameron to fill it and named Edwin Stanton to head the War Department. In a private letter, however, Lincoln extolled Cameron for his "ability, patriotism, and fidelity to public trust." [7]

Before leaving office, Cameron tried to defend himself: on January 15 he informed the Senate that he had never made "a single contract for any purpose whatever." At that, Representative Henry L. Dawes of Massachusetts produced documents proving that all but 64,000 of 1,903,000 arms contracted for between August, 1861, and January, 1862, had been ordered under Cameron's direction. On April 30, 1862, the House censured him for entrusting men like Alexander Cummings with public money and for adopting a policy which damaged the public service. [8]

In a message to Congress on May 26, 1862, Lincoln responded to the censure of Cameron, insisting that the President and all other department heads were "equally responsible with him for whatever error, wrong, or fault was committed in the premises." When war broke out, Lincoln explained, Congress was not in session, the capital was threatened with occupation, the nation was on the brink of disaster. Therefore Lincoln had met with his cabinet, and they had decided that they must assume broad emergency powers or let the government fall. Accordingly, the President had directed that Secretary of the Navy Gideon Welles empower several individuals—including Welles's own brother-in-law—to forward troops and supplies to embattled Washington. The President had allowed Cameron to authorize Alexander Cummings and the governor of New York to transport troops and acquire supplies for the public defense. Since the President believed that government departments were alive with disloyal persons, the President himself had chosen private citizens known for "their ability, loyalty, and patriotism" to spend public money without security, but without compensation either. Thus Lincoln had directed that Secretary of the Treasury Salmon P. Chase advance $2,000,000 to John A. Dix, George Opdyke, and Richard M. Blatchford of New York for the purpose of buying arms and making military preparations. All these emergency actions, the President stated, had received the unanimous approval of his cabinet.

Lincoln conceded that these measures were "without authority of law," but argued that they were absolutely necessary to save the government in the crisis that followed Fort Sumter. He did not deny that misdeeds had occurred in War Department operations, nor did he claim that the House censure was unjustifiable. But he was not willing, he said, to let that censure fall on Cameron alone.[9]

Meanwhile, at Lincoln's urging, Stanton set about reorganizing the War Department, centralizing its activities, and conducting an official audit of its contracts. By canceling many of these and adjusting others, Stanton's auditors saved the government almost $17,000,000. At the same time, with the administration's full support, Congress enacted laws that required open and competitive bidding in government purchasing and that subjected contractors to court-martial in case of fraud.[10]

Welles's Navy Department

The House committee on contracts, while it found no outright corruption in navy purchasing, did discover that George D. Morgan—Welles's brother-in-law—had amassed a personal fortune as Welles's New York agent. Charging a commission of 2.5% on all contracts he arranged,

Morgan had made $95,000 in four and a half months in 1861. Though the commissions came from the sellers, several shipowners testified that the government actually paid them. It was standard practice, they said, to add commissions to the sale price for boats.

The Morgan affair brought considerable flak from Congress, where John P. Hale, chairman of the Senate Committee on Naval Affairs and an adamant political foe of Welles, promised an investigation. On January 11, 1862, the Senate demanded a full report on Morgan's purchases, and Welles responded with a thorough accounting in which he concealed nothing, altered nothing. In his defense, the Secretary insisted that in the crisis of 1861 there had been neither time nor opportunity to use competitive bids in buying privately owned vessels. To enforce the blockade, the navy needed a fleet in a hurry and the best way to acquire one, Welles argued, was to centralize purchases in the hands of a businessman like Morgan, whose loyalty and integrity Welles could guarantee. Welles argued that Morgan was entitled to his commission, which was the usual rate charged by New York ship brokers. And the Secretary gave evidence that Morgan had driven hard bargains and that the boats he had purchased were excellent.

Unimpressed with Welles's arguments, Senator Hale charged him with nepotism and corruption and went on to imply that the entire Lincoln administration was infested with graft. When newspapers joined Hale in demanding Welles's resignation, the President stood by his secretary and refused to dismiss him. For one thing, with the public in an uproar over Union military procrastination and ineptitude, Lincoln could ill afford another admission of weakness in his official family. For another, Welles was a capable man, and on the whole he ran an honest and reliable department. In the Senate, meanwhile, Hale insisted that Welles be censured. A week later, on February 14, 1862, the Senate rejected the motion by a vote of 31 to 5. Welles—and Lincoln—had been exonerated.[11]

Chase's Treasury Department

Most of the charges of misconduct in the Treasury Department focused on the controversial trade in the southern states. Although commerce with the Confederacy itself was illegal, the government adopted an intricate system of licenses and permits to regulate business in occupied areas. Much of it was done under the supervision of the Treasury Department, with Chase himself issuing permits, drawing up regulations, and appointing Treasury agents to enforce them. The trouble was that huge profits could be made in exchanging vital supplies for southern cotton, which commanded an extraordinary price in cotton-starved Boston. As a result, the system of trade (in the words of one historian) "became an open invitation to corruption," as speculators swarmed into occupied territories and set about bribing army officers and Treasury agents alike.[12]

Chase, for his part, was appalled at the amount of chicanery going on, but insisted that he could not possibly "look after all the agents of the department." But when informed of some delinquency, he asserted, "I institute proper investigations, and, if the delinquency is found actually to exist, take proper measures."[13]

Chase's political opponents—especially the Blairs—claimed that he was blind to the misdeeds of his own appointees. In 1864, Frank Blair, Jr., stood up in Congress and proclaimed "that a more profligate administration of the Treasury Department never existed, that the whole Mississippi Valley is rank and fetid with the frauds and corruptions of its agents."[14] Still, nobody at the time questioned Chase's personal honesty and integrity. And if there were field agents who accepted bribes, specialists now conclude that Chase's major appointees were among the most capable in Lincoln's administration.[15]

Lincoln and Congressional Investigating Committees

No evidence has been found that Lincoln ever obstructed any congressional investigation of his civil or military departments. On the contrary, when called upon to furnish documents regarding administrative misconduct, the President responded fully, if sometimes defiantly. For example, when Blair inveighed against Chase's department and demanded a congressional inquiry, Chase's friends in Congress countered with an investigation of Blair and Lincoln as well. As it happened, Blair had been elected to Congress while holding a commission in the army. Although it was illegal for him to serve, he came to Congress anyway—some said at Lincoln's urging, since at the time the President and Chase were rivals for the 1864 Republican nomination. After Blair's attack on Chase, some representatives spoke of impeachment, and the Senate officially rebuked both Lincoln and Stanton for allowing Blair to function in what appeared to be a dual and unlawful capacity. When the House demanded that Lincoln provide information about the matter, the President sent over a complete report, including a letter he had written advising that Blair could help the Union cause more as Speaker of the House than as an army officer. Therefore Lincoln suggested that Blair give the President his commission, help organize the House, and resign from the army if elected Speaker; if not, he could have his commission back and return to the field (Blair was not chosen Speaker, but lingered on in Congress nevertheless). Lincoln disclaimed any responsibility for Blair's conduct there and gladly returned his commission when Blair called for it on his way back to Sherman's army.[16]

While Lincoln and Congress clashed several times, the President nevertheless worked closely with numerous congressmen—chief among them Charles Sumner, who acted as Lincoln's principal adviser on foreign affairs. On the domestic front, Lincoln maintained personal contact with the Joint Committee on the Conduct of the War, composed mainly of "radical" Republicans whose job it was to ferret out disloyalists and incompetents in both the administration and the armed services. Lincoln met frequently with the worried patriots who served on the committee, hearing out their complaints about generals and cabinet members alike—and even listening to criticisms of his own war policies, which they often thought too indecisive and conciliatory. The President and the committeemen disagreed, sometimes emphatically but they had a mutual regard for one another and kept the lines of communication open between the White House and Capitol Hill.

One example is Mary Todd Lincoln's alleged disloyalty. Since Mrs. Lincoln came from a prominent family of Kentucky slaveholders and since her sister was married to a Confederate officer, rumors flourished in Washington that Mary was a Confederate spy. The story goes that the members of the Joint Committee took up the charges in a secret morning session. To their astonishment, Lincoln came into the committee room alone. "No one spoke," recalled one member, "for no one knew what to say. The President had not been asked to come before the Committee, nor was it suspected that he had information that we were to investigate reports, which, if true, fastened treason upon his family in the White House."

At last Lincoln said: "I, Abraham Lincoln, President of the United States, appear of my own volition before this Committee of the Senate to say that I, of my own knowledge, know that it is untrue that any of my family hold treasonable communication with the enemy." Then the President left as quietly as he had come. "We sat for some moments speechless," the committee member related. "Then by tacit agreement, no word being spoken, the Committee dropped all consideration of the rumors that the wife of the President was betraying the Union. We were so greatly affected that the Committee adjourned for the day." [17]

Mary Todd Lincoln and the Renovation of the White House

In 1861 Congress appropriated $20,000 for refurnishing the White House, but Mrs. Lincoln, "who had no money sense," exceeded the budget by some $6,700. Certain that "Mr. Lincoln will not approve it," she prevailed on Benjamin French, commissioner of public buildings, and begged him in tears to see the President "and tell him it is common to overrun appropriations." When French interceded in Mary's behalf, Lincoln became furious and refused to cover the excess bill with government funds. "It can never have my approval," the President stormed. "I'll pay it out of my pocket first—it would stink in the nostrils of the American people to have it said the President of the United States had approved a bill overrunning an appropriation of $20,000 for *flub dubs*, for this damned old house, when the soldiers cannot have blankets." [18]

Congress finally settled the problem by burying an extra appropriation in the White House budget for the ensuing year.

Internal Security and Arbitrary Arrests

From the outset, Lincoln dealt harshly with "the enemy in the rear"— with what he called "a most efficient corps of spies, informers, suppliers, and aiders and abettors" of the rebellion who took advantage of "Liberty of speech, Liberty of the press and *Habeas corpus*" to disrupt the Union war effort. [19] Consequently, he suspended the writ of habeas corpus and authorized army commanders to declare martial law in various areas behind the lines and to try civilians in military courts. Lincoln openly defended such an invasion of civil liberties, contending that strict measures were imperative if the laws of the Union—and freedom itself—were to survive the war.

At first, responsibility for suppressing disloyal activities was divided among the State, War, and Navy Departments, with William H. Seward's State Department playing the largest role. Seward not only censored the telegraphs and the mails, but utilized government agents, U.S. marshals, city police, and some private informers to maintain surveillance of "suspicious" persons and to help arrest them. Still, Lincoln was troubled by such activities; and in May, 1861, he issued an executive memorandum that "unless the *necessity* for these arbitrary arrests is *manifest*, and *urgent*, I prefer they should cease."[20]

In 1862 Lincoln centralized jurisdiction over internal security matters in Stanton's War Department. To deal with such matters, Stanton created a corps of civilian provost marshals, but allowed them too much independence in policing and jailing alleged disloyalists. Their zealous, far-ranging operations led to widespread criticism of the Lincoln administration. At the same time, Stanton empowered army officers to apprehend anybody who discouraged volunteering or otherwise helped the enemy. And he got up dragnets in which state militia, home guards, police chiefs, and vigilantes all participated. All told, some 13,000 persons—most of them antiwar Democrats—were seized and imprisoned under Stanton's authority. The outcry against arbitrary arrests—most of it from antiwar Democrats—was so strident that Lincoln and Stanton both tried to restrain excessive use of power whenever they could. Both speedily ordered the release of people unwarrantably arrested, especially political prisoners. Also, when General Ambrose E. Burnside suspended the antiadministration Chicago *Times*, the President promptly revoked the order.[21]

The most controversial military arrest was that of Clement L. Vallandigham, an Ohioan and a leading antiwar Democrat. In 1863 he stumped Ohio denouncing the draft, the despotism of the Lincoln government, and the war itself and calling for a negotiated peace with the Confederacy. During one of his orations, an officer in civilian dress, detailed from General Burnside's headquarters, leaned against the platform taking notes. Three days later the army arrested Vallandigham, and a military commission sentenced him to imprisonment for the duration of the war. When Ohio Democrats cried out in protest, Lincoln replied, "Must I shoot a simple-minded soldier boy who deserts, while I must not touch a hair of a wily agitator who induces him to desert?" Though Lincoln actually may have regretted the arrest, he refused to pardon Vallandigham, instead ordering him banished to the Confederacy.[22]

Clearly, in the complex area of internal security in the midst of civil war, government agents often confused antiwar rhetoric for traitorous designs, and innocent people suffered. Lincoln, for his part, conceded that errors and excesses had occurred and did what he could to correct them. Yet throughout the conflict he maintained a tough line on disloyalty; and Congress—and most Republicans—generally supported him.

NOTES

[1]J. G. Randall, *Lincoln the President* (paperback ed., New York, 1945), II, 18–19.

[2]Lorenzo Thomas to Simon Cameron, October 21, 1861, in U.S. War Department, *The War of the Rebellion: A Compilation of the Official Records of the Union and Confederate Armies* (70 vols. in 128, Washington, D.C., 1880–1901), ser. I, vol. III, 540–549.

[3]*House Report 2,* 37th Cong., 2nd Sess., xxxvi, xlii, lxi–lxiv, 37–99; Report of the Commission on War Claims, *House Executive Document 94,* 37th Cong., 2nd Sess., 11–18, 25–26, 34, and *passim.*

[4]Lincoln to David Hunter, September 9, 1861, in Roy P. Basler, ed., *Collected Works of Abraham Lincoln* (9 vols., New Brunswick, N.J., 1953–1955), IV, 513.

[5]Allan Nevins, *The War for the Union* (4 vols., New York, 1959–1971), I, 307–327, 331–341, 374–382. In April, 1863, the Joint Committee on the Conduct of the War released a somewhat incomplete report on Frémont's Western command. The report largely absolved him of blame in the contracts imbroglio and lauded his emancipation decree. *Report of the Joint Committee on the Conduct of the War* (1863), pt. III, 5–6 and *passim.*

[6]Charles H. Van Wyck chaired the committee. *House Report 2,* 37th Cong., 2nd Sess., pp. iv–xi, 34–54, and *passim;* A. Howard Meneely, *The War Department, 1861* (New York, 1928), 252–269; Fred A. Shannon, *The Organization and Administration of the Union Army* (2 vols., Cleveland, 1928), 61–62.

[7]Basler, *Collected Works,* V, 96–97.

[8]*Congressional Globe,* 37th Cong., 2nd Sess., 1840–1841, 1888.

[9]Basler, *Collected Works,* V, 240–243.

[10]*Senate Executive Document 15* (January 14, 1862), 37th Cong., 2nd Sess., *passim;* *Senate Report 9* and *15,* 37th Cong., 2nd Sess., *passim;* and *Congressional Globe,* 37th Cong., 2nd Sess., app., 124ff.

[11]John Niven, *Gideon Welles: Lincoln's Secretary of the Navy* (New York, 1973), 374–377.

[12]David Donald, ed., *Inside Lincoln's Cabinet: The Civil War Diaries of Salmon P. Chase* (New York, London, and Toronto, 1954), 32.

[13]*Ibid.*

[14]Quoted in Benjamin P. Thomas, *Abraham Lincoln* (New York, 1952), 415.

[15]Donald, *Inside Lincoln's Cabinet,* 32–33; and Harry J. Carman and Reinhard H. Luthin, *Lincoln and the Patronage* (New York, 1943), 57.

[16]Lincoln to Montgomery Blair, November 2, 1863, in Basler, *Collected Works,* VI, 554–555; J. G. Randall and Richard N. Current, *Lincoln the President* (New York, 1955), IV, 181–182. Frank Blair returned to the army in April, 1864. Officially, he served in Congress from March 4 to June 10, 1864, when his opponents there succeeded in unseating him.

[17]Quoted in Carl Sandburg, *Abraham Lincoln: The War Years* (4 vols., New York, 1939), II, 199–200. See also Thomas, *Abraham Lincoln,* 298.

[18]Benjamin Brown French to Pamela French, December 24, 1861, in Justin G. Turner and Linda Levitt Turner, *Mary Todd Lincoln: Her Life and Letters* (New York, 1972), 89.

[19]Lincoln to Erastus Corning and others, June 12, 1863, Basler, *Collected Works,* VI, 263.

[20]*Ibid.,* IV, 372.

[21]*Ibid.,* VII, 361, 363–364; Benjamin P. Thomas and Harold Hyman, *Stanton: The Life and Times of Lincoln's Secretary of War* (New York, 1962), 157–158, 280–281, 375.

[22]Basler, *Collected Works,* VI, 215n–216n, 266; Gideon Welles, *Diary,* ed. by Howard K. Beale (3 vols., New York, 1960), I, 321.

ANDREW JOHNSON
1865–1869

William S. McFeely

The administration of Andrew Johnson, which began upon Lincoln's assassination in April, 1865, was predominantly concerned with redefining the status and rights of people, both black and white, living in the defeated Confederate states. The strong differences over racial policies between Johnson and his opponents in Congress lie outside the scope of this study. Johnson asserted an ideological and constitutional position of great importance on May 29, 1865, when he issued his Amnesty Proclamation. Under its terms, the President used his pardoning power to restore effectively the political and economic rights of virtually all white southerners.[1]

Of concern here is not this stand by Andrew Johnson, but allegations that Johnson abused his powers as president by not executing the laws of Congress. Many important expressions of Johnson's defiance were made without notice to Congress or the public. Charges of such abuses of power formed the subject of extensive hearings in 1867 held by the Judiciary Committee of the House of Representatives. The committee heard more than eighty-five witnesses conversant with conditions in the South and enforcement of federal law and took 1,154 pages of testimony.[2]

The first major case of failure to carry out the presidential duty of enforcing an act of Congress occurred on August 16, 1865. Congress, on March 3, 1865, had passed legislation creating the Freedmen's Bureau in the executive branch. President Lincoln signed the bill. Under its terms, "the Commissioner, under the direction of the President," was authorized to "set apart" for "loyal refugees and freedmen" for the period of three years "not more than forty acres of lands abandoned within the insurrectionary states."[3] This implied a promise of forty acres for about 20,000 freedmen families in the South. On August 16, with notice only to the assistant commissioner of the bureau in Tennessee and to subordinate officers in the bureau headquarters in Washington (the commissioner was on vacation), Johnson ordered lands covered by the act of March 3 restored to a former landowner, B. B. Leake. On the back of a request for guidance in the matter, Johnson added that the "same action will be had in all similar cases."[4] Almost casually, Congress's act was abrogated.

The appointive power lies with the president and extended, of course, over the Freedmen's Bureau.[5] Investigating congressmen, however, charged that the power of appointment was abused when appointments were made for the specific purpose of frustrating rather than facilitating the enforcement of the law. Johnson replaced Thomas Conway, assistant commissioner for Louisiana, with James Scott Fullerton, and instructed Fullerton to report directly to him. The President did this because Conway was prepared to execute the congressional land redistribution plan; Fullerton, as instructed, did not do so.[6] The former assistant commissioner for South Carolina, Rufus Saxton, who had refused to resign and had to be fired so that lands could be restored, testified that a prominent white planter, William Whaley, "told me that the President had told him this property [held by freedmen] would be given up."[7] That restoration of land was Andrew Johnson's intent was made completely clear when Freedmen's Bureau Commissioner O. O. Howard, in the company of Whaley, relayed the same message to the freedmen of Edisto Island.[8]

By extending the pardoning power to include the restoration of lands that the freedmen were farming and by issuing orders to the bureau to evict freedmen from such lands, Johnson set aside the land provisions of the act of March 3, 1865.[9] As House Judiciary Chairman George S. Boutwell stated, "In violation of law and without authority of law he [President Johnson] has restored them [abandoned lands covered by the act] to their former rebel owners."[10]

When Congress reconvened in December, 1865, it began work on a congressional form of Reconstruction. The program comprised the Fourteenth Amendment as well as a series of bills, including the Civil Rights Bill of 1866 that upheld land ownership by blacks and the Reconstruction Acts of 1867 that enfranchised Negroes in the South. In

veto messages and other statements, Johnson vigorously spoke his ideological and constitutional objections to the congressional program. The
bills were carried over his vetoes, and he was constitutionally required
to execute them.

This he did not do fully.[11] Two of Johnson's cabinet members repeatedly ignored the Test Oath Act of July 2, 1862, which required federal
officeholders to affirm that they had not sympathized with, or contributed to, the Confederate cause. One cabinet member, Attorney General
James Speed, did comply with the provisions of this law; but Hugh Mc-
Culloch, Secretary of the Treasury, abandoned the oath requirement
and staffed departmental posts in the South with former Confederates,
and William Dennison, Postmaster General, had by March, 1866, appointed to post office positions in the South 2,042 people, of whom only
1,177 were able to qualify under the Test Oath Act.[12]

Not only were former Confederates unable to take the oath restored
to office, but they could not be counted on to protect the lives of the
black citizens of the South. One such incident was the New Orleans riot,
which caused General Philip Sheridan to speak critically of the role of
the President. Sheridan called the violence in the city, which resulted
in the death of many black citizens by a marauding band that included
some of the city's police, a "massacre." Johnson's refusal to order an alert
of nearby federal troops and his reliance instead on a pardoned Confederate mayor and the local law enforcement officials were regarded by the
majority of a special congressional investigation committee in 1866 as
abuses of powers by Johnson.[13]

On December 6, 1867, Chairman Boutwell reported the Judiciary
Committee's recommendation for impeachment. He listed among numerous allegations of presidential misconduct Johnson's failure to enforce the act calling for the distribution of the abandoned lands to the
freedmen, his disregard of the Test Oath Act, and the failure to keep the
peace in New Orleans. Calling for impeachment in a speech on the floor
of the House, Boutwell said, ". . . when you consider all these things can
there be any doubt as to his purpose, or doubt as to the criminality of
his purpose?"[14] His colleagues did have doubts; they defeated the recommendation for impeachment on December 7, 1867, by 57 votes for
impeachment, 108 against.[15]

Michael Les Benedict is one recent historian who, like the House

Judiciary Committee, takes seriously the compound effect of Johnson's acts in the South. Benedict does not accept the long-standing view that Andrew Johnson's acquittal in the later Senate trial was just reward for a man beleaguered by vindictive radicals. Not unlike Boutwell, Benedict ponders the nature of Johnson's offenses. At one point, he says, "Yet Johnson had broken no law; he had limited himself to his constitutional powers," but in another place he states, "Johnson had already shown his willingness to nullify Congressional legislation" by failing to enforce it. The consequence of Johnson's actions, he believes, was that by 1868 the "Reconstruction program enacted by Congress lay in utter ruin." To such incidents as the New Orleans riot, he adds interference with, and removal of, federal officials charged with carrying out congressional programs and stresses as a major abuse of power Johnson's having "appointed provisional governors of vast territories without the advice and consent of the Senate." [16]

Johnson placed no obstacles in the way of the Judiciary Committee's investigation of the many witnesses and its examination of many executive documents, including letters, telegrams, and memoranda sent to federal officials in the South. The President complied with requests for personal data. For example, William S. Huntington, cashier of the First National Bank of Washington, was allowed to give full information on the President's personal account. Huntington reported that the President "said he had no early objection to have any of his transactions looked into; he had done nothing clandestinely. . . ." [17]

Dropping the effort to establish the President's guilt by a collectivity of abuses, the House of Representatives turned to a specific act of defiance of Congress. It voted impeachment on Johnson's removal of Secretary of War Edwin M. Stanton in violation of the provisions of the Tenure of Office Act.[18] This alleged abuse of power by the President was one for which he took open public responsibility. The impeachment was approved by the House of Representatives on February 24, 1868, by a vote of 126 to 47.[19] The eleven articles of impeachment on which the Senate had to judge Johnson focused on the narrow issue of the removal of Secretary Stanton, and not on the earlier charges of failure to uphold congressional laws, but it should be noted that the removal of Stanton was closely tied to the earlier abuses.

By 1867 Stanton was the only remaining member of the cabinet critical of the President's reactions to congressional Reconstruction. His position with respect to carrying out the program was crucial. The only administrative payroll available for carrying out federal policies in the South was the army's. The Freedmen's Bureau was a part of the War Department. Thus the seemingly narrow issue of the removal of Secretary of War Stanton was not totally a deflection from the congressional concern with the broader matter of Johnson's frustration of its Reconstruction program.[20]

In the eyes of Johnson's opponents, the removal of Stanton was not dissimilar to the removal of Conway from Louisiana in 1865; of Saxton from South Carolina in 1866; of Wager Swayne, who had supported some of the acts favorable to the freedmen while assistant commissioner of the Freedmen's Bureau in Alabama in 1867; and of General Philip Sheridan from Louisiana.[21] Chairman Boutwell pointed to such acts as prime examples of the multiplicity of offenses for which Johnson was culpable. In 1868 the House concentrated on only one highly specific issue, the Stanton removal.

Article Ten, which quoted from speeches in which President Johnson defied Congress, and the first section of Article Eleven, which accused Johnson of challenging the authority of Congress to act at all (on the ground that former Confederate states were not represented), alluded to the abuses of power catalogued in the earlier House Judiciary Committee report.[22] The other nine articles and the balance of Article Eleven related explicitly to the Stanton removal. The subject of the trial was the Stanton matter and, more fundamentally, constitutional questions of presidential and congressional authority, rather than misconduct and abuse of power. In May, 1868, the President was acquitted when, for the lack of one vote, the two-thirds majority was not attained.

In areas outside Reconstruction, the Johnson administration underwent the usual congressional scrutiny. In investigations of frauds in the collecting of taxes in the distillery industry and customs in the collector's offices in the various ports, many local officers were found culpable.[23] The 1867 Congressional Investigating Committee found no substantiation for allegations that payments of $5,000 each were offered to Senators James R. Doolittle and David T. Patterson (Johnson's son-in-law), both of whom were to vote for Johnson's acquittal, and to Robert Johnson, the President's son, and that such sums were not received by the three men.[24] Neither Secretary of the Treasury Hugh McCulloch nor President Johnson was accused of knowledge of such abuses or of failure to act to prevent them.

The acrimony between Johnson and his congressional opponents was intense.[25] His accusers were not apt to have overlooked any evidence of abuses involving financial corruption, and none of substance was presented. Andrew Johnson generated hatred on ideological issues, but personally he was scrupulously honest.[26]

NOTES

[1]James Richardson, *A Compilation of the Messages and Papers of the Presidents, 1789–1897* (10 vols., Washington: Government Printing Office, 1896–1899), VI, 310–312.

[2]*House Report 7: Impeachment of the President*, 40th Cong., 1st Sess., November 25, 1867, 1–1154.

[3]*13 U.S. Statutes at Large*, March 3, 1865, 504–509.

[4]*House Report 7*, 88.

[5]Raoul Berger, *Executive Privilege: A Constitutional Privilege—A Myth* (Cambridge, Mass., 1974), 52.

[6]*House Report 7*, 100–101; William S. McFeely, *Yankee Stepfather: General O. O. Howard and the Freedmen* (New Haven, 1968), 176–187.

[7]*House Report 7*, 114.

[8]Oliver Otis Howard, *Autobiography of Oliver Otis Howard* (2 vols., New York, 1908), 238; and actual eyewitness account quoted in *Congressional Globe*, 39th Cong., 1st Sess., pt. 1, 517.

[9]Howard, *Autobiography*, 237; and chart of lands restored, *House Report 7*, 128–148.

[10]*Congressional Globe*, 40th Cong., 2nd Sess., vol. 39, pt. 5, app., 61 (December 6, 1867).

[11]Michael Les Benedict, *The Impeachment and Trial of Andrew Johnson* (New York, 1973), 40.

[12]Ellis Paxson Oberholtzer, *A History of the United States since the Civil War* (5 vols., New York, 1917–1937), vol. I, 174. Benedict disagrees and claims that Dennison did comply; Benedict, *Impeachment*, 40; *12 U.S. Statutes*, July 2, 1862.

[13]*House Report 16: New Orleans Riots Report*, 39th Cong., 2nd Sess.; P. H. Sheridan to U. S. Grant, August 2, 1866, Andrew Johnson Papers, Library of Congress.

[14]*Congressional Globe*, 40th Cong., 2nd Sess., vol. 39, pt. 5, app. 54–62, 61; Benedict, *Impeachment*, 78.

[15]*Congressional Globe*, 40th Cong., 2nd Sess., vol. 39, pt. 1, 68.

[16]Benedict, *Impeachment*, 22, 39, 60, 180.

[17]*House Report 7*, 183.

[18]The Tenure of Office Act was passed over presidential veto on March 2, 1867. Benjamin P. Thomas and Harold M. Hyman, *Stanton: The Life and Times of Lincoln's Secretary of War* (New York, 1962), 527. Eric L. McKitrick, *Andrew Johnson and Reconstruction* (Chicago, 1960), 495–499.

[19]David Miller Dewitt, *The Impeachment and Trial of Andrew Johnson, Seventeenth President of the United States: A History* (New York, 1903), 370, 373.

[20]Raoul Berger, *Impeachment: The Constitutional Problem* (Cambridge, Mass., 1973), 259.

[21]McKitrick, *Johnson*, 494–495.

[22]*Trial of Andrew Johnson* (3 vols., Washington, 1868), I, 6–10.

[23]*House Report 30: New York Custom-House*, 39th Cong., 2nd Sess., March 2, 1867; *House Report 25, New Orleans Custom-House*, 39th Cong., 2nd Sess., February 25, 1867 (Doc. 1305); *House Report 24: Frauds on the Internal Revenue*, 39th Cong., 2nd Sess., February 25, 1867.

[24]*House Report 30*, 8.

[25]John H. Cox and Lawanda Cox, *Politics, Principle and Prejudice, 1865–1866: Dilemma of Reconstruction America* (New York, 1963).

[26]Claude G. Bowers, *The Tragic Era: The Reconstruction after Lincoln* (Cambridge, Mass., 1929).

ULYSSES S. GRANT
1869–1877

William S. McFeely

Ulysses S. Grant had to respond to more charges of misconduct that took the form of financial corruption than any other president. No department escaped congressional investigation. The only cabinet post ignored in the following account is that of the postmaster general, and the omission is deliberate; charges of continuing misappropriations of funds in the postal service will be treated in the analysis of the Star Routes under Presidents Hayes, Garfield, and Arthur. In addition to cabinet members, Grant's secretaries, members of his family, and the President himself were accused of abusing power that derived from his office.

This is not the place for an interpretation of Grant the man and the job he did as president. However, a note or two might lend perspective: (1) All of the events narrated below are separate acts. With the possible exception of the still enigmatic Orville Babcock, there is no man who links the events one to another. There is no conspiracy that connects them. (2) All the accusations of misconduct in the Grant administration, with two exceptions that are discussed, involve making money in rather small amounts so that others outside the government could make a good deal more.

Historians H. Wayne Morgan, Ari Hoogenboom, and others re-evaluating the Grant administration find its reputation for unbridled, unprecedented, and unsurpassed corruption exaggerated. Hoogenboom suggests that one of the reasons there was so much talk about corruption at the time was that at last some people, including Ulysses S. Grant, wanted to do something about it. He stresses, for example, abolition of the moiety system during Grant's administration rather than the notorious abuse of it by one of its last practitioners, John Sanborn, whose contract is discussed below. He credits Grant with appointing the first Civil Service Commission rather than blaming him for abuses that made later civil service reform essential.[1]

These points acknowledged, President Grant, as the facts will suggest, had a good many allegations to which to respond.

Black Friday: Gold Panic of 1869

In 1869 speculators on the New York gold market sought to drive up the price of gold. In March gold was selling at $130 an ounce; by Black Friday, September 24, it was selling at $160.[2] Essential to the scheme of the speculators to raise the price of gold was the absence of the U.S. Treasury from the market. If the government were to sell large quantities of gold, the price would drop.

The two chief speculators were Jay Gould and James Fisk, Jr. They enlisted as an ally Abel Rathbone Corbin, whose wife was Virginia Grant, the President's sister. President Grant, on his way to Boston, was entertained on June 15, 1869, on one of Fisk's steamers. At dinner Gould tried both to deduce what the President's monetary policy would be and to persuade him not to sell government gold. Grant appeared inclined toward selling.[3] Later Corbin, without giving any suggestion that he had himself invested heavily in gold, sought to persuade Grant that the sale of gold by the government would harm the sale of American agricultural products on world markets.[4]

Gould successfully persuaded Wall Street that Grant would not order a sale. Throughout the period, Grant and Secretary of the Treasury George S. Boutwell appeared committed to neutrality between the contesting speculators in the gold market. As Grant said in a letter of September 12, "You will be met by the bulls and bears . . . to induce you to sell gold . . . on the one side, and to hold fast on the other. . . . I write . . . to put you on your guard."[5] Concern about the rise of the price of gold caused pressure on Boutwell to sell government holdings. On September 14 rumors that the Secretary would sell made Fisk and Gould highly nervous.[6]

Gould persuaded Corbin to write on September 17, 1869, to President

Grant, who was in Pennsylvania. The letter (and a cover letter) was delivered by hand to one of the President's secretaries, General Horace Porter, who gave it to Grant. Grant having read it, the messenger wired Corbin, "letters delivered all right."[7] The letters were then destroyed.[8]

Corbin interpreted the words "all right" as a reply meaning acquiescence with his suggestion that Treasury gold not be sold. The message meant only that the letter had been duly delivered. This presumed word of acquiescence was circulated on Wall Street, and prices continued to rise.

That night Mrs. Grant wrote Mrs. Corbin that the President was disturbed that Corbin was speculating in gold. This much discussed letter, signed "Sis" and referred to as the "Sis letter," was written in haste, read only by the Corbins and possibly Gould, and was reported to have been destroyed. It was subject to many interpretations. Opinion differed over whether it was a strong, if indirect, presidential rebuke of a speculating brother-in-law, a warning from Julia Grant that Corbin had better quit the market, or a suggestion that she too was a speculator and wanted them all to get out of the market. Corbin read the letter in Gould's presence on September 22, 1869, and insisted on selling his gold to Gould so that he could truthfully tell Grant that he was not investing in gold. The letter was also a signal to Gould, who secretly began to sell his gold.[9]

Returning to Washington, D.C., Grant conferred with Boutwell, and on September 24, with prices still rising rapidly, Boutwell telegraphed an order that $4,000,000 be sold. Boutwell recommended sale of $3,000,000. Grant $5,000,000. This suggests that a major sale was on the President's mind; he was not merely reflecting Boutwell's advice. When word of the telegram reached the gold room, panic selling began and the price fell in an hour from $160 to $155.[10] Many speculators were ruined, and the economy seriously disturbed. Boutwell's previous indecision, followed by this necessary but rash large sale, has been criticized by historians.[11] Democrats on the investigating committee, however, held that Grant had disrupted Boutwell's plan for an orderly entrance into the market.[12]

The congressional investigation into the matter, chaired by Representative James Garfield, concentrated on the gold market in New York rather than on the federal government, but there were suggestions of misconduct close to the president. Corbin admitted to speculations in gold. The assistant treasurer of the United States, General Daniel

Butterfield, appointed by Grant with Corbin's sponsorship, and a co-ordinator of a testimonial fund of $105,000 given Grant in 1866, was shown to have perjured himself, and admitted to borrowing in order to speculate in the gold market to the extent of $1,500,000 (enough to produce a profit of $25,000). Grant had him fired in October.[13]

Fisk asserted that of Corbin's account of $1,500,000, the sum of $500,000 was invested for the account of Julia Dent Grant, and $500,000 for General Porter. This Gould denied, and Corbin produced evidence that his profit from the sale of his gold was used immediately to repay a personal loan. Hence it is to be presumed that no funds went to Mrs. Grant or Porter, and that they had not been speculating. There is only Fisk's word that Porter and Julia Grant were among the speculators.[14]

A majority of eight of the investigating committee, all Republicans, completely exonerated Grant.[15] Two minority members (both Democrats) thought Mrs. Corbin and Mrs. Grant should have been interrogated. Requests for the "taking of their testimony" were refused by the "Executive Mansion."[16]

Chairman Garfield, on instruction of the committee, called on the President and said that the committee had testimony that made reference "to himself, and to some members of his family, and that the committee had authorized me to lay before him that portion of the testimony, that he might make any suggestions or statements concerning it." The President replied that he did not want to see the testimony. One committee member then postulated that Grant might prefer a more "formal" relationship with Congress: "Thereupon, believing that he would be glad to appear and afford us his explanations, (as his Secretary [of the Treasury] had, and as President Lincoln had to a former committee)," Congressman Samuel S. Cox, a Democrat on the committee, moved that Grant be "summoned." This was voted down by the committee.[17] In addition to Treasury Secretary Boutwell's testimony, the committee heard from the President's secretary, Horace Porter. Grant remained aloof.

James Ford Rhodes states there was "absolutely no ground for the least suspicion of the complicity direct or indirect of the President, Mrs. Grant or Horace Porter."[18] Most authorities follow Rhodes in viewing Grant as not personally involved and as being unlucky in his choice of a brother-in-law. Excessive chivalry, which Congressman Cox would have eschewed, leaves Julia Dent Grant's role in doubt.

Santo Domingo Annexation

The complex story of President Grant's effort to annex Santo Domingo (as the Dominican Republic was then called) lies largely outside the limits of this study. Hamilton Fish, Grant's able secretary of state, was dismayed but acquiesced when Grant entrusted the negotiations to Orville E. Babcock, a personal aide of the President. Critics have asked whether Grant and Fish were fully exercising their responsibilities for the conduct of foreign affairs when they entrusted a matter as consequential as the absorption of one nation by another to a person of no official standing in the government.

Fish's biographer regards Grant's attention to Santo Domingo as salutary because it deflected the President from intervention on the side of oppressed insurgents in Cuba and permitted Fish to pay undivided attention to settling the Alabama Claims and thus bettering relations with England.[19]

Babcock had been on Grant's staff since 1863 at Vicksburg. An attractive, gregarious man, he commanded Grant's loyalty almost to the end of the administration. The Santo Domingo affair, however, was only the first time he was accused of being corrupt. From then through the Whisky Fraud investigation and Safe Burglary Conspiracy trial in 1876, discussed below, he was the focus of many of the accusations of corruption in the Grant administration. Babcock went to Santo Domingo in 1869 and secretly negotiated a treaty of annexation with President Buenaventura Baez. The debate over ratification was the occasion of a famous dispute between Grant and Senator Charles Sumner, who led the successful fight to defeat annexation.

There was also an investigation by a Senate committee that brought charges from Senator Carl Schurz and others that various promoters, including Babcock, had financial stakes in the annexation. Indeed, the suggestion was strong that annexation had no value save for the private gains to be made by its promoters. Though dubious of his motivation, Schurz conceded that Babcock when offered a large tract of land by Baez "in consideration of a 'great kindness' . . . declined, saying 'it would ruin the treaty.' " There is no conclusive evidence that Babcock stood to gain from the treaty, but clearly other speculators did.[20]

In a minority report, three senators, Schurz and O. S. Ferry, Republicans, and George Vickers, Democrat, made a charge of an uglier sort. Davis Hatch was an American entrepreneur living in Santo Domingo. He had favored another Dominican leader who had led insurgents against Baez. For this, Hatch was condemned to die, but his sentence of execution was converted to one of banishment. At the time of Babcock's visit to Santo Domingo, Hatch—despite the banishment decision—was still in jail, and hence in danger. The three senators, in their report, claimed that Babcock acquiesced in the imprisonment because Hatch, if liberated, might speak against Baez and jeopardize the treaty. The senators closed, "declaring our most emphatic dissent . . . that the imprisonment of an American citizen abroad or at home, on the ground that he might exercise an influence this or that way with regard to a question of public interest, can be justified or excused under any circumstances."[21]

President Grant's response to the accusations of Babcock's possible misconduct was to assume that they came both from Democrats and, worse, from dissident voices within his own party. He clung to the belief that his close friend Babcock was innocent. He saw him as a target for those who either lacked the courage or the evidence to attack Grant himself. Babcock's influence rose rather than fell subsequent to the Santo Domingo affair. He became Grant's principal secretary controlling, albeit not exclusively, access to the President.

If promoters, perhaps including Babcock, saw the annexation of the Caribbean republic as a chance for pecuniary gain, it is clear that Grant conceived of it in different terms. In 1885, looking back on his presidency, he singled out the Santo Domingo annexation for special attention and wrote: "It is possible that the question of a conflict between races may come up in the future. . . . It was looking to a settlement of this question that led me to urge the annexation of Santo Domingo during the time I was President of the United States."[22] If black Americans were to become frustrated in the states and territories of the continental United States, they would have the black island in the Caribbean to which to go. The merits of such an argument lie outside the scope of this study, but for some the Santo Domingo annexation was not simply a matter of speculative opportunism.

Washington, D.C., and Freedmen's Affairs

The participation of President Grant in the administration of the city of Washington and in the closely related subject of the administration of federal programs for the freedmen largely lies beyond the boundaries of these essays. There were related scandals, known pejoratively as the Washington Ring, the Freedmen's Ring, and the Safe Burglary Conspiracy. They involved complex matters in the developing and governing of the capital city and disagreements over what the responsibilities of the federal government for its black citizens were. Very few of these complex affairs touched President Grant directly.

In three instances, however, the President became personally engaged and had to respond to the predicaments of men under grave attack: Alexander Robey Shepherd, Oliver Otis Howard, and Orville E. Babcock. These three men, very different one from another, illustrate Grant's dilemma in facing attacks made on men under his jurisdiction. In one case, that of Shepherd, he made what was seen as a brazen reappointment; in another, Howard's, a skillful shift of assignment; and in the third, Babcock's, he was silent. This last was because the President had already gone the limits of personal loyalty, as will be seen below in the discussion of the Whisky Frauds.

In the late 1860s, certain citizens of Washington complained of open sewers and other evidences of mismanagement in a rapidly growing city, and argued for the end of electoral government. Some of these complaints reflected the fact that more and more of those people elected to govern the city were black. The Negro population of the city was 32% of the total in 1870.[23]

In 1871 Congress made the city a territory under the jurisdiction of the executive branch. An unanticipated byproduct of this was to bring the White House into city hall politics. Henry D. Cooke of the First National Bank of Washington, and a brother of Jay Cooke, the country's leading banker, was named territorial governor. Both Cookes were prominent Republicans. Alexander Robey Shepherd, a highly successful entrepreneur in the plumbing business, was named vice president of the

Board of Public Works, and became the active manager of the District government.[24]

There were significant improvements made in the rapidly growing city; many of the adornments we think of today as characterizing Washington date from Shepherd's day. But the debt of the city rose, and there were charges of corruption and favoritism involving real estate developers and road builders.[25]

In 1873 the country suffered one of its most severe economic panics. The focal event was the failure of Jay Cooke & Co. In its wake, many other banks failed, including the Freedman's Savings Bank, almost all of whose depositors were former slaves struggling to get an economic foothold. The question of federal responsibility for this congressionally chartered bank lies outside this inquiry, other than to note that the congressional investigators in 1876 condemned the disastrous portfolio policy of Henry Cooke, the bank's chief investment officer, and thus held him responsible for the failure. Cooke, under criticism for maladministration of both the bank and the city, resigned as territorial governor of Washington in 1873.[26]

The congressional investigation of the Freedman's Bank followed an even more exhaustive study in 1874 of the administration of the city by a joint select committee of Congress. Both Shepherd and Cooke were very severely criticized. Cooke, having retired to private life, required no action by Grant. Shepherd, however, had no intention of leaving the city government. Likened by Congressman Robert B. Roosevelt to New York's "Boss" Tweed (William Marcy Tweed), and about to be investigated by Congress, "Boss" Shepherd nevertheless was named governor of Washington, D.C., in 1873 by Grant to replace Cooke.[27] When in 1876 on the recommendation of the investigating committee, the District of Columbia was changed to a commission form of government, Grant again ignored criticism of Shepherd and named him commissioner. The Senate rejected the nomination.[28]

Not only was the Freedman's Savings Bank's failure in 1873 under scrutiny, but also the defunct Freedmen's Bureau. General O. O. Howard, its commissioner, was charged with poor administration. Explicitly, his disbursement officer, responsible for paying bounties due Negroes who had fought in the Civil War, was charged with misuse of the funds set aside for that purpose. Grant, protecting an old soldier and fellow wartime commander, saw to it that Howard's case was heard by a military court of inquiry, and that the members of the court were not from that wing of the army dominated by General William W. Belknap, Secretary of War, which was highly antagonistic to Howard. Most modern authorities would agree that much of the attack on Howard masked a desire to discredit any federal efforts to assist black citizens.

Howard was cleared by the 1874 court of inquiry, but was still highly controversial. He would have liked to stay in Washington and remain involved in Freedmen's Bureau affairs. In Howard's case, Grant, rather than defy criticism, took the advice of another old soldier, William T. Sherman, under whom Howard had commanded the Army of the Tennessee, and transferred Howard to duty in the Northwest—as far from Washington, D.C., and Freedmen's affairs as possible.[29]

Also in 1874 Shepherd and his associates remained under severe criticism for their management of the city. One of these associates was Orville E. Babcock, the President's private secretary, who had another job as well. He was commissioner of public buildings for the District of Columbia. The citizens group criticizing the Shepherd administration was known as the Memorialists. Columbus Alexander was their leader.[30] Under particular fire in 1874 for alleged frauds was the United States attorney for the District of Columbia, Richard Harrington. He was later indicted for heading what was known as the Safe Burglary Conspiracy.

As the story was told in the *New York Times,* Harrington—working with H. C. Whitley, Chief, United States Secret Service, a division of the Treasury Department—secured the services of William Benton and George E. Miles. Miles, known under several aliases, was a professional safe cracker. On April 23, 1874, Harrington notified the Washington chief of police, Major A. C. Richards, that he had received a note warning that his office safe might be broken into. That night a small detachment of police covered the several doors of the building housing the United States attorney's office. Governor Alexander Shepherd's brother, Thomas M. Shepherd, chanced to pass by and was posted across the street.

Harrington, meanwhile, arranged for Miles and Benton to open the safe and remove documents thought by the Memorialists to be of value in their investigation. Miles then blew the safe. The police (not part of the conspiracy) moved in, but Miles left by the back door. Thomas Shepherd pursued him, but Miles escaped.

Benton, with the documents, also exited. Richards wanted to seize him, but Harrington persuaded the police chief not to, on the assumption that he would lead them to a bigger culprit. They followed Benton to Columbus Alexander's house.

There, the intention was to catch Alexander in the act of receiving stolen documents. The next day's newspapers would carry the story, complete with the blowing of the safe. Benton was to be arrested, but Harrington was to see to it that his prosecution was not pressed. Unluckily for the conspirators, Alexander proved to be a sound sleeper. There was no response to Benton's repeated rings. Why Alexander did not hear or respond to the loud rings is not known.

Richards became suspicious and began an investigation. This led to an inquiry by a committee of the House of Representatives, who interrogated several witnesses thoroughly. Columbus Alexander was cleared, but the committee declined to go further because of (1) conflicting testimony, (2) absence of some essential witnesses, and (3) the fact that the case would go before the courts. The committee sent its report to both Secretary of the Treasury Benjamin Helm Bristow (new to the job since the safe burglary and not sympathetic to Whitley) and Attorney General George W. Williams for action.[31]

In September, 1874, Harrington, Whitley, and three other men (including another Secret Service man, Ichabod C. Nettleship) were indicted for conspiracy. In December, due to a technicality involving the indictment, the government withdrew the case. Asked why they had not reopened the case more promptly, former attorney general George H. Williams testified on April 10, 1876, that he alone had made the decision, and that President Grant had not ordered abandonment of the case. (It should be noted that both Attorney General Williams and his predecessor, Amos T. Akerman, were also interrogated in 1876 in a congressional investigation of the Justice Department.)[32]

Harrington was reindicted and on April 9, 1876, Whitley, who had been granted immunity by Attorney General Edwards Pierrepont and turned witness for the prosecution, implicated Orville E. Babcock. (Babcock had recently been acquitted in the Whisky Frauds case discussed below.) The allegation was that it was Babcock who had introduced Whitley into the conspiracy because he feared Columbus Alexander's inquiry would lead to misdeeds in his handling of the office of commissioner of public buildings. Babcock was accused of having used Whitley to maintain surveillance of reporters who were making charges against the President's secretary during the Whisky Fraud cases. Babcock admitted telling Whitley to report to Harrington, but denied knowing what assignment the United States Attorney had in mind. Babcock flatly denied Whitley's claim that he (Babcock) said Harrington had bungled the matter and that Whitley could have done it better alone.

Babcock was indicted for conspiracy to "injure and oppress Columbus Alexander" on April 15, 1876. The government's case against him was based largely on the theory that he was the only man involved who was of sufficiently high place to be able to obtain the cooperation of Secret Service men. Witnesses, other than Whitley, however, also implicated Babcock. The defense lawyer contended that Babcock's only involvement was in directing Whitley to report to Harrington. Babcock was acquitted on September 29, 1876.[33] In fairness, it should be noted that about the only facts that are firm are that the safe was blown and that Babcock, when in the executive mansion, could command the assistance of the head of the Secret Service. Babcock had been off the President's staff since the previous March.

Collectors of Customs

The collectors of customs in the various ports were particularly prone to corrupt practices. In the guise of regular fees or warehouse storage charges for goods held past the usual unloading period, bribes could be accepted. Such practices predated and postdated the Grant administration. There was, however, a full-scale investigation of what was called the Collectors Ring conducted by the Senate in 1872.

On July 1, 1870, Grant, at the insistence of Senator Roscoe Conkling, appointed Thomas Murphy as the collector of the Port of New York.[34] Murphy hired George K. Leet, a member of Grant's wartime staff, and turned over to him part of the general business, which involved collecting storage charges on imported goods not picked up by merchants within two days.[35] Grant had written a letter of introduction for Leet to Murphy's predecessor as collector stating, "I cheerfully commend him as possessing all the qualities necessary to inspire confidence."[36] When in Washington in 1869–1870, Leet had roomed with Grant's personal secretaries, Horace Porter and Orville E. Babcock.[37]

Merchants soon complained to Grant that because of the monopoly held by Leet's firm, Leet & Co., storage charges became exorbitant.[38] Because of these criticisms and Grant's previous association with Leet, the President told Murphy in October, 1871, "Mr. Murphy, there is so much noise, and talk, and scandal, about this young man Leet . . . on account of his being with me during the war, that I think I had better stop that, and I think that young man had better leave."[39] Moreover, Grant's secretary, General Porter, in a letter to Murphy on October 31, 1870, wrote that the President felt that "if any persons have been employed in the custom house upon representations that they are his particular friends and favorites, he hopes they may be discharged; and, that if any persons ever apply for positions under you, upon such a pretense, he requests that they may not be employed."[40] Murphy, however, momentarily convinced Grant that it was not essential to fire Leet.[41]

The Senate Committee on Investigation and Retrenchment held a series of hearings to examine charges against the New York Custom House of fraud, bribery, and high rates. Hearings began on January 3, 1872, and the committee submitted a majority report on June 4, 1872.[42] The authors of a minority report noted that all but one of the custom house inspectors before the committee testified they had taken bribes.[43] Two of the witnesses were accused of having perjured themselves before the committee; in addition, none of the principal officers of the New York Custom House voluntarily furnished information.[44] However, neither the majority nor the minority report directly implicated Grant in the scandal.[45]

As a result of the investigation, Grant removed Leet from his position. Earlier, in November, 1871, Murphy had resigned and Grant appointed Chester A. Arthur, another Conkling man, as his successor.[46] A student of civil service reform contends that the "administration of the New York Custom-house improved steadily" after Arthur replaced Murphy. He also points out that the worst abuses had occurred in the administration of Andrew Johnson when, according to Grant's Civil Service Commission, headed by reformer George William Curtis, "the evils of the 'spoils' system culminated."[47]

In New Orleans the Collector of the Port was James F. Casey. He was married to a sister of Julia Dent Grant, the President's wife. On July 12,

1870, George S. Boutwell, Secretary of the Treasury, complied with a formal request from the Senate that he supply a compendium of letters calling for the removal of the President's brother-in-law.[48]

The letters from Louisianans do not talk of corrupt practices but instead, with complete frankness, say that as Republicans they view with dismay the fact that Casey had not replaced the Democrats on his staff.[49]

In the investigation that followed, serious charges of fraud were made against Casey and his associates. Citing one of Casey's political rivals and hence a somewhat dubious source, Hamilton Fish recorded in his diary that Casey had had available to him large sums for the purpose of political bribery.[50] The report of the congressional committee, completed in 1872, was held back in the hope that Casey would resign. He did not do so, so the report was released. In March, 1873, Grant reappointed him to a three-year term. He was confirmed by the Senate.[51]

Credit Mobilier

Perhaps the most notorious political scandal of the era was Crédit Mobilier, but it touched the area of presidential misconduct only tangentially. Crédit Mobilier was a corporation established in connection with the construction of the Union Pacific Railroad. It was headed by Congressman Oakes Ames and served as a corporate funnel through which moved huge subsidies from Congress for the building of the Union Pacific, with which Ames was also closely associated. Ames and others, acting as principals of Crédit Mobilier, spent the subsidies on construction contracts with other companies they controlled. They received profits upward of $20,000,000.

To forestall a congressional investigation, the chief promoter, Ames, sold stock in Crédit Mobilier to his colleagues in Congress at less than its market value, and in some cases deferred payment for the shares.[52] Entered into somewhat casually, none of these deals seems to have profited the congressmen by more than a few hundred dollars.

When the story became known in 1872, the careers of several congressmen were severely affected. Vice President Schuyler Colfax was exposed as having accepted shares in 1867–1868 while serving as Speaker of the House of Representatives. The House considered impeachment of Colfax, but his act was viewed as a non-impeachable offense, since it took place before he became vice president.[53] President Grant's response was to deny Colfax renomination in 1872. His new vice president, Henry Wilson, admitted that his wife paid $2,000 and received a receipt for stock, but when he learned legislative favors might be expected by the company, he had the money refunded. He claimed she refused to accept the profit of $814 due her and that he paid it to her from his own pocket.[54] Congressman James Garfield also accepted stock and was often reminded of it by political opponents.[55] Garfield's career, unlike Colfax's, was not blighted. He was elected president in 1880.

Sanborn Contract

The corruption of John D. Sanborn, a tax collector, was made possible by the abuse of both executive and congressional power. The payment to informers of portions (called moieties) of the taxes collected from delinquents was an ancient practice that had been under debate as a federal tax collecting device since 1853.[56] The obvious dangers of false accusations and blackmail led to the repeal of the practice in the Revenue Act of 1872. This legislation of the Grant administration is regarded by the chief authority on the subject as an important step toward civil service reform.[57]

Through the efforts of Representative Benjamin F. Butler of Massachusetts, however, a rider to an appropriations bill empowered the Treasury Department to make no more than three contracts with private third parties for the collection of delinquent taxes. The private party would receive a percentage of any delinquent taxes which were detected and collected.[58] The contracts were made while George Boutwell was secretary of the Treasury (March, 1869–March, 1873). The August, 1872, contract authorizing Sanborn to retain as commission 50% of any delinquent taxes he collected was signed by then acting secretary of Treasury, William A. Richardson.[59] Sanborn, a special agent of the Treasury since 1869, was an associate of Butler. It was Butler who suggested to Richardson that Sanborn collect internal revenue taxes evaded by railroads, distillers, and others.[60]

Richardson became secretary of the Treasury in March, 1873, and it was during his incumbency that the congressional investigation was held. The report of the House Ways and Means Committee held that Sanborn's methods were improper, the profit was considerable, $213,500, and circumstances pointed to negligence, if not actual connivance, on the part of Secretary Richardson.[61]

The committee report following the investigation determined that the Treasury had encouraged negligence on the part of its own collectors so that Sanborn would have more to collect, and that most of the $427,000 he collected would in due course have come to the government without pressure.[62] Sanborn's methods were "unorthodox": armed with a letter from Richardson, he entered the Internal Revenue Bureau's Boston office, demanded a list of delinquent taxpayers, and proceeded to collect the taxes while deducting his 50% commission.[63] With railroads, he was even more direct: he simply sent a demand letter, along with a false oath to the effect that he had received information of tax evasion, to the 592 railroads listed in Appleton's Railway Guide. Of Sanborn's total profit, $213,500, he claimed to have paid $156,000 in "expenses" to men whom he would not name.[64]

The congressional report included copies of letters from Boutwell and Richardson which served to show that "the whole power of the Internal Revenue Bureau, as well as the entire machinery of government for the collection of taxes, was placed at the disposal of Sanborn."[65] While the congressmen stated that Richardson and Boutwell deserved "severe condemnation for the manner in which they have permitted the law to be administrated," the members of the committee "find nothing impeaching the integrity of Secretary Boutwell's or Richardson's action; and the testimony does not prove that the Secretaries or any of their associates were influenced by corrupt motives."[66] Boutwell does not discuss the matter in his memoirs.

The presidential connection with this unsavory matter was remote. Nevins suggests that the Sanborn contract had been a quid pro quo for Butler's support for Richardson's confirmation as secretary of the Treasury. And that Grant, therefore, had paid the price. With a motion to censure Richardson on the floor of the House, the Secretary resigned. Grant appointed him a judge on the Court of Claims.[67] Richardson was replaced as Treasury secretary by former solicitor general Benjamin Helm Bristow, a man with the highest reputation for honesty.

Emma Mine and Robert C. Schenck

Robert C. Schenck, an Ohio Republican congressman, was named minister to Great Britain in December, 1870.[68] He was closely associated with Jay Cooke and with the Northern Pacific Railroad, and was remarkably frank in his belief that his own economic development and the nation's went hand in hand. While chairman of the House Ways and Means Committee, he wrote his daughter: "Yesterday I got down town to meet Mr. Jay Cooke. I am gradually willowing the ground and personally putting in seed for profitable enterprises."[69] Confirmed by the Senate, he took up his post in June, 1874.

In November Schenck became a stockholder and promoter at the Emma Silver Mining Company, a British corporation; the mine was in Utah. Schenck's name was used prominently on promotional material in Great Britain and, in effect, he was using his position as minister to promote the mine. His friends at the house of Jay Cooke were also sponsors of the enterprise.[70]

On November 27, 1871, Secretary of State Hamilton Fish advised Schenck "to withdraw your name from the management of the company."[71] Schenck resigned from Emma Mine on December 6, 1871, but delayed announcement until January 12, 1872, reportedly so that his friends could sell their shares before his announcement shook confidence in the company and the price of Emma's stock declined.

In 1873 Emma Mine failed. In 1876 Congressman Abram Hewitt conducted an exhaustive study of the history of the Emma Mine corporation. Schenck's highly favorable arrangements with the company were exposed, but the committee concluded that the minister "was not guilty of a fraud or any fraudulent intention."[72] Schenck, under threat of legal action in England, resigned as minister in May, 1876.

The committee did not address itself to the question of what should be the proper response of either the Secretary of State or the President to such a use of a diplomatic post. Schenck was greatly criticized for his attempt to induce people in the country to which he was accredited to invest in a speculation in his home country.

Interior Department and Columbus Delano

In 1870 President Grant appointed Columbus Delano, former Ohio congressman and head of the Internal Revenue Bureau, to succeed Jacob D. Cox as secretary of the interior. In matters pertaining to possible abuses of power, Cox is considered by authorities to have been less susceptible to corruption than his successor.[73]

In 1875 various westerners charged Columbus Delano and his son John with corruption, bribery, and fraud. Governor E. M. McCook of Colorado claimed that Jerome B. Chaffee, Colorado banker and future senator, had secured land patents from the Department of the Interior after he had paid John Delano $1,200. In March, 1875, L. C. Stevens, former chief clerk in the Surveyor's Office, told Benjamin Helm Bristow, Secretary of the Treasury, that the surveyor general, Silas Reed, made several corrupt contracts to benefit John Delano and that Reed and John Delano had blackmailed five deputy surveyors for $5,000. Stevens also claimed to have seen a letter from Columbus Delano to Reed in which Delano thanked him for what he had done for his son.[74]

Although Stevens forwarded his charges to Grant, the President was disinclined to fire Delano. On April 29, 1875, Grant told Secretary Hamilton Fish, who favored the Interior Secretary's resignation, "If Delano were now to resign, it would be retreating under fire and be accepted as an admission of the charges." Grant secretly accepted Delano's resignation in mid-August, but did not make it public until Bristow threatened to resign if Delano were not removed. In October, 1875, Grant appointed Zachariah Chandler, former Michigan senator, to succeed Delano.[75]

On March 17, 1876, Chandler reported to the cabinet that he had found extensive fraud in Delano's Interior Department, including at least 800 fraudulent entries of land grants. The chief clerk of the Land Bureau was implicated and, according to Hamilton Fish, Grant offered him immunity to gain his cooperation in testifying. Fish wrote: "The President directs every effort to be made to obtain evidence, and protection for the Clerk from prosecution to the extent of the law if he can furnish evidence which will convict persons more guilty than himself."[76]

War Department and William W. Belknap

William W. Belknap, a Civil War general, was appointed secretary of war on the death of Grant's close associate, John A. Rawlins, in October, 1869. In 1870, during the Franco-Prussian War, Senators Carl Schurz and Charles Sumner, frequent critics of the Grant administration, accused Belknap of having "violated the neutrality laws by selling government arms to agents of the French." Schurz, not entirely unmindful of the German vote, further charged that Belknap received bids from Remington and Sons for obsolete guns and, on learning that Remington was an agent for the French, sold the guns to a neighbor of the Remington family. Belknap also arranged for the army to sell the French 54,000,000 cartridges to fit the guns. The charges, investigated by a congressional committee, were substantiated, but no criminal act was cited or impeachment proceedings initiated.[77]

In 1870 Mrs. Belknap persuaded her husband to give a friend, Caleb P. Marsh, a New York contractor, the post-tradership at Fort Sill in the Indian Territory. John S. Evans, holder of the valuable tradership, wanted to retain it. Belknap suggested a partnership. A contract executed in New York and witnessed by Marsh's lawyer called for Evans to pay Marsh $15,000 annually. It was amended to an amount of $12,000. This contract was given to a congressional committee in February, 1876, as part of an investigation in which Marsh revealed that Mrs. Belknap received half the amount.[78] As Marsh recounted the conversation, Mrs. Belknap told him, "If I can prevail upon the Secretary of War to award you a post you must be careful to say nothing to him about presents, for a man once offered him $10,000 for a tradership of this kind and he told him that if he did not leave the office he would kick him down stairs."[79] When Mrs. Belknap died in 1870, Marsh continued payments for the benefit of a Belknap child, who died in 1871. Payments then came to Mrs. Belknap's sister and continued to do so after she married the Secretary. Belknap claimed ignorance of these funds that helped pay his domestic expenses. Marsh told investigating congressmen, after admitting and documenting his bribe: "The money was sent according to the instructions of the Secretary of War; sometimes in bank-notes. . . . I think on one or more occasions by certificate of deposit on the National Bank of America in New York. Sometimes I paid him in New York in person."[80]

Marsh told his story and presented the confirming evidence to the House Committee on Expenditures in the War Department on February 29, 1876. At 11 a.m. on March 1, and again at 3 p.m., the committee met. Secretary Belknap appeared in the afternoon. Belknap withdrew, leaving his counsel, who made a "verbal proposition" with respect to the report the committee would make the next day to the full House. The proposition was not defined; it may have been an offer of resignation if impeachment were not asked.[81]

That evening the committee met in the rooms of one of its members. The next morning, Secretary of the Treasury Bristow, already at work exposing other corruption within the administration, learned that there was "incontrovertible" evidence of Belknap's guilt. He hurried to the executive mansion to suggest that the President listen to the committee's case for impeachment. As Bristow left, Belknap arrived. Learning that the committee would that day ask for impeachment, the Secretary of War had rushed to the President. At 10:20 a.m. he offered Grant a two-sentence letter of resignation; Grant's acceptance took one sentence.[82]

At 11 a.m. the committee received copies of these letters. The members, deeply distressed that the substance of their deliberations the previous evening had reached Belknap, promptly passed unanimously three resolutions: (1) that Belknap be impeached, (2) that the House Committee on the Judiciary prepare articles of impeachment "without undue delay," and (3) "that five members of the House proceed immediately to the bar of the Senate, and there impeach William W. Belknap, late Secretary of War."[83]

Grant expressed surprise at the expressions of criticism in the press and outrage in Congress at the suggestion that he had made a prosecution by the House difficult. In the Senate trial, Belknap was acquitted by a vote of 37 to 24. Twenty-three of the senators who saved Belknap from the disgrace of a sentence of guilt, expressible in a requirement of removal, did so for want of jurisdiction. Belknap had, with the swift assistance of Grant, removed himself, and the Senate was trying a former, not a sitting, member of the cabinet.[84] Belknap was replaced as secretary of war by Alphonso Taft.

One further aspect of the scandal was the report in the *New York Tribune* that on March 9, 1876, before the Committee on Expenditures in the War Department, Orvil Grant admitted obtaining four Indian posts from his brother and sharing with partners in their profits.[85] President Grant took no action against his brother, who retained the posts.

Navy Department and George M. Robeson

George Robeson became secretary of the navy in 1869. His net worth was $20,000, and he had what Allan Nevins called "a slender law-practise."[86] As secretary, he began dealing with a grain and feed firm in Philadelphia, A. G. Cattell & Co. The firm, with capital of $30,000, had not previously done business with the navy. Soon it was earning commissions from other suppliers who, through Cattell, received navy contracts. A congressional investigation of great thoroughness revealed that the Cattell firm had become highly successful since 1869. Robeson cooperated with the investigating committee by testifying and by supplying his bank book that showed that he made deposits totaling $320,000 in the years 1872–1876. Nevins further reports that one of the members of the Cattell family purchased a house at Long Branch, where the Grants summered, for Robeson. There was no direct evidence of cash payments to Robeson in the books at A. G. Cattell & Co. The books of the firm were found to be in disorder.[87] Circumstantial evidence all, but damning.

In July, 1876, the investigating committee reviewed the voluminous testimony taken and issued a long report detailing misconduct and saying that "a system of corruption has grown up . . . likely to be known hereafter as 'Cattellism.' It should be checked and in the vigorous manner rebuked." The committee recommended courts-martial for naval officers implicated and debated the question of punitive action against Secretary Robeson. The final section of the long report of the seven majority members (all Democrats) was a resolution referring the matter to the Judiciary Committee either to "report articles of impeachment against George M. Robeson, Secretary of the Navy" or to prepare legislation to make laws, such as those requiring report to Congress of any fines levied over $1,000, "sufficiently punitive to protect the public service." Three Republican minority members issued a dissenting resolution completely exonerating Robeson.[88] Grant did not call for the

Secretary's resignation. With the administration coming to a close, the impeachment action was not pursued.

Whisky Frauds

Whisky distillers and Internal Revenue Commission agents often made false reports of production to avoid tax. Such practices were common as far back as the Lincoln administration.[89] Investigation later made it clear that a large number of government employees joined people in the industry in depriving the country of revenue. In St. Louis virtually every agent was believed to be involved. And complicity either in the frauds themselves or in the acceptance of bribes to prevent the exposures of the frauds reached to President Grant's closest associate, his secretary, Orville E. Babcock, and perhaps the Grant family itself.

It must be acknowledged that there was a partisan component to the investigation of the Whisky Frauds. Benjamin Helm Bristow, Secretary of the Treasury, wanted to be president. His reputation was based largely on his relentless exposure of the Whisky Frauds, and he became a hero of a major anti-Grant wing of the Republican Party. There is little to suggest that Bristow slanted the investigation to embarrass the Grant wing of the party, but many, including the President, believed he did.

There had always been strong political opposition to Grant within his own party in the state of Missouri. In February, 1870, he appointed a loyalist, General John A. McDonald of St. Louis, supervisor of revenue for Missouri and six other states. Grant knew McDonald socially but not well; Babcock supported the appointment.[90]

On June 3, 1874, Bristow, on being named secretary of the Treasury, began his investigation of records dating back to 1870. He determined that 12,000,000 to 15,000,000 gallons of whisky escaped tax annually.[91] Congress appropriated $125,000 for an investigation by the Secretary.[92] On February 11, 1875, Bristow received a letter from George W. Fishback, publisher of the St. Louis *Democrat*: "If the Secretary wants to break up the powerful ring which exists here, I can give him the name of a man who, if he receives the necessary authority and is assured of absolute secrecy about the matter, will undertake to do it, and I will guarantee success."[93] The man, Myron Colony, was a writer for the newspaper.

On March 1, 1875, Bluford Wilson, Solicitor of the Treasury and Bristow's chief assistant in the investigation, appointed Colony as an agent of the Secret Service division of the Treasury Department. Colony and Wilson worked out a complex and successful system of catching the perpetrators of the frauds.

Wilson told the House of Representatives Select Committee Concerning the Whisky Frauds that in late April, 1875, John McDonald broke down in Bristow's office and confessed to a central role in the Whisky Frauds. He did so because of strong evidence amassed by Colony and Wilson. Regaining his composure, McDonald now called on Wilson and, in return for immunity, offered to obtain delinquent revenues from the distillers. He urged Wilson not to seize the distilleries, in a full-scale prosecution of the case, because "the party interests in his state and his district would be greatly damaged. . . ." McDonald, according to Wilson, "spoke of his own great and powerful influence in the West. . . ." Wilson heatedly responded that if it were in his power he would "dismiss him [McDonald] from the public service."[94]

McDonald, in a book carrying his version of the story, ignored the Wilson conversation, but referred to similar hints of damage to the party in a talk with Bristow. He claimed that Bristow "with some anxiety . . . in his face, . . . inquired if I intended talking with the President. . . ." McDonald said that he did and reported that he repeated to Grant that damage would be done the party if the cases were prosecuted. He urged that the evidence be burned; Grant reportedly thought sealing it would be better. McDonald alleged that he received assurances that only distillers and not government men (and hence not party men) would be prosecuted.[95] There is no corroborative evidence with respect to this conversation.

Wilson told a different story. He testified that he was instructed to prepare a digest of firm evidence. With this dossier, Wilson and Bristow visited the President. Asked by a committee member if Bristow said explicitly at that meeting that McDonald was a confessed guilty party, Wilson replied, ". . . he did not, for the reason that it appeared at the interview that the President and the Secretary had previously been in conference touching that subject and that the President understood that branch of the case quite as well as General Bristow did." There is no firm evidence that Grant had been given McDonald's name. Wilson refused to elaborate on the conversation: "I wish now to say to the committee that I have taken the best advice within my reach . . . as to what would be my course in answering interrogators calling for what took place between the Secretary of the Treasury and the President, and while the advice I have received has been various and conflicting, my own judgment and preference is that so long as the President of the United States and the Secretary of the Treasury do not themselves choose to go into questions touching the subject of this inquiry, I ought not to be expected to do so."[96] Under relentless questioning, Wilson did violate this position somewhat, but he closed by intimating strongly that President Grant supported prosecution unimpeded by favoritism.

By May 13, 1875, some 350 men, from Galveston to Boston, in both the government and distillery industry, were arrested. When the cases were discussed in the capital, Bristow told Hamilton Fish "that Babcock is as deep as any in the Whiskey Ring, [and] that he has most positive evidence. . . ." Bristow also told the Secretary of State that McDonald was the "centre pin of the plot." When Bristow and Fish broached the subject of the ring in general terms with the President, Grant said: "Well, Mr. Bristow, there is at least one honest man in St. Louis on whom we can rely—John McDonald. I know that because he is an intimate acquaintance and confidential friend of Babcock's." Bristow responded: "Mr. President . . . McDonald is the head and centre of all the frauds. He is at this very time in New York ready to take a steamer on the first indication at any effort to arrest him."[97] In July, 1875, Attorney General Edwards Pierrepont and Bristow went to Long Beach and reportedly told Grant that Babcock also was criminally involved in the case. Grant did not comment on this accusation, but wrote: "Let no guilty man escape if it can be avoided. Be specially vigilant . . . against all those who insinuate that they have high influence to protect, or to protect them."[98]

In August Bristow confronted Babcock with a telegram, signed "Sylph," the order for which was in Babcock's handwriting. Babcock admitted he had sent it to McDonald, but claimed it did not refer to the Whisky Ring matter. Evidence is strong that in the telegram Babcock was telling McDonald that he (Babcock) had successfully deflected the prosecution. Bristow, by citing a date discrepancy, gave evidence of Babcock's complicity to Grant, who nonetheless believed Babcock's explanation.[99] Wilson marked Grant's hostility toward the prosecution from these events in August.

Grant clearly was troubled by the whole matter. He was told by friends of Babcock that Wilson was spying on the President. He appeared to think that somehow Babcock was being made a scapegoat.[100] He did not fire or suspend his secretary, but he sought to help him defend himself. On December 2, 1875, General Babcock wrote Grant formally requesting a military court of inquiry. In the cabinet this was acceded to by even dubious members, since none felt that such a hearing would supersede a civil court action. Grant had three generals appointed who were believed to be sympathetic to Babcock. Grant also ordered Attorney General Pierrepont to direct the prosecutor, United States Attorney David P. Dyer, to turn over to the court of inquiry evidence relevant to Babcock's case that had been gathered for the grand jury.[101] Dyer's response was to go to the grand jury which, on December 9, 1875, returned a true bill accusing Babcock of conspiracy.[102] With Babcock now before a civilian court, the military tribunal was disbanded.

With respect to others under indictment, Grant expressed distaste for grants of immunity to gain testimony against greater offenders. He stated to Bristow's chief aide, Solicitor of the Treasury Wilson, that he (Wilson) was obtaining convictions on the word of "confessed perjurors and felons." On January 26, 1876, Attorney General Pierrepont, siding with Grant against Bristow, ordered no further grants of immunity. One authority views this as reflecting Grant's determination to protect his "endangered secretary."[103] The failure to use grants of immunity, which the President did permit in other investigations, was regarded by Wilson as the reason few major cases were successfully prosecuted.

Accusations reached ever closer to Grant. In January newspapers implicated Frederick Dent Grant, the President's oldest son, and Orvil Grant, his brother, in the Whisky Ring. Grant asked Pierrepont to get the reporters before a grand jury and act on their evidence if they had any, and publish the reporters' names if the charges proved false.[104]

By February 8, 1876, Grant felt besieged. Manifesting "a great deal of excitement," he confided to his cabinet his feelings about those pursuing him: ". . . they had taken from him his secretaries and clerks, his messengers and doorkeepers; that the prosecution was aimed at himself, and they were putting him on trial; that he was as confident as he lived of Babcock's innocence. . . ."[105]

Grant spoke of going to St. Louis to testify in Babcock's behalf. Fish and others urged that he not do so. Instead he gave a deposition, taken February 12, 1876, by Lucien Eaton, for the prosecution, with cross-examination by W. Cook, for the defense. Secretary Bristow and Attorney General Pierrepont were present as was Chief Justice Morrison R. Waite, who notarized the document.[106] Read at the trial on February 17, it was believed to have contributed significantly to Babcock's acquittal on February 28, 1876. He was then replaced as Grant's secretary by U. S. Grant, Jr., the President's second son. Babcock, who apparently had put aside no substantial savings, became an inspector of lighthouses and drowned at Mosquito Inlet, Florida, in 1884.

Benjamin Helm Bristow appeared before the Congressional Investigating Committee in July, 1876. By then he had left the cabinet and was estranged from Grant, but at the hearing he refused to testify about "what occurred between the President and myself, . . . which . . . I think is a matter of the highest privilege, of which I have no right to speak at all." Bristow was pressed repeatedly to tell the committee about Grant's role while the cases were being prosecuted. He said this would require him to discuss conversations with the President and, concluding his testimony, said, "I decline to do so."[107]

General McDonald went to jail. In the book he wrote to prove that others should have been there instead, he made a strong case for Babcock's guilt. Many of the documents he cited, and others, are in the Bristow Papers in the Library of Congress. This evidence suggests that Babcock was guilty.

McDonald also said Grant was guilty of criminal involvement. In this accusation he could cite no documents similar to those implicating Babcock. One authority, William Hesseltine, wrote, "McDonald attempted to prove Grant a member of the ring, but failed to establish his contention."[108]

NOTES

[1]H. Wayne Morgan, "Toward National Unity," and Ari Hoogenboom, "Civil Service Reform and Public Morality," in H. Wayne Morgan, ed., *The Gilded Age* (Syracuse, 1970), 1–12, 77–95.

[2]*Gold Panic Investigation,* 41st Cong., 2nd Sess., House Report 31, March 1, 1870, 2.

[3]*Ibid.,* 171.

[4]*Ibid.,* 243.

[5]*Ibid.,* 359.

[6]*Ibid.,* 9.

[7]*Ibid.,* 232.

[8]*Ibid.,* 445.

[9]*Ibid.,* 251–252, 474. In her unpublished memoirs Julia Dent Grant acknowledged writing the letter; John Y. Simon, Executive Director, Ulysses S. Grant Association, to Author, June 14, 1974.

[10]*Gold Panic Investigation,* 17.

[11]John A. Carpenter, *Ulysses S. Grant* (New York, 1970), 97.

[12]*Gold Panic Investigation,* 476–479.

[13]Allan Nevins, *Hamilton Fish: The Inner History of the Grant Administration* (2 vols., New York, 1957), I, 285; *Gold Panic Investigation,* 6, 259.

[14]*Gold Panic Investigation,* 173, 258–259.

[15]*Ibid.,* 1–23.

[16]*Ibid.,* Minority Report, 461–479.

[17]*Gold Panic Investigation,* 472.

[18]James Ford Rhodes, *History of the United States,* (8 vols., New York, 1896–1919), VI, 256.

[19]Nevins, *Fish,* II, 501.

[20]*Investigation of the Davis Hatch Memorial,* 41st Cong., 2nd Sess., Senate Report 234, June 25, 1870, p. xlvi.

[21]*Ibid.,* 35–38.

[22]Ulysses S. Grant, *Personal Memoirs of U.S. Grant* (2 vols., New York, 1886), II, 550.

[23]Constance McLaughlin Green, *The Secret City: A History of Race Relations in the Nation's Capital* (Princeton, 1967), 63; Washington *Evening Star,* June 7 and 9, 1869.

[24]William B. Hesseltine, *Ulysses S. Grant* (New York, 1935), 321; Nevins, *Fish,* II, 657–658.

[25]James G. Blaine, *Twenty Years of Congress: From Lincoln to Garfield* (2 vols., Norwich, Conn., 1884–1886), II, 548.

[26]*Freedman's Savings and Trust Company,* 44th Cong., 1st Sess., House Report 502, May 19, 1876 (see particularly Minority Report); Hesseltine, *Grant,* 321–322.

[27]Report of the Joint Select Committee on the District of Columbia, 43rd Cong., 1st Sess., Senate Report 453, June 16, 1874.

[28]Hesseltine, *Grant,* 321–322; Constance McLaughlin Green, *Washington: Village and Capital, 1800–1878* (Princeton, 1962), 360–362.

[29]George R. Bentley, *A History of the Freedmen's Bureau* (Philadelphia, 1955), 213–214; O. O. Howard to S. P. Lee, Howard Papers, Bowdoin College; Diary of Willard Saxton, February 25, 1874, Historical Manuscripts, Yale University; John A. Carpenter, *Sword and Olive Branch: Oliver Otis Howard* (Pittsburgh, 1964), 220–243.

[30]H. V. Boynton, "The Washington 'Safe Burglary' Conspiracy," *American Law Review, 1876–1877,* II (Boston, 1877), 401–446.

[31]*Alleged Safe-Burglary at the Office of the United States Attorney, Washington, D.C.,* 43rd Cong., 1st Sess., House Report 785, June 23, 1874.

[32]*Disbursements under the Registration Act,* 44th Cong., 1st Sess., House Report 800, August 5, 1876.

[33]*New York Times,* May 10, June 16, 19, 22, August 25, September 16, October 21, November 28, December 10, 1874, and January 5, April 10, 11, 13, 16, September 25, 29, October 1, 1876 and *passim; Nation,* December 3, 1874; New York *Evening Post,* July 1, December 1, 5, 1874.

[34]Hesseltine, *Grant,* 211; Nevins, *Fish,* I, 368.

[35]Carpenter, *Grant,* 118.

[36]*New York Custom-House Investigation,* 42nd Cong., 2nd Sess., Senate Report 227, June 4, 1872, I, p. viii.

[37]Hoogenboom, "Civil Service Reform," 77–95, 91.

[38]Nevins, *Fish,* II, 594.

[39]*New York Custom-House Investigation,* III, 349.

[40]*Ibid.,* I, p. x.

[41]Carpenter, *Grant,* 118.

[42]*New York Custom-House Investigation,* I, pp. i–cxlvi.

[43]*Ibid.,* p. lxxix.

[44]*Ibid.,* pp. cxl–cxli.

[45]*Ibid.,* pp. i–cxlvi.

[46]Hesseltine, *Grant,* 256–265.

[47]Hoogenboom, "Civil Service Reform," 80, 90.

[48]*Removal of James F. Casey,* 41st Cong., 2nd Sess., Senate Executive Document 109, July 12, 1870.

[49]*Ibid.,* 1–18.

[50]Nevins, *Fish,* I, 599.

[51]*Ibid.,* 657; Hesseltine, *Grant,* 346.

[52]Hesseltine, *Grant,* 309–312; *Credit Mobilier Investigation,* 42nd Cong., 3rd Sess., House Report 77, February 18, 1873.

[53]*Credit Mobilier Investigation,* 82; *Inquiry as to Impeachment in Credit Mobilier Testimony,* 42nd Cong., 3rd Sess., House Report 81, February 24, 1873, 2.

[54]*Credit Mobilier Investigation,* 187–188.

[55]*Ibid.,* p. vii.

[56]Hesseltine, *Grant,* 383; *Discovery and Collection of Monies Withheld from the Government,* 43rd. Cong., 1st Sess., House Report 559, May 4, 1874.

[57]Hoogenboom, "Civil Service Reform," 77–95 (Hoogenboom refers to related legislation in 1874).

[58]*Monies,* 1.

[59]*Ibid.,* 2.

[60]Nevins, *Fish,* II, 708.

[61]Ross A. Webb, *Benjamin Helm Bristow: Border State Politician* (Lexington, 1969), 134; *Monies,* 3.

[62]*Monies,* 1–9.

[63]Hesseltine, *Grant,* 364; *Monies,* 559.

[64]Nevins, *Fish,* I, 708.

[65]*Monies,* 5, 559.

[66]*Ibid.,* 8, 559.

[67]Nevins, *Fish,* II, 708, 714.

[68]Hesseltine, *Grant,* 321; Carpenter, *Grant,* 108.

[69]Robert C. Schenck to his daughter Sally, New York, July 27, 1870, in Schenck Papers, Rutherford B. Hayes Library, Fremont, Ohio.

[70]*Emma Mine Investigation,* 44th Cong., 1st Sess., House Report 579, May 25, 1876, p. x; Nevins, *Fish,* II, 650; Carpenter, *Grant,* 159.

[71]Nevins, *Fish,* II, 651.

[72]*Emma Mine,* pp. i, v–vi, xv–xvi.

[73]Carpenter, *Grant,* 114–115.

[74]Webb, *Bristow,* 171–172.

[75]*Ibid.*, 172–174; Nevins, *Fish*, II, 775; Carpenter, *Grant*, 146.

[76]Nevins, *Fish*, II, 796, citing Fish diary.

[77]Hesseltine, *Grant*, 265; Nevins, *Fish*, I, 404.

[78]*Malfeasance of W. W. Belknap, Late Secretary of War*, 44th Cong., 1st Sess., House Report 186, March 2, 1876, 1–11.

[79]*Ibid.*, 3.

[80]*Ibid.*, 4.

[81]*Ibid.*, 2.

[82]*Ibid.*, 2, 10, 11; Nevins, *Fish*, I, 804.

[83]*Malfeasance*, 1.

[84]*Impeachment of W. W. Belknap* (Report of the Judiciary Committee), 44th Cong., 1st Sess., House Report 222, March 8, 1876; *Impeachment of William W. Belknap* (Report of the Judiciary Committee), 44th Cong., 1st Sess., House Report 345, March 30, 1876; *Report of the House Managers on the Impeachment of W. W. Belknap, Late Secretary of War*, 44th Cong., 1st Sess., House Report 791, August 2, 1876.

[85]Nevins, *Fish*, I, 807.

[86]*Ibid.*, II, 815.

[87]*Ibid.*, II, 816.

[88]*Investigations of the Navy Department*, 44th Cong., 1st Sess., House Report, 784, July 25, 1876, 1–198; *Investigation by the Committee on Naval Affairs*, 44th Cong., 1st Sess., House Miscellaneous Document 170, pts. 1–5, April 27, 1876.

[89]Nevins, *Fish*, II, 762.

[90]Hesseltine, *Grant*, 207–219; Carpenter, *Grant*, 148.

[91]Webb, *Bristow*, 187.

[92]*Whisky Frauds: Testimony before the Select Committee Concerning Whisky Frauds*, 44th Cong., 1st Sess., House Miscellaneous Document 186, July 25, 1876.

[93]H. V. Boynton, "The Whisky Ring," *North American Review*, CXXIII (October 1876), 280–327.

[94]*Whisky Frauds*, 353–355.

[95]John McDonald, *Secrets of the Great Whisky Ring: And Eighteen Months in the Penitentiary . . .* (St. Louis, 1880), 140–145.

[96]*Whisky Frauds*, 355.

[97]Typescript of Diary of Hamilton Fish, Library of Congress, May 22, 1875.

[98]*Whisky Frauds*, 485; Hesseltine, *Grant*, 384.

[99]Fish Diary, September 17, 1875.

[100]*Whisky Frauds*, 358–362.

[101]Nevins, *Fish*, 791; Boynton, "Whisky Ring," 311.

[102]*Whisky Frauds*, 39.

[103]Nevins, *Fish*, II, 796–797.

[104]*Ibid.*, *Fish*, II, 793.

[105]Fish Diary, February 8, 1876.

[106]McDonald, *Secrets*, 256–275; *New York Times*, February 18, 1876.

[107]*Whisky Frauds*, 28, 324.

[108]Hesseltine, *Grant*, 382.

RUTHERFORD B. HAYES
1877–1881

John G. Sproat

The Disputed Election

Rutherford B. Hayes entered the White House under the cloud of the disputed election of 1876 and the ensuing electoral crisis, and the cloud did not dissipate during his four years in office. To many voters—some Republicans as well as most Democrats—Hayes's title to the presidency was a fraudulent one, resting upon an unjust claim to electoral votes that rightfully should have been cast for his opponent in the election, Samuel J. Tilden. Historians today generally agree that the election was marked by sufficient confusion, especially in the southern states, to warrant the raising of honest questions about which candidate won in several states. In the winter of 1876–1877, the matter was highly charged with partisan emotion, and the champions of neither candidate were inclined to concede honest motives to their opponents. Hayes never doubted the legitimacy of his victory, and certainly his supporters never acknowledged that fraud had marked their efforts to secure him the presidency. But from the start of his administration, Hayes suffered from what is today known as a "credibility gap" in his relations with Congress, the press, and much of the public. He was seldom permitted to forget the tenuousness of his claim to office, and his more vengeful enemies at times pitilessly taunted him with such epithets as "His Fraudulency" and "Rutherfraud."[1]

In the presidential election, Tilden had won a clear popular majority and claimed 184 electoral votes.[2] Republican leaders immediately challenged the announced results in Florida, Louisiana, and South Carolina, charging that wholesale fraud and intimidation of black voters by the Democrats had invalidated the apparent Tilden victory. If the Republicans could reverse the announced results in the three states, Hayes would win the election with 185 electoral votes. Both parties sent "visiting statesmen" to the South, the Democrats to protect their victories, the Republicans to challenge the results. Although the Republican effort was initiated and directed by Senators Zachariah Chandler and William E. Chandler, chairman and secretary respectively of the Republican National Committee, Hayes fully supported the challenges and kept himself in close touch with the situation as it developed through the winter.

In all his communications with the principals in the challenges, Hayes was careful to insist that honesty and fairness characterize the resolution of the dispute. But many "visiting statesmen" paid little or no attention to this instruction, and the history of the struggles between Republicans and Democrats in the three contested states is rife with instances and rumors of fraudulent activities. The key state turned out to be Florida, and four electoral votes there probably should have gone to Tilden, enough to elect him. But the evidence upon which to make a definitive judgment was slim in 1876–1877, and it remains so today. How much Hayes himself knew at the time or learned later about questionable activities on the part of his supporters in the three states, it is impossible to say with certainty. Once in office, however, he rewarded many of them with government jobs, much to the dismay of the civil service reformers.[3]

Hayes won the presidency ultimately because a specially constituted electoral commission decided along strict party lines in his favor, and because in the Compromise of 1877 Republican negotiators in his name promised to withdraw federal troops from the South and work for federal funding of internal improvements in that section. At times during the negotiations, the spokesmen for Hayes appeared to compromise as well his ethical position by committing him to details beyond their knowledge of his intentions. Part of the understanding involved the abandonment of what remained of the goals of racial equality of Reconstruction with the delineation of racial relations left in the hands of local white leaders in the South. The extent to which Hayes himself was involved in the compromise is not fully known. He was determined in any event to pursue a "new departure" policy toward the South and toward southerners a generous share in his administration's functions.

His conciliatory attitude, once he became president, fed the suspicions of those who questioned the legitimacy of his tenure.[4]

In 1878 Democrats in the House of Representatives made a major effort to impugn finally Hayes's title to office, when they established a select committee to investigate the disputed election. The Potter Committee, as it was known, uncovered no evidence of substance to link Hayes with any irregularities and, ironically, the investigation cast more doubt upon Tilden's conduct than on Hayes's.[5]

Political Assessments in 1878 and 1880

On June 22, 1877, Hayes issued a sweeping executive order designed to halt the use of officeholders in political activities and the practice of assessing them for political "contributions." Applicable to all departments in the federal government, the order was the strongest word yet on the subject from a chief executive:[6]

> No officer should be required or permitted to take part in the management of political organizations, caucuses, conventions, or election campaigns. Their right to vote and to express their views on public questions, either orally or through the press, is not denied, provided it does not interfere with the discharge of their official duties. No assessments for political purposes on officers or subordinates should be allowed.

That part of the order banning political activity caused much confusion and alarm in many departments, and especially in the postal service, for local postmasters traditionally held key positions in the party organizations and were thought to be indispensable figures in local campaigns. In the face of pressure to modify his order, Hayes stood firm. Acknowledging that the order would disrupt party organizations at first, he concluded that the problem would disappear after volunteers had replaced the postmasters.[7]

In the matter of assessments, Hayes was considerably less consistent. During the congressional elections of 1878, he permitted abuses of the letter as well as the spirit of his executive order. In May of that year, George C. Gorham as secretary of the Republican Congressional

Committee sent letters to all employees of the federal government earning a salary in excess of $1,000 a year, soliciting contributions for the campaign of not less than 1% of their salaries and assuring them that such "voluntary" contributions would meet with no "official objections." Testifying in 1879 before a select committee of the Senate, Gorham insisted that President Hayes had seen and approved the letter and that two follow-up letters had also gone out to the officeholders. Democrats on the committee claimed that Gorham had violated the law of 1876, which prohibited officeholders from soliciting contributions from other officeholders. Hayes was silent on the matter, even in the face of complaints from civil service reformers, and Gorham was never indicted.[8]

During the campaign of 1878, Gorham's committee raised $106,000, of which $93,000 came from officeholders. In 1880 the committee again asked officeholders for contributions and took in more than $100,000. There is no evidence that Hayes either condoned or condemned the 1880 activities; rather he appears to have ignored the matter.[9]

The New York Custom House

Hayes came into office pledged to work for effective civil service reform. He established a good record in the matter of patronage in some departments (Interior, for example, where the reformer Carl Schurz held sway), even as he continued in the ways of his predecessors in other matters. As the historian John A. Garraty notes:

> He did not entirely reject the claims of the spoilsmen, cheerfully rewarding politicians who had helped swing the disputed electoral votes his way, interpreting very leniently his executive order requiring government workers who were concurrently holding party offices to relinquish one or the other, and devoting many hours to the distribution of petty political plums.[10]

Some of his fellow Republicans were exasperated by Hayes's habit of picking and choosing his way through the patronage jungle. Garfield, in effect, charged him with hypocrisy in dealing with the spoilsmen and asked that the President exercise the same self-denial in making appointments that he demanded in other officials. Hayes was uneasy about his failure to comply strictly with good civil service principles and admitted making some bad appointments, especially in rewarding his supporters of 1876–1877. To most historians today, it appears that Hayes's record of inconsistency on reform rested less on any inclination on his part to subvert effective reform than on the practical necessity of working within a system that was not yet prepared to accept reform.[11]

To Hayes, the first step in bringing about effective reform was the divorce of the legislature from the nominating power. "With this, reform can and will successfully proceed," he observed. "Without it, reform is impossible."[12] Almost immediately upon assuming office, he opened a subtle but persistent attack to gain this first step, an attack made easier in the long run because it was directed at an institution in which misconduct, fraud, and corruption were almost endemic—the New York Custom House.

Custom houses in general were natural targets for civil service reformers, for they controlled an enormous share of the federal patronage and in turn were usually under the thumb of powerful local political bosses. The New York house, in particular, had long been known as a focal point of corruption, and Congress periodically had mounted more or less futile investigations of its activities. At the time Hayes became president, it was controlled by Roscoe Conkling, a powerful senator and leader of the Republican Stalwarts—a man who despised reformers in general and Hayes in particular. Conkling's men in the custom house included Chester A. Arthur and Alonzo B. Cornell, respectively collector of customs and naval officer.[13]

At Hayes's order, Secretary of the Treasury John Sherman in April, 1877, appointed commissions to investigate all the custom houses. In New York the commission of civilians was chaired by John Jay, an old Conkling enemy. On May 24 the Jay Commission submitted its first report, in which Arthur was charged with the "settled practice" of making appointments for political reasons rather than for competency in matters of revenue collecting. It was largely on the basis of this report that Hayes issued his "no assessment" order of June 22, and in notifying Sherman of the order he referred specifically to conditions in the revenue service:

It is my wish that the collection of the revenues should be free from partisan control, and organized on a strictly business basis, with the same guaranties for efficiency and fidelity in the selection of the chief and subordinate officers that would be required by a prudent merchant. Party leaders should have no more influence in appointments than other equally respectable citizens. No assessments for political purposes on officers or subordinates should be allowed. No useless officer or employee should be retained.

Further reports by the Jay Commission included charges that 200 petty politicians were supported by the custom house though they performed no public service; that both Arthur and Cornell were guilty of dereliction of their official duties; and that Cornell, in holding a political position (chairman of the Republican State Committee) as well as a public office, was in violation of an executive order.[14]

Knowing that any interference from Washington in New York politics would arouse Conkling's ire, Secretary Sherman somewhat reluctantly advised Arthur to effect reforms and cut his staff forthwith by 20%. Arthur made some substantive changes in procedures at the custom house, even though his formal response to Sherman accused the administration of appointing a partisan commission. At best his options were limited by his ties to Conkling, who did indeed view the investigation as a personal challenge to his power in New York.[15]

Hayes had no desire to force a showdown with Conkling, yet he was determined to bring about a major change in the revenue service. Quiet efforts were made to urge Arthur and Cornell to resign voluntarily. As Sherman recalled, "The President was quite willing to base his request for their resignation, not upon the ground that they were guilty of the offenses charged, but that the new officers could probably deal with the reorganization of the custom-house with more freedom and success than the incumbents." That attitude earned for Hayes sharp criticism from reformers, who preferred to have him throw out the wrongdoers without ceremony. But Hayes continued to move cautiously in pursuit of his larger goal: the removal of appointments to office from the patronage control of senators and representatives. Ignoring a barrage of insults from Conkling, he waited patiently until Congress met in special session in October, 1877, then sent to the Senate his nominations for new officials in the New York Custom House.[16]

Challenged thus directly on their "right" to control patronage, a majority of Republican senators rallied to Conkling's assistance in blocking
the appointments. In the next session of Congress, the President again
submitted the names of new officers and was again rebuffed. But when
Congress adjourned in 1878 for the summer, Hayes summarily removed
Arthur and Cornell from office and appointed Edwin A. Merritt and
Silas W. Burt to the posts. No charges were levied against the ousted officers; rather they were removed simply because the "interests of the service" required change. But when the new names were sent to the Senate
after Congress reconvened in December, they were accompanied by the
specific charges of fraud and corruption in the custom house reported
earlier by the Jay Commission. After a bitter struggle, the Senate voted
to confirm the appointments.[17]

Hayes won an important victory for reform in this struggle, for the
New York Custom House was a cynosure of the spoils system. Unhap-
pily for him, the victory cost him precious support within his party and
further weakened his presidency.

The Indiscretion of Secretary Thompson

In 1879 the French engineer Ferdinand de Lesseps tried to promote a
scheme for the building of a canal in Panama. President Hayes resolved
to stay clear of the de Lesseps scheme because of its French origin and
probable orientation. To Congress on March 8, 1880, he asserted that
any isthmian canal must of necessity be an American canal, for it would
clearly impinge upon this nation's vital interests.[18]

De Lesseps next sought to create an "advisory committee" in this
country to woo support for his plan and disarm American suspicions of
the plan's French connections. In seeking a prominent man to head the
committee, he turned first to General Grant, who refused him, and then
to Richard W. Thompson, Hayes's secretary of the navy. Hayes warned
Thompson not to accept such a position. But the Secretary, attracted by
the nominal duties and the annual salary of $25,000, overcame an initial
reluctance and accepted de Lesseps's offer. Apparently, he thought that
his employment by a canal company with foreign connections would be
no bar to his remaining in Hayes's cabinet. Hayes dealt with the problem

swiftly. Thompson was informed that his (unsubmitted) resignation had been accepted by the President, and he quickly accepted the inevitable and formally resigned. The matter was closed with no repercussions.[19]

The Star Route Frauds

During the period of rapid national growth after the Civil War, extraordinary demands were put on many traditional government services, including the postal system. Especially in the West, the problem of providing mail service to isolated and sparsely populated regions, or to areas subject to rapid and fluctuating population change, had to be met by expedient, flexible means. Railroad and steamship deliveries were supplemented by pony express, wagon trains, and stagecoaches. In a relatively short period of time, the Post Office Department underwent a considerable expansion in budget and personnel, and by the end of 1876 some 134 stagecoach lines and pony expresses were in operation. In the department's directory, these routes were identified by asterisks; hence the term Star Routes.

Star Routes were contracted to private individuals who agreed to transport the mails with "certainty, celerity, and security." The contracts stipulated the number of trips and speed of deliveries, and the second assistant postmaster general was empowered to alter contracts at his discretion to meet changing conditions in the West. In the postwar era, both Congress and the executive were inclined to liberality in extending postal services, and a pattern developed wherein generous grants of money were awarded with a minimum of supervision from Washington.[20]

The second assistant postmaster general during the Hayes administration was Thomas J. Brady, who had been appointed by Grant in 1876. He performed valuable (and questionable) services for the Republicans in the southern states during the electoral crisis of that year. Sometime after entering the postal service, Brady initiated a combination, "ring," in Washington to defraud the government of Star Route revenues. The method was simple enough: Contractors who were parties to the fraud and who had obtained their contracts legally would petition the Post Office Department for alterations to permit them to offer more and faster service at greatly increased rates, and Brady would approve the alterations. The cost to the government soared, even though no improvement in service came about. The "postal ring" included individuals in both the Post Office and Treasury Departments. Among its top leaders was Stephen W. Dorsey, a prominent Stalwart Republican and sometime "carpetbag" senator from Arkansas, who in 1880 became secretary of the Republican National Committee and virtual manager of James A. Garfield's presidential campaign in that year.

The operations of the ring did not become public knowledge until after Garfield entered the White House, and there is no evidence on record to indicate that Hayes, as president, had any direct knowledge of the corruption. Why he had no such knowledge, however, is a question that has never been satisfactorily answered. The suspicion that something was amiss in the postal system was rife in Washington throughout Hayes's term, fed anew each year as Brady came up with huge deficits that had to be covered by special congressional appropriations. In 1880 he asked Congress for a deficiency appropriation of $2,000,000 for inland transportation of the mails, and the press demanded an investigation. Congress undertook an inquiry; but, as with similar earlier undertakings, it was conducted in a halfhearted manner. Both Congress and Hayes appeared to view the matter as a problem of extravagance, not of possible fraud.[21]

If Hayes knew nothing of the corruption, other leading Republicans were very much aware of the Brady-Dorsey combination. On February 11, 1881, Dorsey was honored at a dinner in New York for his services in the recent presidential contest. Former president Grant presided; and the highlight of the evening was a rambling, rather cryptic, speech by Chester A. Arthur, Vice President-elect, in praise of Dorsey's deft use of money in the campaign, especially in the crucial state of Indiana:

Indiana was really, I suppose, a Democratic State. It had been put down on the books always as a State that might be carried by close and perfect organization and a great deal of—(laughter)—I see the reporters are present, therefore I will simply say that everybody showed a great deal of interest in the occasion and distributed tracts and political documents all through the State.[22]

Arthur's remarks sparked rumors in the press that Indiana had been "bought" in the election with money obtained by fraud. To a puzzled

President-elect Garfield, Senator James G. Blaine wrote several days later, "I am afraid the true intent and meaning of the Dorsey dinner was to enable him to make demands which will in the end modestly center in the Second Assistant-Postmaster Generalship, through which channel there are cunning preparations being made by a small cabal to steal half a million a year during your administration." No evidence exists to suggest that either Blaine or Garfield brought this astonishing intelligence to the attention of President Hayes.[23]

After he left Washington and when the full story of the frauds came to light, Hayes's reaction suggests that the matter deeply troubled him. "One thing you may be sure of," he wrote to a friend, "I am not a party to covering up anything. Brady and his Stalwarts were always my enemies as you know." He noted that several times he had alerted his postmaster general to extravagance in the postal system. To his diary he confided troubled thoughts: "Enemies blame me for not discovering the fraud and putting a stop to it. When I took office the Post-Office Department was believed to be well conducted, with honesty and efficiency. . . . I did not wish to change what was in good condition." It is evident that Hayes, in office, had seen the problem as one of policy only—that is, whether the discretionary power to adjust contracts on Star Routes should be exercised in a liberal or a restrictive manner. His only action in the matter was to direct that all increases in contracts be made by the Postmaster General in consultation with the President and cabinet. This extraordinary action suggests that Hayes suspected something more than mere extravagance, but he made no specific mention of fraud or corruption. When Garfield as president learned of the extent and baldness of the frauds, he commented, "I am surprised that it could have so long escaped the notice of President Hayes's Administration."[24]

Removal of the Ponca Indians

In the last days of the Grant administration, the Ponca Indians had been removed from their ancestral homelands in the Dakotas and resettled in the Indian Territory in the Southwest. The removal had been carried out forcibly by the army with incredible hardship and misery, resulting in the death of many Poncas. The lands in which they were resettled turned out to be unsatisfactory, so preparations were made in 1879 to remove them again, this time under the direction of the Department of the Interior, headed by Carl Schurz. The Poncas protested bitterly and were joined in their outcry by concerned whites, especially in New England, including Helen Hunt Jackson. Schurz refused to modify his order or to permit the Poncas to return to the Dakotas, and when members of the tribe tried to flee northward they were resisted and their leader, Standing Bear, was jailed.

Schurz admitted that the Indians had been wronged, but insisted that they were the "victims of unfortunate circumstances rather than of evil designs." President Hayes, too, acknowledged that a "grievous wrong" had been committed. But rather than show a lack of confidence in Schurz, the President simply took over the matter from his interior Secretary, appointed a commission to investigate it, and ultimately developed a compromise to which the Poncas agreed.[25]

NOTES

[1]The best biography of Hayes is Harry Barnard, *Rutherford B. Hayes and His America* (Indianapolis and New York, 1954), which is especially good on the disputed election. Kenneth E. Davison, *The Presidency of Rutherford B. Hayes* (Westport, Conn., 1972), focuses on the presidential years and is a good survey.

[2]Three histories dealing with the disputed election should be consulted in order to understand the intricacies of the crisis. Paul L. Haworth's older account, *The Hayes-Tilden Disputed Presidential Election of 1876* (Cleveland, 1906), remains useful and informative. C. Vann Woodward, in *Reunion and Reaction: The Compromise of 1877 and the End of Reconstruction* (Boston, 1951), changed the thinking of a generation of historians about the crisis. This book remains the standard account of the compromise negotiations, even though some of its conclusions have been intelligently challenged by Keith I. Polakoff, *The Politics of Inertia: The Election of 1876 and the End of Reconstruction* (Baton Rouge, 1973).

[3]Haworth, *Hayes-Tilden*, 57, 76; John Bigelow, *The Life of Samuel J. Tilden* (2 vols., New York, 1895), II, 26, 29–31, 53–55; Polakoff, *Politics of Inertia*, 209–210, 242–244, 261–264.

[4]Woodward, *Reunion and Reaction*, 118.

[5]*House Miscellaneous Document 31*, 45th Cong., 3rd Sess., iv.

[6]James Richardson, *A Compilation of the Messages and Papers of the Presidents, 1789–1897* (10 vols., Washington, 1896–1899), X, 4402–4403.

[7]Dorothy G. Fowler, *The Cabinet Politician: The Postmasters General, 1829–1909* (New York, 1943), 170–171; Charles R. Williams, ed., *Hayes Diary and Letters*, III, 495.

[8]*Senate Report 427*, 46th Cong., 1st and 2nd Sess., 2–3, 20; Ari Hoogenboom, *Outlawing the Spoils: A History of the Civil Service Reform Movement, 1865–1883* (Urbana, 1961), 163–166; Fowler, *Cabinet Politician*, 171–172; Harrison C. Thomas, *The Return of the Democratic Party to Power in 1884* (New York, 1919), 83ff.

[9]Fowler, *Cabinet Politician,* 171–172; Louise Overacker, *Money in Elections* (New York, 1932), 102–103.

[10]John A. Garraty, *The New Commonwealth, 1877–1890* (New York, 1968), 261–262.

[11]Theodore Clarke Smith, *The Life and Letters of James Abram Garfield* (2 vols., New Haven, 1925), 654; Davison, *Presidency of Hayes,* 159–160. The views of historians about the civil service reformers range from the generally sympathetic, as in Ari Hoogenboom, *Outlawing the Spoils,* to the critical, as in John G. Sproat, *"The Best Men": Liberal Reformers in the Gilded Age* (New York, 1968).

[12]Williams, *Hayes Diary and Letters,* III, 513–514.

[13]A still reliable account of the confrontation between Hayes and Conkling is Venila L. Shores, *The Hayes-Conkling Controversy* (New York, 1919). Recently, a definitive biography of Conkling has appeared: David M. Jordan, *Roscoe Conkling of New York: Voice in the Senate* (Ithaca, 1971). Relevant documents are *House Executive Document 8,* 45th Cong., 1st Sess., and *House Executive Document 25,* 45th Cong., 2nd Sess.

[14]Richardson, *Messages and Papers,* X, 4402; *House Executive Document 8,* 15; and *25,* 7ff.

[15]Shores, *Hayes-Conkling,* 221ff; Jordan, *Conkling,* 270–275; John Sherman, *Recollections of Forty Years in the House, Senate and Cabinet* (2 vols., Chicago and New York, 1895), II, 674.

[16]Sherman, *Recollections,* II, 677, 681; Barnard, *Hayes,* 450–452; Jordan, *Conkling,* 275–280.

[17]Williams, *Hayes Diary and Letters,* III, 454, 514; Sherman, *Recollections,* II, 684.

[18]Richardson, *Messages and Papers,* X, 4537–4538.

[19]Charles R. Williams, *The Life of Rutherford B. Hayes* (2 vols., Boston and New York, 1914), II, 218ff; Davison, *Presidency of Hayes,* 114, 120.

[20]The Star Route story is best followed in *Appleton's Annual Cyclopaedia* (1882), 753–767, and (1883), 777; and in *House Miscellaneous Document 38,* 48th Cong., 1st Sess. The fullest historical treatment is J. Martin Klotsche, "The Star Route Cases," *Mississippi Valley Historical Review,* XXII (1935), 406–416. See also George F. Howe, *Chester A. Arthur: A Quarter-Century of Machine Politics* (New York, 1934), 180.

[21]Further information regarding Brady and Dorsey may be found in the discussions of the Garfield and Arthur administrations.

[22]Klotsche, "Star Route Cases," 414ff; Williams, *Hayes Diary and Letters,* IV, 11–13; *House Miscellaneous Document 31,* 46th Cong., 1st Sess., 1.

[23]Howe, *Arthur,* 129–131; *New York Times,* February 13, 1881, and May 19, 1881; *Nation,* XXXII (February 21, 1881), 122; Smith, *Garfield,* II, 1085–1086; Robert G. Caldwell, *James A. Garfield, Party Chieftain* (New York, 1931), 334ff.

[24]Williams, *Hayes Diary and Letters,* IV, 12–13; Smith, *Garfield,* II, 1157. Davison, *Presidency of Hayes,* 169–170, is a good examination of Hayes's confusion. Leonard D. White, *The Republican Era, 1869–1901: A Study in Administrative History* (New York, 1958), 376ff, concludes that Hayes acted indecisively in the entire matter and "solved" the problem only at a heavy administrative cost to himself and his cabinet.

[25]Williams, *Hayes Diary and Letters,* III, 626, 629–631; Carl Schurz, *Speeches, Correspondence, and Political Papers,* ed. by Frederic Bancroft (6 vols., New York, 1913), IV, 50–78. The best account of the incident is Davison, *Presidency of Hayes,* 188–189, although Schurz's defense of his own action illumines the larger story as well.

JAMES A. GARFIELD
1881

John G. Sproat

The Star Route Frauds, Continued

Two days before he took office as president, James A. Garfield offered the postmaster generalship in his administration to Thomas L. James, a Stalwart Republican from New York. As James testified later, Garfield at the time warned him that there appeared to be "something very wrong" in the Post Office Department and that if this was indeed the case "he expected me to find it out, and then put the plow in to the beam, and after that to subsoil it." On March 9, after James's appointment to the position, the President again spoke with him, this time to order a full investigation of apparent willful waste and gross corruption in the department. James was instructed to search the records of the contract office for evidence of corruption, to effect immediate reforms in the postal system, and to pursue the matter until all the facts had been ascertained. The President also approved James's choice of P. H. Woodward, a special postal agent, to conduct the investigation.[1]

One month later, James and Woodward reported to the President about their discoveries concerning the Star Route contract service. As Garfield noted that day in his journal, "Great frauds have been discovered and I will clear out the contract office." Wayne MacVeagh, the Attorney General, was immediately informed of the findings and instructed to cooperate with the Postmaster General in the investigation. On April 14, after further talks with his two cabinet officers, Garfield observed, "The corruption and wrongdoing has been of a very gross and extensive kind." At a cabinet meeting on the 19th, he insisted upon

"immediate action" within the Post Office Department to effect personnel changes. The next day brought the resignation of Thomas W. Brady,
the chief conspirator in the frauds, from his high position. On the 26th,
Brady's chief clerk was cashiered; and several weeks later the sixth audi-
tor of the Treasury, the man in charge of Post Office accounts, resigned.[2]

The investigation had indeed uncovered evidence of gross misdeeds.
Over a five-year period, an estimated $4,000,000 had been stolen from
the postal service. Several "rings" of crooked contractors were identified,
and in one of the most audacious of these Stephen W. Dorsey was clearly
implicated. Evidence showed that 24 contracts awarded to Dorsey and
his associates on bids totaling $55,264 had ultimately put $501,092 into
their pockets. Dorsey's brother held contracts worth $14,497, a sum that
soared to $147,273; his brother-in-law with a contract worth $30,396
got away with $218,141; one of his partners inflated a $10,371 contract
to $135,678.[3]

In discussing the prosecution of the offenders with Garfield and the
cabinet, the Attorney General warned the President of the possible political consequences of further action:

> Before a final decision, remember that these proceedings may
> strike men in high places; that they may result in changing a Re-
> publican majority in the United States Senate into a Democratic
> majority; that it may affect persons who claim that you are under
> personal obligations to them for service rendered during the last
> campaign—and one person in particular who asserts that without
> his management you could not have been elected.

MacVeagh warned Garfield to "look these facts squarely in the face"
before authorizing action, for "neither the Post-master General nor myself will know friend or foe in this matter." After a moment's reflection,
Garfield responded: "No, I have sworn to execute the laws. Go ahead
regardless of where or whom you hit. I direct you not only to probe this
ulcer to the bottom, but to cut it out."[4]

Doubtless, Garfield was troubled by the prospect of having to order
criminal proceedings against an old and valued political ally, the more
so because he knew the action would hurt his party. Dorsey had indeed
been responsible for Garfield's victory in 1880, and after the election the

winner had written of his manager that he was a "man of great ability and with strong and decisive views of the merits of men." MacVeagh testified that the prosecutions were "a source of very great anxiety and I might almost say of distress to President Garfield. It would be very strange if it had been otherwise." As the scandal broke, Dorsey demanded of Garfield a special separate investigation to replace the Attorney General's probe. On one occasion, the President noted that he was "kept up until midnight by business connected with Dorsey's troubles. I have great sympathy with him and some doubts." On May 15, after consulting closely with members of his cabinet, Garfield gave orders that "no prosecution should be begun without my orders."[5]

The pressure on the President to abort the investigation and prosecution was heavy. Brady, for example, released to the press an injudicious letter Garfield had written earlier to Jay Hubbell, of the Republican Congressional Committee, that appeared to countenance assessments: "Please say to Brady that I hope he will give us all the assistance he can. I think he can help effectively. Please tell me how the Depts generally are doing." Brady insisted that he interpreted this letter as an appeal to him to use the profits of the Star Routes for campaign purposes, but there is no evidence either that Garfield meant any such thing or that he knew of the tainted revenues at the time. As owner of the Washington newspaper *National Republican*, Brady also mounted a vicious journalistic attack on Garfield and the investigation, an attack that was maintained at fever pitch throughout the ensuing trials as well.[6]

Although Garfield may have been reluctant to prosecute Dorsey, he did not really waver in his determination to see justice done. MacVeagh put together a team of able investigators and prosecutors, including Benjamin H. Brewster and George Bliss, and methodically prepared the cases for court. "Everything was carried on with his constant knowledge and sympathy," he testified of the President's role. On June 28 Dorsey and his counsel conferred with Garfield and audaciously tried to turn the case against James and MacVeagh, but the President received their petition coldly. His last mention of the affair in his journal came the next day: a notation that he had complained to James that the agents in the cases were too slow, that "they should be more earnest in their work, and that they should have the accused parties indicted and tried."[7]

On July 2 President Garfield was shot by Guiteau; and, after a long struggle for survival, he died on September 19. During the summer of illness, James and MacVeagh had no choice but to act on their own. The investigation continued, but at the time Arthur succeeded to the presidency no court action had as yet been taken.

NOTES

[1]James's testimony is in *House Miscellaneous Document 38,* 48th Cong., 1st Sess., pt. 2, pp. 1–4, hereinafter referred to as *Star Route Investigation.* The standard biographies of Garfield are Robert G. Caldwell, *James A. Garfield: Party Chieftain* (New York, 1931), and Theodore Clarke Smith, *The Life and Letters of James Abram Garfield* (2 vols., New Haven, 1925).

[2]*Appleton's Annual Cyclopaedia* (1881), 848; Smith, *Garfield,* II, 1156ff; George F. Howe, *Chester A. Arthur: A Quarter-Century of Machine Politics* (New York, 1934), 180ff; *Star Route Investigation,* 6.

[3]Caldwell, *Garfield,* 235; Leon B. Richardson, *William E. Chandler, Republican* (New York, 1940).

[4]Smith, *Garfield,* II, 1158; *Star Route Investigation,* 4.

[5]Smith, *Garfield,* II, 1053–1054, 1159; *Star Route Investigation,* 6.

[6]Smith, *Garfield,* II, 1159; J. Martin Klotsche, "The Star Route Cases," *Mississippi Valley Historical Review,* XXII (1935), 407–413; Howe, *Arthur,* 181.

[7]Smith, *Garfield,* II, 1161ff.

CHESTER A. ARTHUR
1881–1885

John G. Sproat

Prosecution of the Star Route Cases

President Chester A. Arthur had in the past been an intimate of several principals in the Star Route scandal, particularly Dorsey. Together with other leading Republicans, Arthur had known in 1880 that Dorsey's election funds came from sources outside the "normal" channels of political fund-raising, and the probability is great that he shared with James G. Blaine and William E. Chandler at least a suspicion that Dorsey was involved in corrupt activities within the Post Office Department. During his first few weeks as president, Arthur moved slowly in dealing with the matter; and some historians have suggested that his repugnance at the thought of prosecuting old comrades influenced him to hold back and do less than his duty. One Arthur biographer implies that the resignation of Attorney General MacVeagh on November 8, 1881, was prompted in part by that officer's fear that the Star Route cases would not be prosecuted willingly by the new administration and that he, MacVeagh, would end up as the scapegoat in the mess.[1]

But there is no solid evidence that Arthur unduly delayed the prosecution of the cases or that he interceded in any way on behalf of the principals. His delay in proceedings, doubtless, resulted from his determination to familiarize himself thoroughly with the matter and evaluate the men who would take the cases to court. In naming Benjamin H. Brewster to succeed MacVeagh as attorney general, he signaled clearly his intent to take the cases to court. Brewster had been chief legal counsel for the government in the Star Route investigation. In his annual message to Congress a few weeks later, Arthur noted the instructions he had given the Justice Department:

> The investigations of the Department of Justice and the Post Office Department have resulted in the presentation of indictments against persons formerly connected with that service, accusing them of offenses against the United States. I have enjoined upon the officials who are charged with the conduct of the cases on the part of the Government, and upon the eminent counsel who before my accession to the Presidency were called to their assistance, the duty of prosecuting with the utmost vigor of the law all persons who may be found chargeable with frauds upon the postal service.[2]

Dorsey, Brady, and six other defendants were indicted and brought to trial in February, 1882. All pleaded not guilty and put up stubborn defenses, characterized by persistent efforts to disrupt the proceedings, intimidate witnesses, impugn the integrity of the court, and, ultimately, approach witnesses with an intent to bribe. At the trial's conclusion, the jury stood 10 to 2 for conviction of Brady and 9 to 3 for conviction of Dorsey. In September a second trial began. Commenting upon the proceedings in his second annual message, Arthur noted, "If any guilty person shall finally escape punishment for their offenses, it will not be for lack of diligent and earnest efforts on the part of the prosecution." Nine months after the second trial opened, the jury brought in a verdict of "not guilty as indicted."[3]

No third trial was ordered. Several individuals were indicted for bribery, and a number of minor officials were dismissed from government positions for various offenses in connection with the trials. Responsible observers at the time and historians since agree that the trials of the Star Route principals were handled badly by the prosecution, perhaps because the prosecutors conducted the cases under pressure of the statute of limitations. They also had the difficult task of proving conspiracy, the only crime for which the defendants were charged. Brewster always insisted that Arthur cooperated fully with the prosecution. To a congressional committee in 1884, he reported Arthur's instructions as follows:

I want this work to be done as you are doing it, in the spirit in which you are doing it; I want it to be done earnestly and thoroughly. I desire that these people shall be prosecuted with the utmost vigor of the law. I will give you all the help I can. You can come to see me whenever you wish to, and I will do all I can to aid you.

And, Brewster added, "he did so all the way through; without a moment's hesitation—always stood by me and strengthened me and gave me confidence."[4]

Political Assessments

Despite the law of 1876 and Hayes's executive order of 1877 prohibiting assessments, the practice continued under Arthur. In 1882 the Republican Congressional Committee sent out its usual solicitation letter, inviting contributions of specified sums (usually 2% of the individual's annual income) and assuring contributors that their "gifts" would "not be objected to in any official quarter." The letter went to every employee of the federal government, including military personnel, congressional page boys, and scrubwomen. Civil service reformers protested vigorously and warned government workers that they would be subject to prosecution if they complied with the assessment. But Attorney General Brewster ruled that members of Congress were not "officers" in the sense intended by the law of 1876, hence the antiassessment prohibition did not apply to them. In July President Arthur announced that officeholders might give or not give, as they chose, without fear for their jobs. His remarks may not have inspired great confidence in the officeholders, for the campaign committee collected a sizable fund for use in the elections. George William Curtis in an address to the National Civil Service Reform League that fall sharply criticized Arthur's handling of patronage and assessments, accusing the President, in effect, of violating the spirit of his declared support for reform.[5]

In one instance, at least, Arthur took decisive action on the side of the antiassessment reform. While serving simultaneously as a Treasury agent and member of the New York Republican State Committee, General Newton M. Curtis was convicted for violating the law of 1876. Appealed to by old friends to pardon Curtis for doing what "most of us have ourselves done," Arthur refused. Curtis's conviction ultimately was upheld by the Supreme Court.[6]

Politics in the Pensions Office

During the campaign of 1884, the commissioner of the Pensions Office, William W. Dudley, took a "leave of absence" to engage in political activity in Indiana and Ohio. With 100 special examiners from the office, most of them also on "leaves of absence," Dudley worked to persuade pensioners to support the "soldier ticket" of the Republicans. Especially among pensioners with claims awaiting adjudication, the word was passed that a vote for Blaine and Logan would mean an expedited claim. The work was done openly and news of it spread rapidly. On October 20 the *New York Times* condemned Dudley for "outrageous violations of duty." Carl Schurz, addressing voters in Ohio, called the Dudley work "one of the most shameless and infamous abuses of official power on record, for which those guilty of it should be driven out of office in disgrace."

No action was taken by the administration to halt the practice. Dudley, who had planned to resign in any event, left office on November 10 and subsequently became treasurer of the Republican National Committee. Arthur's biographer concludes that the President "could probably have halted this electioneering but preferred to avert further disastrous dissensions in his party."[7]

NOTES

[1]George F. Howe, *Chester A. Arthur: A Quarter-Century of Machine Politics* (New York, 1934), 161, 181ff. Howe's is the standard biography of Arthur. Forthcoming is a biography by Thomas C. Reeves based upon an exhaustive survey of recent manuscript finds and scholarship. Professor Reeves was kind enough to discuss the Arthur administration with me and to point up the paucity of instances of misconduct associated with it.

[2]First Annual Message, in James Richardson, *A Compilation of the Messages and Papers of the Presidents, 1789–1897* (10 vols., Washington, 1896–1899), X, 4640.

[3]Howe, *Arthur,* 187ff; Matthew Josephson, *The Politicos, 1865–1896* (New York, 1938), 323–335; Second Annual Message, in Richardson, *Messages and Papers,* X, 4730.

[4]Brewster, quoted in Howe, *Arthur,* 192. Howe notes that if Arthur had been inclined to influence the trials on behalf of the defendants, his inclination could only have been

exercised through the Post Office Department or the Justice Department; thus the importance of Brewster's remarks.

[5]Charles Eliot Norton, ed., *The Orations and Addresses of George William Curtis* (3 vols., New York, 1894), III, 205–225. Howe, *Arthur,* chap. xviii, is a good discussion of Arthur and civil service reform. The definitive study of the civil service reform movement is Ari Hoogenboom, *Outlawing the Spoils.* Somewhat sardonic, but nonetheless informative, treatments are Josephson, *The Politicos;* Fred A. Shannon, *The Centennial Years: A Political and Economic History of America from the Late 1870's to the Early 1890's* (Garden City, N.Y., 1967), chap. v.

[6]Richardson, *Message and Papers,* X, 4748; Howe, *Arthur,* 206; Hoogenboom, *Outlawing the Spoils,* 226–227.

[7]Howe, *Arthur,* 216; John W. Oliver, *History of the Civil War Pensions, 1861–1885* (Madison, Wis., 1917), 104–112, 115; *New York Times,* October 20, 1884.

GROVER CLEVELAND
1885–1889

FIRST TERM

R. Hal Williams

Elected mayor of Buffalo in 1881, governor of New York in 1882, and president of the United States in 1884, Grover Cleveland owed his rapid rise in politics to his reputation for honesty, retrenchment, and administrative reform. In 1884 he ran as the clean candidate against James G. Blaine, the Republican nominee, who had an unsavory reputation. Already known for the slogan "A Public Office Is a Public Trust," Cleveland set his stamp on the campaign when, threatened by a scandal involving his illegitimate child, he instructed friends, "Whatever you do, tell the truth."[1] Historians have differed over the nature of Cleveland's contributions to the politics of the 1880s, but none has ever seriously questioned the President's personal integrity or the essential honesty of his administration. As one writer has put it: "His distinguishing characteristic was plain honesty. . . . he made integrity the first virtue of political life."[2]

Only two incidents of importance involving charges of misconduct occurred during Cleveland's first administration.

Augustus H. Garland and the Pan-Electric Telephone Company

In 1885, in making up his cabinet, Cleveland selected as his attorney general Augustus H. Garland, a senator from Arkansas. Two years before, while a senator, Garland had been given shares to a nominal value of $500,000 in a new corporation named the Pan-Electric Telephone Company. At the same time he had been made an attorney for the company. The Pan-Electric Company's main asset was the Rogers telephone patent, a rival of the Bell telephone patent. The Rogers patent had value only if the Bell patent could be declared invalid.

When Garland took office as attorney general, he did not give up his stock, even though it was a potential embarrassment. Soon he was asked by the company to begin a government suit to test the validity of the Bell patent. Properly, he refused. But a few weeks later, while he was in Arkansas on vacation, the solicitor general, John Goode, decided to file the suit. The decision aroused considerable public outcry. Critics investigated Garland's stockholdings, revealing that he owned about one-tenth of all the stock in the company. Should the Bell patent be invalidated, the Attorney General's stock would be worth millions of dollars.

Alerted to the situation, President Cleveland ordered the solicitor general to halt the suit. He also instructed L. Q. C. Lamar, the Secretary of the Interior, to look into the whole matter, and he called on Garland for an explanation. On October 8, 1885, Garland replied in a long letter, in which he acknowledged his close relationship with the company but insisted that the solicitor general's decision had been reached entirely without his knowledge or consent. Cleveland appeared to accept the explanation, and the issue died down until early in 1886 when Secretary Lamar, his inquiry completed, recommended that the suit be pressed. Lamar's recommendation set off renewed public criticism of Garland.

The House of Representatives appointed a committee to investigate. Holding public hearings, the committee heard numerous witnesses, including Garland himself, who testified at length on April 19, 1886. Garland again contended that he had not used his official influence in behalf of the Pan-Electric Company. Dividing on party lines, the committee issued a report in which the Democratic majority concluded that Garland, the solicitor general, and Lamar had done nothing "dishonest, dishonorable, or censurable"—while the Republican minority charged that Garland and the solicitor general had been engaged in a speculative scheme for their own enrichment.[3]

After November, 1886, when a circuit court at Cincinnati dismissed the case against the Bell patent, the question of Garland's stockholdings no longer aroused much controversy. President Cleveland had apparently been satisfied by Garland's explanations, and the Attorney General served out the remainder of his term. Solicitor General Goode was not so fortunate: his nomination to the office, still pending when the issue arose, failed to clear the Republican-dominated Senate. For the most part, historians agree that Garland was guilty of no criminal wrongdoing, but that he had committed a serious indiscretion and had shown bad judgment in not surrendering his stock on taking office.[4]

William F. Vilas and the Lumber Industry

William F. Vilas, a businessman and prominent Democratic politician from Wisconsin, became secretary of the interior in 1887. Shortly after his appointment, several Republican senators charged that Vilas, a stockholder in the Superior Lumber Company, was profiting from rulings in his department that facilitated logging on Indian reservations in northern Wisconsin. In March, 1888, the Senate Select Committee on Indian Traders began an investigation, with which Secretary Vilas cooperated fully. Vilas turned over pertinent correspondence within his department and at the committee's request suspended all logging activity on the reservations until the matter was resolved. He also sent to the area a special investigator of his own, with instructions to look into the charges.

After a lengthy investigation, the Senate committee reported in 1889. The Republicans in the majority found evidence of neglect of duty and abuse of official power (though not corruption) on the part of several local officials in Wisconsin. They also called Vilas, as head of the department, "fully responsible" and "censurable" for his subordinates' misconduct. The Democrats in the minority disagreed. They exonerated the local officials of misconduct and cleared Vilas of any wrongdoing.[5]

There is no evidence that President Cleveland played any role in the affair, though Vilas, a close friend and collaborator, undoubtedly consulted him and received his permission to cooperate with the investigation. On the most important accusation—that Vilas had personally profited from the lumbering activity—the committee (both majority and minority) cleared Vilas completely, finding that the Superior Lumber Company was not involved in the logging and that Vilas in no way benefited personally from it.[6]

NOTES

[1]H. Wayne Morgan, *From Hayes to McKinley: National Party Politics, 1877–1896* (Syracuse, N.Y., 1969), 210, 214.

[2]Rexford G. Tugwell, *Grover Cleveland* (New York, 1968), p. xi. See also Allan Nevins, *Grover Cleveland: A Study in Courage* (New York, 1932), 4; Morgan, *From Hayes to McKinley*, 246–276; Matthew Josephson, *The Politicos, 1865–1896* (New York, 1938), 352; Richard Hofstadter, *The American Political Tradition and the Men Who Made It* (New York, 1948), 180.

[3]House Report 3142, 49th Cong., 1st Sess., ser. 2444 (Washington, 1886), 1–125. Testimony in the case is in *House Miscellaneous Document 355*, 49th Cong., 1st Sess., ser. 2424 (Washington, 1886).

[4]Nevins, *Cleveland*, 293–295; Horace Samuel Merrill, *Bourbon Leader: Grover Cleveland and the Democratic Party* (Boston, 1957), 86. For the defeat of the solicitor general's nomination, see *Nation*, XLIII (July 15, 1886), 43.

[5]*Senate Report 2710*, 50th Cong., 2nd Sess., ser. 2624 (Washington, 1889), pp. i–xc.

[6]*Ibid.*; Horace Samuel Merrill, *William Freeman Vilas: Doctrinaire Democrat* (Madison, Wis., 1954), 140–150, and his *Bourbon Leader*, 85–86.

BENJAMIN HARRISON
1889–1893

R. Hal Williams

Like Cleveland, Benjamin Harrison entered the White House with a widespread reputation for personal and official integrity. Like Cleveland, too, he left office with that reputation largely intact, even though opposing Democrats scrutinized closely every action of his administration. With his party in control of Congress—an advantage few presidents had in the late nineteenth century—Harrison presided over an active administration that worked to advance the Republican Party's program: a higher tariff, some measure of control over corporate consolidations, a compromise adjustment of the troublesome silver issue, an attempt to safeguard voting rights in the South, and a commitment to distribute pensions liberally to Civil War veterans. These policies aroused great controversy, both then and later, but no historian has raised serious questions about Harrison's own integrity or the integrity of his administration.

In regard to official misconduct, four incidents of some importance touched the Harrison administration.

W. W. Dudley and the 1888 Campaign

In 1888 William Wade Dudley, a one-legged Union army veteran and a friend and supporter of Harrison, occupied the position of treasurer of the Republican National Committee. Dudley was noted for his eagerness to win elections, and in this particular race he took a special interest in the campaign in his home state of Indiana. On October 24— late in the campaign—he allegedly wrote a letter of instructions to Republican county leaders there. A Democratic mail agent on the Ohio

& Mississippi Railroad, his curiosity aroused by the large number of envelopes from the Republican National Committee, opened one. On October 31 the Indianapolis *Sentinel* published the letter, and other newspapers promptly picked it up. The letter created a sensation, for in it Dudley had apparently instructed the county leaders to pay the "floaters" and other doubtful voters to vote for Harrison, to ensure a Republican victory. "Divide the floaters into blocks of five," the letter read, "and put a trusted man with necessary funds in charge of these five and make him responsible that none get away and that all vote our ticket."[1]

The Republicans responded with denials. The party's national chairman attacked the letter's authenticity, as did other party leaders. Dudley himself labeled the letter a forgery, and he instituted libel actions against four New York newspapers that had printed it. When the story broke, Benjamin Harrison hesitated. Then a day or so later, he issued a short public statement denying any knowledge of, or complicity in, the matter. Harrison avoided taking a position on Dudley's guilt or innocence, on the grounds that he had not yet seen the actual letter. Pressured to defend Dudley, he refused. Harrison's statement satisfied few people: Dudley felt betrayed, while for their part the Democrats assailed Harrison's failure to repudiate Dudley. With only a few days remaining in the campaign, Harrison allowed Dudley to stay in his position at the committee, but he never spoke to him again.[2]

After the election Dudley won retractions from the newspapers he had sued, though most historians have since agreed that in fact he probably had written the letter. In 1889–1890 the Democrats—apparently with some help from Indiana Republicans—tried to indict him for ballot fraud, but a grand jury called for that purpose refused to indict. During the early 1890s, Dudley attempted to involve the administration in a small bit of land speculation, but President Harrison promptly quashed the attempt. Mutual friends occasionally tried to reconcile the two men, but without success. The "blocks of five" incident ended their political and personal relationship.[3]

James R. Tanner and the Pensions Bureau

On March 23, 1889, Harrison named James R. Tanner to head the Bureau of Pensions within the Interior Department. An energetic veteran who had lost both legs at the Second Battle of Bull Run, Tanner vowed to manage the bureau in a way that would produce maximum benefits for veterans. Working quickly, he did just that. He raised pension rates, reduced the amount of proof needed to show eligibility for a pension, and even reviewed old rates—with the result that he sent thousands of dollars in back pensions to surprised veterans who had not requested such a review. The generosity was spread around, and a portion of the proceeds went to employees in the Pensions Bureau, though apparently not to Tanner himself.

Amid growing publicity, Secretary of the Interior John W. Noble, Tanner's superior and a Union army veteran himself, ordered a probe. He found evidence of lavish and illegal handouts, but Tanner denied Noble's authority to interfere in the operation of the Pensions Bureau. Fed up, Noble protested to President Harrison and also cited Tanner for disrespect and insubordination in his annual report. Apprehensive of Tanner's support in the influential Grand Army of the Republic, Harrison delayed action for a time, but then on September 11, 1889, he sent a mutual friend to Tanner's Georgetown home to ask the commissioner to resign. Tanner refused, Harrison immediately gave him the choice of resignation or suspension, and on September 12 Tanner submitted his resignation. Accepting it to take effect with the appointment of a successor, Harrison told Tanner, "Your honesty has not at any time been called into question." To others Harrison acknowledged that Tanner had been a bad appointment, and he expressed relief at Tanner's departure from office.[4]

Green B. Raum and the Pensions Bureau

Harrison had difficulty finding a replacement for Tanner. After several candidates turned him down, he finally settled on Green B. Raum, an Illinois veteran who had Secretary Noble's support. Unfortunately, Raum also conducted the office in a manner that gave rise to charges of misconduct. Critics accused Raum of accepting sizable loans from pension lawyers in return for expediting their cases through the Pensions Bureau. House committees twice investigated the charges, in each case submitting a report that divided on party lines. In 1891 a Republican-dominated committee cleared Raum (with the two Democratic members dissenting), while in 1892 a Democrat-dominated committee concluded that Raum "has prostituted his office for the purposes of private gain" and (with the two Republican members dissenting) urged his removal.[5] On each occasion, despite considerable evidence that the commissioner had misused his office, President Harrison chose to accept the conclusions of the Republicans on the investigating committee. Commissioner Raum served out the remainder of the administration.[6]

The Cape May Cottage

In early June 1890, John Wanamaker, the Postmaster General, and several Philadelphia friends presented to Mrs. Harrison a large new cottage at Cape May Point, in New Jersey. Many observers protested, suggesting that such gifts were improper and might amount to a bribe. Harrison's exact intentions are unclear. When the matter first arose, he made no comment; a few weeks later he contended that he had always intended to purchase the cottage once Mrs. Harrison had had an opportunity to visit it to give her approval. Mrs. Harrison made the visit during June, and on July 2 Harrison sent Wanamaker a check for $10,000 in payment for the cottage.

Harrison's biographer accepts the President's explanation. He concludes: "Harrison was unlikely to use his high office to gain monetary profit. Perhaps a little tardily, but no less earnestly, he acted so as to avoid any suspicion of it."[7]

NOTES

[1]Harry J. Sievers, *Benjamin Harrison: Hoosier Statesman, From the Civil War to the White House* (New York, 1959), 418.

[2]*Ibid.*, 417–421; H. Wayne Morgan, *From Hayes to McKinley: National Party Politics 1877–1896* (Syracuse, N.Y., 1969), 311–312; Matthew Josephson, *The Politicos, 1885–1896* (New York, 1938), 422–423, 431–433; Richard J. Jensen, *The Winning of the Midwest: Social and Political Conflict, 1888–1896* (Chicago, 1971), 27–30; Allan Nevins, *Grover Cleveland: A Study in Courage* (New York, 1932), 436–449; Robert D. Marcus, *Grand Old Party: Political Structure in the Gilded Age, 1880–1896* (New York, 1971), 143–144.

[3]Harry J. Sievers, *Benjamin Harrison: Hoosier President, The White House and After* (Indianapolis, 1968), 149, 200; Matilda Gresham, *Life of Walter Quintin Gresham, 1832–1895* (2 vols., Chicago, 1919), II, 604–618.

[4]Harrison's letter to Tanner quoted in Sievers, *Benjamin Harrison: Hoosier President*, 124. For the Tanner story, see *ibid.*, 117–128; Mary R. Dearing, *Veterans in Politics: The Story of the G.A.R.* (Baton Rouge, 1952), 393–396; Donald L. McMurry, "The Bureau of Pensions during the Administration of President Harrison," *Mississippi Valley Historical Review*, XIII (December, 1926), 343–364.

[5]*House Report 3732*, 51st Cong., 2d Sess., ser. 2887 (Washington, 1891), pp. i–xix; *House Report 1868*, 52nd Cong., 1st Sess., ser. 3049–3050 (Washington, 1892), p. xxxix.

[6]McMurry, "Bureau of Pensions," 358–362; Leonard D. White, *The Republican Era, 1869–1901: A Study in Administrative History* (New York, 1958), 217–218; Dearing, *Veterans in Politics*, 396–397, 436.

[7]Sievers, *Benjamin Harrison: Hoosier President*, 155–158.

GROVER CLEVELAND
1893–1897

SECOND TERM

R. Hal Williams

Grover Cleveland's second administration, beset by the hardships and discontent born of the economic depression of the 1890s, differed in essential respects from his first, which had been marked by a certain placidity. But in one respect it did not differ: once again contemporaries questioned Cleveland's policies and vision, but almost never his integrity. Historians have echoed this judgment.

James J. Van Alen and the Italian Mission

One case in which Cleveland's intentions did come under attack involved James J. Van Alen, a wealthy resident of Rhode Island who in 1892 contributed almost $50,000 to the Democratic Party's campaign fund. Early in 1893 reports circulated that Cleveland planned to appoint Van Alen minister to Italy, and even Cleveland's close friends and supporters protested. Conscious of his own rectitude to the point of self-righteousness, Cleveland could not believe that anyone would question the purity of his motives. "No one will accuse me of such a trade," he wrote a friend.[1]

In October, 1893, Cleveland made the appointment, which the Senate quickly confirmed. But a few weeks later Van Alen, embarrassed by the furor, resigned. Cleveland urged him not to—"We should not yield to the noise and clamor which have arisen from these conditions," he told Van Alen—but Van Alen stuck by his decision. There the matter ended.[2]

The Sugar Trust and the Wilson-Gorman Tariff of 1894

Campaign contributions also led to a second accusation of misconduct within the Cleveland administration. On May 14, 1894, as Congress debated the Wilson-Gorman tariff bill, the Philadelphia *Press* and other newspapers stated that the American Sugar Company, which had a virtual monopoly of the industry, had helped to write the sugar schedules in the bill. Specifically, the papers charged, the company through its notorious head, Henry O. Havemeyer, had given a large contribution in 1892 (reported at $100,000 or more) in return for tariff aid. Finally, it was alleged that John G. Carlisle, Cleveland's secretary of the Treasury, had participated in the bargain and had assisted in carrying it out.

As soon as the allegations were published, the Senate appointed an investigating committee, which took testimony from government officials and from Havemeyer and other officers in the American Sugar Company. Cleveland and Carlisle cooperated with the committee, and Carlisle testified at length before it. The committee implicated several senators in sugar stock speculation, censured the American Sugar Company for improper activity, but exonerated Carlisle. Carlisle, the committee found, had participated as secretary of the Treasury in compiling the sugar and other schedules, but in doing so he had acted properly and without reference to any campaign contribution by the sugar company. Historians have confirmed this finding.[3]

Later one additional charge emerged in connection with the 1894 tariff bill. An official in the Interior Department told a reporter that Daniel S. Lamont, Cleveland's close friend and the Secretary of War, had given him inside information on the sugar schedules and that this information enabled him to speculate in sugar stocks. Following Lamont's advice, he told the reporter, he had made $34,000 on an investment of $5,000.

There is no independent evidence either to corroborate or contradict the reporter's statement. Several historians have accepted it.[4]

The Sale of Bonds to Protect the Gold Reserve

During the depression Cleveland devoted most of his efforts to saving the gold standard, under attack, he thought, by economic conditions and free silver advocates. On several occasions he was forced to sell bonds to obtain gold for the Treasury. Angered by the policy, opponents frequently charged that there was a corrupt alliance between Cleveland, Carlisle, and other government officials, on the one hand, and eastern and European financiers such as J. P. Morgan, on the other. Investigations were made, including an extensive one by a Senate committee in 1896. No hard evidence was found of such an alliance, or of dishonest proceedings of any kind, and historians have agreed that the Cleveland administration's fervid defense of the gold standard stemmed from conviction, not corruption.[5]

NOTES

[1]Grover Cleveland to Oscar S. Straus, October 20, 1893, in Allan Nevins, *Letters of Grover Cleveland, 1850–1908* (Boston, 1933), 338–339. Also, Cleveland to Richard Watson Gilder, September 1, 1893, and Cleveland to Gilder, October 8, 1893, *ibid.*, 333, 336.

[2]Cleveland to Van Alen, November 22, 1893, *ibid.*, 339–340; Mark D. Hirsch, *William C. Whitney: Modern Warwick* (New York, 1948), 417–420; Nevins, *Cleveland*, 518; Matthew Josephson, *The Politicos, 1885–1896* (New York, 1938), 514.

[3]*Senate Report 606*, 53rd Cong., 2nd Sess., ser. 3188 (Washington, 1894), pp. i–xiii. The testimony is in *Senate Report 457, pt. 2*, and *Senate Report 485*, both *ibid.* Historians' conclusions can be found in James A. Barnes, *John G. Carlisle: Financial Statesman* (New York, 1931), 333–338; Nevins, *Cleveland*, 577–578.

[4]For the reporter's statement, see Arthur Wallace Dunn, *From Harrison to Harding: A Personal Narrative, Covering a Third of a Century, 1888–1921* (2 vols. New York, 1922), 127–128. Historians accepting it include Josephson, *The Politicos*, 548n; Nevins, *Cleveland*, 578.

[5]*Senate Document 187*, 54th Cong. 2nd Sess., ser. 3471 (Washington, 1896), 1–332.

WILLIAM McKINLEY
1897–1901

John G. Sproat

Secretary Alger and the Conduct of the War Department

On September 8, 1898, Secretary of War Russell A. Alger formally petitioned President William McKinley for an investigation into the War Department's conduct of the war with Spain. For months Alger had been the target of a crescendo of criticism and verbal abuse arising out of the confusion that marred the American war effort from start to finish. The range of criticism is suggested in Alger's request that the inquiry examine such matters as mobilization, supply transportation, military contracts, all expenditures, orders emanating from the War Department—in short, everything connected with the army during the brief conflict except grand strategy and tactics. McKinley quickly approved the request, and on September 24 he announced that a voluntary commission of military men and civilians would conduct the investigation. His first choice to head the commission, Lieutenant General John M. Schofield, suspected that the inquiry was a political ploy and declined to serve. McKinley then recruited General Grenville M. Dodge, a prominent Republican businessman and Civil War veteran, who had long been a friend and defender of Alger.[1]

Alger was a poor choice to head the War Department. A former governor of Michigan and past commander in chief of the Grand Army of the Republic, he had been picked purely for political reasons. Genial and self-confident, he knew nothing about the War Department, and during the year following his appointment he did almost nothing to prepare the army for a war whose coming he could hardly have failed to anticipate.

Admittedly, the task he faced was a gargantuan one. For decades the American people had badly neglected the army. By 1898 it was riddled with stuffy traditionalism, petty jealousies, and bureaucratic lethargy. The wonder is that it performed as well as it did and managed to reform itself pragmatically as the war progressed. Given the American military posture in 1898, it was all but inevitable that the war effort should have been marked by confusion and bungling. Of his own role in the disarray, Alger plaintively observed that "the life of the Secretary of War was not a happy one in those days of active military operations."[2]

Early in the war, McKinley began to suspect that Alger was an ineffective war minister—and so did the press and members of Congress. As early as May 18, the *New York Times* demanded that Alger be removed. But while McKinley lost confidence in him and consistently bypassed him in dealing with the army command, especially in matters of strategy, he retained him in office and publicly supported him.[3]

The earliest indications that the outdated military system was in serious trouble came in July and August in the badly neglected medical department. Shortages, low priorities, poor distribution, nightmarish sanitary conditions, and epidemic tropical diseases mounted to inflict upon the army what one authority has called a "shattering medical disaster."[4] At Santiago, Cuba, the Fifth Corps suffered so badly from medical, supply, and morale problems that McKinley prepared orders to return the unit to the United States. But before he could act, a group of officers in Cuba, including Theodore Roosevelt, circulated a round-robin letter to newspapers at home in which they warned that the Fifth Corps "must be moved at once or it will perish" and accused the government of inefficiency and corruption. The letter so upset McKinley that he hastened the unit's return and billeted the sick and demoralized soldiers at a half-completed camp on Long Island, where new chaos quickly set in.[5]

Alger bore the blame in the public's eye for this and other misadventures during the war. Even as the army began to pull itself together and overcome its early difficulties, he remained the butt of bitter resentment and outrage, within the army and without. Indeed, the term "Algerism" became a popular synonym for incompetence. Despite a rising cry for his ouster, Alger refused to step aside, and McKinley did nothing to force him out of office. Probably the President realized that the firing of

Alger could be construed as an admission that the administration had mismanaged the war.

As the Dodge Commission prepared to undertake its inquiry, McKinley gave it instructions akin to a charge to a grand jury:

> The people of the country are entitled to know whether or not the citizens who so promptly responded to the call of duty have been neglected or maltreated by the Government to which they so willingly gave their services. If there have been wrongs committed, the wrongdoers must not escape conviction and punishment.

He assured Dodge that he would put no limit on the scope of the investigation. Doubtless, McKinley was concerned about possible corruption and criminal negligence in the war effort, although his views as to what the inquiry might achieve in a positive way were vague.[6]

In February, 1899, the Dodge Commission issued a nine-volume report, containing an enormous body of conflicting testimony and very little in the way of conclusions as to why the war had been mismanaged. The commanding general of the army, Nelson A. Miles, proved to be the witness most unfriendly to Alger and McKinley, with both of whom he had been at odds on practically everything throughout the war. Miles's testimony included a sensational charge that the War Department had foisted tainted and grossly inferior meat—"embalmed beef"—on the troops, and the commission spent long hours running down the charge before concluding that Miles could not substantiate it. The report noted that many complaints and charges against the army were rooted in the rumors and tall tales that soldiers naturally circulate among themselves. The commission concluded, finally, that the army was guiltless of deliberate negligence and major corruption and that, under very difficult circumstances, it had probably done its best in the war. As for Alger, the commissioners could not agree among themselves as to his competence or incompetence. The report acknowledged that he was an honest and hard-working official, but also noted that he had failed sufficiently to understand the need for efficiency and discipline in the army.[7]

Thus cleared of official wrongdoing, Alger remained only a political problem for McKinley, rather than a possible source of major scandal and embarrassment. Alger persisted in his refusal to give up his cabinet post, holding on with a tenacity that exasperated other members of the administration. When he finally resigned in August, 1899, it was under conditions totally unrelated to the war and the investigation.[8]

Corruption in the Cuban Post Office

Early in 1900 the new military governor of Cuba, General Leonard Wood, uncovered evidence of fraud in the Cuban Post Office, an agency that was at that time under the direct supervision of the United States Post Office Department. Acting on a tip that the chief of the office's Bureau of Finance had absconded with public funds, Wood received authorization from Secretary of War Elihu Root to apprehend the man, Neely, and hold him in Cuba. Neely subsequently implicated Estes G. Rathbone, the director general of the Cuban Post Office, and the Postmaster General in Washington ordered a full investigation. To track down the frauds, he selected his fourth assistant, Joseph L. Bristow, a man with a reputation as a zealous investigator.[9]

Before leaving for Havana, Bristow conferred with the President and was treated to some plain speaking:

> Mr. Bristow, I have been more pained by this scandal than by anything that has occurred during my Administration. These people are our wards. They have had great confidence in our integrity and a reverence for the American name, and to think that the trusted officials whom we have sent there should plunder their revenues and steal their money is a great humiliation to me.

Bristow was instructed to do his duty and to leave any complaints about his activities to the White House.[10]

Bristow's job was complicated by Rathbone's close ties to Senator Marcus A. Hanna, the President's long-time adviser and intimate friend. Hanna did not hesitate to put pressure on the investigation on behalf of Rathbone. To Wood, for example, he issued a direct challenge: "If you bring *my friend* to trial, you will never get to be more than a captain doctor in the army." Throughout the McKinley administration, Hanna had demonstrated a cavalier disdain for civil service rules in securing appointments to the postal service, and the President could hardly have been unaware of his friend's circumvention of the laws, even though he took no action against him. In the case of the Cuban scandal, however, McKinley acted without regard to Hanna's feelings. As Bristow remarked later, the President gave him "cordial support" throughout the inquiry, and "as the months passed my gratitude increased as I learned that this support had been given in the face of the intense hostility of Hanna and Heath and all of Rathbone's friends." Rathbone ultimately was arrested and charged with appropriating government funds for personal use. Bristow remained with the department and several years later exposed a nest of fraud and corruption in the postal service that had gone unperceived through Cleveland's second term and on through McKinley's term and into Roosevelt's.[11]

NOTES

[1]The fullest treatment of the army during the war years is Graham A. Cosmas, *An Army for Empire: The United States Army in the Spanish-American War* (Columbia, Mo., 1971). Cosmas documents Alger's incompetency fully, but he is also sharply critical of McKinley, picturing the President as evasive, hypocritical, and dissembling throughout the Alger affair. H. Wayne Morgan, *William McKinley and His America* (Syracuse, 1963), is much more sympathetic to the President, although Morgan does not examine the Alger affair and investigation in great detail. Margaret Leech, *In the Days of McKinley* (New York, 1959), suggests that the Dodge Commission did not uncover the whole truth about the War Department, an opinion that public opinion at the time shared. Alger told his own story in his book *The Spanish-American War* (New York and London, 1901).

[2]Walter Millis, *The Martial Spirit* (Boston and New York, 1931), 160; Cosmas, *Army for Empire*, 245ff. The report of the Dodge Commission is in *Senate Document 221*, 56th Cong., 1st Sess., hereafter referred to as *Dodge Report*.

[3]*New York Times*, May 18, 1898; Cosmas, *Army for Empire*, 281; Morgan, *McKinley*, 384.

[4]Cosmas, *Army for Empire*, 274.

[5]*Ibid.*, 245ff; Morgan, *McKinley*, chap. 7.

[6]*Dodge Report*, I, 237–238; Morgan, *McKinley*, 424ff. Leech, *In the Days of McKinley*, 315–316, notes that McKinley did not grant the commission authority to compel witnesses to appear before it or to require the swearing in of witnesses, although the President may only have been recognizing that army officers would have been reluctant to testify fully if put under oath for fear of jeopardizing their careers. Most witnesses voluntarily took the oath.

[7]General Miles did not take the oath before testifying. The investigation resulting from his sloppy testimony is reported in "Food Furnished by the Subsistence Department to Troops in the Field," *Senate Document 270*, 56th Cong., 1st Sess. See also Cosmas, *Army for Empire*, 284ff, on Miles. *Dodge Report*, I, 116.

[8]Charles G. Dawes, *A Journal of the McKinley Years, 1893–1913* (Chicago, 1950), 187–188; Leech, *In the Days of McKinley,* chap. 16.

[9]The incident is related in some detail in Bristow's own book, *Fraud and Politics at the Turn of the Century* (New York, 1952). See also Leech, *In the Days of McKinley,* 384, 534, 554–555.

[10]Bristow, *Fraud and Politics,* 100.

[11]*Ibid.,* 97ff; Philip C. Jessup, *Elihu Root* (2 vols., New York, 1938), 290–291; Leonard D. White, *The Republican Era, 1869–1901: A Study in Administrative History* (New York, 1958), 270–271.

THEODORE ROOSEVELT
1901–1909

John W. Chambers

Postal, Land, and Indian Service Scandals, 1902–1910[1]

In view of Theodore Roosevelt's high sense of morality and national purpose, his administration was greatly embarrassed by the discovery in his second year in office of corruption in the Indian Service, the Land Office, and the Post Office Department. The swindling of the Creeks and other Indian tribes out of parcels of their territory involved only a few relatively minor federal agents and was investigated and eventually prosecuted.[2] Higher officials were involved in fraudulent exchange and speculation in federal timberlands in Oregon. In November, 1902, Secretary of the Interior Ethan A. Hitchcock and President Roosevelt forced the resignation of Binger Hermann as commissioner of the General Land Office when they learned that he had been suppressing reports of an extensive land fraud ring. After a year-long investigation disclosed widespread violation of the law, Attorney General Philander Knox on November 6, 1903, appointed Francis J. Heney as special prosecutor. The California Democrat obtained indictments against 146 persons, including several leading Oregon Republicans—U.S. Senator John H. Mitchell and Representatives John Williamson and Binger Hermann. Senator Mitchell, who was charged with accepting a bribe in 1902 in return for conspiring with Hermann, then head of the Land Office, to expedite illegal land patents, was convicted in July, 1905, and sentenced to six months in prison. Hermann was accused of conspiring to defraud the government, and Williamson with subornation of perjury; however, the cases against both men were dismissed in 1910 and 1913 when jurors were unable to reach a verdict.[3]

Even more widespread corruption was uncovered in the Post Office. Rumors of misconduct in the department led the President in December, 1902, to consult with top postal officials who confirmed the reports. Roosevelt, Postmaster General Henry C. Payne, and Eugene F. Loud, chairman of the House Committee on Post Offices and Post Roads, agreed on the need for an investigation, but delayed its initiation three months until after Congress adjourned. On March 7, 1903, the President sent official instructions to the investigator, Fourth Assistant Postmaster General Joseph L. Bristow. In May a former cashier at the Washington post office told reporters of the corruption and blamed high Republican Party officials. When Postmaster General Payne, despite his initial support of the inquiry, dismissed the accusations as "hot air," the press accused him of attempting a cover-up. The President promised a full investigation and that month appointed two special investigators to aid Bristow. When extensive corruption was found, one of the investigators, Charles J. Bonaparte, was appointed a special prosecutor. The President informed him that "my first purpose is to do exact justice in all these matters. My next is, so far as practicable, to show people that I am doing exact justice; and if possible I should like to prevent men getting the idea that I am shielding anyone. . . ."[4]

By mid-October, 1903, charges had been brought against twenty-nine men; eventually forty-four government employees, including several important officials, were indicted. John Tyner, assistant attorney general for the Post Office Department, who had served as postmaster general under President Grant, was charged with fraud and receiving a bribe. After his wife and sister-in-law had secretly visited his office and retrieved documents from his safe, Tyner was acquitted because of lack of evidence. George W. Beavers, general superintendent of the Division of Salary and Allowances, was not so fortunate; he spent two years in prison. August W. Machen, general superintendent of the Free Delivery System, received a sentence of four years and a fine of $10,000. Two others in the Post Office Department were convicted of offering bribes to government employees.[5]

President Roosevelt defended himself by pointing out that the corruption in the various governmental departments occurred among men appointed by his predecessors and that he had moved quickly and decisively to prosecute those guilty of misconduct when he had learned about their actions. Historians have, on the whole, agreed with him.[6]

Irregularities in the Payment for the Panama Canal Rights

The acquisition of the Panama Canal, one of the most important accomplishments of the Roosevelt administration, also proved to be one of the most controversial. Debate focused on the decision for the Panama route, the method of acquiring the canal territory, and the payment for the rights to build an interoceanic waterway. After first considering a Nicaraguan route, the United States government decided to buy the rights and equipment of the French entrepreneurs who had partly completed a canal on the isthmus in the late nineteenth century. The original Panama Canal Company, founded by Ferdinand de Lesseps, the Suez canal engineer, had gone bankrupt, but it had been succeeded by the New Panama Canal Company. In 1904 the American government's payment of $40,000,000 was divided between them, with $25,000,000 going to the original company and $15,000,000 to its successor. Critics called the amount excessive and the method of distribution secretive. They also charged that some American representatives of the company had exerted an improper influence upon the United States government.

Even before the actual transaction took place, critics attacked the U.S. government's plan to pay $40,000,000 to the French companies. In October, 1903, Henry Watterson, owner-editor of the Louisville *Courier-Journal,* charged corruption and stockjobbing in connection with the adoption of the Panama rather than the Nicaragua route. After the successful Panamanian revolution and the signing on November 18, 1903, of the Hay-Bunau-Varilla Treaty giving the United States sovereignty over the Canal Zone, the Kentucky editor stepped up his campaign against "The Forty Thieves of the Forty Millions."[7] He separately suggested that President Roosevelt had been influenced in choosing the Panamanian route by the French company and its chief engineer, Philippe Bunau-Varilla, who became the first minister from the Republic of Panama to the United States.[8] In a message to Congress on January 8, 1906, President Roosevelt denied these and other allegations of corruption in construction of the canal. He blamed the accusations on disappointed office seekers, rejected contractors, and "sensation mongers." However, as a result of the controversy, the Senate determined to investigate the entire Panama Canal situation, including its acquisition.[9]

On January 11, 1906, Senator John T. Morgan of Alabama, chairman of the Senate Committee on Inter-Oceanic Canals and a long-time partisan of the Nicaraguan route, began a year-long series of hearings on the relationship of the United States to the Panama Canal. The main witness was William Nelson Cromwell, the American attorney and lobbyist for the French company. Though Cromwell testified about some aspects of his work on behalf of his clients, he refused to answer a number of questions about the company on the basis of the privileged relationship between lawyer and client. A majority of the committee supported him, and the investigation proved inconclusive.[10]

Two years later, during the 1908 campaign, the first public suggestions were made that at least one of the President's relatives might have been enriched by the United States purchase of the French rights to the Panama Canal. The New York *World* reported on October 3, 1908, that two days earlier a complaint had been filed with the U.S. district attorney in New York charging that efforts were being made by unnamed persons to blackmail Cromwell for his alleged corrupt handling of the Panama transaction. At the same time, the paper quoted the complaint as stating that the Democratic National Committee had under consideration an accusation that Cromwell and Bunau-Varilla had organized a syndicate which purchased the French canal stock for approximately $3,500,000 on the Paris exchange and later sold it to the United States for $40,000,000. The alleged syndicate was said to include, among others, Cromwell, Bunau-Varilla, Charles P. Taft, the brother of the Secretary of War and Republican presidential nominee, and Douglas Robinson, brother-in-law of President Roosevelt.[11]

Although all of the alleged members of the syndicate denied the allegations, the *World*'s story and additional insinuations that higher authorities were involved were given wide publicity among both Republican and Democratic newspapers. After a search in Paris and Washington by *World* reporters failed to uncover the records of the French company and of the disbursement of the $40,000,000 to specific stockholders, many newspapers suggested that the administration was deliberately withholding evidence. "If the brother of W. H. Taft participated in this big steal," the Chicago *Journal* asserted, "then the American public has the right to know it."[12] The Indianapolis *News* declared that the

Chief Executive's failure to produce the evidence "is the equivalent to something like a confession." The main question, according to the *News,* was "Who Got the Money?" [13]

A month after the election of his chosen successor, William Howard Taft, President Roosevelt responded to the newspaper charges in a letter released to the press on December 7, 1908. Denouncing the newspaper accusations as totally false, the Chief Executive said that the relevant documents had been readily available in Washington since they were received in 1904. Furthermore, he denied that the United States had paid one cent of the $40,000,000 to any American citizen. The entire sum, according to the President, had gone directly to the French government, which then distributed it. "The mere supposition that any American received from the French Government a rakeoff," Roosevelt declared, "is too absurd to be discust [*sic*]." As to the alleged syndicate of Americans, he insisted that "so far as I know there was no syndicate: there certainly was no syndicate in the United States that to my knowledge had any dealings with the Government, directly or indirectly." [14] The President declared that neither Robinson nor Charles Taft belonged to any such syndicate, nor did they have the slightest connection with the Panama matter.

Still not content, Roosevelt sought to obtain additional information about the stockholders of the French company from Cromwell and Senator Philander Knox, who had been attorney general and had handled the mechanics of the Panama transaction. By December 10, 1908, the President had received from Cromwell what were purported to be certified copies of the French company records from its books in Paris. These included a complete list of stockholders of the New Panama Canal Company as of January 15, 1900; a list of all stockholders present on February 28, 1902, when the company decided to sell its property to the United States; and a certified copy of the final report of the liquidation of the predecessor, the old de Lesseps Panama Canal Company, filed on June 25, 1907. [15]

On December 8, 1908, the New York *World* accused the President of making "deliberate misstatements" in his defense of the Panama Canal transaction. It called for a full congressional investigation of the canal purchase. The editors claimed that Roosevelt's assertions were untrue and that he must have known that they were untrue. In refutation, the *World* declared that the $40,000,000 had not been paid directly to the French government but to J. P. Morgan and Company, the fiscal agent.

The French government had not distributed the funds; rather, Cromwell divided the payment between the old and new Panama Canal companies, as he had testified before the Morgan Committee in 1906. Rejecting the President's denial that any American syndicate existed, the *World* charged that Roosevelt could have read the "syndicate subscription agreement" in the published hearings of the Morgan Committee "if he had cared for the truth."[16]

The *World* then posed a series of questions. Why did the United States pay $40,000,000 for a bankrupt property whose control could probably have been bought on the open market for less than $4,000,000? Who were the real stockholders of the Panama Canal Company? Among whom was the $15,000,000 payment to the New Panama Canal Company divided? The editors argued that the question of whether Charles Taft or Douglas Robinson had profited from the "Panama exploitation" had become incidental to the larger issue of the veracity of the President of the United States.[17]

President Roosevelt sought first to exonerate himself by supplying evidence to bolster his explanation. On December 15, 1908, he sent a special message to Congress in which he denounced the New York *World* and Indianapolis *News,* recounted the steps in the canal purchase (more precisely than on December 7), and, after stating that the documents had always been accessible, turned them over to Congress as addenda to his message. These papers included the material submitted by government departments and by Cromwell, as well as the report and hearings of the 1906–1907 investigation by the Senate Committee on Inter-Oceanic Canals, 250 cards on State Department diplomatic papers, documents from Paris (in French), and a large volume containing the names of the stockholders which was said to have been used as the basis for liquidation by the New Panama Canal Company. With this evidence in the hands of the legislature, the President asserted, another congressional investigation would be superfluous.[18]

After this effort to vindicate himself, the Chief Executive initiated criminal libel proceedings against his major accusers, Joseph Pulitzer's New York *World* and Delavan Smith's Indianapolis *News.* Not since the expiration of the Sedition Act in 1801 had the federal government held jurisdiction in regard to libel against national officials. Instead, libel had been the province of the states. However, with Roosevelt determined to exert the power of the federal government against his attackers, Attorney General Charles J. Bonaparte pressed the case in the U.S. District Courts under an 1898 statute to "Protect the Harbor Defenses and Fortifications Constructed or Used by the United States from Malicious Injury, and for Other Purposes." Federal grand juries were impaneled on January 17, 1909, in Washington, D.C., and in New York City. A month later, they returned criminal libel indictments against the newspaper editors and owners. They reasoned that federal jurisdiction was involved because copies of the papers containing the alleged libel had been mailed in post offices and had been sold on national property in the District of Columbia and at the U.S. Military Academy at West Point. Although the U.S. attorney in Indianapolis resigned in protest against what he considered a tortured interpretation of the 1898 law, the government continued its prosecution and sought to extradite the executives of the *News* from Indiana to Washington to stand trial.[19]

The federal judiciary, which received the case after Theodore Roosevelt left the White House in March, 1909, rejected the government's attempt to prosecute the press for criminal libel in the U.S. courts. In October, 1909, Judge Albert B. Anderson of the U.S. District Court for Indiana ruled against the government's application to extradite the defendants of the Indianapolis *News* and bring them to trial. The prosecution, he stated, had shown neither prima-facie evidence of libel (since suspicion about the Panama Canal transaction had been widespread) nor proof of malice. He also denied the applicability of the 1898 statute.[20]

The case against the *World* met a similar fate. Judge Hough of the U.S. District Court in New York City also held the federal statute inapplicable and quashed the indictment. This time, however, the government appealed the case. On January 3, 1911, the Supreme Court of the United States ruled unanimously in support of the defendants. Chief Justice Edward D. White's opinion rejected the administration's interpretation of the 1898 law and instead upheld the autonomy of the states and the adequacy of their libel legislation. If Roosevelt, his brother-in-law, and the other aggrieved parties wanted to file suit for damages, the Chief Justice declared, they would have to do so in state courts under existing libel provisions.[21] None chose to do so, and in the spring of 1911 the cases pending in the District of Columbia were dismissed upon the motion of Taft's attorney general, George W. Wickersham.[22]

Neither court case dealt with the substantive question of corruption or misconduct in the American acquisition of the Panama Canal rights, and there has never been a conclusive judicial finding in regard to the *World*'s charges and President Roosevelt's defense.[23] The House Committee on Foreign Affairs, however, made an extensive investigation between January, 1912, and February, 1913.[24] Yet, despite the two congressional investigations and two federal libel cases, contemporaries failed to establish conclusively whether there had been any corruption or deception of American officials, or even who received the $40,000,000 in payment.

Though no historian has ever accused Theodore Roosevelt of profiting financially from United States acquisition of the canal, the historical assessment of the newspaper's charges of irregularities and presidential untruthfulness and of the President's response to them has been mixed. Those who have been critical of the President have emphasized the secrecy involved in the payment for the canal. George Mowry and Henry Pringle noted that the lists of stockholders in the French company in 1900 and 1902, which Cromwell provided Roosevelt and Knox, were never made public and have disappeared from both men's papers.[25] Mowry commented that "it is perhaps significant that afterward Roosevelt had 'a most uncomfortable feeling' about Cromwell and his part in the Panama affair."[26] Other historians have dismissed such implications and exonerated the administration from any direct or indirect misconduct in regard to the financial transaction. The most authoritative historical defense of the President was made by the editors of Roosevelt's letters, who concluded in 1952 that the *World*'s claims "had no basis of truth and were, in fact, libelous. . . ."[27]

Historians of both persuasions have, almost without exception, sharply criticized the President's prosecution of the *News* and the *World* for criminal libel. If Roosevelt had been successful, such an extension of federal power, they have suggested, might have seriously jeopardized freedom of the press.[28]

Improper Campaign Financing

In the 1904 presidential election, Theodore Roosevelt confronted Judge Alton Parker of New York, the Democratic candidate. The campaign lacked excitement until the Democrats charged that the Republican leadership was extorting campaign contributions from the giant corporations, many only recently organized during the great merger movement at the turn of the century.

On October 1 three Democratic newspapers, the *New York Times,* the *World,* and the Brooklyn *Eagle,* launched an assault upon what they called "Cortelyouism." The object of their attack was George B. Cortelyou, Roosevelt's secretary of commerce and labor (whose department included the new Bureau of Corporations, the forerunner of the Federal Trade Commission). Cortelyou was currently serving as chairman of the Republican National Committee and the President's campaign manager. The editorial writers accused Cortelyou of using his position in government to extract large donations for the G.O.P. campaign chest from big business. They also assailed Senator Nelson Aldrich of Rhode Island for encouraging the trusts to believe that they were buying the President. Theodore Roosevelt bore the ultimate responsibility, the editors declared, because he allowed these men to offer implied invitations to bribe the executive and obtain immunity from prosecution.[29]

Greatly angered by this assault upon his integrity, Roosevelt that afternoon directed his campaign manager not to be put on the defensive but to launch "the most savage counterattack possible" upon the Democratic leaders, accusing them of "pandering to the trust people" by advocating state rather than federal regulation of corporations. At the same time, he privately reassured Republican editors of the falsity of the opposition's charges.[30]

Three weeks later, the President was told confidentially by two reporters that executives of the Standard Oil Company had been coerced into contributing $100,000 to his campaign fund. On October 26 he wrote a confidential letter to Cortelyou directing him to tell Cornelius Bliss, the Republican Party treasurer, to return the donation if it had been accepted. Though Roosevelt defended the propriety of corporate contributions as long as they entailed no specific obligation, he feared that because of Standard's hostility to the Bureau of Corporations (which he considered one of his major accomplishments), its contribution would be viewed as placing his administration under an improper obligation.[31]

By the end of October, Judge Parker had joined in the attack upon "Cortelyouism." In a speech on November 3, he went even further and described the Republican actions as "blackmail." He charged that

Roosevelt and Cortelyou were extorting large donations from the trusts in exchange for pledges of continued confidentiality of potentially damaging facts gathered by the Bureau of Corporations in its investigations. Three days later he publicly invited Roosevelt to join him in rejecting contributions from the trusts.[32]

Smarting under the Democratic onslaught, the President decided to reply personally. On November 4 he publicly denounced Parker's charges that he and Cortelyou were guilty of gross misconduct as "monstrous," and declared that the opposition candidate had not produced any proof because the accusations were "unqualifiedly and atrociously false." Both parties, he added, had received contributions from corporations, which was perfectly proper. "If elected," Roosevelt announced, "I shall go into the Presidency unhampered by any pledge, promise, or understanding of any kind, sort, or description, save my promise, made openly to the American people, that so far as in my power lies[,] I shall see to it that every man has a square deal, no less and no more."[33] Cortelyou and Secretary of War Elihu Root joined the presidential denunciation and asserted further that the Republican presidential campaign fund of 1904, which had been donated by more than 4,000 persons, was the smallest in twelve years and less than half the size of McKinley's in 1896.[34]

Neither Roosevelt's rebuttal nor his overwhelming electoral victory put an end to the accusations. In September, 1905, during an investigation of the insurance industry by the Armstrong Committee of the New York legislature, several company executives testified that they had contributed tens of thousands of dollars to the Republican National Committee the previous year. As a consequence, the Democratic press revived Judge Parker's accusations.[35]

Two years later the issue of the 1904 Republican campaign contributions became front-page news. On April 2, 1907, the New York *World* announced that President Roosevelt had asked Edward H. Harriman, head of the Union Pacific and other railroads and a wealthy New York Republican, to help finance the G.O.P. campaign in the Empire State. The newspaper said that Harriman had contributed $50,000 and collected an additional $200,000 for the party. The evidence was contained in a letter from the millionaire to his attorney, Sidney Webster, in late December, 1905, which had been stolen and sold to the *World* by one of the financier's former stenographers. In the letter, Harriman recalled that the President had sent for him before the election at a time when many feared that New York would swing into the Democratic column in the state elections and therefore possibly in the presidential contest as well. "[The President] told me that he understood the campaign could not be carried on without sufficient money," Harriman wrote, "and asked me if I would help them in raising the necessary funds."[36] In Harriman's view, the financial problem in New York stemmed from factionalism within the party caused by Senator Chauncey Depew. He recalled that Roosevelt had agreed that if it were found necessary, he would appoint Depew ambassador to France to remove him from domestic politics.

Returning to New York, Harriman quickly raised the money and gave the checks to Cortelyou, who turned them over to Governor B. B. Odell, who was running his chosen successor's gubernatorial campaign. After the election, when the Republicans had won both the governor's mansion and the White House, Harriman visited Roosevelt again, but in their December meeting, the President informed the financier that he had decided it was not necessary to send Depew to Paris and would keep him in the Senate instead.[37]

Although Harriman confirmed the authenticity of the letter to Webster, President Roosevelt rejected the millionaire's interpretation of their pre-election meeting, and he denied any implication of misconduct. On April 2, 1907, when the *World*'s story reached the White House, Roosevelt handed reporters a copy of a letter he had written months before on October 6, 1906, to the chairman of the Republican Congressional Campaign Committee, who had claimed Harriman was so angry with Roosevelt that he would not contribute to the party in 1906. In his letter, Roosevelt declared that he had never asked the New Yorker "to raise a dollar for the presidential campaign of 1904." He suggested that Harriman himself had requested the meeting to solicit Roosevelt to ask Cortelyou to aid the Republican gubernatorial candidate (which Roosevelt said he did) and to get the President to send Senator Depew to Paris (which Roosevelt said he refused to do).[38] Though Roosevelt's explanation convinced many of his innocence, his phrase "Now, my dear sir, you and I are practical men" from a letter to Harriman after their meeting was taken out of context by his critics and offered as evidence that the President had made a secret and sinister bargain with the financier.[39]

Additional suggestions of undue corporate influence in politics were raised in the following year. Speaking in support of the presidential candidate of his little-known Independence Party, publisher William Randolph Hearst, on September 17, 1908, released the first of a series of purloined letters which indicated that the Standard Oil Company had bribed a number of important senators from both parties over the previous half dozen years. The correspondence of John D. Archbold, vice president and chief lobbyist for the giant petroleum corporation, had been sold to Hearst by two company employees. Although the Archbold letters did not implicate the President, they raised again the issue of improper campaign donations by the trusts.[40] Informed that the treasurer of William Howard Taft's current campaign for the presidency had requested contributions from both Archbold and Harriman, Roosevelt fired off a vigorous protest. He reiterated that in 1904 he had directed his campaign manager to reject or to return the contribution by "the representatives of the Standard Oil Company." The current Republican treasurer, George R. Sheldon, responded that in 1904 a large contribution had been made under the authority of the executive committee of the Standard Oil Company, and that G.O.P. Treasurer Cornelius Bliss had not returned it. Roosevelt expressed surprise at this since, he said, Cortelyou had told him that Bliss had said no Standard Oil money had been received or would be accepted. But the President added that after the election he had heard from someone else that "certain individuals who had contributed had Standard Oil as well as other interests."[41]

A month before the 1908 election, the issue of the Standard Oil contribution of 1904 popped up again. Governor Charles N. Haskell of Oklahoma, who had resigned as treasurer of the Democratic National Committee, charged in an open letter to the President on October 14 that senators beholden to the corporation had persuaded Roosevelt to authorize the lease of Indian oil lands to subsidiaries of the giant refining combine. He said the President had overruled his secretary of the interior in the summer of 1904 in order to grant a pipeline franchise through Osage lands to the Prairie Oil and Gas Company, and he suggested that Roosevelt had succumbed to oil companies' protests against an adverse decision by his subordinate. Roosevelt returned Haskell's letter of accusation along with a stinging denial of the charges. On November 15, after the election, the New York *Sun* made a similar claim and asserted that a $150,000 Standard Oil contribution had been given after the reversal. Branding the allegation "a lie, pure and simple," Roosevelt obtained from his former secretary of the interior a denial of either improper pressures or being overruled.[42]

After Theodore Roosevelt announced in February, 1912, that he would challenge William Howard Taft for the Republican nomination for president, the issue of the 1904 campaign contributions was raised once again—this time by members of his own party. When Senator Boies Penrose, a member of the G.O.P. Old Guard, charged that eight years earlier Roosevelt had taken $150,000 from Standard Oil and then asked for more, the former president reiterated his denial and his instructions to Cortelyou. One result of this controversy was a congressional investigation into campaign finance since 1900. A Senate committee, headed by the progressive Republican Moses E. Clapp of Minnesota, began the work in June, 1912, and continued it almost until the inauguration of the Wilson administration the following year. The committee listened to dozens of witnesses, including the principals in the campaign of 1904 except for Cornelius Bliss, who had died in 1911.

The senators learned that despite Roosevelt's fears in 1904, the Republicans had a much larger campaign fund than the Democrats and that it had been amassed primarily from big business. Testimony revealed that 72½% of the $2,195,000 collected by the G.O.P. National Committee in that year had come from giant corporations. The major contributors included the following:

Edward T. Stotesbury (U.S. Steel, a Morgan Company) . . $166,000
John Archbold & H. H. Rogers (Standard Oil)   150,000
J. P. Morgan (J. P. Morgan & Co., investment banking) . .   150,000
George J. Gould (railroads)   100,000
C. S. Mellen (Morgan's N.Y., New Haven & Hartford RR.) .   50,000
Henry Clay Frick (U.S. Steel)   50,000
James H. Hyde (insurance).   25,000
James Speyer (investment banking)   25,000
William Nelson Cromwell (corporation lawyer).   5,000

In contrast, the Democratic National Committee had raised only $700,000—one-third of the Republican war chest. Judge Parker's largest benefactors, each contributing well over $100,000, were the financiers

August P. Belmont and Thomas Fortune Ryan, and the vice-presidential candidate, Henry G. Davis, a West Virginia industrialist.[43]

Testimony conflicted over whether President Roosevelt knew of the controversial Standard Oil contribution in 1904. Archbold stated on August 23, 1912, that when he gave the company's donation to the Republican treasurer in 1904, "I said to Mr. Bliss 'We do not want to make this contribution unless it is thoroughly acceptable and will be thoroughly appreciated by Mr. Roosevelt,' and Mr. Bliss smilingly said we need have no possible apprehension on that score."[44] Five days later Roosevelt rushed a letter to the committee denouncing Archbold's assertion that Bliss acted with Roosevelt's knowledge and consent as "an unqualified falsehood." The former president declared that any contribution from the company "was done not merely without my knowledge, but was done against my express direction and prohibition and in spite of the fact that I was assured that no such request had been made and that no such contribution had been or would be received."[45]

Under questioning before the Senate committee on October 4, 1912, Roosevelt said that until Archbold testified on August 23, 1912, he had not known that the Standard Oil Corporation itself (in contrast to individuals with Standard Oil as well as other interests) had contributed to his election fund. It appears that the former president was dissembling. For he had been informed as early as September 22, 1908, by Taft's campaign treasurer that the Standard Oil contribution of 1904 had been made "under the authority of its executive committee."[46]

Historians who are critical and those who are sympathetic toward Roosevelt generally agree that the President was probably unaware before the election of 1904 that the Standard Oil Company's contribution had been received and spent by the party. Bliss may have kept that information from him, and perhaps from Cortelyou as well, at least until after the election. He would not have been the first or the last campaign treasurer or manager to guard his candidate against becoming fully aware of the financing of the campaign.[47]

The question of Roosevelt's 1904 dealings with Harriman has remained unresolved. Before the Clapp Committee, the testimony conflicted, as had the recollections of the two principals five years earlier. On August 14, 1912, Governor Odell confirmed Harriman's interpretation as the financier had recounted it to him a few days after his controversial meeting at the White House. However, on October 4, 1912, Roosevelt reiterated his own previous assertions about what had transpired that day.[48] Like the participants, historians have disagreed over the incident. Some writers have suggested that Harriman perhaps unconsciously distorted the President's meaning. More critical historians and biographers have been less generous to the President. One of the harshest, Henry Pringle, accused Roosevelt of distorting evidence to prove his point and discredit his adversary.[49]

After the Clapp Committee revelations, no one could deny the preponderance of generous contributions from the corporations in a relatively ample campaign chest. Though Cortelyou and Root had been technically correct in asserting in 1904 that the Republican presidential campaign fund of that year was the party's smallest since 1892, they had been disingenuous about its size and its source.[50] Nevertheless, the accusations of extortion, promises of future influence, or other improper conduct on the part of the President and his immediate subordinates have remained unproved. Historians continue to debate the larger question of the degree to which Roosevelt's policies were designed to aid big business, but no direct evidence has yet been produced which conclusively linked corporate contributions to specific favorable treatment of particular trusts. Indeed, the reverse was sometimes true. Harriman became disgruntled over the Hepburn railroad regulation act, and Standard Oil was successfully prosecuted for violating the antirebate and antitrust laws. Standard's vice president John Archbold testified angrily in 1912 about Roosevelt's postelection business policy. "There never was a more outrageous course of action taken on the part of any administration in any nation of the world," the corporation's lobbyist insisted. "Darkest Abyssinia never saw anything like the course of treatment we experienced at the hands of the administration following Mr. Roosevelt's election in 1904."[51]

The continuing controversy over the 1904 Republican campaign fund contributed to reforms of campaign financing in the first decade of the twentieth century. In his first message to Congress after the election, Roosevelt had called for a law requiring publicity for the expenditures by political committees and candidates. A year later on December 5, 1905, he repeated this suggestion and, after the insurance scandals, recommended that corporations be prohibited from making political contributions.[52] On January 26, 1907, as a result of the efforts of the National Campaign Publicity Association (headed primarily by Democratic leaders), Congress prohibited contributions by national banks and corporations (but not by their officers as individuals) in the election of federal officials. That December Roosevelt went beyond the concept of disclosure to suggest payments directly from the public treasury to the major parties for "proper and legitimate [campaign] expenses." Although Congress ignored Roosevelt's proposal, it did adopt in 1910 the first federal campaign fund disclosure law which, with a 1911 amendment, required primary, convention, and preelection statements of contributions and limited the amounts that could be legally spent by candidates for Congress.[53]

The Steel Merger of 1907 and Charges that the President Helped Violate the Antitrust Law

During the recession and Wall Street panic of late 1907, President Roosevelt acquiesced in the merger of two steel companies as a means of averting further economic dislocation, but his action haunted him politically for the rest of his life.

The decision had been made in haste but within an overall attempt to help the financial community and the banking system weather the liquidity crisis. Although the Roosevelt administration pumped cash and credit into New York, the money shortage continued, and by the beginning of November, it appeared that one of the larger New York brokerage houses, Moore & Schley, was on the verge of a bankruptcy, which would have placed additional strain upon credit institutions and further depressed the financial situation. Later Grant B. Schley testified that $5,000,000 or $6,000,000 would have saved his firm, and Judge Elbert H. Gary, president of United States Steel Corporation, concurred. But at the time, the brokerage house rejected J. P. Morgan's offer of a $5,000,000 loan as inadequate. Hence, Morgan sought to provide the firm with liquid assets by having U.S. Steel purchase Moore & Schley's large holding of stock in the Tennessee Coal and Iron Company, the major steel producer in the South with plants and enormous reserves of iron and coal in northern Alabama and southern Tennessee. Moreover, before Judge Gary and Henry Clay Frick, the heads of Morgan's U.S. Steel Corporation, agreed to buy the stock of their southern competitor, they insisted on first obtaining governmental assent that the arrangement would not violate the antitrust laws.

The two executives sped from New York to Washington on a special single-car train to put the proposal before President Roosevelt on Monday morning, November 4, 1907, and telephone his answer to Wall Street before the Stock Exchange opened at 10 a.m. Interrupting the President at breakfast, they explained that an important business firm (they did not tell him the name, and Roosevelt testified in 1911 that he thought they had meant a trust company) would fail during the coming week without help. U.S. Steel had been asked to purchase the majority of Tennessee Coal and Iron, which the firm in difficulty held as collateral, as the only way of saving the firm. In one of his characteristic "posterity" letters sent to his attorney general that day, Roosevelt explained:

Judge Gary and Mr. Frick inform that as a mere business transaction they do not care to purchase the stock; that . . . but little benefit will come to the Steel Corporation from the purchase. . . . They further informed me that . . . the acquisition of the property in question will not raise [their proportion of America's steel properties] above sixty per cent. But they feel that it is immensely to their interest, as to the interest of every responsible businessman, to try to prevent a panic and general industrial smashup at this time. . . . I answered that while of course I could not advise them to take the action proposed, I felt it no public duty of mine to interpose any objection.[54]

The recollection of the meeting by Judge Gary, in a letter sent three days later for the files of the Justice Department, agreed with that of the President. Gary also said that he had mentioned that U.S. Steel would be acquiring Tennessee Coal and Iron Company at a price "somewhat in excess" of its real value, but that the purchase "would be of great benefit to financial conditions and would probably save from failure an important business concern. . . ."[55] Testifying before a House committee four years later, Gary recalled that the President had concluded, "I do not believe that anyone could justly criticize me for saying that I would not feel like objecting to the purchase under the circumstances." The steel executive considered this "tacit acquiescence" by the Chief Executive.[56]

Although the details of the White House meeting did not become public until a year later, the fact that it was held was reported by the press that afternoon. Immediately after the early morning conference, Judge Gary telephoned New York, and news of the President's acquiescence in the proposed merger was leaked to Wall Street. The following day U.S. Steel purchased majority control of Tennessee Coal and Iron Company from Moore & Schley, and by the end of the week, the market had rallied sufficiently to prove that the panic had subsided.

The President had misjudged his critics, however. William Jennings Bryan found fault with Roosevelt's action in the next issue of his publication, *The Commoner,* less than two weeks later. In the presidential election the following year, Bryan, as the Democratic candidate, again charged Roosevelt with favoritism to a monopolistic corporation. He argued that U.S. Steel, with the President's express consent, had bought one of its largest rivals and acquired over 50% of the total steel production of the nation. Bryan's accusation of improper presidential authorization was echoed by a number of newspapers. During the 1908 campaign, the President responded swiftly and directly. In a public letter to Bryan on September 27, he declared that there had been no violation of the law. Contending that the merger increased the Steel Corporation's share of total output by only 4%, the President assured the public that it did not significantly alter the standing of the company. It had, he asserted, prevented a crash which would have turned the financial panic into a widespread disaster.[57]

Following the election, the lame-duck Congress began an investigation of United States Steel, the 1907 merger, and the President's role in the transaction. On January 4, 1909, the Senate directed the Attorney General to explain why the government had not instituted antitrust proceedings against the Steel Corporation. Two days later the President released the memorandum-rationale which he had prepared for Attorney General Charles Bonaparte on November 4, 1907. Roosevelt also informed the Senate that the head of the Justice Department concurred that there were no grounds for an antitrust suit. However, the Chief Executive said he had instructed the Attorney General not to respond to that part of the Senate resolution which called for a statement of his reasons for nonaction. The President said he did this

> because I do not conceive it to be within the authority of the Senate to give directions of this character to the head of an executive department or demand from him reasons for his action. Heads of the executive departments are subject to the Constitution, and to the laws passed by the Congress in pursuance of the Constitution, and to the directions of the President of the United States, but to no other direction whatever.[58]

In response, the Senate passed a resolution authorizing the Judiciary Committee to determine whether the President was empowered to permit the steel acquisition and whether the merger had violated the antitrust laws. A special subcommittee, headed by Clarence D. Clark (R–Wyo.), the Judiciary Committee chairman, began hearings on January 22, 1909. Commissioner of Corporations Herbert K. Smith balked when the committee attempted to obtain from him confidential business information which U.S. Steel had earlier given voluntarily to investigators from the Bureau of Corporations. Noting that the law creating the agency stated that confidential information could only be made public by the President, Smith refused to provide the material to the senators. He enlisted the support of the Attorney General and of the President, who ordered him to send all papers relating to U.S. Steel and Tennessee Coal and Iron to the White House. Roosevelt told his son on January 23 that he had warned the chairman of the committee that he would not turn the confidential documents over to Congress. Dramatically, the Chief Executive had informed the Senator that the legislature would have to impeach him to obtain the documents.[59] In practice, however, the President modified his position. A few days later, after examining the material, he released a number of papers to the committee with the claim that "no part of any such confidential information hereby withheld had any bearing whatever upon the subject matter of the Senate resolution referred to [the legality of Roosevelt's action and the steel merger]."[60]

The Senate subcommittee had questioned George Perkins, a Morgan partner, and Grant Schley of Moore & Schley, among others, but had been unable to reach agreement among its own members. The Judiciary Committee issued no report, but three Democrats, led by Senator Charles A. Culberson of Texas, and one Republican published their views. They concluded that Roosevelt had been deceived about the situation on Wall Street and about the value of the southern company to United States Steel. In their opinion, the merger violated the Sherman Antitrust Act, and the President should not have permitted it:

> ... the President is without authority to annul or suspend a law or to direct its non-enforcement either generally or in a particular case. The principle involved, in its broadest sense, is inherent in our form of government and is essential to the preservation of the rights and liberties of the people. This view is strengthened, if such were necessary, by the fact that the President is the one official who is by the Federal Constitution expressly enjoined to "take care that the laws be faithfully executed."[61]

The controlling majority of Republicans on the Judiciary Committee and in the Senate dismissed this contention as irrelevant. Roosevelt had not authorized the purchase, they said; he had merely declared his refusal to "interpose any objection" to the arrangement.[62]

On March 3, 1909, Roosevelt was succeeded as president by the man he had chosen to continue his policies, William Howard Taft. Yet within two years the two were completely estranged, partly over the issue of Roosevelt's acquiescence in the 1907 steel merger. Prodded by a congressional resolution, the Taft administration in June, 1910, reinvigorated the federal investigation of U.S. Steel, which had been languishing for five years. The following summer a committee of the first Democrat-dominated House since 1895 began an inquiry into the giant steelmaking company. Testifying on August 5, 1911, before what he privately considered a group of "dishonest jacks," former president Roosevelt described his part in the absorption of the Tennessee Coal and Iron Company and again denied that he had been deceived by Gary and Frick. His duty, he said, had been to stop the panic and prevent widespread misery, not to determine whether the steelmen's main motive was acquiring their competitor or stemming the financial slump. Actually, Roosevelt thought both motives had been in their minds.[63]

Nevertheless, on October 26, 1911, the Taft administration began anti-trust proceedings against United States Steel. The acquisition of the southern company was cited by the government as one of the major steps contributing to the Steel Corporation's monopoly. In his petition, special counsel Jacob M. Dickinson, Secretary of War, argued explicitly that Gary and Frick had deceived President Roosevelt.[64] The former chief executive indignantly defended his action and assailed Taft's antitrust policy in an article in *Outlook* magazine. He also broke with his old friend and let it be known that he might challenge Taft for the presidency.[65]

The national legislature, the federal courts, and subsequent historians all have passed judgment on Theodore Roosevelt's decision of November 4, 1907. But they have differed in their assessments.

In 1912 the majority of the Stanley Committee submitted a report to the House of Representatives sharply critical of the Steel Corporation and of Roosevelt's action. It asserted that the panic had subsided by October 26, 1907, and the President had been deceived about conditions on Wall Street, as well as the adverse effect that the merger would have upon the steel industry. Implying that the merger violated the antitrust laws, the majority asserted that the President had no right to condone or encourage such a violation. The congressmen concluded bluntly that since 1907 the dominance of U.S. Steel had been "due in no small measure to the sudden, ill-considered, and arbitrary fiat of the Chief Executive."[66]

Like the Republican minority on the Stanley Committee, which had dissented from the majority report, the federal judiciary was more sympathetic to the former president and the steelmakers. On June 3, 1915, the U.S. District Court of New Jersey, dismissing as unproved the government's charge that U.S. Steel was a combination in restraint of trade, concurred with Roosevelt that the purchase of the southern company had been in the judges' words "made in fair business course" without "a wrongful motive to injure others."[67] Following the government's appeal and new arguments by both sides, the Supreme Court of the United States on March 1, 1920, agreed that "the law does not make mere size an offense" and that President Roosevelt had not been guilty of any wrongdoing.[68]

Historians and biographers have disagreed over the answers to the questions raised by the Chief Executive's action at the White House meeting. Some historians have endorsed Roosevelt's defense of his decision not to object to the acquisition and have argued that it was one of a series of steps taken to stabilize the financial situation. The editors of his letters concluded that the significance of the decision had been exaggerated by hostile politicians and by most historians. They also claimed that Roosevelt was apparently correct in his assessment of the purpose of the steel executives. The editors quoted Roosevelt's subsequent assertion that U.S. Steel's share of the nation's steel production dropped from 58% in 1906 to 54% in 1910, of which 2% was produced by the former Tennessee Coal and Iron Company.[69]

A number of historians have been more critical of Roosevelt's role in the incident. They emphasized that the White House meeting lasted less than an hour and that the President had not been apprised of all the details or alternatives. He was unaware that the institution in jeopardy was only a brokerage house (not a major trust company or bank) and that it had other collateral (including large holdings of stock in American Tobacco, Guggenheim Copper, and a number of other firms, in addition to its holdings in Tennessee Coal and Iron). The President did not know that Moore & Schley could have survived on a loan of $6,000,000 rather than the $45,000,000 which U.S. Steel eventually paid for Tennessee Coal and Iron. Furthermore, the critics claim, Roosevelt was deceived or "imposed upon" by the denial of self-interest expressed by Gary and Frick.[70]

Charges of Misuse of the Secret Service, 1908–1909

President Roosevelt's last months in office were dominated by a controversy over congressional accusations that he had misused the United States Secret Service. A number of lawmakers charged that the Chief Executive had expanded these federal detectives from a small group created to locate counterfeiters and protect the president into an "army of federal spies" probing, without legal authority, into business, agriculture, conservation, and other fields. Likening them to Napoleon's secret police, some congressmen claimed they were used by Roosevelt to coerce and intimidate members of the national legislature, in violation of the separation of powers, by keeping them under surveillance.

A confrontation between Congress and the outgoing president over the issue developed during the winter of 1908–1909. Led by Speaker Joseph Cannon and Representative James A. Tawney, an Old Guard Republican from Minnesota, the lawmakers adopted an amendment to the Sundry Civil Appropriation Bill limiting the Secret Service to Treasury Department matters. Defending what he considered an essential enforcement agency, the President chastised the legislators in his annual message of December 8, 1908, for taking action which "could be of benefit only to the criminal classes." The chief argument in favor of the amendment, Roosevelt said, "was that congressmen did not themselves wish to be investigated by Secret Service men."[71]

Embittered by the implication of congressional corruption, the House of Representatives rebuked the President. On January 8, 1909, it voted 211 to 36 to lay on the table the sections which dealt with the Secret Service in his last two messages to Congress. With considerable exaggeration, Speaker Cannon claimed it was the most important legislative victory over the executive since the adoption of Henry Clay's resolution censuring Andrew Jackson for his policy toward the Bank of the United States. But it was a hollow triumph. Though Congress curbed the Secret Service, Roosevelt and Attorney General Bonaparte on July 26, 1908, had created within the Department of Justice an entirely new detective agency which eventually came to be known as the Federal Bureau of Investigation.[72]

Historians have pictured the conflict over the Secret Service as a reassertion of prerogative by a Congress resentful of an aggressive chief executive. They have pointed out that though many legislators opposed the expansion of the federal detective force on civil liberty grounds, others were retaliating for the administration's earlier prosecution and imprisonment of several members of Congress in connection with the postal and land frauds. Some sought to protect business or agricultural interests from national inquiry. Historians have agreed that Roosevelt sought primarily to strengthen his ability to prosecute criminals, but the most thorough student of the controversy concluded that congressional suspicions were not completely unwarranted. While seeking to maintain the Secret Service to hunt down violators of federal law, Roosevelt went out of his way in 1908 and 1909 to incriminate members of Congress who had been persistent critics of his administration.[73]

NOTES

[1]The author of this section acknowledges his indebtedness to the research assistance provided by Stewart Levy, a student at Yale Law School, who gathered much of the information regarding the postal, land, and Indian Service frauds, and campaign financing issue in the Roosevelt administration, and the Bryan, Pindell, Caminetti, and Sullivan affairs in the Wilson administration.

[2]*Senate Document 26* and *189*, 58th Cong., 2nd Sess. See also Angie Debo, *And Still the Waters Run* (Princeton, 1940), 117–125; Elting E. Morison et al., eds., *The Letters of Theodore Roosevelt* (8 vols., Cambridge, Mass., 1951–1954), III, 503n, 692n, IV, 740n, VI, 1252, hereafter referred to as Morison, *Roosevelt Letters.*

[3]S.A.D. Puter and Horace Stevens, *The Looters of the Public Domain* (Portland, Ore., 1908); Morison, *Roosevelt Letters*, IV, 1127–1128n.; J. A. O'Callaghan, "Senator Mitchell and the Oregon Land Frauds, 1905," *Pacific Historical Review*, XXI (1952), 255ff; John Messing, "Public Lands, Politics, and Progressives: The Oregon Land Fraud Trials, 1903–1910," *ibid.*, XXXV (1966), 35–66; H. S. Brown, "Punishing Land Looters," *Outlook*, LXXXV (1907), 427–439.

[4]Roosevelt to Charles Joseph Bonaparte, personal, October 24, 1903, in Morison, *Roosevelt Letters*, III, 637.

[5]On the postal scandals, see *New York Times*, November 24, 1903; *Literary Digest*, XXVIII (March, 1904), 393–394; Morison, *Roosevelt Letters*, III, 444n, 500n, 636n, VI, 741–742n, 975n; Dorothy G. Fowler, *The Cabinet Politician, The Postmaster General, 1829–1909* (New York, 1943); Gerald Cullinan, *The Post Office Department* (New York, 1968), 115–117.

[6]Roosevelt to Lemuel C. Davis, October 5, 1903, in Morison, *Roosevelt Letters*, III, 444, 620–621; Theodore Roosevelt, *An Autobiography* (New York, 1913), 402–404; Henry F. Pringle, *Theodore Roosevelt: A Biography* (New York, 1931), 343; George E. Mowry, *The Era of Theodore Roosevelt and the Birth of Modern America, 1900–1912* (New York, 1962) 171; John M. Blum, *The Republican Roosevelt* (New York, 1966), 53–54n; William H. Harbaugh, *The Life and Times of Theodore Roosevelt* (rev. ed., New York, 1966), 212.

[7]The issue of the complicity of President Roosevelt in the Panamanian Revolution of 1903 has not been included in this essay because the contemporary criticism involved policy decisions rather than charges of corruption of American officials.

[8]"An Attempt at an American 'Panama Canal Scandal,' " *Literary Digest*, XXVI (October 17, 1903), 494–495; Philippe Bunau-Varilla, *Panama: The Creation, Destruction, and Resurrection* (London, 1913), 423–424; Arthur Krock, comp., *The Editorials of Henry Watterson* (Louisville, Ky., 1923), 296–299.

[9]*Congressional Record*, 59th Cong., 1st Sess., 1906, XL, pt. 1, 79; "Our First Panama Canal Investigation," *Literary Digest*, XXXII (January 20, 1906), 78–79.

[10]U.S. Senate, Committee on Inter-Oceanic Canals, *Investigation of Panama Canal Matters: Hearings*, 59th Cong., 2nd Sess. (4 vols., Washington, D.C., 1907), Senate Document 401, ser. 5097–5100. Cromwell's testimony is on 1041–1251, 3029–3207.

[11]*New York World*, October 3, 1908.

[12]Chicago *Journal* quoted in Clyde Peirce, *The Roosevelt Panama Libel Cases* (New York, 1959), 52.

[13]Indianapolis *News*, October 20 and November 1, 1908, quoted in Peirce, *Roosevelt Libel Cases*, 54, 56.

[14]Roosevelt to W. D. Foulke, December 1, 1908, released December 7, in Morison, *Roosevelt Letters*, VI, 1394.

[15]Roosevelt to P. Knox and W. N. Cromwell, December 8, 1908, and Roosevelt to Knox, December 10, 1908, in Morison, *Roosevelt Letters,* VI, 1414–1419.

[16]New York *World,* October 8, 1908.

[17]*Ibid.*

[18]Theodore Roosevelt, *Presidential Addresses and State Papers* (4 vols., New York, 1905), VIII, 1987ff.

[19]Pringle, *Roosevelt,* 337; *The Roosevelt Panama Libel Case against the New York World* (New York, 1911), 1–15; Peirce, *Roosevelt Libel Cases,* 84–85.

[20]Peirce, *Roosevelt Libel Cases,* 93–96.

[21]*U.S. v. Press Publishing Co.,* 219 U.S. 1 (1910).

[22]Peirce, *Roosevelt Libel Cases,* 99.

[23]For additional criticisms, see New York *World,* December 15 and 16, 1908; October 17, 1910; Peirce, *Roosevelt Libel Cases,* 79, 83.

[24]U.S. House, Committee on Foreign Affairs, *The Story of Panama: Hearings on the Rainey Resolution* (H.R. 32), 62nd Cong., (Washington, D.C., 1912–1913).

[25]Mowry, *Era of Theodore Roosevelt,* 153; Pringle, *Roosevelt,* 332.

[26]Mowry, *Era of Theodore Roosevelt,* 154, quoting Roosevelt to W. H. Taft, June 3, 1905. Also critical but not directly accusing the President of complicity is Peirce, *Roosevelt Panama Libel Cases.*

[27]Morison, *Roosevelt Letters,* VI, 1315–1316n, 1415–1416n. Similar judgments were made in Roosevelt, *Autobiography,* 517, 566; Joseph B. Bishop, *Theodore Roosevelt and His Time Shown in His Own Letters* (2 vols., New York, 1920), I, 306; Arthur H. Dean, *William Nelson Cromwell* (New York, 1957), 145–146; Harbaugh, *Theodore Roosevelt,* 197.

[28]Morison, *Roosevelt Letters,* VI, 1425–1426n; John Morton Blum, *The Republican Roosevelt* (paperback, New York, 1966), 123; Harbaugh, *Roosevelt,* 345–346; Pringle, *Roosevelt,* 334.

[29]*New York Times,* October, 1904; Morison, *Roosevelt Letters,* IV, 963n.

[30]Roosevelt to G. B. Cortelyou, October 1, 1904, and to Lyman Abbott, October 7, 1904, in Morison, *Roosevelt Letters,* IV, 963–964, 975–976.

[31]Roosevelt to G. B. Cortelyou, letter of October 26, 1904, and telegram of October 27, 1904; Roosevelt, "Memorandum," October 27, 1904; and Roosevelt to Cortelyou, (October 27, 1904; all in Morison, *Roosevelt Letters,* IV, 995–998.

[32]*New York Times,* November 4 and 5, 1904.

[33]Roosevelt to G. B. Cortelyou, November 2, 1904, in Morison, *Roosevelt Letters,* IV, 1009–1013, and IV, 995n; *New York Times,* November 5, 1904; *Washington Post,* November 5, 1904; *Presidential Addresses and State Papers* III, 97–100.

[34]*New York Times,* November 5 and 6, 1904.

[35]New York *Herald,* September 21, 1905, in Pringle, *Roosevelt,* 356.

[36]E. H. Harriman to Sidney Webster, December, 1905, quoted in New York *World,* April 2, 1907. For Roosevelt's actual invitation, see Roosevelt to Edward H. Harriman, October 10, 1904, in Morison, *Roosevelt Letters,* IV, 979.

[37]Harriman to Webster, December, 1905, in New York *World,* April 2, 1907.

[38]Roosevelt to James S. Sherman, October 6, 1906, in Morison, *Roosevelt Letters,* V, 447–452; the letter was released to the press on April 2, 1907.

[39]Roosevelt to Edward H. Harriman, October 14, 1904, in Morison, *Roosevelt Letters,* V, 448–449; see also Pringle, *Roosevelt,* 453–454.

[40]John K. Winkler, *W. R. Hearst: An American Phenomenon* (New York, 1928), 224–232; Pringle, *Roosevelt,* 504–506.

[41]Roosevelt to W. H. Taft, September 19, 1908; Roosevelt to George R. Sheldon,

September 21, 1908; Roosevelt to William Jennings Bryan, September 23, 1908; Roosevelt to George R. Sheldon, September 25, 1908, in Morison, *Roosevelt Letters*, VI, 1243–1268.

[42]Roosevelt to Charles N. Haskell, October 16, 1908; Roosevelt to Ethan Allen Hitchcock, April 16, 1908; "Statement drawn up in the presence of ex-Secretary Hitchcock . . . ," November 15, 1908; both in Morison, *Roosevelt Letters*, VI, 1291, 1353–1395.

[43]U.S. Senate, Committee on Privileges and Elections [Clapp Committee], *Campaign Contributions: Testimony . . . June 14, 1912 to February 25, 1913 pursuant to Sen. Res. 79*, 62nd Cong., 3rd Sess. (2 vols., Washington, D.C., 1913), I, 204–206. Hereafter cited as Clapp Committee, *Testimony*. The list of contributors was compiled from evidence produced by the Clapp Committee and in an unsuccessful libel suit filed in 1914 against Roosevelt by William F. Barnes, the political boss of Albany.

[44]Clapp Committee, *Testimony*, I, 123.

[45]*Ibid.*, I, 177–178.

[46]Roosevelt, testimony of October 4, 1912, *ibid.*, I, 491; compare with Roosevelt to George R. Sheldon, September 25, 1908, in Morison, *Roosevelt Letters*, VI, 1256–1257.

[47]Pringle, *Roosevelt*, 356–358. Roosevelt's lack of knowledge during the 1904 campaign of the size and sources of the Republican campaign fund is supported by Bishop, *Roosevelt*, I, 328–334, and II, 96–98; Morison, *Roosevelt Letters*, IV, 995n; and Benjamin T. Ford, "A Duty to Serve: The Governmental Career of George B. Cortelyou" (doctoral dissertation, Columbia University, 1963, copyrighted 1967), 132–134. Mowry, *Era of Theodore Roosevelt*, 179, stated that "it is practically certain that Roosevelt at the time knew a portion of the truth and suspected a good deal more." Mowry criticized Roosevelt for not raising the issue of contributions from other corporations in addition to Standard Oil with Cortelyou. Harbaugh, in *Theodore Roosevelt*, 221, and in "Election of 1904," in Arthur M. Schlesinger, Jr., and Fred L. Israel, eds., *History of American Presidential Elections, 1789–1968* (4 vols., New York, 1971), 1992, agreed with Mowry's criticism.

[48]Clapp Committee, *Testimony*, I, 112–113, 504.

[49]Pringle, *Roosevelt*, 452–453, pointing to Roosevelt's 1908 release of his 1904 correspondence with Harriman. By omitting earlier letters between the two men and by dropping a phrase from one of his letters when he released the documents, Roosevelt made it appear as though he were merely consenting to see Harriman at the financier's request, whereas, in fact, Roosevelt had proffered the invitation. Also critical of Roosevelt are George Kennan, *E. H. Harriman* (2 vols., Boston, 1922), II, chaps. 25 and 26, and Matthew Josephson, *The President Makers* (reprint ed., New York, 1964), 165. Morison, *Roosevelt Letters*, IV, 979n, surmised that "there is reason to suspect that Roosevelt did not commit himself as firmly as Harriman said he had."

[50]Virtually the only figures available on Republican campaign expenses before 1900 were printed in C. G. Dawes, *Journal* (1950), 389–390, which relied upon a letter from Cornelius Bliss to Harry New, June 6, 1908. The veteran Republican treasurer recalled the G.O.P. expenditures as being $1,700,000 in 1892, $3,450,000 in 1896, slightly below $3,000,000 in 1900, and $2,096,000 in 1904. Ford, "Cortelyou," 126.

[51]John D. Archbold, August 23, 1912, in Clapp Committee, *Testimony*, I, 133; Morison, *Roosevelt Letters*, IV, 996n. For other rejections of the "blackmail" charge, see Ford, "Cortelyou," 140–141; John M. Blum, *The Republican Roosevelt* (New York, 1954), 69.

[52]*Congressional Record*, 58th Cong., 3rd Sess. (December 6, 1904), XXXIX, 17; *ibid.*, 59th Cong., 1st Sess. (December 5, 1905), XL, 96.

[53]Act of January 26, 1907, U.S. *Statutes at Large*, XXXIV, 864; *Congressional Record*,

60th Cong., 1st Sess. (December 3, 1907), XLII, 78; Act of June 25, 1910, amended August 19, 1911, U.S. *Statutes at Large*, XXXVI, 822; Louise Overacker and Victor J. West, *Money in Elections,* (New York, 1932), 236; Herbert E. Alexander, *Money in Politics* (Washington D.C., 1972), 199.

[54]Roosevelt to Charles J. Bonaparte, November 4, 1907, in Morison, *Roosevelt Letters,* V, 830–831.

[55]Elbert Gary to Elihu Root, November 7, 1907; Root to Gary, November 13, 1907; both in the Elihu Root Papers, quoted in Mowry, *Era of Theodore Roosevelt,* 218–219.

[56]U.S. House, Committee on Investigation of United States Steel Corporation [chaired by Augustus O. Stanley], *United States Steel Corporation, Hearings . . . May 27, 1911–April 13, 1912,* 62nd Cong., 2nd Sess. (8 vols., Washington, D.C. 1911–1912), June 2, 1911, pt. 3, 139; June 7, 1911, pt. 4, 167. Hereafter referred to as Stanley Committee, *U.S. Steel Hearings.*

[57]*The Commoner,* November 15, 22, 1908; W. J. Bryan to Roosevelt, September 26, 1908, in Paolo Coletta, *William Jennings Bryan* (3 vols., Lincoln, Neb., 1964–1969), I, 393, 421; Roosevelt to W. J. Bryan, September 27, 1908, in Morison, *Roosevelt Letters,* VI, 1260–1261, 1481n.

[58]Roosevelt to the Senate, January 6, 1909, in U.S. Senate, *Absorption of the Tennessee Coal & Iron Co. Views of Messrs. Culberson . . . together with the Hearings . . . ,* 60th Cong., 2nd Sess., 1909, Report 1110, pt. 2, reprinted in Stanley Committee, *Hearings,* 1121–1122. The inquiry to the Attorney General was authorized by *Senate Resolution 240,* 60th Cong., 2nd Sess., 1909.

[59]*Ibid.,* 1159–1162; Roosevelt to Kermit Roosevelt, January 23, 1909, in Morison, *Roosevelt Letters,* VI, 1481.

[60]Morison, *Roosevelt Letters,* VI, 1481n.

[61]U.S. Senate, *Absorption of the Tennessee Coal & Iron Co.,* reprinted in Stanley Committee, *Hearings,* 1121–1143, the quotation is from 1135. Three members of the five-man subcommittee, Senators Charles A. Culberson, A. B. Kittredge, and Lee S. Overman, were joined by Senator Isidor Rayne when they submitted their views on March 2, 1909. More limited concurring opinions were filed by Senators A. O. Bacon, Knute Nelson, and Joseph B. Foraker.

[62]Morison, *Roosevelt Letters,* VI, 1481n.

[63]Stanley Committee, *U.S. Steel: Hearings,* II, 1123, 1391–1392.

[64]Morison, *Roosevelt Letters,* VII, 429n.

[65]Theodore Roosevelt, "The Trusts, the People, and the Square Deal," *Outlook,* XCIX (November 18, 1911), 649; Mowry, *Era of Theodore Roosevelt,* 291. See also Roosevelt to Everett P. Wheeler, and Roosevelt to James Garfield, both on October 30, 1911, in Morison, *Roosevelt Letters,* VII, 429–431.

[66]U.S. House Committee on Investigation of U.S. Steel Corporation, 62nd Cong., 2nd Sess., 1912, Report 1127, pt. 1, 206–212, the quotation is from 207.

[67]"Minority Report" by Representative August P. Gardner, *ibid.,* pt. 2, especially 6, 58–65. The District Court's opinion is quoted in Bishop, *Roosevelt,* II, 58.

[68]*U.S. v. United States Steel Corp.,* 251 U.S. 416 (1920). Regarding the President's action in connection with the acquisition, the Court held, "His approval, of course, did not make it legal, but it gives assurance of its legality, and we know from his earnestness in the public welfare he would have approved of nothing that had even a tendency to its detriment."

[69]Morison, *Roosevelt Letters,* V, 830–831n, VII, 321–322n, 429–430n; see also Roosevelt, *Autobiography,* 477–483, 607–609, and Bishop, *Roosevelt,* II, 56–59. Mowry, *Era of Theodore Roosevelt,* 218–219, 288–290, provided a detailed account but avoided

making judgments. John A. Garraty, *Right-Hand Man: The Life of George W. Perkins* (New York, 1960), 210–214, 248–249, also eschewed evaluation but implied that Roosevelt's action ended the panic.

[70]Critical historians include Pringle, *Roosevelt*, 444–445, 552; Robert H. Wiebe, "The House of Morgan and the Executive, 1905–1913," *American Historical Review*, LXV (October, 1959), 55–56; Harbaugh, *Roosevelt*, 298–301, 380–381; Gabriel Kolko, *The Triumph of Conservatism: A Reinterpretation of American History, 1900–1916* (Chicago, 1963), 37–38, 114–117, 170–171; and Coletta, *Bryan*, I, 393.

[71]Hermann Hagedorn, ed., *The Works of Theodore Roosevelt* (24 vols., New York, 1924–1926), XVII, 620–621. The Secret Service, which had increased from 1,200 to 1,900 under Roosevelt, took on enforcement of the Pure Food and Meat Inspection, and of Safety Appliances laws, protection of the public land and timber, and the investigations by the Bureau of Corporations.

[72]*Congressional Record*, 60th Cong., 2nd Sess., 1909, 373–375, 615, 719–739, 1167–1168, 3121–3136, 3795–3801, 5554–5559; *Inquiry Pursuant to Resolution Authorizing Investigation of Secret Service . . . ,* 60th Cong., 2nd Sess., 1909, Senate Report 970, ser. 5383; *Hearings before Subcommittee of House Committee on Appropriations*, 60th Cong., 2nd Sess., House Report 2205, I, 126, 185–193, 773–781; U.S. *Statutes at Large*, 60th Cong., 2nd Sess., pt. 1, 1014.

[73]Willard B. Gatewood, Jr., "The Secret Service Controversy," in Gatewood, *Theodore Roosevelt and the Art of Controversy: Episodes of the White House Years* (Baton Rouge, 1970), 236–287, especially 256. See also Harbaugh, *Roosevelt*, 344–345, and Morison, *Roosevelt Letters*, VI, 1019n, 1424–1425n, 1460n.

WILLIAM HOWARD TAFT
1909–1913

John W. Chambers

Fearful that natural resources were dwindling and confident in the management abilities of national government experts, Theodore Roosevelt had launched an extensive conservation program during his second administration. Reversing the traditional federal policy of opening up public lands to private development as quickly as they were claimed and settled, Roosevelt removed millions of acres from public entry on the theory that regulated access would provide more efficient utilization of the nation's resources.

Part of the program involved the removal of hundreds of thousands of acres of coal land in Alaska and was contested by local claimants. Among those petitioning for exemption from this action was Clarence Cunningham, the head of a Seattle group which had acquired some 5,000 acres of coal land along the Bering River since 1902. A dispute over the petition erupted in 1907 in the General Land Office between the commissioner, Richard A. Ballinger, former reform mayor of Seattle, and twenty-four-year-old Louis R. Glavis, who was investigating the legitimacy of the claims. The young man considered the claims illegal, but he was overruled by his superior. However, Secretary of the Interior James Garfield, who agreed with Glavis, rescinded the approval and continued the investigation. During 1908 Ballinger retired to resume his law practice and to head the Taft campaign in the state of Washington. In the spring of 1909, President William Howard Taft appointed him as his first secretary of the interior.

When Ballinger returned to head the department, the earlier conflict with Glavis smoldered and then erupted as part of a larger clash between the policies of westerners, like Ballinger, who favored rapid distribution of public lands to private entrepreneurs in mining, lumbering, ranching, and farming, and eastern conservationists, like Chief Forester Gifford Pinchot. By 1909 Glavis had become convinced that the Cunningham claimants were guilty of collusion and fraud and were secretly acting on behalf of the Morgan-Guggenheim mining syndicate, the most powerful economic interest group in Alaska. He also believed the claims impinged on a national forest preserve which came under the jurisdiction of Pinchot's Forest Service. Glavis was partly right. A later investigation disclosed a contract dated July 20, 1907, between the two groups under which David Guggenheim agreed to purchase half-interest in the Cunningham claims. However, in the summer of 1909 before the document was discovered, Ballinger curtailed the investigation and sought to hold a hearing on the petition as soon as possible. Glavis, who was removed from the case, determined that the department was seeking to avoid starting criminal prosecution against the claimants. In July, 1909, he appealed over his superiors' heads to Pinchot's bureau in the Department of Agriculture to delay the hearings and continue the investigation. On August 9 Glavis told Pinchot that Ballinger, his land commissioner, Fred Dennett, and several other Land Office employees were guilty of official misconduct, including collusion with fraudulent land claimants.

Already critical of Ballinger for his attacks on the legality and wisdom of the Roosevelt administration's conservation policy, Pinchot accepted Glavis's accusations, wrote a letter of endorsement, adding some concerns of his own, and sent the investigator to the President. On August 18, 1909, Glavis called on William Howard Taft at the vacation White House in Beverly, Massachusetts. In a fifty-page report, Glavis noted that Ballinger was a personal friend of many of the Cunningham claimants, that he had clear-listed the claims in 1907 despite Glavis's assertion that they were illegal, that he prevented a full investigation of their legitimacy, and that he was in an undue hurry to have the hearing before Glavis thought the government's case was ready. Glavis's most damaging assertion was that in 1908, between the time he resigned as commissioner of the Land Office and was appointed secretary of the interior, Ballinger had acted as an attorney for the Cunningham claimants before the Land Office. Glavis cited this as evidence of Ballinger's bias.

It was only later that he learned of an 1873 statute which prohibited former government employees from representing claimants for a fee before the agencies by whom they had been employed.[1]

The President on August 22 sent copies of the charges to Ballinger and the others accused and asked for their responses. On September 6 the Secretary of the Interior delivered a thousand-page explanation and rebuttal to the President. After looking over the documents, Taft turned them over to Attorney General George Wickersham for investigation and analysis. On September 11 Wickersham returned to Beverly and discussed the matter with the President during the next three days. On September 13 the Chief Executive sent a thirteen-page letter to Ballinger and the others exonerating them from what he called Glavis's ill-founded accusations. At the same time, the President ordered Glavis be dismissed "for disloyalty to his superior officers in making a false charge against them. . . ."[2]

Glavis and Pinchot carried the accusations to a larger audience. With the help of members of the Forester's staff, Glavis wrote an article which appeared in *Collier's Weekly* in November. The next issue contained a scathing editorial condemning the Morgan-Guggenheim interests and suggesting that Taft had been deceived into "whitewashing Ballinger." Other muckraking magazines such as *Hampton's* and *McClure's* took up the campaign. On January 5, 1910, Pinchot broke with the administration. In a letter to Senator Jonathan P. Dolliver, which was read in the Senate, Pinchot praised Glavis as "the most vigorous defender of the people's interests." He admitted that some of his own staff members had supplied information against Ballinger and his policies to the press, but he defended their actions as being motivated by "a high and unselfish sense of public duty. . . ."[3] Pinchot hoped his action would force the President to dismiss him, thus focusing public attention on the issue and freeing him to make a full-scale attack upon Ballinger's reversal of the Roosevelt-Pinchot conservation program. He was not disappointed. On January 7 Taft ordered the Forester removed from office because of his "improper appeal to Congress and the public."

A special joint committee of senators and representatives was authorized on January 19 to begin an inquiry into the charges of Ballinger's alleged misconduct. The Secretary of the Interior had requested it in an attempt to clear his name, and the President had supported him. The case received widespread press coverage during the forty-five days of hearings between January 26 and May 20, 1910.

The most sensational aspect of the hearings was the discovery that members of the administration had predated one important document, dealing with Glavis's dismissal, and attempted to suppress another. The brilliant advocate Louis D. Brandeis, who had been hired by *Collier's Weekly* to represent Glavis, made the revelations. Studying the chronology of events, Brandeis suspected that Taft had not given adequate attention to the mass of documents that had been presented to him by Glavis and the men he accused. The President had sent to the Senate on January 6 the documents "upon which he acted in reaching his conclusions" on the charges and in writing his letter of September 13, 1909, exonerating Ballinger and dismissing Glavis.[4] Among the materials submitted by the Chief Executive were Glavis's documented allegations, detailed replies from Ballinger and his subordinates (717 printed pages), plus an eighty-seven-page memorandum summarizing and analyzing this material prepared by the Attorney General for Taft's use. The Wickersham Memorandum was dated September 11, 1909. That was only five days after Ballinger had delivered his briefcase load of documents and rebuttals to Taft, on September 6. Brandeis correctly concluded that the Attorney General could not have read all the material and prepared such a detailed and polished summary in such a brief period.

Brandeis's suspicions were confirmed by a private stenographer from the Interior Department who confided to him that Ballinger had been accompanied to Beverly on September 6 by Oscar Lawler, an assistant attorney general in the Interior Department, who was asked by the President at the meeting to prepare an opinion. Lawler, a loyal supporter of Ballinger, returned to Washington and in the Secretary's own office wrote a memorandum exonerating his friend. Lawler even incorporated suggestions from the Interior Secretary in the final draft which he gave to the Attorney General, who delivered it to Taft on September 11. Aware that the Lawler Memorandum had been omitted by the government, Brandeis tried repeatedly to require the Attorney General to forward all the documents involved in the case to the Senate. When the chairman of the House Judiciary Committee added his request for information, Wickersham claimed executive privilege and continued to withhold the controversial Lawler Memorandum. Yet he admitted that his summary had not been written until after the President's decision of September 13, 1909 (Taft acknowledged receipt of it on October 28), and had been predated September 11. However, the Attorney General insisted that this later summary was based upon documents and rough notes which had been in the President's possession when he acted upon the charges.[5]

Continuing his hunt for the elusive Lawler Memorandum, Brandeis cross-examined Ballinger on May 13, 1910. The Secretary could not remember what the document said, even though he admitted having read it and approved it. He denied that the memorandum had played a significant role, although he reluctantly conceded that Lawler had prepared a résumé for the President before the Chief Executive made his decision.[6] Backed at last by the Joint Committee, Brandeis asked the administration directly for the Lawler Memorandum. The Attorney General sent it to the committee chairman the next day with the explanation that it had been in the files all the time, but had not been submitted previously because "it seems to have been overlooked in collecting papers in answer to your previous communications."[7]

On May 15, 1910, President Taft finally elaborated on the basis for his decision in the Glavis case. In a letter to the committee chairman, he admitted that he had asked Lawler to "prepare an opinion as if he were president." But he said that he had been disappointed in the thirty-page document when it arrived in Beverly on September 11. It was too critical of Pinchot as well as Glavis, and Taft said he had used only a few general paragraphs from it. He insisted that his conclusions about Ballinger were

based on my reading of the record and were fortified by the oral analysis of the evidence and the conclusions which the Attorney General gave me during his visit [between September 11 and 13]. I was very sorry not to be able to embody this analysis in my opinion but time did not permit [Taft was scheduled to leave on a long western trip in a week]. I therefore directed him to embody in a written statement such analysis and conclusions as he had given me, file it with the record, and date it prior to the date of my opinion, so as to show that my decision was fortified by his summary of the evidence and his conclusions therefrom.[8]

Thus as finally admitted by the administration, the complete chronology of events in the summer of 1909 had occurred as follows:

Aug.   18   Glavis's charges given to Taft.

Aug.   22   President sent charges to Ballinger to answer.

Sept.   6   Ballinger delivered his rebuttal and evidence to Taft.

Sept. 11   Attorney General Wickersham brought Lawler Memorandum and other notes to Taft and discussed the matter with the President for three days.

Sept. 13   Taft wrote letter exonerating Ballinger and directing that Glavis be dismissed.

Oct.   28   Taft acknowledged receipt of Wickersham Memorandum, predated September 11.

Administration stalwarts in Congress had maintained control of the selection of the investigating committee, which was headed by Senator Knute Nelson of Minnesota, one of Taft's chief legislative leaders, so its conclusion was virtually predetermined.[9] The seven regular Republicans issued the majority report, which exonerated Ballinger, endorsed his land-use politics, and recommended that the Cunningham coal claims be granted. The four Democrats and an insurgent Kansas Republican sustained Glavis's charges and condemned the Secretary of the Interior.[10]

Although the administration won its case before the committee, it lost it before much of the country. The progressive magazines were almost unanimous in their opposition to Taft and Ballinger during the controversy and so was much of the press. Thousands of progressives rallied around Pinchot, who became for a time one of the most popular men in America. Despite increasing pressure for his resignation, Ballinger remained in the cabinet with Taft's support for nearly a year. When Ballinger stepped down on March 7, 1911 (as much over policy differences as a result of pressure for his resignation), Taft publicly endorsed him but selected an ardent conservationist, Walter L. Fisher, as his successor. Within a few months, the new secretary directed the cancellation of the Cunningham claims.

Over half a century of research and analysis has produced both consensus and disagreement over various aspects of one of the most emotional *causes célèbres* in American history. Partisanship of some degree has almost always played a part as each generation has reargued the Ballinger-Pinchot controversy.[11] On some issues, however, the advocates of both sides have reached agreement. In recent years, few consider that Richard Ballinger and the Taft administration were guilty of actual fraud or corruption, as many progressives once did. Indisputably, the connection between the Morgan-Guggenheim syndicate and the Cunningham claimants has been proven, but there has been no evidence that the Secretary of the Interior was aware of such proof at that time. Certainly, Ballinger did violate a governmental regulation when, as a former employee, he represented the Cunningham claimants before the General Land Office in 1908. Yet his sympathizers excuse this as a relatively minor infraction involving only a $250 fee.[12] Most historians and biographers question some aspect of the conduct of the major administration figures in the episode, but some also criticize Glavis and Pinchot for insubordination and exaggeration. One recent historian condemned the press for conducting a trial by newspaper that was comparable to a "smear" campaign against the administration.[13] Some historians have sought to abandon traditional descriptions of the controversy as a struggle between personalities and to view it instead as a conflict between officials trying to carry out two different kinds of resource policy and also between two opposing forces within the Republican Party in the early twentieth century.[14]

To various degrees, virtually all historians have been critical of President Taft's role in the Ballinger-Pinchot controversy. The most severe have questioned his judgment in several matters: in asking an assistant attorney general who was also one of Ballinger's friends to prepare a brief, in not allowing Glavis a chance to reply to Ballinger's rebuttal and charges against him, and in attempting to conceal the Lawler Memorandum and predating the Wickersham Memorandum. They also find fault with his underestimate of the seriousness of the dispute (until late September Taft considered it merely an interdepartmental squabble) and his failure to realize the larger issues of conservation and political policy involved.[15]

Even scholars sympathetic to Taft admit that the President "mishandled" the affair. However, they deny any malice or disingenuousness on his part. Instead, they view Taft as a political blunderer, unconcerned about public opinion, which he considered ill-informed on the issue, waiting too long in dismissing Pinchot and in responding to the charges of predating the Wickersham Memorandum, and reluctant to launch a counterattack against his opponents. He took, they contend, a narrow view of the president's powers, and he was sometimes more concerned with legal points than with the political power of his administration. Having determined that his Secretary of the Interior was innocent, Taft refused to sacrifice him for political gain. "If I were to turn Ballinger out, in view of his innocence and in view of the conspiracy against him," Taft confided to a friend, "I should be a white-livered skunk. I don't care how it affects my administration and how it affects the administration before the people; if the people are so unjust as this I don't propose to be one of them."[16] Long after Ballinger had become a political liability, Taft stood by him out of a sense of justice.

Dr. Harvey Wiley and the Manipulation of a Salary, 1911–1912

A year after the Ballinger-Pinchot controversy, another incident threatened to explode in the nation's headlines, but this time President Taft averted political disaster while sustaining justice. In April, 1911, a personnel committee of the U.S. Department of Agriculture decided that Dr. Harvey W. Wiley, chief chemist of the Food and Drug Administration, and two other government employees had conspired to violate the law by hiring a chemical expert for a full year rather than on a per diem basis as required by statute. The committee charged that the expert had been hired for $1,600 a year to cloak a secret agreement to pay him $20 a day in deliberate defiance of the $9 statutory limit. It recommended that he be dismissed, that the chief of the Drug Division be demoted, and that Dr. Wiley and the assistant chief chemist be given the opportunity to resign.

Secretary of Agriculture James Wilson endorsed the recommendation at a cabinet meeting, and Attorney General George Wickersham approved the suggestion on May 13 after reviewing the case. However, President Taft delayed action until July 7, when he instructed Secretary Wilson to show the Attorney General's conclusions to the accused and give them a chance to make a full defense. A few days later, the story broke in the press, and the supporters of the popular Dr. Wiley, considered by many to be the chief protector of America's health, rallied to his aid. On September 14 the President overruled the Attorney General's opinion as based upon insufficient evidence, and personally expressed sympathy for Dr. Wiley's efforts to obtain expert assistance for law enforcement. A House investigating committee concurred in a report of January 22, 1912, and the charges against the men were dropped.[17]

NOTES

[1]Glavis's charges are recorded in U.S. Senate, *Investigation of the Department of the Interior and of the Bureau of Forestry*, 61st Cong., 3rd Sess. (13 vols., Washington, D.C., 1911), Senate Document 719, II, 4–62. These volumes, ser. 5892–5903, are hereafter referred to as Senate, *Investigation*. The most detailed recent accounts of the Ballinger-Pinchot controversy, published since the Ballinger papers were made available in the early 1960s, are Elmo R. Richardson, *The Politics of Conservation: Crusades and Controversies, 1897–1913* (Berkeley, 1962); James Penick, Jr., *Progressive Politics and Conservation: The Ballinger-Pinchot Affair* (Chicago, 1969); Paolo E. Coletta, *The Presidency of William Howard Taft* (Lawrence, Kan., 1973).

[2]Senate, *Investigation*, IV, 1187–1189.

[3]*Ibid.*, IV, 1283–1285.

[4]*Ibid.*, II, 3.

[5]*Ibid.*, VII, 4139; VIII, 4395–4397, 4416–4417, 4455–4458, 4507–4524.

[6]*Ibid.*, VII, 3862–3869.

[7]*Ibid.*, VII, 4364.

[8]*Ibid.*, VIII, 4393–4394.

[9]M. Nelson McGeary, *Gifford Pinchot: Forester-Politician* (Princeton, 1960), 181.

[10]Senate, *Investigation*, I.

[11]Those sympathetic to Pinchot and Glavis have included Rose Stahl, "The Ballinger-Pinchot Controversy," in *Smith College Studies in History*, XI (Northampton, Mass., 1926), 65–126; Alpheus T. Mason, *Bureaucracy Convicts Itself: The Ballinger-Pinchot Controversy of 1910* (New York, 1941); George Mowry, *Theodore Roosevelt and the Progressive Movement* (Madison, Wis., 1946); Gifford Pinchot, *Breaking New Ground* (New York, 1947); and McGeary, *Gifford Pinchot*. Those sympathetic to Ballinger and Taft have included Henry F. Pringle, *The Life and Times of William Howard Taft* (2 vols., New York, 1939); John T. Ganoe, "Some Constitutional and Political Aspects of the Ballinger-Pinchot Controversy," *Pacific Historical Review*, III (1934), 323–333; Harold Ickes, "Not Guilty: Richard A. Ballinger," *Saturday Evening Post*, May 25, 1940; Ickes, *Not Guilty: An Official Inquiry into the Charges Made by Glavis and Pinchot*

against Richard A. Ballinger, Secretary of the Interior, 1909–1911 (Washington, D.C., 1940); Penick, *Progressive Politics.*

[12]Coletta, *Presidency of Taft,* 90; Pringle, *Taft,* I, 500–501.

[13]Ickes, *Not Guilty;* Penick, *Progressive Politics,* 163–164.

[14]Samuel P. Hays, *Conservation and the Gospel of Efficiency: The Progressive Conservation Movement, 1890–1920* (Cambridge, Mass., 1959); Richardson, *The Politics of Conservation;* Penick, *Progressive Politics;* see also Lawrence Rakestraw, "Conservation Historiography: An Assessment," *Pacific Historical Review,* XLI (August, 1972), 271–288.

[15]Mason, *Bureaucracy Convicts Itself,* 178–200; McGeary, *Gifford Pinchot,* 181–189.

[16]Taft to P. A. Baker, May 21, 1910, Taft Papers, in Donald F. Anderson, *William Howard Taft: A Conservative's Conception of the Presidency* (Ithaca, 1973), 76. For sympathetic views of Taft, see *ibid.,* 72–78; Coletta, *Presidency of Taft,* 98–100; Pringle, *Taft,* I, 491, 494, 504, 511–514.

[17]"Expenditures in the Department of Agriculture," *Hearings,* 1911; "Expenditures in the Department of Agriculture," 62nd Cong., 2nd Sess., 1912, *House Report 249;* Oscar E. Anderson, Jr., *The Health of a Nation: Harvey W. Wiley and the Fight for Pure Food* (Chicago, 1958), 243–250.

WOODROW WILSON
1913–1921

John W. Chambers

Compared to the two preceding administrations, Woodrow Wilson's government was relatively untouched by any major scandal involving its highest officeholders. However, during the first two years that the Democrats were in the White House, several comparatively minor incidents involving new appointees caused some embarrassment. Subsequently, somewhat larger episodes would develop, especially with respect to conduct of the war.

The Caminetti-Diggs Affair of 1913

On June 20, 1913, the Federal District Attorney in San Francisco resigned with a public telegram to the President accusing Attorney General James McReynolds of "yielding to influence" in delaying a federal prosecution under the Mann Act. At the urging of Labor Secretary William B. Wilson, McReynolds had postponed the trial of two young Californians, Drew Caminetti and Maury I. Diggs, because Caminetti's father, the new head of the Immigration Service, was needed in Washington to reorganize his bureau. Republicans urged a congressional investigation, and even the nation's leading Democratic journal suggested that the Attorney General resign. Though admitting privately that the cabinet officers had made a serious mistake, the President publicly defended McReynolds's judgment and integrity. On June 23 he ordered the Justice Department to press the trial "with the utmost diligence and energy." The controversy soon died away when it became clear that the young men would be prosecuted despite the prominence of Caminetti's father. They were convicted and imprisoned in 1917.[1]

William Jennings Bryan and Lectures for Profit, 1913–1914

Despite his appointment as secretary of state in 1913, William Jennings Bryan continued his annual summer lecture series for profit on the Chautauqua circuit. The spectacle of the head of the U.S. State Department leaving Washington on alternate weeks between July 15 and September 20 to give his stock speeches in the company of acrobats and vaudeville performers under the big tent led to a major controversy. The criticism which began in July was most vociferous among eastern newspapers and journals and Republican members of Congress. The Secretary of State was chastised for unprofessional conduct which demeaned his high office and for violation of ethics by spending so long a period away from his official duties in order to enrich himself.[2]

Bryan retorted that his cabinet salary of $12,000 a year was inadequate to support him and to pay his expenses which, including insurance premiums and contributions to schools, charities, and churches, came to almost $7,000, approximately what he earned during a lecture season. The President had given Bryan permission beforehand on the condition that he would receive only his share of receipts from season tickets and that no charge would be levied upon others who wished to hear him. Despite the attacks, the President held fast to his position and allowed the Secretary of State to tour the circuit in the summers of 1913 and 1914.[3]

U.S. Minister to the Dominican Republic, 1913–1915

In December, 1913, the *New York Times* and other newspapers reported that the U.S. minister to the Dominican Republic, James M. Sullivan, was suspected of misusing his position by transferring deposits collected by the American receiver general from Dominican customs into a bank whose owner had helped obtain Sullivan's appointment. The minister's brother, a contractor, was reportedly receiving a large share of the government's construction contracts. A few days later, Secretary of State Bryan defended his appointee and called the criticism entirely unjustified.[4]

The following year, however, Sullivan became the center of a public scandal. In March, 1914, Walter Vick, the receiver general of Customs, took his accusations to both the Secretary of State and the President, but they would neither investigate nor recall Sullivan. Frustrated, Vick went to the New York *World,* which after conducting its own investigation ran a series of articles in early December alleging that Sullivan had corrupt connection with local banks and construction companies. Forced into action, Wilson on December 8, 1914, ordered an investigation into the charges.[5]

Bryan appointed Senator-elect James D. Phelan (D–Calif.), a friend of the administration, to head the inquiry. His report, acquitting Sullivan of charges of intemperance and graft, acknowledged that his diplomatic appointment had indeed been arranged primarily by several New Yorkers who were financially interested in Dominican affairs, especially the bank on the island to which Sullivan had transferred the customs receipts after his appointment. The report, which had been submitted in May, 1915, was not published until July 21, after the New York *World* had suggested the report was being suppressed by the administration.[6]

Under pressure from the President, who may also have been disturbed by the minister's intervention in island politics, Sullivan resigned July 8, 1915, some two weeks before the Phelan report was released to the press.[7] Up to the end, Wilson continued to believe that Sullivan had been "very foolish rather than anything worse." But Bryan surmised "that we were deceived as to the interests which supported Mr. Sullivan's candidacy."[8] Arthur S. Link has concluded that the extent to which Sullivan profited financially from his position and his friendship with the Dominican president remains unknown, but since Sullivan's cousin received a large share of the government's construction contracts, it is not inconceivable that the minister himself may have also been the recipient of favorable treatment.[9]

Secretary of the Interior Franklin K. Lane, 1916–1920

Differences over natural resources policy between easterners and westerners, which helped to fuel the Ballinger-Pinchot controversy during the Taft administration, generated another heated, if less extreme, confrontation during President Wilson's years in the White House. Once again, the conservationist forces assailed a secretary of the interior from the West who favored making governmental mineral resources more readily available to private entrepreneurs.

At issue was the policy of Secretary of the Interior Franklin K. Lane, a former San Francisco lawyer and civic reformer, who favored opening up government oil lands. In 1916 Lane supported proposals endorsed by western oil companies to validate claims to petroleum rights within the government's Elk Hills, California, reserves. He also endorsed plans for relief for oil operators already producing oil in the California naval reserves under claims made improperly but in good faith. Lane's efforts were blocked by the Secretary of the Navy and eastern conservationists, but not before a bitter dispute had ensued. Gifford Pinchot launched the assault in July by publicly accusing Lane of lying and of betraying the cause of conservation.[10] The New York *Herald* joined in by publishing a series of articles seeking to show that the Secretary was in collusion with the oil operators.[11]

Charges of misconduct against Lane were raised again two years later by a government officer during an interagency fight between the Interior and Justice Departments. In the so-called Kearful Affair in February, 1918, Assistant Attorney General Francis J. Kearful testified before the House Committee on Public Lands that he believed the Secretary of the Interior would permit leases in cases "where charges of fraud had been made and without [further] investigation."[12]

Historians have differed in their assessment of Franklin K. Lane, his conservation policy, his relationship to the oil companies, and his integrity. Some have been severely critical. John Ise suggested that Lane was "one of the most dangerous men that have ever held the office of Secretary of the Interior because, while he was working persistently to promote the ends of exploiting interests, he was writing articles on conservation, and in general preserving an attitude of impenetrable sincerity and respectability."[13] Other scholars have been more sympathetic. J. Leonard Bates concluded that there was no evidence that Lane was dishonest or lacking in integrity. Instead, Bates believed Lane was a man of poor judgment; he cited the Secretary's acceptance of a $50,000-a-year job with the Doheny oil interests when he left the Wilson administration early in 1920 as proof of this. Bates asserted that Lane's views had been determined by geography rather than by corruption as he responded to the needs of his section of the country. Additionally, Arthur Link insisted that Lane's oil proposals should be put in perspective and that his overall achievements provided a sizable contribution to the cause of wise conservation.[14]

World War I Mobilization and Conflict of Interest

The dramatic expansion of governmental activity and spending during the mobilization of America's resources during World War I provided many possibilities for misconduct and corruption, but with the exception of the Alien Property Custodian's Office, relatively few actual instances of malfeasance occurred.[15]

In its plans for wartime economic mobilization, the Wilson administration decided to employ business volunteers to aid the government in coordinating American production during the 1917–1918 emergency. Before the United States declaration of war, businessmen served only as part-time consultants to the Council of National Defense, but after April, 1917, as the United States moved to a war footing, several hundred came to work full-time in Washington either without compensation or as "dollar-a-year" men on leave, but still on salary, from their companies. Though many praised the businessmen for their patriotism, others were more critical of the arrangement. A number of southern Democrats and Republican progressives in Congress served as the major source of criticism of the advisory committees and the opportunities they created for a dollar-a-year man to recommend a contract to the government as an industry adviser, and then to accept the recommendation in his governmental capacity. Senator Kenneth McKellar of Tennessee made specific charges of actual misconduct through the letting of contracts to favorites and relatives at exorbitant fees.[16] Senator James K. Vardaman of Mississippi alleged that some men had used their official positions to enrich themselves.[17] However, such specific allegations of malfeasance were rare.

Much more common was the concern that companies with representatives in the government's war agencies would benefit unfairly because of their connection with "insiders." Senator James A. Reed of Missouri launched a blistering attack upon Arthur V. Davis, who served simultaneously as chairman of the government's Advisory Commission's aluminum committee and president of the Aluminum Company of America, for ruling on contracts made between the government and his firm. According to the *Washington Post,* the organizational arrangement "lends itself to favoritism, overcharge, and graft. . . ."[18] Senator Lawrence Y. Sherman accused Howard D. Coffin, vice president of Hudson Motor Car Company and chairman of a subcommittee on automotive transport, of limiting farm machinery manufacturers to less than 50% of the sheet steel supply they needed, while allowing the automobile industry supply to remain unrestricted.[19]

The president and his subordinates defended the businessmen from such imputations. The business advisers, Wilson wrote to Senator McKellar, provided essential information and cooperation for the government's mobilization program. In the forthcoming reorganization of the war agencies, he asserted, they would not be connected with either the initiation or the conclusion of contracts.[20] Despite extensive lobbying the administration was unable to defeat an amendment to the Lever Act of August 10, 1917, which made it illegal for a government agent or employee, including agency advisers, to contract for supplies in which he was financially interested.[21] It was able, however, to prevent a more drastic proposal by Senator McKellar in January, 1918, which would have taken mobilization out of the hands of the dollar-a-year men altogether and given it to fully compensated government employees. Attempting to deal with the conflict-of-interest issue through reform rather than rejection of the business volunteer program, the War Industries Board in June, 1918, adopted a resolution requiring its members to file declarations of all their business connections and financial interests. But the business members of the agency were not required to resign from their companies while working for the government.

The most serious charges of actual misconduct were raised against officials in the government's aircraft production program, and included accusations of deception, corruption, and attempted cover-up. In part, they stemmed from disappointment when the government failed to fulfill its exaggerated promise in the spring of 1917 to provide an air force of 100,000 planes (the War Department later trimmed this goal to 22,000) to smash German defenses and reduce the need for costly infantry assaults. Despite large doses of publicity and public funds, the program flopped.[22]

Charges of inefficiency and corruption in the program put the administration under increasing pressure for an investigation and corrective measures. As early as November, 1917, Gutzon Borglum, a sculptor, aviator, and acquaintance of Wilson, warned the President of the failure and blamed it on an automobile manufacturers' conspiracy to prevent the growth of a competitive aircraft industry. In response, the Chief Executive gave Borglum a free hand to investigate and make recommendations. However, the President and Secretary of War suppressed Borglum's preliminary report of January 21, 1918, when it blamed the program's failure on the dishonesty of prominent industrialists. But the sculptor-aviator only intensified his efforts. Two months later he publicly assailed the program for squandering $840,000,000 without producing a single combat aircraft. Blaming speculators using their government jobs for profit, he accused Colonel Edward A. Deeds, head of the aircraft program in the Signal Corps Equipment Division, of giving enormous contracts to men without any connection with aircraft production, solely because of their influence with him. These charges, together with revelations that some contracts had gone to mysterious companies with no existing plants, equipment, or capital, increased public suspicion of corruption and fraud.[23]

The administration responded by attempting to put its house in order. When a quasi-official inquiry by a New York lawyer and Democrat supported many of Borglum's charges, the President insisted upon a shake-up in the War Department and the Council of National Defense. Both the chief of the Army Signal Corps and the chairman of the Council's Aircraft Production Board (who was also the vice president of Hudson Motor Car Company) were removed from their positions on April 18. The President also jettisoned Borglum, who by mid-April had become an embarrassment to the administration. On May 2 the deposed investigator publicly accused high War Department officials of deliberate deception in trying to cover up what he called the shady practices of some private contractors. This was followed by an immediate public demand—from the press, the Aeronautical Society of America, and the Senate—for an investigation. On May 6 the President directed the Department of Justice to make a "searching inquiry" into every phase of the program. At the same time, he released to the press the documents he considered pertinent to the Borglum case.[24]

Borglum's charges of suppression of scandal had, however, made an internal investigation unacceptable. Suspecting a "whitewash," the Senate refused to condone one department investigating another. Instead, on May 10 it passed a resolution authorizing its Military Affairs Committee "to inquire into and report to the Senate the progress of aircraft production in the United States, or into any other matters relating to the conduct of the war."[25] Unable to defeat what he considered an authorization for a partisan and disruptive dragnet, the President outflanked his enemies on Capitol Hill. On the advice of his intimate adviser Colonel Edward House, the Chief Executive invited his Republican opponent in the 1916 presidential campaign to participate in the Justice Department probe. Assured that he would have an absolutely free hand in the search for evidence, Charles Evans Hughes, who was also a former justice of the Supreme Court and a former governor of New York, accepted on May 16. The administration also mollified Borglum by asking him to join the inquiry.[26]

During the summer of 1918, the Hughes investigation held its hearings in secret in order to avoid embarrassing the war effort or disclosing military secrets. After listening to 280 witnesses and taking 17,000 pages of testimony Hughes submitted his report, which was released by the President on October 31, 1918. Although he had discovered incompetence, confusion, a lack of central responsibility in the aircraft program, and some minor violations of the law, he disclosed no evidence of thievery or major corruption. Colonel Deeds had been cleared of major corruption or lawbreaking, but Hughes charged him with "reprehensible conduct" and recommended that he be disciplined through court-martial. Deeds, who had been head of United Motors Company, vice president of Dayton Metal Products Company, and a founder (although not a stockholder) of the Dayton Wright Aircraft Company, had served as a dollar-a-year adviser before being commissioned a colonel in charge of the Signal Corps aircraft program in 1918. Yet, according to the Hughes Report, Deeds had continued to act as a confidential adviser to his former business colleagues in Ohio despite his military appointment. In order to avoid criticism, he had also falsified his report to the Secretary of War in regard to his stockholdings in companies producing aircraft equipment. Furthermore, Hughes charged him with misleading the public about the progress of the aircraft production program.[27]

Although the President praised the Hughes Report, there was some criticism of it. Gutzon Borglum believed its author had been forced to suppress evidence derogatory to Henry Ford and his Liberty Motor program. Even greater criticism came from aircraft industry proponents after a special War Department review board exonerated Colonel Deeds in January, 1919.[28]

Beginning with the Sixty-sixth Congress in 1919, a number of Republican-controlled investigating committees scrutinized the records of the Council of National Defense, the War Industries Board, and the Aircraft Production Board seeking evidence of misconduct. Though they uncovered many instances of ignorance, error, and inefficiency in the government's economic mobilization program, the investigators found few and relatively unimportant evidences of malfeasance. Even though a House Committee called the procedure in Deeds's exoneration "astonishing and significant," it took no steps to reverse it. Generally, most historians agree that confusion plagued the mobilization, but they also conclude, as one recent commentator observed, that "despite the abandon with which money was spent, the war was conducted without major scandal, and, in the closing months, with increasing efficiency."[29]

Collusion and Fraud in the Office of the Alien Property Custodian

The major area of misconduct and corruption during World War I was the Alien Property Custodian's Office. However, the instances of wrongdoing were not revealed until the 1920s and therefore did not become a major scandal during the Wilson administration.

The Office of the Alien Property Custodian had been created in October, 1917, to take over and administer enemy-owned property in the United States. A. Mitchell Palmer, a Pennsylvania lawyer-banker and reform congressman, had been appointed to head the agency. Most of the criticism of Palmer's administration which arose in the 1920s was directed at the sale of German property to his friends and political associates as well as the alleged misconduct of some of his subordinates. The alien property custodian had obtained from Congress the power to dispose of enemy-owned property. After Palmer warned that German agents might buy companies which produced essential war goods if the firms were sold at public auction, the President on July 15, 1918, gave him the power to sell property worth less than $10,000 privately, without public announcement and bidding.[30]

Probing such sales under Palmer, subsequent Republican administrations exposed a number of scandals and in several cases initiated criminal proceedings. In 1922 Joseph Guffey, Palmer's director of sales, was accused of holding back both the sales proceeds and the interest earned by placing these funds in New York banks and of using the money to speculate on the stock market. He was indicted on twelve counts of embezzlement although the indictment was later quashed under suspicious circumstances.[31] Another scandal involved disposal of German property in the Philippine Islands, where the local manager of alien property had rigged the transactions so that the items went to a small group of friends. Learning of this, Palmer revoked the sales, and President Wilson supported his decision when it was appealed. However, when Palmer appointed a new agent in Manila, the man proceeded to approve the resale of the properties to the original purchasers. Although the Republicans in the 1920s uncovered abundant evidence of fraud, no one was ever brought to trial.[32]

Palmer himself was involved in two controversial episodes. In December, 1918, rumors began in the business world that the auction sale of Bosch Magneto Company, the largest producer of magnetos in the United States, had been rigged. The suspicions had been aroused when the firm was sold to a friend of Palmer's who owned a truck manufacturing company in Allentown, Pennsylvania. According to the biographer Stanley Coben, Palmer lied about the transaction in 1919 when he testified before a Senate committee holding hearings on his nomination as attorney general. Even though three officers of Bosch Magneto were charged in 1926 with defrauding the government, no indictments were obtained because the Justice Department was unable to prove that Palmer or any of his staff members had benefited from the sale. Forty years later Coben concluded that the original rumors had been correct; the sale had been improperly conducted.[33] In 1920 Palmer came under attack because of the disposal of more than 5,000 German chemical patents to a special independent, nonprofit corporation, the Chemical Foundation. The corporation had purchased the chemical patents from the Custodian's Office and licensed American producers to use them. Critics charged that Palmer had sold the patents too cheaply. In 1925

Coolidge's attorney general filed suit against the foundation, but the federal judiciary, including the Supreme Court of the United States, upheld the legitimacy of the transaction.[34]

In judging the record of the alien property custodian between 1917 and 1919, Palmer's biographer concluded that although evidence existed that he closed his eyes to the manipulation and dishonesty of some of his friends, the custodian himself seemed to have "walked successfully the fine line which separates the legal from the illegal."[35] During his administration, Woodrow Wilson, like the general public, had been unaware of most of these incidents. The President was, however, concerned about the possibility that the power of private sale granted by his executive order of July 15, 1918, might be misused. In a letter to the alien property custodian on September 4, 1918, the Chief Executive expressed his hope that Palmer would use it "in the most sparing manner and only where no other sort of sale is possible."[36]

NOTES

[1]Arthur S. Link, *Wilson: The New Freedom* (Princeton, 1956), 117–118.

[2]"Public Office and Public Duty," *Outlook*, CIV (July 26, 1913), 646–647; "Secretary Bryan and the Chautauqua Lectures: A Poll of the Press," *ibid.* (August 2, 1913), 746–748; "The Bryan Scandal," *Nation*, XCVII (September 18, 1913), 256–257.

[3]Paolo E. Coletta, *William Jennings Bryan* (3 vols., Lincoln, Neb., 1964–1969), II, 104–107; Link, *Wilson: The New Freedom*, 111–113.

[4]*New York Times,* December 10 and 12, 1913.

[5]New York *World*, December 7, 9, 10 and 11, 1914.

[6]*Ibid.,* July 27, 1915.

[7]Link, *Wilson: The New Freedom*, 107–109, 110n; Arthur S. Link, *Wilson: The Struggle for Neutrality, 1914–1915*, (Princeton, 1960), 511–512.

[8]Wilson to Robert Lansing, June 22, 1915; W. J. Bryan to Wilson, May 19, 1915, quoted in Link, *Wilson: The New Freedom*, 110.

[9]Arthur S. Link, *Woodrow Wilson and the Progressive Era*, (New York, 1954), 98. The administration was also embarrassed in the winter of 1914–1915 by accusations of impropriety in the appointment of Henry M. Pindell as ambassador to Russia. See "The Pindell Incident," *Outlook*, CV (November 22, 1913), 607–608; "The Case of Brother Pindell," *North American Review*, CXCVIII (December, 1913), 752–758.

[10]*New York Times,* July 1 and August 14, 1916.

[11]Link, *Wilson: The New Freedom*, 133.

[12]J. Leonard Bates, *The Origins of Teapot Dome: Progressives, Parties, and Petroleum, 1909–1921* (Urbana, Ill., 1963), 154.

[13]John Ise, *The United States Oil Policy* (New Haven, Conn., 1926), 336.

[14]Bates, *Origins of Teapot Dome*, 197, 202–203; Link, *Wilson: The New Freedom*, 135.

See also Gerald T. White, *Formative Years in the Far West: A History of Standard Oil Company of California and Predecessors through 1919* (New York, 1962), 446–449.

[15]Only charges of misconduct and malfeasance against officials in the Wilson administration will be considered in this study.

[16]*New York Times*, March 1, 1918.

[17]*Ibid.*, June 29, 1918.

[18]*Ibid.*, July 3, 1917; *Congressional Record,* 65th Cong., 1st Sess., 1917, LV, pt. 5, 4596; *Washington Post,* July 2, 1917. See also the criticism from progressives such as Amos Pinchot and Harry Slattery in Bates, *Origins of Teapot Dome,* 99.

[19]*Congressional Record,* 65th Cong., 1st Sess., 1917, LV, 5031.

[20]Wilson to Kenneth D. McKellar, July 6 and July 13, 1917, both in Ray S. Baker, *Woodrow Wilson: Life and Letters* (8 vols., Garden City, N.Y., 1927–1939), VII, 150–151, 164–165.

[21]Section 3 of *U.S. Statutes at Large,* XL, 276. For the debate on the amendment to the Food and Fuel Act, see Robert Cuff, "Woodrow Wilson and Business-Government Relations during World War I," *Review of Politics,* XXXI (July, 1969), 385–407.

[22]The best accounts of the controversy are in Seward W. Livermore, *Woodrow Wilson and the War Congress, 1916–1918* (Seattle, 1968), 125–130; Daniel R. Beaver, *Newton D. Baker and the American War Effort, 1917–1919* (Lincoln, Neb., 1966), 161–165, 169–170; Merlo J. Pusey, *Charles Evans Hughes* (2 vols., New York, 1952), I, 374–382.

[23]Gutzon Borglum to Wilson, November 22, 1917, and Wilson to Borglum, December 5, 1917, January 2, 1918, all in Wilson Papers, Library of Congress; New York *World,* March 21, 1918; *Literary Digest,* LVII (April 27 and May 15, 1918); Beaver, *Baker;* 161–162; Livermore, *Wilson and Congress,* 125–128.

[24]Wilson to Gutzon Borglum, April 15, 1918, Howard Coffin to Wilson, Wilson to Coffin, May 6, 1918, Wilson to Newton D. Baker, May 7, 1918, all in Baker, ed., *Wilson: Life and Letters,* VIII, 92, 122, 126; notes of cabinet meeting of March 9, 1918, in E. David Cronon, ed., *The Cabinet Diaries of Josephus Daniels, 1913–1921* (Lincoln, Neb., 1963), 289; *New York Times,* April 30, 1918; H. Snowden Marshall, "Report to the President," April 12, 1918, Baker Papers; Livermore, *Wilson and Congress,* 128–129.

[25]*Congressional Record,* 65th Cong., 2nd Sess., 1918, 6642.

[26]*New York Times,* May 17, 1918; Edward M. House to Wilson, May 9, 1918, Wilson Papers; Livermore, *Wilson and Congress,* 132–133; Pusey, *Hughes,* I, 374–376.

[27]U.S. Department of Justice, *Report of the Aircraft Inquiry* (Washington, D.C., 1918). Pusey, *Hughes,* I, 378–382.

[28]*New York Times,* January 17, February 6, 1919; Livermore, *Wilson and Congress,* 133, 273; Pusey, *Hughes,* I, 381–382. For a defense of Edward Deeds, see Isaac F. Marcosson, *Colonel Deeds: Industrial Builder* (New York, 1947), 278–280. The Senate Military Affairs Committee issued its own report on the aircraft production program. See "Why American Airplanes Are Not Winning the War," *Literary Digest,* LVIII (September 7, 1918).

[29]William E. Leuchtenburg, *The Perils of Prosperity, 1914–1932* (Chicago, 1958), 39. See also Frederic L. Paxson, *America at War, 1917–1918* (Boston, 1939), 40; Robert D. Cuff, *The War Industries Board: Business-Government Relations during World War I* (Baltimore, 1973), 100, 106–109, 154, 160–161, 171, 221; G. B. Clarkson, *Industrial America in the World War* (Boston, 1923); Preston W. Slosson, *The Great Crusade and After, 1914–1928* (New York, 1930), 55–56; Michael D. Reagan, "Serving Two Masters: Problems in the Employment of Dollar-a-Year and Without Compensation Personnel" (doctoral dissertation, Princeton University, 1959), 2–19, 217. For the House Select Committee's judgment, see U.S. House, 66th Cong., 2nd Sess., 1920, *House Report 637,* 19.

[30]*New York Times,* March 10, 12, and 13, 1918; Baker, *Wilson: Life and Letters,* VIII, 382. The most complete account is in Stanley Coben, *A. Mitchell Palmer, Politician* (New York, 1963), 127–154.

[31]*New York Times,* December 29, 1922; Coben, *Palmer,* 140–141, 298n.

[32]Wilson to Francis B. Harrison, July 22, 1918, Harrison to Wilson, July 23, 1918, in "Report of Philippine Investigation," 68, 71–85; Alien Property Custodian Records (RG 131); Coben, *Palmer,* 142.

[33]U.S. Senate, Committee on the Judiciary, *Hearings on the Nomination of A. Mitchell Palmer,* 65th Cong., 1st Sess., 1919, I, 128; for later investigations, see *New York Times,* December 29, 1922, April 10, April 17, 1924, October 2, 1926, December 6, 1927, January 26, 1930; Coben, *Palmer,* 143–146.

[34]*U.S. v. Chemical Foundation Inc.,* 272 U.S. 1 (1926); Coben, *Palmer,* 147–148.

[35]Coben, *Palmer,* 139.

[36]Wilson to A. Mitchell Palmer, September 4, 1918, in Baker, *Wilson: Life and Letters,* VIII, 382–383.

WARREN G. HARDING
1921–1923

Robert P. Ingalls

Historians have long regarded Warren G. Harding's administration as the most corrupt in the twentieth century.[1] Ultimately, three of the President's appointees, including a cabinet officer, went to jail. His attorney general was tried twice by juries that failed to reach a verdict after the defendant refused to testify. The Attorney General's closest friend and confidant committed suicide, as did the chief counsel of the Veterans' Bureau.

In addition to these instances of corruption, the Harding administration was troubled by allegations of government by crony. Harding claimed that in selecting his cabinet he sought the "best minds," which was undoubtedly the case in the choice of men such as Charles Evans Hughes, Herbert Hoover, and Henry Wallace. But the cabinet also included Harry M. Daugherty, whose background made him an object of suspicion as attorney general. Daugherty, a lawyer originally from Washington Court House, Ohio, had served briefly in the state legislature during the 1890s, but his chief association with politics was through his activities as a lobbyist and his long-time friendship with Harding. The lawyer had first met Harding around the turn of the century at a Republican rally, and according to Daugherty, he immediately thought to himself, "What a President he'd make."[2] The relationship between the two deepened as Harding moved up in Ohio politics and Daugherty boosted him for the presidency. After serving as Harding's campaign manager in 1920, Daugherty became attorney general.

Below the cabinet level, Harding appointed other friends to government posts. Dr. Charles E. Sawyer from Harding's home town of Marion became a brigadier general and White House physician. Ed Scobey, a one-time county sheriff and old friend, was selected as director of the Mint. Harding picked his brother-in-law, Reverend Heber H. Votaw, for superintendent of federal prisons after removing the position from the civil service lists. Daniel Crissinger, a Marion lawyer with little banking experience, was named controller of currency and, subsequently, governor of the Federal Reserve Board. At the time these appointments attracted little attention, but they were later cited as evidence of Harding's questionable standards, despite the fact that most of his friends in government were never implicated in any wrongdoing.

Although the Harding administration produced some of the worst examples of corruption in the history of the federal government, much of the evidence of misconduct did not surface until after Harding died on August 2, 1923. Therefore, this section treats only Harding's responses to charges aired before August, 1923, and the discussion of the Coolidge administration examines the reaction of Coolidge to subsequent allegations of official misconduct which reportedly occurred under Harding.

Harry M. Daugherty and Jesse W. Smith

In 1922 critics of Attorney General Harry M. Daugherty tried unsuccessfully to impeach him. Daugherty first came under attack in the spring of 1922 because of his failure to pursue war fraud cases brought against companies that had allegedly engaged in profiteering during World War I. Congressional criticism increased after the Attorney General obtained a sweeping injunction against railway strikers in September, 1922. The executive committee of the American Federation of Labor immediately demanded Daugherty's impeachment, and Republican congressman Oscar E. Keller of Minnesota spoke out against the Attorney General in the House. When Congress reconvened in December after the midterm elections, Keller called for Daugherty's impeachment and filed a list of fourteen charges with the House Judiciary Committee. Keller accused Daugherty of failing to pursue war fraud cases, refusing to prosecute bootleggers, obtaining pardons for favored criminals, putting congressmen under surveillance, diverting funds illegally, failing to enforce antitrust laws, and using his influence to obtain the injunction against railway strikers.

The House Judiciary Committee considered the allegations during December. Daugherty denied any misconduct on his part and questioned the motives of his opponents. "Back of this so-called impeachment," he declared, "stand arrayed certain radical leaders of certain organizations seeking to serve notice upon every future Attorney General that if he dare enforce the laws of the United States against such organizations he does so under the pain and penalty of being haled before the Senate of the United States, sitting as a high court of impeachment under the Constitution."[3] At public hearings which lasted two days, Keller declined to submit evidence to support most of his accusations. The Judiciary Committee then voted 12 to 2 to dismiss the charges as unsubstantiated, and in January, 1923, the House upheld the decision by a vote of 204 to 77.[4] Throughout 1922 President Harding had defended Daugherty and expressed confidence that any investigation undertaken by Congress would absolve the Attorney General of any wrongdoing.

Then, on May 30, 1923, Daugherty's closest friend and constant companion, Jesse W. Smith, committed suicide amid rumors that he was involved in shady deals. Although Smith had never held a government job in Washington, he had worked out of the Justice Department, where he had an office near that of the Attorney General, and had given the impression of being a department official. Smith had also been a friend of Harding, with whom he regularly played poker, but the President had apparently become increasingly concerned about friends like Smith.[5] According to the recollection of Emporia, Kansas, editor William Allen White, Harding declared during the winter of 1923: "I can take care of my enemies all right. But my damn friends, my God-damn friends, White, they're the ones that keep me walking the floor nights!"[6] The following spring Harding had informed Daugherty that Smith could not join the presidential party for an upcoming trip to Alaska because of his improper conduct. After hearing this, Daugherty told Smith that he would have to return to Ohio.[7] Shortly thereafter Smith killed himself in the Washington apartment he shared with Daugherty. At the time of Smith's death, Daugherty was a guest at the White House. One of his special assistants discovered Smith's body and notified William J. Burns, head of the Justice Department's Bureau of Investigation, who lived in the same apartment building. The two officials then called the White House, and Harding sent a doctor to the scene. After examining Smith, the physician publicly ascribed the suicide to depression resulting from an acute case of diabetes.

In 1924, after Harding's death, a Senate investigation revealed that Jesse Smith had acted illegally in concert with other men from Ohio, popularly known as the Ohio Gang. Working out of a "little green house on K Street" in Washington, the group had sold influence, liquor withdrawal permits, and immunity from prosecution. Witnesses testified that they had spent thousands of dollars for permits allowing them to withdraw liquor from bonded government warehouses. The alcohol, supposedly intended for medicinal purposes, wound up in the hands of bootleggers. A convicted bootlegger, George Remus, swore that he had paid Jesse Smith more than $250,000 for protection from prosecution, although he was ultimately indicted for violation of the Volstead Act. Smith had reportedly used his access to the Justice Department to help people, like Remus, who paid the Ohio Gang for favors. However, none of these hangers-on from Ohio was a government employee, and the exact nature of their activities remained hidden until the Senate inquiry in 1924.[8]

Prohibition Enforcement

Referring to the Volstead Act in his message to Congress of December 8, 1922, President Harding declared, "There are conditions relating to its enforcement which savor of nation-wide scandal."[9] That law, which had gone into effect in January, 1920, had empowered the Treasury Department to enforce the ban on the manufacture, sale, or transportation of alcoholic beverages. When the law was widely violated under Harding, some prohibitionists blamed Secretary of the Treasury Andrew W. Mellon for not taking sufficient interest because he had previously owned part of a leading distillery.[10] One of the biggest problems in enforcing the law was the Volstead Act itself, which excluded the agents in the department's Prohibition Unit from the civil service. As a result, they were political appointees, and they soon won a reputation for being corrupt. The poorly paid agents and investigators, numbering about 2,000 men, fell victim to the temptation of overlooking violations of the law in return for payoffs. In October, 1922, the federal grand jury for the Southern District of New York declared in a publicized letter to the Secretary of the Treasury, "Apparently the agents selected for the active work of suppressing illegal traffic in whisky have been chosen principally for political reasons when it was necessary to select men for this work who are worthy of confidence and of such stable character that they would not yield to the temptations to which it was well understood they would be subjected."[11] Although bribery and similar offenses were difficult to discover and prove, the Prohibition Unit dismissed 752 enforcement officers, agents, and inspectors during the years 1920–1926. In the same period, 23 employees were convicted for violating the Volstead Act and 118 for other offenses. The agents also became unpopular because they killed innocent victims in gun battles with bootleggers. A number of agents were indicted for murder, but convictions were rare.[13]

Whatever the causes of lax enforcement of the Volstead Act—and historians point to many reasons—Harding responded to the "nation-wide scandal" by appealing for individual compliance and more state action. When the President called for obedience to the law, it was known that he himself drank liquor in the White House. However, in January, 1923, Harding announced that he had become a total abstainer. Since the President took no other action, the enforcement of the Volstead Act remained ineffective.[14]

E. Mont Reily in Puerto Rico

Late in 1921 E. Mont Reily, governor general of Puerto Rico, was accused of misconduct in office.[15] Upon assuming his post in July, 1921, Reily had dismissed proindependence Puerto Ricans from office, and he had publicly attacked his local opponents. In November, after protests against Reily reached Washington, his immediate superior, Secretary of War John Weeks, wrote the President, "I think the Governor has lacked discretion in many of his acts . . . and some of his removals cannot be justified."[16] The following month Harding told Weeks, "I am frank to say [the complaints] do not impress me [and are] unworthy of any serious consideration."[17] However, criticism of Reily continued. Early in 1922 the Puerto Rican Senate adopted a resolution calling for Reily's removal, and a grand jury on the island indicted him for illegally appropriating funds.[18] During the summer of 1922, the President admitted to Secretary Weeks that "the Governor has very largely destroyed his usefulness by the series of blunders which have been brought to our attention," but Harding took no action.[19] In December Reily conferred with Harding in Washington and then returned to his post in Puerto Rico. On February 16, 1923, after a car accident and a nervous breakdown, Reily resigned as governor general for reasons of health.

Veterans' Bureau

During the winter of 1922–1923, several officials reported to Harding that they suspected that his director of the Veterans' Bureau, Charles R. Forbes, was involved in illegal activities.[20] Late in November, 1922, Harding was told by his personal physician, Brigadier General Charles E. Sawyer, that Forbes was selling off valuable hospital supplies as surplus material. The President stopped shipment of the goods to a Boston firm which had paid $600,000 for them, but he permitted their transfer to continue after receiving assurances from Forbes that the supplies were damaged. Meanwhile, Sawyer related his suspicions to Attorney General Harry M. Daugherty, who, according to his recollection, looked into the Veterans' Bureau. Finding a number of questionable transactions, Daugherty told the President about them.[21] With complaints against Forbes increasing, Harding called him to the White House at the end of January and apparently asked for his resignation. Following this meeting, Forbes sailed for Europe, and after arriving there, he resigned from his post on February 15, 1923. Despite evidence of illegal practices in the Veterans' Bureau, Harding took no further action.

Congress, however, pursued the matter. On March 2 the Senate initiated its own inquiry into the Veterans' Bureau. Two weeks later Charles F. Cramer, general counsel of the bureau and a close friend of Forbes, committed suicide in his Washington home. After collecting evidence for six months, the Senate investigating committee began public hearings on October 22, 1923. The panel's chief witness, Elias H. Mortimer, was a representative of the Thompson-Black Construction Company of St. Louis. He testified that after meeting Charles Forbes in February, 1922, the two had traveled around the country inspecting prospective sites for veterans' hospitals. Mortimer paid most of the bills on these trips, and in June he gave Forbes $5,000 from John W. Thompson. At the time the Veterans' Bureau director was helping Thompson's company get government contracts by letting its owners know in advance about construction sites and building plans. In return for these considerations, Forbes allegedly received a share of the profits from Thompson-Black. The director also bought up land that his bureau later purchased for hospitals, and he reportedly split some of the profits from such deals with the bureau's legal adviser, Charles Cramer. In addition, the committee discovered that Forbes had sold several million dollars worth of supplies for $600,000 under the pretext that they were damaged goods. Forbes, however, testified that he had done no wrong.[22]

After two months of hearings, the Senate committee turned its evidence over to the Department of Justice, which got indictments against Charles Forbes and John Thompson for conspiracy to defraud the government. In 1924 each was found guilty and sentenced to two years in prison and a $10,000 fine.[23]

Teapot Dome and the Origins of the Investigation

In April, 1922, rumors reached Senator John Kendrick of Wyoming that the government had secretly leased private drilling rights for Naval Oil Reserve Number Three, known as Teapot Dome. Kendrick asked the Interior Department for information and was told on April 10 that no contract for a lease had been made. Four days later the *Wall Street Journal* reported that the Interior Department had leased Teapot Dome to Harry Sinclair's Mammoth Oil Company. Kendrick then introduced a resolution in the Senate calling for "all proposed operating agreements" for the Teapot Dome, and the Senate adopted the resolution on April 15. Three days later the Interior Department formally announced the leasing of the entire Teapot Dome oil reserve and indicated that an additional lease would be awarded for parts of California reserves to Edward L. Doheny's Pan-American Petroleum and Transport Company. On April 21 the Department of the Interior complied with the Kendrick resolution by sending the Senate a copy of the contract with Sinclair's company.

A long history of government oil policy lay behind Teapot Dome, the name associated with the worst scandal of the Harding administration. In 1912 President William Howard Taft had created the first two naval oil reserves, encompassing over 60,000 acres, at Elk Hills and Buena

Vista Hills in California. Taft had acted after receiving warnings from conservationists and scientists that unrestricted tapping of petroleum could lead to critical shortages in the future. Three years later President Woodrow Wilson set aside almost 10,000 acres of oil-bearing land in Wyoming for the exclusive use of the United States Navy. This Naval Oil Reserve Number Three was called Teapot Dome because the oil dome lay under an outcropping of rock shaped like a teapot. Although conservationists strongly supported the policy of petroleum reserves, oil men and many westerners continued to fight for private development of natural resources on all public lands. In part as a result of this pressure, Congress passed the Oil Land Leasing Act of 1920, which permitted the government to lease private drilling rights on public lands. Moreover, the country's three naval oil reserves were included in the law in order to allow the tapping of government petroleum to prevent drainage into neighboring private lands. Another law adopted in 1920 gave the secretary of the navy control over the three reserves "to conserve, develop, use, and operate the same in his discretion, directly or by contract, lease or otherwise." [24]

Early in the Harding administration, the Navy Department relinquished its jurisdiction over the naval oil reserves. In an executive order dated May 31, 1921, the President transferred the reserves to the Interior Department. [25] According to a public announcement, Harding acted at the request of both Interior Secretary Albert B. Fall and Navy Secretary Edwin L. Denby. Fall, a New Mexican who had previously served in the Senate, had long favored expanded private development of the country's resources, and he had clashed before with conservationists. In July, 1921, Fall awarded the first drilling contract to Edward Doheny for offset wells at the Elk Hills reserve, but this lease generated little criticism because it resulted from publicized competitive bidding and served to prevent drainage.

After the revelation of additional leases in April, 1922, conservationists sought a full Senate inquiry. Although they had no evidence of any wrongdoing, conservationists distrusted Fall, and several of them persuaded Senator Robert M. La Follette to introduce a resolution authorizing the Senate Committee on Public Lands to investigate the entire subject of leases on naval oil reserves. The Senate adopted the La Follette resolution by a unanimous vote on April 29, 1922. [26] In response to the resolution, which called for all material in the Interior Department files concerning the leases, Secretary Fall sent a truckload of documents to the Senate in June, 1922. In a letter of transmittal accompanying the records, President Harding declared that the oil policy of Fall and Denby "was submitted to me prior to the adoption thereof, and the policy decided upon and the subsequent acts have at all times had my entire approval."[27]

Public hearings on Teapot Dome, which ultimately produced evidence that sent Albert Fall to jail, did not begin until sixteen months later, in October, 1923. By that time, Fall had resigned from the cabinet, and Harding had died. When Fall left the Interior Department in March, 1923, his name was still untarnished. Harding was probably unaware that Fall had done anything wrong.[28]

Allegations about Harding after His Death

On August 2, 1923, President Harding died in San Francisco while on a tour of the West.[29] Americans turned out by the millions to mourn Harding as his funeral train crossed the country to Washington and back to Marion, Ohio, where he was buried. At the time, people could pour out their grief for a beloved president because there was little reason to question his integrity. One observer recollected that "the country thought of Harding as a capable and deserving President who had died mid-term of a worthy administration."[30] Only later would investigations gradually reveal the extent of previously undetected corruption within the administration.

As congressional and legal proceedings subsequently uncovered evidence of misconduct by Harding appointees, stories began circulating about alleged scandals in the former president's official and private affairs.[31] Charges relating to Harding's official conduct focused on allegations about the buying of his presidential nomination and possible political payoffs in the 1923 sale of his newspaper, but historians have found no conclusive evidence that Harding was personally involved in any corrupt activities.[32]

In addition to the gossip spread by several notorious books, doubts about Harding were sown by his old friend, Harry Daugherty. After the President's death, Daugherty destroyed the records of a bank account he had shared with Jesse Smith, and in 1927 he refused to testify about its contents. When Daugherty's lawyer then intimated that the former attorney general had taken these steps to protect someone else, speculation grew that Daugherty might have sought to hide the details of Harding's financial transactions with others, perhaps women friends. However, any possible link between the bank account and Harding remains uncertain since Daugherty destroyed the evidence.[33]

Harding's reputation declined rapidly as a result of the exposure of corrupt activities in his administration. Shortly after the President's death, the Harding Memorial Association was formed to raise money for a monument to be built in Marion. The association, with President Coolidge as honorary chairman and all cabinet officers on its executive board, soon collected almost $1,000,000. But after its completion in 1927, the monument remained undedicated because neither Coolidge nor his successor, Herbert Hoover, could find the time to preside over the ceremonies. When, belatedly in June, 1931, Hoover formally dedicated the memorial, he referred directly to the scandals associated with Harding:

> Here was a man whose soul was seared by a great disillusionment. . . . Harding had a dim realization that he had been betrayed by a few of the men whom he had trusted, by men whom he believed were his devoted friends. It was later proved in the courts of the land that these men had betrayed not only the friendship and trust of their staunch and loyal friend but that they had betrayed their country. That was the tragedy of the life of Warren Harding.[34]

Most studies of the Harding presidency have viewed it as a tragedy— at best. During the 1920s and 1930s, writers produced several widely circulated books which related in colorful detail the corruption of the Harding era. However, most of these early works were by journalists who accepted uncritically the gossip surrounding Harding and his years in the White House.[35] Historians later attempted to separate fact from fiction in assessing Harding. Yet they reached much the same conclusion as the newspapermen; namely, the Harding administration was a failure because its salient characteristic was corruption which reached proportions unrivaled in the twentieth century up to that time.[36]

The 1960s marked a milestone in the studying of Harding. In 1964 the Harding Memorial Association opened its vast collection of Harding papers to scholars. Until that time, the rumored destruction of Harding's correspondence by his widow had been cited as evidence of the President's possible involvement in the corruption of his administration. Several works drawing on the Harding papers have appeared. One, a popular study by Francis Russell, emphasized the reported scandals in Harding's life.[37] Andrew Sinclair, one of the first historians to examine the Harding papers, concluded, "Harding believed in the nineteenth-century system of corrupt politics and unrestricted business opportunity, because this was the university of his youth and middle age. Although, in the White House, he began to learn painfully the duties and the role of a modern President, his education came too late."[38] On the other hand, Robert K. Murray, who has written a recent and fully documented study of the Harding presidency, has sought to revise the standard interpretation. Stressing the "tremendous economic and social change" of the postwar period, Murray declared: "Harding was able to secure a general consensus during this period which facilitated national progress rather than blocked it. By all standards of political compromise, the Harding administration was a success."[39] Pointing to Harding's achievements, Murray has minimized the importance of the well-known scandals. "Some corruption existed, to be sure, but it was not the most significant aspect of this period of American history."[40] There is, however, resistance to this interpretation of an administration marred by such flagrant corruption.

NOTES

[1]The author and editors wish to acknowledge the generosity of Robert K. Murray who prepared a thirty-eight-page manuscript about corruption in the Harding administration to assist in the preparation of this document.

[2]Daugherty quoted in Robert K. Murray, *The Harding Era: Warren G. Harding and His Administration* (Minneapolis, 1969), 19.

[3]*Reply of the Attorney General . . . to Charges Filed with the Committee on the Judiciary . . .* , quoted in Andrew Sinclair, *The Available Man: The Life behind the Masks of Warren Gamaliel Harding* (New York, 1965), 261.

[4]*House Report 1372,* 67th Cong., 4th Sess.; *Congressional Record,* 67th Cong., 4th Sess. (January 25, 1923), 2451–2452.

[5]In his biography of Harding, Samuel Hopkins Adams suggested that the President's regular poker games might have somehow involved corruption because "in Harding's Ohio days, poker was one method of repaying political obligations" by letting a politician win. Samuel Hopkins Adams, *Incredible Era: The Life and Times of Warren Gamaliel Harding* (Boston, 1939), 214. Robert K. Murray has disputed Adams, declaring that "there was nothing sinister or sinful about [the card sessions]." Murray, *The Harding Era,* 117. Francis Russell also presented the games as essentially innocent and apolitical. Russell, *The Shadow of Blooming Grove: Warren G. Harding in His Times* (New York, 1968), 446–448.

[6]William Allen White, *Autobiography* (New York, 1946), 619.

[7]Harry M. Daugherty, *The Inside Story of the Harding Tragedy* (New York, 1932), 248–249.

[8]*Investigation of the Attorney General,* Hearings before the Senate Select Committee on the Investigation of the Attorney General, 68th Cong., 1st Sess. (Washington, 1924), *passim.* The extent of President Harding's knowledge about the activities of Jesse Smith and the Ohio Gang is open to question, but historians agree that Harding was not personally involved in their dealings. Adams, *Incredible Era,* 239–241; Sinclair, *The Available Man,* 262–263; Robert K. Murray, *The Politics of Normalcy: Governmental Theory and Practice in the Harding-Coolidge Era* (New York, 1973), 104.

[9]Harding Address to Congress, December 8, 1922, reprinted in *Congressional Record,* 67th Cong., 4th Sess. (December 8, 1922), 215.

[10]Before entering the cabinet, Mellon had put his stock in the Overholt distillery in trust to be sold, but he showed little interest in enforcing prohibition. Harvey O'Connor, *Mellon's Millions: The Biography of a Fortune* (New York, 1933), 236–237.

[11]Quoted in Laurence F. Schmeckebier, *The Bureau of Prohibition: Its History, Activities and Organization* (Washington, 1929), 45.

[12]*Ibid.,* 51–53.

[13]According to a recent historian, "Harding served liquor in the private rooms of the White House, although not at public gatherings or in the social rooms on the first floor." Murray, *The Harding Era,* 119.

[14]Charles Merz, *The Dry Decade* (New York, 1931), 101–110; Andrew Sinclair, *Era of Excess: A Social History of the Prohibition Movement* (New York, 1964), 183–185.

[15]Reily, a Harding appointee from Missouri, had first met the future president during the 1920 campaign.

[16]Weeks to Harding, November 12, 1921, quoted in Murray, *The Harding Era,* 336.

[17]Harding to Weeks, December 16, 1921, quoted *ibid.,* 337.

[18]According to Murray, there "were indications that the grand jury charges against Reily were almost pure hokum (and they were)." *Ibid.,* 338.

[19]Harding to Weeks, August 11, 1922, quoted *ibid.*

[20]Harding had first met Forbes on a visit to Hawaii in 1915.

[21]Daugherty, *Inside Story,* 181–184. Daugherty did not give the dates of his conversations with Sawyer or the President, and subsequent testimony by other participants is often either imprecise or contradictory in reference to dates. Historians have not yet examined this episode in detail.

[22]*Investigation of Veterans' Bureau,* Hearings before the Senate Select Committee on Investigation of Veterans' Bureau, 67th Cong., 4th Sess (Washington, 1923), *passim.*

[23]The convictions of Forbes and Thompson were upheld on appeal. *Thompson et al. v. U.S.,* 10 F. 2d 781 (1926). Thompson never served his sentence because of bad health.

[24]Quoted in J. Leonard Bates, *The Origins of Teapot Dome: Progressives, Parties, and Petroleum, 1909–1921* (Urbana, Ill., 1963), 207.

[25]Executive order reprinted in *Leases upon Naval Oil Reserves,* Hearings before the Senate Committee on Public Lands and Surveys, 67th and 68th Cong. (3 vols., Washington, 1923–1924), I, 177–178.

[26]Investigators did not find any proof of wrongdoing until more than a year and a half later, but they remained suspicious, in part because La Follette's office was ransacked, and Senator Thomas J. Walsh, leader of the inquiry, thought his phones were tapped. In 1924 Gaston Means admitted to a Senate committee that he had broken into La Follette's office while working for the Justice Department's Bureau of Investigation. Murray, *Politics of Normalcy,* 110. Means's testimony before Select Committee on the Investigation of the Attorney General, quoted in Fred J. Cook, *The FBI Nobody Knows* (New York, 1964), 130–132.

[27]Harding to the President of the Senate, June 7, 1922, reprinted in *Leases upon Naval Oil Reserves,* Hearings, 67th and 68th Cong., 25.

[28]In June, 1923, Harding met privately with Emma Fall, wife of the former interior secretary. William Allen White later wrote that he was told Harding emerged from the meeting "obviously frustrated, worried, and excited." White, *Autobiography,* 623–624. Mrs. Fall subsequently denied that she had discussed oil leases with the President. However, Samuel Hopkins Adams "assumed with certitude" that Mrs. Fall had told Harding about the Teapot Dome scandal. Adams, *Incredible Era,* 340. Recent historians, citing statements by Mrs. Fall and Senator Arthur Capper, who saw the President after the encounter, have discounted White's story and concluded that Harding probably died unaware of any misconduct by Fall. David B. Stratton, "Behind Teapot Dome: Some Personal Insights," *Business History Review,* XXXI (Winter, 1957), 399–401; Russell, *The Shadow of Blooming Grove,* 576; Murray, *The Harding Era,* 442, 483.

[29]No autopsy was performed on Harding, but his doctors concluded that he probably had suffered a cardiac collapse on July 27 and died of a cerebral hemorrhage on August 2. In a 1930 book, *The Strange Death of President Harding,* Gaston Means claimed that Mrs. Harding had poisoned her husband, but historians have uniformly dismissed the book as a fabrication by a confessed perjurer. Means, *The Strange Death of President Harding* (New York); Sinclair, *The Available Man,* 286–287; Russell, *The Shadow of Blooming Grove,* 638–639; Murray, *The Harding Era,* 448–451, 490–491.

[30]Mark Sullivan, *Our Times: The United States, 1900–1925* (6 vols., New York, 1926–1935), VI, 272.

[31]The most sensational story about Harding's personal life appeared in a 1927 book, *The President's Daughter* (New York), by Nan Britton, who claimed to have been the President's mistress. Whatever their relationship might have been, there is no evidence that Harding's possible extramarital affairs affected his official duties as president. Murray, *The Harding Era,* 532.

[32]After Teapot Dome became a scandal in 1924, a friend of deceased oil man Jake Hamon testified before a Senate committee that Hamon had bragged that the Harding nomination had cost him a million dollars in 1920. However, other witnesses discounted the story. In 1928 another Senate inquiry discovered that after Harding's death the Republican National Committee had used money from oil men to pay off the 1920 campaign debt. *Leases upon Naval Oil Reserves,* Hearings, 67th and 68th Cong., 2995, 3037–3094; *Leases upon Naval Oil Reserves,* Hearings before the Senate Committee on Public Lands and Surveys, 70th Cong., 1st Sess. (Washington, 1928), *passim.* William Allen White, an observer of the 1920 convention, later wrote, "I have never seen a convention . . . so completely dominated by sinister predatory economic forces." White,

Autobiography, 584. Despite White's comment, historians have found no evidence of a conspiracy behind Harding's nomination. Wesley M. Bagby, *The Road to Normalcy: The Presidential Campaign and Election of 1920* (Baltimore, 1962), 97–99; Burl Noggle, *Teapot Dome: Oil and Politics in the 1920's* (Baton Rouge, 1962), 141–143, 186–197; Murray, *The Harding Era*, 67–68. All writers on the subject have rejected the charge that Harding's 1923 sale of his newspaper for $550,000 involved any kind of political payoff.

[33]For the background of the bank account in question, see the episode entitled "Harry M. Daugherty and the Alien Property Custodian," discussed under the Coolidge administration.

[34]Quoted in Murray, *The Harding Era*, 493.

[35]William Allen White, *Masks in a Pageant* (New York, 1928); Frederick L. Allen, *Only Yesterday: An Informal History of the Nineteen Twenties* (New York, 1931); Adams, *Incredible Era*.

[36]See, for example, Arthur M. Schlesinger, Jr., *The Crisis of the Old Order* (Boston, 1957), 49–53; William E. Leuchtenburg, *The Perils of Prosperity, 1914–32* (Chicago, 1958), 89–95.

[37]Russell, *The Shadow of Blooming Grove.*

[38]Sinclair, *The Available Man*, 298.

[39]Murray, *The Harding Era*, 533–534.

[40]Murray, *The Politics of Normalcy*, 129.

CALVIN COOLIDGE
1923–1929

Robert P. Ingalls

E arly in the morning of August 3, 1923, Calvin Coolidge received the news that he had succeeded to the presidency as a result of Warren Harding's death. Coolidge inherited a number of problems related to corruption within the Harding administration. Congressional investigations of the Veterans' Bureau scandal and the Teapot Dome allegations were already in progress. Furthermore, Coolidge temporarily retained all members of the Harding cabinet, some of whom subsequently came under suspicion. Coolidge's responses to charges of misconduct within the Harding administration are treated here. In addition, this section covers allegations of wrongdoing that occurred during the Coolidge administration.

Teapot Dome and the Conclusion of the Investigation

Late in 1923 the Senate Committee on Public Lands heard testimony that former secretary of the interior Albert B. Fall had started making expensive improvements on his New Mexican ranch at about the time he awarded Harry Sinclair a contract for drilling on Teapot Dome, Naval Oil Reserve Number Three.[1] In a letter dated December 26, 1923, Fall explained to the committee that he had borrowed $100,000 in cash from Edward B. McLean, publisher of the *Washington Post*, in November, 1921, and he had used the money to enlarge his ranch holdings. Fall added that he had never asked Edward Doheny or Harry Sinclair for money, "nor have I ever received from either of said parties one cent."[2]

Fall's explanation appeared to settle the matter, but his story soon fell apart. In an interview in Palm Beach, Florida, on January 11, 1924, the ailing McLean told Senator Thomas J. Walsh, leader of the Senate inquiry, that he had not lent $100,000 to Fall. Under pressure from Walsh, Fall then admitted in a letter that he had obtained the money from "other sources," which he refused to identify.[3] Fall's confession that he had previously lied to the committee turned Teapot Dome into a scandal. The appearance of misconduct deepened when, on January 24, Edward Doheny testified before the Senate committee that he had lent Fall $100,000, which had been delivered in a little black bag in November, 1921. Five months later a company owned by Doheny had won a contract for drilling rights on the naval oil reserve at Elk Hills, California, but Doheny denied any connection between the lease and his personal loan to the Secretary of the Interior, who had been a close friend for thirty years.[4]

In the midst of these disclosures, President Coolidge entered the controversy for the first time. Until January, 1924, Coolidge had held that, as summarized on January 18, "It wouldn't be natural to take any action until the [Senate Public Lands] Committee had made their investigation, in order to find out whether anything develops that would appear to warrant any further investigation of action by any other part of the Government."[5] Four days later he told newspaper reporters that the previous day he had directed the Department of Justice to observe the hearings of the Public Lands Committee. "I don't suppose it needs to be stated," he added, "that if any irregularities are disclosed, or any misdeeds on the part of any one, they will be subject to investigation by the Department of Justice, and such action taken as the laws of the country require."[6] On January 24, the day Doheny revealed he had lent Fall $100,000, the President confirmed previous verbal instructions directing Attorney General Harry M. Daugherty to have someone from his staff attend the hearings. Coolidge also ordered Daugherty to "examine all evidence disclosed at the hearings in the most careful manner, and make any additional investigation suggested by any disclosures [sic] or discrepancies in such evidence, in order to take appropriate action for the same purpose."[7]

Demands for an independent inquiry soon led to the appointment of special counsel. On January 23 Thomas Walsh suggested in a Senate debate that the President should appoint a special counsel to investigate and prosecute since Attorney General Daugherty was an old friend of Fall and was himself under suspicion of misconduct in office. Charges also circulated in Washington that Harding's cabinet, most of whom still served under Coolidge, may well have considered the oil leases; however, on January 25 Coolidge declared in a press conference that he could not recall any such discussions while he had been vice president.[8] Nevertheless, Senator Walsh informed the Public Lands Committee, meeting in executive session on January 26, that he would offer a resolution authorizing the President to cancel the leases, to enjoin further tapping of oil, and to appoint special counsel to prosecute any violators of federal law.

President Coolidge, who may have learned of Walsh's proposal, took the initiative.[9] In a statement drafted during the evening of January 26 and telephoned to the press, Coolidge stated, "Having been advised by the Department of Justice that it is in accord with the former precedents, I propose to employ special counsel of high rank drawn from both parties to bring such actions for the enforcement of the law." The President promised that criminal and civil cases would be pursued, any fraud uncovered, and any illegal contracts canceled.[10] Despite this announcement, Walsh went ahead and introduced his resolution, which passed the Senate unanimously.

The process of installing special prosecutors took several weeks. On January 29 the President named former attorney general Thomas W. Gregory, a Democrat, and Silas H. Strawn, a Republican. But Gregory soon withdrew from consideration because of his firm's ties with Edward Doheny, and Coolidge withdrew Strawn's name when opposition to him developed in the Senate Public Lands Committee. The President then nominated Atlee Pomerene, a former Democratic senator from Ohio, and Owen J. Roberts, a Republican lawyer. The Senate confirmed their appointments, and Coolidge handed them their commissions as special counsel on February 19, 1924.

While the President and the Senate were considering the nominees for special counsel, pressure mounted in Congress for the dismissal of Navy Secretary Edwin Denby because he had agreed to let Fall's Interior Department take charge of the naval oil reserves in 1921. On January 28, 1924, Senator Joseph T. Robinson, a Democrat, introduced a resolution calling for Denby's resignation. Senator Thomas Walsh supported the measure, although he did not think Denby had committed an impeachable offense since, he said, "stupidity" was not a ground for impeachment. On February 11 ten Republicans joined Democrats to pass the Robinson resolution. Coolidge rejected the Senate's advice. "No official recognition," the President declared, "can be given to the passage of the Senate resolution relative to their opinion concerning members of the Cabinet or other officers under Executive control." Quoting James Madison and Grover Cleveland on the separation of powers, Coolidge said: "The President is responsible to the people for his conduct relative to the retention or dismissal of public officials. I assume that responsibility." He concluded that he would "take such action as seems essential" as soon as special counsel advised him about the case of the oil leases, and he would "deal thoroughly and summarily with every kind of wrong doing." [11] A week later Denby sent his resignation to Coolidge in order, he said, to save the President "embarrassments." Insisting that he had done nothing wrong, the Secretary of the Navy delayed the effective date of his departure for one month so that the Congress could institute impeachment proceedings if it doubted him. Accepting Denby's resignation, Coolidge responded that "your honesty and integrity have not been impugned." [12]

Soon thereafter, Coolidge himself came under suspicion. Late in February the Senate Public Lands Committee questioned C. Bascom Slemp, Coolidge's private secretary, about the possibility that he had tried to persuade Edward McLean to back up Fall's lie about the source of the $100,000. Slemp admitted that he had seen McLean and Fall in Palm Beach at the time Senator Walsh had gone there in January to interview McLean, but the President's secretary declared that he had not discussed the money with McLean. When asked by Walsh if he had communicated with the White House during his stay in Palm Beach, Slemp replied that "all communications that I would make to the White House I would have to reserve as confidential." However, Slemp emphasized that he objected only to having his personal correspondence published, and he told Walsh, "I would like you to see these [communications] so that if there is any public matter really pressing about it, you can see them." [13] Assured by Slemp that the messages contained nothing pertinent, Walsh did not pursue the matter. Several days later, however, Walsh introduced a series of telegrams, subpoenaed from Western Union, which had been exchanged between Washington and Palm Beach during January and

February, 1924. Among them were two from Coolidge sent to McLean on January 12 and February 12. The President immediately issued a statement explaining that the messages were quite innocent.[14]

During March, 1924, Coolidge rejected a Senate request for information from the Bureau of Internal Revenue. A Senate resolution, adopted on February 29, asked the President to direct the Secretary of the Treasury to furnish the Public Lands Committee with the income tax returns of Albert Fall, Edward Doheny, and Harry Sinclair. Coolidge refused on the ground that his compliance would violate the Revenue Act of 1921, but he promised to cooperate with the Treasury Secretary in amending department rules so that committee representatives could inspect the tax returns in question.[15] There is no indication that either the President or the committee pursued the matter any further.

After completing its hearings on May 14, 1924, the Public Lands Committee adopted a majority report which the Senate subsequently approved. The committee majority charged Fall with disregarding the law, and it condemned the "essentially corrupt" deals surrounding the oil leases.[16]

The final judgment rested with the courts, but it took years to conclude the litigation growing out of the oil leases. During 1927, as a result of civil suits initiated by the President's special counsel, the Supreme Court unanimously upheld lower court decisions canceling the leases held by Edward Doheny's Pan-American Petroleum Company for the Elk Hills reserve and the lease held by Harry Sinclair's Mammoth Oil Company for Teapot Dome. In each case, the Supreme Court found that the contracts resulted from a conspiracy between Fall and the holder of the lease.[17] In criminal cases brought by the special prosecutors, juries acquitted Fall, Doheny, and Sinclair of charges that they had conspired to defraud the government.[18] Sinclair, however, was found guilty of both contempt of court for putting jurors under surveillance and contempt of the Senate for refusing to answer questions during the Teapot Dome inquiry. Sinclair received sentences totaling nine months for the two contempt charges.[19] In 1929 Fall was convicted of accepting a bribe from Doheny.[20] The following year, oddly enough, Doheny was found innocent of bribing the Secretary of the Interior.[21] Fall, the first cabinet member convicted and sent to jail for a crime committed in office, served nine months and nineteen days of a one-year sentence.

Harry M. Daugherty and the Alien Property Custodian

During early 1924, in the midst of revelations about former interior secretary Albert B. Fall, Attorney General Harry M. Daugherty once more came under attack. On February 19, 1924, Democratic senator Burton K. Wheeler introduced a resolution calling for a Senate investigation of Daugherty because of his alleged failure to prosecute corruption. The following day a group of Republican senators called on President Coolidge and told him that Daugherty should resign for the good of the party. Coolidge for the moment took no action, and Daugherty declared publicly that he would not resign under fire lest it be interpreted as a confession of guilt. On March 1 the Senate adopted the Wheeler resolution by a vote of 66 to 1.

The five-man investigating committee began public hearings on March 12. The lead-off witness, Roxy Stinson, was the divorced wife of Jesse Smith, who had committed suicide the previous year. She testified that Smith and the so-called Ohio Gang had sold liquor permits and arranged shady stock deals from their headquarters on K Street. When asked if Smith's closest friend, Attorney General Daugherty, had been involved in these transactions, Roxy Stinson answered yes. Her knowledge was based on conversations with her late ex-husband, which Daugherty's counsel dismissed as hearsay testimony. Other witnesses, including a convicted bootlegger and an indicted former member of the Justice Department's Bureau of Investigation, gave similar evidence about deals and payoffs negotiated by Jesse Smith, who at the time had free access to the Justice Department although he was not a government employee.[22]

As the hearings continued, Daugherty issued denials of any involvement in illegal activities, but throughout March the pressure against him increased. On March 20 the committee looking into the Justice Department asked that Daugherty allow a member of the committee staff to examine department records. The Attorney General rejected the request because, he said in a letter dated March 27, "To permit a general fishing expedition among the files of the department by a representative of your committee, with power to withdraw from the files such papers and documents as the examiner might choose, would lead to endless confusion."[23] On the same day Daugherty refused to open department files, he received a letter from the President, who wrote: "I do not see how you can be acting in your own defense in this matter, and at the same time and on the same question acting as my attorney general. . . . I am sure that you will see that it is necessary for me to have the advice of a disinterested attorney general."[24] In another letter to Daugherty that day, Coolidge's secretary wrote: ". . . the President does not understand the delay in complying with his request. He directs me to notify you that he expects your resignation at once."[25] On March 28 Daugherty resigned, telling the President that he did so "solely out of deference to your request." The retiring attorney general also sent Coolidge a six-page defense of his record.[26]

Before leaving office, Daugherty had tried to frustrate the Senate inquiry in a number of ways. He had agents from the Bureau of Investigation, headed by William Burns, follow witnesses. The department also looked into the background of Senator Wheeler, the driving force behind the investigation of the Justice Department. As a result of this probing by Burns's agents, Wheeler was indicted in April, 1924, for conspiracy to defraud the government because he had allegedly practiced law before a federal agency during the period between his election and his swearing in as a U.S. senator. A jury took ten minutes to acquit Wheeler of the charge in 1925.[27]

The Senate panel ultimately uncovered evidence of a conspiracy to defraud the government for which Daugherty and another official were indicted. The charge concerned the activities of the Office of Alien Property Custodian, which had been created during World War I to take possession and dispose of property in the United States held by persons residing in enemy countries. In 1921 Harding's appointee as alien property custodian, Thomas W. Miller, had turned over to private claimants the American Metals Company, a firm the government had seized during the war because of German ownership. The group that gained control of the company in 1921 paid $441,000 to John T. King, a Republican National committeeman, for arranging the transfer. Out of the money, most of which was in traceable Liberty bonds, King gave $50,000 to Miller and $224,000 to Jesse Smith for helping with the deal. Smith deposited $50,000 of his share in an Ohio bank headed by Harry Daugherty's brother. The funds went into an account, known as "Jess Smith Extra No. 3," which Smith and Daugherty held jointly. This connection with the payoff led to the indictment in 1926 of Daugherty, along with King and Miller, for conspiracy to defraud the government. King died before the first trial, which resulted in a deadlocked jury. At a second trial in 1927, Miller was found guilty and sentenced to eighteen months in prison and a $5,000 fine. The jury again failed to reach a decision on Daugherty, who had destroyed the ledger sheets for "Jess Smith Extra No. 3" and who refused to take the stand. He made a statement to explain his reasons for not testifying:

> Having been personal attorney for Warren G. Harding before he was Senator from Ohio and while he was Senator, and thereafter until his death,
>
> And for Mrs. Harding for a period of several years, and before her husband was elected President and after his death, . . .
>
> And having been attorney for the Midland National Bank of Washington Court House, Ohio, and for my brother, M. S. Daugherty,
>
> And having been Attorney General of the United States during the time that President Harding served as President,
>
> And also for a time after President Harding's death under President Coolidge,
>
> And with all of those named as attorney, personal friend and Attorney General, my relations were of the most confidential character as well as professional,
>
> I refuse to testify and answer questions put to me because: The answer I might give or make and the testimony I might give might tend to incriminate me.[28]

After the second hung jury, the government dropped the charge against Daugherty.[29]

"Ford-Coolidge Deal"

In addition to coping with allegations of wrongdoing that had their origin in the Harding years, President Coolidge confronted certain charges with respect to his own administration. In late 1923 he backed Henry Ford's offer to buy Muscle Shoals, the government project in the

Tennessee Valley, in what appeared to be an agreement with Ford for his support in the upcoming presidential election. The industrialist had first submitted a bid for the project in 1921, when the Harding administration proposed selling the facilities, which had been built during the war to produce hydroelectric power and nitrates. After Harding's death, Coolidge talked to Ford in October, 1923, about his plans for Muscle Shoals, but the President took no position on the bid. Meanwhile, Ford-for-president clubs had sprung up around the country. On December 3, 1923, Coolidge and Ford again met for a discussion which was never made public. Three days later the President delivered his first message to Congress and outlined a plan for Muscle Shoals which seemed to fit Ford's offer. On December 19 Ford declared that he would not run for president on any ticket because he supported Coolidge's election to a full term. Rumors immediately circulated that these announcements were part of a Ford-Coolidge deal.

Senator George Norris, an opponent of selling Muscle Shoals, subsequently investigated the charge. In April, 1924, at Senate hearings on Muscle Shoals legislation, Norris introduced a telegram, dated October 12, 1923, from one Ford employee to another. "In private interview had with President Coolidge this morning," the message read, "he said incidentally: 'I am friendly to Mr. Ford, but wish some one would convey to him that it is my hope that Mr. Ford will not do or say anything that will make it difficult for me to deliver Muscle Shoals to him, which I am trying to do.'"[30] The day after the telegram was produced in the Senate, Coolidge denied the statement attributed to him. "I have never said I was trying to deliver Muscle Shoals to Mr. Ford or anyone else. I do not think his favor is for sale."[31] Norris found no additional evidence of a bargain, but he blocked Senate approval of Ford's bid, which the industrialist withdrew in October, 1924.[32]

Andrew W. Mellon and the Bureau of Internal Revenue

In 1924 a dispute between Secretary of the Treasury Andrew W. Mellon and Republican Senator James Couzens led to a probe of tax administration. The row originated in a series of published exchanges between the two men regarding Mellon's tax proposals. After the Treasury secretary questioned the millionaire senator's investments in tax-exempt government bonds, Couzens introduced a Senate resolution on February 21, 1924, calling for an investigation of the Bureau of Internal Revenue, which was under Mellon's jurisdiction. The following month the Senate adopted the resolution and named Couzens to the special committee. The Secretary of the Treasury cooperated by obtaining waivers from firms so that he could turn over to the panel their files from the Bureau of Internal Revenue. The records showed that a number of companies, in which Mellon had some financial interest, had received large tax rebates and deferential treatment from the bureau. Mellon insisted that the rebates were routine. However, President Coolidge tried to stop the inquiry, according to Couzens, by offering the Senator the ambassadorship to Great Britain.[33]

Determined to continue the investigation, Couzens encountered opposition. After he had won committee approval to pay personally the cost of retaining counsel, Couzens and the Senate came under attack from the executive branch. "If the interposition of private resources be permitted to interfere with the executive administration," Mellon wrote Coolidge, "the machinery of government will cease to function." In support of Mellon's complaint about the committee's use of privately paid counsel, Coolidge told the Senate, "I enter my solemn protests and give notice that in my opinion the departments ought not to be required to participate in [such inquiries]."[34] Angered by this criticism, the Senate authorized funds to employ counsel for the investigating committee. While the panel was pursuing its task, Couzens suddenly found himself accused by the Bureau of Internal Revenue of owing over $10,000,000 in back taxes as a result of a stock sale in 1919. After considering the government's suit, the Board of Tax Appeals ruled in 1928 that Couzens had paid $900,000 too much and was entitled to a refund.[35] Meanwhile, after almost two years of work, the Senate committee investigating the Bureau of Internal Revenue had reported in 1926 that the tax rebates, amounting to millions of dollars to large firms, were completely legal.[36]

The Rejection of Charles Beecher Warren as Attorney General

In March, 1925, Coolidge's nominee for attorney general, Charles Beecher Warren, came under attack in the Senate because of his ties to a company charged with violating antitrust laws. As a representative of the American Sugar Refining Company between 1902 and 1906, Warren had bought the stock of a number of small sugar refineries and organized the Michigan Sugar Company. Warren had then become president of the Michigan firm, which was largely owned by the American Sugar Refining Company, the so-called Sugar Trust. Warren had remained with the Michigan company until shortly before his nomination as attorney general on March 4, 1925. Senators opposed to Warren pointed out that the Federal Trade Commission had recently cited the Michigan Sugar Company and fifteen similar firms for illegally contracting to control the marketing of sugar pulp in violation of the Sherman Antitrust Act. Defenders of Warren argued that his actions twenty years earlier had been considered perfectly legal at the time. In a tie vote on March 7, 1925, the Senate failed to confirm Warren.[37] President Coolidge immediately renominated Warren and indicated to the press that Warren would be given a recess appointment if the Senate again rejected him. On March 18 the Senate voted 46 to 39 against Warren, who shortly thereafter turned down a recess appointment.[38]

Prohibition Enforcement

Coolidge inherited from Harding a legacy of law enforcement of the Volstead Act and of corruption among prohibition agents. Coolidge, who personally abstained from liquor, called on citizens to obey the law. In his first message to Congress, he also recommended increased state action and the extension of the federal civil service to cover prohibition against the Treasury Department. Enactment of the latter proposal in 1927 helped reduce corruption, but enforcement of the Volstead Act remained ineffective.[39]

Conclusion

In assessing Coolidge as president, historians have emphasized that he did little but that he symbolized purity in government. Coolidge inherited an administration that quickly fell into disrepute because of the revelations of corruption. Although he was sometimes slow to respond to charges of misconduct, he restored public confidence in the presidency.[40]

NOTES

[1]Until learning of Fall's sudden display of wealth, the committee had uncovered no evidence of wrongdoing since it had begun investigating the oil leases in April, 1922.

[2]Fall to Members of the Senate Committee on Public Lands, December 26, 1923, reprinted in *Leases upon Naval Oil Reserves,* Hearings before the Senate Committee on Public Lands and Surveys, 67th and 68th Cong. (3 vols., Washington, 1923–1924), 1433.

[3]Fall to Walsh, January 11, 1924, *ibid.,* 1699.

[4]*Leases upon Naval Oil Reserves,* 1771ff. Called before the Public Lands Committee on February 2, 1924, Fall refused to answer any questions on the ground that it might tend to incriminate him. *Ibid.,* 1961–1963.

[5]Howard H. Quint and Robert H. Ferrell, eds., *The Talkative President: The Off-the-Record Press Conferences of Calvin Coolidge* (Amherst, Mass., 1964), 59.

[6]*Ibid.,* 59–60.

[7]Coolidge to Daugherty, January 24, 1924, quoted in Burl Noggle, *Teapot Dome: Oil and Politics in the 1920's* (Baton Rouge, 1962), 81.

[8]Quint, *The Talkative President,* 60. Charles Evans Hughes, Herbert Hoover, and John W. Weeks, cabinet members who had also served in the Harding cabinet, issued statements supporting Coolidge's claim that oil leases had never been discussed. Noggle, *Teapot Dome,* 83.

[9]Noggle assumed in his study of Teapot Dome that the terms of Walsh's plan leaked to the President. Coolidge's recent biographer expressed no opinion. Noggle, *Teapot Dome,* 90–91; Donald R. McCoy, *Calvin Coolidge: The Quiet President* (New York, 1967), 208.

[10]Coolidge statement, January 26, 1924, quoted in Noggle, *Teapot Dome,* 92.

[11]Coolidge statement, February 11, 1924, reprinted in *New York Times,* February 12, 1924.

[12]Denby to Coolidge, February 17, 1924, Coolidge to Denby, February 18, 1924, quoted in Noggle, *Teapot Dome,* 116–117. Denby, who was never indicted in connection with the oil leases, was subsequently exonerated in cases brought against others. *Pan-Am. v. U.S.,* 273 U.S. 456 (1927); *Mammoth Oil Co. et al. v. U.S.,* 275 U.S. 13 (1927).

[13]*Leases upon Naval Oil Reserves,* 2348. Though quoting Slemp's reference to "confidential" material, historians have failed to point out that he offered to let Walsh see his messages from Florida to the White House. Noggle, *Teapot Dome,* 130–131; McCoy, *Calvin Coolidge,* 218.

[14]The telegram of January 12 told McLean: "Prescott is away. Advise Slemp with whom I shall confer. Acknowledge." Coolidge explained that he had wanted advice about a political appointment, and since Samuel J. Prescott, the usual source of such information, was unavailable, he wanted to know from Slemp with whom he should confer. The second message to McLean read in part: "Thank you for your message. You have always been most considerate." This was an acknowledgment of a congratulatory note which McLean had sent after Coolidge refused to dismiss Denby. Telegrams quoted in Noggle, *Teapot Dome,* 131–132. In his study, Noggle concluded that no one gave "any testimony that could link Calvin Coolidge to Teapot Dome's complex intrigues." Coolidge "emerged from the McLean episode with no noticeable tarnish on his reputation." *Ibid.,* 132, 136.

[15]*New York Times,* March 1 and 7, 1924.

[16]*Senate Report 794,* 68th Cong., 1st Sess., reprinted in *Congressional Record,* 68th Cong., 1st Sess. (June 6, 1924).

[17]*Pan Am. v. U.S.*, 273 U.S. 456 (1927); *Mammoth Oil Co., et al. v. U.S.*, 275 U.S. 13 (1927).

[18]The trials are discussed in Francis X. Busch, *Enemies of the State* (Indianapolis, 1954), 117–170.

[19]*Sinclair v. U.S.*, 279 U.S. 263 (1929); *Sinclair v. U.S.*, 279 U.S. 749 (1929).

[20]49 F.2d 506 (1931). By the time Fall came to trial for bribery, investigators had determined that he had received some $300,000 from Harry Sinclair in addition to the $100,000 from Doheny. Prosecutors cited the Sinclair money as evidence that Fall intended to use his government job for personal gain.

[21]For a discussion of the federal statues on bribery which take intent into consideration, see Charles G. Hagland, "The Naval Reserve Leases," *Georgetown Law Journal*, XX (March 1932), 327.

[22]*Investigation of the Attorney General*, Hearings before the Senate Select Committee on the Investigation of the Attorney General, 68th Cong., 1st Sess. (Washington, 1924), *passim*.

[23]Daugherty to Smith W. Brookhart, March 27, 1924, reprinted in *New York Times*, March 28, 1924.

[24]Coolidge to Daugherty, March 27, 1924, quoted in McCoy, *Calvin Coolidge*, 217.

[25]C. Bascom Slemp to Daugherty, March 27, 1924, quoted in Noggle, *Teapot Dome*, 128.

[26]Daugherty to Coolidge, March 28, 1924, quoted *ibid.*

[27]Daugherty's successor as attorney general, Harlan Fiske Stone, forced Burns to resign in May, 1924. Alpheus T. Mason, *Harlan Fiske Stone: Pillar of the Law* (New York, 1956), 150.

[28]For Daugherty's statement to the court, see Mark Sullivan, *Our Times: The United States, 1900–1925* (6 vols., New York, 1926–1935), VI, 354.

[29]Daugherty always insisted that he was innocent of any wrongdoing while attorney general, but his destruction of bank records and his refusal to testify were considered suspicious acts for an innocent man. In any event, Mark Sullivan was certain that Daugherty did not receive any of the illicit money from Jesse Smith because the Attorney General was too loyal to Harding to risk discrediting him. Sullivan, *Our Times*, VI, 355–356. Samuel Hopkins Adams implied in his study of Harding that Daugherty was probably guilty. Adams, *Incredible Era: The Life and Times of Warren Gamaliel Harding* (Boston, 1939), 416–421. Francis Russell found the evidence ambiguous but seemed to conclude that Daugherty was innocent. Russell, *The Shadow of Blooming Grove: Warren G. Harding in His Times* (New York, 1968), 512–513. Robert K. Murray found it "almost inconceivable . . . that the many activities of Smith, especially his involvement with the alien property custodian, could have remained completely hidden from Daugherty." Murray, *The Harding Era: Warren G. Harding and His Administration* (Minneapolis, 1969), 484. Yet Murray concluded that Daugherty "was not involved in Smith's corrupt activities in any direct way." Murray, *The Politics of Normalcy: Governmental Theory and Practice in the Harding-Coolidge Era* (New York, 1973), 126.

[30]James M. Miller to E. G. Liebold, October 12, 1923, reprinted in *Muscle Shoals*, Hearings before the Senate Committee on Agriculture and Forestry, 68th Cong., 1st Sess. (Washington, 1924), 389.

[31]Coolidge statement, April 29, 1924, reprinted *ibid.*, 457.

[32]In a report, dated May 31, 1924, Senator Norris implied that an agreement had been reached between Ford and Coolidge. *Senate Report 734*, 68th Cong., 1st Sess., 26. After a detailed study of the alleged deal, Preston J. Hubbard took no position on the validity of the charge. Preston J. Hubbard, *Origins of the TVA: The Muscle Shoals Controversy,*

1920–1932 (Nashville, 1961), 112–146. According to Coolidge's recent biographer, who noted the lack of conclusive evidence, "Coolidge had thought that he had made a good arrangement for himself and for the country, but the apparent fact that a deal had been made left him vulnerable to attack." McCoy, *Calvin Coolidge,* 228.

[33]Harry Barnard, *Independent Man: The Life of Senator James Couzens* (New York, 1958), 162.

[34]Mellon to Coolidge, April 10, 1924. Coolidge Message to the Senate, April 11, 1924, reprinted in *Congressional Record,* 68th Cong., 1st Sess. (April 12, 1924), 6087–6088.

[35]Barnard, *Independent Man,* 166–167.

[36]*Senate Report 27,* 69th Cong., 1st Sess. (Washington, 1926). Following Andrew Mellon's retirement as secretary of the Treasury in 1932, he was charged by the Roosevelt administration with having evaded income taxes in 1931. After hearing the evidence, a grand jury issued no criminal indictment. The Bureau of Internal Revenue then filed a civil claim for unpaid taxes on questionable deductions. The complicated case was finally decided by the Board of Tax Appeals on December 7, 1937, four months after Mellon's death. The board ruled that no fraud was involved but that Mellon owed $600,000 of the $3,000,000 in back taxes claimed by the government. *A. W. Mellon, Petitioner v. Commissioner of Internal Revenue, Respondent,* 36 B.T.A. 977 (Docket No. 76, 499); Eugene C. Gerhart, *America's Advocate: Robert H. Jackson* (Indianapolis, 1958), 72–80.

[37]This was the first Senate rejection of a cabinet appointment since 1868.

[38]Joseph P. Harris, *The Advice and Consent of the Senate* (Berkeley, 1953), 119–124.

[39]Charles Merz, *The Dry Decade* (New York, 1931), 104–105, 236, 246; Andrew Sinclair, *Era of Excess: A Social History of the Prohibition Movement* (New York, 1964), 278; McCoy, *Calvin Coolidge,* 303.

[40]William Allen White, *A Puritan in Babylon: The Story of Calvin Coolidge* (New York, 1938); Claude M. Fuess, *Calvin Coolidge: The Man from Vermont* (Boston, 1940), 498–499; McCoy, *Calvin Coolidge,* 413–414.

HERBERT HOOVER
1929–1933

Robert P. Ingalls

B efore assuming the presidency, Herbert Hoover had served as secretary of commerce under both Harding and Coolidge. Despite
this link with the Harding administration, Hoover had emerged with
his reputation untarnished since none of the charges of misconduct had
been leveled against him or any members of the Department of Commerce. During his years in the White House, Hoover was under the close
scrutiny of the Democratic National Committee, which hired a full-time
publicity director to keep an eye on the Republican administration.

Summer Camp

When President Hoover established a summer camp for himself in the
mountains of Virginia during 1929, some newspaper reports implied
that public money had paid the cost of the retreat. After the appearance
of press headlines such as "MARINES BUILDING CAMP FOR HOOVER,"[1]
the President's secretary declared, "Every nail and every board in the
President's camp was paid for by Herbert Hoover out of his own pocket."
Following this announcement on July 19, 1929, the President released
a letter dated August 2, 1929, to the chairman of the Virginia Conservation Commission, which gave more details about the camp. Located
near the headwaters of the Rapidan River, the site of 164 acres lay close to
the new Shenandoah National Park. "My contribution," Hoover wrote,
"has been the purchase and preparation of the building materials, together with some labor costs." In addition, the Marine Corps furnished
the labor for building the cabins. "I desire," the President concluded,

"that the camp shall ultimately become the property of the Shenandoah National Park, so that . . . they [sic] may hold it for the use of my successors."[2] At the end of his term, Hoover deeded the camp to Virginia, which in turn was to transfer it to the national park. The state trustee reported that Hoover had spent about $114,000 on the camp.[3]

Sugar Lobbyists

In December, 1929, a Senate committee investigating lobbyists produced letters that appeared to implicate President Hoover in the activities of sugar lobbyists. Herbert C. Lakin, who wrote the letters, lobbied in Washington on behalf of Cuban sugar interests. After Hoover's victory in 1928, Lakin had retained Edwin P. Shattuck, a lawyer, to help with the campaign to keep down the duty on imported sugar. Shattuck was hired because he was thought to be a close friend of the President-elect. Following Hoover's inauguration, Lakin reported positive results in correspondence to Cuba. "I have not yet had a second interview with Senator [Reed] Smoot [chairman of the Senate Finance Committee]," Lakin wrote on March 15, 1929. "Both he and Shattuck have had conferences on this subject with President Hoover who has instructed them to confer together."[4] In another message Lakin declared: "President Hoover has taken a direct hand. He has already suggested a possible solution to Senator Smoot and to Mr. Shattuck."[5]

When questioned nine months later about the basis of these statements, Lakin proved less knowledgeable than his letters implied. Testifying before a subcommittee of the Senate Judiciary Committee in December, 1929, he could not verify that Shattuck and Hoover had ever discussed the duty on sugar. Shattuck himself denied that he had approached the President directly about the issue. "I have discussed [sugar matters] with Senator Smoot and others," he told the committee, "but I have had no directions from Mr. Hoover about the sugar tariff, nor have I discussed the sugar tariff with Mr. Hoover."[6]

Within a month after looking into the matter, the Senate panel issued an interim report which completely exonerated President Hoover. The committee concluded that it found "no impropriety nor anything open to censure or criticism."[7]

Oil Shale Lands

In September, 1930, the resignation of a member of the Interior Department raised the specter of another scandal like Teapot Dome. The official, Ralph S. Kelley, had served with the department for twenty-five years, and for the previous six years he had headed the field division of the U.S. General Land Office in Denver. In his letter of resignation, dated September 28, 1930, which he released to the press, Kelley charged that "the large oil interests are endeavoring to secure titles by fraud" to parts of "the public domain in western Colorado [which contain] an immense oil reserve embracing an area of approximately 800,000 acres, in which the oil occurs in a rock called shale." Kelley estimated that "this oil field contains more than 40,000,000,000 barrels of petroleum, of a potential value . . . of $40,000,000,000." The private companies attempting to wrest these oil fields from the public included, according to Kelley, "several of the very concerns whose fraudulent practices have so recently been exposed in the investigation and trials of former Secretary of the Interior Albert B. Fall and Harry Sinclair." Asserting that his protests had been ignored or overruled by the Secretary of the Interior, Kelley resigned so that "public opinion can be focused upon the practices by means of which titles to billions of dollars of Colorado oil property have already wrongfully passed out of the hands of the Government."[8]

Refusing to accept Kelley's resignation, the Secretary of the Interior, Ray Lyman Wilbur, demanded that Kelley supply specific information to substantiate his charges. On September 29 Wilbur also asked the Attorney General to conduct an investigation. Meanwhile, Kelley was suspended from his post pending resolution of the matter. On October 2 the assistant attorney general put in charge of the investigation invited Kelley to make a full statement of the facts. Kelley, however, refused to cooperate with the Justice Department because, he said, "members of the President's Cabinet are much too closely bound together to permit impartial investigations of each other." Kelley advised the assistant attorney general that "I have made arrangements whereby the principal facts supporting the allegations contained in my letter of resignation will at once be presented for the consideration of the public."[9]

These "arrangements" turned out to be a series of articles in the New

York *World.* On September 11 Kelley had signed a contract with the newspaper, in which he promised a 22,000-word story in return for $12,000, more than three times his annual salary of $3,600. The week before beginning publication on October 6, the *World* attempted to syndicate the series by advertising an exposé about the "theft of oil lands that will rival Teapot Dome." [10]

On October 24 the Department of Justice reported that it found Kelley's charges baseless. Oil shale, it was pointed out, had no commercial value since the cost of extracting oil from shale greatly exceeded the value of the product. Of the more than 8,000,000 acres of public land containing oil shale, less than 200,000 acres, about 3% of the total, had been patented by private interests. Of the 43,000 acres patented during the Hoover administration, 23,000 were approved by Kelley himself. Furthermore, the Secretary of the Interior had put Kelley in charge of all pending oil shale claims. On the basis of these findings, the Justice Department concluded, "There is no merit or substance in Kelley's charges." [11] After receiving this report, Secretary Wilbur dismissed Kelley from the Interior Department on October 28.

That same day President Hoover spoke publicly about the charges for the first time. He declared, "I hope that the American people realize that when reckless, baseless, and infamous charges in the face of responsible denial, with no attempt at verification . . . are broadcast, reflecting upon the probity of public men, such as Secretary Wilbur, the ultimate result can only be damaging to public service as a whole." [12]

Prohibition Enforcement

President Hoover made the first sustained attempt to enforce the Volstead Act. In his inaugural address, he warned, "Our whole system of self-government will crumble either if officials elect what laws they will enforce or citizens elect what laws they will support." [13] The following year a national commission appointed by Hoover reported that during the previous nine years the federal government had failed to enforce prohibition. To improve obedience to the law, the commission made a series of recommendations, including transfer of the Prohibition Bureau from the Treasury Department to the Justice Department. [14] Enactment of this proposal, which Hoover had already endorsed in late 1929, aided the President in his effort to curb the illegal use of alcohol. By the end of the Hoover administration, the number of convictions and jail sentences for liquor offenses had risen sharply.[15]

RFC Loan to Charles G. Dawes

In 1932 questions arose about a loan by the Reconstruction Finance Corporation (RFC) to a bank directed by Charles G. Dawes, former head of the RFC. Created in February, 1932, the RFC was a government lending agency authorized to provide emergency credit to banks, railroads, and other large institutions in need of capital as a result of the depression. On June 27, 1932, three weeks after resigning as president of the RFC, Dawes announced that the Central Republic Bank of Chicago, which he had taken over after leaving the RFC, had received loans to keep it solvent. He did not give the source of the money, but reports from Wall Street indicated that the RFC had put up $80,000,000. The following day Congressman Fiorello La Guardia questioned the propriety of such a large loan, which turned out to be $90,000,000, to a bank led by someone so recently connected with the RFC.[16] When the charge of possible misconduct resurfaced during the 1932 election campaign, the President defended Dawes in a speech on November 4. Hoover explained that two Democratic members of the RFC board and other bankers, not Dawes, had suggested the loan on June 26, almost three weeks after Dawes's retirement from the RFC.[17]

Air Mail Contracts

Less than a year after Hoover completed his term as president, his Postmaster General, Walter F. Brown, faced charges of collusion and other illegal acts in the granting of air mail contracts during the years 1929–1932. When allegations of wrongdoing first surfaced at the end of Hoover's term, the Senate authorized an inquiry by a special committee, which became known as the "Black Committee" after its chairman, Senator Hugo L. Black. At its public hearings which began in September, 1933, the Black Committee listened to conflicting testimony about the legality of the former postmaster general's methods.

Brown's leading critics were small independent operators who complained that he had favored big airline companies in awarding air mail contracts. At a series of so-called spoils conferences in May and June, 1930, the Postmaster General and airline executives had allegedly divided up the country's air mail routes among the largest operators. When one participant in the conferences expressed concern about their legality, another executive said, "I quite agree with you; if we were holding this meeting across the street in the Raleigh Hotel, it would be an improper meeting; but because we are holding it at the invitation of a member of the cabinet, and in the office of the Post Office Department, it is perfectly all right." [18] After these meetings, Brown awarded air mail contracts to the highest bidder in several cases, and he also avoided competitive bidding in a number of instances by approving the "extension" of existing airlines, which almost doubled the routes of some companies.

To this list of charges catalogued by independent operators, James A. Farley, Brown's successor as postmaster general, added several others. In 1929 Brown had extended five air mail contracts for six months to avoid competitive bidding, which was allegedly illegal. Before Brown left office, he had also reportedly destroyed incriminating Post Office files in violation of the law. Farley concluded that "all the present domestic air-mail carriers secured contracts based on conspiracy and collusion." [19]

Appearing before the Black Committee, former postmaster general Brown defended his methods. His goal had been a national air transportation system capable of carrying passengers safely, profitably, and on schedule, and he used government air mail contracts, on which fledgling airlines depended for survival, as a lever to achieve consolidation and improved service. Brown helped subsidize both air mail service and the construction of larger planes for passengers by winning enactment of legislation which required the government to pay for air mail according to the airplane space available for mail. Explaining his policy to the committee, Brown declared:

> I could think of no other way to make the industry self-sustaining, . . . than to compel the air mail contractor to get some revenue from the public. Almost all of them were refusing to carry passengers and were depending wholly upon the Post Office Department and we were getting nowhere in the development of

airplanes. . . . I believe that it was my duty to force them, if I could under the law, to get revenue from nonpostal sources, and the obvious one was passengers; and . . . the purpose of it was altogether to help develop an industry that could live without a subsidy.[20]

The Black Committee heard sensational revelations, but ultimately it could find nothing illegal in Brown's practices, which may have stretched the law but did not break it. Postal laws permitted the Postmaster General to extend contracts for up to six months. Press reports from 1930 showed that the spoils conferences were not secret, and subsequent events indicated that the airlines had not developed a plan for dividing air mail routes. The Watres Act of 1930 gave the postmaster general the right to consolidate and extend routes in the public interest. The Black Committee never received any proof that Brown had destroyed incriminating files before leaving the Post Office Department.[21]

Conclusion

Despite a spate of charges, investigations turned up no evidence of official misconduct within the Hoover administration. Historians have only begun to examine the Hoover presidency. Thus far they agree that his four-year term was free of corruption.[22]

NOTES

[1] *Time*, July 29, 1929.

[2] Hoover to William E. Carson, August 2, 1929, reprinted in *New York Times*, August 8, 1929. Hoover later said that he had also paid for the land for the camps. Hoover, *The Memoirs of Herbert Hoover: The Cabinet and the Presidency, 1920–1933* (New York, 1952), 322.

[3] *New York Times*, January 11, 1933.

[4] Lakin to Gerardo Machado, March 15, 1929, reprinted in *Lobby Investigation*, Hearings before a Subcommittee of the Senate Committee on the Judiciary, 71st Cong., 2nd Sess. (Washington, 1930), 1583.

[5] Lakin to Chadbourne, Manas and Rodriguez, March 15, 1929, reprinted *ibid.*, 1601.

[6] *Ibid.*, 1727.

[7] *New York Times*, January 15, 1930.

[8] Kelley to Ray Lyman Wilbur, September 28, 1930, reprinted in *Oil Shale Lands*, Hearings before the Senate Committee on Public Lands and Surveys, 71st Cong., 2nd Sess. (Washington, 1931), 320–321.

[9]Kelley to Seth W. Richardson, October 3, 1930, reprinted *ibid.*, 328–329.

[10]New York World Syndicate to St. Paul *Pioneer Press et al.*, October 2, 1930, quoted *ibid.*, 348. Kelley's contract with the *World* is reprinted *ibid.*, 316–318. For his articles, see New York *World*, October 6–19, 1930.

[11]William D. Mitchell to Wilbur, October 24, 1930, reprinted in *Oil-Shale Lands*, 333–334.

[12]Hoover statement, October 28, 1930, reprinted *ibid.*, 335–336. After Congress reconvened in December, the Senate Public Lands Committee looked into Kelley's charges, but hearings came to an abrupt end in February, 1931, when Kelley failed to appear, due to illness, for his second day as a witness. *New York Times*, February 28, 1931.

[13]Hoover Address, March 4, 1929, reprinted in *Congressional Record*, 71st Cong., 1st Sess. (March 4, 1929), 5.

[14]National Commission on Law Observance and Enforcement, Preliminary Report, reprinted in *New York Times*, January 14, 1930.

[15]As a result of Hoover's efforts, according to Andrew Sinclair, "Prohibition had developed from a joke into a threat to all." Sinclair, *Era of Excess: A Social History of the Prohibition Movement* (New York, 1964), 192.

[16]*New York Times*, June 28–29, 1932.

[17]Hoover Address, November 4, 1932, reprinted *ibid.*, November 5, 1932. Years later, Jesse H. Jones, one of the Democratic members of the RFC who recommended the loan to Dawes's bank, confirmed Hoover's version of events surrounding the loan. Jones, *Fifty Billion Dollars: My Thirteen Years with the RFC, 1932–1945* (New York, 1951), 72–81.

[18]Testimony of William McKee, *Investigation of Air Mail and Ocean Contracts*, Hearings before the Senate Special Committee on Investigation of Air Mail and Ocean Mail Contracts, 73rd Cong., 2nd Sess. (Washington, 1933–1934), 1450.

[19]Farley to Hugo L. Black, February 14, 1934, reprinted in *Air Mail*, Hearing before the House Committee on the Post Office and Post Roads, 73rd Cong., 2nd Sess. (Washington, 1934), 88.

[20]*Investigation of Air Mail Contracts*, 2569–2570.

[21]In 1941, a commissioner of the U.S. Court of Claims concluded that there had been no fraud or collusion in Brown's administration of the Post Office Department. Henry Ladd Smith, *Airways: The History of Commercial Aviation in the United States* (New York, 1942), 276–277. Historians have agreed that the evidence supports Brown's contention that he acted in the public interest, as he interpreted it. *Ibid.*, 276; Arthur M. Schlesinger, Jr., *The Coming of the New Deal* (Boston, 1959), 450.

[22]Eugene Lyons, *Herbert Hoover: A Biography* (New York, 1964), 220–333; Arthur M. Schlesinger, Jr., *The Crisis of the Old Order* (Boston, 1957), 224–269.

FRANKLIN D. ROOSEVELT
1933–1945

James Boylan

During his 1936 campaign for reelection, Franklin D. Roosevelt boasted of the handling of emergency relief funds by his administration: "... in spite of all the demand for speed, the complexity of the probable, and all the vast sums of money involved, we have had no Teapot Dome."[1] That claim remained a generally accurate one for Roosevelt's entire term in office, the longest tenure of any American president. No scandal produced the conviction, indictment, or even the forced resignation of a member of the White House staff or any other major New Deal administrator. This record was made in the face of twelve years of scrutiny by critics of unsurpassed vigilance.

Roosevelt may have been favored by circumstance to the extent that a time of depression and social change may inhibit corruption. Although the New Deal lifted domestic government expenditures to five times their pre-depression level, the nature of the outlays, concentrated on relatively small-scale aid to individuals, offered limited opportunities for windfalls. Moreover, the early Roosevelt years attracted to Washington a type of public servant less interested in the usual rewards of politics, including monetary rewards, than in social objectives. There was something of a change in atmosphere when the New Deal was put on the shelf during the war years. Standards of conduct, especially in handling government contracts and funds for the military, became notably looser. Nonetheless, the administration escaped the taint of any scandal at its upper levels.[2]

Air Mail Contract Inquiry

Roosevelt's first problem with corruption was a leftover from the previous administration. In September, 1933, a Senate committee under Hugo L. Black, Democrat of Alabama, began hearings on the award of air mail contracts by Walter F. Brown, President Hoover's postmaster general. Senator Black took to the White House his findings that the contracts had been obtained by collusion. On February 9, 1934, President Roosevelt abruptly canceled the contracts and ordered the Army Air Corps to fly mail on an emergency basis. The White House paid for its hasty action with the loss of five pilots and six planes in a week, and was forced to return air mail service to commercial lines in May.[3]

Allegations Against Howe

Minor accusations of misconduct brushed a member of Roosevelt's inner official family, Louis McHenry Howe, secretary to the President until his death in 1936, and a long-time adviser. Roosevelt had given Howe, among other assignments, the task of overseeing the Civilian Conservation Corps (CCC) on his behalf. Early in 1934 a Senate committee turned up a story that a CCC contract for 200,000 toilet kits had been awarded without competitive bidding; General Robert Fechner, head of the CCC, blamed Howe. But there was no damning evidence, and Senator Morris Sheppard of Texas, chairman of the Senate committee, sent Howe a letter exonerating him. Secretary of the Interior Harold L. Ickes later complained that the matter had been "hushed up," and Howe's biographer says tersely, "Louis managed to squirm out." Yet only a month after that squall, Howe got into contract trouble again when he tried to steer a navy award to the Bath Iron Works, which was not the low bidder, believing the move might help the administration in Maine's midterm elections. Roosevelt, experienced in such business from his Navy Department post in World War I, squelched the idea by notifying Howe that giving a contract to a high bidder would be "indefensible."[4]

Roosevelt vs. Long

Roosevelt regarded Senator Huey P. Long of Louisiana, who had become a national figure in the roles of radical reformer, tireless demagogue, and state political boss, as a serious threat to the nation and to his own political future. For his part, Long had cast off his earlier support of Roosevelt almost as soon as Roosevelt was settled in the White House. Their rivalry produced political combat that was fierce and occasionally unscrupulous, with Roosevelt using official powers for political ends and Long, in return, broadcasting charges of corrupt behavior in the administration.[5]

Besides pursuing such routine strategies as cutting off Long's sources of federal patronage, the Roosevelt administration sought to expose the Long regime as corrupt. The Treasury Department already had on hand a report on a preliminary tax inquiry conducted in the last days of the Hoover administration by Elmer Irey, head of the department's intelligence division. When Henry Morgenthau, Jr., became secretary of the Treasury in January, 1934—almost at the same time that Long founded his national "Share Our Wealth" organization—he ordered Irey's division back on the case, and soon at least fifty investigators were busy in Louisiana.[6]

Long struck back in February, 1935, with an assault designed to cause consternation in the Roosevelt cabinet. Taking the Senate floor on February 11, he ran through a long disconnected list of charges suggesting corruption in the Post Office Department, which was headed by James A. Farley, who was also Democratic national chairman. Many of the charges proved ephemeral—that Farley had given free stamps to collectors, that he had blocked investigation of a Nashville bank, that he had protected a wire gambling service. But Long gave special emphasis to an accusation that Farley was interested financially in companies doing construction work for the Public Works Administration and had used his influence to push contracts their way.[7]

Three days later Long made his next move. He called on the Senate to ask Harold L. Ickes, Secretary of the Interior and head of the Public Works Administration, to transmit information gathered by a department investigator, Louis Glavis (see "Controversies about Work Relief" below), concerning New York post office construction. Glavis had found that two lower-level officials, one in the Treasury and one in the Post Office Department, had destroyed two documents dealing with the construction contract, and thus concealed a possible irregularity. There was no indication that the heads of the departments, Farley and Morgenthau, had been involved.[8]

Long had revealed a matter of which the President himself had not been aware, and Roosevelt's response was prompt. He summoned Glavis to the White House, looked at his findings, and evidently decided that the administration had little to fear. He did not attempt to hold up the Senate's unanimous approval of Long's resolution, and he directed Ickes, Morgenthau, and Farley to send to the Senate any material their files contained on the matter. He also urged Farley to testify before a Senate committee, but Farley agreed only to send a letter responding to the charges. Meanwhile, the President also nipped any animosity that might have arisen from Glavis's trespassing into other departments.[9]

This immediate action had the effect of blunting Long's onslaught. Not that he had given up: he announced on March 4 that Farley was about to resign and that Roosevelt had chosen a successor. The prophecy proved to be false. Farley remained, and within a week the proposed investigation collapsed, with senators rallying to Farley's support and the House Post Office Committee dropping its inquiry. Roosevelt had won the skirmish.[10]

The final episode of the Roosevelt-Long conflict took place after Long's assassination in September, 1935. That event occurred almost at the culmination of the tax investigation of Long and his associates. Roosevelt personally persuaded a former governor of Texas, Dan Moody, to serve as prosecutor, and twenty-five indictments were handed up. Yet, curiously, the government moved early in 1936 to dismiss most of the criminal indictments and to settle for recovery of back taxes in civil suits, to the chagrin both of the Treasury investigators and of members of the grand jury. The apparent result of this action was the dissolution of the Long machine and the transfer of allegiance of Louisiana's political leadership to Roosevelt. The columnist Westbrook Pegler dubbed the purported transaction "the Second Louisiana Purchase." Still, the notion of buying the Long machine is improbable, for as James Farley remarked: "If there was 'purchase,' it is only fair to ask what was purchased." As soon as Senator Long died, thus ending the threat of his running on a third ticket, it was apparent to everyone in politics that Louisiana would vote Democratic in 1936."[11]

The rivalry with Long, however, does not reveal Roosevelt in an altogether favorable light. His response in the attack on Farley was exemplary, but the attack on Long via the Bureau of Internal Revenue was questionable. The timing of the resumption of the investigation, of the indictments, and of the settlements suggests strongly that politics dictated to law enforcement.

Controversies about Work Relief

The New Deal originated a constellation of agencies to stimulate the economy, increase employment, and render aid to millions stricken by the depression. The most important of these were the agencies run by two men of contrasting temperament who became vigorous rivals: Harold L. Ickes, who headed the Public Works Administration (PWA), and Harry Hopkins, who ran at different times the Federal Emergency Relief Administration (FERA), the Civil Works Administration (CWA), and the Works Progress Administration (WPA). In dealing with the possibility of corruption in their agencies, Ickes was prudent above all; Hopkins, who placed a higher priority on immediate results, was more vulnerable.

As head of the Department of the Interior and of the PWA, Ickes ran what Arthur M. Schlesinger, Jr., has called "traditionally the most corrupt of government departments and . . . what seemed potentially to be the most corruptible of emergency agencies." To check on all PWA transactions, he brought back into government Louis Glavis as head of a division of investigation—the same Glavis whose work had revealed the land frauds of the Ballinger-Pinchot affair a quarter century before. The PWA's chief of personnel, moreover, was a former private detective, E. K. Burlew. Ironically, Ickes proceeded so deliberately with PWA projects to make sure there was no possibility for scandal that the agency appears to have done little in its role of stimulating the economy.[12]

When even a hint of misconduct surfaced, Ickes strained to deal with it. The Long accusations against Farley arose because Ickes had set Glavis on the trail of a minor contract irregularity. Similarly, Ickes showed great concern over an accusation that the PWA had mishandled $47 worth of cement in the Virgin Islands, a charge that arose in connection with a dispute between political factions in that dependency. This kind of fussiness helped Ickes run an agency that remained almost free of any misconduct. In his diary, Ickes quoted Roosevelt as saying on December 27, 1934: "There have been a good many complaints about the slowness of the Public Works program and Harold's caution. I never expected it to be any faster than it has been and we can stand criticism of caution. There hasn't been even a minor scandal in Public Works, and that is some record."[13]

By contrast, each of the successive work-relief programs managed by Hopkins confronted charges. The CWA, hurriedly formed in 1933, provided direct federal relief until the FERA once more took over the burden in the spring of 1934; even its brief existence was troubled by accusations of waste and corruption. The FERA ran on authority divided between the state administrations, many of them headed by governors, and Washington headquarters. Hopkins fought stoutly to keep the FERA nonpolitical, but he had to deal with several governors in the effort. Floyd Olson of Minnesota stepped out of the FERA in the wake of charges that he had made political use of the relief organization. William Langer of North Dakota was rebuked by Hopkins for soliciting political funds from relief recipients; he was tried and acquitted on related charges.[14]

The most explosive incident occurred in Ohio, where Governor Martin Davey, a Democrat, headed the FERA and tried to make the agency perform political functions. A clash with Hopkins was touched off on March 4, 1935, when Davey urged replacement of nonpolitical FERA personnel with Democrats. Hopkins, already armed with a report from his field representative that Ohio politicians had been raising campaign funds through FERA offices, responded with heat. On March 15, 1935, he drafted two letters for the President's approval. One, to be signed by Roosevelt, instructed Hopkins as follows:

> I wish you to pursue these investigations diligently and let the chips fall where they may. This Administration will not permit the relief population of Ohio to become the innocent victims of either corruption or political chicanery.

You are authorized and directed forthwith to assume entire control of the administration of Federal relief in the State of Ohio.

The other letter, from Hopkins to Davey, ousted the governor from the FERA and excoriated him at length. Davey responded with a warrant charging Hopkins with criminal libel, but ultimately withdrew it. Hopkins's new relief administrator in Ohio moved promptly, with the removal of thirty-five FERA employees who had also been working for the Davey organization.[15]

Hopkins largely succeeded in keeping the FERA nonpolitical, but its successor, the WPA, carried seeds of political trouble in its founding legislation. When the WPA was established under the Emergency Relief Appropriations Act of 1935, Congress insisted on presidential appointment and congressional confirmation of all relief officials receiving more than $5,000 a year. In effect, this meant that the Democratic Party would have to approve all WPA appointments, because presidential nominees would be cleared through Democratic chairman Farley and through individual senators, more than two-thirds of whom were Democrats in that Congress.[16]

The WPA quickly became one of the country's largest employers and biggest bureaucracies, and also a sizable political target. Critics charged that WPA workers were lazy, that their projects were make-work, and, above all, that they were being recruited into a pro–New Deal voting bloc. Hopkins tried to anticipate criticism by issuing directives throughout the 1936 election year that forbade WPA employees to run for office or to engage in any political activity whatever. The more substantial charge that year centered less on political corruption, however, than on possible manipulation of the relief rolls for electoral purposes. Roosevelt is vulnerable to this charge, for he was quoted as saying, when told that WPA rolls might be reduced on October 1, 1936, for lack of funds, "You tell Corrington Gill [a top WPA deputy] that I don't give a goddam where he gets the money from but not one person is to be laid off on the first of October." Yet, as John Morton Blum notes, to have gone through with the dismissal would not only have been "politically stupid" but "cruel." Nor are statistics conclusive: an article in the *Atlantic Monthly* in 1938 stated unequivocally, "The relief rolls expand during

election campaigns, and decline almost uniformly during the corre-
sponding months of non-election years"; Arthur M. Schlesinger, Jr., has
reached just the opposite verdict—that campaigns had no discernible
effect on the rolls.[17]

The WPA became more deeply entangled in the hard-fought midterm
campaign of 1938. It was fought in two phases: the first came in the
primaries, in which Roosevelt tried unsuccessfully to "purge" anti–New
Deal Democrats in Congress and, with better success, to renominate
his allies; there were widespread charges that administration candidates
had enlisted the WPA to bolster their finances and their support at the
polls. The second was the general campaign in which the Republicans,
rebounding from their 1936 setbacks, developed the alleged politiciza-
tion of the WPA into a full-blown issue.[18]

Assertions that political pressure was being put on WPA recipients
accompanied at least ten primary contests. (Senator Claude Pepper of
Florida was alleged to have benefited from a last-minute allocation of
relief funds to his state.) The Pennsylvania Democratic organization run
by Senator Joseph F. Guffey had its own man, Edward Jones, running
the WPA in the state; Jones had been severely criticized in 1936, and in
1938 similar charges of political manipulation led to court action. The
most publicized accusations emanated from Kentucky. There Senator
Alben W. Barkley, Senate majority leader and Roosevelt spokesman, was
challenged by Albert B. Chandler (who later became baseball commissioner). On May 23, 1938, Chandler's campaign manager charged that
the Barkley camp had been squeezing contributions from relief recipients. There was substance to the charges; twenty-two instances of such
pressure were documented in a series for the Scripps-Howard newspapers by Thomas L. Stokes—among them, that the state administrator
had sent out a letter describing ways to collect from WPA workers contributions amounting to 2% of their annual wages. However, there was
no evidence that Barkley himself was personally aware of these efforts.[19]

Such charges had a substantial impact both on the public and in Congress. A Gallup poll published on June 10, 1938, showed that 54% of
those interviewed believed that the WPA was playing a role in politics.
Immediately after Chandler's camp made its charges in Kentucky, Senator Carl A. Hatch, Democrat of New Mexico, offered an amendment
to the 1938 relief bill to bar anyone receiving relief funds from political

activity; the amendment was defeated, but Hatch planned to try again. In the meantime, the Senate ordered an investigation of the use of federal relief funds in states holding senatorial elections; the inquiry was placed under the campaign expenditures committee of Senator Morris Sheppard of Texas. On August 3, 1938, the committee issued an interim report that charged coercion of workers in Kentucky and Tennessee and contradicted as well Hopkins's denial of all but two of the charges in Stokes's articles.[20]

It was difficult for the administration to respond effectively. Hopkins had contributed to this difficulty himself by participating actively in the Roosevelt purge, most notably in his endorsement of an unsuccessful candidate to oppose Senator Guy M. Gillette in his native Iowa. Moreover, many of the abuses stemmed from the actions of candidates and party leaders, not WPA officials; as Hopkins declared in May, 1938, "I cannot control a politician who does not work for me." The President echoed this plaint in a news conference a few days before the election when he said, "No administration can be wholly responsible for the actions of either Republican or Democratic local political leaders." For his part, Hopkins had to be content with repeated directives aimed at enforcing a policy of noninterference with WPA workers' allegiances, voting, or paychecks. But his efforts were often greeted with skepticism, not only in the opposition press, but in the administration; his long-time rival, Ickes, observed in his diary after the election, "WPA is more than ever on the verge of an open scandal in so many places that I wonder whether suppression will work in the long run." Ickes did not describe the nature of the "suppression."[21]

The final report of the Sheppard Committee, issued on January 3, 1939, contained serious but not surprising charges. It found abuses in three states—Kentucky, Tennessee, and Pennsylvania—but no basis, on the other hand, for upholding similar accusations in Maryland, Missouri, New York, Indiana, New Jersey, and Ohio. It noted as well that not only Senator Barkley, who won the Kentucky primary, but his opponent, Chandler, had taken contributions from government employees. In Pennsylvania it found apparently systematic solicitation of WPA workers by the Guffey organization. Hopkins, who had resigned as WPA administrator on December 24, 1938, to become secretary of commerce, escaped direct criticism. Only one member of his staff, Aubrey

Williams, was rebuked for telling relief workers in June, 1938, "We've got to keep our friends in power." However, Arthur Krock noted in the *New York Times*, "The report is an indictment of Mr. Hopkins for—if nothing more—stubbornly defending and giving clean bills of health to the WPA when the newspapers were full of proof to the contrary."[22]

The initiative in taking corrective measures after the report was assumed, not by the administration, but by Senators Hatch, Sheppard, and Warren R. Austin of Vermont, a Republican. They sponsored a bill "to prevent pernicious political activities" that placed restrictions on non–civil service federal employees similar to those already barring civil service employees from political participation; the bill ultimately exempted policymaking officials. The administration claimed such credit as it could: Hopkins declared himself in favor of such legislation, and Roosevelt praised Congress for its efforts to take politics out of relief. He also placed WPA employees under the civil service. After Congress completed action in July, 1939, Roosevelt considered a veto because the bill did not include state and municipal employees, but ultimately signed the measure and claimed, without much proof, that it had originated in his January message to Congress.[23]

Despite the Sheppard investigation and an even sterner inquiry in 1939, under Representative Clifton Alexander Woodrum of Virginia, no significant evidence emerged of corruption among WPA personnel. Representative Woodrum volunteered in the House that his committee had found nothing that raised "any question upon the personal character or integrity of any high WPA official in Washington." One historian of relief notes that "in four and one-half years there had not been one case of a really responsible official of the WPA who had gone crooked" and that no dishonesty had been found at any level higher than that of district manager.[24]

Nonetheless, critics persisted in trying to lay the WPA's political troubles at the feet of the President. Stanley High, a journalist, wrote in May, 1939, "The administration of work relief, which is now America's biggest business, can be not better than the President of the United States insists it shall be." Indeed, fault could be found with his lack of an active role in meeting the 1938 charges; the record appears singularly lacking in any outright presidential condemnation of abuses during the campaign, and the Chief Executive left it to Congress to meet the need for reform with a bill he did not consider entirely satisfactory. Even so, Roosevelt has not generally been blamed for the WPA's shortcomings, especially when these shortcomings are weighed against the size and expenditure, as well as the achievements, of the relief program.[25]

The TVA Investigation

The New Deal's most noteworthy experiment in regional development, the Tennessee Valley Authority, was more frequently subjected to constitutional challenges than to charges of misconduct. Yet accusations by one of the TVA's three directors against his associates figured in a broad congressional inquiry in 1938. Arthur E. Morgan, "a Yankee moralist and mystic,"[26] found himself at odds with his more down-to-earth colleagues, Harcourt Morgan and David E. Lilienthal. So determinedly did Morgan pursue these differences, both in private and in the public press, that President Roosevelt called the directors to the White House for a showdown. When Arthur Morgan proved unable to support his charges, Roosevelt summarily removed him from office, whereupon Morgan took his complaints to Congress.[27]

The investigation that took place through the fall of 1938 encompassed not only Morgan's complaints but the general administration of the TVA. The hearings were enlivened by the appearance of Wendell L. Willkie, a utilities executive who became the Republican presidential candidate two years later. Little interest was shown in the investigation by the press thereafter, however, and the committee's report, on April 3, 1939, received only passing attention. The committee found that internal dissension had handicapped the functioning of the TVA board, but that contrary to Morgan's allegations, "no member of the Board aided or assisted directly or indirectly a private company or other private interest in the institution or defense of suits and injunctions affecting the administration of the functions of the Authority." It also dismissed Morgan's contention that there had been corruption involved in the claims by Senator George L. Berry of Tennessee to damages for the flooding of land containing marble deposits. In effect, the committee confirmed the President's action in dismissing Morgan.[28]

The Roosevelt Family

Because members of his family played prominent public roles during Roosevelt's years in the White House, they were frequently subject to criticism. Eleanor Roosevelt, the President's wife and *ad hoc* adviser, carried on a lively and remunerative career as a radio commentator, lecturer, and newspaper columnist; a hostile critic estimated her earnings for the fifteen years after 1933 at more than $3,000,000. The size of her earnings led to accusations by Representative Hamilton Fish, Republican of New York, that the Roosevelts had not filed straightforward income tax returns. Within weeks, a congressional committee charged with looking into the matter gave the First Family a clean bill of health; the committee's ranking Republican member called the President's "an eminently fair return." [29]

Another member of the family may have been more vulnerable. Since 1930 James Roosevelt, one of the President's sons, had been in the insurance business; his company had come to serve a variety of large corporate clients. By his own account, James Roosevelt had earned as much as $44,000 a year before 1937. John T. Flynn charged, in *The Roosevelt Myth*, that the President's son had used his father's name and the influence of the White House to develop his business. Flynn asserted: "This was graft. . . . It was graft fully known to the President." Attacks of this nature reached a peak when James Roosevelt joined the White House staff, at his father's request, as an administrative assistant, but lessened after he replied to one hostile article by permitting reproduction of his tax returns in a national magazine. The authors of a study of criticisms of the Roosevelt administration term the charges against James Roosevelt a "slander." [30]

Elliott Roosevelt, another son, was subjected to embarrassing charges involving his work for the government, but only after his father's death. Elliott, as an army–air force officer assigned to aid in the development of a photo-reconnaissance plane, accepted the hospitality of one manufacturer, Howard Hughes, and then recommended immediate procurement of Hughes's F-11 reconnaissance plane, which was made of plywood. There were sharp differences of opinion in the Air Force on its merits. The plane was not ready to fly until a year after the war, and Hughes was seriously injured in a crash of the first test model. In 1947 the Senate's special defense investigating committee summoned Elliott Roosevelt, who denied that Hughes's entertainment had influenced him, insisted that he had never discussed procurement with his father, and charged that the investigation was aimed at smearing the late President. In its subsequent report, the committee did not charge Elliott Roosevelt with wrongdoing, but questioned his technical qualifications for a procurement position.[31]

World War II and Defense Contracts

From 1940 to 1945, the focus of the Roosevelt administration was shifted from easing economic crisis to the enormous effort of waging a global war. New Dealers had to make room for men with the required business and industrial expertise. The administration revived the World War I policy of employing businessmen without compensation, on the dollar-a-year arrangement, while leaving them free to continue drawing salaries from private employers. Such positions offered opportunity for favoritism toward one company or industry, as well as other abuses.

The administration took steps to reduce such hazards, most notably in the War Production Board, which had more than a thousand uncompensated employees. The President instituted the practice of a Federal Bureau of Investigation check on each man, as well as a policy of refusing to appoint any men involved in antitrust suits. The dollar-a-year men were not assigned to key positions in branches that dealt primarily with their own industries. To prevent conflict of interest in legal matters, no lawyers were hired as dollar-a-year men; they were required to sever private connections and to serve on a regular government salary.[32]

Congress provided a further deterrent to misconduct when it established in 1941 a special committee to oversee the defense program, under the chairmanship of Senator Harry S. Truman of Missouri. In general, the Truman Committee in its early days heard more of conflict, confusion, and delay in the mobilization program than of outright misconduct. However, late in 1941 it heard charges of influence peddling in the award of defense contracts. Thomas G. Corcoran, who had made his name in Washington drafting New Deal legislation, had received, as a lawyer in private practice, $100,000 in fees connected with defense contracts in a single year. Similarly, Charles G. West, a former under secretary of the interior under Ickes, admitted that he had collected fees from the Empire Ordnance Company based on a percentage of the anticipated contract awards.[33]

In its seven years of existence under Truman and the chairman who succeeded him, the committee turned up abundant evidence of fraud in private companies, but only two major cases of official misconduct, neither directly involving the executive branch. One was the connection between Representative Andrew J. May, chairman of the House Military Affairs Committee, and the Garsson brothers, munitions manufacturers. The other was the case of Brigadier General Bennett E. Meyers, who was revealed to have led a double life as an army–air force officer while drawing a salary for running the Aviation Electric Company of Dayton, a government subcontractor. He was convicted of subornation of perjury (for instructing his nominal "president" to lie) and served a prison sentence.[34]

Among war agencies not directly connected with the defense effort, none was more important or more pervasive than the Office of Price Administration (OPA), which supervised price control and rationing of scarce goods. When Chester Bowles became head of the OPA in 1943, President Roosevelt directed him to see that the agency remained strictly nonpolitical. Bowles notified all OPA employees that they must either stay out of politics or resign. Within a week, according to Bowles, he heard of two violations—one a speech against Roosevelt, the other an oration supporting him—and he demanded the resignation of both offenders.[35]

Bowles correctly was much more concerned over the possibility of corruption among OPA officials, for, as he observed, "By deliberately misplacing a digit in a single price control order . . . a member of our OPA staff could put several million dollars into someone's pocket." After finding the FBI unwilling to undertake general surveillance, Bowles adopted a plan suggested to him by Mayor Fiorello La Guardia of New York, and formed his own investigatory division, staffed with agents borrowed, with the President's approval, from the Secret Service. He then notified all OPA employees of the existence of the policing body and urged cooperation. The OPA came through the war with a record untarnished by corruption. Bowles observed with pride that the Republican Eightieth Congress sought evidence of war-time wrongdoing in the OPA but was "unable to come up with a single charge." In these efforts, he made clear, he had the full cooperation of President Roosevelt.[36]

In general, historians of America in the war years have not given concerted attention to charges of official misconduct, despite the acknowledged and widespread existence of laxness in handling materials and money. But occasional threads of evidence appear to touch the White House. It came out in 1951, for example, as a result of a dispute between President Truman and Senator Richard M. Nixon of California, that Roosevelt's White House had suppressed a Securities and Exchange Commission report on the same Empire Ordnance Company that had been a subject of Truman Committee hearings.[37] Late in the war, there were similar scattered charges concerning the Commodity Credit Corporation and the Reconstruction Finance Corporation that foreshadowed the more serious scandals of the Truman years.

Such shadows do not diminish the scale of Roosevelt's achievement in managing the diplomatic, military, and industrial strategy of the country's greatest war effort, and doing so without the occurrence of a major scandal. Clearly unable to keep in touch with all facets of wartime policy, he was not alone responsible for the good record. Yet the precedents he set in the peacetime years and the New Dealers he kept on to serve in the war effort helped forestall, although not altogether to obliterate, the consequences of wartime prosperity and of the enlargement of government in the depression and war years. Those consequences would fall primarily on the Truman administration.

Conclusion

In general, historians have had little to say about the personal and official honesty of Franklin D. Roosevelt and those who served with him in his three terms, with the exceptions noted in this essay. Even these do not constitute a major blemish on his administration's record, for, in the words of William E. Leuchtenburg, "no corruption was ever traced back to any national New Deal administrator."[38] Indeed, it would appear that a majority of historians and biographers have taken this record for granted. As a consequence, it is difficult to assay Roosevelt's precise role in countering corruption, aside from scattered instances—much more difficult than it would be, for example, in the case of a president who had permitted corruption to flourish. The silence of historians may be a kind of tribute.

NOTES

[1]Franklin D. Roosevelt, *Public Papers*, V (New York, 1938), 484.

[2]Arthur M. Schlesinger, Jr., *The Age of Roosevelt: The Coming of the New Deal* (Boston, 1959), 16–20.

[3]*Ibid.*, 448–451; Henry Ladd Smith, *Airways: The History of Commercial Aviation in the United States* (New York, 1942) 249–277. For other details on the air mail contracts, see section on Hoover.

[4]Patrick Anderson, *The Presidents' Men* (Garden City, 1969), 19; Alfred B. Rollins, Jr., *Roosevelt and Howe* (New York, 1962), 405, 427.

[5]Rexford G. Tugwell, *The Democratic Roosevelt* (New York, 1957), 349; Arthur M. Schlesinger, Jr., *The Age of Roosevelt: The Politics of Upheaval* (Boston, 1960), 48–56; William E. Leuchtenburg, *Franklin D. Roosevelt and the New Deal, 1932–1940* (New York, 1963), 96–99.

[6]T. Harry Williams, *Huey Long* (New York, 1969), 794–796; Schlesinger, *Politics of Upheaval*, 56–57.

[7]Williams, *Long*, 803–804; George Wolfskill and John A. Hudson, *All but the People: Franklin D. Roosevelt and His Critics, 1933–1939* (New York, 1969), 49; James A. Farley, *Jim Farley's Story* (New York, 1948), 50–51.

[8]Williams, *Long*, 804–805; Harold L. Ickes, *Secret Diary*, I: *The First Thousand Days, 1933–1936* (New York, 1953), 294–297.

[9]Williams, *Long*, 805–807; Ickes, *Diary*, I, 298–300.

[10]Farley, *Story*, 50–51; Williams, *Long*, 807.

[11]Schlesinger, *Politics of Upheaval*, 250; John T. Flynn, *The Roosevelt Myth* (New York, 1948), 73–74; Harnett T. Kane, *Louisiana Hayride* (New York, 1941), 182–184. Farley is quoted in Kane, 184.

[12]Schlesinger, *Coming of the New Deal*, 285–286; Leuchtenburg, *Roosevelt*, 70.

[13]On the Virgin Islands, see Ickes, *Diary*, 394–408; Harold B. Hinton in *New York Times*, sec. IV, July 14, 1935. Roosevelt quotation (fuller than the edited version in Ickes, *Diary*, I, 256) is in Schlesinger, *Coming of the New Deal*, 287.

[14]Searle F. Charles, *Minister of Relief: Harry Hopkins and the Depression* (Syracuse, 1963), 76; Leuchtenburg, *Roosevelt*, 121–124.

[15]Roosevelt-Hopkins letter is quoted in Charles, *Minister*, 79; see also analysis by N. R. Howard, *New York Times*, sec. IV, March 24, 1935.

[16]Charles, *Minister*, 175–176; Schlesinger, *Politics of Upheaval*, 355.

[17]John Morton Blum, *From the Morgenthau Diaries: Years of Crisis, 1928–1938* (Boston, 1959), 272–273; Lawrence Sullivan, "Relief and the Election," *Atlantic Monthly*, November, 1938, 607–615; Schlesinger, *Politics of Upheaval*, 590.

[18]Milton Plesur, "The Republican Congressional Comeback of 1938," *Review of Politics*, XXIV (October, 1962), 525–562; Charles M. Price and Joseph Boskin, "The Roosevelt 'Purge': A Reappraisal," *Journal of Politics*, XXVIII (August, 1966), 660–670.

[19]Charles, *Minister*, 197; James T. Patterson, *Congressional Conservatism and the New Deal* (Lexington, 1967), 238; Hal Borland in *New York Times*, sec. IV, June 12, 1938;

"T.R.B." and "WPA and the Politicos," *New Republic,* July 6, 1938, 249–250; Stokes, *Chip off My Shoulder* (Princeton, 1940), 534–536.

[20]Gallup poll, *New York Times,* June 19, 1938; Charles, *Minister,* 196–198.

[21]Hopkins quotation in Charles, *Minister,* 181. Roosevelt quotation in *Complete Presidential Press Conferences* (New York, 1972), XII, 207–208. Ickes, *Diary,* II: *The Inside Struggle, 1936–1939* (New York, 1954), 501. See also Robert E. Sherwood, *Roosevelt and Hopkins: An Intimate History* (New York, 1948), 78–104.

[22]Sheppard Committee text is printed in *New York Times,* January 4, 1939. Krock quotation, *ibid.* See also Patterson, *Conservatism,* 293.

[23]Dorothy Ganfield Fowler, "Precursors of the Hatch Act," *Mississippi Valley Historical Review,* XLVII (September, 1960), 247–262.

[24]Charles, *Minister,* 204.

[25]Stanley High, "The W.P.A.: Politician's Playground," *Current History,* May, 1939, 23–25, 62. For a contrary opinion, see the editorial "WPA Scandals of 1938," *New Republic,* January 18, 1939, 300–301. See also Leuchtenburg, *Roosevelt,* 332–333.

[26]Schlesinger, *Coming of the New Deal,* 327.

[27]Thomas K. McCraw, *TVA and the Power Fight, 1933–1939* (Philadelphia, 1971), 132–133; Francis Biddle, *In Brief Authority* (Garden City, 1962), 56–57.

[28]Biddle, *Authority,* 68–71; U.S. Congress, Joint Committee on the Investigation of the Tennessee Valley Authority, *Investigation of the Tennessee Valley Authority,* Senate Document 56, 76th Cong., 1st Sess., April 3, 1939, 7–9.

[29]Joseph P. Lash, *Eleanor and Franklin* (New York, 1973), 551–570; Flynn, *Myth,* 248; Wolfskill and Hudson, *All but the People,* 42.

[30]Wolfskill and Hudson, *All but the People,* 46–47; Flynn, *Myth,* 237–239; Alva Johnston, " 'Jimmy's Got It,' " *Saturday Evening Post,* July 2, 1938, 8–9, 57; Walter Davenport, "I'm Glad You Asked Me," (interview with James Roosevelt), *Collier's,* August 20, 1938, 9–12, 57.

[31]Flynn, *Myth,* 243; U.S. Senate, Special Committee Investigating the National Defense Program, *Investigation of the National Defense Program: Aircraft: Hughes Photo-Reconnaissance Plane,* Senate Report 440, pt. 3, 80th Cong., 2nd Sess., April 14, 1948, 11–23.

[32]George A. Graham, *Morality in American Politics* (New York, 1952), 207–208. For a general account of businessmen's participation in mobilization, see Bruce Catton, *The War Lords of Washington* (New York, 1948).

[33]Donald H. Riddle, *The Truman Committee: A Study in Congressional Responsibility* (New Brunswick, 1964), 141–165; David Hinshaw, *The Home Front* (New York, 1943), 145; *New York Times,* December 19, 1941.

[34]Riddle, *Truman Committee,* 148–149; *Investigation of the National Defense Program,* 1–2.

[35]Chester Bowles, *Promises to Keep* (New York, 1971), 72.

[36]*Ibid.,* 83–85. See also Harvey C. Mansfield and Associates, *A Short History of OPA,* Historical Reports on War Administration: Office of Price Administration, General Publication No. 15, 1947.

[37]*New York Times,* January 11, 1952; see also Riddle, *Truman Committee,* 147, and Blair Bolles, *How to Get Rich in Washington* (New York, 1952), 250–251.

[38]Leuchtenburg, *Roosevelt,* 270n. Compare Schlesinger, *Age of Roosevelt,* and Tugwell, *Democratic Roosevelt,* as well as such treatments as John Gunther, *Roosevelt in Retrospect* (New York, 1950); James MacGregor Burns, *Roosevelt: The Lion and the Fox* (New York, 1970); Walter Johnson, *1600 Pennsylvania Avenue* (Boston, 1963); and even such a critical account as Raymond Moley, *After Seven Years* (New York, 1939).

HARRY S. TRUMAN
1945–1953

James Boylan

Harry S. Truman became president of a country much changed from the prewar America of Franklin D. Roosevelt. War-born prosperity had replaced depression, and government had turned its attention from combatting hardship to underwriting an immense military enterprise. In the aftermath of war, leftover property, ready money, and improvised policies offered opportunity for personal gain at public expense.

Such opportunity had an unfortunate effect on official behavior. Whatever his achievements in other fields, President Truman was unable to enforce high standards of conduct throughout his administration, nor did he invariably select appointees capable of observing high standards. As Truman's time in office lengthened, their indiscretions came increasingly into public view and provided the opposition with ammunition for its 1952 election-year charge that there was a "mess in Washington." That there was a mess, to the extent that misconduct extended to several agencies and touched the White House itself, is indisputable; what has remained in dispute is the effectiveness of the President's responses.[1]

The Pauley Nomination

The most controversial episode involving ethical standards in the early Truman administration centered not on overtly illegal activity but on a political "deal." When Truman nominated Edwin W. Pauley, former treasurer of the Democratic National Committee, for undersecretary of the navy early in 1946, there were charges that Pauley's closeness to the oil industry unsuited him for the post, which could involve administering naval oil reserves. Pauley, himself a former oil producer, had been active during the war in the campaign to frustrate the federal claim to underwater ("tidelands") oil fields; the campaign was opposed by the Department of the Interior, which sought to establish the federal claims in the courts. During the hearings on Pauley's nomination, Secretary of the Interior Harold L. Ickes, who as "Honest Harold" personified the integrity of New Deal progressives, accused Pauley of trying to forestall his department's filing of a tidelands suit in order to salvage political contributions from oil interests.

The President responded with tactics that soon became familiar in his administration: he supported the man while taking action against his policy. At the time of the nomination, Truman had already disapproved of a congressional resolution supporting the claims of the states; Pauley had lobbied for its passage. Nor did the President waver thereafter in his support of federal ownership. But neither did he waver in his support of Pauley. He answered Ickes by suggesting that the Secretary had been mistaken; Ickes resigned with a letter that not only challenged Truman's truthfulness but warned him of the danger of a Teapot Dome–like scandal. Truman accepted the resignation and stood by Pauley until, with little hope of receiving confirmation, Pauley withdrew his name.[2]

The Kansas City Election Inquiry

Truman was vulnerable to more serious allegations after he intervened in August, 1946, in the politics of his home state. In an effort to rid Missouri's Fifth Congressional District, in Kansas City, of an unfriendly congressman, the President endorsed Enos Axtell and enlisted the old Pendergast Democratic political organization in Axtell's behalf against Representative Roger S. Slaughter. In the voting in the Democratic primary on August 6, Axtell carried four Kansas City wards in which the Pendergast organization was dominant, by a ratio of 5 to 1, and thereby won a narrow victory in the district. (He was defeated by a Republican in November.) An immediate investigation by the Kansas City Star produced evidence of voting improprieties.

The U.S. Department of Justice gradually became involved in the case. The Federal Bureau of Investigation had received word of possible frauds only eight days after the primary, but the department did not institute an investigation until October 16 after the *Star* had published its findings. Even then, the inquiry was limited to interviews with *Star* reporters. On January 6, 1947, the Justice Department, having found no basis for grand-jury action, declared the case closed.

But there were repercussions. Spurred by Senator James P. Kem, Republican of Missouri, a committee of the Eightieth Congress undertook an inquiry in the spring of 1947. However, on the day before public hearings began, the ballots and other records of the primary disappeared from the vaults of the Kansas City Board of Elections. Two federal grand juries, sitting later in the year in Kansas City, handed up a total of twenty-four indictments, but convictions were almost impossible without the records.

Suspicion lingered concerning the role of the Justice Department. The 1947 investigating committee narrowly rejected an investigation of the part played by Attorney General Tom C. Clark, and the minority criticized him for representing inaccurately to the committee the nature of the original investigation. As was conceded much later by Theron Lamar Caudle, assistant attorney general in charge of the criminal division, the FBI effort had been carefully limited and had received "top-level attention." A member of a House subcommittee investigating the Department of Justice in 1952 charged further that Clark had removed reports on the primary from the FBI files for two years, until 1949. That same subcommittee noted that Justice Department officials who were involved in the case "fared unusually well in their subsequent careers." Most notably, Caudle was moved to a more desirable post in the tax division. It is almost impossible to determine, however, to what extent such advancement was a reward, or what role, if any, the White House played in either the investigation or the promotions.[3]

Commodity Speculation

A pattern that persisted through the Truman administration was the President's refusal to disavow associates whose actions had threatened to embarrass him. A striking instance occurred in October, 1947, when the President criticized speculation in the grain market, only to have the

White House physician, Dr. Wallace H. Graham, admit two days later that he was one of the speculators. (Dr. Graham also asserted falsely that he had pulled out of the market; he did not actually withdraw until December 18, 1947, a day before the names of speculators were revealed to Congress.) Another speculator, on a much larger scale, was Edwin Pauley, who had been named a special assistant to the Secretary of the Army. He was accused by Harold Stassen, a potential Republican presidential candidate, of having "profiteered" in grain to the amount of a million dollars on the basis of inside information. Pauley denied obtaining such information but conceded that he had made profits of $932,703 in three years of speculation. He resigned from the Department of the Army on January 11, 1948.

The commodity investigation spread well beyond the White House. The Senate Appropriations Committee, seeking further information on trading by insiders, asked the Commodity Exchange Authority for the names of speculators. The Department of Agriculture denied the request on the ground that publishing such names was illegal, but Secretary Clinton P. Anderson agreed that he would be responsive to a joint resolution of Congress, which was duly approved. On December 29, 1947, the Agriculture Department released a list of a hundred federal, state, and municipal officials involved in commodity speculation. In 1948 a House select committee reported that 823 federal employees had made a net of $10,000,000 to $20,000,000 in speculation during 1946 and 1947, but did not charge that these employees had used inside information illegally or unethically.[4]

General Vaughan and "5-Percenters"

The President was even more seriously embarrassed by the continuing activities of his military aide, Brigadier General Harry H. Vaughan, a Missourian who had served on Truman's senatorial staff. Even in Truman's first weeks in the White House, Vaughan resumed the kinds of "referrals" he said had been part of his earlier job. On May 1, 1945, he wrote a note on White House stationery to obtain a wartime travel priority for a perfume manufacturer. That summer he secured Air Transport Command space for John F. Maragon of Kansas City, who was caught on his return from Europe in attempting to smuggle perfume raw materials.

Nonetheless, Vaughan successfully recommended Maragon that fall for a position with an American mission to Greece.

Vaughan was the key participant as well in the celebrated incident that made "deep freeze" a symbol of corruption in the Truman administration. As Vaughan described the matter: "In 1945 I had a talk with two old friends of mine—Mr. Harry Hoffman and Mr. David Bennett. The subject of deep-freeze units came up, and I said that I would like one for my house and that I would also like to send one to the Little White House in Independence [the Truman residence in Missouri]." Hoffman, a Milwaukee manufacturer, sent not merely a freezer for Vaughan and for Mrs. Truman but four more for other members of the administration—John W. Snyder, federal loan administrator; Fred Vinson, Secretary of the Treasury; and James K. Vardaman and Matthew Connelly of the White House staff. Only Vinson sent his back.[5]

Another incident that earned Vaughan notoriety was his effort to assist Tanforan racetrack, a California enterprise controlled by gambling interests. By exerting heavy pressure on the housing expediter, Vaughan cleared the way for Tanforan to receive an allocation of $150,000 worth of scarce building materials. The columnist Drew Pearson, who sought to find the reason for the allocation, was unable to obtain the facts, and concluded later that Vaughan had contrived to keep the matter secret.[6]

Until mid-1949 Vaughan's activities had been carried on largely in secret, but a wave of revelations exposed not only his efforts but a far larger game that one observer called *How to Get Rich in Washington.*[7] The object was the peddling of influence—the sale of contacts in the government by numerous free-lance agents who came to be known, from their customary fee, as "5-percenters." The story surfaced with charges by a New England furniture manufacturer, aired in the New York *Herald Tribune,* that he had bought the influence of one James V. Hunt, a paid consultant to the War Assets Administration, who worked through General Alden H. Waitt of the Army Chemical Corps, Quartermaster General Herman Feldman, and General Vaughan. In short order, an inquiry under Senator Clyde R. Hoey, Democrat of North Carolina, got under way. Hearings in August and September, 1949, and a committee report on January 18, 1950, produced not only a perjury conviction for John Maragon, but severe criticism of Vaughan for making Maragon's "fixing" operations possible. Yet in none of his activities, save that of the freezers, was Vaughan accused of accepting personal payment, although it was alleged that he collected political contributions.[8]

For his part, President Truman refused to criticize, much less rid himself of, General Vaughan. In his news conference of August 18, 1949, he specifically declined to discuss the Hoey investigation and suggested to reporters that they "suspend judgment on General Vaughan until he has been heard by the committee." Even after the committee had chastised Vaughan, Truman did not publicly discipline him; in fact, the general remained in the White House to the end of the Truman administration. Nor did the administration undertake major reforms as a result of the 5-percenter investigation, beyond a hasty announcement by the Department of Defense that it had altered procurement procedures to permit business people to deal directly with the Pentagon without intermediaries.[9]

The RFC Investigation

Although defense procurement had been the focus of the 5-percenter inquiry, it soon became clear that undercover influence was at work in other areas of government as well, in particular the Reconstruction Finance Corporation (RFC).[10] On February 8, 1950, the Senate—voting only a few days after the RFC had filed suit to foreclose on the Lustron Corporation, which had defaulted on loans of $37,500,000—ordered an investigation of the RFC. The subsequent inquiry produced evidence that well merited the title of one of the subcommittee's reports, "Favoritism and Influence." RFC directors were revealed to have been manipulated not only by influence peddlers but by party officials and at least one member of the White House staff. Two directors in particular were found to be so controlled: Walter L. Dunham, a token Republican who owed his appointment to the Michigan Democratic national committeeman, and William E. Willett, who had risen through the RFC ranks. Five influences affected their official decisions:

(1) Goodwin, Rosenbaum, Meacham and Bailen, a Washington law firm whose chief partner, Joseph H. Rosenbaum, boasted that he had Willett and Dunham in his "hip pocket."

(2) E. Merl Young, husband of a White House secretary and a former RFC examiner who joined the Lustron Corporation, a prefabricated

housing enterprise, on the day after approval of one of its loans. He also went on the payroll as a vice president of the F. L. Jacobs Company (see below) and worked for the Democratic National Committee in 1948. His wife was the recipient of the "genuine royal pastel mink coat" with which the Republican vice-presidential candidate in 1952, Richard Nixon, contrasted his own wife's "Republican cloth coat." The coat was the gift of Rosenbaum. The minority report on the RFC noted: "Happily, the friendly Mr. Rosenbaum had represented the furrier sometime earlier in a loan application to the RFC, so the coat was charged to his account, at a discount of $1,000."

(3) Rex C. Jacobs, president of the R. L. Jacobs Company of Detroit, who allegedly joined Young and Dunham in a plot to drive Lustron into receivership and to take over the remains.

(4) Donald Dawson, personnel adviser to the President, former personnel officer of the RFC, and husband of the chief custodian of the RFC files.

(5) William M. Boyle, Jr., Democratic national chairman and a former secretary to Senator Truman. He was revealed as having helped the American Lithofold Corporation of St. Louis obtain a $565,000 RFC loan and as having maintained his ties with Lithofold after becoming party chairman. Although cleared of doing anything illegal in this case, he resigned on October 13, 1951. (It was found in the course of the investigation that the Republican national chairman, Guy G. Gabrielson, had also represented a loan applicant before the RFC.)

The operations within the RFC gradually emerged under the scrutiny of a Senate subcommittee headed by Senator J. William Fulbright, Democrat of Arkansas. An interim committee report on May 19, 1950, was designed to cut off an RFC loan of $10,100,000 to the Texmass Petroleum Company, which had used the services of both Young and Boyle; both the RFC's Dallas office and its review committee had opposed the loan, but the RFC directors had approved it, 2 to 1. The committee's criticism failed to stop it. A second interim report, on August 11, found fault with RFC supervision of a Lustron transportation contract that had permitted the milking of Lustron funds. In September the committee discovered that two potential purchasers of RFC properties were under indictment and forced the agency to call off the sale.[11]

President Truman made his initial response to the inquiry by means of his appointive powers. With three vacancies on the board as of August, 1950, he reappointed Dunham and Willett, the directors most under suspicion. But he also named C. Edward Rowe; Rowe was to become vice chairman and, according to his later testimony, was to clean up the RFC. Rowe came to the post from the Harrington & Richardson Arms Company of Massachusetts, which had received a $300,000 RFC loan in April, 1950.

The Fulbright committee's report brought it into direct conflict with the President. "Favoritism and Influence" revealed the pressures on directors, most notably from the White House aide Dawson, to whom Dunham and Willett owed their appointments in part. The report recommended that the agency be placed under a single administrator because of "deterioration of the top management structure . . . attributable to the equal division of the management responsibility among the members of the five-man Board of Directors." After discussing the situation with the President in private, the committee, dissatisfied with his response, made the text public on February 2, 1951. The President asserted at a news conference that he had long since proposed such a change "and that reorganization plan was rejected at the behest of this committee that has written this asinine report."[12]

The President also took a controversial action that smacked of retaliation. On February 23, 1951, two days after the Fulbright subcommittee opened public hearings, the White House admitted that it had requested and received from the RFC copies of letters by members of Congress concerning RFC business. Subcommittee members charged that the correspondence was merely being used in connection with study of a reorganization plan.

In fact, a presidential reorganization plan was soon submitted. Despite determined efforts by the Republican minority to do away with the RFC altogether, Congress voted to forego its option of rejecting the President's plan. As of April 30, 1951, the board of directors was abolished in favor of a single administrator. Four days later, Stuart A. Symington filled that post.

But the President's action failed to resolve the controversy with Congress. Although RFC officials and such outsiders as Young testified in public hearings, Truman declined to permit his personnel aide, Dawson, to appear for more than two months, and indeed apparently tried to obtain cancellation of the committee's summons via an indirect approach to one of its members. Ultimately, he permitted Dawson to testify, and on May 10, 1951, interrogation began. Dawson denied that he had exerted influence in favor of specific loans, but admitted that he had accepted the hospitality of the Saxony Hotel in Miami Beach, which had received a loan of $1,500,000. Despite this and other damaging admissions, Dawson was retained on the White House staff.

The subsequent report on the RFC by the Senate Banking and Currency Committee did not discuss the role of the White House in creating the conditions that made the scandal possible, nor is that role easy to evaluate. Even the hostile minority report conceded, "Other than the direct intervention in the ill-starred Lustron venture, there is no evidence that the Offices of the President were officially and responsibly used in influencing lending policies of the Corporation." Nor did that single "direct intervention" necessarily reflect on the President: when Lustron wanted to fire Young, Dawson called the matter to the President's attention and Truman made the "very proper response" that Lustron should do what was best for the company. However, the very fact that the employment of an influence peddler was checked with a President is suggestive of an unhealthy relationship between the RFC and the White House. Clearly, Truman made sound enough moves toward reform of the RFC, but he made them while neglecting to remove at once those officials who had made the reforms necessary.[13]

The Bureau of Internal Revenue Allegations

The expansion of federal tax collections in the war and postwar years offered an even more fertile field for those seeking special favors from the government, or those willing to dispense them. During the Truman administration, the Bureau of Internal Revenue was collecting taxes at eight times the prewar level. But the bureau's organization was antiquated and ill-adapted to such a load; much responsibility was dispersed among sixty-four district collectors who were customarily political appointees. The commissioner of internal revenue himself usually had political ties: Robert Hannegan, named commissioner in 1943, became Democratic national chairman and Truman's first postmaster general. Joseph D. Nunan, his successor, was a New York legislator who had joined the bureau after failing of reelection. Nunan's successor was George D. Schoeneman, who had preceded Donald Dawson in the patronage-clearing position of White House personnel officer. After mid-1947 the tax division of the Justice Department, charged with prosecuting tax violations, was under Theron Lamar Caudle, who had handled the politically sensitive Kansas City election investigation. Flexible, complex tax laws, administered by officials customarily selected on bases other than their expertise, and the confidentiality afforded transactions between the bureau and the taxpayer, resulted in the most widespread and serious official misconduct of the Truman years.

The scent of scandal began to rise in 1950 as a result of the efforts of Senator John J. Williams, Republican of Delaware. An informant had told Senator Williams of irregularities in the office of the New York third district. (Unknown to Williams, Commissioner Schoeneman had already asked Secretary of the Treasury John W. Snyder to remove the district collector, James W. Johnson.) Williams asked for records of the New York office; refused, he gave his information to the Senate Finance Committee in executive session. Despite damning evidence against him—including the bribery of eight of his subordinates by taxpayers—Johnson clung to office for a year, defying both an informal presidential request and a resolution, introduced by Williams, calling for his removal.[14]

By 1951 allegations of abuses in the Bureau of Internal Revenue brought about a congressional inquiry. The House Committee on Ways and Means established a subcommittee on administration of the internal revenue laws under the chairmanship of Representative Cecil R. King, Democrat of California; through 1951 and 1952 it uncovered illegal activity in collectors' offices and in Washington headquarters. The investigation resulted in the removal of nine of the sixty-four district collectors. The subcommittee reported:

> Two of the nine Collectors separated from service had extorted large sums from delinquent taxpayers. Several evaded personal income taxes while in office and at least one Collector used his authority to prevent audit of his returns. The total confusion which reigned in the office of two Collectors demonstrated their incompetence as administrators. . . . Field investigations by this subcommittee

disclosed that in a number of these offices conditions had been allowed to deteriorate as long as 16 years, because Bureau officials were unwilling to offend the politically appointed Collectors.[15]

The most noted of these collectors was James P. Finnegan of the first Missouri (St. Louis) district, successor to Hannegan in that position and a friend of President Truman and Secretary of the Treasury Snyder. His name had come up in the Fulbright subcommittee hearings on the RFC, not only because he had associated with the Dunham-Dawson-Young circle, but because he had acted, while collector, as attorney for American Lithofold Corporation, which had paid him $45,000 for his services in unsuccessfully seeking a loan.

Finnegan's abuses of taxpayers were revealed in 1950. An FBI informant led Commissioner Schoeneman to send investigators to St. Louis. They found that Finnegan had taken part in a racket that involved referring tax delinquents to an insurance company that split its receipts with the collector, but this investigation produced no formal charges against him. In March, 1951, a former employee complained to a federal judge in St. Louis that the district office had failed to act on tax-fraud cases that involved clients defended by lawyers with political connections. Although a grand jury brought no immediate indictments, Finnegan resigned on April 14, 1951, and the President accepted his action "with regret."[16]

But this was not the end of his case. Senator Williams urged Secretary Snyder to take further action and underlined his request by reading into the record the 1950 report on Finnegan by Treasury agents. The grand jury was reconvened and, despite an apparent effort by the Justice Department to hamstring the investigation, began to hand up indictments. In October, 1951, a week after he had admitted to congressional investigators that he had taken insurance proceeds and had accepted fees from a St. Louis law firm that owed back taxes, Finnegan was indicted on two counts of bribery and three counts of misconduct in office, and found guilty in 1952 on the misconduct charges. He served eighteen months in prison in the 1950s but was pardoned, by President Lyndon B. Johnson, shortly before his death in 1967. One question concerning his departure remained unclear: had he tried to resign but stayed on at the urging of the White House, or had he resisted, as the President suggested in a subsequent news conference?[17]

Substantial as they were—166 Internal Revenue officials fired or forced to resign in 1951 alone—the casualties of the investigation were not confined to lower levels. One former commissioner, Nunan, was exposed as a tax evader and convicted in 1954. His successor, Schoeneman, while not subject to charges of wrongdoing, nonetheless resigned effective July 31, 1951, after having failed to persuade his superior, Secretary Snyder, to take sterner measures. Charles Oliphant resigned as the bureau's general counsel on December 4, 1951, a day after a disgruntled Chicago taxpayer had mentioned him as a member of a purported government ring attempting a half-million-dollar shakedown. Caudle, mentioned as another member of the ring, had been removed as head of the Justice Department's tax division less than three weeks before. (For details of Caudle's removal, see "Department of Justice Investigation" below.)

Cutting even closer to the President—and, in fact, producing the only criminal charge against a member of Truman's White House staff—was the involvement in the Internal Revenue scandals of Matthew Connelly, presidential appointments secretary. Connelly had worked for Truman on the Senate War Investigating Committee, and had been in the White House since April, 1945. In September, 1952, Caudle, testifying before the subcommittee investigating the Department of Justice, mentioned Connelly's name in connection with the tax case of Irving Sachs of St. Louis. According to later charges, Connelly had accepted from H. J. Schwimmer, Sachs's lawyer, a topcoat, two suits, and an oil royalty worth $7,000, for unspecified assistance; Connelly, moreover, had accepted these gratuities in 1951 and 1952 at the height of the tax investigation. Despite Connelly's purported aid, Sachs was convicted and fined. On December 1, 1955, Schwimmer, Caudle, and Connelly were indicted for conspiracy, and Ellis Slack, a Caudle subordinate, was named a co-conspirator but not indicted. All three were convicted. Connelly served a term of less than a year in federal prison in 1960, and was pardoned by President John F. Kennedy in 1962.[18]

The administration's countermeasures against this scandal resembled those taken in the RFC investigation—willingness to make institutional changes combined with slowness to admit the fault of erring appointees. When John B. Dunlap succeeded Schoeneman as commissioner, he was given powers to investigate bureau employees, and one of his first steps was to order a check on employees' tax returns for the previous three years. Six months later, on January 2, 1952, the President announced a reorganization of the bureau as "part of a program to prevent improper conduct in the public service, to protect the Government from the insidious influence peddlers and favor seekers, and to expose and punish any wrong doers." The plan set the following changes: (1) Abolition of the sixty-four collectors' offices. (2) Appointment of only one officer, the commissioner, by the president, with all other positions to be filled through civil service. (3) Establishment of twenty-five district offices, headed by district commissioners responsible only to the commissioner. (4) Establishment of an inspection service independent of the rest of the bureau. The House of Representatives approved the plan on January 30, 1952, as did the Senate on March 13.

But if the administration hoped to escape further criticism of the bureau, it was disappointed. The investigating subcommittee issued a report in February, 1952, after hearings on misconduct in the San Francisco offices, asserting that abuses there had been "encouraged and protected by the complacency and indifference of an inept top administration in Washington." The subcommittee later got into a dispute with the White House when it demanded a copy of the log kept by the former counsel, Oliphant. The log was not made available to the committee until November 18, 1952, after the presidential election, but it still furnished the basis for further investigations by the successor to the King subcommittee in the next Congress. There was a further brief dispute when the subcommittee became convinced in 1952 that a New York grand-jury inquiry had been instigated to divert evidence from the congressional investigation.[19]

More important than this friction was the question of whether the administration's action in seeking and ousting wrongdoers had been appropriately prompt and severe. The President defended himself stoutly in a news conference on December 13, 1951:

The collector in Boston was fired before anybody began to look into his situation, except the Treasury Department. The collector of revenue in St. Louis was dispensed with long before anything was looked into by any committee. The collector in San Francisco was fired before any committee went into it, and a grand jury right now in California has just indicted him. The necessary action in all these things has been taken by the executive branch of the Government whenever it was necessary.

Yet the chronology of the investigation shows that the sequence was more complicated than the President indicated. Finnegan of St. Louis had indeed resigned early, but the administration had taken no initiative to look into his misconduct, despite a damning Treasury agents' report. James G. Smyth of San Francisco was dismissed more than a month after—not *before*—the subcommittee began its investigation of his office. Nor is the picture clear with respect to a number of other resignations or dismissals, for they often just preceded or followed public testimony by the individual.[20] Although the housecleaning was eventually widespread and thorough, the timing suggests that much of it was done in response to the heat of publicity.

Special Corruption Inquiry

By the closing weeks of 1951, the confluence of scandal had become so dominant in the news media that the administration could no longer respond wholly on a case-by-case basis. Not only had the RFC and the Bureau of Internal Revenue been subject to exposure, but charges had been made against at least six other executive agencies and departments: the Office of the Alien Property Custodian, the Federal Power Commission, the antitrust division of the Justice Department, the Maritime Commission, the Securities and Exchange Commission, and the Civil Aeronautics Board. The touring committee under Senator Estes Kefauver had pointed out the relationships between local Democratic officials and organized crime, most notably in New York City, whose mayor, William O'Dwyer, had retired and had been appointed ambassador to Mexico in 1950. A new scandal was brewing in the Department of Agriculture, where perhaps $10,000,000 worth of government-stored grain had been "converted" to private hands—or, more bluntly, stolen. All these, combined with the approach of an election year, increased pressure on the administration for dramatic action.[21]

In his news conference of December 13, 1951, the President was questioned persistently about the steps he might take. One reporter asked whether he might appoint special counsels like Owen J. Roberts and Atlee Pomerene, whom President Coolidge had named to investigate the Teapot Dome allegations in 1924. Truman turned aside the question, but there were reports thereafter that he was considering a special commission or the appointment of a federal judge, Thomas F. Murphy of New York, as a special prosecutor.[22]

Ultimately, the President was forced back into existing channels of command, Judge Murphy backed out, and the President sought then to place the inquiry under a new attorney general. After repeated refusals, he found a candidate willing to serve—Justin Miller, a former federal judge. But when Truman asked the incumbent, J. Howard McGrath, to resign (via a messenger, Clark M. Clifford), McGrath resisted. On January 10, 1952, Truman gave in and announced, not only that there would be no special commission to investigate misconduct, but that any investigation would be under McGrath. Critics doubted that McGrath was the right man for the job: chairman of the Democratic National Committee before entering the cabinet after the 1948 election, he had demonstrated no great skill in running his department, and had drawn heavy fire in December for defending the work of his department in an appearance before tax investigators. Nonetheless, he made the gesture of getting an inquiry under way when, on February 1, Newbold Morris, an independent Republican from New York, was named his special assistant and placed in charge of the investigation.[23]

Morris's two-month stay in Washington proved disastrous. Senator Hoey, who had headed the 5-percenter investigation, pointed out that Morris's law firm and a foundation he headed faced possible legal action because of their involvement in suspect trading for government-surplus tankers. Morris antagonized members of Congress by charging them with character assassination, and Congress in turn refused to grant him the subpoena power he had requested. Moreover, he encountered frustration in the Department of Justice itself. After he had prepared a financial questionnaire for all Department of Justice employees earning more than $10,000 a year, the Attorney General blocked its delivery. A week later a request for department records by Morris's office was rejected by McGrath, and the Attorney General confided to a congressional committee that he regretted the decision to employ Morris.[24]

Morris's days were numbered. Despite the special assignment he had been given, McGrath considered him a subordinate and, on April 3, 1952, fired him. It later appeared that McGrath believed he had won the President's assent to his action. If so, Truman had not revealed the consequences, for later the same day he removed McGrath from office and replaced him with James P. McGranery, a federal judge and former Democratic congressman with earlier experience in the Justice Department. The new attorney general declared the special corruption inquiry at an end. Of this episode, the House subcommittee that later studied the Department of Justice concluded:

> Although the investigation assigned to Newbold Morris was soundly conceived, and strongly indicated as desirable within the executive branch, the selection of Morris himself was astonishing, in view of the fact that he was subject to pressure, from the very outset, on account of a possible criminal prosecution being considered against him by the Criminal Division of the Department. Morris' experiences are replete with indications of bad faith toward his work on the part of his superiors.[25]

Department of Justice Investigation

Even before Morris's appointment, the House of Representatives had authorized an investigation of the Department of Justice and the Office of the Attorney General "relating to and limited to specific allegations and complaints based upon credible evidence." The assignment was given to a subcommittee of the Committee on the Judiciary, chaired by Representative Frank L. Chelf, Democrat of Kentucky. Initially, the cooperation of the White House was reluctant, and that of the Justice Department even more so. At first, the President rejected the subcommittee's general request for data on cases referred to the department for action, complaining that such a sweeping request would hinder government business; later, he relented to permit release of data on specific cases. Further, a memorandum to agency heads on April 12, 1952, urged cooperation with the subcommittee and called attention to an executive order empowering the subcommittee to examine tax returns under specified conditions. The subcommittee complained that as long as McGrath was in office, the department engaged in "outright obstructionist tactics." The accession of McGranery led to an easing of this situation.[26]

It was appropriate that the Department of Justice be the subject of the final major investigation of misconduct in the Truman administration, for the work of that department had figured prominently in previous investigations. Most strikingly, the figure of T. Lamar Caudle had appeared repeatedly in the background. Even before he came to Washington in 1945, Caudle had been the subject of an FBI inquiry because of his handling, as a federal attorney in North Carolina, of Office of Price Administration prosecutions. Nonetheless, Attorney General Clark installed him as head of the criminal division, where he supervised the limited investigation and dropping of the Kansas City voting case.

Caudle's transfer to the tax division, despite his lack of experience in tax law, placed him in a position critical to the administration, for it fell to him to decide in many instances which tax cases should be prosecuted. From his testimony before the Chelf subcommittee, there emerged a pattern of what might be called bending enforcement— handling of tax cases responsive to pressure or favors, delays, failures to prosecute, dismissals for "health" reasons. In one instance, associates of Caudle represented tax-case defendants. In another Caudle was instrumental in dismissal of charges against a client represented by the Democratic National committeeman of that state. A third case was allegedly dampened in a way that produced a contribution to the 1948 Democratic campaign.

Despite his vulnerability, Caudle remained in Truman's good graces as late as October, 1951. But within the next month, it came out that Caudle had received a $5,000 commission on the sale of a friend's airplane to a relative of a man involved in a tax case; Caudle later recommended against prosecution. The President removed Caudle from office on November 16, 1951, and replaced him with Ellis Slack (who was later named a co-conspirator in the St. Louis tax investigation). Caudle appeared before the Chelf subcommittee and emerged unaccused but scarcely unscathed. Chelf and the senior minority member, Kenneth B. Keating of New York, declared, "We feel that he is an honest man who was indiscreet in his associations and a pliant conformer to the peculiar moral climate in Washington."[27] In 1955, however, he was indicted in the same St. Louis case as Matthew Connelly and convicted; he was pardoned in 1965 by President Lyndon B. Johnson after serving a brief prison term.

By the time the Chelf-Keating subcommittee issued its report, President Truman's Republican successor had been in office six months, and the findings could have no effect on Democratic administration of the Department of Justice. Yet the subcommittee's conclusions summarized aptly, for the record, endemic malfunctions that had led to misconduct not only in the Department of Justice but elsewhere in the administration. Among other points, the subcommittee concluded:

II. For a number of years past the Department of Justice has been weakened by the tenure in high posts of persons whose administrative and professional competence was dubious. At lower levels, though there are many fine public servants, unwarranted emphasis has been placed on conformity and political regularity, rather than initiative and professional contributions to the work of the department. . . .

V. The handling of contract fraud cases, involving substantial losses of public funds, provides a shocking measure of inefficiency within the Department; the Government has actually recovered much more in voluntary refunds, from contractors who were merely overpaid, than the Department of Justice has succeeded in collecting in a vastly larger number of cases where the Government had absolute rights to recovery against contractors who had defrauded it.

VI. Some department officials have been notably lax in associating with, and accepting favors from, persons against whom they were supposed to be defending the Government's interests. The department itself and its top leadership are partly responsible, since no effort has been made to prescribe or enforce standards of propriety in such relationships. . . .

VIII. In the recent case of a St. Louis grand jury called to investigate improprieties in the enforcement of the tax laws, the Department of Justice, and the Attorney General through his subordinates . . . interfered improperly with the work of the jury to an extent which merits grave censure.

IX. It has been possible . . . for defendants in civil and criminal cases to play the field officers of the Department against Washington, and to impose delays, bring pressure, and secure favors until the processes of law enforcement and the collection of Government claims have been totally defeated.[28]

In general, neither contemporary commentators nor historians of the Truman administration have found that the President met such failings with alacrity, or that he met fully his responsibility for setting the administration's standards.[29] The only work devoted entirely to the scandals goes even further in suggesting that there was "a general conspiracy to obstruct justice." However, it does not elaborate on the operation of such a conspiracy, and the possibility of its existence is not supported elsewhere.[30] A recent treatment by Cabell Phillips observes:

The five-percenters, the influence peddlers, and the tax fixers had been put to flight—temporarily at least—but it was Congress that had flushed them out and wielded the whip. The President on his own had followed up by drastically reorganizing the RFC and the tax service and by his abortive enlistment of Mr. Morris with his mop and pail. But in the minds of most of the public these gestures looked as futile as locking the barn door after the horses are gone.[31]

Alonzo L. Hamby, though highly critical of Truman, also makes the reasonable suggestion that the President's attitude changed as his perception broadened. He points to Truman's changed attitude between 1951 and 1952 on the need to force disclosure of government officials' incomes. Hamby credits Truman with making sound institutional reforms, but he condemns him for creating "an impression of White House complacency which obscured the practical constructive steps he was taking."[32] Indeed, Hamby hints that perhaps Truman, despite his background in machine politics, may have been relatively uneducated in the types of misconduct possible in his postwar government, and that the tardiness of his responses was a product of the slowness of his education.

While this education was taking place, there occurred misconduct on a scale that may not have harmed the functioning of the government in most fields of policy, but certainly shook the confidence of the public in the executive branch and the President himself. The ultimate toll in his official family was heavy: a secretary who went to jail for deeds committed in the White House; two White House aides censured for persistent intervention in matters beyond their legitimate responsibilities; an assistant attorney general fired and later tried and jailed; a commissioner of internal revenue appointed by Roosevelt and held over by Truman jailed for lawbreaking while in office; many lower-level tax officials removed and tried for various offenses. President Truman has not been found directly to have ordered or otherwise to have caused any of these transgressions. Yet many of them clearly took place in circumstances in which the transgressor gave the impression that the power of the President was behind him. The loyalty he gave so unstintingly to his associates was not always returned in the same measure.

NOTES

[1]Patrick Anderson, *The Presidents' Men* (Garden City, 1969), 113.

[2]On Pauley's career, see Edward W. Harris in the St. Louis *Post-Dispatch*, October 16–19, 1945. On the tidelands, see Ernest R. Bartley, *The Tidelands Oil Controversy* (Austin, 1953), 101–161. For Truman's account of the controversy, see his memorandum to Charles G. Ross, February, 1946, Ross Papers, Harry S. Truman Library, Independence, Mo. A general account also appears in Robert Engler, *The Politics of Oil* (Chicago, 1967), 343–353.

[3]Kansas City case: see U.S. Senate, Subcommittee of the Committee on the Judiciary, *Hearings, Kansas City Vote Fraud*, 80th Cong., 1st Sess., May 28, June 5 and 6, 1947; Memorandum, "Report of the Activities of the Department of Justice in Connection with the Kansas City Primary Elections of 1946," n.d., box 6, Clark M. Clifford papers, Truman Library; and, for later phases, U.S. House, Committee on the Judiciary, Subcommittee to Investigate the Department of Justice, *Investigation of the Department of Justice*, House Report 1079, 83rd Cong., 1st Sess., August 1, 1953, 91–93.

[4]The Graham case is discussed in Blair Bolles, *How to Get Rich in Washington* (New York, 1952), 41–42.

[5]See Vaughan's explanation in Harry S. Truman, *Public Papers . . . January 1–December 31, 1949* (Washington: Government Printing Office, 1964), 425–426n; Jules Abels, *The Truman Scandals* (Chicago, 1956), 43–48; and, for the version of White House associate James K. Vardaman, Drew Pearson, *Diaries, 1949–1959* (New York, 1974), 485–487.

[6]U.S. Senate, Committee on Expenditures in the Executive Departments, Subcommittee on Investigations, *Hearings, Influence in Government Procurement*, 81st Cong., 1st Sess., August 8–September 1, 1949; Pearson, *Diaries*, 65.

[7]By Blair Bolles (cited above).

[8]U.S. Congress, *Hearings, Influence in Government Procurement, passim;* and *The 5-Percenter Investigation*, Report 1232, 81st Cong., 2nd Sess., January 18, 1950.

[9]Truman, *Public Papers . . . 1949*, 424–426.

[10]U.S. Senate, Committee on Banking and Currency, *Study of the Reconstruction Finance Corporation and Proposed Amendment of RFC Act*, Senate Report 649, 82nd Cong., 1st Sess., August 20, 1951.

[11]General accounts of the RFC influence ring can be found in Abels, *Scandals*, 83–121, and Bolles, *How to Get Rich*, 127–219. Quotation on mink coat is from U.S. Congress, *Study of the RFC*, 50.

[12]See U.S. Senate, Committee on Banking and Currency, *Study of the Reconstruction Finance Corporation*, Interim Report; *Favoritism and Influence*, 82nd Cong., 1st Sess., February 5, 1951. Truman, *Public Papers . . . 1951* (Washington: Government Printing Office, 1965), 145.

[13]U.S. Congress, *Study of the RFC*, August 20, 1951, 43, 44.

[14]For Williams's account, see "Story of Tax Scandals," interview in *U.S. News & World Report*, December 7, 1951, 24–31.

[15]U.S. House, Committee on Ways and Means, *Internal Revenue Investigation*, House Report 2518, 82nd Cong., 1st Sess., January 3, 1953, 26–27.

[16]On Finnegan, see especially Bolles, *How to Get Rich*, 279–285. His obituary is in *New York Times*, September 6, 1967.

[17]News conference of December 13, 1951, Truman, *Public Papers . . . 1951*, 643.

[18]Connelly's case is summarized in Anderson, *Presidents' Men*, 125–126. Anderson notes that associates of Truman still believe Connelly was "framed."

[19]Truman, *Public Papers . . . 1952* (Washington: Government Printing Office, 1966), 1–2; U.S. Congress, *Internal Revenue Investigation*.

[20]Truman, *Public Papers . . . 1951*, 642; U.S. Congress, *Internal Revenue Investigation*, 35–37.

[21]Alonzo L. Hamby, *Beyond the New Deal: Harry S. Truman and American Liberalism* (New York, 1973), 460–461. On grain thefts, see Allen J. Matusow, *Farm Policies and Politics in the Truman Years* (Cambridge, Mass., 1967), 238.

[22]Roberts-Pomerene: Truman, *Public Papers . . . 1951*, 641.

[23]See the account of this episode in Hamby, *Beyond the New Deal*, 462–465; also *New York Times*, January 11, 1952.

[24]*Ibid.*; Abels, *Scandals*, 15–18.

[25]U.S. Congress, *Investigation of the Department of Justice*, 1.

[26]"Obstructionist tactics": *Ibid.*

[27]Quoted in Congressional Quarterly Service, *Congress and the Nation, 1945–1960* (Washington, 1961), 1712. Caudle is also discussed in Abels, *Scandals*, 158–194.

[28]U.S. Congress, *Investigation of the Department of Justice*, 1, 2.

[29]George A. Graham, *Morality in American Politics* (New York, 1952), 170; Bert Cochran, *Harry Truman and the Crisis Presidency* (New York, 1973), 249.

[30]Abels, *Scandals*, 315.

[31]Phillips, *The Truman Presidency* (New York, 1966), 403, 413.

[32]Hamby, *Beyond the New Deal*, 461, 464.

DWIGHT D. EISENHOWER
1953–1961

Mark I. Gelfand

B ecause of the heavy barrage of criticism the Republicans had tell-
ingly directed at the scandals in the Truman administration during
the 1952 campaign, both the executive and legislative branches were
particularly sensitive to the issue of corruption in government for the
duration of Dwight D. Eisenhower's tenure. At an early meeting in February, 1953, the President instructed cabinet members to be alert to
conditions that might breed charges of favoritism or conflict of interest,
and to be quick about calling on the Department of Justice to investigate
dubious situations.[1] The President's emphatic action was prompted, in
part, by clear signals from Congress that it intended to maintain the
vigorous oversight role that had helped uncover the "mess" of the preceding regime. After the Democrats regained control of the legislature
in 1955, the President and his aides would be under steady pressure
about corruption, and before the end of Eisenhower's term allegations
about the improper use of public office had reached deep into the White
House itself.

The Nixon "Slush Fund"[2]

Charges of official misconduct were leveled at the Eisenhower entou-
rage even before the November, 1952, election. On September 18 the
New York *Post* claimed that Republican vice-presidential candidate
Richard M. Nixon had received some $16,000 to $17,000 from a group
of wealthy California businessmen since his election to the Senate in
1950. Under the headline "Secret Rich Men's Trust Fund Keeps Nixon

in Style Far Beyond His Salary," the *Post* announced the "existence of a 'millionaires club' devoted exclusively to the financial comfort of Senator Nixon." Given the stress that the Eisenhower campaign had placed on condemning corruption in Truman's government, the allegations about Nixon were explosive, but few on Eisenhower's staff immediately grasped the danger. Not until Nixon ran into hostile demonstrators at his rallies, and two influential newspapers supporting the Republican ticket, the New York *Herald Tribune* and the *Washington Post,* called for Nixon's withdrawal from the race, did Eisenhower and his advisers realize that some action was necessary.

The initial strategy was to play for time. Public reaction had to be gauged and all options considered before any decision could be reached. It would be difficult, the Eisenhower staff concluded, to retain Nixon if there were many more Republican demands for his ouster, but dismissal also had its liabilities. Eisenhower reportedly told a top aide, "If Nixon has to go, we cannot win." With the various wings of the Republican party split over what should be done, Eisenhower delayed making up his mind. In one speech he told his audience that "knowing Nixon as I do, I believe that when the facts are known to all of us, they will show that Dick Nixon would not compromise with what is right." But in talking to reporters the next day, Eisenhower denied that he planned any "whitewash" and said, "Of what avail is it for us to carry on this crusade against this business of what has been going on in Washington if we ourselves aren't as clean as a hound's tooth."

A television address by Nixon was finally agreed upon as the best way out of the impasse. Eisenhower would have additional time to determine the popular mood. In his speech on the night of September 23, Nixon defended the fund by arguing that it had been used solely to defray political expenses which he said could not be charged to the federal government, and gave a detailed accounting of his finances in an effort to prove that none of the money had ended up in his pocket. After declaring that he was no "quitter" and that he was dedicated to Eisenhower, he asked the American people to decide his future by wiring or writing the Republican National Committee.

The massive outpouring of national sympathy for Nixon's plight shaped Eisenhower's response. Appearing before a crowd shouting, "We like Dick," a few minutes after the speech was over, Eisenhower praised his running mate as a courageous and honest man who, in a showdown fight, would be more useful than a "whole boxcar of pussy-footers." Although he announced that no final decision on Nixon's fate could be made until he talked to him in person, the flood of telegrams to the National Committee settled the matter before the interview could take place. When Eisenhower met Nixon at the Wheeling airport on the night of September 24, he put his arm around him and said, "You're my boy."

Conflict of Interest and Sub-Cabinet Officials

Eisenhower ran into conflict-of-interest difficulties when he attempted to staff his administration with successful businessmen. A portent of the troubles to come was provided in January, 1953, by the delay of the Senate Armed Services Committee in confirming the President's nominees for secretary of defense, deputy secretary of defense, secretary of the army, secretary of the navy, and secretary of the air force until each man agreed to dispose of any business holdings which might lead to possible conflict-of-interest situations. Eisenhower reportedly regarded the episode as the "first test of the administration's ability to distinguish right from wrong,"[3] but stiffer trials lay ahead.

Between 1955 and 1960 Eisenhower was obliged to accept the resignations of a number of sub-cabinet officials whose conduct, under probing by congressional committees, raised ethical, if not legal, questions. These appointees included the Secretary of the Air Force (the use of his position to help direct business toward his own firm); the assistant secretary of defense for legislative and public affairs (impropriety in having firms controlled by his wife and brother-in-law bid for and receive military procurement contracts); the administrator of the General Services Administration (political favoritism in awarding of government insurance business); a member of the Federal Communications Commission (acceptance of loans and other favors from the attorney for a successful applicant for a television station license); and the chairman of the Federal Communications Commission (receiving of gratuities from the broadcast industry). In addition, a second-echelon, nonpresidential appointee, the commissioner of public buildings, resigned under fire when it was disclosed that he had given federal contracts to firms which were clients of a company in which he held a 90% partnership. Generally, the White House staff, frequently Assistant to the President Sherman Adams, requested the official to resign when it appeared that the revelations might embarrass the President. Except in the instance of the FCC commissioner, who was indicted on charges of conspiracy to defraud the United States government (later dismissed because of his physical inability to stand trial), none of these officials faced any court action, since there was no obvious violation of the conflict-of-interest statutes. Nor was the President, with the exception of the allegations regarding the Air Force Secretary, drawn into these matters.[4]

The controversy surrounding Secretary of the Air Force Harold E. Talbott caused Eisenhower "a good deal of personal dismay." Although the President and Talbott were not close friends, they had come to know each other well and had played bridge together at the White House on a few occasions.[5] When the Senate Permanent Subcommittee on Investigations revealed in the summer of 1955 that Talbott had utilized his position and Air Force stationery to solicit business for a company of which he was half owner, Eisenhower was confronted with the first high-level scandal of his administration. Asked to comment on the disclosures at his July 27 news conference, the President refused to pass judgment on Talbott until the evidentiary record was complete, adding, however, that "I do not believe that any man can properly hold public office merely because he is not guilty of any illegal act." A public servant's actions, Eisenhower declared, have "to be impeccable both from the standpoint of law and the standpoint of ethics. . . . [He must] avoid any indiscretion that even leans in that way or even gives the appearance that an office might be used."[6] Three days later, after discussions with Sherman Adams, Talbott resigned in order not to embarrass the President any further politically. In his letter to Eisenhower asking to be relieved of his duties, Talbott complained about "distorted publicity" and asserted, as he had throughout, that his behavior had been "within the bounds of ethics." Eisenhower's reply complimented Talbott on his management of the Air Force, but noted that "under the circumstances your decision [to resign] was the right one."[7]

Democratic National Committee Chairman Paul M. Butler accused Eisenhower of sidestepping an "unpleasant responsibility" with his "friendly acceptance" of Talbott's resignation. The President's handling of the matter, Butler argued, made "a mockery" of his campaign pledges to have uncompromising honesty in government: "The new rule seems to be 'don't get caught' or 'if you get caught, we'll let you resign.' " But the Democratic majority on the Permanent Subcommittee on Investigations indicated that its inquiry had been "satisfactorily resolved" by the Secretary's departure, and the Talbott episode disappeared from political debate.[8] Upon leaving the Pentagon, Talbott received the Defense Department's highest civilian award, the Medal of Freedom.

The House Judiciary Committee raised a different issue, that of the denial of records to Congress by the executive branch. This occurred in the committee's 1955 investigation of charges that members of the Business Advisory Council of the Department of Commerce were using their position to influence government policy to the advantage of their own firms. Demands by the chairman of the committee that the council's files be turned over to the panel for study were discussed at the July 29, 1955, meeting of the cabinet. Reaffirming the principle of executive privilege he had laid down during the U.S. Army–McCarthy confrontation, Eisenhower said it was up to the departments involved to draw a line between what should and should not be made available to congressional committees. Although the President expressed the wish to release as many government papers as possible, Eisenhower told the cabinet that he wanted it clearly understood that he was never going to yield to the point where he would become known as a President who had practically crippled the presidency.[9]

Operating within these guidelines, the Commerce Department refused to hand over the files. "We cannot permit any individual," the department's general counsel announced on August 5, "to conduct a fishing expedition among the private papers of the Department, exposing to possible misunderstanding, misrepresentation, and hit-and-run smears the confidential counsel of the executive branch."[10] When the committee responded by issuing a subpoena for the records, the Secretary of Commerce wrote a letter to the chairman explaining why he could not comply:

> Such files contain individual business statistics and forecasts the disclosure of which is made a crime by law. They contain the advice of advisers and subordinates solicited, given and received in confidence. The publication of such materials would tend to dry up

some of the sources of information which this Department must consult in fulfilling its basic statutory responsibilities and would be contrary to the public interest.

"I am bound," the Secretary concluded, "to honor such confidences and my conclusions in this regard are supported by the established constitutional principle of the separation of powers in the Government." [11] A majority of the committee disputed these contentions, but the Secretary refused to change his position.

In the face of the department's stand, the committee's investigation ceased. "Since the Department of Commerce has not disclosed the records of the Business Advisory Council," the panel's report observed, "this subcommittee at this time is in no position to evaluate the benefits afforded by its services to the Government." [12] But the subcommittee's activities did prod the President into issuing an executive order later in 1955 tightening the conflict-of-interest regulations for part-time experts, consultants, and workers without compensation.

Conflict of Interest and Dixon-Yates

The Dixon-Yates contract precipitated "one of the most celebrated, hard-fought and bitter disputes of the whole Eisenhower administration." [13] At immediate issue was whether the demands of the city of Memphis for more electricity would be met by the federally financed Tennessee Valley Authority (TVA) or, as the Dixon-Yates agreement provided, by private enterprise. Implicitly at stake in the controversy was the future of the TVA and, indeed, of public power. Although the President's role in the origins of the contract is both distinct and crucial, his responsibility for subsequent developments during 1954 and 1955 remains obscure.

Eisenhower viewed the TVA as an example of the "creeping socialism" which he believed threatened the foundations of the American way of life. Referring to the TVA at a cabinet meeting in the summer of 1953, Eisenhower exclaimed, "By God, if ever we could do it, before we leave here, I'd like to see us sell the whole thing, but I suppose we can't go that far." [14] When the question of supplying electrical needs of Memphis came to the President's attention later that fall, he rejected the TVA's proposal to expand its generating capacity, and opted instead to have private business undertake the project. All available evidence tends to substantiate Sherman Adams's explanation that Eisenhower's "only motive in sponsoring the privately owned power plant was to check further growth of the TVA, which he regarded as a product of the 'whole-hog' theory of the previous Democratic administrations—the idea that the Federal Government must undertake great resource development projects alone, freezing out the energy and initiative of local government and local people engaged in private enterprise." [15]

Having made the basic decision on private versus public power, the President left the details of implementation to the director of the Bureau of the Budget (BOB), at first Joseph M. Dodge and then Rowland Hughes. Working in conjunction with the chairman of the Atomic Energy Commission (AEC),[16] Dodge and Hughes held preliminary negotiations during the winter of 1954 with the executives (Edgar H. Dixon and Eugene A. Yates) of two large private power companies operating in the Memphis region on how to take care of the city's electrical requirements. In April Hughes recommended to the President that the AEC be instructed to conclude a final agreement with the newly formed Dixon-Yates corporation.[17] Documents later released by the Budget Bureau indicated that this was the first time Eisenhower had been informed of the identity of the private parties and of the nature of the plan for meeting his power policy objectives. After a session with Republican congressional leaders in June, Eisenhower issued the directive to the AEC.

Announcement of this decision mobilized the friends of the TVA and public power, prompted charges of a "give-away" to private interests, and led to accusations by Democratic National Chairman Stephen A. Mitchell that the President was guilty of "cronyism." Mitchell's allegations hinged on the fact that Bobby Jones, the famous golfer and Eisenhower's frequent companion on the Augusta National Golf Course, was a director of one of the two firms in the Dixon-Yates syndicate. The Democratic Chairman was careful to hedge his remarks, but the charges created a political sensation which propelled the Dixon-Yates contract onto the front pages. Jones emphatically denied having any conversations about his business dealings with the President, and at his August 17 press conference Eisenhower confessed only to being "a little astonished that any kind of such innuendo should include a private citizen of the character and standing of Bob Jones." [18]

The Jones story soon faded, but Mitchell's attack had important ripple effects. Besides defending the golfing hero and reaffirming his approval of the order to the AEC at his August 17 press conference, the President also made what the political scientist Aaron Wildavsky has called a "dramatic and unusual gesture."[19] Noting that "every single official action I take involving the contractual relationship of the United States with anybody, except only when the question of national security is directly involved, is open to the public," Eisenhower told the reporters that "any one of you here present may, singly or in an investigation group, go to the Bureau of the Budget, to the chief of the Atomic Energy Commission, and get the complete record from the inception of the idea to this very minute; it is all yours."[20]

If the President believed that his sweeping offer, which appears to have been made in good faith, would put an end to the Dixon-Yates controversy, he was to be greatly disappointed. The material contained in the chronologies prepared by the BOB and the AEC raised questions about the administration's handling of the negotiations with Dixon-Yates, about the administration's treatment of an unsolicited bid from another private firm which would have saved the government money, and about the administration's failure to keep the TVA informed about the progress of the talks with Dixon-Yates. These disclosures were sufficient to keep the Dixon-Yates contract a burning issue on Capitol Hill through the early winter of 1955, but what was to prove even more embarrassing to the White House was what the BOB and AEC chronologies had not included: the name of the man the Supreme Court was later to characterize as "the real architect of the final contract."[21]

On February 18, 1955, Senator Lister Hill (D–Ala.), a supporter of the TVA, announced in a Senate speech that one Adolphe Wenzell, a vice president and director of the First Boston Corporation, a large New York underwriting firm which specialized in utility issues, had advised the Budget Bureau on the Dixon-Yates contract for which his company was arranging the financing. The absence of Wenzell's name from the supposedly complete chronology put out by the BOB and the AEC in the summer of 1954 made it clear, according to Hill, that "facts have been deliberately concealed from the Congress and the American people." Furthermore, Hill contended, the cover-up of Wenzell's role was continuing. In a letter sent to Hill the week before, BOB Director Hughes had acknowledged that Wenzell had served as an unpaid consultant to the Budget Bureau, but neglected to mention Wenzell's participation in the Dixon-Yates negotiations.[22]

Hughes denied the Senator's charges in a statement released shortly after Hill spoke. However, although the Budget director claimed that all important documents and information in the bureau's possession relative to Dixon-Yates had been made public previously, he also made an addition to that record. Wenzell, he conceded, had taken part, at BOB's request, in a few meetings where the "technical" aspects of the Dixon-Yates proposal were being discussed. Aided by these revelations, opponents of the Dixon-Yates contract were able to launch a congressional investigation of the case.

The evidence collected in open hearings during the summer of 1955 by a special three-man panel[23] of the Antitrust and Monopoly Subcommittee of the Senate Judiciary Committee convinced the unit's members that "a broad effort was made to conceal Mr. Wenzell's role in the Dixon-Yates matter." The BOB and AEC chronologies of events leading to the Dixon-Yates deal, they concluded, "were false. Important names, documents and many important meetings held and attended by government officials in regard to the matter were deleted, despite President Eisenhower's pledge of the 'complete record.' " Nor had the administration been cooperative with the subcommittee in its attempts to bring out the facts. An AEC letter to the panel, for example, while "not technically untruthful, was typical of the sly formulations, clever language and legalistic characterizations which have been repeatedly used to prevent our committee from getting the whole truth." The testimony of Budget Director Hughes, perhaps the key government figure in the controversy, "defie[d] understanding." In sum, the subcommittee declared, it had been "completely blocked from getting to the bottom of the Dixon-Yates contract by the very men in the White House who were involved in the negotiations."[24]

Particularly disturbing to the subcommittee were the frequent claims of executive privilege by administration witnesses. Hughes refused to describe his discussions with the President and to hand over a report Wenzell had prepared for the BOB; the AEC rejected the panel's request for records concerning the preparation of the commission's chronology and the AEC chairman declined to answer questions relating to his conversations with other executive branch officials; and the chairman of the Securities and Exchange Commission (SEC) attempted to avoid testifying on his telephone talks with Assistant to the President Sherman Adams, while the SEC was holding hearings on the Dixon-Yates deal. After a ruling by the Attorney General that executive privilege did not extend to the commission in its quasi-judicial proceedings, the chairman did give the details of his chat with Adams, but he balked at revealing the substance of subsequent conversations with Adams concerning his testimony before the subcommittee. When the subcommittee asked Adams to appear, the White House aide declined the invitation, citing his "official and confidential relationship to the President." [25] Decrying the "loose practices" followed by the executive branch "with respect to its claims of privilege," the subcommittee argued that "privilege is being asserted for the purpose of hiding and covering up unsavory aspects of this Dixon-Yates matter which would seriously embarrass the executive branch if exposed to public scrutiny." The executive branch, the panel's report concluded, "has demonstrated contempt of Congress and its constitutional powers, as well as disregard of the democratic processes." [26]

By all accounts, Eisenhower was not familiar with the specifics of the Dixon-Yates affair, particularly the scope of Wenzell's involvement. The *New Yorker*'s Washington correspondent, Richard Rovere, summed up the opinion of most contemporary observers as well as later students of the episode when he wrote in December, 1955, that the President's "personal responsibility in Dixon-Yates is unclear, but his ignorance and innocence are quite evident." [27] The Senate Antitrust Subcommittee noted, "One of the shameful things about the Dixon-Yates deal is the way the President's staff apparently has played fast and loose with facts, even where he [the President] is concerned." [28]

The President's inability to keep abreast of developments in the Dixon-Yates affair caused him troubles at his press conferences. At his June 29, 1955, news session, more than four months after Hughes had conceded publicly that Wenzell had served as a Budget Bureau consultant on Dixon-Yates, Eisenhower told reporters: "Mr. Wenzell was never called in or asked a single thing about the Yates-Dixon contract. . . . My understanding is that quickly as the Dixon-Yates thing came up he resigned . . . because he was connected with a great Boston finance company." [29] According to Sherman Adams, "Immediately after the press conference the President found out, of course, to his great irritation that his information was neither wholly accurate nor quite complete." [30] Eisenhower's press secretary, James Hagerty, issued an amplifying statement later in the day which, while reaffirming the administration's contention that Wenzell never took part in any government policy decision, advised that "one exception" to the President's remarks "should be noted to keep the public record exactly straight." The one exception referred to was the entire period from January 14 to April 3, 1954, [31] when the Dixon-Yates contract was being negotiated and Wenzell was serving as technical consultant to the Budget Bureau on various financial matters involved in the agreement. [32]

Eisenhower also had difficulty answering questions about Dixon-Yates at two press conferences the following month. Queried at his July 6 session about Budget Director Hughes's invoking executive privilege to prevent the Antitrust Subcommittee from hearing testimony from five BOB staff members, the President was unable to recall if Hughes had talked to him about it. But Eisenhower did defend the principle of executive privilege, contending that failure to protect the "ability of the commander to get the free, unprejudiced opinions of his subordinates" would "wreck the Government." [33] The question of the President's awareness that Wenzell's name had been "knowingly eliminated" from the AEC chronology at the recommendation of the Budget Bureau came up at the July 27 news conference. "Leaning across a desk and flushing noticeably," according to one newspaper story, the President asserted: "I don't intend to comment on it any more at all. I think I have given to this conference, time and again, the basic elements of this whole development, and everything that I could possibly be expected to know about it. . . . I don't know exactly such details as that. How could I be expected to know? I never heard of it." [34]

By the time of his second July news session, the President had ordered the AEC to cancel its signed agreement with Dixon-Yates. This decision came not because the White House believed that Wenzell's activities raised any legal doubts about the validity of the contract, but because the city of Memphis had decided to build a power plant of its own and thus no longer needed the electricity to be supplied by Dixon-Yates. Since a project along these lines had been Eisenhower's objective from the start, he felt vindicated. The President also saw nothing irregular in his administration's handling of the Dixon-Yates episode. Asked at his July 6, 1955, news conference whether, "on the basis of what you have been told about Wenzell's role," he regarded that role as "proper," Eisenhower answered, "Indeed, yes." [35]

The Supreme Court reached a different verdict. Because of the protracted congressional debate over the propriety of Wenzell's activities, the administration had found it advisable to refuse to pay the cancellation costs called for in the AEC's contract with Dixon-Yates. It argued that Wenzell's conflict of interest (which Eisenhower had consistently denied existed) had rendered the contract "unlawful, null and void." [36] Dixon-Yates took its case to the Court of Claims and won a $1,870,000 judgment, a decision Eisenhower considered "right." [37] But for political reasons the Justice Department appealed, and in January, 1961, a six-judge majority of the Supreme Court ruled in favor of the government, declaring that it was "quite likely that the contract would never have come into fruition had Wenzell not participated on behalf of the Government." The records, the Court wrote, "disclose numerous instances in which Wenzell seemed to be more preoccupied with advancing the position of First Boston or the sponsors (Dixon-Yates) than with representing the best interests of the Government." Wenzell's "primary allegiance was to First Boston" and his "loyalty to the Government was a fleeting one." Finding Wenzell's performance in violation of the conflict-of-interest law, a possibility Wenzell had raised with Budget Directors Dodge and Hughes while he was serving as the bureau's consultant, the Justices observed, "The statute is directed at an evil which endangers the very fabric of a democratic society, for a democracy is effective only if the people have faith in those who govern, and that faith is bound to be shattered when high officials and their appointees engage in activities which arouse suspicion of malfeasance and corruption." [38]

The Sherman Adams–Bernard Goldfine Affair

The Sherman Adams scandal, observed an experienced Washington reporter in 1961 in a review of the former White House aide's reminiscences, "still defies explanation." [39] In the years before 1958, a legend had grown in Washington that Adams, the Assistant to the President, was as "cold and clean as New Hampshire granite—a barrier against the corrupting influence of personal and political favoritism."[40] "No one who has ever seen Sherman Adams plain," wrote Richard Rovere in February, 1958, "could possibly think of him as an influence peddler. The idea is ludicrous; the imagination will not put up with it." Politics, Rovere went on, "is full of surprises, but for Sherman Adams to be caught in some sordid little mess is beyond the realm of the possible."[41]

With the disclosures by the House Special Subcommittee on Legislative Oversight in the winter and spring of 1958, the impossible became a reality. The first allegations of impropriety on Adams's part surfaced in February when the former chief counsel to the subcommittee presented evidence that in 1953 Adams had, at the request of the prominent Republican attorney Murray Chotiner, discussed a Civil Aeronautics case, involving a client of Chotiner's, with the acting chairman of the Civil Aeronautics Board (CAB). In one of his letters to Chotiner, Adams had relayed some advice on legal strategy which had been given to him by the CAB official.[42] Although Adams's contact with the board chairman was in apparent violation of CAB rules, the revelation aroused little attention since the subcommittee was then investigating Federal Communications Commissioner Richard Mack. But in June the panel made public additional material on Adams's activities. It produced records showing that New England industrialist Bernard Goldfine had paid some $1,600 in hotel bills at Boston's Sheraton-Plaza for Adams between November, 1955, and May, 1958. Furthermore, the subcommittee announced that it had witnesses who were ready to testify that Goldfine had received preferential treatment from the Federal Trade Commission (FTC) and the Securities and Exchange Commission as a result of his close association with Adams.[43]

Returning quickly to Washington from a Maine fishing vacation, Adams sent a letter to the subcommittee on June 12 terming its insinuations about his relationship with Goldfine "unwarranted and unfair." Although acknowledging that Goldfine had paid his bill at the Sheraton-Plaza, as well as at a hotel in Plymouth, Massachusetts, and conceding that he had made inquiries with the FTC and SEC on behalf of Goldfine, Adams categorically denied that there was any chain of cause and effect between the favors and the calls, or that he had interfered in the agencies' proceedings in any fashion. All he did for Goldfine, Adams contended, was to obtain some information for him and to help arrange an appointment between Goldfine and the chairman of the FTC—assistance that Adams considered both routine and proper.[44]

Adams's hope that his letter would end the matter was dashed by new revelations appearing over the next few days. Newspapers reported that Adams had accepted expensive gifts from Goldfine, including a $700 vicuña coat and a $2,400 oriental rug. Subcommittee investigators disclosed that Goldfine had paid one of Adams's bills at New York's Waldorf-Astoria in 1954, thereby casting doubt on the explanation Adams had offered for his frequent stays at the Boston hotel at Goldfine's expense—that the businessman had maintained the Sheraton-Plaza apartment on a continuing basis. Most damaging, however, was the testimony of an FTC attorney concerning Goldfine's meeting with the FTC chairman in the spring of 1955, which had been set up by Adams. According to the witness, when the conference was over Goldfine told the chairman's secretary, in a tone clearly intended for others in the room to hear, to "get Sherman Adams on the phone." Then, again so that no one could fail to comprehend what was going on, Goldfine said, "Sherm, I'm over at the Federal Trade Commission. I have been well received over here."[45]

Realizing that his position was becoming increasingly untenable, Adams sought to silence his critics by appearing voluntarily before the House panel. On previous occasions, most notably in the Dixon-Yates case, Adams had cited executive privilege in declining invitations to testify before congressional committees, but in this instance the Assistant to the President believed that, as he wrote later, since the subcommittee wanted "to cast reflections on my personal conduct in my position in the White House . . . the usual restrictions against testimony by a White House staff member did not apply." Eisenhower approved this decision.[46] Accompanied by the President's special counsel, Adams took the witness chair on June 17 and in his prepared remarks contended that if his conduct had caused any doubts, "the error was one of judgment and not of intent." "No call of mine, no appointment that I have ever requested to be made, or any inquiry that has been made by me," Adams declared, "has ever been intended to be made to affect the decision of any official in the Government of the United States." Making light of the vicuna coat (actually worth only $69 at Goldfine's mills) and the rug (not a gift but a loan), and noting that he considered Goldfine a personal friend and had given him presents, Adams compared his aid to Goldfine to that congressmen afforded their constituents and rejected the idea that agency officials "might allow themselves to be influenced in their decisions by a White House telephone call, letter or statement."[47]

Under questioning by the subcommittee, Adams conceded that some of his actions might have been unwise. When the panel's chief counsel pointed out that the information Adams had received from the FTC chairman and then passed on to Goldfine was confidential and that therefore the FTC chairman may have violated federal law, Adams confessed to having no knowledge of the relevant statute. It was also brought out that Adams had "recommended" the FTC chairman's appointment to his position and that in the past Adams had found it necessary to ask some of the regulatory agencies' commissioners to resign.[48] Asked if he thought that, in view of the position he occupied, he had "overstepped the bounds of propriety" in seeking to help Goldfine, Adams replied: ". . . if there were any errors here . . . they were errors perhaps of inexperience. . . . If I had the decisions now before me to make, I believe I would have acted a little more prudently."[49]

Two weeks later Bernard Goldfine testified before the subcommittee. Admitting that he had given a lot of gifts to a lot of public officials, Goldfine claimed that he had "never asked Governor Adams to do anything out of line, and he never did anything for me that was out of line. . . . What I asked Governor Adams was done openly without any attempt to hide." An examination of Goldfine's federal tax returns by the subcommittee's staff, however, revealed that Goldfine had charged off as a business expense the cost of the rug and the hotel bills. Also damaging to Adams was Goldfine's refusal to answer a series of questions the subcommittee posed on the financial operations of two of his companies. He was cited for contempt of Congress and subsequently convicted.[50]

Throughout all of the almost daily revelations about Adams's activities, the President maintained the utmost confidence in his chief of staff and repeatedly defended him. Within the White House, Adams had acquired such a sturdy reputation for being careful not to abuse the material prerogatives of his office that when the allegations about him began to appear, Eisenhower was, as he wrote later, "not only astounded but unbelieving, to say the least."[51] The President's response to a question at his February 26, 1958, news conference about the

Chotiner-CAB incident seems to indicate that Eisenhower was not familiar with the episode,[52] but when the Adams-Goldfine relationship became known in June, the White House almost immediately jumped to Adams's aid. The day following the subcommittee's initial disclosures, with Adams still en route from Maine to Washington and unable to consult with the President, Eisenhower's press secretary, James Hagerty, released a statement expressing the view that the panel's "insinuations . . . will be quickly disposed of and proved completely false." The next day, June 12, when Adams sent his letter to the subcommittee, Hagerty told reporters, "Sherman Adams says he has done nothing improper, and President Eisenhower agrees that he has done nothing improper." Four days later the White House reaffirmed the President's faith in Adams.[53]

Eisenhower's strongest expression of support for Adams came in remarks he prepared for his news conference on the day after Adams testified before the subcommittee. Two years earlier the President had told a similar gathering that he could not believe that "anybody on my staff would ever be guilty of an indiscretion. But if ever anything came to my attention . . . that individual would be gone." In June, 1958, however, with Adams under fire, Eisenhower began his statement by suggesting that "a gift is not necessarily a bribe. One is evil, the other is a tangible expression of friendship." The President explained:

The circumstances surrounding the innocent receipt by a public official of any gift are therefore important, so that the public may clearly distinguish between innocent and guilty action.

Among these circumstances are the character and reputation of the individual, the record of his subsequent actions, and evidence of intent or lack of intent to exert undue influence. Anyone who knows Sherman Adams has never had any doubt of his personal integrity and honesty. No one has believed that he could be bought; but there is a feeling or belief that he was not sufficiently alert in making certain that the gifts, of which he was the recipient, could be so misinterpreted as to be considered as attempts to influence his political actions. To that extent he has been, as he stated yesterday, "imprudent."

On the basis of these considerations, Eisenhower drew his "own conclusions of this entire episode":

I believe that the presentation made by Governor Adams to the congressional committee yesterday truthfully represents the pertinent facts. I personally like Governor Adams. I admire his abilities. I respect him because of his personal and official integrity. I need him.

Eisenhower finished by declaring, "Now, ladies and gentlemen, so far as I am concerned, this is all that I can, all that I shall, say."[54]

And the President did say nothing more publicly until September, when he accepted Adams's resignation. Questions about Adams were raised at Eisenhower's news conferences of June 18, July 2, and August 6, but he declined to answer them, citing his June 18 remarks as definitive.[55] Eisenhower's September 22 letter to Adams confirming the latter's departure from the White House had nothing but praise for his aide's activities: "Your performance has been brilliant; the public has been the beneficiary of your unselfish work. After six years of intimate association you have, as you have had throughout, my complete trust, confidence and respect." The only reference in the letter to the controversy swirling around Adams came in the opening sentence where the President "deeply deplore[d] the circumstances" that had led Adams to resign.[56]

Adams elaborated on those "circumstances" in a nationwide television address, arranged by the White House, that same evening. Claiming that all the "responsible" testimony presented to the subcommittee "clearly established that [he] had never influenced nor attempted to influence any agency or any official or employee of any agency in any case, decision or matter whatsoever," Adams accused the subcommittee of engaging in "a calculated and contrived effort to attack and to discredit" him. According to Adams: "A campaign of vilification by those who seek personal advantage by my removal from public life has continued up to this very moment. These efforts, it is now clear, have been intended to destroy me and so doing, to embarrass the Administration and the President of the United States."[57]

Although Eisenhower vehemently denied that he had asked Adams to resign,[58] it is generally accepted that the President had, by late August, come to the conclusion, albeit very reluctantly, that Adams would have to leave the administration. Eisenhower reportedly felt it was "the hardest, most hurtful decision" he had made as President,[59] but it was one that he believed that he had to make for the good of the Republican Party.[60]

The President's Finances

With a single fleeting exception, no touch of scandal ever attached itself to Eisenhower's personal finances, although the media showed occasional interest in the unusually large number of gifts the President received. In December, 1955, *Newsweek* estimated that in the first three years of his administration Eisenhower had accepted more than $40,000 worth of gifts, most of them animal stock and equipment for his Gettysburg farm.[61] The same month *U.S. News & World Report,* in an article prompted by the presentation of a tractor and cultivator to Eisenhower by three farm cooperatives, observed that the White House had no "rigid policy" on gifts; there was no limit on the value of the objects the President might accept—no cash, however, would be taken. Asked to explain how Eisenhower could justify his actions in view of the strict standards on gifts he had set for other federal officials, a White House aide declared, "The office of the President is too big to be influenced by any gift."[62] The gifts did not become an important political issue.[63]

The President's only public comments on his attitude concerning gifts came in the summer of 1957 after the Cowles newspapers ran a series of articles on his personal finances. Queried at his July 31 news conference about the great many gifts he had received, Eisenhower noted that since he was an elected official, "the conflict of interest law does not apply to me."[64] This remark led Senator Wayne Morse (D–Ore.) to declare on August 2 that the Eisenhower administration was following a "shocking code of political immorality":

Acceptance [Morse argued] of a $4,000 tractor with a cigarette lighter attached; the acceptance of a $1,000 bull, or one of even greater value; the acceptance of a large part of the rest of the livestock and the machinery for the farm, along with thousands of dollars' worth of other gifts for his farm cannot be regarded by the President as falling within the spirit and intent of the conflict of interest policy, which the American people have a right to expect all Government officials to respect.[65]

The Oregon senator's blast generated a question at Eisenhower's August 7 news session on what philosophy guided the President when people offered him gifts. Most presents, Eisenhower replied,[66]

come to me from large organizations, voluntary organizations, and I make this stipulation: anything that is given me is right out on the record, and it is given for a particular purpose. People have put bushes on the farm on the theory that they want to build that up as a good-looking place some day to be sort of a public property.

Now, as far as I am concerned, I need no gifts and I never accept gifts that I believe have any personal motive whatsoever behind them, I mean any selfish motive of any kind. If they are not those—I never have accepted one from a corporation or business firm. I merely try to keep my relations with people on what I think is a friendly, decent basis.

With these remarks, the issue of Eisenhower's finances disappeared from public view, except for a few stories by the syndicated columnist Drew Pearson. In a May, 1960, article, Pearson estimated that the President had received $300,000 worth of machinery, livestock, and horticultural goods for his Gettysburg farm, but perhaps Pearson's most interesting revelation occurred after Eisenhower left the White House. Pearson reported in the winter of 1961 that during his presidency Eisenhower had leased the farm to three wealthy oilmen who apparently made no serious effort to turn a profit on their investment. Indeed, one of the lessees claimed a sizable tax deduction each year for the losses incurred in running the farm.[67]

Another allegation of Pearson's, this one in 1958, seemed for a time to be more damaging to Eisenhower. On the day that Adams went before the Legislative Oversight Subcommittee to explain his relations with Goldfine, the Pearson column carried a story, which the *Washington*

Post ran under an eight-column, front-page headline, that Eisenhower had accepted a vicuna coat from the New England industrialist. The President's press secretary had previously denied rumors of such a gift, but after Pearson made his charges, Hagerty conceded that Eisenhower had received vicuna material from Goldfine and had sent him a "thank you" letter. But, Hagerty went on, the President had not kept the material, giving it instead to a friend, whose name Eisenhower could not recall.[68] Neither the press nor Congress followed up on the disclosure, however, as both were engrossed in unraveling the far more complicated Adams-Goldfine relationship.

What some commentators interpreted as implied criticism of Eisenhower's attitude toward gifts[69] was delivered by a special committee of the Association of the Bar of the City of New York in February, 1960. Creation of the Association's Committee on the Federal Conflict of Interest Laws in 1958 was itself a sign that the "mess in Washington" which Eisenhower had promised to clean up in 1952 had not disappeared. Included among the committee's comprehensive proposals for remedying the situation was the indirect suggestion that perhaps Eisenhower was partly responsible for the continuing problem. Noting that "in all matters [of conflict of interest] within the executive branch, the key figure must be the Chief Executive," the committee emphasized the role the President could play by the "power of example":[70]

> The President must set the general tone of the administration—the standard of sensitivity to ethical problems that will govern the conduct of millions of subordinates. The behavior of department heads, and of their juniors, will be powerfully influenced by the standards of behavior set by example in the White House. For example, although the flow of gifts, most of them symbolic in nature, to 1600 Pennsylvania Avenue probably cannot and should not be stemmed, the matter of how the White House disposes of these gifts is very delicate. The soundest approach to this problem appears to be an invariable practice of passing such gifts along to charity or to national museums. In all other aspects of personal behavior in relation to those who may be regarded as seeking to advance their particular economic interests, the greatest circumspection should be used by all Presidents.

NOTES

[1]Robert J. Donovan, *Eisenhower: The Inside Story* (New York, 1956), 79–80.

[2]This section is based upon the accounts in Barton J. Bernstein, "Election of 1952," in *History of American Presidential Elections*, ed. by Arthur M. Schlesinger, Jr. (New York, 1971), 3243–3244; and Herbert S. Parmet, *Eisenhower and the American Crusades* (New York, 1972), 134–141.

[3]Donovan, *Eisenhower*, 26. For a review of the confirmation hearings, see Association of the Bar of the City of New York, *Conflict of Interest and Federal Service* (Cambridge, Mass., 1960), 97–103.

[4]The most convenient summary of these and other cases is David A. Frier, *Conflict of Interest in the Eisenhower Administration* (Ames, Iowa, 1969).

[5]Donovan, *Eisenhower*, 333.

[6]*Public Papers of the Presidents: Dwight D. Eisenhower, 1953–1961* (Washington, 1958–1961), *1955*, 734.

[7]"The End of the Talbott Story," *U.S. News & World Report*, XXXIX (August 12, 1955), 72.

[8]*Congressional Quarterly Almanac, 1955* (Washington, 1956), 513.

[9]Donovan, *Eisenhower*, 341–342.

[10]Quoted in U.S. House Committee on the Judiciary, 84th Cong., 1st Sess., *Hearings on WOC's and Government Advisory Groups* (Washington: Government Printing Office, 1955), 940.

[11]*Ibid.*, 941.

[12]U.S. House Committee on the Judiciary, 84th Cong., 1st Sess., *Interim Report on the Business Advisory Council* (Washington, 1955), 31.

[13]*Congress and the Nation, 1945–1964* (Washington: Congressional Quarterly, 1965), 913.

[14]Quoted in Emmet John Hughes, *The Ordeal of Power* (New York, 1963), 152.

[15]Sherman Adams, *First-Hand Report* (New York, 1961), 317.

[16]For the background of the AEC's involvement, see Aaron Wildavsky, *Dixon-Yates: A Study in Power Politics* (New Haven, 1962), 31–49. Unless otherwise noted, all other statements of fact in the Dixon-Yates discussion come from the Wildavsky study.

[17]The actual name of the enterprise was the Mississippi Valley Generating Company, but everyone invariably referred to it as Dixon-Yates, which is the term used here.

[18]Eisenhower, *Public Papers, 1954*, 717.

[19]Wildavsky, *Dixon-Yates*, 124.

[20]Eisenhower, *Public Papers, 1954*, 717–718.

[21]*U.S. v. Mississippi Valley Generating Co.*, 364 U.S. 520, 552 (1961).

[22]*Congressional Record*, 84th Cong., 1st Sess., 1714–1716.

[23]All three members, chairman Estes Kefauver (D–Tenn.), Joseph O'Mahoney (D–Wyo.), and William Langer (R–N.D.), were outspoken opponents of the Dixon-Yates contract.

[24]U.S. Senate, Committee on the Judiciary, 84th Cong., 1st Sess., *Interim Report of the Subcommittee on Antitrust and Monopoly Legislation* (mimeographed), 15, 17, 22; U.S. Senate, Committee on the Judiciary, 84th Cong., 2nd Sess., *Power Policy: Dixon-Yates Contract* (Washington, 1956), pp. xviii, xxviii.

[25]Quoted in Wildavsky, *Dixon-Yates*, 274.

[26]U.S. Senate, Judiciary Committee, *Interim Report*, 22, 24. Shortly before Wenzell was to appear before the subcommittee, Hughes invited him to his apartment and told

him that any time he did not feel like talking about his relationship with various administration officials, he could refuse to answer on the grounds of the President's directive concerning executive privilege. Wenzell testified freely, much to the discomfort of the administration. He claimed that the Dixon-Yates proposal could not have been submitted without the information he supplied on the cost of borrowing money.

[27]Richard Rovere, *Affairs of State: The Eisenhower Years* (New York, 1956), 353, 355, 356. That Eisenhower was not familiar with the facts in the Dixon-Yates case is the conclusion of Wildavsky, *Dixon-Yates*, 301–302; Frier, *Conflict of Interest*, 76; and Clark R. Mollenhoff, *Washington Cover-up* (Garden City, N.Y., 1962), 68–74, 78. Raoul Berger, who relies heavily on Mollenhoff, writes: "Throughout, Eisenhower exhibited a lamentable unawareness of the scandal his subordinates sought to sweep under the rug. Eisenhower is not, of course, to be charged with knowing concealment of scandals in his administration; rather his trust was abused by his subordinates; though it can hardly be gainsaid that he was bumbling throughout, making no attempt to come to grips with the facts and charges that were constantly being aired in the newspapers and brought directly to his attention by a lively press corps." Berger, *Executive Privilege: A Constitutional Myth* (Cambridge, Mass., 1974), 239, 239n. 30. Eisenhower's political opponents generally accepted the notion that the President was simply uninformed on the Dixon-Yates issue; see Marquis Childs, *Eisenhower: Captive Hero* (New York, 1958), 178. Parmet, *Eisenhower and the American Crusades,* provides only a cursory treatment of the Dixon-Yates affair, but overall he gives the President good grades for his political sense. For two other attempts to revise the usual image of Eisenhower as uninformed and nonpolitical, see Murray Kempton, "The Underestimation of Dwight D. Eisenhower," *Esquire*, LXVIII (September, 1967), 108–109; and Garry Wills, *Nixon Agonistes* (New York, 1971), 114–135.

[28]U.S. Senate, Judiciary Committee, *Interim Report,* 15.

[29]Eisenhower, *Public Papers, 1955,* 653, 657.

[30]Adams, *First Hand Report,* 315.

[31]Eisenhower, *Public Papers, 1955,* 657–658 n. 1.

[32]On two earlier occasions, Eisenhower had made news conference statements about facets of the Dixon-Yates controversy which contradicted those of his subordinates; see Wildavsky, *Dixon-Yates,* 110, 135–136.

[33]Eisenhower, *Public Papers, 1955,* 672–674.

[34]*Ibid.,* 743; Wildavsky, *Dixon-Yates,* 271.

[35]Eisenhower, *Public Papers, 1955,* 678. Eisenhower reaffirmed this opinion in his memoirs; *Mandate for Change* (Garden City, N.Y., 1963), 383.

[36]Wildavsky, *Dixon-Yates,* 274–280, 285.

[37]Eisenhower, *Mandate for Change,* 384.

[38]*U.S. v. Mississippi Valley Generating Co.,* 364 U.S. 520, 554, 558, 559, 562. For a critque of the decision's failure to "reconcile the claims of law and justice," see Wildavsky, *Dixon-Yates,* 288–292.

[39]Wallace Carroll, "Light on Yesterday's Headlines," *New York Times Book Review,* June 25, 1961, 1.

[40]Mollenhoff, *Washington Cover-up,* 122.

[41]Richard Rovere, "Letter from Washington" [February 20, 1958], *New Yorker,* XXXIV (March 1, 1958), 98.

[42]U.S. House Committee on Interstate and Foreign Commerce, Special Subcommittee on Legislative Oversight, 85th Cong., 2nd Sess., *Hearings on the Investigation of Regulatory Commissions and Agencies* (Washington, 1958), 525.

[43]*Ibid.,* 3484–3489.

[44]*Ibid.*, 3591–3593.

[45]*Ibid.*, 3595–3597, 3634; Frier, *Conflict of Interest*, 20.

[46]Adams, *First Hand Report*, 439, 443.

[47]U.S. House, Subcommittee on Legislative Oversight, *Hearings on Regulatory Commissions*, 3712–3717.

[48]*Ibid.*, 3724, 3736.

[49]*Ibid.*, 3738.

[50]*Congressional Quarterly Almanac, 1958* (Washington, 1959), 695, 698–699.

[51]Dwight D. Eisenhower, *Waging Peace* (Garden City, N.Y., 1955), 312.

[52]Eisenhower, *Public Papers, 1958*, 186; Mollenhoff, *Washington Cover-up*, 122–123; Bernard Schwartz, *The Professor and the Commissions* (New York, 1959), 226–228.

[53]Frier, *Conflict of Interest*, 16; *Congressional Quarterly Almanac, 1958*, 691–692.

[54]Eisenhower, *Public Papers, 1958*, 479–480.

[55]*Ibid.*, 480, 485, 511–512, 589. The President's May 4, 1956, comments are in Eisenhower, *Public Papers, 1956*, 457.

[56]Eisenhower, *Public Papers, 1958*, 704–705.

[57]Robert L. Branyan and Lawrence H. Larsen, eds., *The Eisenhower Administration, 1953–1961: A Documentary Record* (New York, 1971), 924.

[58]Eisenhower, *Public Papers, 1958*, 719.

[59]Quoted in John L. Steele, "How the Pros Shot Sherm Adams Down," *Life*, XLV (September 29, 1958), 28.

[60]Eisenhower, *Waging Peace*, 316. All accounts of this episode agree that it was politics that forced the resignation of Adams.

[61]"To the President with Very Best Wishes," *Newsweek*, XLVI (December 12, 1955), 34. This article, like most on the subject, noted that all the presidents had received many gifts while in office, but that Eisenhower was receiving them at a rate far higher than any of his predecessors.

[62]"It's Christmas All the Time for U.S. Presidents," *U.S. News & World Report*, XXXIX (December 16, 1955), 39–41.

[63]Fletcher Knebel, article reprinted in *Congressional Record*, 85th Cong., 1st Sess., 13435.

[64]Eisenhower, *Public Papers, 1957*, 580–581.

[65]*Congressional Record*, 85th Cong., 1st Sess., 13434.

[66]Eisenhower, *Public Papers, 1957*, 592–593. One item out of Eisenhower's financial past not brought up during his White House tenure was the special tax ruling he had received, before becoming president, on the royalties from his book, *Crusade in Europe*. Congress subsequently passed the "Eisenhower Amendment" to prevent similar rulings in the future; *New York Times*, September 15, 1953, 35.

[67]Frier, *Conflict of Interest*, 209–211. Eisenhower later called Pearson's allegations "one man's tissue of lies." *New York Times*, January 30, 1964, 1.

[68]*New York Times*, June 18, 1958, 1, 23.

[69]*Ibid.*, February 23, 1960, 1, 23.

[70]Association of the Bar, *Conflict of Interest*, 189. In 1964, when President Johnson was being attacked by Republicans for allegedly receiving a stereo set from an insurance broker who had sold him a life insurance policy, Eisenhower said he did not "think we should be too ready to throw stones at public officials for accepting gifts." *New York Times*, January 30, 1964, 1.

JOHN F. KENNEDY
1961–1963

Mark I. Gelfand

The Kennedy administration took office under a small political cloud. Allegations of fraud and vote-stealing filled the air in the days following John F. Kennedy's narrow victory in November, 1960, but as president-elect and as president, Kennedy avoided any extended comment on this sensitive subject. He would have something to say, however, about the charges concerning more common varieties of official misconduct that were leveled at his aides.

Secretary Udall and Political Contributions

In early May, 1961, less than a week after Kennedy had presented Congress with his comprehensive proposals for a tightening of the conflict-of-interest laws, the newspapers carried stories that Secretary of the Interior Udall had requested an oil company executive to solicit $100 contributions for tickets to a Democratic fund-raising dinner from other oil and gas industry businessmen. The Interior Secretary immediately denied any wrongdoing, contending that the executive had misunderstood his intentions, and demanded that the material carrying his name be withdrawn. When the President was asked at his next news conference if he believed, in light of the Udall incident, that "ethical standards have appeared to falter," Kennedy launched into an attack upon the present methods of campaign financing. Observing that he had spoken to Udall and was satisfied with the Secretary's explanation, the President expressed the thought that such embarrassing situations were inevitable under the existing system. Kennedy coupled his call for governmental assumption of campaign costs with a warning that "no one should contribute to any campaign fund under the expectation that it will do them the slightest bit of good." The President wrote a final, humorous note to the episode a few weeks later at the fund-raising dinner when he prefaced his formal speech by complimenting all those responsible for the banquet and thanked "Mr. Udall, who handled the publicity."[1]

Billie Sol Estes

For a time in 1962, the Kennedy administration appeared to be seriously threatened politically by the business dealings of a schemer who had built a "paper empire centered on an inverted pyramid of personal credit, at whose base lay government crop and storage guarantees." Billie Sol Estes was a Pecos, Texas, entrepreneur who had ambitions of cornering the fertilizer market in his region. Operating with a little of his own cash and extensive lines of credit backed by chattel mortgages on nonexistent anhydrous ammonia tanks, fraudulently transferred federal cotton allotments, and lucrative federal grain warehouse contracts, Estes had become a figure to be reckoned with in the political economy of West Texas by 1960. But after a local newspaper disclosed the details of the tank mortgages in February, 1962, the rickety Estes financial structure began to shake, and in April a federal grand jury indicted Estes on three counts of mail fraud, three counts of illegally transporting securities in interstate commerce, and one count of conspiracy.[2]

The legal action in El Paso set off tremors in Washington, especially at the Department of Agriculture. A week after Estes was indicted, the deputy administrator of the department's Stabilization and Conservation Service, which ran the cotton allotment program, resigned when it was revealed that Estes had taken him shopping for clothing in Dallas's fashionable and expensive Neiman-Marcus department store. A few days later the department fired an aide to a former assistant secretary of agriculture for failing to make himself available to a Texas inquiry for questioning about his ties to Estes. The following month the former assistant secretary, then in training for a government assignment abroad, was dismissed when the FBI reported that he had charged personal long-distance telephone calls to Estes's credit card. At about the same time, an assistant secretary of labor submitted his resignation after it was disclosed that he had accepted a $1,000 cash gift from Estes.[3]

By mid-May the developing Estes scandal had attracted the attention of two congressional committees and Republican leaders. Subcommittees of the Government Operations panels on both sides of Capitol Hill launched investigations of Estes's improper use of government subsidy programs and of allegations that the Texan had received favored treatment from the Department of Agriculture. Former president Eisenhower, noting that, unlike the situation which had prevailed for most of his White House tenure, all of the investigatory agencies of the government were under the control of one political party, called upon Kennedy to set up a nonpartisan group to study the Estes case. Other Republican spokesmen demanded the ouster of Secretary of Agriculture Orville Freeman.

Although promising to lend all assistance to the legislative inquiries, Freeman and Kennedy tried their best to play down the charges of political favoritism. Claiming that the affair had been "ballooned out of all proportion," Freeman told an early May news session that only three Agriculture Department employees had "possibly received" gifts from Estes, and there was no evidence that he had gained special consideration in return. Freeman's only concession to the department's critics was the admission that the agency's scrutiny and subsequent cancellation of Estes's cotton allotments should have been handled "more expeditiously." But, Freeman reminded the reporters, "the Government hadn't lost . . . a single dime to Estes."[4]

At his news conference on May 17, the President backed up his agriculture secretary all along the line. "I have the greatest confidence in the integrity of Secretary Freeman," declared the President. Taking credit for the fact that it was "this administration" that had indicted Estes, Kennedy went on to assure the newsmen and his television audience that "if any members of the executive branch are involved, any improprieties shown, they will be immediately . . . disciplined appropriately." Kennedy answered a query about favoritism in the Estes case by seconding Freeman's denial that any extraordinary treatment had been given Estes, although he added: "I don't take anything for granted in this matter. . . . That's why we have seventy-six FBI agents working on it." Turning aside Eisenhower's suggestion of an independent inquiry, Kennedy expressed his "great respect" for Senate Permanent Investigations Subcommittee Chairman John L. McClellan (D–Ark.) and promised that "all the information which we have will be made available to the committee."[5]

The congressional hearings, which ran from late spring to late summer, revealed serious organizational problems within the Agriculture Department but no misconduct at the top. Secretary Freeman testified before the committees and provided them with relevant department documents. He said everyone who had improperly accepted gifts from Estes had left the department, and he took "full responsibility" for the mistakes that had been committed in the department's dealings with Estes. Though not absolving Freeman of blame for the "woeful lack of supervision and direction" in the agency's operations, Chairman McClellan commended the Secretary for the prompt remedial steps he took once he became acquainted with the facts of the Estes case.[6] The committees' reports, released in the fall of 1964, were sharply critical of the department's "faulty, inefficient and ineffective" auditing and investigatory procedures, but praised the agency for acting "with alacrity in attempting to correct weaknesses as soon as they came to light."[7] The only political casualties of the Estes affair, which in "its early stages was hailed as a political issue that would rival the Goldfine scandal of the Eisenhower administration,"[8] were two congressmen defeated for reelection after having been identified as recipients of Estes's largesse.

TFX Fighter-Bombers

On November 24, 1962, the Department of Defense announced that it was awarding the $6,500,000,000 contract for 1,700 TFX fighter-bombers, "the most coveted prize the Pentagon ever dangled before bidders,"[9] to the General Dynamics Corporation. The competition for the contract had been intense for a number of reasons: the utilization of the novel variable-sweep wing would give the winner extremely helpful experience in employing this new technology; it appeared likely that the TFX would be the last major military airplane procurement for the rest of the decade; the huge dimensions of the Pentagon's purchase would keep the successful firm and its subcontractors busy for years. Secretary of Defense Robert S. McNamara had begun accepting applications for the contract in the fall of 1961, and by the spring of 1962 the contest had narrowed down to two companies: General Dynamics and Boeing. Soon after it was disclosed that General Dynamics had won, Senator Henry Jackson, a Democrat of Washington, the site of Boeing's home offices, asked the Permanent Subcommittee on Investigations to examine the circumstances leading to the decision. A preliminary inquiry was started in early December.

Thus commenced "one of the longest and most extensive congressional investigations ever undertaken." [10] The subcommittee conducted two comprehensive sets of hearings, the first in 1963 and the second in 1970, and it did not submit its report until eight years after the TFX contract had been signed. The 1963 hearings were held on forty-six days between February 26 and November 20 and filled 2,740 pages of printed record. Almost all of the sessions were behind closed doors, as requested by the Pentagon, because specific details about the TFX were highly classified; censored transcripts of the proceedings, however, were made public the same day.

Jackson sought the investigation because he had found out that the Pentagon's Source Selection Board, composed of top generals and admirals, had been unanimous in its finding that the Boeing proposal was technically superior to, and less expensive than, the General Dynamics version of the TFX. What Jackson and the subcommittee wanted to know was why McNamara and the civilian secretaries of the air force and the navy had overruled the board and decided "to buy the second best airplane at the higher price." [11]

The political implications of Jackson's request for an inquiry were obvious. General Dynamics would build the TFX at its Fort Worth plant, and the Vice President, the former secretary of the navy, and the new secretary of the navy were all Texans. Together, Texas and New York—where General Dynamics' primary subcontractor, Grumman, had its facilities—had far more electoral votes (sixty-nine) than Washington (nine) and Kansas (eight), where Boeing would have produced the TFX at its Wichita factory. Both Texas and New York had gone for Kennedy in 1960: neither Washington nor Kansas had. Furthermore, General Dynamics was in serious economic trouble: its contract for the B-58 bomber was winding up, and it had just suffered severe losses on its commercial jets. Republicans and Democrats wondered if the contract had been awarded as a result of political and regional pressures, possibly in conflict with national security and economy interests.[12]

Relations between the Defense Department and the subcommittee started off amicably, but deteriorated after the Senate panel began to question the judgment of Secretary McNamara and his civilian subordinates. The subcommittee was initially given access to all pertinent department records, but these were later closed to its investigators. This does not seem to have been a problem for the subcommittee, since the staff had already seen most of what it wanted.[13] When testimony by uniformed personnel proved extremely critical of the Secretary's decision, McNamara declassified a five-page memorandum for the record, dated November 21, 1962, which explained the reasons for giving the contract to General Dynamics. The rationale was essentially technical, and it came under heavy fire from Defense Department witnesses, both military and civilian. On three occasions in March, high Pentagon officials made statements to reporters, on- and off-the-record, which some observers viewed as designed to discredit the subcommittee with the public. In his appearance before the panel on March 21, McNamara declared: "There is a lot of harm that will accrue from this investigation. I cannot see any good that will accrue from it. I can see only harm."[14]

At his press conference the same day, Kennedy took a different stance. "I see nothing wrong with the Congress looking at these matters," he said. Declaring that he thought McNamara had decided correctly, the President noted that "this contract involves a large amount of money and naturally some people would prefer it to go another place than the place which the Secretary chose." McNamara had done the right thing, he repeated, "and I think this investigation will bring that out, and I have no objection to anyone looking at this contract as long as they feel that a useful function is served." Kennedy affirmed his faith in the fairness of the subcommittee and expressed confidence that as a result of the hearings "we all know a lot more about the TFX than we did before, and that's a good thing."[15]

How much the President knew about the TFX contract before it was signed was a question the subcommittee could not answer. At his March 21 news conference, Kennedy denied making any suggestions as to who should get the contract and said that the award was made "completely" by the Defense Department.[16] Documents presented to the subcommittee by the department indicated that McNamara planned to discuss his recommendation with Kennedy before the contract was let, and that, indeed, the Secretary did inform the President of the pending award a week before the public announcement. That Kennedy approved the contract is certain; whether he indicated any preferences in his talks with McNamara did not come out in the evidentiary record compiled by the subcommittee. "What part the White House meetings played in the decision," the panel's report concluded, "is not known." [17]

Nor could the subcommittee determine if the choice of General Dynamics had been politically inspired. McNamara categorically denied that socio-economic factors or Vice President Johnson's Texas background had any bearing on his decision, but the panel was something less than impressed by the "cursory deliberations" of the Secretary which led to his reversal of the Source Selection Board's expert opinion. "Secretary McNamara's efforts in arriving at the decision," declared the panel in its report, "can at best be described as capricious, lacking in depth and without factual substantiation." But, beyond saying the department's actions involved "inexcusable procedures by high ranking Government officials," the subcommittee was unable to go. [18] A political scientist who has studied the TFX decision and is inclined to accept McNamara's stated technical reasons for picking General Dynamics writes, "On the basis of the evidence available to the public, it is not possible to conclude either that political pressures influenced the awarding of the contract or that they did not." [19]

If the subcommittee failed to confirm or allay Jackson's suspicions on the political issue, its probe of the TFX did raise some doubts about the propriety of two Defense Department officials' behavior. Evidence gathered by the panel's staff revealed that Deputy Secretary of Defense Roswell L. Gilpatric had performed a number of legal services for General Dynamics and had attended many of the corporation's board meetings while he was in private practice during the late 1950s. The investigators also disclosed that soon after the TFX contract had been awarded, General Dynamics chose Gilpatric's old law firm, Cravath, Swaine & Moore, to be the company's counsel, and elected a senior partner of the firm to its board of directors. Gilpatric had "resigned" from Cravath, Swaine & Moore upon joining the Defense Department in 1961, but he received $20,000 annually under a severance agreement, and as far as the firm's insurance underwriters were concerned, Gilpatric was merely on a leave of absence. Some of the subcommittee's members believed that this relationship should have led Gilpatric, who was responsible for implementing the Kennedy administration's tightened code of ethics within the Defense Department, to remove himself from the TFX decision.[20]

Gilpatric denied any wrongdoing and was supported by the President. Noting that McNamara was fully acquainted with his career, the deputy secretary explained that Cravath, Swaine & Moore represented a great many firms in the defense industry, and that it was impossible for him to disqualify himself from participation in all contracts involving the firm's clients. Denying any conflict of interest, Gilpatric said that all of his actions dealing with defense contracts had been "predicated on considerations of national defense, and nothing else."[21] Kennedy expressed his "highest regard" for Gilpatric at an August news conference,[22] and in November the Justice Department sent a letter to the subcommittee clearing him of any conflict-of-interest charges. New material which challenged Gilpatric's earlier testimony on his relations with General Dynamics and Cravath, Swaine & Moore was brought up at hearings on November 19 and 20, but with the suspension of hearings after the latter date the matter was not pursued until 1970, when the subcommittee's report declared that Gilpatric had been "guilty of a flagrant conflict of interest" in the TFX decision.[23] In the meantime, Gilpatric had left the Defense Department to rejoin Cravath, Swaine & Moore.

More embarrassing to the administration were the subcommittee's revelations about Secretary of the Navy Fred Korth. At the panel's hearings in July, the staff brought out the fact that Korth had retained $160,000 of stock in a Fort Worth bank which did business with General Dynamics. Three months before becoming navy secretary, Korth, as president of the bank, had approved a $400,000 loan to the aerospace company. An examination of the log of visitors and telephone calls to Korth's Pentagon office also disclosed that the Secretary had contacts sixteen times with representatives of General Dynamics, as compared to only two with Boeing's, during the contract competition in 1962. Korth denied any "predisposition" toward General Dynamics in the TFX award, and in the same news conference in which he had defended Gilpatric, the President also supported the Navy Secretary. In September the Justice Department backed up Korth's contention that there had been no conflict of interest.[24]

Additional evidence uncovered by the subcommittee forced the President to request Korth's resignation the next month. Korth had testified that he had severed his relationship with the Fort Worth bank, but a check of the institution's records showed that while at the Pentagon, Korth had received letters of praise from the bank's officers for bringing them new accounts. Some of the letters written by Korth to promote the bank's business were on navy stationery and included an offer to invite some of the bank's "extra good customers" for a ride on the navy's official yacht, the *Sequoia*. Subcommittee Chairman McClellan brought the letters to the attention of Attorney General Robert F. Kennedy, who in 1955, as counsel to the same subcommittee, had been instrumental in causing the ouster of the Secretary of the Air Force, Harold Talbott, under similar circumstances. Although the Justice Department found no illegal acts by Korth, the Attorney General believed that the President had no choice but to demand Korth's resignation. In mid-October Korth asked to be relieved, citing the need to attend to his "pressing business affairs." The President's acceptance letter, while omitting the usual "regrets," thanked Korth for his contributions to the improvement of the navy.[25]

It appears that the administration attempted, unsuccessfully as it turned out, to conceal the real reasons for Korth's departure. Wishing to avoid any inference that questionable activities had touched the awarding of the TFX contract, the Pentagon spread the story that Korth had left because of a dispute with the Defense Secretary over the latter's decision not to proceed with development of a nuclear-powered aircraft carrier.[26] Korth's letter-writting activities came out a few days later, however, and at his October 31 press conference the President was asked if the Secretary's resignation had been requested. "I think the letters which Mr. Korth and I exchanged," replied Kennedy, "explain the situation as I would like to see it explained." He went on:[27]

> I have no evidence that Mr. Korth acted in any way improperly in the TFX matter. The fact of the matter is, I have no evidence that Mr. Korth benefited improperly during his term of office in the

Navy. And I have no evidence, and you have not, as I understand it—the press has not produced any, nor the McClellan committee—which would indicate that in any way he acted improperly in the TFX. I always have believed that innuendoes should be justified before they are made, either by me, in the Congress, or even in the press.

Writing in his column the next day, James Reston commented, "Korth wasn't crooked; he was morally insensitive and stupid, but the President insists Korth wasn't fired, which raises the question: Why not?"[28]

On the morning of November 22, Kennedy spoke before the Fort Worth Chamber of Commerce and referred to the TFX as "the best fighter system in the world" and promised that it would save taxpayers at least $1,000,000,000 in costs.[29]

NOTES

[1]*New York Times*, May 3, 1961, 1, 26, and May 28, 1961, 39; *Public Papers of the Presidents: John F. Kennedy, 1961–1963* (Washington, 1962–1964), *1961,* 357–358.

[2]"A Scandal Hot as a Pistol," *Life,* LII (June 1, 1962), 78; "Estes: Three-Sided Country Slicker," *Fortune,* LXVI (July, 1962), 166–170; Julius Duscha, *Taxpayers' Hayride* (Boston, 1964).

[3]*Congressional Quarterly Almanac, 1962* (Washington, 1963), 990–992.

[4]*Ibid.,* 991.

[5]Kennedy, *Public Papers, 1962,* 400–401, 404, 407. Kennedy was upset at the New York *Herald Tribune's* coverage of the Estes case, particularly with what he believed was its unfair treatment of Freeman, and ordered the White House's subscription to the newspaper canceled. Pierre Salinger, *With Kennedy* (Garden City, N.Y., 1966), 118.

[6]*Congressional Quarterly Almanac, 1962,* 997, 999–1000.

[7]U.S. House, Committee on Government Operations, 88th Cong., 2nd Sess., *Operations of Billie Sol Estes* (Washington, 1964), 27; U.S. Senate, Committee on Government Operations, 88th Cong., 2nd Sess., *Department of Agriculture Handling of Pooled Cotton Allotments of Billie Sol Estes,* Senate Report 1607 (Washington, 1964), 152.

[8]*Congressional Quarterly Almanac, 1962,* 988. Estes was convicted of the federal charges in 1963.

[9]Clark R. Mollenhoff, *The Pentagon* (New York, 1972), 385.

[10]U.S. Senate, Committee on Government Operations, 91st Cong., 2nd Sess., *TFX Contract Investigation,* Senate Report 1496 (Washington, 1970), 2.

[11]*Ibid.,* 17.

[12]Henry L. Trewhitt, *McNamara* (New York, 1971), 139.

[13]U.S. Senate, Government Operations Committee, *TFX Contract,* 3–4.

[14]*Ibid.,* 24–27; Trewhitt, *McNamara,* 142–146.

[15]Kennedy, *Public Papers, 1963,* 274–275, 281. Theodore Sorensen later reported that

Kennedy was unhappy with the Senate probe; an internal government memorandum quoted by Sorensen stated: "What we are really dealing with in the TFX investigation is the spectacle of a large corporation, backed by Air Force Generals, using the investigatory power of Congress to intimidate civilian officials just because it lost out on a contract. If . . . successful, it will be impossible for any civilian official ever again to exercise judgment . . . [without] measuring the influence of large corporations with Congress or . . . to control the military men who are theoretically under his direction." Sorensen, *Kennedy* (New York, 1965), 416–417.

[16]Kennedy, *Public Papers, 1963,* 281.

[17]U.S. Senate, Government Operations Committee, *TFX Contract,* 51; Trewhitt, *McNamara,* 139–140. There is nothing in the record which indicates that the subcommittee sought materials from the White House or that any administration witness invoked executive privilege.

[18]U.S. Senate, Government Operations Committee, *TFX Contract,* 50, 90.

[19]Robert J. Art, *The TFX Decision* (Boston, 1968), 3. Art contends that the crucial issue in the TFX controversy was civilian vs. military control, and that McNamara had sound reasons for choosing General Dynamics.

[20]*Congressional Quarterly Almanac, 1963* (Washington, 1964), 1094–1095; Mollenhoff, *Pentagon,* 404–407.

[21]Mollenhoff, *Pentagon,* 407; *Congressional Quarterly Almanac, 1963,* 1095.

[22]Kennedy, *Public Papers, 1963,* 636.

[23]U.S. Senate, Government Operations Committee, *TFX Contract,* 51.

[24]*Ibid.,* 37–38; Mollenhoff, *Pentagon,* 407–410. In its 1970 report, the subcommittee said Korth had committed an "impropriety" by not removing himself from the deliberations on the TFX; *TFX Contract,* 51.

[25]Mollenhoff, *Pentagon,* 410–411.

[26]Clark R. Mollenhoff, *Despoilers of Democracy* (Garden City, N.Y., 1965), 221; *New York Times,* October 15, 1963, 1, 33.

[27]Kennedy, *Public Papers, 1963,* 829, 833.

[28]*New York Times,* November 1, 1963, 32. At his November 14, 1963, news conference, Kennedy was asked his opinion of the moral and ethical climate in Washington in light of the Korth and Bobby Baker cases. He replied: "I think that this administration has been very vigorous in its actions, and I think that we have tried to set a responsible standard. There are always going to be people who fail to meet that standard, and we attempt to take appropriate action dealing with each case." *Public Papers, 1963,* 851.

[29]Kennedy, *Public Papers, 1963,* 887, 889.

LYNDON B. JOHNSON
1963–1969

Mark I. Gelfand

E xcept for one insignificant instance,[1] the charges of misconduct that swirled around the Johnson administration were directed at the President's immediate staff and the President himself. The President's political career stretched back more than a quarter century, and much of his past behavior came under attack while he occupied the White House. Effective Democratic control of the congressional investigatory machinery, plus the Senate's concern for its own image, kept the legislature's probe of Johnson's actions within tolerable limits for the President. The media proved more difficult for Johnson to manage, however; indeed, there arose the first cries about a "credibility gap" that would plague the President's domestic and foreign policies.

Robert G. (Bobby) Baker

What has been called "the most bizarre Washington scandal of the 1960's"[2] broke out into the open just as Johnson assumed the presidency. On September 9, 1963, a private suit had been filed in a District of Columbia court charging that Robert G. Baker, the secretary to the Senate Majority, had improperly used his influence to obtain contracts in defense plants for his vending machine firm. The *Washington Post* reported the legal action three days later and then followed up with a story on Baker's extensive and complicated business activities. Over the next few weeks a number of publications carried articles on the details of the Senate official's financial wheeling-and-dealing, as well as rumors of fast-and-loose living in the higher circles of the government. Baker resigned his post on October 7 rather than answer questions at an executive session of Senate leaders, and on October 10 the Senate authorized an investigation of its former aide. Closed-door hearings by the Committee on Rules and Administration were started on October 29 and were in progress on November 22.

Because of Johnson's previous intimate ties with Baker, his name was linked to Baker's as soon as the case began to unravel. Baker had been selected as majority secretary in 1955 by Johnson, then majority leader, and Baker had over the next six years established himself as an important figure in the so-called Johnson System. In referring to Baker during this period, Johnson had said: "I have two daughters. If I had a son, this would be the boy. . . . [He is] my strong right arm, the last man I see at night, the first one I see in the morning."[3] The two men appear to have drifted apart after Johnson left the Senate in 1961 for the vice presidency, but when the disclosures about Baker came out in the fall of 1963 they were immediately seen as politically damaging to Johnson. There was speculation that President Kennedy might use the Baker scandal as an excuse to drop Johnson as his running mate in 1964 and, indeed, Johnson, according to one account, suspected that Attorney General Robert Kennedy was hounding Baker so as to embarrass the Vice President and to force him off the ticket.[4]

The continuing Senate investigation of Baker's affairs awaited Johnson as he moved into the White House. However, since all of the testimony heard by the Rules Committee in December was in executive session, the new president enjoyed a short respite from additional headlines. Johnson had avoided comment on the Baker case while he was vice president, but some of his aides now counseled him "to repudiate Baker promptly and thoroughly with a statement to the effect that he had trusted and been fond of this bright young man and was sorry he had turned bad."[5] The President decided against this course and said nothing, although on December 17 he did issue, at the request of the Rules Committee, an executive order allowing the panel to inspect income and other tax returns relevant to its probe of Senate employees.

Allegations made before the Rules Committee and released to the public in mid-January, 1964, would force Johnson to break his silence on the subject. Don B. Reynolds, a suburban Maryland insurance salesman, claimed that shortly after he sold Majority Leader Johnson

$100,000 of life insurance in 1957, Walter Jenkins, Johnson's administrative assistant, suggested that Reynolds purchase advertising time on KTBC, the Austin, Texas, television station owned by the President's wife, Lady Bird Johnson. The clear implication was that Johnson was demanding a kickback on the broker's commission Reynolds had received on the majority leader's policy. Reynolds bought the commercial spots at a cost of $1,208, which he then resold, for a fraction of that amount, to someone who could use them. The insurance man also testified that in 1959 Baker, whom Reynolds had taken into his firm as a vice president, urged that he give Johnson the particular model of a high-fidelity stereophonic phonograph in which Mrs. Johnson had expressed interest. The $584.75 phonograph was sent to the Johnsons' home in Washington along with invoices, according to Reynolds, that indicated he was the buyer. Two years later, after becoming vice president, Johnson bought another $100,000 life insurance policy from Reynolds.[6]

Learning of Reynolds's charges before they appeared in the press, Johnson and his aides attempted to delay their disclosure and minimize their impact. When a Washington newspaper sent an advance copy of its article breaking the Reynolds story to the White House with a request for its reaction, Abe Fortas, one of the President's most trusted confidants, telephoned the paper's editor and urged that publication be withheld because additional material to be brought out later would give a different picture of the whole incident. The newspaper went ahead anyway.[7] Fortas, along with Clark Clifford, another Johnson intimate, also advised the President not to let Walter Jenkins, now a key figure on the White House staff, testify in person before the Rules Committee, as the Republican members of the panel demanded. Rather than risk having the hostile cross-examination Jenkins was sure to face generate even more publicity for the insurance man's accusations, Johnson restricted Jenkins's rebuttal to a sworn statement to the committee, in which he denied knowing that Baker was associated with Reynolds's firm, denied suggesting to Baker or Reynolds the purchase of television time, and claimed that he thought the stereo was a gift to Johnson from Baker, not Reynolds.[8]

Soon after the Reynolds testimony hit the front pages, Johnson raised the issue at his next news conference. Avoiding any mention of the television advertising allegation, the President explained the life insurance policy as a regular business deal taken as a precautionary measure to protect the interests of his wife and two daughters. Johnson said he had believed the stereo was a present from the Baker family and noted that the Bakers and Johnsons had exchanged gifts before. Baker, the President told reporters, "was an employee of the public and had no business pending before me and was asking for nothing, and so far as I know expected nothing in return any more than I did when I had presented him with gifts." Declining to take any questions on the subject, Johnson concluded, "That is all I have to say about and all I know about it."[9]

Johnson discussed the Baker controversy only one more time during the eighteen months that it occupied the attention of the Senate. In a March, 1964, television interview conducted by correspondents from the three networks, the President tried to separate himself as much as possible from the man who had once been his closest aide on Capitol Hill. Asked if they were still friends, Johnson declared, "I haven't seen him . . . or haven't talked to him since he resigned from the Senate." Calling Baker a former "employee of the Senate," which was true in a technical sense but not in a practical one since Baker had worked for the majority leader, Johnson rejected the idea that Baker had been his "protégé": ". . . he was there before I came to the Senate for ten years, doing a job substantially the same as he is doing now, he was elected by all the Senators and appointed by no one, including the Republican Senators." The President also claimed "unfamiliarity" with the evidence that had been accumulated against Baker, but beyond saying that everyone was entitled to a fair trial and that he favored a full investigation of Baker's activities, Johnson refused to comment on the revelations.[10]

The public-relations offensive inaugurated by the President's rebuttal of Reynolds's allegations at the news conference was followed up by a vigorous White House campaign to create doubts about Reynolds's character. "Persons within and close to the Johnson administration," reported the *New York Times* in February, 1964, "have attempted to use secret Government documents to impugn" Reynolds's testimony. The *Times* noted that a number of newsmen and editors had been read excerpts by White House aides from what were purported to be air force intelligence and FBI files on Reynolds. This material indicated that Reynolds had engaged in black-market activities overseas, as well as other kinds of immoral and improper conduct. The derogatory information on Reynolds received a wide distribution in the February 5 column of Drew Pearson, in which Reynolds was described as a man who "has brought reckless charges in the past against people who crossed him, accusing them of being Communists and sex deviates." Both Pearson and the President's press secretary categorically denied that the White House was responsible for these leaks from confidential records.[11]

Most of the facts that the Senate committee uncovered about Baker's affairs in no way touched Johnson, but 1964 was an election year and so the President wanted the investigation wrapped up as soon as possible. By repeated party-line votes, the Democratic majority on the Rules Committee turned back Republican efforts to expand the scope and duration of the inquiry. Hearings were suspended on March 25, and on July 8 the panel's report was issued. Although the majority disapproved of Baker's numerous business activities, finding him "guilty of many gross improprieties," its review of the Johnson insurance episode concluded with an attack on the man who had brought the charges: "It appears rather obvious that Mr. Reynolds in his effort to enjoy the limelight of this investigation was not reluctant to draw on his imagination and to add to his store of knowledge as time passed."[12] For their part, the Republican minority complained that the probe had never been completed, stressing that Jenkins should have been called to testify in person.

But the Baker case would not disappear. As the presidential campaign got under way, Republicans spoke frequently of a "whitewash" (according to Barry Goldwater, "Bobby Baker's affairs lead right straight into the White House"), and in September Senator John Williams (R–Del.), who had been investigating Baker on his own for nearly a year, presented new evidence of wrongdoing by Baker—involvement in an illegal contribution to the 1960 Democratic campaign fund. President Johnson immediately ordered an FBI investigation of the charges, and a few days later the Senate voted to reopen its probe of Baker. After two days of testimony in early October, however, the Rules Committee's hearings were suspended indefinitely for lack of a quorum. Following this announcement, the panel's chairman, B. Everett Jordan (D–N.C.), left Washington to join Mrs. Johnson on her whistle-stop campaign tour of the South.[13]

The Rules Committee picked up its work after the elections, but the partisan divisions persisted. Republicans revived their demand that

Jenkins, who had resigned from the White House staff in October, be called as a witness, but the Democrats, acting on the advice of Jenkins's physician, who said that he was in no condition to appear before the committee, permitted him to give testimony by means of written interrogatories. With some modifications, Jenkins reaffirmed his earlier statement. In March, 1965, the committee released an FBI report which found no basis for the allegations Reynolds had made concerning the TFX contract, a "big sex party" in New York, and the lavish use of government counterpart funds in Hong Kong by Vice President Johnson. By a 6–3 party-line vote, the panel declared that the FBI study "makes it obvious beyond a doubt that the testimony of Don B. Reynolds is unworthy of belief." Senator Williams contended that the FBI report represented "a continuation of an organized attempt to discredit Mr. Reynolds rather than an effort to establish the truth," but Senator Jordan announced that with the FBI's findings in hand the committee's investigation was completed.[14] The committee's supplemental report, presented in June, 1965, acknowledged the cooperation of executive branch agencies in the panel's work and cleared Jenkins and Johnson of any impropriety in the life insurance deal. As they had the year before, the members of the Republican minority argued that the task of the committee was unfinished.[15]

On January 5, 1966, a District of Columbia grand jury indicted Baker on nine counts of fraud, conspiracy to defraud the government, and evasion of income taxes in 1962–1964. None of the charges was connected to Baker's relationship with Johnson. A year later Baker was convicted on seven of the counts.

Walter Jenkins

Just a month before Election Day, 1964, White House Chief of Staff Walter Jenkins was arrested in the men's room at the Washington, D.C., YMCA, one block west of the executive mansion, on a morals charge. Jenkins told no one at the White House of his run-in with the law, or of a similar incident in 1959, but within a week rumors of Jenkins's problem had reached the newsrooms of Washington's three dailies. When an editor at one of these papers attempted to reach Jenkins to confirm the story, Jenkins called Abe Fortas.

Unable to contact the President, who was in New York on a campaign trip, Fortas acted quickly on his own. After discussing the matter with Jenkins, the Washington attorney had Jenkins check into a hospital and then, accompanied by Clark Clifford, Fortas visited the editors of the newspapers to plead that they hold up publication of their articles on the arrest. Fortas and Clifford pointed out that this was not the type of story the papers usually ran, asked that disclosure of the arrest be delayed so that the Jenkins family could be informed privately, revealed that Jenkins was presently under medical attention, and promised that he would be requested to resign his post. As a student of Fortas's career has observed, "The mere fact of his presence at the [newspapers'] offices, along with another of the President's close advisers, amounted to pressure which any editor would have found difficult to resist."[16] Although the three papers did agree to the Fortas-Clifford bid for more time, United Press International broke the story later that day. By then Jenkins had been admitted to a hospital, and Johnson was about to accept his resignation.[17]

The Jenkins episode disappeared almost as swiftly as it had surfaced. Johnson moved rapidly to allay fears that his aide's vulnerability to blackmail had endangered national security by publicly calling upon the FBI to make an investigation. In a week, an unusually short time, the FBI reported that there had not been any compromising of United States security interests. Not answered in the report was the question of why Jenkins had not been subjected to a full FBI investigation either in 1961 or 1963, when Johnson became vice president and then president.[18] Apparently deeply shaken by what had happened to one of his oldest friends, Johnson called in reporters to a private room in the White House and started making insinuations about leading Republicans, hinting that he would use the material "if they keep after my people." On another occasion, Johnson charged that Eisenhower had suffered from "the same type of problem" with one of his White House aides, an allegation quickly denied by the former president.[19] Barry Goldwater sprinkled his speeches with references to the "curious crew" around Johnson, but in the excitement created by the ouster of Khrushchev and the explosion of Communist China's first nuclear device, Walter Jenkins dropped out of the news.

The Johnson Fortune

The Johnsons were among the wealthiest families ever to occupy the White House, and the manner in which they made their fortune fascinated the media. Unlike his predecessor in the White House, who had inherited his money, Johnson amassed his riches almost entirely while he was in public office, mainly after he entered the Senate and began his rise to national power in 1948. To what extent the Johnsons enjoyed their prosperity—built as it was upon favorable rulings by the Federal Communications Commission because of the Senator's political prominence—would take, as one newspaper noted in 1964, "a subtle scientist to measure precisely,"[20] but the matter unquestionably invited a great deal of conjecture.

Johnson's disposition of his family's fortune when he assumed the presidency contributed to the interest of the press in how the money was made. Some of the President's aides reportedly urged prompt and total disassociation with the multimillion-dollar radio-TV station KTBC in Austin, which was the keystone of the Johnsons' financial empire. These aides argued that since KTBC enjoyed a television monopoly in the Austin area, and since radio and TV were regulated by a federal agency, any continued connection of the Johnson family with the station would be harmful to the President's image. But Mrs. Johnson, who has generally been credited with making KTBC such a successful enterprise and who actually held the stock in the broadcasting company, could not bear to part with the business.[21] Thus the Johnsons' response to their glaring conflict-of-interest problem was the creation of a blind trust, whereby all of the family's broadcasting properties were placed under the control of an outside party. That the Johnsons' choice for trustee happened to be an old family friend who saw the Johnsons frequently on social occasions raised doubts as to the propriety of the arrangement.

An FCC decision in December, 1963, involving KTBC kept the President's finances in the news. Thanks to earlier FCC rulings over a period of ten years, KTBC was the only television station in the Austin viewing area, one of the largest such single-market regions in the nation. However, an application by a community antenna television service threatened KTBC's dominance. The commission's twice-delayed judgment in the CATV case did not break from its past record: KTBC retained its status as the only commercial TV station in a city of nearly 200,000 people. Somewhat defensively the FCC pointed out that the ruling was based upon a principle laid down a year before and applied in all similar cases since and upheld by the courts. But some of the facts in the Austin situation set it apart from the precedents, thereby posing anew the question of whether the FCC could ever completely erase from its deliberations the knowledge that it was deciding the fate of the Johnson family's fortune.[22]

In his only public comments on his finances, at two press conferences in April, 1964, Johnson was something less than candid in describing the sources of his wealth. At one session he said, "I have no interest in any television any place," and at the other, "I don't have any interest in Government-regulated industries of any kind and never have had." Both statements were technically accurate: the television stock was in the name of Mrs. Johnson and their two daughters. Johnson conceded that fact, but employed such terms as would make it difficult for anyone not acquainted with his wife's business background to realize that a television station was involved.[23]

By the summer of 1964, Johnson's fortune had become, as James Reston observed, an "underground issue poisoning the atmosphere" of the election campaign.[24] Important publications such as the Washington Evening Star,[25] the Wall Street Journal[26] (whose correspondent won the Pulitzer Prize for National Reporting for his two-part article), U.S. News & World Report,[27] and Life[28] carried features on the President's wealth. None of the pieces alleged that Johnson had done anything illegal or unethical, but the authors did not hide their suspicions that what was in the public record was not the entire story. The Life article, for example, in describing the Johnsons' real estate deals, observed:[29]

> Following the trail of some of these transactions resembles the action in a Western movie, where the cowboys ride off in a cloud of dust to the south, the herd stampedes northeastward, the Indians start to westward but, once out of sight, circle toward the north, the rustlers drift eastward and the cavalry, coming to the rescue, gets lost entirely—all over stony ground leaving little trace.

Nor were the media prepared to accept the contention, favored by the family, that Mrs. Johnson was responsible for the creation of the fortune.

Instances of Johnson's participation in conferences and strategy moves were cited, and there were even suggestions, quickly denied by the White House, that the President continued to engage in and discuss the family's businesses.[30]

Failing to quiet the mounting public discussion of the issue by his silence, Johnson attempted to end the speculation by releasing some figures of his own. When *Life*, "after thorough and painstaking research (with no help from Johnson)" estimated the President's fortune at $14,000,000, the White House sought to have the article dropped or revised before it was published. The magazine's editors were "alternately appealed to and argued with in a long night session," but they decided to go ahead.[31] A few days later, the President distributed copies of an audit, prepared by one of the nation's largest accounting firms, which placed the Johnson family's assets at $3,500,000. This figure was somewhat misleading, since it was based on the purchase price of Johnson's holdings, which bore no relationship to their market value some two decades after they were acquired.[32]

However, the audit had the desired effect of muffling debate on the subject, and the Republicans could not capitalize on Johnson's wheeling-and-dealing image in the campaign. The question of the Johnson family's wealth ceased to be newsworthy after 1964 because, as the *New York Times* noted in that year, "a thorough combing of the records of the Johnsons' enterprises failed to turn up any creditable evidence that Mr. Johnson has ever misused his political fortune to enhance his personal fortune."[33]

NOTES

[1]In April, 1965, Assistant Secretary of Commerce Herbert W. Klotz resigned when it was disclosed that he had profited on his transactions in Texas Gulf Sulphur stock because of a tip that had come to him indirectly from a company insider. Although he was not charged with doing anything illegal, and despite the fact that his stock dealings were in no way connected with his official duties, the White House asked the Assistant Secretary to resign. *New York Times*, April 23, 1965, 1, 53.

[2]Rowland Evans and Robert Novak, *Lyndon B. Johnson: The Exercise of Power* (New York, 1966), 332.

[3]Eric F. Goldman, *The Tragedy of Lyndon Johnson* (New York, 1969), 83.

[4]Evans and Novak, *Johnson*, 332–333. The authors did not believe that Johnson's suspicions were justified.

[5]Goldman, *Johnson*, 26–27. One former Johnson aide doubted that Johnson "knew much about Baker's enterprises," but added, "No doubt he should have tried to know; politicians are willfully obtuse about such things where a valuable friend is involved." Harry McPherson, *A Political Education* (Boston, 1972), 200.

[6]Evans and Novak, *Johnson*, 413.

[7]Charles B. Seib and Alan L. Otten, "Abe, Help!—LBJ," *Esquire*, LXIII (June, 1965), 88. Baker had hired Fortas as his lawyer in the summer of 1963 when his legal troubles began, but Fortas resigned when Johnson became president.

[8]Evans and Novak, *Johnson*, 413.

[9]*Public Papers of the Presidents: Lyndon B. Johnson, 1963–1969* (Washington, 1965–1969), *1963–1964*, 220–221.

[10]*Ibid.*, 365, 857, 1057.

[11]*New York Times*, February 6, 1964, 15, and February 8, 1964, 1, 10.

[12]U.S. Senate, Committee on Rules and Administration, 88th Cong., 2nd Sess., *Financial and Business Interests of Officers or Employees of the Senate*, Senate Report 1175 (Washington, 1964), 58, 45.

[13]*Congressional Quarterly Almanac, 1964* (Washington, 1965), 963.

[14]*Ibid.*, 969.

[15]U.S. Senate, Committee on Rules and Administration, 89th Cong., 1st Sess., *Supplemental Report*, Senate Report 388 (Washington, 1965), 15, 18–19, 28, 33.

[16]Robert Shogan, *A Question of Judgment* (Indianapolis, 1972), 103.

[17]Seib and Otten, "Abe, Help!—LBJ," 87.

[18]Clark R. Mollenhoff, *Despoilers of Democracy* (Garden City, N.Y., 1965), 351.

[19]Goldman, *Johnson*, 252; Alfred Steinberg, *Sam Johnson's Boy* (New York, 1968), 689.

[20]Louis M. Kohlmeier, "The Johnson Wealth: How President's Wife Built $17,500 into Big Fortune in Television," *Wall Street Journal*, March 23, 1964, 12.

[21]Goldman, *Johnson*, 27.

[22]Louis M. Kohlmeier, "Johnson & FCC: Agency Curb on Rival of Wife's TV Station Spotlights Touchy Issue," *Wall Street Journal*, March 24, 1964, 1, 14.

[23]Johnson, *Public Papers, 1963–1964*, 458, 470–471.

[24]*New York Times*, August 12, 1964, 34.

[25]Washington *Evening Star*, June 9, 1964.

[26]See notes 20 and 22.

[27]"New Political Issue: Mrs. LBJ's Property," *U.S. News & World Report*, LVI (May 25, 1964), 12.

[28]Keith Wheeler and William Lambert, "How L.B.J.'s Family Amassed Its Fortune," *Life*, LVII (August 21, 1964), 62–72.

[29]*Ibid.*, 69.

[30]*New York Times*, June 10, 1964, 25.

[31]Hugh Sidey, *A Very Personal Presidency* (London, 1968), 183–184.

[32]*New York Times*, August 20, 1964, 1, 16.

[33]*Ibid.*, August 23, 1964, IV, 12.

RICHARD M. NIXON
1969–1974

Kathryn S. Olmsted and Eric Rauchway

Long familiar to American voters as the Republican Congressman from California who attacked Alger Hiss as an agent of the Soviet Union, as the Senator who won office by claiming his opponent, Helen Gahagan Douglas, was "pink down to her underwear," and as the dour Vice President to the smiling Dwight D. Eisenhower (as well as a losing candidate for the presidency and the California governorship), Richard M. Nixon ran for the White House in 1968 as a "new Nixon," a man who had matured out of his old roles of Red-baiter and attack dog, a once-fierce Cold Warrior who now promised "an honorable end to the war in Vietnam."[1]

In pursuing that campaign promise, Nixon reverted to his old ways even before winning office by seeking to ensure that the outgoing administration of Lyndon B. Johnson would fail in its efforts to negotiate its own peace treaty to end the war in Southeast Asia. Once in office, Nixon—without congressional warrant—first secretly and then openly expanded the Vietnam War into neighboring Cambodia. In the face of growing protest and in response particularly to military analyst Daniel Ellsberg's unauthorized release in 1971 of the Defense Department's internal studies of the Vietnam War (the series of documents better known as "the Pentagon Papers," which revealed the analysts' conviction that the war could not be won), Nixon established a team of operatives devoted to stopping such leaks by criminal means. Throughout the Nixon administration, recourse to illegal behavior became not only an available option but central to the President's conception of the office of chief executive of the United States.

The Chennault Affair

President Johnson announced on March 31, 1968, that he would not seek re-election so that he could work on bringing an end to the war in Vietnam. Even before Nixon won the Republican presidential nomination, Johnson sought Nixon's support for these peace overtures, telling the former Vice President in late July about his plans to begin negotiations. Johnson would call a halt to the U.S. bombing of North Vietnam if (and only if) the North Vietnamese government acquiesced to three conditions: keeping out of the demilitarized zone between the North and the South, ending the shelling of South Vietnamese cities, and agreeing to peace talks with the United States and the South Vietnamese government. Nixon told the President that he supported this proposal and stated publicly his intention to back the administration's efforts to end the war in Vietnam.[2]

Privately, Nixon told Bui Diem, the South Vietnamese Ambassador to the United States, to regard Anna Chan Chennault, a Chinese-born U.S. citizen and the widow of celebrated World War II general Claire L. Chennault, as his spokesperson. Through Chennault, Nixon instructed the South Vietnamese that they could expect better peace terms from an incoming Nixon administration than they could get from the outgoing Johnson administration. The Saigon government, he urged, should therefore delay engaging in negotiations until after the election. Nixon made a vague but public statement to the same effect on October 7, 1968, reversing his previous remarks in support of the Johnson peace efforts, and saying instead of his possible inauguration in January, "We might be able to agree to much more then than we can do now."[3]

On October 12, through Soviet diplomats, Hanoi signaled its willingness to reach terms with the U.S. government. Johnson secured approval from South Vietnam's President Nguyen Van Thieu to halt the bombing under the previously agreed-upon conditions. The North Vietnamese negotiators said they were prepared to agree to those conditions.

Public opinion polls showed Nixon's lead over the Democratic candidate, sitting Vice President Hubert H. Humphrey, Jr., shrinking. Nixon feared that news of peace negotiations would further boost Humphrey's fortunes. On October 22, Nixon told his aide H.R. "Bob" Haldeman to "keep Anna Chennault working on SVN [South Vietnam]" and (according to Haldeman's notes) asked if there were "any other way to monkey wrench it? Anything RN can do."[4]

Learning from a third party of Nixon's efforts, Johnson ordered Federal Bureau of Investigation (FBI) surveillance of Chennault and the South Vietnamese embassy and wiretaps on both. With approval from his advisers, Johnson announced a bombing halt on October 31.

Then, on November 2, South Vietnamese President Thieu issued a statement saying that peace talks could not begin without further concessions. That night, a wiretap caught Chennault calling South Vietnamese Ambassador Diem and urging his government to continue this course of deferring negotiations. "Hold on," she said, "we are gonna win." She said "her boss" had instructed her to urge the South Vietnamese to remain firm in their resistance to peace negotiations.[5]

Johnson privately told the Republican Senate leader Everett M. Dirksen of Illinois that this strategy of delay was "killing four or five hundred a day waiting on Nixon." Nixon's communications might have violated the Logan Act, which bars private citizens' negotiations with foreign governments; it might also have constituted (as Johnson said) "treason." Dirksen replied, "I know." Johnson said that only Nixon's encouragement was permitting the South Vietnamese to continue their intransigence.[6]

Nixon won the election by less than 1 percent of the popular vote. For lack of proof, Johnson did not reveal all he knew, but sketchy versions of the Republican's efforts to stop peace negotiations surfaced soon after the election. Early analyses identified this sabotage of diplomacy as sufficiently significant to have put Nixon over the top and into the White House. Johnson was among these early analysts. In his own 1971 memoir, the former President claimed Nixon's treachery "cost Hubert Humphrey the election." Johnson retained his own records of the episode rather than leave them for Nixon's staff to find, and instead entrusted them to an aide who in turn lodged them with the Lyndon Baines Johnson Presidential Library, which kept them sealed until 1994, when at last a satisfactory chronology of these events began to emerge.[7]

FBI Director J. Edgar Hoover informed Nixon of the surveillance shortly after the election and, indeed, exaggerated its extent. The incoming President now feared the existence of copious incriminating records in the hands of his political opponents.[8]

Operation Menu and Associated Wiretaps

In February after his inauguration, Nixon, together with his National Security Adviser Henry A. Kissinger, began planning an expansion of the Vietnam War into the neutral neighboring nation of Cambodia. Nixon officials wanted to bomb the North Vietnamese supply chain, which ran through that nation and carried materiel to the Viet Cong in South Vietnam. Although the United States had struck some targets in Cambodia under the Johnson administration, the proposed new assaults would be much vaster. The White House kept this project, code-named "Operation Menu," secret, fearing Congress would not support expanding the war, especially given Nixon's campaign promise of bringing the war to an honorable end. Haldeman, now Chief of Staff to Nixon, wrote in his diary of his astonishment at the scope and secrecy of the plan, feeling he was "entering an entire new world." To make the plan work, the U.S. Army Commander of Military Operations in Vietnam, Creighton W. Abrams, Jr., identified targets in Cambodia, and Air Force Colonel Ray B. Sitton delivered them to Kissinger and his military aide Colonel Alexander M. Haig, Jr., in a basement room at the White House. Kissinger reviewed, sometimes changed, and approved the targets, returning the list to Sitton, who in turn conveyed it to Saigon. Airborne B-52s, bound for targets in Vietnam, routinely received diversion orders redirecting them to targets in Cambodia. The officers involved then destroyed records of the diversions, producing fraudulent reports of the air raids that concealed their true objectives.

Nixon boasted of his role in the operation to Treasury Secretary John B. Connally, Jr., in May 1972, saying he himself had come up with the name. The secret aerial missions had originally been referred to as "Breakfast"; Nixon insisted the bombardment had to entail a full menu of damage done to the enemy. The bombing continued for years, thus contributing to the destabilization of Cambodia and opening the way for the later genocidal campaigns of the Khmer Rouge. The House Judiciary Committee considered the concealment of bombing in Cambodia among potential articles of impeachment against Nixon, although ultimately its members rejected it in favor of more narrowly defined crimes. Operation Menu's full enormity was not made public until 2000, when President William J. Clinton declassified data revealing that the United

States had dropped almost 2.8 million tons of bombs on Cambodia during the Nixon administration, which was nearly five times as much as previously believed.[9]

A prolonged campaign of such scope could not remain entirely secret, and by May 1969 news of it appeared on the front page of the *New York Times*, whose reporter cited "Nixon Administration sources."[10] Nixon asked Hoover, with the approval of Attorney General John N. Mitchell, to identify those sources. With Kissinger's help, Hoover drew up a list of suspects. Mitchell signed orders for the FBI to wiretap, without judicial warrant and outside the ordinary procedures of oversight, thirteen officials and four reporters. The FBI sent surveillance reports from these wiretaps to Kissinger and Nixon.[11]

One of the officials wiretapped was Morton H. Halperin, a Kissinger aide. Although the surveillance turned up no evidence of Halperin's involvement in leaks, the FBI continued to listen to his conversations for almost two years, long after he left the administration and became an adviser to Maine Senator Edmund S. Muskie, a candidate for the Democratic presidential nomination in 1972. This illegal surveillance, originally begun to protect a secret war, thus continued as illegal surveillance in the name of acquiring political intelligence.

The more Nixon and Kissinger learned about the private observations of their subordinates, the more worried they became about the lack of loyalty among administration staff members, as well as other members of the defense community who had access to confidential information. Eventually these suspicions came to center not only on Halperin but on his former colleague at the Defense Department Leslie H. Gelb; Johnson's Secretary of Defense, Clark M. Clifford; and his Deputy Assistant Secretary of Defense, Paul C. Warnke, all of whom had worked on the Pentagon's internal study of the Vietnam War, which had concluded that continuation of the war lacked rational justification. To assist with that project, Halperin had recruited an analyst from the RAND Corporation named Daniel Ellsberg.[12]

Surveillance, Enemies, and the Plumbers

To monitor and harass Americans protesting the war in Vietnam, Nixon ordered the Central Intelligence Agency (CIA) to expand its Operation

CHAOS, a program of surveillance and infiltration of domestic dissident groups.[13] The operation, which had begun during the Johnson administration, was illegal because the CIA's charter prohibited it from spying on Americans in the United States. In addition to the CHAOS expansion, one of Nixon's aides, Tom Charles Huston, proposed the creation of a new interagency committee to monitor and neutralize domestic protesters. Called the Huston Plan, the program called for agents of the National Security Agency (NSA), CIA, and FBI to use several illegal methods, including surreptitious entries, warrantless wiretaps, and secret mail opening. Nixon withdrew his approval of the plan only after FBI Director Hoover objected to it. But Nixon did not forget the essence of the proposal and later returned to it.[14]

Nixon's top aides systematized the administration's hatred and fear of its opponents with the "Enemies List." The White House Counsel John W. Dean III first proposed creating the list in the summer of 1971 in a memo urging the administration to "maximize the fact of our incumbency" by using "the available federal machinery to screw our political enemies." The federal machinery might include "grant availability, federal contracts, litigation, prosecution, etc."[15] Other Nixon staff members supplied names for the list, which grew to include two hundred reporters, columnists, movie stars, prominent academics, and even famous athletes known to oppose the President. Nixon and his aides also tried to politicize the Internal Revenue Service (IRS) by using the agency to target his political enemies on the left. In discussing whom to choose for a new director of the IRS, Nixon explained that he wanted someone who would "go after our enemies, and not go after our friends" and "do what he's told. Every income tax return I want to see, I see!" However, his choice for director successfully resisted many of the President's orders.[16]

Nixon officials came to view Daniel Ellsberg as one of their most significant enemies and set out to destroy him. Ellsberg, the defense analyst who helped write the Pentagon's internal assessment of the war, suddenly rose to prominence in 1971 when he leaked that study to the *New York Times*. Persuaded that the Kennedy and Johnson administrations had systematically lied to the American public about the war, continuing the fight solely because they lacked the courage to admit defeat, Ellsberg came to believe that Nixon was doing the same. Ellsberg tried to convince antiwar senators to release the documents, but they refused. So he went to the press.[17]

When the *Times* began publishing the Pentagon Papers, Nixon and his aides debated how to respond. The study, after all, covered only previous administrations and did not necessarily reflect on the current president. Initially, the Nixon men thought they could only benefit from this revelation of Democratic presidential incompetence and perfidy. But one of Nixon's advisers, former Illinois Congressman Donald H. Rumsfeld, argued that the leak of the classified documents threatened the presidency itself. Haldeman summarized Rumsfeld's argument to the President this way: "The implicit infallibility of presidents, which has been an accepted thing in America, is badly hurt by this, because it shows that people do things the president wants to do even though it's wrong, and the president can be wrong."[18] Moreover, the leak might inspire other would-be whistle-blowers—including some who might have access to Nixon administration secrets—to go public. Nixon soon came to see Ellsberg as part of a conspiracy to undermine his own power as well as the power of the U.S. presidency. "We're up against an enemy, a conspiracy," Nixon said on July 1, 1971. "They're using any means. We are going to use any means. Is that clear?" Nixon identified the conspirators principally as intellectuals and Jews. "I was hoping one of them would be a Gentile. But gee, they're all . . . All Jews."[19]

To find and punish conspirators and leakers like Ellsberg, the President ordered the creation of a secret group in the White House later known as the "Plumbers" (so named because they looked for leaks) but more properly referred to as the Special Investigations Unit (SIU). "I need a man, a commander, an officer in charge here at the White House . . . ," Nixon said on July 1, 1971. "I really need a son-of-a-bitch like Huston who'll work his butt off and do it dishonorably." Charles W. "Chuck" Colson suggested E. Howard Hunt, Jr., who, Colson said, "spent 20 years in the CIA overthrowing governments. Ideologically, he is already convinced this is a big conspiracy."[20] In addition to Hunt, the Plumbers included G. Gordon Liddy, a former FBI agent and Treasury aide. SIU lacked congressional warrant and was expressly tasked with committing crimes.[21]

In a futile attempt to find damaging information on Ellsberg, the Plumbers broke into the office of Ellsberg's psychiatrist. The President also told them to burglarize the liberal Brookings Institution, which Huston told him held a secret Johnson file on the bombing halt, which possibly implicated Nixon in the Chennault affair.[22] Liddy proposed firebombing the building to get the files, but Haldeman rejected the plan as too costly.

As Nixon began to organize his campaign for re-election, his focus on enemy action shifted to his electoral opponents. Liddy and Hunt moved from the White House to the Committee to Re-elect the President (CRP, popularly known as CREEP), where they oversaw a massive espionage and sabotage operation directed against several Democratic presidential aspirants. Liddy's first plan, code-named "Gemstone," targeted the Democratic National Convention. At a meeting in Attorney General Mitchell's office in January 1972, Liddy proposed a million-dollar operation that included break-ins at the headquarters of Democratic presidential candidates Muskie and George S. McGovern, a Senator from South Dakota, wiretaps on the phones of Democratic candidates and their staffs, the use of sex workers for entrapment, and the kidnapping of radical leaders such as "Yippies" Jerry C. Rubin and Abbot Howard "Abbie" Hoffman.[23] Concerned about its expense, Mitchell did not initially approve Gemstone. Liddy ultimately won approval from campaign officials for a scaled-down, $250,000 operation.

In addition to Liddy's sabotage and espionage programs, CRP also employed an operative to undermine and destroy the campaigns of various Democratic presidential aspirants. The agent, Donald H. Segretti, hired spies who forged documents on the letterheads of Democratic candidates, spread false rumors about their sex lives, infiltrated and spied on their campaigns, and planted fake information in the media about them. These pranks, referred to by Nixon staffers as "ratfucking," had a dramatic effect on the campaign. After Nixon's tricksters wrote that Muskie had laughed at a joke that used a pejorative word for Americans of French Canadian descent, Muskie's intense emotional reaction to this and another scurrilous charge that his wife was an alcoholic helped doom his campaign. Moreover, dirty tricks committed during primary season aroused suspicion among Democrats of their fellow partisans. Thus the Nixon campaign sowed dissension within the Democratic Party and made it difficult for the opposition to unite after the convention.

CRP paid for these surveillance and sabotage operations using a slush fund of illegal campaign contributions. In April 1972, Nixon had signed a new campaign fund-raising law that, among other requirements, forced campaigns to report the source of their money. In the months before the new law went into effect, the CRP raised more than $20 million in unreported contributions. Much of this money came from extortion and bribery. CRP officials threatened corporate leaders with retaliation by the IRS, the Commerce Department, or the Justice Department's antitrust division if they did not contribute. The re-election committee also dangled federal employment, particularly ambassadorships, in front of potential contributors, providing they gave enough. In one conversation with Haldeman in June 1971, Nixon stated that "anyone who wants to be an ambassador must give at least $250,000." Haldeman agreed: "Yeah, I think any contributor under $100,000 we shouldn't consider for any kind of thing." [24]

Watergate Break-In, Cover-Up, Exposure

In mid-June 1972, police discovered evidence of one part of the Nixon administration's many illegal programs. The break-in at the Democratic National Committee headquarters in a Watergate complex office building that day was actually the second Watergate burglary. The first occurred in late May 1972, when a team of former CIA agents under Hunt and Liddy's direction secretly entered DNC headquarters and placed wiretaps on two phones. When one of the taps failed to work and perhaps also to search for documents that could damage or help Nixon's campaign, the team returned to replace the defective wiretap. During the burglars' second trip, a security guard discovered evidence of the illegal entry and alerted the police. Reporters jumped on the story when they realized that one of the burglars was James W. McCord, Jr., the chief of security for the CRP, although Press Secretary Ronald L. Ziegler dismissed the incident as a "third-rate burglary attempt." [25]

Nixon and his advisers immediately understood that if they let the investigation proceed, their many illegal activities would be revealed. They thus embarked on a cover-up, seeking to delay or altogether stymie an investigation lest it reveal the creation of the Plumbers, the break-in at Ellsberg's psychiatrist's office, the Huston Plan, the Cambodia wiretaps, the Enemies List, the espionage and sabotage efforts against several Democratic presidential candidates, the bribery and extortion committed by the campaign's fund-raisers, and other embarrassments.[26] To avoid exposure, Nixon and his aides began to consider how to foil investigators and ensure that the burglars refused to cooperate with prosecutors. On June 23, 1972, Nixon met with Haldeman to discuss how to handle the break-in. The White House taping system recorded the President ordering Haldeman to use the CIA to pressure the FBI to drop its investigation.[27]

Nevertheless, the FBI continued its inquiry, and one bureau official, Associate Director W. Mark Felt, began to leak information about the inquiry to the *Washington Post*. The *Post*'s reporters, especially Carl Bernstein and Robert U. "Bob" Woodward, who would soon be celebrated for their coverage of the entire scandal, dubbed Felt "Deep Throat."[28] His leaks kept the story alive in the press. The President, however, stated categorically that "no one in this administration, presently employed, was involved in this very bizarre incident."[29] A federal grand jury indicted the five burglars, Hunt, and Liddy, but no other administration officials.

In January 1973, the trial of the "Watergate Seven" opened in federal district court in Washington. Although the defendants continued to play along with the cover-up during the trial itself, the presiding judge, John J. Sirica, doubted that the trial had exposed the real truth about Watergate. He threatened the defendants with long prison sentences if they did not tell all they knew. McCord then shocked the court and the rest of the country by writing a letter to Sirica claiming that the witnesses had perjured themselves and that unidentified "others" were involved in the Watergate conspiracy.[30] After McCord chose to reveal his role in the cover-up, other conspirators soon followed.

Senate Democrats and Justice Department lawyers insisted that Nixon's incoming Attorney General, Elliot L. Richardson, appoint a special prosecutor to investigate the break-ins and cover-up, and they forced Richardson to promise that he would fire the prosecutor only if there were "extraordinary improprieties on his part."[31] Richardson chose Archibald Cox, Jr., a Harvard Law School professor who had served as Solicitor General in the Kennedy administration, as Special Prosecutor.

In addition, the Senate established a select committee to investigate any "illegal, improper, or unethical activities" that occurred during the presidential election of 1972.[32] The committee's nationally televised hearings would command the nation's attention.

Under pressure from the Special Prosecutor, Dean began cooperating with Cox and, suggesting that the President had been involved in the cover-up from the beginning, gave damning testimony against Nixon in the Senate hearings. The most dramatic moment in the hearings came when Alexander P. Butterfield, Haldeman's chief assistant, revealed in July 1973 that Nixon had been taping conversations in the White House since early 1971. The voice-activated tapes could potentially prove whether the President or Dean was telling the truth about the Watergate cover-up—or, in other words, what the President knew and when he knew it, in the memorable phrase of Republican Senator Howard H. Baker, Jr., of Tennessee. The Senate Watergate Committee subpoenaed several tapes—the first time in history that Congress had issued a subpoena to a president. Cox also issued his own subpoenas.

Entering battle with the Senate Watergate Committee and Cox over control of the tapes, the President resisted these subpoenas. He claimed that he could withhold the tapes on the grounds of executive privilege. Cox, however, insisted that the tapes contained evidence of crimes and therefore must be turned over to investigators. Nixon proposed a compromise in which Senator John C. Stennis, a conservative Mississippi Democrat known to be hard of hearing, would listen to the audiotapes and report on their contents. When Cox declined this dubious compromise, Nixon decided to fire him. Attorney General Richardson and Deputy Attorney General William D. Ruckelshaus resigned rather than carry out the President's order. Ruckelshaus advised Solicitor General Robert H. Bork, the next in command at the Justice Department, to carry out the President's order "if his conscience would permit." It did; Bork finally fired Cox, and the press dubbed the episode the "Saturday Night Massacre."[33] The incident galvanized opposition to the President, as newspaper editorial boards around the country called for his impeachment or resignation. Public support for impeachment doubled to 38 percent.[34]

Acting Attorney General Bork replaced Cox with Houston lawyer

Leonidas "Leon" Jaworski, who afforded Nixon no relief and continued Cox's proceedings to secure the tapes. When Nixon relinquished some of them, prosecutors discovered that there was an eighteen-and-a-half-minute gap on one recording of a conversation between Haldeman and Nixon on June 20, 1972, just three days after the Watergate burglars had been caught. Technical experts testified that someone had manually erased the tape. Jaworski and his staff grew convinced of Nixon's complicity in the cover-up, and they subpoenaed more tapes.[35]

The President suffered other reverses and accusations of misconduct in the fall of 1973. Vice President Spiro T. Agnew was forced to resign after he pleaded no contest to charges of accepting bribes and failing to pay taxes on those bribes as Governor of Maryland. Members of Congress also raised questions about Nixon's personal finances. He had made questionable, backdated deductions on his tax returns which allowed him to avoid hundreds of thousands of dollars in taxes. The President blamed the financial chicanery on his lawyers and accountants. In addition, investigations revealed that his private homes in Florida and California had increased in value largely because of taxpayer-funded improvements. The President angrily rebutted accusations of financial impropriety, telling a November 1973 press conference, "I am not a crook. I earned everything I got." The President finally paid $284,000 in back taxes in April 1974 but did not pay an additional $150,000 he owed because the statute of limitations had expired.[36] The scandals regarding Nixon's personal finances were not directly related to the story of misconduct in the 1972 election, but revelation of them in the middle of the Watergate investigation contributed to the growing consensus that the President could not be trusted.

In March 1974, the federal grand jury investigating Watergate crimes indicted seven top presidential aides, including Haldeman and Mitchell, along with more than thirty other people. Ultimately more than forty individuals associated with the Nixon scandals would plead guilty or be convicted of crimes. Jaworski asked the jury to name Nixon as an unindicted co-conspirator, rather than charge him with crimes, because the prosecutor doubted that a president could be indicted while in office. An impeachment process should be finished first, he believed.

As Jaworski continued to demand more tapes, the President offered another compromise. Instead of releasing all the actual tapes, he would give the special prosecutor edited transcripts of some of them. In April 1974, he announced his delivery of these transcripts in a nationally televised address in which he was flanked by stacks of blue notebooks representing the conversations. Rather than ending the controversy as Nixon had hoped, the transcripts only emboldened the President's critics. Some transcripts, with creative edits that benefited the President, differed markedly from the actual recordings that Congress had already obtained. The transcribed conversations quickly became a cultural phenomenon. Some television and radio shows staged dramatic readings, newspapers ran them as special inserts, and paperback editions sold over a million copies. The transcripts laid bare the vulgarity of the Oval Office conversations, with "expletive deleted" becoming a Watergate catchphrase. Supporters of the President, including many Republicans, expressed disgust both with the foul language and with the matter-of-fact discussion of crimes like paying hush money to the burglars. The Senate Minority Leader, Pennsylvania's Hugh D. Scott, Jr., said that the conversations revealed "a deplorable, shabby, disgusting and immoral performance" by everyone involved.[37]

Impeachment Debate and Resignation

The House Judiciary Committee began to consider articles of impeachment against Nixon in May 1974. After a brief public session, the committee met behind closed doors for the next two months as its members studied the massive factual record of Watergate that had been prepared by the committee's staff members. As they read through the documents, seven Southern Democrats and moderate Republicans—soon dubbed the "fragile coalition"—began to support removing Nixon from office. The President tried to demonstrate his mastery of foreign policy by embarking on a major diplomatic journey in June 1974, traveling to Egypt, Syria, Israel, and the Soviet Union. But critics argued that he was just trying to distract Americans from Watergate, and momentum for impeachment continued to build.

On the committee's first day of public deliberations on impeachment, July 24, 1974, the Supreme Court announced its unanimous ruling that Nixon must turn over all the subpoenaed tapes to the special prosecutor.

Without knowing the content of those conversations, the committee members began to debate and vote on articles of impeachment. Strong majorities approved articles for obstruction of justice (27–11) and abuse of power (28–10). A third article on contempt of Congress also secured a majority (21–17). One-third of all committee Republicans voted for at least one of the three articles. Articles that the committee considered on the secret bombing of Cambodia and Nixon's failure to pay his taxes did not win majority support. The decision by some Southern Democrats and moderate Republicans to vote for impeachment signaled that a majority of the entire House would almost surely follow suit. But Nixon still had a chance of retaining the support of one-third of the senators, which was all he needed to stay in office. Even at this late date, some Republicans—mostly conservatives who saw Nixon as a victim of the "liberal media"—fiercely defended the President.

Nixon's support all but evaporated on August 5, when the White House released the transcripts of the other subpoenaed tapes, including one that Nixon had thus far withheld even from his own lawyers and top aides. The tape recorded on June 23, 1972, provided what became known as the "smoking gun": evidence that the President had been involved in the Watergate cover-up from the beginning. The entire country could now read how the President and Haldeman had tried to use the CIA to end the FBI investigation of the Watergate break-in.

The revelation of the smoking-gun tape destroyed the President's last chance of staying in office. Even his strongest defenders on the House Judiciary Committee said they would support impeachment for obstruction of justice, and key Republican senators said they would vote to convict. On August 7, a delegation of prominent congressional Republicans led by Senator Barry M. Goldwater of Arizona visited Nixon in the White House and told him that he would almost certainly be removed from office if the Impeachment Inquiry followed its likely course.

To avoid impeachment and removal, on August 9, 1974, Nixon resigned, the only president in American history to do so. Shortly before he boarded a helicopter to depart the White House, he delivered an impromptu speech to staff in which he offered, perhaps inadvertently, a clear summation of the reasons for his downfall. "Always remember, others may hate you," he said, "but those who hate you don't win unless you hate them, and then you destroy yourself." [38]

Defense and Legacy

The word "Watergate," often used to summarize the illegal actions of the Nixon administration, unhelpfully reduces them to a story centered on the break-in. But in truth, power unfettered by law characterized Nixon's entire understanding of the Oval Office and indeed constitutes possibly his most important influence on later constitutional law and U.S. politics. Nixon articulated his views most bluntly after his presidency when offering a defense of his crimes in office. In a series of interviews with the British journalist David Frost in 1977, Nixon allowed that his principal error had not been in violating the law but in failing to destroy evidence. "If the tapes had been destroyed . . . I believe that it is likely that I would not have had to go through the agony of resignation." Nixon also offered a general theory of misconduct in the presidency: "When the president does it, that means it is not illegal." [39] The former President considered the power of the presidency to confer lawfulness on actions taken by the occupant of the office.

Over time, as Nixon's expansive understanding of presidential power became clear, Congress passed a series of laws in an effort to restrict the office. The War Powers Act of 1973 curtailed unilateral presidential military action. The provision for an independent counsel in the 1978 Ethics in Government Act sought to institutionalize and protect investigations of the President and thus to prevent any future Saturday Night Massacres. The investigations of a Senate select committee under the chairmanship of Idaho Senator Frank F. Church III exposed misuse of the nation's intelligence resources, leading to the Foreign Intelligence Surveillance Act of 1978, which imposed a judicial barrier that the President must surmount before spying on U.S. citizens. [40]

But Nixon's theory of the presidency had influential and persistent adherents, including Richard B. Cheney, who almost immediately after Watergate worked to restore to the White House the power that in their view had never rightfully left it. These efforts reached their culmination during the presidency of George W. Bush, in—as one scholar writes—"asserting that Congress does not have the right to enact laws that limit the president's powers as chief executive or commander in chief." This view supported the Bush administration's legal justifications of warrantless surveillance and expansion of war powers. Lawyers for the President, using this theory, concluded along Nixonian lines that "the president can interpret the law and unilaterally decide to ignore it, without legal sanction or redress." What President Clinton called Nixon's "incredibly sharp and vigorous and rigorous mind" continued to affect the lives of Americans and people around the world for decades after his death. Nixon's understanding of presidential power remains an important and living legacy of his efforts to defend his hold on office, irrespective of the law.[41]

NOTES

[1]Herbert Mitgang, "Nixon's Enemy in 1950 Had the Last Laugh in '74," *New York Times,* May 25, 1992, 15; Theodore H. White, *The Making of the President 1968* (New York: HarperCollins, 2010), 387–388; "Transcripts of Acceptance Speeches by Nixon and Agnew to the G.O.P. Convention," *New York Times,* August 9, 1968, 20.

[2]Ken Hughes, *Chasing Shadows: The Nixon Tapes, the Chennault Affair, and the Origins of Watergate* (Charlottesville: University of Virginia Press, 2014), 11–12.

[3]Hughes, *Chasing Shadows,* 25.

[4]John A. Farrell, *Richard Nixon: The Life* (New York: Doubleday, 2017), 342–343. Also John A. Farrell, "When a Candidate Conspired With a Foreign Power to Win an Election," *Politico,* August 6, 2017, www.politico.com/magazine/story/2017/08/06/nixon-vietnam-candidate-conspired-with-foreign-power-win-election-215461.

[5]Hughes, *Chasing Shadows,* 46.

[6]Farrell, *Nixon,* 342; Hughes, *Chasing Shadows,* 47.

[7]Farrell, "When a Candidate Conspired"; Lyndon Baines Johnson, *The Vantage Point: Perspectives of the Presidency, 1963–1969* (New York: Holt, Rinehart, Winston, 1971), 548. For an early and, in the author's own description, unsatisfactory sketch of this episode, see White, *Making of the President,* 439–445.

[8]Hughes, *Chasing Shadows,* 66–67.

[9]Greg Grandin, *Kissinger's Shadow: The Long Reach of America's Most Controversial Statesman* (New York: Metropolitan, 2015), 53–55; Hughes, *Chasing Shadows,* 91; Tim Weiner, *One Man Against the World: The Tragedy of Richard Nixon* (New York: Henry Holt, 2015), 40–42.

[10]William Beecher, "Raids in Cambodia by U.S. Unprotested," *New York Times,* May 9, 1969, 1.

[11]Fred Emery, *Watergate: The Corruption and Fall of Richard Nixon* (London: Jonathan Cape, 1994), 11–13.

[12]Hughes, *Chasing Shadows,* 93.

[13]On the Nixon administration's mind-set in this era, see Joan Hoff, *Nixon Reconsidered* (New York: Basic Books, 1994), 283–285.

[14]On the Huston Plan, see U.S. Congress, Senate Select Committee to Study Governmental Operations with Respect to Intelligence Activities, Hearings, vol. 2, *Huston Plan* (Washington, D.C.: U.S. Government Printing Office, 1976).

[15]Stanley Kutler, *The Wars of Watergate: The Last Crisis of Richard Nixon* (New York:

Knopf, 1990), 104; Michael Koncewicz, *They Said No to Nixon: Republicans Who Stood Up to the President's Abuses of Power* (Berkeley: University of California Press, 2018), 46.

[16]Koncewicz, *They Said No*, chapter 1, quote at 41.

[17]Hughes, *Chasing Shadows*, 101.

[18]Conversation between Nixon and Haldeman, June 14, 1971, cited in Daniel Ellsberg, "Truths Worth Telling," *New York Times*, September 28, 2004.

[19]Stanley Kutler, *Abuse of Power: The New Nixon Tapes* (New York: Free Press, 1997), 8; Hughes, *Chasing Shadows*, 108.

[20]Hughes, 127–128.

[21]Hughes, 129.

[22]Hughes, 70.

[23]J. Anthony Lukas, *Nightmare: The Underside of the Nixon Years* (New York: Viking Press, 1973, 1976), 172.

[24]"Nixon Set Minimum Contribution for Choice Diplomatic Posts," *Washington Post*, October 30, 1997.

[25]Farrell, *Nixon*, 471; Emery, *Watergate*, 161.

[26]Hughes, *Chasing Shadows*, 153.

[27]The smoking-gun tape and its transcript are available at the Miller Center's website, millercenter.org/the-presidency/educational-resources/the-smoking-gun.

[28]Max Holland, *Leak: Why Mark Felt Became Deep Throat* (Lawrence: University Press of Kansas, 2012).

[29]"Campaign," *Chicago Tribune*, August 30, 1972.

[30]Kutler, *Wars of Watergate*, 270.

[31]"Richardson's Guidelines for Special Prosecutor," *New York Times*, May 18, 1973.

[32]U.S. Congress, Senate Select Committee on Presidential Campaign Activities, *The Final Report of the Select Committee on Presidential Campaign Activities* (Washington, D.C.: U.S. Government Printing Office, 1974), xxiii.

[33]See Koncewicz for the most recent and thorough discussion of the Saturday Night Massacre. Also William D. Ruckelshaus, "Watergate and Me," *Crosscut*, December 26, 2012, crosscut.com/2012/12/best-2012-bill-ruckelshaus-watergate-and-me.

[34]Andrew Kohut, "How the Watergate Crisis Eroded Support for Richard Nixon," Pew Research Institute, August 8, 2014, www.pewresearch.org/fact-tank/2014/08/08/how-the-watergate-crisis-eroded-public-support-for-richard-nixon/.

[35]Kutler, *Wars of Watergate*, 449.

[36]Kutler, *Wars of Watergate*, 434.

[37]"Scott Labels All Transcript Talks 'Shabby, Immoral,'" *Los Angeles Times*, May 8, 1974.

[38]"Remarks on Departure from the White House," August 9, 1974, www.presidency.ucsb.edu/documents/remarks-departure-from-the-white-house.

[39]Farrell, *Nixon*, 549–550.

[40]Bruce J. Schulman, "Restraining the Imperial Presidency: Congress and Watergate," in *The American Congress: The Building of Democracy*, ed. Julian E. Zelizer (Boston: Houghton Mifflin Company, 2004), 644–647. On the Church committee, see especially Kathryn S. Olmsted, *Challenging the Secret Government: The Post-Watergate Investigations of the CIA and FBI* (Chapel Hill: University of North Carolina Press, 1996).

[41] Richard W. Waterman, "The Administrative Presidency, Unilateral Power, and the Unitary Executive Theory," *Presidential Studies Quarterly* 39, no. 1 (March 2009), 5–9; "'He Had an Incredibly Sharp and Vigorous and Rigorous Mind,'" *New York Times*, April 28, 1994, A20.

GERALD R. FORD, JR.
1974–1977

Joan Hoff

Gerald R. Ford, Jr., Republican Congressman from Michigan and House Minority Leader, became Vice President to Richard M. Nixon under the provisions of the Twenty-Fifth Amendment when, in 1973, Spiro T. Agnew resigned the vice presidency after pleading guilty to tax evasion. Upon Nixon's own resignation from the presidency, Ford became President. He thus served as both Vice President (selected by Nixon and confirmed in that office by Congress) and President without having been elected to either office—an unprecedented distinction. Besides having to assume a president's normal responsibilities upon Nixon's resignation, Ford faced the additional challenge of overcoming the consequences of the Nixon administration's corruption, clearing the political atmosphere of the bitter controversies of Watergate, and restoring Americans' confidence in their government. No significant misconduct marred his presidency, which proved to be—because of Ford's failure to be elected in 1976 to a full term—a short one.

Ford's Pardon of Nixon

After Nixon resigned on August 9, 1974, Ford sought to decide whether to pardon the disgraced former President, a decision forced upon him by powerful Republicans and Nixon supporters and his own desire to return the nation's governance to normality. Ford's situation was complicated by the fact that his constitutional authority lacked the backing of the nation's voters. Accordingly, he had to act judiciously. He also realized that, without a pardon, his administration might be consumed in responding to a prosecution and trial of his predecessor, which would have contributed to more national divisiveness and prevented him from concentrating on other domestic and foreign policy problems, including his chances of election to the presidency in his own right in 1976.[1]

Consequently, after thirty-one days as President, on September 8, 1974, Ford unconditionally granted Nixon "a full, free, and absolute pardon . . . for all offenses against the United States which he, Richard Nixon, has committed or may have committed or taken part in" while in office. Because Nixon had been named only as a co-conspirator in charges brought against others in the Watergate scandal without having been indicted for any of them, he was thus freed from the threat of all criminal charges growing from his presidency. Ford maintained that his pardon of the former President was in the nation's best interests. Although the pardon raised suspicions that a "deal" had been struck between the two men in the last days before Nixon's resignation—or even, it was rumored, as early as eight months before, when Ford succeeded Agnew as Vice President—no evidence has ever emerged to confirm this suspicion, and historians now absolve Ford of the charge. The only known political agreement between Nixon and Ford was the latter's 1973 concession not to seek the presidency in 1976 because Nixon hoped that John B. Connally, Jr., former Democratic Texas Governor and Secretary of the Treasury under Nixon, and by 1973 a Republican, would succeed him.[2]

Yet Ford's action could not escape controversy as unwise and part of a "corrupt bargain," and his press secretary, Jerald F. terHorst, resigned in protest over it. The consensus among historians is that while his pardon of Nixon weighed on Ford's chances of winning the 1976 election, it was among many factors contributing to his loss.[3]

Presidential Papers Controversy

The disposition of Nixon's presidential papers proved another troublesome issue. Ford consulted on the matter with Henry A. Kissinger, who was serving as both Secretary of State and National Security Adviser, holdover White House Chief of Staff Alexander M. Haig, Jr., and other officials, many of whom had been implicated in the corruption of the previous administration. Some of these figures sought to keep Nixon's presidential papers and tapes under the former President's control out of fear that the release of documents from the papers might hold incriminating evidence about their own activities.

On the day that Ford announced his pardon of Nixon, he also disclosed the Nixon-Sampson agreement between the former President and the head of General Services Administration (GSA), Arthur G. Sampson, that allowed Nixon to retain ownership and control—that is, unprecedented latitude, including possible destruction—of his presidential papers and Watergate-related tapes. These documents were stored in the Executive Office Building, and Ford had instructed his staff to prevent any destruction of Nixon's papers. However, the Justice Department informed Ford that since the beginning of the Republic it had been understood by all three branches of government that presidential papers were considered the private property of occupants of the Oval Office. Accordingly, both the tapes and print documents remained Nixon's personal property to be disposed of as he wished. The Watergate Special Prosecutor's Office did not concur. Because these two entities disagreed, Haig began at Nixon's request—and without the knowledge of the National Archives and Records Administration, then a subsidiary of the GSA—to prepare Nixon's papers for shipment to the former President.[4]

The Nixon-Sampson agreement quickly became a source of embarrassment to the administration. The revelation caused such furor that in December 1974 Congress passed the Presidential Recordings and Materials Preservation Act, which rescinded the Nixon-Sampson agreement and made the Nixon records and those of all future presidents the property of the U.S. government. In 1977 the Supreme Court declared the 1974 act constitutional, and in 1979 the National Archives and Records Administration began processing and opening to the public previously classified documents of the Nixon administration. However, Nixon and his attorneys fought from 1974 to 1987 to prevent the release of most of his papers and tapes, until the National Archives finally won the exclusive right to release this material.[5]

Intelligence Agency Misconduct

During Ford's presidency, investigations by a Senate Select Committee headed by Idaho Senator Frank F. Church III disclosed numerous illegal activities conducted by the intelligence community, including the CIA, the FBI, and the National Security Agency. The agencies' transgressions up to 1974 included efforts to assassinate foreign leaders and over-throw foreign governments, gather intelligence on American political dissidents, open domestic mail intended for foreign destinations, and arrange with U.S. telecommunications companies to obtain phone re-cords.[6] Since the agencies had long engaged in these activities and their transgressions were not tied to any policies or decisions formulated by Ford, none of them directly implicated his administration.

In response to allegations against the intelligence agencies, the President appointed an investigative commission headed by Vice President Nelson A. Rockefeller. However, critics at the time said that the fail-ure of the commission to probe alleged CIA assassination plots called into question its credibility and the motives of the Ford administration. Researchers later found that Deputy White House Chief of Staff Rich-ard B. Cheney had edited the commission's report to soften its findings. The President himself had sought to limit the testimony of CIA officials, including acting Director William H. Colby, and Ford's staff members tried to restrict information the commission received.[7] He also had tried, but failed, to prevent the release of certain classified parts of the Church Committee report, most of whose essential findings became public. The report, issued in April 1976, led to several reforms, includ-ing expanded congressional oversight of intelligence activities and the eventual passage of the Foreign Intelligence Surveillance Act (FISA) of 1978, which established a special court to review surveillance requests by intelligence agencies.[8]

The administration of Gerald Ford is unlikely to be remembered with-out its association with the President's controversial pardon of Richard Nixon. Ford's pardon inadvertently created a lasting double standard of justice for presidents and high government officials in signaling that they might not have to fear being held accountable for illegal and cor-rupt acts while in office. Yet in the context of the history of presidential behavior, Ford's two-and-a-half-year presidency is notable for its absence of executive misconduct.

NOTES

[1] Stanley I. Kutler, *The Wars of Watergate: The Last Crisis of Richard Nixon* (New York: Knopf, 1990), 553–560; and Clark R. Mollenhoff, *The Man Who Pardoned Nixon* (New York: St. Martin's Press, 1976), 91.

[2] Gerald R. Ford, *A Time to Heal: The Autobiography of Gerald R. Ford* (New York: Harper & Row, 1979), 105, 164–165, 1981–99; Richard M. Nixon, *The Memoirs of Richard Nixon* (New York: Grosset & Dunlap, 1978), 674, 924–927; and Edward Schapsmeier and Frederick H. Schapsmeier, *Gerald Ford's Date with Destiny: A Political Biography* (New York: Peter Lang, 1989), 168, 173–175, 177 (quotation), 180.

[3] Allan J. Lichtman, *Predicting the Next President: The Keys to the White House 2016* (Lanham, MD: Rowman & Littlefield, 2016), 139–142; Scott Kaufman, *A Political Biography of Gerald R. Ford* (Lawrence: University Press of Kansas, 2017), 264–302.

[4] Joan Hoff, *Nixon Reconsidered* (New York: Basic Books, 1994), 323–325; Ford, *A Time to Heal*, 164–169; and Schapsmeier and Schapsmeier, *Ford's Date with Destiny*, 174–175, 180. The Nixon-Sampson agreement can be found in the Ford Presidential Papers, John Marsh Files, Box 24, especially Phillip Areeda to Ford, December 2, 1974; Buchen to Ford, December 13, 1974; Sampson to Marsh, January 14, 1975; Casselman to Marsh, January 24, 1975; and in Buchen Files, Boxes 30, 32. Of particular importance is Buchen to Ford, August 25, 1975 (reviewing the controversy over Nixon's papers), Box 30.

[5] James J. Hastings, "The Status of the Nixon Presidential Materials," in Leon Friedman and William F. Levantrosser, eds., *Watergate and Afterward: The Legacy of Richard M. Nixon* (Westport, CT: Greenwood Press, 1992), 253–262; and Melvin Small, *The Presidency of Richard Nixon* (Lawrence: University Press of Kansas, 1999), 301–303.

[6] Loch Johnson, *A Season of Inquiry: The Senate Intelligence Investigation* (Lawrence: University Press of Kansas, 2004).

[7] Robert L. Jackson, "Credibility Issue Raised as Ford Gets CIA Report," *Los Angeles Times*, June 7, 1975, 1; John Prados and Arturo Jimenez-Bacardi, "The Rockefeller Commission, the White House and CIA Assassination Plots," National Security Archive, February 29, 2016, nsarchive.gwu.edu/briefing-book/intelligence/2016-02-29/gerald-ford-white-house-altered-rockefeller-commission-report; U.S. Department of Justice, "The Foreign Intelligence Surveillance Act of 1978," it.ojp.gov/privacyliberty/authorities/statutes/1286.

[8] Kathryn S. Olmsted, "Reclaiming Executive Power: The Ford Administration's Response to the Intelligence Investigations," *Presidential Studies Quarterly* 26:3 (summer 1996), 725–737; and Johnson, *A Season of Inquiry*.

JAMES E. CARTER, JR.
1977–1981

Kevin M. Kruse

From the start, Jimmy Carter (as he was always known) presented himself as an "outsider." Though he had relatively little government experience for a presidential candidate—just four years in Georgia's state senate and four more as its Governor—Carter turned his thin résumé into an asset. His total lack of involvement in national government, he argued, meant that he was untainted by it, too. When he announced his presidential campaign in December 1974, the longshot candidate emphasized that he was much more than a politician. Presenting his role in government as just one of his identities, he introduced himself to the nation as "a farmer, an engineer, a businessman, a planner, a scientist, a governor, and a Christian." And in the years that followed, Carter downplayed his past in politics. Instead, he emphasized his simple roots in the rural South of Plains, Georgia, where his family ran a peanut farm and warehouse and he served as a Baptist Sunday school teacher.[1]

Distancing himself from Washington, Carter presented himself as the antithesis of its political culture of cronyism and corruption. This "outsider" trope became more common in the wake of the Watergate crisis of the Nixon administration, but Carter laid an early claim to the territory. "The strongest feeling in this country today," an adviser noted in a 1972 memorandum, "is the general distrust of government and politicians at all levels. The desire and thrust for strong moral leadership was not satisfied with the election of Richard Nixon."[2] Accordingly, Carter worked to associate himself with the values of trust, honesty, integrity, and responsibility. "I will never make a misleading statement," he promised voters. "I will never tell a lie or avoid a controversy. I will never let you down."[3]

After he won the presidency, Carter immediately worked to make his promises manifest. In January 1977, he announced that he was placing his interest in his family's farm and peanut warehouse into a blind trust. Moreover, the President-elect made it clear that he expected everyone in his administration to follow his personal example. The Carter White House soon instituted stricter rules for financial disclosures and conflicts of interest and worked to curb the practice of "revolving-door" government, in which officials left office and then went to work for businesses in the industries they had dealt with in their government roles. The new ethics rules, Press Secretary Joseph L. "Jody" Powell explained, were meant "to restore the confidence of the American people in their own government."[4]

Jimmy Carter thus built his presidency on a promise to maintain the highest standards of ethical behavior. But because of that promise, those closest to him—his family, his friends, and his business associates—would come under intense scrutiny. The Carter administration experienced a series of seeming scandals, as one figure after another found himself under investigation. The President, seeking to keep his promise of transparency and honesty, had no choice but to submit to public scrutiny. In the end, the scandals resulted in no serious charges, but the steady stream of investigations hurt the administration all the same.

Bert Lance

The first scandal of the Carter administration stemmed, ironically enough, from the ethical standards set down by the new President.

In keeping with his directive that appointees disclose their financial holdings and divest themselves of anything that might represent a conflict of interest, Carter asked Thomas B. "Bert" Lance, his longtime friend and incoming Director of the Office of Management and Budget (OMB), to dispose of his considerable stock holdings in the two Georgia banks he once ran. Lance initially agreed to put his stock in the National Bank of Georgia (NBG), valued at some $3.3 million, into a blind trust, which would then divest itself completely of the stock by that December. However, the stock's value soon began to fall and by the summer of 1977 was reportedly down to half its earlier valuation. Hoping to avoid a significant loss, Lance asked the President for assistance. Carter obliged by writing a letter to Senator Abraham A. Ribicoff, Chairman of the Senate Governmental Affairs Committee, which had overseen Lance's confirmation hearings, to ask for an unlimited extension of the divestment deadline.[5]

The request for an extension prompted renewed scrutiny in the press. First, there were reports that Lance, who had promised in his confirmation hearings to steer clear of any matters involving banking regulation as long as he held NBG stock, had nevertheless done exactly the opposite. Reports showed that Lance had met with NBG officials in his OMB office and had also written the chairman of the Senate Banking Committee to advance the banking industry's position on another matter. Second, and more seriously, the columnist William L. Safire charged that Lance had used his political influence to secure a $3.4 million personal "sweetheart loan" from the First National Bank of Chicago. "Jimmy Carter's Broken Lance," Safire wrote in one of his many columns on him, "is a walking conflict of interest."[6]

Initial investigations seemed to clear Lance of any wrongdoing. In a return appearance before the Ribicoff committee, Lance explained to the senators that the loan was part of a long-standing NBG relationship with the Chicago bank and noted that he was paying 0.75 percent above the prime interest rate on it. Satisfied with his testimony, the committee approved the request for an extension of the stock divestment deadline. Meanwhile, the U.S. Comptroller of the Currency, John G. Heimann, released a 394-page report that declared that Lance had done nothing illegal. The White House took the report as a sign of vindication. At a press conference, President Carter turned to his friend and said, "Bert, I'm proud of you."[7]

But it soon became clear that the President had misread the Comptroller's report. While the document noted that Lance had not done anything technically illegal, it laid out in detail how the OMB director had regularly engaged in "borderline shoddy banking practices." Rather than putting the matter to rest, the report launched a new round of revelations about Lance's past improprieties. These included misuse of NBG aircraft and a loose handling of overdrafts on accounts, which Heimann said showed Lance ran the bank "as a personal fiefdom rather than as a trustee for other people." [8]

By late August 1977, the White House had become consumed by the Lance scandal. The President stubbornly stood by his old friend, but the political costs soon became clear. "Every time we tried to talk about other issues, we would be asked, but what about Bert Lance?" an aide remembered. "We ended up being paralyzed by it." The media seized on the issue, with former Republican aides taking particular delight in highlighting the Carter team's shortcomings. Safire, a former Nixon speechwriter, kept up a steady drumbeat of columns on what he now called "Lancegate." Likewise, Jerald F. terHorst, who had briefly served as President Gerald Ford's press secretary, wrote, "Time and again, candidate Carter pledged that he would restore public trust after Watergate by requiring appointees to be free of the appearance of wrongdoing, as well as the fact of it. But his handling of the Lance matter suggests that his bottom line is not so stringent, after all." [9]

The press attention prompted a renewed round of inquiries. After a second report, Comptroller Heimann alerted the White House that he would be referring several matters to the Justice Department and Internal Revenue Service for further investigation. With growing demands for the appointment of a special prosecutor, the Ribicoff committee summoned Lance for another appearance. On September 17, 1977, Lance fared well in a nationally televised hearing.

Carter's aides seized on the moment to tell the President that Lance had "won a great victory and now should step down." Carter reluctantly agreed and, four days later, announced Lance's resignation in a press conference. Lance would be acquitted in a later trial, but the administration nevertheless suffered considerably as a result. The President's approval rating, as measured in a Gallup poll, dropped twelve points in the weeks between mid-August and mid-September 1977. As Carter later reflected, "It is impossible to overestimate the damage inflicted upon my administration by charges leveled against Bert Lance." [10]

Carter's Warehouse

As the "Lance affair" came to a close, concerns about the Carter family's peanut warehouse in Plains began to mount.

Upon taking office, Carter had placed his share of the family-owned warehouse—62 percent—in a blind trust under the control of Atlanta lawyer Charles H. Kirbo. The remainder was maintained by Carter's mother, Lillian, and his younger brother, Billy (as he was commonly called), who oversaw daily operations. Over the course of 1977, the business fell on hard times, partially due to an unwise expansion of operations and partially due to a drought that hurt local crops. The President's blind trust lost more than $300,000 during that period, and Kirbo soon announced that he was looking to sell the warehouse entirely.[11]

The attention to the failing family enterprise brought to the surface details about past mismanagement of the warehouse and concerns about possible misappropriation of funds. In November 1978, newspapers reported that the National Bank of Georgia, under Bert Lance's direction, had lent Carter's Warehouse $1 million without full collateral. Further inquiries in January 1979 revealed that Lance had also, in early 1976, directed bank officials to lower interest rates on loans and lines of credit to Carter's Warehouse totaling nearly $4 million in all. While the issuing of the loans came under scrutiny, so did the terms of their repayment. In March 1979, a former bonded warehouseman who was employed by NBG to supervise the collateral on the warehouse loan reported that, at Billy Carter's direction, he had sent misleading reports to the bank. It soon became clear that the warehouse was roughly $500,000 behind in its repayment schedule.[12]

Though the President had divested himself of the business, these reports raised questions about his possible role in securing the loan and soon questions about whether any money from the loan had been diverted to his 1976 presidential campaign. On March 20, 1979, with pressure for a full investigation mounting, Attorney General Griffin B. Bell appointed former U.S. Attorney Paul J. Curran, a New York Republican, to serve as Special Counsel to investigate the loans. (Initially, Curran's powers fell short of those of a special prosecutor as outlined in the recently passed Ethics in Government Act of 1978, the post-Watergate legislation that instituted new policies and procedures for investigations of the executive branch. Under pressure from Republicans in Congress, Bell expanded Curran's authority and effectively made him a special prosecutor in everything but name.)[13]

The Special Counsel's investigation unfolded over seven months during the summer of 1979. "I want to do the investigation as quickly as possible," Curran told reporters, "but obviously it has to be thorough." The Special Counsel's legal team reviewed 80,000 documents and took grand jury testimony from 64 witnesses, including Billy Carter. Most significantly, President Carter himself provided a sworn deposition in an interview that lasted four hours, marking the first time in American history that a sitting president was interviewed under oath in a criminal investigation. "Curran is looking for the smoking peanut, if there is one," a reporter for the *Atlanta Constitution* noted, "and if there isn't, he wants to be very sure."[14]

In October 1979, the Special Counsel issued his findings in a 179-page public report. Curran concluded that there was no evidence that any money had been diverted from Carter's Warehouse to the Carter presidential campaign. Moreover, he declared that, while he was not "exonerating" Billy Carter, he had found no grounds for federal criminal charges over the handling of the NBG loans at the warehouse either. Asked how it felt to be declared "clean," the President responded, "I knew it all the time."[15]

"Billygate"

In addition to his supporting role in the Carter's Warehouse scandal, Billy Carter took center stage in a scandal of his own.

When his older brother ran for President, Billy Carter found himself thrust into the national spotlight. Once business at Carter's Warehouse sputtered, the President's brother tried to capitalize on his newfound fame. He hired a Nashville talent agent, made appearances on talk shows, and collected fees on the lecture circuit. He even promoted a variety of products, including "Billy Beer." For nearly two years, the younger Carter stood out as a folksy curiosity, but little more.[16]

That began to change in September 1978, when Billy Carter took a highly publicized trip to Libya with a collection of Georgia politicians and business leaders seeking to make deals with the government there.

Although the Libyan regime of Muammar Gaddafi was widely regarded at the time as anti-American, anti-Israel, and a sponsor of international terrorism, media reports initially treated the trip as just another colorful misadventure of the First Brother. (The *Washington Post* ran a short item noting the irony of the heavy drinker heading to a Muslim nation that barred alcohol.)[17]

The following January, however, the relationship turned into a new scandal, when Billy Carter returned the hospitality of the Libyan government by holding a posh reception in Atlanta for a "friendship delegation" from the regime. When reporters asked why he was aligning himself with the Libyans, the President's brother replied, "The only thing I can say is there is a hell of a lot more Arabians than there is Jews." Waving away charges that the Libyans had sponsored terrorism, he charged that the "Jewish media [tore] up the Arab countries full-time." In addition to the anti-Semitic comments, the media soon reported that, while waiting for the Libyans at the Atlanta airport, Billy Carter stepped out of a limousine and urinated on the tarmac in full view of a former ambassador to the United Nations and several reporters.[18]

Billy Carter quickly became a major embarrassment to the Carter administration. "If he's not working for the Republican Party," an *Atlanta Constitution* columnist marveled, "he should be. He's turning out to be the dirtiest trick played on Jimmy Carter since the '76 campaign." The White House immediately distanced itself from Billy Carter's comments, but the President, as in the Lance affair, was reluctant to rebuke his brother publicly. As the controversy lingered, he eventually offered indirect criticism. In a late February comment that was pointedly leaked to the press, the President relayed that he had found his brother's statements "objectionable" and was "terribly concerned" about Billy's health. Soon, Billy Carter entered a hospital for treatment of alcohol abuse.[19]

Billy Carter's relationship with Libya burst back into the news in July 1980, when the Department of Justice announced that the President's brother had been required to register as a foreign agent due to his relationship with the Middle Eastern nation. Reports soon revealed that, well after his initial trip in September 1978, the younger Carter had continued to travel to Libya and had received payments of hundreds of thousands of dollars from the Libyan government and oil interests there. The President claimed he knew nothing about his brother's travels, save for a November 1979 trip that resulted from First Lady Rosalynn Carter's suggestion that Billy might use his Libyan connections to help secure the release of Americans taken hostage in Iran. Revelations that the President's brother was on the payroll of a hostile nation and, moreover, might have influenced the administration's policies sparked a new stage in the scandal. William Safire dubbed it "Billygate."[20]

In late July 1980, the Senate acceded to demands from Republican members and established a special nine-member subcommittee to investigate Billy Carter's connections to Libya and the Carter administration's role in that relationship. Anxious to clear the air in an election year, the President announced he was eager to appear before the subcommittee and "the sooner, the better." Over the first week of August 1980, Carter released a number of diplomatic cables, issued a lengthy report to the Senate, and held an hour-long press conference in which he addressed the scandal directly. Insisting there had been no "impropriety," Carter contrasted his response with the Nixon administration's handling of Watergate. "It was much better to have the information come out as we determined it," he asserted, "than it would be if we had withheld information and, in effect, stonewalled the question for two or three weeks."[21]

The Senate investigation began as a major inquiry. "The early hearings had all the trappings of the famous Watergate hearings," the *New York Times* noted. "Ten or 12 separate television crews covered those first hearings, the press tables resembled subway cars at rush-hour, and tourists waited in line for hours to get a glimpse of history." But the initial fascination faded as testimony revealed little of consequence. In early October 1980, the subcommittee released its findings. In their 249-page report, the senators unanimously asserted that the Carter administration had shown poor judgment in its handling of the matter. Billy Carter, the report noted, "merits severe criticism," but there was no evidence of illegal or clearly unethical actions on the part of the President or his administration.[22]

In the end, the three main scandals of the Carter administration followed the same general pattern, in which sloppy financial practices and suspect business dealings invited close investigation but ultimately proved to have fallen short of outright criminal misdeeds.

NOTES

[1]Stuart E. Eizenstadt, *President Carter: The White House Years* (New York: Thomas Dunne Books, 2018), 48; James T. Wooten, "Carter Bids 'Men of Faith' Take Greater Public Role," *New York Times*, June 20, 1976; James P. Gannon, "Carter's Character," *Wall Street Journal*, July 12, 1976.

[2]Burton I. Kaufman, *The Presidency of James Earl Carter, Jr.* (Lawrence: University Press of Kansas, 1993), 13.

[3]Curtis Wilkie, "Democrats Have a Front Runner," *Boston Globe*, February 26, 1976.

[4]David S. Broder, "Ethics Code Is Outlined by Carter," *Washington Post*, January 5, 1977; Aldo Beckman, "Carter Discloses Ethics Guidelines for Self, Aides," *Chicago Tribune*, January 5, 1977.

[5]Robert Shogan, "Lance Caught Up in New Political Ethics," *Los Angeles Times*, August 14, 1977; Kaufman, *The Presidency of James Earl Carter, Jr.*, 59–60.

[6]Kaufman, *The Presidency of James Earl Carter, Jr.*, 60; William Safire, "Carter's Broken Lance," *New York Times*, July 21, 1977; William Safire, "Boiling the Lance," *New York Times*, July 25, 1977.

[7]"Carter to Get Comptroller's Report on Lance," *Hartford Courant*, August 18, 1977; James Coates, "Bank Probe Clears Lance," *Chicago Tribune*, August 19, 1977; Kaufman, *The Presidency of James Earl Carter, Jr.*, 60–61.

[8]Eizenstadt, *President Carter*, 127–128.

[9]Julian E. Zelizer, *Jimmy Carter* (New York: Times Books, 2010), 68; William Safire, "Lancegate," *New York Times*, August 11, 1977; J. F. terHorst, "Carter's Taste of Scandal," *Atlanta Constitution*, August 28, 1977.

[10]Kaufman, *The Presidency of James Earl Carter, Jr.*, 62–63; Nicholas M. Horrock, "Variety of Charges Caused Bert Lance's Decline and Fall," *New York Times*, September 22, 1977; news.gallup.com/interactives/185273/presidential-job-approval-center.aspx; Zelizer, *Jimmy Carter*, 69.

[11]Robert Lezner, "Carter Peanut Business Faces a Slump This Year," *Boston Globe*, October 8, 1977; "Peanuts a Pain to Carter," *Newsday*, November 7, 1977; "Carter's Blind Trust Had Loss Last Year Totaling $306,271," *Wall Street Journal*, June 16, 1978.

[12]Jeff Gerth, "Lance Bank Lent Carter Business $1 Million Without Full Collateral," *New York Times*, November 19, 1978; Nicholas M. Horrock, "Lance Told Bank to Cut Loans for Carter Concern, Audit Reports," *New York Times*, January 18, 1979; Ted Gup and John F. Berry, "Carter Warehouse Loan Scheme in '76 Is Alleged," *Washington Post*, March 11, 1979; Nicholas M. Horrock, "Former Carter Warehouseman Says He Sent Misleading Data to Bank," *New York Times*, March 19, 1979.

[13]Nicholas M. Horrock, "Bell Names Former U.S. Attorney to Investigate Carter Peanut Loans," *New York Times*, March 21, 1979; Patrick J. Sloyan and Anthony Marro, "The Peanut Probe," *Newsday*, April 1, 1979; "Carter Loan Probe Gets 'Special' Chief," *Chicago Tribune*, March 21, 1979; Wendell Rawls, Jr., "Bell Increases Curran's Authority to Examine Carter Business Loans," *New York Times*, March 24, 1979.

[14]Nicholas M. Horrock, "Billy Carter Says Peanut Money Wasn't Diverted to '76 Campaign," *New York Times*, May 19, 1979; Anthony Marro, "Carters Cleared in Probe of Family Peanut Farm," *Newsday*, October 17, 1979; Margaret Shannon, "Paul Curran and the Peanut," *Atlanta Constitution*, July 8, 1979.

[15]Marro, "Carters Cleared in Probe of Family Peanut Farm"; John F. Berry and Ted Gup, "Inquiry Clears Carter Family's Peanut Business," *Washington Post*, October 17, 1979.

[16]Kaufman, *The Presidency of James Earl Carter, Jr.*, 136; Bill Montgomery, "Billy, Like Beer, May Become Stale," *Atlanta Constitution*, January 14, 1979.

[17]"Billy Carter, Georgians Visit Libya," *Baltimore Sun*, September 30, 1978; "No Beer for Billy on Libyan Visit," *Washington Post*, September 29, 1978.

[18]Carole Ashkinaze, "Billy Carter Invites 400 to Bash for Libyans," *Atlanta Constitution*, January 9, 1979; Norman Kempster, "Billy Carter's Bid to Help Libyans Fails," *Los Angeles Times*, January 11, 1979; Kaufman, *The Presidency of James Earl Carter, Jr.*, 136–137; "Relieving Himself in Public Latest Billy Carter Caper," *Hartford Courant*, January 13, 1979; Montgomery, "Billy, Like Beer, May Become Stale."

[19]Bill Shipp, "Is Billy Working for KGB or GOP?" *Atlanta Constitution*, January 10, 1979; "White House Disavows Billy Carter's Libya Views," *Los Angeles Times*, January 11, 1979; Martin Schram, "Billy Is a Real Pain, Carter Finally Says," *Atlanta Constitution*, February 25, 1979; Ted Thackrey, Jr., "Billy Carter in Alcoholic Unit," *Los Angeles Times*, March 7, 1979.

[20]Zelizer, *Jimmy Carter*, 108–109; Robert G. Kaiser and Edward Walsh, "Billy Carter Used by Brzezinski as Libya Go-Between," *Washington Post*, July 23, 1980; "Billy Carter and the Libyans—From the 1978 Beginning," *Boston Globe*, July 25, 1980; William Safire, "None Dare Call It Billygate," *New York Times*, July 21, 1980.

[21]John H. Averill and Robert L. Jackson, "Senate Votes to Probe Billy Carter Affair," *Los Angeles Times*, July 25, 1980; Jack Nelson, "Carter Seeks to Speed Up Senate Probe," *Los Angeles Times*, July 30, 1980; "President Releases Libya Cables; Senate Sets Probe Hearings," *Hartford Courant*, August 1, 1980; "Text of Carter's Report to Senate on His Actions on Brother's Ties with Libya," *New York Times*, August 5, 1980; "Carter Defends White House Stand on Brother's Links with Libyans," *Wall Street Journal*, August 5, 1980.

[22]David E. Rosenbaum, "Senate Unit Assails President and Aides in Billy Carter Case," *New York Times*, October 3, 1980.

RONALD REAGAN
1981–1989

Jeremi Suri

Ronald Reagan defined his presidency as an antidote to what he called "big government." His argument was persuasive because it was moralistic: "Man is not free unless government is limited."[1] Limited government for Reagan did not mean fewer services for citizens: government spending on Social Security and other programs increased during his presidency. Limited government meant less regulation and oversight of economic activities. During Reagan's presidency, the federal government reduced its efforts to reverse inequality, the dominance of large corporations, and greed.

A modest man in his habits and attitudes, Reagan did not succumb to greed himself. In fact, he conducted himself in a remarkably simple, often abstemious, manner as President. Reagan did not profit from the presidency, and he sought—with the notable exception of the illegal Iran-Contra maneuvers—to act within the constitutional expectations of a public servant accountable to the other branches of government and, ultimately, to the American people.

Reagan's dislike of government regulation, however, enabled a pervasive diversion from strict ethical rules of conduct within his administration. There were fewer daily checks from the Oval Office on self-interested behavior among various aides. The President trusted his loyalists, and he empowered them to act with little oversight. Although he followed a strong personal ethical code, Reagan did not articulate one for those who worked around him. Administration employees received little guidance from the President and suffered few immediate consequences for misbehavior. When legal and ethical concerns about the executive branch came to his attention, Reagan largely avoided discussing the topic with his advisers. He was averse to personal conflict, and he preferred to avoid the appearance of presidential interference. Enforcing ethics in government, according to Chief of Staff James A. Baker III, was not a "big thing" for Reagan. "I don't think it was something in the big picture."[2]

Reagan's negligence in promoting ethics among his subordinates made his administration the most scandal-ridden since Watergate. At times, it appeared to replay some of that same history, with televised congressional investigatory hearings and serious talk of impeachment. In contrast to Nixon, however, Reagan was generally a law-abiding president. Yet he did not punish (and he sometimes rewarded) those around him who flagrantly broke the law. As a result, numerous prominent Reagan administration officials were convicted of crimes, some went to jail, and many ended their careers in disrepute. Independent Counsel investigations and prosecutions multiplied throughout his term in office.

The gravest irony of the Reagan administration was that its aversion to big government swelled the coffers of those privileged officials who controlled government. Managerial negligence and deregulation encouraged corruption and lawbreaking. Anti-communist zealotry empowered unconstitutional militarism. The government did not diminish in size during Reagan's presidency, but instead grew larger than before. And it became less tethered to the law.

Corruption at the Environmental Protection Agency

Created by President Nixon in 1970, the Environmental Protection Agency (EPA) was a priority target for the Reagan administration's efforts to shrink government. Speaking to the nation on February 5, 1981, the President explained, "Regulations of every kind, on shopkeepers, farmers, and major industries, add $100 billion or more to the cost of the goods and services we buy."[3] Too many of these regulations, he believed, emanated from EPA rules to protect clean water and air. Large oil and chemical companies, in particular, resented EPA constraints on their production, distribution, and disposal of key ingredients.

Reagan appointed two leaders of the EPA who promised to cut back on the agency's regulatory work. Anne M. Gorsuch—a strong advocate of deregulation and a former Colorado state legislator—became the administrator of the agency. Rita M. Lavelle, a California Republican Party activist, former assistant to then Governor Reagan, and lobbyist for large chemical companies, became the EPA's assistant administrator.

Immediately, Gorsuch and Lavelle curtailed EPA actions against companies and cut personnel to the point of reducing the agency's budget by 25 percent. The EPA had on its books $700 million in outstanding fines due from businesses that violated environmental laws, but under Gorsuch and Lavelle the agency collected only $40 million. EPA leaders began meeting frequently, often in secret, with industry leaders, and they sought to use the agency to facilitate company activities, not hold them accountable to environmental laws. In many cases, the EPA intentionally neglected law enforcement that would be costly to corporate allies. This was an obvious and extreme case of "regulatory capture"— the use of government resources for profit, not public protection. It was clearly illegal.[4]

As evidence of the EPA's collusion with industry spread, the leaders of the agency attacked whistle-blowers, which was also illegal. Hugh Kaufman, a longtime EPA employee who revealed some of the illegal meetings, was followed to a hotel where agency investigators alleged he was having an affair with a woman. In fact, the woman at the hotel was his wife. "They thought they could squeeze me by checking out my sex life," Kaufman recounted.[5]

Gorsuch went further in her cover-up efforts. Even when subpoenaed, she refused to share documents on industry meetings and environmental cleanup efforts with Congress. Reagan initially backed Gorsuch, claiming "executive privilege" over the documents. Members of both parties in Congress, however, rejected this claim as an abuse of executive power. On December 16, 1982, the House of Representatives voted overwhelmingly (204 Democrats and 55 Republicans in favor) to cite Gorsuch for contempt of Congress. She was the first Cabinet-level official ever held in contempt.[6]

The political costs of Gorsuch's scandalous behavior had now grown too high for the President. With the encouragement of the White House, she resigned in March 1983. The EPA also turned over the subpoenaed documents to Congress, which brought further attention to the agency's illegal behavior. President Reagan brought back William D. Ruckelshaus, the founding administrator of the EPA in 1970, to restore the agency to its mission of public service.

Reagan had also fired Rita Lavelle in February 1983, a rare move by a President who avoided personnel conflicts. Six different congressional committees had begun investigations of her alleged negligence in administering EPA "superfunds" for toxic waste cleanups as well as her favoritism to chemical industry leaders. Less than a year later, Lavelle became the first convicted Reagan administration felon. A federal judge sentenced her to six months in prison and a $10,000 fine for lying to Congress. Lavelle also received a sentence of five years' probation and mandatory community service for obstructing a congressional investigation. The judge spoke for many observers when she demanded that Lavelle and other Reagan appointees at the EPA recognize the "injury you have caused to the Federal Government, to yourself, and to all of us as citizens."[7]

Grant Rigging at the Department of Housing and Urban Development

A similar assessment applied to the officials Reagan appointed at the Department of Housing and Urban Development (HUD). In 1989, an Inspector General's report revealed that HUD's Section 8 Moderate Rehabilitation Program, budgeted at more than $350 million each year during the Reagan presidency, had been captured by developers and politicians, who used the government's resources to enrich themselves and support their chosen candidates, not the needs of those living in poor housing conditions. The Inspector General documented how seventeen well-connected individuals in the Republican Party had received direct payments for their assistance in procuring HUD contracts for real estate developers. More than $2 billion of taxpayer money had been diverted from housing assistance to corrupt purposes.[8]

Samuel R. Pierce, Jr.—a prominent attorney, longtime Republican official, and the only African American in Reagan's Cabinet—served as Secretary of Housing and Urban Development during both presidential terms. His leadership came under close scrutiny from Congress, the Justice Department, and the Inspector General. Despite his evident negligence, Pierce escaped prosecution. Seventeen others—including Pierce's executive assistant, Deborah Gore Dean—were convicted of fraud, bribery, and perjury. In 1990 the House Government Operations Committee concluded, "At best, Secretary Pierce was less than honest and misled the subcommittee about his involvement in abuses and favoritism in HUD funding decisions. At worst, Secretary Pierce knowingly lied and committed perjury during his testimony." An Independent Counsel investigation reported that Pierce "created an atmosphere at HUD that allowed influence-peddling to go on."[9]

The most prominent Reagan administration adviser convicted in the HUD scandals was Interior Secretary James G. Watt. An outspoken critic of environmentalists, Watt was a controversial Reagan Cabinet appointment; strongly opposed by Democrats, he had firm support from Western Republicans who sought fewer restrictions on land usage. Watt resigned from the Reagan administration on October 9, 1983, after two stormy years at the Department of the Interior, following a particularly offensive remark about how he populated government commissions: "We have every kind of mixture you can have. . . . I have a black, I have a woman, two Jews and a cripple. And we have talent." Watt resigned before the likely passage of a Senate resolution calling for his removal.[10]

Watt was not deterred from his continued aggressive and self-serving behavior. Immediately after leaving the Department of the Interior, and against federal prohibitions, he worked as a high-paid lobbyist for real estate developers seeking contracts from HUD. When investigated, he lied about his activities and sought to hide subpoenaed documents. Watt was indicted on twenty-five felony counts, and he ultimately pleaded guilty to a single misdemeanor. He was sentenced to five years' probation, a $5,000 fine, and 500 hours of mandatory community service. The punishment was light, but few doubted his active participation in HUD corruption.[11]

Illegal Lobbying by Reagan Confidants

Federal regulations prohibit government officials and those who have recently left office from using their positions to enrich themselves, their families, and their associates. Violation of these regulations by Reagan's close advisers was a systemic problem, and it was an area in which the President's ethical reticence encouraged corrupt behavior. Chief of Staff

Baker was the notable exception. He was one of the few people around the Oval Office who escaped prosecution.

The same could not be said for Michael K. Deaver. He had worked with Reagan since his governorship in California and, serving officially as Deputy Chief of Staff, had done more than anyone else to manage the President's image. Deaver left the White House in 1985, the beginning of Reagan's second term, to form his own lobbying firm. He used his personal connections with the White House to arrange meetings for wealthy clients from South Korea, Puerto Rico, and the United States. When questioned by Congress and a grand jury, Deaver lied and withheld information. When prosecuted, Deaver's only defense was alcoholism. He received a three-year suspended prison sentence, was placed on probation, and fined $100,000. Another close associate of Reagan and Deaver, Lyn C. Nofziger, received a similar punishment for illegal lobbying, including ninety days in prison and a $30,000 fine.[12]

Edwin Meese III went even further in his abuse of government influence for private gain. He had also worked for Reagan since 1967, and he became Counselor to the President with cabinet rank in 1981. During Reagan's second term, beginning in 1985, he served as Attorney General. In both these roles, Meese was continually surrounded by scandals of his own making.

In April 1988, Deputy Attorney General Arnold I. Burns and Assistant Attorney General William F. Weld (later Governor of Massachusetts) advised Reagan that Meese was so corrupt that he should be fired and prosecuted immediately. A report by the Justice Department's Office of Professional Responsibility concurred, explaining that Meese had pursued "conduct which should not be tolerated of any government employee, especially not the attorney general." Reagan inexplicably allowed Meese's illegal conduct to continue, and he never fired him. Meese resigned in July 1988, following a fourteen-month criminal investigation of his activities that did not result in prosecution but revealed extensive evidence of misdeeds.[13] Meese's illegal activities included failure to report reimbursements on more than thirty trips as White House Counselor, and, even more suspicious, failure to report personal loans he received from individuals (John R. McKean and Edwin W. Thomas) whom he helped appoint to government positions.

Meese also repeatedly used his White House influence to promote businesses in which he had a personal financial interest. Meese helped a
small New York manufacturer, Wedtech, obtain a number of no-bid
defense contracts. This was bad enough, but Meese once again failed
to report important information: his personal $60,000 investment with
one of Wedtech's principals.[14]

In 1985 Meese, then Attorney General, intervened in complex negotiations between Israel, Iraq, Jordan, and the Bechtel Corporation in California to build an oil pipeline through the Middle East. Meese lobbied
National Security Adviser Robert C. McFarlane as well as Israeli Prime
Minister Shimon Peres on behalf of business associates at Bechtel, from
whom he personally profited. Meese may have been the least ethical of
Reagan's closest advisers; he relied on the President's continuing willingness to excuse his behavior.[15]

Pentagon Bribes and Kickbacks

Reagan's tolerance of Meese and other unethical figures in the White
House contributed to a wider culture of illegality throughout the administration, particularly in the Pentagon. Reagan's military buildup meant
that the Department of Defense received a quick and enormous infu-
sion of money for procurement of weapons and related technologies.
This was especially true in the U.S. Navy, where the President pledged
to build the largest force ever—one of 600 ships. Vast ambitions, massive funding, and limited ethical enforcement created many predictable
temptations to corruption.

Melvyn R. Paisley, Reagan's Assistant Secretary of the Navy with
primary responsibility for procurement, exploited the circumstances.
Colluding with an arms sales consultant, William M. Galvin, Paisley
received secret kickbacks on large contracts offered to industry giants,
including Unisys, Loral, Martin Marietta, United Technologies, and
Paisley's former employer Boeing. Millions of dollars flowed through a
shell company, Sapphire Systems, which Paisley and Galvin had created.
In addition to these illegal kickbacks, Paisley demanded direct bribes
in cash and in kind for his influence in awarding an ever-growing list
of Navy contracts. This corrupt process raised costs for the Pentagon,
and it limited innovation and quality. The Reagan buildup became a

boondoggle for military contractors, consultants like Galvin, and corrupt officials, especially Paisley.[16]

The Federal Bureau of Investigation (FBI) and the Naval Investigative Service (NIS) received information about Paisley's activities in 1986. Working secretly with defense contractors and Pentagon employees, as well as with partners in the Air Force and Internal Revenue Service, the FBI and NIS oversaw the largest and most successful investigation of Pentagon fraud in U.S. history. Code-named "Operation Illwind," the investigation led to more than sixty prosecutions of contractors, consultants, industry leaders, and Pentagon officials. The investigation also yielded $622 million in fines, recoveries, restitutions, and forfeitures. It led to the passage of stricter oversight measures for federal procurements and new limits on lobbying activities. Paisley received a four-year prison sentence and a $50,000 fine.[17]

Savings and Loan Crisis

The Pentagon scandal had an even more costly and corrupt analogue in banking. Ronald Reagan was one of many Americans who revered the image of the local savings bank that paid a modest interest rate to small depositors and invested generously in families buying their first homes. Since 1933, when President Franklin D. Roosevelt created federal insurance for these banks, they had fueled the rise in family home ownership across the United States. With stable interest rates through the mid-twentieth century, savings banks continued to attract depositors who provided the capital for family mortgages, with additional subsidies to them from federal programs like the G.I. Bill and the Federal National Mortgage Association (FNMA, commonly known as Fannie Mae).

The high inflation and market volatility of the 1970s undermined this system. Depositors began to place their money in alternative investments, where they could receive higher rates of return. Long-term mortgages held by savings banks with low interest rates no longer covered the cost of acquiring capital for new mortgages at much higher rates. As part of its commitment to deregulation, the Reagan administration worked with a Democratic Congress to make savings banks more competitive. The consequence was that they became less secure and more open to corruption.

Donald T. Regan led the administration's efforts. The former CEO of Merrill Lynch, one of the largest investment firms in the United States, Regan served as Secretary of the Treasury in Reagan's first term then the President's Chief of Staff from February 1985 to February 1987. Regan saw obvious value in a more freewheeling banking system, and he had faith in the wisdom of bank leaders. At the same time, he wanted the federal government to continue to insure against risk.

Regan worked with Congress in the early 1980s to reduce the capital reserve requirements for banks, permit savings banks to make riskier (and thus potentially more rewarding) investments, and allow wealthy individuals to run savings banks—the result being less anchoring in local communities and less public transparency. These freer banking activities received additional government protection when Congress raised the federal insurance for each depositor from $40,000 to $100,000. Troubled savings banks could now pursue more income with less government interference since the government did more to guarantee against risk.

The new laws created what economists call "moral hazard"—when risk taking is incentivized but the risk takers do not bear the costs. Moral hazard in banking encourages bubbles, the situations in which investors are tempted to pursue ever-higher returns beyond reasonable valuations for real estate and other commodities. Numerous officials within the Reagan administration—including Edwin J. Gray (Chairman of the Federal Home Loan Bank Board) and L. William Seidman (Chairman of the Federal Deposit Insurance Corporation)—warned of this imminent problem, but Regan and his allies ignored them, condemning cautious voices as "re-regulators."[18]

One of the reasons administration officials ignored warnings was because they had personal interests of their own in the growth of a freewheeling savings and loan industry. Regan had led a large investment bank and remained closely tied to it. Richard T. Pratt, the Chairman of the Federal Home Loan Bank Board before Gray, was also an investment banker who left the administration in 1983 to run Merrill Lynch's mortgage loan division. With the knowledge of the White House, savings bank leaders used their new freedom to lobby members of Congress directly and to offer large campaign donations and other perquisites to Republicans and Democrats, who continued to support deregulation and cover up public risks.[19]

The cover-ups widened as savings banks were taken over by well-connected risk-seeking entrepreneurs, including Charles H. Keating, Jr., and Neil M. Bush (son of Vice President George H.W. Bush), who invested depositor money in overpriced real estate and other schemes doomed to failure. The banks had become what two journalists called "huge casinos," offering "cash for trash."[20] The new proprietors of these banks paid themselves large salaries with generous travel and housing benefits. They drove more than one thousand savings institutions to bankruptcy, and the federal government had to pick up the bill. Repaying depositors and recovering misused assets at the deregulated banks ultimately cost American taxpayers $124 billion.[21]

The Reagan administration's deregulation efforts distorted the entire savings and loan industry by encouraging irresponsible risk-taking, institutional corruption, influence peddling, waste, and lawbreaking. Men close to Reagan and numerous members of Congress from both parties personally benefited from this financial plundering, and taxpayers paid the bill. This was a bipartisan scandal.

The Iran-Contra Affair

The biggest scandal of the Reagan years, and the most significant constitutional crisis since Watergate, was the Iran-Contra affair. In the spring and summer of 1987, millions of Americans watched forty-one days of televised joint hearings from the House Select Committee to Investigate Covert Arms Transactions with Iran and from the Senate Select Committee on Secret Military Assistance to Iran and the Nicaraguan Opposition. The "Iran-Contra Hearings," as they were called, had all the elements of made-for-television drama: powerful elected representatives, eloquent defenders of constitutional checks and balances, zealous anti-communists, and attractive supporting actors. The tangled web of illegal activities that connected Washington, Israel, Saudi Arabia, Iran, Panama, Honduras, Nicaragua, and other countries was often hard to follow, but the plotline was evident: high-level figures in the Reagan administration, perhaps including the President, had broken numerous laws to pursue deeply held foreign policy goals. The key question was not whether they had acted illegally, but who should be punished and how.

From its first days in office, the Reagan administration prioritized reversing perceived advances by communist regimes, supported by the Soviet Union and Cuba, in Central America. William J. Casey, Reagan's former campaign manager and Director of Central Intelligence, focused immediately on Nicaragua—a small, strategically located country on the Central American isthmus with a pro-Cuban and pro-Soviet government (under the Sandinista Liberation Front) that came to power in 1979 following the overthrow of longtime pro-American dictator Anastasio Somoza. Casey and others in the U.S. government were alarmed by the spread of communist influence, which they ascribed to President Carter's weak policies, and they believed that a Nicaraguan counterrevolutionary paramilitary force, the "Contras," could lead a region-wide reversal, beginning in this small country.[22]

In 1981 the Central Intelligence Agency (CIA) began secretly channeling weapons and money to the Contras. When Casey reluctantly shared this information with Congress a year later, the House of Representatives placed restrictions on U.S. aid. Representative Edward P. Boland, a Massachusetts Democrat, authored the first of a series of amendments to federal appropriations, which prohibited the use of covert resources to overthrow the Sandinista government in Nicaragua. The amendment passed the House (unanimously) and the Senate and President Reagan signed it into law.[23]

Despite these restrictions, the CIA and the U.S. military increased their support for the Contras, claiming dishonestly that the aid was not designed to overthrow the Sandinista regime. In 1983, CIA-supplied aircraft bombed the Sandino Airport near Nicaragua's capital. In 1984, the CIA helped the Contras mine the main harbors of Nicaragua—a violation of international law for which the International Court of Justice ruled against the United States.[24] These escalatory actions, combined with news coverage of human rights atrocities committed by the Contras and their supporters in neighboring Honduras, motivated Congress to write still more restrictive legislation. A new Boland amendment, passed by the House and Senate in late 1984 and signed by President

Reagan that December, prohibited all military assistance to the Contras or other groups in and around Nicaragua. The Reagan administration had defied congressional intent since 1982; after 1984 continued aid to the Contras was clearly illegal.

The center for U.S. strategy toward the Contras was the National Security Council (NSC), located in the White House, staffed by Robert C. McFarlane, Admiral John M. Poindexter, and Lieutenant Colonel Oliver L. North, among others. These men believed that President Reagan wished to continue funding the Contras despite congressional prohibition. McFarlane also responded to Reagan's personal demand to help secure the release of American hostages held in the Middle East despite a stated U.S. policy of not negotiating with terrorists. These two priorities—continued support for the Contras and the negotiated return of American hostages—merged in the NSC as a secret illegal plan for arms sales to Iran (the sponsor of many hostage-taking groups in the Middle East) and diversion of the revenue from the Iranian arms sales to the Contras.[25]

Diverting weapons and cash across two continents required a long chain of secret deals with shady arms dealers, mercenaries, money changers, drug runners, and terrorists. The White House worked with all of these groups as it lied to Congress and the American people. American anti-tank and anti-aircraft missiles, originally sent to Israel, made their way to Iran, and cash for the diversion of those missiles made its way to dictators in Panama and Honduras. These figures in turn skimmed off their share of the funds before sending what was left to the Contras. The U.S. military then, at White House request, replenished the weapons Israel had diverted. This was American-sponsored organized crime.

The scheme revealed the self-defeating consequences of covert White House zealotry. Iranian-supported groups released some American hostages, but then they took more. If they could ransom hostages for weapons, why not increase their leverage? And the diverted cash to the Contras had little positive effect. Most of the money was stolen before it reached its target, and it encouraged the most corrupt elements of the Contra leadership. Since the money was secret, the recipients were not held accountable for how they used it.

These criminal maneuvers involved White House thievery of weapons and money from American taxpayers, as well as the premeditated violation of congressional legislation. The Reagan administration intentionally and flagrantly broke the law. The revelation of these facts by enterprising journalists led to the joint congressional Iran-Contra hearings, preceded by a special review board (the "Tower Commission," named after its chairman, Texas Republican Senator John G. Tower), whose findings were preliminary and based on limited investigation. In December 1986 a panel of three judges from the U.S. Court of Appeals for the Federal Circuit—empaneled as a Watergate-era check on executive abuses—appointed an Independent Counsel, Lawrence E. Walsh.[26]

Walsh was a lifelong Republican who had served with distinction under numerous presidents. He had been a prosecutor in the New York District Attorney's office (serving under Thomas E. Dewey), a federal judge (appointed by President Dwight D. Eisenhower), and a Deputy Attorney General (serving under William P. Rogers, later Nixon's Secretary of State). Walsh was known as an honest and dogged pursuer of justice. He lived up to that reputation.[27]

Over more than six years, he and his team of lawyers unraveled the lurid details of hidden NSC conversations, exotic CIA meetings, and repeated cover-ups rising to the level of the President himself. Reagan knew about the arms sales to Iran, which, at the very least, violated the Arms Export Control Act. Reagan also knew that his staff was continuing to support the Contras despite the Boland amendments—although it is not clear that the President understood how money from the Iranian arms sales was making its way to Nicaragua.[28] Like many of his closest advisers, Reagan lied to Congress and the American people when he falsely claimed he was unaware of nearly everything. Walsh's final report concluded: "President Reagan created the conditions which made possible the crimes committed by others by his secret deviations from announced national policy as to Iran and hostages and by his open determination to keep the contras together 'body and soul' despite a statutory ban on contra aid. . . . [T]he crimes committed in Iran/contra were motivated by the desire of persons in high office to pursue controversial policies and goals even when the pursuit of those policies and goals was inhibited or restricted by executive orders, statutes or the constitutional system of checks and balances."[29]

Walsh chose not to prosecute the President, especially in light of Reagan's declining health after he left office.[30] He also chose not to prosecute

Vice President George H.W. Bush, who became President after Reagan. Walsh charged fourteen high-level officials with criminal behavior, including McFarlane, Poindexter, North, Defense Secretary Caspar W. Weinberger, and Assistant Secretary of State Elliott Abrams. In a move that echoed President Gerald Ford's pardon of Richard Nixon, President Bush pardoned Weinberger, Abrams, and three others on Christmas Eve 1992—just before the end of his presidency.

The Iran-Contra Affair embodied the profound and systemic ethical lapses at the heart of the Reagan administration. The President did not benefit personally from the lawbreaking around him, but he did almost nothing to stop it. Out of greed and zealotry, his closest advisers repeatedly broke the law, lied to Congress, and stole government funds. More than one hundred high-level Reagan administration officials faced prosecution, and more than $130 billion was embezzled. Reagan's commitment to deregulation, aggressive military spending, and diminished oversight created a cocktail of corruption that was, in many ways, worse than Watergate.[31]

NOTES

[1]Ronald Reagan, Farewell Address to the Nation, January 11, 1989, available at: www.reaganfoundation.org/media/128652/farewell.pdf.

[2]James Baker interview, quoted in Lou Cannon, *President Reagan: The Role of a Lifetime* (New York: Simon & Schuster, 1991), 795.

[3]Ronald Reagan, Address to the Nation on the Economy, February 5, 1981, available at: www.reaganlibrary.gov/research/speeches/20581c.

[4]See Jonathan Lash, *A Season of Spoils: The Reagan Administration's Attack on the Environment* (New York: Pantheon Books, 1984); Joel Dyer, "How Reagan and the Largest EPA Scandal in History May Explain Why Valmont Butte Is Still Contaminated," *Boulder Weekly*, February 9, 2012. On "regulatory capture," see Daniel Carpenter and David A. Moss, *Preventing Regulatory Capture: Special Interest Influence and How to Limit It* (New York: Cambridge University Press, 2014).

[5]Scott Tong, "What Happened When an Industry-Friendly EPA Leader in the '80s Went Too Far," *Marketplace*, May 2, 2017, www.marketplace.org/2017/05/02/sustainability/what-happened-when-industry-friendly-epa-leader-80s-went-too-far.

[6]Philip Shabecoff, "House Charges Head of EPA with Contempt," *New York Times*, December 17, 1982.

[7]Philip Shabecoff, "Rita Lavelle Gets 6-Month Term and Is Fined $10,000 for Perjury," *New York Times*, January 10, 1984.

[8]"Still Rising: The H.U.D. Bill and Smell," *New York Times*, July 13, 1989; "Housing

and Urban Development (HUD) Influence-Peddling Scandal Unfolds Before Hill Panels," *CQ Almanac*, 1989, available at: library.cqpress.com/cqalmanac/document.php ?id=cqal89-1139712.

[9]Tad DeHaven, "Three Decades of Politics and Failed Policies at HUD," *Policy Analysis*, November 23, 2009, available from the Cato Institute at: object.cato.org/sites/cato .org/files/pubs/pdf/pa655.pdf; Stephen Labaton, "Ex-Official Is Convicted in HUD Scandal of '80s," *New York Times*, October 27, 1993; Gwen Ifill, "After Years of Obscurity, HUD Emerges in Scandal," *Washington Post*, May 30, 1989.

[10]Steven Weisman, "Watt Quits Post: President Accepts with Reluctance," *New York Times*, October 10, 1983.

[11]David Johnston, "Former Interior Secretary Avoids Trial with a Guilty Plea," *New York Times*, January 3, 1996; Cannon, *President Reagan*, 823.

[12]Philip Shenon, "Deaver Is Sentenced to Suspended Term and $100,000 Fine," *New York Times*, September 24, 1988.

[13]Cannon, *President Reagan*, 800–802; Philip Shenon, "Meese Says He'll Step Down, Contending He Is Vindicated by the Special Prosecutor," *New York Times*, July 6, 1988.

[14]"Meese's Three Years in Office: A Calendar of Troubles," *New York Times*, March 30, 1988.

[15]"Meese and the Pipeline: The Story So Far," *New York Times*, February 24, 1988.

[16]Irwin Ross, "Inside the Biggest Pentagon Scam," *Fortune*, January 11, 1993; Christopher Marquis, "M.R. Paisley, 77, Dies; Bid-Rigging Figure," *New York Times*, December 26, 2001.

[17]Federal Bureau of Investigation, "Operation Illwind," case summary, available at: www.fbi.gov/history/famous-cases/operation-illwind; Marquis, "M.R. Paisley, 77, Dies."

[18]Cannon, *President Reagan*, 824–828.

[19]William Greider, *Who Will Tell the People: The Betrayal of American Democracy* (New York: Simon & Schuster, 1992), 60–78.

[20]Steven Roberts and Gary Cohen, from *U.S. News and World Report*, quoted in Cannon, *President Reagan*, 826–827.

[21]Adam Tooze, *Crashed: How a Decade of Financial Crises Changed the World* (New York: Viking, 2018), 44–45.

[22]Bob Woodward, *Veil: The Secret Wars of the CIA, 1981–1987* (New York: Simon & Schuster, 1987), 221–236.

[23]Malcolm Byrne, *Iran-Contra: Reagan's Scandal and the Unchecked Abuse of Presidential Power* (Lawrence: University Press of Kansas, 2014), 8–27.

[24]Paul Lewis, "World Court Supports Nicaragua After U.S. Rejected Judges' Role," *New York Times*, June 28, 1986.

[25]Byrne, *Iran-Contra*, 28–207.

[26]Byrne, *Iran-Contra*, 208–306.

[27]Joe Holley, "Lawrence E. Walsh, Iran-Contra Special Prosecutor, dies at 102," *Washington Post*, March 20, 2014.

[28]Final Report of the Independent Counsel for Iran/Contra Matters, August 4, 1993, available at: fas.org/irp/offdocs/walsh/.

[29]Final Report of the Independent Counsel, August 4, 1993.

[30]Byrne, *Iran-Contra*, 324.

[31]See Byrne, *Iran-Contra*, 331–339; Theodore Draper, *A Very Thin Line: The Iran-Contra Affairs* (New York: Farrar, Straus and Giroux, 1991).

GEORGE H.W. BUSH
1989–1993

Kathryn S. Olmsted and Eric Rauchway

When George H.W. Bush won election to the presidency, he was serving as Vice President in the administration of Ronald Reagan, and he entered an Oval Office still occupied by his predecessor's political agenda and legacy of misconduct. In particular, the effort to resolve the episode generally described as the Iran-Contra Affair continued through the entirety of Bush's term in office, while Bush's determination to appoint at least one Supreme Court justice whose politics reflected Reagan's conservatism put him in the position of dealing afresh with illegal actions that occurred under the administration of the previous President.

Iran-Contra

Judge Lawrence E. Walsh and his associates in the Office of the Independent Counsel continued their seven-year investigation of the Iran-Contra scandal through the Bush administration with mixed results. On the one hand, Walsh succeeded in winning convictions or guilty pleas in eleven of the fourteen cases he brought.[1] On the other, he was repeatedly stymied by partisan attacks, appellate rulings, legal challenges, recalcitrant witnesses, and, ultimately, the President's pardon power.

The Iran-Contra scandal tainted both the Reagan and Bush administrations. Reagan officials had broken a law that prohibited aid to counterrevolutionaries—the Contras—in Nicaragua. They had also violated the Arms Export Control Act by secretly selling arms to the Islamist government of Iran as part of a scheme to ransom American hostages in the Middle East. The profits from the Iranian arms deals had been secretly and illegally diverted to the Contras. Although Congress had held its own investigation of the Iran-Contra Affair during the Reagan administration, Independent Counsel Walsh began his prosecutions in the Bush administration. He also continued to investigate whether other Reagan White House officials not previously proved to be complicit in the scandal—including Vice President Bush—had been implicated in some of the Iran-Contra crimes.

Walsh originally wanted to prosecute several Iran-Contra figures on broad conspiracy charges for violating the Boland amendments to a series of Defense Appropriations Acts, which banned U.S. aid to the Contras.[2] As Representative Edward P. Boland declared of his legislative intent on the floor of Congress, "To repeat, the compromise provision clearly ends U.S. support for the war in Nicaragua."[3] Walsh soon found himself foiled in his efforts to prove this case because government agencies refused to allow the prosecutors or defendants to introduce classified material in public court. As a result, lawyers for Lt. Col. Oliver L. North, the National Security Council staffer who had overseen the illegal operations, complained that they could not defend him against broad charges without access to classified documents, and Walsh was forced to drop two conspiracy counts. Instead, the Independent Counsel charged North with more easily provable crimes like obstruction of the work of Congress and a presidential inquiry, perjury, making false statements to investigators, and personal enrichment. Walsh would follow the same model in subsequent prosecutions.

North's trial began in Washington, D.C., federal district court in January 1989. Walsh's office charged North, a linchpin of the conspiracy who had won a popular following during the televised congressional hearings two years earlier, with obstruction of Congress, deception, and corruption. The colonel did not dispute many of the prosecutors' facts but insisted that he had been "a pawn in a chess game being played by giants."[4] Nevertheless, the jury convicted him in May 1989 on three counts—two related to obstruction and deception, another to personal corruption.[5] But an appeals court threw out North's conviction, ruling 2-1 that the testimony of witnesses in his trial might have been influenced by North's immunized congressional testimony. The panel's sole dissenting judge wrote that the ruling "makes a subsequent trial of any congressionally immunized witness virtually impossible."[6]

Walsh turned next to an even more significant target: former National Security Adviser John M. Poindexter, whose trial could potentially require the testimony of a former, as well as the current, President. The judge ruled that President Bush did not have to testify but that former President Reagan had to give a deposition. It was the first time that a former U.S. President testified in a trial about crimes committed during his time in office. Reagan tried to help Poindexter, but his videotaped testimony was notable mostly for raising suspicions about the former President's mental decline. He could not recall that, while he held office, his National Security Adviser Robert C. McFarlane had pleaded guilty to withholding information from Congress; he could not remember, either, the name of the Chairman of the Joint Chiefs of Staff who served him.[7]

In April 1990, Poindexter became the highest-ranking White House official since Watergate to receive prison time. The jury convicted him on five counts of obstructing justice and lying to Congress, and the judge sentenced him to six months in jail. However, an appeals court overturned his conviction on now familiar grounds—that his immunized congressional testimony had compromised his ability to receive a fair trial.

Throughout Walsh's long quest for convictions of participants in the Iran-Contra scandal, defenders of Reagan and Bush accused the Independent Counsel of making crimes out of policy differences and, although Walsh was a lifelong Republican, of pursuing a partisan vendetta. In essence, the Walsh critics did not believe that Congress had the right to set the nation's foreign policy; therefore, they contended, the Boland amendments and the Arms Export Control Act were illegitimate, and the men who broke those laws were not really criminals.

Walsh's prosecutions proceeded slowly in part because his targets and witnesses claimed falsely that they did not have contemporaneous notes that would be relevant to his inquiry; they even insisted that they had never received his requests for these notes. Walsh's office did not see former Defense Secretary Caspar W. Weinberger's 7,000 pages of notes until late 1991, and it did not gain access to Bush's diary, which contained Iran-Contra material, until November 1992, after Bush had lost his re-election bid.[8]

Because of the difficulty in obtaining the relevant documents, it was not until June 1992 that Walsh's office indicted Weinberger on five counts of obstruction, perjury, and making false statements to investigators. The trial was potentially historic because of Weinberger's stature as a Cabinet member and because his notes and his testimony could potentially reveal much more about Iran-Contra—and about President Bush's involvement in the scandal.

After the judge in Weinberger's trial threw out one charge for technical reasons, the Independent Counsel's office decided to file an additional charge on October 30, 1992, just four days before the presidential election in which Bush was seeking a second term. The indictment included quotations from Weinberger's notes showing that President Bush had lied when he claimed that he did not know about the arms-for-hostages trades. Republicans were furious about the additional charge, seeing it as a politically motivated attempt to harm Bush's chances for re-election.

Bush's political opponents hailed the release of Weinberger's notes as proof positive that the President had participated in a cover-up. "This is the smoking gun," said the Democrats' vice presidential nominee, Albert A. Gore, Jr.[9] It was possible that Bush would be forced to testify at Weinberger's trial or that the former Defense Secretary would reveal information that would lead to Bush's indictment.

But Weinberger never went to trial. He and five other alleged Iran-Contra conspirators—former National Security Adviser McFarlane, former Assistant Secretary of State Elliott Abrams, and CIA officers Clair E. George, Alan D. Fiers, and Duane R. Clarridge—received Christmas Eve pardons from the President, just weeks before Bush left office. Bush declared that the Iran-Contra conspirators had acted out of patriotism and that Walsh's prosecution reflected "a profoundly troubling development in the political and legal climate of our country: the criminalization of policy differences."[10]

The pardons effectively ended Walsh's investigation. The Independent Counsel wrote a thorough and scathing final report to Congress in which he suggested, among other things, that President Reagan had known about the diversion of funds. But the report was written for history; there would be no more trials. The former President was now disabled by dementia, and the current President had ensured that the most important trial—that of Weinberger—would be aborted before it began.

Disgusted by the pardons, Walsh suggested that President Bush's failure to produce his own "highly relevant contemporaneous notes, despite repeated requests for such documents" amounted to misconduct and that the President might be using his pardon power to cover up his own crimes. "In light of President Bush's own misconduct, we are gravely concerned about his decision to pardon others who lied to Congress and obstructed official investigations," he wrote in a statement. Walsh concluded that the "Iran-Contra cover-up, which has continued for more than six years, has now been completed." [11]

Clarence Thomas

On July 1, 1991, President Bush nominated Clarence Thomas, then a judge on the U.S. Court of Appeals for the District of Columbia Circuit, to replace Thurgood Marshall as an Associate Justice of the Supreme Court. On October 5, during hearings of the Senate Judiciary Committee into Thomas's fitness for a seat on the high court, news broke of an FBI interview with Anita F. Hill, a law professor at the University of Oklahoma. Hill had told the FBI that in the early 1980s, while she was working as Special Assistant to Thomas at the U.S. Equal Employment Opportunity Commission (EEOC) under the administration of Ronald Reagan, Thomas had repeatedly sexually harassed her by making unwanted sexual advances, crude jokes, and other inappropriately sexual remarks.

The EEOC had held in its 1980 "Guidelines on Discrimination Because of Sex" that Section 703 of Title VII of the Civil Rights Act of 1964 outlawed workplace sexual harassment and defined such behavior to include "verbal . . . conduct of a sexual nature" when "such conduct has the purpose or effect of unreasonably interfering with an individual's work performance or creating an intimidating, hostile, or offensive working environment." [12] As Chairman of the EEOC—Thomas insisted on the title "Chairman," changing it back to the more traditional style from the gender-neutral "Chair"—Thomas bore responsibility for enforcing this law. Hill explained that his conduct therefore not only broke the law, it indicated "his sense of how to carry out his job"; that is, "he did not feel compelled to comply with" the laws he was charged with enforcing.[13] So far as the question of law went, Thomas agreed. He told the Senate that in his view sexual harassment was "illegal" and that it included "unwelcome sexual teasing, jokes, remarks or questions."[14] In a memorandum dated November 14, 1984, Thomas had reinforced the EEOC's commitment to this interpretation of the Civil Rights Act. He pressed Solicitor General Charles Fried to argue this point in the case of *Meritor Savings Bank v. Vinson*, and in their June 19, 1986, opinion the Supreme Court affirmed its legality.[15]

Hill, Thomas, and the Supreme Court all understood that the conduct Hill described would have been illegal. Thomas disputed only—and flatly—the facts at issue. Asked before the Senate Judiciary Committee if he had ever said, "There is a pubic hair in my Coke," he said "No, Senator." He denied boasting of his sexual ability to Hill. He declared he had never spoken to her about the actor known as Long Dong Silver. He said he had never discussed with her, nor described to her, any pornography, and he denied having pressured her to go out on a date with him.[16]

By the time Hill and Thomas had given their testimony, it was clear that if Hill was telling the truth, Thomas had broken the law by sexually harassing her while Chairman of the EEOC, again by lying when interviewed by the FBI about Hill's allegations, and a third time by lying when testifying under oath before the Senate.[17]

The President responded to these charges of misconduct by defending his nominee and hastening the process of getting Thomas onto the Supreme Court. Bush had made Thomas a judge in the first place, nominating him to the federal bench two years earlier, and had stood by his nominee when naming him to succeed Marshall, saying that "the fact that he is black and a minority has nothing to do with this. . . . He is the best qualified at this time."[18] Whatever Thomas's other qualifications, his politics were more conservative than those of Bush's prior nominee to the Supreme Court, David H. Souter. The President's support among conservatives had been waning, thus making it attractive for Bush to choose a nominee who had served the Reagan administration; Thomas, with his stint at the EEOC, fit the bill.[19]

Bush had been told of Hill's allegations early on, but Thomas's flat denial reassured the President and his staff. "The force of Thomas's conviction is what saved it. If he'd given an inch, he would have been dead," one White House official said.[20] During the hearings, as the sordid details of Thomas's alleged conduct gained publicity, the President personally assured his Chief of Staff that he meant to continue backing Thomas. Bush remained apprised of efforts to demonstrate Hill's unreliability.

The Senate confirmed Thomas by a vote of 52–48—at that time, the highest number of nays recorded for a justice heading for the Supreme Court. Thomas would not, according to the calendar, ordinarily have taken the oath of office until November 1, but the White House made sure that he took it earlier, on October 23, in an unusually private ceremony. This haste ensured that even if any other revelations emerged, the press would have less interest in publishing them and the Senate could not reconsider his fitness for the Court. Once Thomas took the oath of office he formally held the title of Justice and enjoyed the protection that the Constitution provides to high office holders, meaning that only the cumbersome process of impeachment could remove him. [21]

Over the years of Thomas's justiceship news did emerge that witnesses who did not appear at his confirmation hearing were prepared to corroborate Hill's testimony and undermine his denials. In 2010, then–Secretary of State Hillary Clinton requested a memorandum to present the evidence and develop the case for impeaching Thomas but no action appears to have been taken.[22]

Catalina Villalpando

Late in October 1992, the FBI conducted a series of raids in pursuit of evidence in the course of an investigation into influence peddling by the United States Treasurer, Catalina V. Villalpando. Her former employer, the telecommunications firm Communications International, had given her a $600,000 severance package just as she took office in the Bush administration and had continued to pay her through her confirmation hearings, which she hid from federal inquiry. During the administration, the company had secured a series of contracts, including one of $3.5 million to help rebuild communications infrastructure in Kuwait after the damage done by the Gulf War. The administration suspended Villalpando with paid leave.[23] In 1994, she pleaded guilty to a set of felonies, including tax evasion, and received a four-month prison sentence.[24]

The Villalpando episode did not implicate the President himself nor his consequential subordinates, beyond a reflection upon their judgment in choosing her for office in the first instance; the President's response of suspending her from duty while she negotiated a settlement with the Justice Department for her official misconduct was unremarkable. By contrast, when the President had to respond to other charges of misconduct that went to the heart of his political agenda and that of his predecessor, such as those regarding the Iran-Contra affair, he took actions to preserve his own and Reagan's legacy, irrespective of the legal implications.

NOTES

[1]Two received pardons before trial, and one avoided trial when the Bush administration would not release relevant documents.

[2]96 Stat. 1830, 1865.

[3]Cited in Peter Raven-Hansen and William C. Banks, "Pulling the Purse Strings of the Commander in Chief," *Virginia Law Review* 80, no. 4 (May 1994): 833–944, 860.

[4]Quoted in Malcolm Byrne, *Iran-Contra: Reagan's Scandal and the Unchecked Abuse of Presidential Power* (Lawrence: University Press of Kansas, 2014), 314.

[5]North was convicted of two counts of aiding and abetting the obstruction of Congress and one count of accepting an illegal gratuity.

[6]"North Convictions Set Aside on Appeal." In *CQ Almanac 1990*, 46th ed., 534–535; *Congressional Quarterly* (Washington, D.C.: 1991), library.cqpress.com/cqalmanac/cqal90-1113274.

[7]Lawrence K. Altman, "While Known for Being Forgetful, Reagan Was Mentally Sound in Office, Doctors Say," *New York Times*, October 5, 1997, 34.

[8]Byrne, *Iran-Contra*, 320, 324–325.

[9]Quoted in Byrne, *Iran-Contra*, 321.

[10]"The Pardons: Text of President Bush's Statement on the Pardon of Weinberger and Others," *New York Times*, December 25, 1992.

[11]"Text of Walsh Response to Bush Pardons," *Los Angeles Times*, December 25, 1992.

[12]Equal Employment Opportunity Commission, "Discrimination Because of Sex Under Title VII of the Civil Rights Act of 1964, as Amended; Adoption of Final Interpretive Guidelines," *Federal Register* 45, no. 219 (November 10, 1980), 74676–74677.

[13]"Excerpt of News Conference on Harassment Accusations Against Thomas," *New York Times*, October 8, 1991, A20.

[14]"Nomination of Judge Clarence Thomas to Be Associate Justice of the Supreme Court of the United States," Hearings Before the Committee on the Judiciary of the United States Senate, 102nd Congress, 1st session, October 11, 12, and 13, 1991, part 4 of 4 (Washington, D.C.: Government Printing Office, 1993), 212–213.

[15]*Meritor Savings Bank v. Vinson*, 477 U.S. 57 (1986).

[16]Hearings, 162–163.

[17]Jill Abramson and Jane Mayer, *Strange Justice: The Selling of Clarence Thomas* (Los Angeles: Graymalkin Media, 2018; orig. 1995), Kindle locations 4097–4135.

[18]"Excerpts from News Conference Announcing Court Nominee," *New York Times*, July 2, 1991, A14.

[19]Abramson and Mayer, *Strange Justice*, 285.

[20]Abramson and Mayer, *Strange Justice*, 4131.

[21]Abramson and Mayer, *Strange Justice*, 5816.

[22]Jill Abramson, "The Case for Impeaching Clarence Thomas," *New York*, February 19, 2018, www.nymag.com.

[23]David Johnston, "The Name on the Dollar: U.S. Treasurer Is Suspended as F.B.I. Raids Ex-Employer," *New York Times*, November 1, 1992, E2.

[24]David Johnston, "U.S. Treasurer Under Bush Pleads Guilty to 3 Felonies," *New York Times*, February 18, 1994, A17; "Former United States Treasurer Gets Prison Term for Tax Fraud," *New York Times*, September 14, 1994, A12.

WILLIAM J. CLINTON
1993–2001

Kathryn Cramer Brownell

By the 1990s, the "golden age" of presidential television had ended. While presidents since Dwight D. Eisenhower had enjoyed the ability to address the majority of the American public by appearing on the three commercial networks, William J. Clinton, known popularly as Bill Clinton, faced a very different media landscape as President. The number of households subscribing to cable television grew from 6 percent in 1969 to 68 percent by the end of the twentieth century.[1] After CNN launched the model of twenty-four-hour news in 1980, its success inspired even more specialized news programming with competing all-news channel MSNBC and then Fox News coming on the scene in 1996. Rather than simply reporting official statements from Clinton's administration, a new group of press commentators, known as the "punditocracy," spent hours examining behind-the-scenes White House operations.[2]

Journalism as a profession also changed. Investigative reporters sought to hold the powerful accountable and fulfill their claimed role as members of the "fourth estate," just as celebrated journalists Carl Bernstein and Bob Woodward had done during the Watergate crisis.[3] They also shared the news stage with a wealth of openly partisan outlets and talk radio hosts such as Rush Limbaugh, who brought brash showmanship and conservative ideals to the airwaves.[4] The internet then further enlarged these alternative media environments, or "echo chambers," in which the consumption of ideological commentary became a form of political activism that took root especially on the right.[5]

In this environment, political scandals that rocked Washington during the 1990s assumed a distinctive shape by connecting conservative media, entertainment, and mainstream journalism. Clinton frequently used this environment to his advantage by carefully cultivating his celebrity through appearances on CNN, MTV, and other outlets.[6] But the media's focus on Clinton's personal life, as well as his partisan opponents' determination to bring his administration under investigation by any available means as a political tactic, created a presidency under siege and consumed by scandals—some serious, others trivial.[7] All of them, however, threatened to derail his policy initiatives and undermine his credibility because, for this President, accusations of misconduct were incessant. No proof of criminal activity on Clinton's part ever surfaced even though a judge held Clinton in civil contempt for evading the truth in testimony before a grand jury. The media's excessive quest to unearth scandal, as well as the partisan and personal nature of accusations against him, did not result in Clinton's removal from office, and it failed to dent his high approval ratings. But, by spending so much time fighting allegations of misconduct, he did not achieve many of the bold initiatives he had planned.

Travelgate

When Clinton entered the White House, he brought with him a dedicated, loyal, and effective team whose members were experienced, from Clinton's Arkansas governorship, in combating charges of misconduct. Throughout the 1992 presidential campaign this team expanded and figures like James Carville, Paul E. Begala, George Stephanopoulos, and Madeleine "Mandy" Grunwald perpetually scanned the landscape for troubling allegations against Clinton, who, since his Arkansas days, had a reputation for sexual dalliances and a tendency to bend the truth to his advantage. As soldiers in Clinton's "War Room," they made a speedy response to scandals a priority. With both an offensive and defensive strategy, they helped Clinton survive allegations that ranged from charges that Gennifer Flowers, a singer, model, and actress, had had an affair with the Governor, to questions about Clinton's avoidances of the Vietnam draft, to his smoking but not "inhaling" marijuana, to concerns about his wife Hillary's legal career and the couple's real estate investments in Arkansas.[8] The media team became noted for its skills in the highly celebrated art of "spin" as they continually beat back damaging allegations of misconduct.[9] In the process, the campaign established what the historian William H. Chafe classifies as the "lasting model for how the Clintons would handle political conflict, including a process of dissembling, avoidance, and obscuring the truth."[10] And yet, while the War Room helped Clinton win the election, it also intensified antagonism between him, the press, and his political opponents and ultimately became an obstacle in his efforts to govern.[11]

Charges of misconduct arose as soon as Clinton took office in 1993. New administrations bring new personnel to the White House. In Clinton's case, loyalty mattered. The President and the First Lady, Hillary Rodham Clinton, rewarded Arkansas friends with White House staff positions.[12] Some smaller agencies, however, were not accustomed to such political shifts in personnel. In particular, the White House Travel Office had long been a bureaucratic haven filled with employees untouched by changes in administrations. This office worked closely with members of the press to secure hotel reservations and charter flights to accompany the President when he traveled. They assisted journalists with passports and even at times helped them skirt customs duties on expensive international gifts.[13] Although it was a small agency in a large executive bureaucracy, the individuals who worked there had become close with the White House press corps.

After taking office, the Clintons noted what a close friend of theirs, Harry Z. Thomason, called "gross financial mismanagement" in the Travel Office.[14] In hopes of making the office more efficient and seeing an opportunity to put people loyal to the Clintons in charge, Hillary Clinton worked with their friend and newly appointed Deputy White House Counsel, Vincent Foster, to fire seven members of the office and replace them with loyal Arkansas supporters.

It was not against the law to fire travel employees for purported financial malpractice. But the press, already suspicious of the Clintons, turned the episode into a management issue and reported and commented on it widely in 1993, giving it the name "Travelgate" despite its being of minor importance compared with the earlier "Watergate" affair. The publicity gave William F. Clinger, Jr., the ranking minority Republican on the House Committee on Government Operations, an opening to call for an investigation by the Justice Department.[15] Although

Clinton had pledged his full cooperation during the investigation, by 1994 the Justice Department reported that the administration had not followed through on its promise. The White House, it said, had repeatedly failed to produce the requested information, in part because the President claimed executive privilege surrounding documents in the White House's possession.

Matters became more complicated in the wake of Vincent Foster's suicide on July 20, 1993. That evening, Clinton learned that one of his closest friends and a loyal White House attorney who had helped "fix" problems like Travelgate had succumbed to depression. Foster's death revealed the pressures facing White House advisers, especially as they were frequently thrust into media scrutiny. Before his death, Foster wrote that "I was not meant for the job or the spotlight of public life. Here ruining people is considered sport." [16]

But rather than generating a national conversation about mental health, it unleashed a wave of conspiracy theories that intensified the partisan polarization of Washington. [17] Speculation about White House foul play abounded, especially when it became known that Bernard "Bernie" Nussbaum, the White House Counsel and Foster's boss, had interfered in a police investigation into the suicide by removing, on the basis of attorney-client privilege, papers related to the Clintons from Foster's office. These efforts, which George Stephanopoulos later called an attempt to "preserve a measure of Foster's privacy," evoked questions of criminal behavior by raising concerns about what suppressed information the documents might hold. [18] Conservative media soon accused the Clintons of a murder as well as a cover-up. [19]

Travelgate, which Foster was dealing with before his death, as well as the investigation surrounding his suicide, eventually merged into a larger investigation of misconduct pursued against the Clintons regarding their real estate dealings in Arkansas, which would soon become known simply as "Whitewater." When the GOP took over Congress in 1995, the House Committee on Government Reform and Oversight made repeated requests to the White House for documents concerning Travelgate, ultimately threatening to hold White House officials in contempt of Congress for noncompliance. [20] The committee's pressure worked, and eventually the Clinton administration released more documents associated with the firings. Eventually, as part of the emergent

Whitewater investigation into the Clintons' real estate holdings, a document was discovered that incriminated the First Lady in having mandated, then covered up, the Travel Office firings.[21] The final investigation about Travelgate, however, concluded only that the White House had created "obstacles to the probe" while "fail[ing] to produce documents on time." That is, no crime had been committed.[22]

Whitewater

Having seen Colorado Senator Gary W. Hart's presidential campaign derailed in 1988 by accusations of adultery, Clinton understood that issues he had skirted in Arkansas—notably marital infidelity—could derail his national campaign, so his War Room kept opposition files on potential accusers and prepared to discredit them quickly.[23] This strategy succeeded with regard to accusations of the President's affair with Gennifer Flowers during his Arkansas governorship. But, during his campaign and early presidency, Clinton encountered unexpected questions about Hillary Clinton's legal career and their joint Arkansas real estate investments that tangled the President in yet more difficulties.

In March 1992, just after the War Room fought through the Flowers situation and questions of draft dodging, a *New York Times* article raised a question about the relationship between the Clintons and their friends and business partners from Arkansas James and Susan McDougal.[24] At issue was a 1978 business deal in which the Clintons and the McDougals purchased real estate in the Ozarks called the Whitewater Development. Available records showed that the Clintons stood to benefit from their investment but risked very little if the venture did not succeed. Questions emerged as to why this was so. It appeared that when the endeavor failed, James McDougal had used another of his new businesses, Madison Guaranty Savings and Loan Association, to cover up the two couples' Whitewater losses as well as shortfalls in other real estate dealings in which the Clintons had not been involved. McDougal also remained a financial supporter of Clinton's gubernatorial bid. Then, when Bill Clinton became Governor, McDougal hired Hillary Clinton and the Rose Law Firm, where she was a billing partner, to manage Madison Guaranty's legal affairs. By 1986—that is, long before Clinton's presidency—evidence emerged about how McDougal's savings and loan institution engaged in irregularities. Consequently, federal regulators investigated the situation and then prosecuted James McDougal for "cooking the books" in 1990 in violation of federal law, but a jury did not convict him.[25] As the *New York Times* noted in its 1992 article, this tangled web of relationships raised "questions of whether a governor should be involved in a business deal with the owner of a business regulated by the state and whether, having done so, the governor's wife through her law firm should be receiving legal fees for work done for the business."[26]

The Clintons responded to the story with an aggressive denial of any wrongdoing. A challenger for the Democratic nomination, the former governor of California Edmund G. "Jerry" Brown, brought up allegations of questionable activities in a primary debate during the 1992 presidential campaign by arguing that the Arkansas Governor was "funneling money to his wife's law firm for state business." Clinton responded angrily, "You're not worthy of being on the same platform as my wife." He then called the accusation "garbage."[27] Hillary Clinton attempted to reshape the conversation by making it about feminism. "I suppose I could have stayed home, baked cookies, and had teas," she said, but had instead pursued a legal career to "assure that women can make the choices that they should make—whether it's a full-time career, full-time motherhood, or some combination."[28] While her response generated public criticism for dismissing homemaking, it did quiet down conversations about her work at the law firm. In December, after winning the election, the Clintons had their counsel Vincent Foster strike a deal to transfer all their interest in the Whitewater venture to James McDougal.[29]

The Whitewater issue, which had originated before Clinton's presidency, came back into the headlines following Foster's 1993 suicide. When Bernie Nussbaum separated the files from Foster's office, he was concerned as much about protecting documents from Hillary Clinton's legal career at the Rose firm, which she was determined to keep private, as he was about protecting Foster's privacy. But such dogged pursuit of secrecy and the refusal to cooperate with law enforcement officials fueled the appetite for more "dirt" on the Clintons. Their claims to secrecy also allowed conservative media's argument about Clinton conspiracies to gain traction rather than to disappear.[30]

The Whitewater issue continued to dog the Clintons, especially when some people tried to exploit their assumed vulnerability for the detractors' own purposes. David Hale, a businessman from Arkansas, sought to cut a deal with prosecutors after being indicted for fraud in September 1993 by feeding the press stories about Governor Clinton's having pressured him to lend money to Susan McDougal. He alleged that the Clintons had been engaged in a "criminal conspiracy... to defraud federal regulators."[31] With such rumors circulating widely in public, the newly appointed White House Counsel to the President, David R. Gergen, a former aide to Presidents Nixon, Ford, and Reagan and a respected figure in Washington, presented the Clintons with an option to lay to rest the controversy over Foster's death and Whitewater by releasing the tightly guarded Whitewater documents to journalists.[32] He then arranged an agreement with the *Washington Post* to close the Whitewater case: the Clintons would make a full disclosure of documents in return for a promise of a fair investigation that would clear the Clintons of wrongdoing if none existed. According to Gergen's later account, President Clinton agreed, but Hillary Clinton refused.[33]

George Stephanopoulos later wrote that "if a genie offered me the chance to turn back time and undo a single decision from my White House tenure," it would be the decision to "stonewall the *Post*" that day.[34] Instead of putting the Whitewater investigation to rest, 1993 ended with the *New York Times* and *Washington Post* declaring a full-scale investigation into the Whitewater affair. Both Democrats and Republicans agreed that such a probe should go forth, even though the Clintons' investment had been made long prior to his presidency. Feeling boxed in, Clinton complied and asked Attorney General Janet W. Reno to appoint an Independent Counsel.[35]

Clinton started the second year of his administration under investigation by a New York Republican, Robert B. Fiske, Jr., whom Reno had appointed as a special prosecutor tasked with examining Foster's suicide and all issues related to Whitewater. The Clintons continued to deny any wrongdoing even as they cooperated with the investigation. Fiske first ruled out any misconduct or cover-up in the Foster suicide case by dismissing allegations of his murder. However, the investigation took a turn in the summer of 1994 when the President signed an act reauthorizing Fiske's investigation. The act required that a three-judge panel, not the Attorney General, appoint the Independent Counsel. Despite requests from Reno for the judges to reappoint Fiske, they decided that such an appointment by a Clinton official constituted a potential conflict of interest. Unhappy with Fiske's report on Foster's suicide, conservatives pressured the judges to replace Fiske with someone who would pursue the investigation more vigorously.[36] Ultimately, the judges decided on Kenneth W. Starr. A lawyer and former federal judge and U.S. Solicitor General under President George H.W. Bush, Starr was an active Republican and critic of President Clinton.[37]

With his personal troubles mounting, the President, viewing the Whitewater investigation as a political attack directed at him by conservative Republicans, became even more determined to protect his and his wife's privacy.[38] Consequently, following the Republican takeover of the House of Representatives in the midterm election of 1994, he hired Richard S. "Dick" Morris, the President's trusted consultant from his gubernatorial days in Arkansas, to manage a strategy of both polling and targeted advertising as well as a shift to the political and partisan center to save the Clinton presidency.[39] It succeeded. The public gradually came to see the President as embracing political moderation and the attacks on the Clintons as mean-spirited and partisan-driven.[40]

In the summer of 1995, the Senate stepped into the Whitewater investigation. Senator Alphonse M. D'Amatoa, a New York Republican, launched hearings on all issues related to the matter, including a subpoena of records removed from Foster's office following his death. In December, the Whitewater legal team found several eyebrow-raising documents: a note in Foster's handwriting calling Whitewater a "can of worms," a memo that discussed Hillary Clinton's role in orchestrating the Travel Office firings and then covering them up, and a set of billing records from her at the Rose Law Firm that had mysteriously appeared at the White House private residence.[41] With this new evidence, as well as questions of obstruction of justice now raised, Kenneth Starr subpoenaed the First Lady in January. In her testimony, she professed an eagerness to cooperate and a desire to find the underlying cause of any billing questions and inconsistencies, but she continued to deny any wrongdoing by her or her husband.[42]

The Whitewater investigation resulted in sixteen convictions for charges that included fraud, conspiracy, and obstruction of justice and included the conviction of Webster L. Hubbell, a law partner of Hillary Clinton and former Clinton appointee to the Justice Department.[43] It did not produce any evidence that either of the Clintons had engaged in wrongdoing, even if their actions raised some ethical questions. Ultimately, both James and Susan McDougal went to prison for fraud and conspiracy. Starr insisted that Susan serve in a windowless cell in hopes that a harsh punishment would make her turn on the Clintons.[44] She did not.

Starr lacked enough evidence to indict either the President or the First Lady, but his investigation did have a longer-term impact by intensifying the animosity between the press, the Independent Counsel, the President, and Congress. Bill Clinton felt intensely that vindictive and partisan forces were out to undermine his presidency. The press on the other hand, remained deeply suspicious of him and continued to report stories questioning his character.[45] Republicans saw the benefit of using their "oversight function" to distract Clinton from pursuing any significant legislative efforts.[46] In the end, the Whitewater investigation's chief consequence was to expand the definition of misconduct to include personal behavior. A new era of presidential scrutiny had opened.

1996 Campaign Finance Violations

Reports of campaign finance abuses—including use of the White House for financial gain and the acceptance of illegal foreign contributions—originated during Clinton's 1996 re-election campaign when the *Los Angeles Times* broke a story that the Democratic National Committee (DNC) had raised international money illegally.[47] In October 1996, the House Committee on Government Reform and Oversight began to investigate the allegation. The committee sent requests for documents to the White House. Rather than insisting on executive privilege as it had during the Travelgate investigation, the White House agreed to comply.[48] Yet by March 1997 the committee still had not received any documents, and it issued the first of several subpoenas. The White House delayed the release of the documents until June 1997.

Its purposeful delay bought the administration time to develop a response. The documents in its possession revealed how donations had helped to secure access to the President through dinners, intimate coffee gatherings, even rounds of golf with the President or a night in the White House's Lincoln bedroom. The Clinton team believed that this did not constitute scandalous behavior, just "sloppiness and bad judgments."[49] So it created "Operation Candor." It would release the files to the press while shaping interpretations about what they meant.

Pressed by journalists, the Senate investigation found that Republicans had used similar uncertainties and loopholes in laws and regulations to raise and spend "soft money" tied to party activities, which were little regulated by the Federal Election Campaign Act.[50] Clinton, a Senate committee concluded, had taken advantage of such loopholes in the system, but so had other campaigns, Republican as well as Democratic. As a result, while the media were taken up by the issue, the public dismissed these questionable fund-raising activities as efforts undertaken by both sides. Consequently, the issue failed to gain the political traction that some hoped it would.[51]

In the end, the White House released the names of donors who had attended coffees and other social functions. When the list of names turned out to include the country's top banking executives and involved meeting with federal regulators, Clinton admitted to having inappropriate conversations during social and official functions but denied that these interactions had shaped public policy. He then committed himself to campaign finance reform.[52] Ultimately, the Clinton strategy of candor worked, and Press Secretary Michael D. McCurry's strategic release of information to the media ultimately weakened the congressional investigation and took the sting out of the hearings.[53] In December 1997, Attorney General Reno announced that she would not seek the appointment of an independent counsel in this matter. Yet, like so many other questions regarding the Clintons, this particular complication in the administration's life lingered into 2001, when President George W. Bush closed it.[54]

Monica Lewinsky

On August 17, 1998, President Clinton addressed the nation and admitted to having "inappropriate relations" with a former White House intern, Monica Lewinsky. He emphasized that his answers in a previous deposition had been "legally accurate" but acknowledged that he had misled the American people and his family.[55] Apologizing for "hurting" people, he ended his address with an adamant defense of his privacy. "I intend to reclaim my family life for my family," he declared. "Even presidents have private lives."

As Clinton's defense makes clear, the line between public and private life, as well as the public's distinction between the two, disappeared during the Clinton administration. While political figures and members of the press had previously treated private affairs with discretion, the post-Watergate environment in which politicians and journalists could exploit scandals to advance their careers turned personal shortcomings into questions of character and thus of fitness for office.[56] The resulting inclination to try to turn a president's personal transgressions into breaches of law reached a peak during the Monica Lewinsky scandal, one that ultimately resulted in a House vote to impeach a president for only the second time in history. Yet while the Impeachment Inquiry revealed that the President had lied and committed marital infidelity, it never proved that he had committed a "high crime" that warranted his removal from office.

The case began not with Monica Lewinsky but with another woman who had alleged sexual harassment by the President. In May 1994, Paula Corbin Jones filed a federal lawsuit against President Clinton and an Arkansas State Trooper, Danny Ferguson, for a 1991 encounter between then-Governor Clinton and Jones in Little Rock, during which she alleged that Clinton made unwanted sexual advances toward her. Jones soon received encouragement from Clifford Jackson, a vocal conservative opponent of Clinton in Arkansas.[57] Once again, partisan enmities resulted in major difficulties for the Clintons.

Clinton's legal team attempted to settle the case out of court by offering $700,000 to Jones without an admission by Clinton of sexual misconduct.[58] When Jones rejected these terms, Clinton's lawyers worked to delay the case by seeking its dismissal or an arrangement by which it could be reopened only after Clinton had left office.[59] In doing so, the Clinton defense relied on a 1982 Supreme Court ruling that the President had "absolute immunity, in civil suits, regarding his official acts."[60] However, Jones's allegations against Clinton were not about his acts while President but instead about private acts while he had served as Governor. The facts of the case were not clearly covered by the Court's 1982 decision.

In December 1994, Federal Judge Susan Webber Wright ruled that since the lawsuit dealt with private matters that had happened before Clinton's election to the presidency, the President did not enjoy absolute immunity from trial in this instance. However, she ruled that Clinton would not have to stand trial in the case until after he had left the White House. Jones's attorneys appealed Wright's decision to the U.S. Court of Appeals for the Eighth Circuit, which in January 1996 upheld her ruling on the President's not having immunity from lawsuits that involved private acts, but reversed the trial court's decision that court proceedings on the matter needed to be delayed until Clinton had left office.[61] The Supreme Court unanimously upheld this decision in May 1997, allowing this private lawsuit to begin its resolution during Clinton's time in office. Justice John Paul Stevens wrote in the majority opinion that "the Court is not persuaded . . . that this decision will generate a large volume of politically motivated harassing and frivolous litigation."[62] Contrary to the Court's prediction, the case quickly generated wide interest and became a partisan tool to undermine Clinton's presidency. While Clinton had successfully delayed hearings on the case until after his re-election in 1996, during his second term the presidency, as well as the President, became tabloid entertainment.[63]

Bill Clinton testified in federal court about the charges raised against him by Paula Jones on January 17, 1998. Unknown to Clinton, Special Prosecutor Ken Starr, initially appointed to investigate the Clintons' role in Arkansas Whitewater investments, had begun to look into newly acquired information about a matter that had nothing to do with real estate. He had received information from Lucianne S. Goldberg, a literary agent with conservative connections, that a disgruntled former White House employee, Linda R. Tripp, possessed information about an affair between Monica S. Lewinsky, a young White House intern, and the President.[64] Hoping to trap Clinton in a lie during his deposition in the Paula Jones case, Starr asked Attorney General Reno to expand the Whitewater investigation to include charges of perjury and obstruction of justice. After Reno agreed to Starr's request, which she believed to be about the Whitewater case, Jones's lawyers included questions about the President's sexual conduct.[65] In so doing, they asked the President not just about Jones but about Lewinsky as well.

The result was a legal spotlight focused for the first time on an

American president's sex life rather than on his official acts. Clinton first turned to his reliable strategist Dick Morris, who took a poll and concluded that the public would not forgive him for lying under oath or obstruction of justice.[66] On the question of adultery, Morris advised Clinton to "gradually sensitize the public to the truth."[67] Clinton, trying to navigate public opinion and guard his legal options, denied all stories about an affair with Lewinsky in ways that gave him legal flexibility. The day before delivering his annual State of the Union Address in January 1998, he turned to the cameras with the statement, "I did not have sexual relations with that woman, Miss Lewinsky."[68]

While Starr continued his investigation, now broadly expanded beyond its Whitewater origins, leaks to the press about his discoveries fed the public's appetite for prurient information. Hoping to demonstrate that Clinton had not just lied under oath but also obstructed justice by encouraging Lewinsky to lie about their affair, he interrogated Lewinsky, her mother, and the Secret Service agents guarding the President who might possess information on the subject now under his prosecutorial microscope. In August 1998, Starr subpoenaed the President and videotaped his testimony in the White House for the grand jury.[69]

But Clinton was not without his own arsenal of tactics. Leading up to his testimony, his War Room "spin team," now battle-tried and experienced, commenced efforts to discredit his enemies and shape public opinion by spreading word that Lewinsky was "obsessed" with the President and "emotionally unstable."[70] Clinton supporters also raised questions about Starr by highlighting his right-wing connections and asking why he cared so much about the President's sex life. Nor did the press escape the lash of the President's anger for publishing rumors, not facts.[71]

Perhaps more important, Hillary Clinton joined the battle. She saved the President's 1992 candidacy from accusations of sexual indiscretion with Gennifer Flowers by appearing with him on television, holding his hand, and defending their marriage.[72] Now she appeared before the American people to charge that the accusations against her husband were just another chapter in a "vast right-wing conspiracy" that went so far as to blame the Clintons for murder.[73] Ultimately, the Clinton administration used its media savvy to turn the issue of sexual misconduct into different questions about a lapse in journalistic values and an expansion of conservative efforts to undermine the administration's policy gains and the presidency.[74] Their attack on Starr for pursuing a moralistic crusade rather than a legal investigation also proved effective.[75] Trust in the news media plummeted. Only 11 percent of the public had a favorable view of Starr, and during a midterm election year, House Republicans nervously looked at polls that showed Clinton's high approval ratings.

Nevertheless, the grand jury testimony in August 1998 forced the President to confront the probability that he would have to confess to an affair with Lewinsky. During his January deposition, he had said that he and Lewinsky never had "sexual relations," which he later clarified such a definition as meaning only intercourse, not oral sex or other intimate acts.[76] In an address to the nation following his deposition that August, Clinton claimed that he had not obstructed justice and that charges that he had done so arose from a "politically inspired lawsuit." Sexual misconduct, he argued, was a personal failing, not a political abuse.

The Office of the Independent Counsel disagreed, seeing Clinton's personal activities as disgracing the office of the presidency.[77] Political and religious conservatives praised Starr for his pursuit of the President for immoral behavior. However, to the majority of Americans immersed in the increasingly sexually permissive culture of the 1990s, Starr's actions seemed self-righteous and unwarranted by his assignment, and they judged Starr to be extreme.[78] Finally, in September 1998, Starr delivered the report of his investigation to the House of Representatives, which, to Starr's surprise, voted to publish it without any member's reviewing it in advance.[79] The report concluded that Clinton's behavior warranted impeachment in four categories: "perjury, witness-tampering, obstruction of justice, and abuse of power."[80] In October of the same year, the House Judiciary Committee, as it had in 1974, commenced hearings on a president's impeachment. At the hearings' conclusion, the committee recommended that the full House pursue articles of impeachment concerning the President's perjury and obstruction of justice related to both the Jones and Lewinsky cases.

In defending the President, House Democrats succeeded in making the Starr investigation itself the focus of debate.[81] Rather than discussing high crimes and misdemeanors such as those of Watergate, the House ended up debating whether or not the President had lied about an affair, a sensitive issue inasmuch as many in Congress, notably House Speaker Newt Gingrich (R-GA) and House Appropriations Committee Chairman (and Speaker-elect) Robert L. Livingston (R-LA), had been guilty of the same offense. While the Starr investigation had emboldened the tabloid, conservative, and mainstream press to pursue steamy stories about Clinton's sexual affairs by straying from its original mandate to pursue knowledge of the Clintons' Whitewater investments, it had also undermined the credibility of the investigation process. Nevertheless, Clinton's defense could not stave off his impeachment. Emboldened with confidential reports about Juanita Broaddrick, a nursing home owner who alleged that Clinton had raped her in 1978, the full House voted along party lines to recommend that the Senate try the President for perjury and obstruction of justice. [82]

Clinton's Senate trial began in January 1999, two months following the midterm elections during which Republicans lost seats in the House. Clinton saw these results as his "vindication" by the public, and so too did his colleagues on Capitol Hill.[83] With public opinion on Clinton's side, the Senate failed to produce a two-thirds majority to convict the President. Clinton's approval ratings remained high throughout the entire length of the Starr investigation and congressional attempts to impeach and convict him.

But that was not the end of it. In April 1999, Judge Wright held the President in civil contempt for having made "intentionally false" statements under oath during his January 1998 deposition in the Jones case. Her ruling, as one political scientist concluded, followed a "long judicial tradition in which judges avoid rendering decision in the midst of political controversy involving executive power, and in which their decisions come down after institutional conflicts between the President and Congress have been resolved."[84] Her rebuke of Clinton for giving "false, misleading, and evasive answers" did have direct consequences for Clinton, however.[85] She ordered him to pay legal fees and referred his legal misconduct to the Arkansas Supreme Court for it to consider the question of his disbarment. Ultimately, Clinton reluctantly agreed to the terms that would close the case for good. He would accept a five-year suspension of his license to practice law in Arkansas, pay a $25,000 fine, and admit that he "knowingly gave evasive and misleading answers" in his January 1998 deposition.[86]

In this entire matter, Clinton used his tried and true political tactics— deny, delay, discredit, distract—to fight allegations of misconduct. While such an approach may not win in courts of law, in the court of public opinion and as a matter of political justice, it often carries the day. By winning the battle to frame the debate by construing it as a partisan and ideological vendetta against him and his administration, Clinton saved his presidency.

Driven by partisan politics and inflamed by the media, the allegations of presidential misconduct in the 1990s spiked television ratings and intensified the partisan polarization that had been growing over the previous decade in Washington. Even as Clinton himself shifted to the political center during his presidency, his scandal-laden administration exacerbated this divisive and distrusting environment. In fact, in one of his final acts in office, he continued to generate controversy with a flurry of last-minute pardons. On January 20, 2001, Clinton issued 140 of them, including one to Susan McDougal and to two fugitives, Marc Rich and Pincus Green, wanted for tax evasion.[87] The sheer number initially stunned the press. The details of what opponents charged was an "aggressive" behind-the-scenes lobbying effort to exonerate people undeserving of pardons, raised new legal questions of misconduct, especially since Rich's ex-wife, Denise Rich, was a Democratic Party fund-raiser. Public reaction was fierce, with former President Jimmy Carter calling the pardon of Rich "disgraceful."[88] Although federal prosecutors concluded that Clinton had not violated the law, the pardons highlighted the ways in which the President courted controversy by trespassing the boundaries of ethical practices.

Clinton's presidency demonstrated that the acceptance of the earlier divide between public acts and private behavior had, by the 1990s, greatly narrowed in the world of American politics; private indiscretions could become political liabilities. The Clinton administration revealed the degree to which questionable accusations can easily distract public officials' attention from governing. A perhaps more serious consequence was the turn toward impeachment as a partisan tool rather than as a last resort to check illegal or out-of-bounds executive action.

Clinton's difficulties also exposed how journalistic—especially twenty-four-hour televised—coverage of the presidency had changed from reporting on official actions and statements to investigative efforts to expose personal presidential misconduct, whether or not such charges were credible or politically and ideologically motivated. These journalistic trends, which had been growing in American political life since the 1970s, became deeply ingrained in the media environment of the 1990s, which by the end of the decade had become even more partisan and more dominated by an increasingly combative "punditocracy."[89] As a result, commentary overtook news programming in ways that highlighted the extremes of political debate surrounding character issues and frequently desensitized the public to allegations of misconduct. As an unintended consequence, subsequent administrations have engaged in an open debate about matters that, until the end of the twentieth century, were considered marginal to a president and his presidency. The 1990s ushered in a new partisan and media environment, dependent on one another, that has intensified political polarization and fundamentally transformed the American presidency.[90]

NOTES

[1]Matthew A. Baum and Samuel Kernell, "Has Cable Ended the Golden Age of Presidential Television?" *American Political Science Review* 93, no. 1 (1999), 99–114.

[2]For a deeper examination of the changing media landscape and political responses to it, see David Greenberg, *Republic of Spin: An Inside History of the American Presidency* (New York: W.W. Norton, 2015). On pages 416–426, he discusses the nuances of this 1990s media environment, the rise of the punditocracy, and the Clinton spin operations.

[3]Michael Schudson, *The Power of News* (Cambridge, M.A.: Harvard University Press, 1995), 142–165; Matthew Pressman, *On Press: The Liberal Values That Shaped the News* (Cambridge, M.A.: Harvard University Press, 2018), 224–231.

[4]Brian Rosenwald, *Talk Radio's America: How an Industry Took Over a Political Party that Took Over the United States* (Boston: Harvard University Press, in press).

[5]Nicole Hemmer, *Messengers of the Right: Conservative Media and the Transformation of American Politics* (Philadelphia: University of Pennsylvania Press, 2016); Kathleen Hall Jamieson and Joseph N. Cappella, *Echo Chamber: Rush Limbaugh and the Conservative Media Establishment* (New York: Oxford University Press, 2010).

[6]Greenberg, *Republic of Spin*, 424. Kathryn Cramer Brownell, *Showbiz Politics:*

Hollywood in American Political Life (Chapel Hill: University of North Carolina Press, 2014), 225–232.

[7]Steven Gillon, *The Pact: Bill Clinton, Newt Gingrich and the Rivalry That Defined a Generation* (New York: Oxford University Press, 2008), 173.

[8]For a discussion of War Room operations, see George Stephanopoulos, *All Too Human: A Political Education* (New York: Back Bay Books, 2000), 51–107; Mary Matalin and James Carville, with Peter Knobler, *All's Fair: Love, War, and Running for President* (New York: Random House, 1994).

[9]The operations of the War Room were eventually filmed and became famous with D.A. Pennebaker's *The War Room*, directed by Chris Hegedus and D.A. Pennebaker, 1993, Criterion Collection, DVD, 2012.

[10]William H. Chafe, *Bill and Hillary: The Politics of the Personal* (Durham, N.C.: Duke University Press, 2014), 142

[11]Matthew J. Dickinson, "No Place for Amateurs: Some Thoughts on the Clinton Administration and Presidential Staff," *Presidential Studies Quarterly* 28, no. 4 (1998), 768–772.

[12]Chafe, *Bill and Hillary*, 164–204.

[13]Joe Conason, "Travelgate: The Untold Story," *Columbia Journalism Review* 34, no. 6 (March 1, 1996), 40–41.

[14]Chafe, *Bill and Hillary*, 178–180.

[15]Mark J. Rozell, *Executive Privilege: Presidential Power, Secrecy, and Accountability*, 3rd ed. (Lawrence: University Press of Kansas, 2010), 125–127.

[16]Ken Gormley, *The Death of American Virtue: Clinton vs. Starr* (New York: Random House, 2010), 86.

[17]Chafe, *Bill and Hillary*, 188–194.

[18]Chafe, *Bill and Hillary*, 192–193. Stephanopoulos, *All Too Human*, 184–187.

[19]On Rush Limbaugh's constant speculation about the murder of Foster, see Rosenwald, *Talk Radio's America*.

[20]Rozell, *Executive Privilege*, 126–127.

[21]Chafe, *Bill and Hillary*, 253–254.

[22]Angie Cannon, "Travelgate: No Charges," *U.S. News & World Report*, July 3, 2000, vol. 129, 19.

[23]Matt Bai, *All the Truth Is Out: The Week Politics Went Tabloid* (New York: Vintage, 2015).

[24]Jeff Gerth, "Personal Finances: Clintons Joined S&L Operator in an Ozark Real-Estate Venture," *New York Times*, March 8, 1992.

[25]Gormley, *The Death of American Virtue*, 58–59.

[26]Gerth, "Personal Finances: Clintons Joined S&L Operator."

[27]"Democratic Candidates Debate," March 15, 1992, www.c-span.org/video/?24986-1/democratic-candidates-debate.

[28]Chafe, *Bill and Hillary*, 149.

[29]Gormley, *The Death of American Virtue*, 66.

[30]Chafe, *Bill and Hillary*, 201.

[31]Gormley, *The Death of American Virtue*, 100; Chafe, *Bill and Hillary*, 201.

[32]David Gergen, *Eyewitness to Power: The Essence of Leadership* (New York: Simon & Schuster, 2000), 286–291.

[33]Gergen, *Eyewitness to Power*, 286–291.

[34]Stephanopoulos, *All Too Human*, 226.

[35]Chafe, *Bill and Hillary*, 219–220.

[36]Gormley, *The Death of American Virtue*, 145–151; For a discussion of all the conflict

of interest charges against Starr, see Deborah L. Rhode, "Conflicts of Commitment: Legal Ethics in the Impeachment Context," *Stanford Law Review* 52, no. 2 (2000), 269–351.

[37]Chafe, *Bill and Hillary*, 222.

[38]On the 1994 election, see Gillon, *The Pact*, 135–145.

[39]Chafe, *Bill and Hillary*, 233–240.

[40]Gillon, *The Pact*, 147–172.

[41]Chafe, *Bill and Hillary*, 253–254.

[42]Francis X. Clines, "Hillary Clinton Tells Grand Jury She Cannot Account for Records," *New York Times*, January 27, 1996.

[43]Scott J. Basinger and Brandon Rottinghaus, "Skeletons in the White House Closets: A Discussion of Modern Presidential Scandals," *Political Science Quarterly* 127, no. 2 (2012), 226.

[44]Chafe, *Bill and Hillary*, 276.

[45]Howard Kurtz, *Spin Cycle: How the White House and the Media Manipulate the News*, 2nd ed. (New York: Touchstone, 1998), 38.

[46]Gillon, *The Pact*, 173.

[47]Kurtz, *Spin Cycle*, 38. Gillon, *The Pact*, 182–183.

[48]Rozell, *Executive Privilege*, 138–141.

[49]Kurtz, *Spin Cycle*, 50–62.

[50]On the pressure from journalists and their pursuit of advocacy journalism, see Kurtz, *Spin Cycle*, 68; Robert Mutch, *Buying the Vote: A History of Campaign Finance Reform* (New York: Oxford University Press, 2014), 164.

[51]Kurtz, *Spin Cycle*, 268.

[52]Kurtz, *Spin Cycle*, 115–126.

[53]Kurtz, *Spin Cycle*, 189.

[54]Rozell, *Executive Privilege*, 141.

[55]William J. Clinton, Address to the Nation on Independent Counsel's Grand Jury Testimony, August 17, 1998, Master Tap 08857, William J. Clinton Presidential Library, www.youtube.com/watch?v=tYZFXi6Ro6k&feature=youtu.be.

[56]For a discussion of how "adversarialism" developed in American journalism, see Pressman, *On Press*, 184–218. For a discussion of how such tactics were cultivated by a new generation of politicians, see Zachary C. Smith, "From the Well of the House: Remaking the House Republican Party, 1978, 1994." PhD dissertation, Boston University, 2012.

[57]Gormley, *The Death of American Virtue*, 130–133.

[58]Chafe, *Bill and Hillary*, 273.

[59]Louis Fisher, " 'The Law': Legal Disputes in the Clinton Years," *Presidential Studies Quarterly* 29, no. 3 (September 1999), 701.

[60]Fisher, " 'The Law,' " 701.

[61]Fisher, " 'The Law,' " 702.

[62]*Jones v. Clinton*, No. 95-1853, United States Supreme Court. Argued January 13, 1997; decided May 27, 1997.

[63]Kurtz, *Spin Cycle*, 210.

[64]Chafe, *Bill and Hillary*, 275; Gormley, *The Death of American Virtue*, 285–292; Jeffrey Toobin, *A Vast Conspiracy: The Real Story of the Sex Scandal that Nearly Brought Down a President* (New York: Random House, 1999), 128–133.

[65]Chafe, *Bill and Hillary*, 277.

[66]Jeffrey A. Engel, Jon Meacham, Timothy Naftali, and Peter Baker, *Impeachment: An American History* (New York: Random House Large Print, 2018), 183.

[67]Greenberg, *Republic of Spin*, 425.

[68]William J. Clinton, "Childcare Initiative," January 26, 1998, www.c-span.org/video/?99463-1/president-clinton-monica-lewinsky-denial.

[69]Chafe, *Bill and Hillary*, 272–299; Fisher, "The Law," 706.

[70]Kurtz, *Spin Cycle*, 294.

[71]Greenberg, *Republic of Spin*, 423.

[72]*60 Minutes*, CBS News, January 26, 1992.

[73]Chafe, *Bill and Hillary*, 282.

[74]Kurtz, *Spin Cycle*, 301.

[75]Gillon, *The Pact*, 230.

[76]Engel, Meacham, Naftalie, and Baker, *Impeachment*, 190–198.

[77]Gormley, *The Death of American Virtue*, 541.

[78]On the sexually permissive culture of the 1990s and the failures of Starr's attacks to resonate with the American people, see Kevin Kruse and Julian Zelizer, *Fault Lines: A History of the United States Since 1974* (New York: W.W. Norton, 2019), 227–231. See, for example, Don Van Natta, Jr., "Even Aides See Starr Wounding Himself," *New York Times*, March 2, 1998, A1.

[79]Gillon, *The Pact*, 239. On Starr's surprise, see Engel, Meacham, Naftali, and Baker, *Impeachment*, 205.

[80]"The Starr Report: The Findings of Independent Counsel Kenneth W. Starr on President Clinton and the Lewinsky Affair," *Public Affairs*, 1998.

[81]Gillon, *The Pact*, 242.

[82]Engel, Meacham, Naftali, and Baker, *Impeachment*, 224; Toobin, *A Vast Conspiracy*, 363–365.

[83]Gillon, *The Pact*, 256–258.

[84]Richard M. Pious,"The Paradox of Clinton Winning and the Presidency Losing," *Political Science Quarterly* 114, no. 4 (Winter 1999–2000), 590.

[85]Gormley, *The Death of American Virtue*, 650–651.

[86]Gormley, *The Death of American Virtue*, 668–669.

[87]Jeffrey Crouch, *The Presidential Pardon Power* (Lawrence: University Press of Kansas, 2009), 111.

[88]"Carter Calls Pardon of Rich 'Disgraceful,'" *Washington Post*, February 21, 2001. www.washingtonpost.com/archive/politics/2001/02/21/carter-calls-pardon-of-rich-disgraceful/47fdc8d4-f4b5-45fd-8ce2-d3f58d0f006c/?utm_term=.033a5c052622 (Accessed February 7, 2018).

[89]Greenberg, *Republic of Spin*, 423–426; Hemmer, *Messengers of the Right*, 264–276.

[90]Rosenwald, *Talk Radio's America*; Kruse and Zelizer, *Fault Lines*.

GEORGE W. BUSH
2001–2009

Kathryn S. Olmsted and Eric Rauchway

While George W. Bush's connections with industry sometimes led to charges of corrupt practices during his time in the White House, his presidency became swiftly and indelibly associated with efforts, often open, to evade and erode laws protecting the civil liberties of U.S. citizens in an effort to combat terrorism. The administration's response to charges of such misconduct, which has become its enduring legacy for the institution of the presidency, amounted in the end to the crafting of new legal justifications superseding older, and sometimes fundamental, law.

Connections to Energy Firms

A Houston-based energy services firm, Enron, boasted of innovative business plans and record profits until it emerged that those gains resulted largely from accounting fictions intended to cover up the failure of its novel plans. Even when legal, the firm's energy trading practices, once publicized, sometimes horrified consumers because the firm knowingly created public energy crises in pursuit of profit. As Enron's lawyers wrote of one Enron energy strategy, it "appears not to present any problems, other than a public-relations risk arising from the fact that [it] contributed to California's declaration of a Stage 2 Emergency yesterday." [1] Enron declared the largest bankruptcy in U.S. history in 2001. Journalistic investigation and legal proceedings revealed its fraudulent accounting and other corrupt business habits. Enron's major executives, including Jeffrey K. Skilling and Kenneth L. Lay, were eventually convicted of felonies.

Enron had close ties with the Bush campaign and administration. Notably, Senior Adviser to the President Karl C. Rove had referred the influential Republican activist Ralph E. Reed, Jr., to Enron for a consulting contract to ensure, aides said, Reed's support for Bush.[2]

Secretary of the Army Thomas E. White had served as Vice President of Enron Energy Services before joining the Bush administration. Enron employees implicated White in the firm's fraudulent overvaluation. At the time of joining the administration, he held tens of millions of dollars' worth of Enron stock. He continued to consult with Enron officers while serving in the administration. Although he defended his actions as legal and proper, he tendered his resignation at the request of Secretary of Defense Donald H. Rumsfeld in April 2003.[3]

Of more lasting concern was the administration's connection to Halliburton, an oil services company, and a firm that was then its construction and engineering subsidiary, Kellogg Brown & Root (KBR). Vice President Richard B. Cheney had served as Chief Executive Officer of Halliburton from 1995 until his departure to serve as Bush's running mate in 2000, and he retained a financial interest in the firm in the form of stock options. When planning for the invasion of Iraq, officials in the Bush administration decided to purchase KBR's services. As the Special Inspector General for Iraq Reconstruction later reported, the officials knew that "hiring KBR, though, could create the appearance of a conflict of interest, because Vice President Cheney was the former CEO of KBR's parent company Halliburton." Under Secretary of Defense for Policy Douglas J. Feith raised this concern and informed the Vice President's office of his worry. From the White House, Feith received the reply that "the mission took priority over whatever political fallout might occur from granting a sole-source contract to KBR."[4] KBR provided services for the U.S. wars in Afghanistan and Iraq during the Bush administration and, as officials anticipated, allegations of improper favoritism in contracting with the firm followed amid reports of misconduct and fraud by KBR. Litigation into these matters continued as of early 2019.[5]

Surveillance of U.S. Citizens

The Bush administration's most public forms of misconduct arose from its responses to the terrorist attacks on New York City and Washington, D.C., on September 11, 2001. Among those responses was an increased surveillance effort within the United States. In seeking to prevent further attacks, the White House expanded its programs for intelligence gathering beyond what the law allowed, while also seeking to expand the law to accomodate the scope of the administration's ambitions.

Early in 2002, John M. Poindexter, freshly appointed head of the Office of Information Awareness in the Department of Defense, publicly declared the Bush administration's intention to spy on Americans, contrary to existing law, in an effort to capture and punish the perpetrators of the terrorist attacks of September 11 and prevent further such assaults. Poindexter had earlier served as National Security Adviser to President Reagan and had been convicted of, among other crimes, lying to Congress in connection with the Iran-Contra Affair, although a court later reversed these convictions. Donald Rumsfeld, named Defense Secretary by George W. Bush, hired Poindexter early in 2002 to develop a program of increased surveillance capability for the purpose of establishing what the administration called "total information awareness" as a safeguard against terrorism. The proposed system would permit federal agencies to accumulate in secret—as well as to cross-reference without a judicial warrant—the data trails Americans left when banking or sending electronic communications, including telephone calls. Acknowledging that the Privacy Act of 1974 would prevent the establishment of such a system, the administration sought legislation from Congress to permit establishing the program.[6]

As public awareness of the program grew, so too did opposition to it. The resistance peaked when Poindexter made public a plan to establish a futures market for terrorist attacks, with the idea that betting patterns might successfully predict these events. Americans from across the political spectrum found the Poindexter proposals unacceptable. Under pressure, he resigned. Congress defunded his office, asking that it be "terminated immediately." The legislators had "turned the lights out on the programs Poindexter conceived," Senator Ronald L. Wyden, Democrat of Oregon, declared.[7]

Wyden was only nominally correct. In seeking public and proper revision of the law, the administration followed an unpopular and unsuccessful policy; having failed, it continued carrying on much the same programs in different offices under different names without congressional or media scrutiny. The *New York Times* reported on December 16, 2005, that the administration had authorized the National Security Agency (NSA) to conduct surveillance of Americans' private communications without seeking the judicial warrants required by the Foreign Intelligence Surveillance Act (FISA) of 1978. FISA created special procedures designed to permit surveillance with minimal judicial review. Its secret court had a history of accommodating requests for electronic eavesdropping, and between its creation in 1978 and 2004, it rejected only five requests as against the 18,761 it granted.[8] The USA PATRIOT Act of 2001 expanded intelligence-gathering capacity in response to the terrorist attacks that year without overturning the legal provisions requiring FISA warrants for domestic surveillance. On behalf of the administration, FBI Director Robert S. Mueller III told Congress in April 2005 that, concerning the NSA, "I would say generally, they are not allowed to spy or to gather information on American citizens."[9]

Contrary to the FISA law and to Mueller's representations, the President had ordered the NSA to gather information within the United States on October 4, 2001, shortly after the September 11 terrorist attacks, and he continued to reauthorize this surveillance periodically over the next several years. Under the President's order, the NSA gained access to the switches of private telecommunications firms so it could intercept information streams routed through those switches. The information collected came from throughout the world but also included information streams originating from Americans talking to their fellow citizens solely within the United States. Having collected the information, the NSA shared it with other law enforcement and intelligence-gathering agencies. Once the *New York Times* revealed the existence of the program, administration officials publicly acknowledged using such means to listen, without warrant, to communications they thought might be going to, or coming from, a terrorist organization, and they referred to the operation as the "Terrorist Surveillance Program." In addition, the administration did not acknowledge and did not disclose other forms of surveillance undertaken by the NSA under the same set of orders.[10]

Early in the history of the surveillance program, John C. Yoo, Deputy Assistant Attorney General in the Office of Legal Counsel, wrote an opinion offering a statutory justification for the program even though it was, in Yoo's words, "in tension with FISA."[11] But Yoo believed that FISA's restrictions could be set aside on the assumption that the law did not apply in wartime and could not restrict the President's constitutional authority as commander in chief. On later review, another administration lawyer found Yoo's reasoning "problematic" because FISA's text makes explicit reference to its wartime validity.[12] Assistant Attorney General Jack L. Goldsmith, appointed to the Office of Legal Counsel near the end of 2003, began to raise doubts about the surveillance program's legality. So did the new Deputy Attorney General, James B. Comey, Jr. In March 2004 these officials came into conflict with White House staff members who wanted the program's authorization to continue. Goldsmith and Comey prevailed. The NSA surveillance program's authorization lapsed and so did the program—at least briefly—owing to these convictions that the existing justifications were not lawful.[13]

But within a short time Goldsmith was able to find a new legal basis for the surveillance program. He reasoned that although FISA barred warrantless surveillance, Congress had implicitly overridden this law in the Authorization for Use of Military Force of September 18, 2001. In this statute the lawmakers declared that "the President is authorized to use all necessary and appropriate force against those nations, organizations, or persons he determines planned, authorized, committed, or aided the terrorist attacks that occurred on September 11, 2001, or harbored such organizations or persons[.]"[14] On the basis of such new reasoning, this broad grant of authority included license for surveillance Congress had otherwise outlawed.[15]

In 2006, after the *New York Times* story led to increased public scrutiny of the administration's intelligence gathering on Americans, the Bush administration sought an authorization from the FISA court for its surveillance. The administration noted that although it might collect information about Americans' communications with each other, it would screen the information it collected by comparing metadata on its swept-up messages with other databases to see if there were any reasons for intelligence agencies to take an interest in the information. The FISA court permitted the program to go forward on this basis and reviewed it periodically thereafter, imposing restrictions on the government's ability to use the data it continued to collect.[16] In 2008 Congress amended FISA to accommodate the surveillance program and render its previous illegality ineffectual. Telecommunications companies thereby gained immunity from legal responsibility for cooperating with the government in breaking the law, and the government was permitted to destroy records relating to the program.[17]

A 2009 internal analysis of the President's Surveillance Program, as it came to be called, concluded that it had yielded little information of use in combating terrorism. This report, declassified in 2015, also detailed the administration's responses to charges, both internal and external, that its surveillance program was unlawful. When urged by legal opinions or by press revelations, the administration sought fresh legal justifications and new procedures that would permit it to continue its program of surveillance within the United States under the thus changed color of law.[18]

Justification for War and Exposing Valerie Plame

In 2003, Bush administration officials faced accusations that they had exposed the identity of a covert CIA operative to punish her husband for criticizing the war in Iraq.

Valerie E. Plame, a longtime CIA employee, had worked for the agency's Weapons Intelligence, Non-Proliferation and Arms Control Center. Although much of her career remains classified, she apparently served the CIA in Europe under nonofficial cover—in other words, as a covert operative pretending to be a private businessperson. Unlike spies who serve in official governmental positions, agents with nonofficial cover are not covered by diplomatic immunity and are therefore more vulnerable to prosecution and retaliation by foreign governments if they are exposed.

Plame moved to Washington in 1997 to work at the CIA's headquarters in Langley, Virginia, and in 2002 she was working as part of a team of CIA operatives charged with investigating accusations that Iraq's President, Saddam Hussein, had sought to buy uranium from the country of Niger as part of his alleged program to build nuclear weapons. The CIA decided to send an investigator to Niger to verify the claims. Plame suggested that the agency use her husband, Joseph C. Wilson IV, a former Ambassador to Gabon and a career Foreign Service officer, for that purpose. During his trip to Niger, Wilson decided that there was little evidence to support the charge that Iraq had tried to buy uranium there. He filed a report of his findings to the CIA and the White House. Two other official U.S. investigations came to similar conclusions.[19]

Wilson was therefore surprised to hear President Bush declare in his 2003 State of the Union Address that Iraq had attempted to purchase radioactive material from Niger. "The British government," the President said, "has learned that Saddam Hussein recently sought significant quantities of uranium from Africa." Bush also linked Hussein with the terrorist group Al Qaeda and suggested that Iraq might pass nuclear material to the group: "Secretly, and without fingerprints, he could provide one of his hidden weapons to terrorists, or help them develop their own."[20]

Knowing that the President had received two other reports besides his own discounting the uranium purchase from Niger, Wilson assumed that Bush must be referring to a different African country. But a few weeks later, on March 7, 2003, Mohamed M. ElBaradei, the Director-General of the International Atomic Energy Agency, told the United Nations Security Council that the Bush administration had based its claims on forged documents about a nonexistent Iraq-Niger uranium deal. Indeed, one member of ElBaradei's staff told the *New Yorker* that the forgeries were shockingly obvious: "These documents are so bad that I cannot imagine that they came from a serious intelligence agency," he said. "It depresses me, given the low quality of the documents, that it was not stopped."[21] The State Department said it had been deceived by the forgeries. Nevertheless, the United States invaded Iraq on March 20, and President Bush cited Iraq's alleged weapons of mass destruction as a major part of the case for the invasion.

Wilson knew that the Bush administration had not been deceived: it had deliberately ignored three different reports on the Iraq-Niger link and had manipulated intelligence to exaggerate the Iraqi threat. In July 2003, he decided to go public with his experience. In an op-ed published in the *New York Times* and headlined "What I Didn't Find in Africa," Wilson described his investigation and his findings and concluded that the Bush administration had twisted intelligence to justify its war. "A legitimate argument can be made," Wilson wrote, "that we went to war under false pretenses."[22]

Plame suffered for her husband's decision to criticize the President. Just over a week after Wilson's op-ed was published, conservative columnist Robert Novak wrote a column attacking Wilson and naming his wife. According to Novak, Wilson had gone to Niger at the behest of his wife, "an Agency operative on weapons of mass destruction." Novak, who attributed his information to "two senior administration officials," implied that she had arranged a junket to benefit her husband and that his findings were therefore less credible.[23]

The Intelligence Identities Protection Act of 1982 establishes that anyone who "learns the identity of a covert agent and intentionally discloses any information identifying such covert agent to any individual not authorized to receive classified information" has committed a crime.[24] Congress passed the law in response to leftist publications that had attempted to destroy the CIA by exposing its agents. Once Novak revealed Plame's name, the CIA notified the Department of Justice that the law might have been violated. In September, the FBI began a formal investigation into the leak. Bush's Attorney General, John D. Ashcroft, initially supervised the inquiry but recused himself because of the appearance of a conflict of interest. Ashcroft's deputy James Comey named Patrick J. Fitzgerald, U.S. Attorney for the Northern District of Illinois, as Special Counsel for the case.

As the leak investigation began, President Bush vowed to punish the leaker. "If there is a leak out of my administration, I want to know who it is. And if the person has violated law, the person will be taken care of," he told reporters.[25] Fitzgerald empaneled a grand jury that spent almost two years hearing testimony related to the purported leak. The proceedings encountered many delays because of reporters' refusal to name their sources. New York Times reporter Judith Miller went to jail for eighty-five days for refusing to identify her source; she finally agreed to testify once her source freed her to do so. The inquiry uncovered evidence that the President's Political Adviser Karl Rove and Vice President Cheney's Chief of Staff I. Lewis "Scooter" Libby had tried to sell the Plame/Wilson story to several reporters. Fitzgerald maintained that Libby had lied about his involvement in the leaks, but he concluded that he did not have enough evidence to charge Rove.

In October 2005, the grand jury returned an indictment against Libby, charging him with two counts of making false statements to the FBI, two counts of perjury, and one count of obstruction of justice. Fitzgerald believed that it would be difficult to prove a violation of the Intelligence Identities Protection Act because he would need to show that Libby knew that Plame was a covert operative when he leaked her name. Instead, the prosecutor decided to focus on the more easily provable crimes of deception and obstruction of justice.

On March 6, 2007, the jury delivered a guilty verdict. Libby was convicted of two counts of perjury, one of lying to the FBI, and one of obstruction of justice. He was the highest-ranking White House official convicted of a crime since John Poindexter, Reagan's National Security Adviser. He was sentenced to 30 months in prison, a $250,000 fine, and 400 hours of community service. But he never served his sentence. When the judge denied Libby bail during his appeal, President Bush commuted his "excessive" prison sentence, though he left in place the felony conviction and the other parts of the sentence. The President's critics were outraged by the commutation. "President Bush and Vice President Cheney deserve the widespread contempt they are receiving for this indefensible decision," said House Oversight and Government Reform Committee Chair Henry A. Waxman (D-CA). "The Libby commutation makes a mockery of our judicial system and our most fundamental values." [26]

In Bush's final days as President in 2008, as he considered his options for presidential pardons, Vice President Cheney pressured the President to pardon Libby, his longtime friend and aide. Bush declined to do so. His aides said that he did not want to send the message that anyone was above the law. Ten years later, President Donald J. Trump took the action that Bush had refused and gave Libby a full pardon.

Torture

In late April 2004, the CBS News show *60 Minutes II* aired a segment about abuse and torture at the Abu Ghraib U.S. detention center in Iraq. TV viewers saw deeply disturbing photos of U.S. soldiers abusing and humiliating prisoners and even one picture of a detainee who appeared to have died from a beating. The next week, the *New Yorker* magazine published an article on Abu Ghraib by reporter Seymour M. Hersh that disclosed more photos of prisoner abuse and included quotations from an official U.S. Army inquiry into the torture. The fifty-three-page report by Major General Antonio M. Taguba, completed a few months earlier, had concluded that there had been many cases of "sadistic, blatant, and wanton criminal abuses" of prisoners at Abu Ghraib.[27] Hersh reported that the Army was prosecuting at least six GIs for their roles in the abuse.[28]

Torture was illegal under U.S. and international law. The United States had signed the Geneva Conventions and the UN Convention Against Torture. In addition, Congress in 1996 passed the War Crimes Act, which made it possible to prosecute grave violations of the Geneva Conventions in U.S. courts. However, in the aftermath of the September 11 terrorist attacks, some military officers and administration officials had become convinced that it might be necessary to use torture to obtain information to stop future attacks.

Military spokesmen insisted that the Abu Ghraib abuses were the actions of a few bad actors who broke the rules. Indeed, eleven American soldiers were convicted of various crimes related to the abuse, including dereliction of duty, abuse of detainees, assault, and committing indecent acts. But Americans soon learned that the torture of detainees had been authorized at the highest levels. Beginning in June 2004, shortly after Hersh's exposé, a series of Bush administration legal documents, soon known as the "torture memos," were leaked to the press. The President's legal advisers (including John Yoo, who also sought to find legal justification for the administration's surveillance of U.S. citizens) had concluded in the memos that the abuse of alleged terrorists was not banned under the Geneva Conventions because the suspects were "unlawful combatants" and not attached to any state. Moreover, they argued that the war on terrorism had rendered international humanitarian laws obsolete and that the President had almost unlimited power to conduct the war as he saw fit. They defined torture very narrowly as techniques that caused the "equivalent in intensity to the pain accompanying serious physical injury, such as organ failure, impairment of bodily function, or even death."[29] Subsequent Justice Department memos specifically approved the use of "enhanced interrogation" methods such as forced nudity, exposure to extreme temperatures, stress positions, sleep deprivation, and waterboarding.

Some officials in the Bush administration had pushed back against the memos' reasoning. Lawyers for the State Department found the decision to disregard the Geneva Conventions as "untenable" and "confused and inaccurate" and suggested that U.S. officials could be prosecuted as war criminals.[30] Secretary of State Colin L. Powell argued that the use of abusive interrogation techniques would "reverse over a century of U.S. policy and practice in supporting the Geneva Conventions and undermine the protections of the law of war for our troops, both in this specific context and in general."[31] When Jack Goldsmith was appointed the head of the Office of Legal Counsel in 2003, he fought vigorously against the memos and began quietly withdrawing some of them—in other words, signaling administration officials that they could no longer rely on their legal reasoning.

When the memos began to leak in 2004, human rights groups expressed outrage. Their concerns extended beyond Abu Ghraib to the U.S. base at Guantánamo, Cuba, where many terrorist suspects were imprisoned. Moreover, the *Washington Post* disclosed in 2005 that the CIA was operating a network of secret prisons, or "black sites," in several cooperative countries, where its agents and their surrogates used harsh methods on prisoners. The disclosure caused an international uproar.

Some Democrats and international human rights groups charged that the interrogation methods amounted to torture and that the U.S. Attorney General should appoint a special prosecutor to conduct criminal investigations of Defense Secretary Rumsfeld and CIA Director George J. Tenet, along with military leaders.

President Bush responded to the charges by attributing the Abu Ghraib scandal to "disgraceful conduct by a few American troops who dishonored our country and disregarded our values" and by denying that U.S. interrogators routinely used torture.[32] Bush also supported Vice President Cheney's efforts to try to block a new congressional ban on torture sponsored by Senator John S. McCain III, a victim of torture during the Vietnam War. Cheney, who had memorably stated five days after the September 11 attacks that the United States needed "to work sort of the dark side, if you will" to combat terrorism, wanted to stop

Congress from passing the law or at least to modify it to exempt the CIA. When Congress did pass the ban, Bush issued a signing statement insisting that he could bypass the law if he thought its prohibitions endangered the nation's security.[33]

When Barack Obama became president, he formally revoked the torture memos, ended the use of harsh interrogation practices, and closed the CIA's black sites (though not the prison at Guantánamo). Yet while the Obama administration also released four more of the Bush-era memos on interrogation guidelines, it declined to press charges against those who relied on their reasoning. "It would be unfair to prosecute dedicated men and women working to protect America for conduct that was sanctioned in advance by the Justice Department," said Attorney General Eric H. Holder, Jr.[34] The Justice Department considered filing charges against those who exceeded the Bush administration's interrogation guidelines but ultimately did not prosecute them either. Top officials at the Justice Department also disagreed with the conclusions of their own ethics experts that the authors of the torture memos were guilty of professional misconduct.[35] In 2014, President Obama addressed the issue again, remarking that "we tortured some folks. We did some things that were contrary to our values. . . . I understand why it happened. . . . There was enormous pressure on our law enforcement and our national security teams to try to deal with this. And it's important for us not to feel too sanctimonious in retrospect about the tough job that those folks had. And a lot of those folks were working hard under enormous pressure and are real patriots."[36] Legal commentary from inside and outside the administration, including a memorandum by Harold H. Koh, chief lawyer for the State Department, held that the UN Convention on Torture applied in such cases, but this finding had no evident effect on the President's view of whether to investigate and prosecute these crimes, the perpetrators of which continued to serve the country.[37]

In 2018, President Trump appointed Gina Haspel, the Deputy Director of the CIA who had at one point run a CIA black site, as CIA Director. Haspel's vindication by promotion, as well as the associated lack of any effort to hold Bush officials responsible for breaking the law, combined to create a powerful and enduring legacy of the Bush administration's response to charges of illegal behavior. In the case of misconduct unrelated to the major aims of the White House, as with Thomas

White and the Enron matter, the administration was generally willing to sever its ties with officials accused of breaking the law. But when the administration's core policies appeared, even to its own appointees, to violate statutes, as with its use of surveillance and torture, the government under Bush proved adroit in discovering new legal rationales and, with the assistance of Congress and later administrations, retrospectively rendering actions lawful even though most lawyers and lawmakers had understood them to be criminal.

NOTES

[1] Bethany McLean and Peter Elkind, *The Smartest Guys in the Room: The Amazing Rise and Scandalous Fall of Enron* (New York: Portfolio, 2004), 277.

[2] Tom Redburn, "A Suicide and a Resignation as the Formal Inquiries Get Under Way," *New York Times*, January 27, 2002, 32.

[3] Richard A. Oppel, Jr., and Thom Shanker, "Army Secretary Steps Down; Had Clashed with Rumsfeld," *New York Times*, April 26, 2003, A17.

[4] Special Inspector General for Iraq Reconstruction, *Hard Lessons: The Iraq Reconstruction Experience* (Washington, D.C.: Government Printing Office, 2009), 29.

[5] Phillip Walter Wellman, "6 Veterans Suing KBR and Former Employer Fluor over Fraud Claims," *Stars and Stripes*, January 25, 2019, 7; see also Seth Harp, "Veterans Go Back to Court Over Burn Pits. Do They Have a Chance?" *New York Times Magazine*, May 17, 2018, www.nytimes.com/2018/05/17/magazine/burn-pits-veterans.html; and *U.S. ex rel. Conyers v. Kellogg Brown & Root, Inc.*

[6] John Markoff, "Pentagon Plans a Computer System That Would Peek at Personal Data of Americans," *New York Times*, November 9, 2002, A12.

[7] Carl Hulse, "Congress Shuts Pentagon Unit Over Privacy," *New York Times*, September 26, 2003, A20.

[8] Samuel Walker, *Presidents and Civil Liberties from Wilson to Obama: A Story of Poor Custodians* (Cambridge: Cambridge University Press, 2012), 370.

[9] James Risen and Eric Lichtblau, "Bush Lets U.S. Spy on Callers Without Courts," *New York Times*, December 16, 2005, A1.

[10] Offices of Inspectors General of the Department of Defense, Department of Justice, Central Intelligence Agency, National Security Agency, and the Office of the Director of National Intelligence, "Unclassified Report on the President's Surveillance Program," July 10, 2009, 1.

[11] Offices of Inspectors General of the Department of Defense, Department of Justice, Central Intelligence Agency, National Security Agency, and the Office of the Director of National Intelligence, "Report on the President's Surveillance Program," vol. 1, 14.

[12] Offices of Inspectors General, "Report," vol. 1, 36.

[13] Charlie Savage and James Risen, "New Leak Suggests Ashcroft Confrontation Was Over N.S.A. Program," *New York Times*, June 28, 2013, A6.

[14] Authorization for Use of Military Force, 115 Stat. 224.

[15] Offices of Inspectors General, "Report," vol. 1, 38.

[16] Offices of Inspectors General, "Report," vol. 1, 55–56.

[17]Walker, *Presidents and Civil Liberties*, 469.

[18]Charlie Savage, "Declassified Report Shows Doubts About Value of N.S.A.'s Warrantless Spying," *New York Times*, April 24, 2015, A12.

[19]The other two reports came from the U.S. Ambassador to Niger, Barbro Owens-Kirkpatrick, and Marine Gen. Carleton Fulford. Joseph Wilson, *The Politics of Truth* (New York: Carroll & Graf, 2004), 2.

[20]George W. Bush, "Address Before a Joint Session of the Congress on the State of the Union," January 28, 2003; 2003 Pub. Papers 82, 88.

[21]Seymour M. Hersh, "Who Lied to Whom?" *New Yorker*, March 31, 2003, 41–48; 42.

[22]Joseph C. Wilson, "What I Didn't Find in Africa," *New York Times*, July 6, 2003, WK9.

[23]Robert D. Novak, "Mission to Niger," *Washington Post*, July 14, 2003, www.washington post.com/wp-dyn/content/article/2005/10/20/AR2005102000874.html.

[24]Intelligence Identities Protection Act of 1982, 96 Stat. 122.

[25]George W. Bush, "Remarks Following a Meeting with Business Leaders and an Exchange with Reporters in Chicago," September 20, 2003; 2003 Pub. Papers 1215.

[26]Chairman Waxman on President Bush's Decision to Commute, July 2, 2007, www.democraticleader.gov/newsroom/chairman-waxman-on-president-bushs-decision-to-commute/.

[27]"Article 15-6 Investigation of the 800th Military Police Brigade," online at fas.org/irp/agency/dod/taguba.pdf.

[28]Seymour M. Hersh, "Torture at Abu Ghraib," *New Yorker*, May 10, 2004, 42–47.

[29]The National Security Archive has placed many of these memos online. See the memos of January 25, 2002, nsarchive2.gwu.edu//NSAEBB/NSAEBB127/02.01.25 .pdf; February 7, 2002, www.pegc.us/archive/White_House/bush_memo_20020207_ed .pdf; and the memo quoted here, August 1, 2002, nsarchive2.gwu.edu/NSAEBB/NSAEBB127/02.08.01.pdf.

[30]William H. Taft IV to John Yoo, January 11, 2002, nsarchive2.gwu.edu/torturingde mocracy/documents/20020111.pdf.

[31]Memo from Colin Powell, January 26, 2002, nsarchive2.gwu.edu/torturingdemoc racy/documents/20020126.pdf.

[32]George W. Bush, "Remarks at the United States Army War College in Carlisle, Pennsylvania," May 24, 2004; 2004 Pub. Papers 929, 923.

[33]Charlie Savage, "Bush Could Bypass New Torture Ban," *Boston Globe*, January 4, 2006, archive.boston.com/news/nation/articles/2006/01/04/bush_could_bypass_new_tor ture_ban/.

[34]"Department of Justice Releases Four Office of Legal Counsel Memos," Department of Justice Office of Public Affairs site, April 26, 2009, www.justice.gov/opa/pr/department-justice-releases-four-office-legal-counsel-opinions.

[35]Eric Lichtblau and Scott Shane, "Report Faults 2 Who Wrote Terror Memos," *New York Times*, February 20, 2010, A1.

[36]"Press Conference by the President," August 1, 2014, Obama White House Archives, obamawhitehouse.archives.gov/the-press-office/2014/08/01/press-conference-pres ident.

[37]"Close the Overseas Torture Loophole," *New York Times*, October 20, 2014, A26.

BARACK OBAMA
2009–2017

Allan J. Lichtman

On January 15, 2017, five days before he left the presidency, Barack Obama proclaimed, "I'm proud of the fact that, with two weeks to go, we're probably the first administration in modern history that hasn't had a major scandal in the White House." Scandals of the magnitude of the "Great Barbecue" under President Ulysses S. Grant, Teapot Dome under President Warren G. Harding, Watergate under President Richard M. Nixon, or Iran-Contra under President Ronald Reagan did not rock the Obama administration. Prosecutors indicted only two officials who served in the administration or in Obama's presidential campaigns. In both cases the infractions occurred after the officials' service in government had ended and had no relation to their official duties. In 2015, more than two years after he resigned as CIA Director, David H. Petraeus pleaded guilty to providing classified information to his intimate partner, who was writing a biography of him. In 2016, General James E. "Hoss" Cartwright, whom President George W. Bush appointed Vice Chairman of the Joint Chiefs of Staff and Obama reappointed, pleaded guilty to falsely denying to the FBI that he had discussed classified information with reporters. The transgression occurred in 2012, a year after Cartwright's retirement.

As candidate and president, Obama was sufficiently free of personal scandal that his political opponents invented a pseudo-scandal, based on the lie that he was a fraudulent president born outside the United States. Critics have also focused on some alleged scandals that erupted during Obama's eight years in office.[1] They are as follows.

Internal Revenue Service Targeting of Conservative Groups Applying for Tax Exemptions

Under U.S. Treasury regulations, certain types of nonprofit organizations can gain tax-exempt status if they are "operated primarily for the purpose of bringing about civic betterments and social improvements." Such tax-exempt groups can engage in political advocacy and lobbying, but not as their primary activities. In effect, these regulations have allowed organizations of both the left and right to pump billions of untaxed dollars into American elections without having to disclose their donors.

After the U.S. Supreme Court's January 2010 decision in *Citizens United v. Federal Election Commission* authorized unlimited political spending by corporations and labor unions, the number of applications for tax-exempt status doubled through 2012. The Internal Revenue Service (IRS) sought to identify political groups posing as civic or social improvement organizations by looking for political trigger words in their titles. Early in the 2012 presidential election cycle, conservatives charged that, like Nixon, Obama had corrupted the IRS to punish his political enemies. They asserted that politically motivated IRS officials had tagged words like "patriot" and "Tea Party" to illicitly target right-leaning groups for extra scrutiny and delay, although not for the outright denial of applications.[2]

Controversy over IRS practices dragged on through the end of the Obama administration. In May 2013, the Treasury Inspector General for Tax Administration issued a report that found that "the IRS used inappropriate criteria that identified for review Tea Party and other organizations applying for tax-exempt status based upon their names or policy positions instead of indications of potential political campaign intervention." Although the report found that the IRS primarily singled out conservative groups for review, it did not find any White House involvement in the IRS's targeting practices or any criminal activity. However, the report led to bipartisan condemnation of IRS practices.[3]

Republican-controlled congressional committees launched their own investigations but claimed that missing documents, which the IRS attributed to a computer crash, and a lack of cooperation from Lois G. Lerner, who led the IRS's tax-exempt division, hampered their investigation. On May 7, 2014, the House held Lerner in contempt of Congress on a nearly straight party vote, but the Justice Department declined to prosecute her.[4]

On August 5, 2015, the Senate Finance Committee completed a bipartisan investigation, which faulted the IRS division that dealt with tax exemptions as understaffed, mismanaged, and unprepared to deal with the surge of applications from new organizations affiliated with the burgeoning Tea Party movement. The committee did not find evidence of criminal activity or a political conspiracy on the part of the Obama administration to punish conservative groups. Two years later, in September 2017, during the administration of President Donald J. Trump, a second Inspector General's report found that beginning in the first term of President George W. Bush and continuing through 2013, the IRS had used political trigger words to target both conservative and liberal organizations for heightened review. That is, the IRS was looking at politics that might be infecting so-called charitable groups but not ones limited to conservative organizations. The report, once again, found no evidence of political pressure from the Obama White House on the IRS.[5]

After release of the first Inspector General's report, Obama acknowledged that "the report's findings are intolerable and inexcusable." He said that "the IRS must apply the law in a fair and impartial way, and its employees must act with utmost integrity. This report shows that some of its employees failed that test." Obama ordered a Justice Department investigation of IRS misconduct. That report, in October 2015, concluded without recommending any criminal charges.[6] The Obama administration pushed Lerner out of government along with Joseph H. Grant, Commissioner of the IRS Tax-Exempt and Government Entities Division, and Steven T. Miller, the Deputy IRS Director, who had become Director in November 2012. It claimed that new leadership had revised procedures to ensure the prompt and fair evaluation of applications for tax exemption.

The Solyndra Loan

Solyndra was a manufacturer of cutting-edge technology for solar cells based on cylindrical panels of copper indium gallium selenide. However, plummeting silicon prices led to the company's being unable to compete with conventional solar panels made of crystalline silicon. Solyndra filed for bankruptcy in 2011. It laid off some 1,100 employees and shuttered its operations. Solyndra had been the first company to receive a government loan under the 2009 American Recovery and Reinvestment Act. The President gave the company his personal seal of approval when he visited Solyndra's new Fremont, California, manufacturing headquarters in May 2010. The Department of Energy lent Solyndra $535 million, almost all of which the government lost when the company crashed.

Critics charged that the administration had ignored red-flag warnings about Solyndra's financial condition and prospects for future profits. They said that the White House had pressured the Office of Management and Budget (OMB) to approve the dubious loan as a demonstration of its commitment to green energy and perhaps as an illicit payoff to George B. Kaiser, a donor to the Obama campaign in 2008 and a White House visitor, whose family foundation owned more than a third of Solyndra.

The Obama administration insisted that it had not made the Solyndra loan for political reasons or pressured the OMB. It pointed to an approval process that had begun in the George W. Bush administration and to investigations that had failed to uncover a payback to Kaiser or anyone with an interest in Solyndra. In a news conference on October 6, 2011, President Obama sought to diffuse responsibility for the Solyndra loan and defend his green-energy initiatives. He said, "Solyndra—this is a loan guarantee program that predates me that historically has had support from Democrats and Republicans as well. . . . If we are going to be able to compete in the twenty-first century, then we've got to dominate cutting-edge technologies, we've got to dominate cutting-edge manufacturing." He said when backing pioneering enterprises that "there were going to be some companies that did not work out; Solyndra was one of them. But the process by which the decision was made was on the merits."[7]

As the allegations of scandal slogged on, a Department of Energy spokesperson cited an August 2015 report from the Energy Department's Inspector General that blamed Solyndra for misleading government officials about its financial stability and profit potential. The spokesperson touted the overall success of the loan guarantee program:

"Losses to date represent approximately 2 percent of the overall loan portfolio, while the successes of the program have supported a host of new jobs and more than $50 billion in total investments. Further, project companies supported by the department's Loan Programs Office have already repaid approximately $6 billion, including more than $1.1 billion in interest payments, to the U.S. Treasury." Ultimately, if fault lay anywhere, according to the Department of Energy, it lay with Solyndra's having misled investors and inspectors and not with any corrupt acts on the part of the Obama administration.[8]

"Fast and Furious"

"Fast and Furious" was a "sting operation" directed against Mexican drug cartels as part of a "gun walking" program that began in 2006 during the administration of George W. Bush. The operation let "straw purchasers" buy tagged firearms including assault weapons, which federal agents knew would be transferred illegally to key figures in Mexican drug cartels. Federal agents would then trace the tagged guns to the cartel traffickers and place them under arrest. In 2010 and 2011, agents from several law enforcement agencies ran the sting operation with approval from the U.S. Department of Justice.

However, agents lost track of more than half of some two thousand tagged guns, some of which turned up at murder scenes. The failed operation emerged as a well-publicized scandal after investigators found two of the tagged guns near the scene of the slaying of Border Patrol Agent Brian Terry by Mexican gang members on December 14, 2010. In the spring of 2011, the Republican-controlled U.S. House Oversight Committee began holding hearings on the Fast and Furious operation. Critics charged that the Obama administration transformed Fast and Furious from a perhaps botched operation into a scandal by withholding critical documents from Congress.

On October 12, 2011, the committee issued a subpoena for documents relating to Fast and Furious. On June 20, 2012, President Obama asserted executive privilege for the first time in his presidency to allow Attorney General Eric H. Holder to withhold some of the sought-after materials. The committee immediately voted along party lines to recommend holding the Attorney General in contempt of Congress. Eight days later, the full House voted 255–67 to cite Holder for criminal contempt. Seventeen Democrats joined nearly every Republican in voting for the measure. In another vote that fell closely along party lines, the House voted 258 to 95 to cite Holder for civil contempt. Many Democrats walked out of the chamber in protest.[9]

This was the first time in U.S. history that Congress had cited a sitting head of an established Cabinet department for contempt. The Department of Justice, however, declined to prosecute the Attorney General. Eventually, under court order, the Obama administration released thousands of additional documents on Fast and Furious.

Attorney General Holder dismissed the investigation and contempt vote as a partisan-driven tactic to embarrass the Obama administration in an election year. He agreed that the Fast and Furious "operation was flawed in its concept and flawed in its execution." However, both Holder and President Obama said that they did not authorize the operation and learned about its details only in 2011. They insisted that the matter had been sufficiently resolved with the ending of Fast and Furious and the retirement or resignation of lower-level officials responsible for the operation. Federal prosecutors did not charge any participant in Fast and Furious with a criminal violation.[10]

Benghazi

The Benghazi scandal involved the killing of J. Christopher Stevens, the U.S. Ambassador to Libya, and three other Americans in two diplomatic compounds in Benghazi, Libya. Stevens was the first U.S. ambassador killed overseas in the line of duty since Adolph Dubbs, the American ambassador to Afghanistan in 1979. The Benghazi controversy exploded during the presidential campaign of 2012 and purportedly implicated President Obama tangentially and his high-profile Secretary of State Hillary R. Clinton directly. What could be considered a political issue and an argument about wise or unwise policy and action instead mushroomed into a battle over the conduct of administration officials, who allegedly failed to protect American diplomats and who misled the American people about the origins of the Benghazi attack.

In March 2011, the United States intervened in a civil war in Libya to back the rebels opposing dictator Muammar Gaddafi, who had ruled the country since 1969. America's military engagement ceased before the year's end, when rebels toppled Gaddafi's government. However, absent any central authority, Libya descended into chaos, with bands of armed militias operating without check across the land. Benghazi, Libya's second largest city, was an epicenter of militia activity. On September 10, 2012, Ambassador Stevens traveled to a State Department compound in Benghazi with the aim of establishing a permanent U.S. presence in this key city. Just three diplomatic security personnel accompanied Stevens. A nearby fortified CIA annex had ten additional security personnel.

On the night of September 11, 2012, eleven years to the day after the 9/11 attacks in the United States, heavily armed members of Islamic militant groups attacked the diplomatic compound in Benghazi. They easily breached the walls of the lightly defended outpost. Officials inside telephoned the U.S. Embassy in the capital of Tripoli, the Diplomatic Security Command Center in Washington, and the CIA annex. The attackers set fire to the compound, killing Ambassador Stevens and Information Management Officer Sean Smith.

A team from the CIA annex drove to the compound to attempt a rescue. They located Smith, who was unconscious and later pronounced dead. They could not locate Stevens in the thick smoke; only later did security personnel find Stevens's body. The rescuers drove back to the annex with Smith and compound survivors. The militants attacked the annex after midnight, although defenders held off the attack until morning, when reinforcements arrived from Tripoli. The augmented contingent managed to evacuate the annex and transport its personnel to the airport. However, mortar fire had also killed CIA operatives Glen Doherty and Tyrone S. Woods, both former Navy Seals.[11]

For several years, critics lambasted the Obama administration for the Benghazi tragedy. They charged that President Obama, Secretary Clinton, and UN Ambassador Susan E. Rice had tried to disguise the administration's weak response to terrorism by misrepresenting the attack as a spontaneous response to an anti-Islamic video produced by an American freelancer rather than as a terrorist assault. They argued that Secretary Clinton had personally rejected requests for enhanced security in Benghazi and issued a "stand-down" order that delayed the dispatch of rescue forces. During the 2016 presidential election campaign, the Republican presidential candidate, Donald Trump, asserted that Clinton "decided to go home and sleep" after hearing of the attack.[12]

President Obama and Secretary Clinton responded that these charges of scandal were politically motivated and had no basis in fact. But the controversy endured through the presidential campaign of 2016 and prompted ten investigations—one each by the FBI and an independent commission established by the State Department, two by the Democratic-controlled Senate, and six by the Republican-controlled House. The final investigation by the House Select Committee on Benghazi lasted for two years, from 2014 until 2016.

The Obama administration repeatedly cited the results of investigations, which showed no wrongdoing on the part of the President or his Secretary of State. Administration officials said that their early description of the attack as something other than a terrorist operation resulted from faulty CIA intelligence, not a deliberate attempt to mislead the public. Clinton, they noted, worked until late that night dealing with the Benghazi crisis. They said that there was no "stand-down" order and that no American troops could have arrived in Benghazi in time to save the American personnel. The administration acknowledged that the State Department should have been more responsive to requests for heightened security at Benghazi but that the decisions were made by lower-level officials, not Secretary Clinton. Eric J. Boswell, the Assistant Secretary of State for Diplomatic Security, resigned under pressure, and the State Department suspended three other officials. None was indicted, and none of the investigations recommended criminal charges for any administration official.[13]

Hillary Clinton's Private Email Server

The U.S. House's Benghazi hearings revealed that Secretary of State Clinton had used a private email server for both personal and official business correspondence. The email controversy plagued Clinton throughout her 2016 campaign for the presidency.

Critics charged that Clinton had sought to avoid transparency and had recklessly exposed classified information to foreign hackers. On March 27, 2016, *Washington Post* reporter Robert O'Harrow, Jr., wrote that Clinton and her staff "paid insufficient attention to laws and regulations governing the handling of classified material and the preservation of government records, interviews and documents show. They also neglected repeated warnings about the security of the BlackBerry while Clinton and her closest aides took obvious security risks in using her basement server."[14] The email controversy received more coverage in the mainstream media than any other topic in the 2016 campaign. It prompted investigations by the FBI, the State Department's Inspector General, and the House Select Committee on Benghazi, which heard eight hours of testimony by Clinton in a one-day marathon session.[15]

A May 2016 report by the State Department's Inspector General found that Clinton had violated State Department procedures, had not received official authorization for her use of a private email server, and had not appropriately ensured the security of her work emails. However, the report found no evidence of criminal conduct.[16]

On July 5, 2016, FBI Director James B. Comey, Jr., released the results of an FBI investigation. He announced that while "there is evidence of potential violations" of criminal statutes covering the mishandling of classified information, "our judgment is that no reasonable prosecutor would bring such a case." In a nearly unprecedented public discussion of the decision not to level any criminal charges against Clinton, Comey publicly castigated her, saying, "Although we did not find clear evidence that Secretary Clinton or her colleagues intended to violate laws governing the handling of classified information, there is evidence that they were extremely careless in their handling of very sensitive, highly classified information." Then, just eleven days before the election, he reported the reopening of the Clinton investigation based on emails discovered in the computer of former U.S. Representative Anthony D. Weiner, whose wife was an aide to Hillary Clinton. Two days before the election, Comey said that the new email review had not changed the FBI's recommendation against prosecution.[17]

Republican presidential candidate Trump and his campaign team assailed Comey for not recommending Clinton's indictment and charged that political bias had tainted the FBI investigation. At campaign rallies and the Republican National Convention, Trump and his surrogates led anti-Clinton chants of "Lock her-up!" In reference to purportedly private emails that Clinton had not turned over to the government, Trump said in July 2016, "Russia, if you're listening, I hope you're able to find the 30,000 emails that are missing. I think you will probably be rewarded mightily by our press."[18]

A final June 2018 report of the FBI's Inspector General concluded that the FBI had conducted a thorough, good-faith investigation and reached the right conclusion untainted by political considerations. The report criticized FBI agents Peter P. Strzok II and Lisa Page for exchanging their own emails critical of Trump, which gave the appearance of political bias, although it found that their political views did not influence the investigation. The report chastised Director Comey for unilaterally deciding to criticize Clinton publicly and for releasing his letter reopening the investigation shortly before the 2016 election.[19]

President Obama had a minimal role in dealing with the email fallout. He said that he did not know about the private email server until its public revelation. In a *Fox News Sunday* interview on April 10, 2016, he defended Clinton, saying, "Hillary Clinton was an outstanding Secretary of State. She would never intentionally put America in any kind of jeopardy." He added, "There's a carelessness, in terms of managing emails, that she has owned, and she recognizes. But I also think it is important to keep this in perspective." He guaranteed that he would not interfere with ongoing investigations into her private email server.[20]

Instead of simply admitting that she had made a mistake and moving on, Clinton struggled with explaining her use of the private email server. She first said that she had set up the server "for the purpose of convenience" and did not recall "specific consultations" with State Department officials about using it for official business. She also stated that "former Secretary of State Colin Powell advised her in 2009 about his use of a personal email account to conduct official State Department business." She also did not recall being warned about the vulnerability of her server to malicious hacking. Clinton alleged in addition that she "does not recall" destroying business emails or "instructing anyone else to do [so] and was not in charge of the process for separating business from personal communications," for the purposes of the FBI investigation. As for classified information, she said, "I am confident that I never sent nor received any information that was classified at the time it was sent and received."[21]

On July 31, 2016, after Comey's press conference, Clinton asserted that he had "said my answers were truthful, and what I've said is consistent with what I have told the American people, that there were decisions discussed and made to classify retroactively certain of the emails." She later attempted to clarify this statement: "I was pointing out in both of those instances, that Director Comey had said that my answers in my FBI interview were truthful. That really is the bottom line here. What I told the FBI, which he said was truthful, is consistent with what I have said publicly. I may have short-circuited and for that I will try to clarify." [22] In the second presidential debate on October 9, 2016, Clinton admitted that she had made "a mistake, and I take responsibility." She added, "I am very committed to taking classified information seriously. And as I said, there is no evidence that any classified information ended up in the wrong hands." [23]

Clinton's use of a private email server raised serious issues. It violated federal regulations and put in jeopardy the preservation of official records. Although investigators uncovered no evidence of foreign hacking, the reliance on the private server at least posed the risk of such a security breach. However, the matter became overblown because of Clinton's candidacy, her inability to put the issue to rest, and the relentless attack strategy of her political opponents. In response to a lawsuit brought by the conservative group Judicial Watch, a federal judge in December 2018 ordered a limited inquiry by the U.S. Justice and State Departments into whether Clinton had used her private email to evade public records laws. An Inspector General's report released in October 2016 also raised questions about whether Obama, in fact, knew about Clinton's use of the private server before it surfaced in news reports. This issue faded away after the election of Donald Trump. [24]

The Clinton Foundation

Former President Bill Clinton founded this eponymous foundation "to create economic opportunity, improve public health, and inspire civic engagement, worldwide." [25] However, critics charged that while Secretary of State, Hillary Clinton had doled out favors to major foreign donors to the Clinton Foundation. Conservative author Peter F. Schweizer leveled these charges against Clinton in his 2015 book *Clinton Cash: The Untold Story of How and Why Foreign Governments and Businesses*

Helped Make Bill and Hillary Rich. The FBI apparently opened an investigation of the foundation in 2015, which the Trump administration renewed in 2017. To date, the bureau has not disclosed any findings of wrongdoing by Clinton or her aides.

The most explosive charge centered on donations to the foundation from persons with an alleged financial interest in Uranium One, a Canadian company that purportedly controlled some 20 percent of America's uranium-producing capacity. Schweizer charged that in return for this donation Clinton approved the sale of Uranium One to the Russian atomic energy agency Rosatom. Although the donation was legal, the foundation did not disclose it at the time. Some critics have attempted to implicate President Obama in the alleged Uranium One scandal by claiming that he pressured the FBI to end the investigation into the deal. However, this allegation has not gained traction beyond right-wing circles.[26]

Hillary Clinton and her supporters denied any quid pro quo with foundation donors. They said that the foundation had improved people's lives across the world and earned top ratings from charitable watchdogs. They pointed to the failure of critics to demonstrate any proof of "pay to play," the practice of paying for participation in an activity, and noted that in a Fox News interview Schweizer had admitted that he hadn't "nailed" his thesis. Bill Clinton's biographer, historian David H. Bennett, dismissed the controversy as another right-wing effort to discredit the Clintons: "All this is to be expected given what happened to Bill in the 1990s. He was accused of corruption of money and corruption of power, but nothing was ever found. Filegate, Travelgate, Whitewater: everybody was digging deeply but as one Clinton aide put it, 'there was no there there.' "[27]

Clinton supporters noted that the Uranium One deal was approved by nine U.S. agencies, of which the Department of State was only one, and that the Secretary herself was not personally involved in the process. They said that the actual amount of uranium production controlled by Rosatom was not 20 percent but only 11 percent of U.S. capacity and could not be shipped outside the United States because Rosatom lacked the needed export license. Jeffrey Lewis, a nuclear nonproliferation expert at the Middlebury Institute and formerly a policy director at the progressive New America Foundation, said that Rosatom's purchase of the company "had as much of an impact on national security as it would have if they set the money on fire. That's probably why [all the U.S. agencies involved] approved it."[28]

Vistria

Vistria was an equity investment firm founded in 2013 and run by President Obama's friend Martin H. Nesbitt and Obama's former Deputy Education Secretary Anthony W. "Tony" Miller. In a 2016 article, *Politico* suggested a link between the Obama administration's effort to curb the abuses of the for-profit educational institution, the University of Phoenix, and Vistria's interest in cheaply buying the parent company, which owned the university. Schweizer, in another book, *Secret Empires: How the American Political Class Hides Corruption and Enriches Family and Friends*, published in 2018, argued more forcefully that the Obama administration deliberately used its regulatory powers to benefit its cronies. He claimed that Obama had cracked down on the University of Phoenix to drive down its value, which enabled Vistria to purchase its parent company for pennies on the dollar.[29]

Schweizer's late-breaking charges failed to gain traction outside conservative media circles and prompted no responses from Vistria or former President Obama. However, mainstream journalists noted that regulating polluting industries, predatory lenders, and exploitative for-profit educational outfits had been a policy priority from the early days of the Obama administration and well before the formation of Vistria. Nancy LeTourneau, writing in the *Washington Monthly*, said that it was "absurd" to believe that Obama "didn't really have an issue with polluters contributing to climate change or the way that payday lenders and for-profit colleges ripped people off." Schweizer's "claims are so absurd that perhaps people are finally beginning to see him for the propagandist he's always been."[30]

None of these seven allegations establishes that the President or any of his associates misused their positions for money, sex, or power, the three hallmarks of serious scandal. As for Solyndra, the Clinton Foundation, and Vistria, allegations of wrongdoing are confined to the Obama administration's harshest political critics, who failed to present credible proof that the President or any officials of his administration corrupted their decision-making in response to financial incentives or the interests of friends and associates. Allegations regarding Fast and Furious, IRS practices, Benghazi, and Hillary Clinton's private email server prompted multiple investigations by the FBI, Congress, and various Inspectors General, which concluded with accusations of poor judgment, mismanagement, and incompetence by senior members of the administration, but not by the President, and not violations of law. All told, these controversies resulted in the disciplining, resignation, or retirement of some federal officials. None involved either of Obama's two presidential campaigns, and none resulted in a criminal indictment.

NOTES

[1] Allan J. Lichtman, *The Case for Impeachment* (New York: Dey Street Books, 2017), 97; Glenn Kessler, "Has the Obama White House Been 'Historically Free of Scandal'?" *Washington Post*, January 19, 2018, www.washingtonpost.com/news/fact-checker/wp/2017/01/19/has-the-obama-white-house-been-historically-free-of-scandal/?utm_term=.8655b4112680.

[2] "The IRS Harassment Scandal: A Timeline of 'Reform,'" *Center for Competitive Politics*, December 15, 2015, www.ifs.org/wp-content/uploads/2013/06/2015-12-07_Timeline_IRS-Scandal_Documenting-Efforts-By-The-Regulatory-Community-To-Police-Political-Speech-Full-Version.pdf; CNN Library, "IRS Controversy: Fast Facts," CNN, October 4, 2018, www.cnn.com/2014/07/18/politics/irs-scandal-fast-facts/index.html.

[3] Treasury Inspector General for Tax Administration, "Inappropriate Criteria Were Used to Identify Tax-Exempt Applications for Review," May 14, 2013, Reference Number: 2013-10-053, www.treasury.gov/tigta/auditreports/2013reports/201310053fr.pdf.

[4] In 2017, the new Justice Department leadership under President Trump likewise decided against prosecuting Lerner.

[5] Committee on Finance, U.S. Senate, "The Internal Revenue Service's Processing of 501(C)(3) and 501(C)(4) Applications for Tax Exempt Status Submitted by 'Political Advocacy' Organizations from 2010–2013, Bipartisan Investigative Report," August 5, 2015, www.congress.gov/114/crpt/srpt119/CRPT-114srpt119-pt1.pdf.

[6] White House News Release, "Statement by the President," May 14, 2013, obamawhitehouse.archives.gov/the-press-office/2013/05/14/statement-president.

[7] White House News Release, "News Conference by the President," October 6, 2011, obamawhitehouse.archives.gov/the-press-office/2011/10/06/news-conference-president.

[8]Daniel Graeber, "Is Post-Solyndra Climate Better for U.S. Solar?" UPI, August 28, 2015, www.upi.com/Energy-News/2015/08/28/Is-post-Solyndra-climate-better-for-US-solar/4301440760183/.

[9]CNN Library, "Fast and Furious Fast Facts," CNN, October 22, 2018, www.cnn.com/2013/08/27/world/americas/operation-fast-and-furious-fast-facts/index.html.

[10]CNN Library, "Fast and Furious Fast Facts."

[11]CNN Library, "Benghazi Mission Attack Fast Facts," CNN, September 4, 2018, www.cnn.com/2013/09/10/world/benghazi-consulate-attack-fast-facts/index.html.

[12]"What We Do Know About the Benghazi Attacks Demands a Reckoning," *National Review*, June 28, 2016, www.nationalreview.com/2016/06/benghazi-scandal-hillary-clinton-state-department-obama-administration-house-committee/; Zack Beauchamp, "9 Questions About Benghazi That You Were Too Embarrassed to Ask," *VOX*, July 18, 2016, www.vox.com/2015/10/12/9489389/benghazi-explained; Robert Farley, "Trump on Clinton's '3 a.m. Call,' "FactCheck.org, April 28, 2016, www.factcheck.org/2016/04/trump-on-clintons-3-a-m-call/.

[13]Farley, "Trump on Clinton's '3 a.m. Call' "; Glenn Kessler, "Fact-Checking the Benghazi Attacks," *Washington Post*, October 15, 2015, www.washingtonpost.com/news/fact-checker/wp/2015/10/21/fact-checking-the-benghazi-attacks-2/?utm_term=.1165cee3181e.

[14]Robert O'Harrow, Jr., "How Clinton's Email Scandal Took Root," *Washington Post*, March 27, 2016, www.washingtonpost.com/investigations/how-clintons-email-scandal-took-root/2016/03/27/ee301168-e162-11e5-846c-10191d1fc4ec_story.html?utm_term=.f7117b38065f.

[15]Duncan J. Watts and David M. Rothschild, "Don't Blame the Election on Fake News. Blame it on the Media," December 5, 2017, www.cjr.org/analysis/fake-news-media-election-trump.php.

[16]Office of the Inspector General, U.S. Department of State, "Office of the Secretary: Evaluation of Email Records Management and Cybersecurity Requirements," May 2016, fas.org/sgp/othergov/state-oig-email.pdf.

[17]FBI National Press Office, "Statement by FBI Director James B. Comey on the Investigation of Secretary Hillary Clinton's Use of a Personal E-Mail System," July 5, 2016, www.fbi.gov/news/pressrel/press-releases/statement-by-fbi-director-james-b-comey-on-the-investigation-of-secretary-hillary-clinton2019s-use-of-a-personal-e-mail-system; Casey Hicks, "Timeline of Hillary Clinton's Email Scandal," CNN, November 7, 2016, www.cnn.com/2016/10/28/politics/hillary-clinton-email-timeline/index.html.

[18]Ashley Parker and David E. Sanger, "Trump Calls on Russia to Find Hillary Clinton's Missing Emails," *New York Times*, July 17, 2016, www.ny.times.com/2016/07/28/us/politics/donald-trump-russia-clinton-emails.html.

[19]Office of the Inspector General, U.S. Department of Justice, "A Review of Various Actions by the Federal Bureau of Investigation and Department of Justice in Advance of the 2016 Election," June 2018, www.justice.gov/file/1071991/download.

[20]Interview with Chris Wallace of *Fox News Sunday*, April 10, 2016, American Presidency Project, www.presidency.ucsb.edu/documents/interview-with-chris-wallace-fox-news-sunday-3.

[21]Hicks, "Timeline."

[22]Hicks, "Timeline."

[23]"Fact Check: Clinton and Trump Debate for the Second Time," NPR, October 9, 2016, www.npr.org/2016/10/09/497056227/fact-check-clinton-and-trump-debate-for-the-second-time.

[24]Spencer S. Hsu, "Judge Orders Justice, State Departments to Reopen Narrow Inquiry

into Handling of Clinton Email Records Lawsuit," *Washington Post*, December 6, 2018, www.washingtonpost.com/local/legal-issues/judge-orders-justice-state-depart ments-to-reopen-narrow-inquiry-into-handling-of-clinton-email-records-law suit/2018/12/06/71d03530-f9a1-11e8-863c-9e2f864d47e7_story.html?utm_term =.5d3dbdb1d2c8; Josh Gerstein and Nolan D. McCaskill, "Obama Used a Pseudonym in Emails with Clinton, FBI Documents Reveal," *Politico*, October 23, 2016, www.politico .com/story/2016/09/hillary-clinton-emails-fbi-228607.

[25]Clinton Foundation, www.clintonfoundation.org/.

[26]Eugene Kiely, "The Facts on Uranium One," *The Wire*, October 26, 2017, www .factcheck.org/2017/10/facts-uranium-one/; "Behind the IG Report—How the Obama Justice Department Tried to Shut Down the FBI's Investigation into the Clinton Foundation," *The Daily Caller*, April 15, 2018, dailycaller.com/2018/04/15/ fbi-clinton-foundation-investigation/.

[27]"Clinton Cash: Errors Dog Bill and Hillary Exposé—but Is There Any 'There' There?" *The Guardian*, May 5, 2015, www.theguardian.com/us-news/2015/may/05/ clinton-cash-bill-hillary-scandal-book.

[28]James Conca, "Claims of Clinton-Russia Uranium Collusion Are a Real Empty Barrel," *Forbes*, October 27, 2017, www.forbes.com/sites/jamesconca/2017/10/27/ claims-of-clinton-russia-uranium-scandal-are-a-real-empty-barrel/#becfdf47b559.

[29]Michael Stratford and Kimberly Hefling, "Bid to Buy For-Profit College by Former Obama Insiders Raises Questions," *Politico*, June 29, 2016, www.politico .com/story/2016/06/former-obama-insiders-seek-administrations-blessing-of -for-profit-college-takeover-224917; "Obama's 'Best Friend' Raises Millions for Private Equity Fund," *Fortune*, August 11, 2014, fortune.com/2014/08/11/obamas -best-friend-raises-millions-for-private-equity-fund/.

[30]Nancy LeTourneau, "This Time Schweizer Went Too Far Even for the *New York Times*," *Washington Monthly*, March 22, 2018, washingtonmonthly.com/2018/03/22/ this-time-peter-schweizer-went-too-far-even-for-the-new-york-times/.

About the Editor

A Guggenheim Award–winning professor of history, James M. Banner, Jr., was on the Princeton faculty in 1974 when he contributed to the presidential misconduct report and is now an independent historian in Washington, DC. He was a co-founder of the History News Service, a moving spirit behind the National History Center, and the author of many books, including *Being a Historian*.

Publishing in the Public Interest

Thank you for reading this book published by The New Press. The New Press is a nonprofit, public interest publisher. New Press books and authors play a crucial role in sparking conversations about the key political and social issues of our day.

We hope you enjoyed this book and that you will stay in touch with The New Press. Here are a few ways to stay up to date with our books, events, and the issues we cover:

- Sign up at www.thenewpress.com/subscribe to receive updates on New Press authors and issues and to be notified about local events
- Like us on Facebook: www.facebook.com/newpressbooks
- Follow us on Twitter: www.twitter.com/thenewpress

Please consider buying New Press books for yourself; for friends and family; or to donate to schools, libraries, community centers, prison libraries, and other organizations involved with the issues our authors write about.

The New Press is a 501(c)(3) nonprofit organization. You can also support our work with a tax-deductible gift by visiting www.thenewpress.com/donate.